OLD VIENNA COOKBOOK

Gourmet's

OLD VIENNA COOKBOOK

A Viennese Memoir

Revised Edition

By
Lillian Langseth-Christensen

Photographs by
Lans Christensen

Illustrations by
Leo R. Summers

GOURMET BOOKS, INC.

New York

GOURMET'S OLD VIENNA COOKBOOK:
A Viennese Memoir (Revised Edition).

New text copyright © 1982 by Lillian Langseth-Christensen,
Niederosterreich, Austria

Photographs copyright © 1982 by Gourmet Books, Inc.

Photographs on pages 113, 288, and 496 copyright © 1978, 1982
by Ronny Jaques.

Manufactured by Dai Nippon Printing Co., Ltd., Tokyo, Japan.

Library of Congress Cataloging in Publication Data

Langseth-Christensen, Lillian.
    Gourmet's Old Vienna cookbook.

    Includes index.
     1. Cookery, Austrian. 2. Menus. I. Gourmet.
II. Title. III. Title: Old Vienna cookbook.
TX721.L35 1982   641.59436   82-15394
ISBN 0-933166-03-6

Contents

5

Menus and Memoirs

Color Photographs

Acknowledgments

Among the many people involved in the revision of the *Old Vienna Cookbook* we wish to thank especially Countess Gabrielle Seefried auf Buttenheim and Diplom-Ingenieur Maria Witwer for letting us photograph in their homes. We are also grateful to those who allowed us to use their hotels as location sites: Direktor Gerhard Paul of the Hotel Bristol in Vienna; Herr Anton Hölzl, manager of the Bristol's Café and Rôtisserie Sirk; Herrn Hans and Frau Rosemarie Danube and Johannes Count Walderdorff of the Hotel Goldener Hirsch in Salzburg; Hans and Rosemarie Thiery of the Hotel Schloss Dürnstein in Dürnstein. Thanks are due, too, to Herrn Helmut Touzimsky of Meinl and to Braun and Company on the Graben for lending us lovely linen accessories.

In closing, I want to thank Kemp Miles for her invaluable assistance with the preparation of food for photography and for her joyful company, Lans Christensen for his good-natured know-how, Evie Righter for her unfailing attention to editorial detail, and Jane Montant, without whose inspiration this project would never have come to pass.

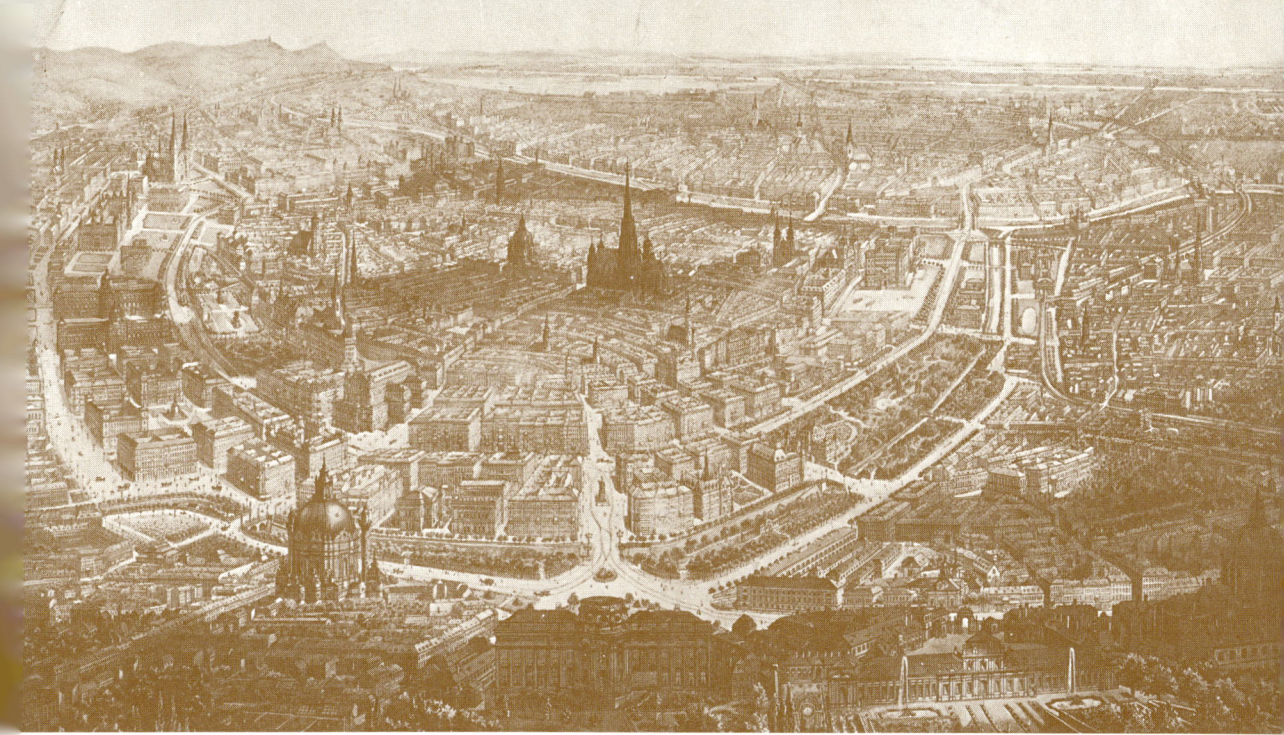

Foreword

To DESCRIBE Vienna is no problem: She is beautiful, gay, and *gemüt-lich*. To describe a Viennese is quite a different undertaking, one which cannot be accomplished in just three words. To be Viennese means more than having a national or municipal allegiance; it is a state of mind, if not actually a mild neurosis. The only reason the Viennese, the *Urwiener*, has been able to survive at all is that Vienna has a population of nearly 1,800,000 others exactly like him, who break umbrellas over one another's heads or kiss the hand, as the case may be, all in complete harmony and understanding. These alternately lovable and exasperating, fascinating and maddening people speak a language of their own called *Wienerisch*, almost incomprehensible to many other Austrians, a language characterized by a loving little diminutive attached to the names of everything from elephants to mice. All Viennese laugh at the same thing, that is, themselves; they are all endowed with an enormous capacity for the enjoyment of life at the instant of living it, and every last one of them, serious-minded men of affairs included, boasts a full set of sweet teeth.

This state of mind and heart and teeth, the state of being Viennese, leaves everyone with something called his individual *Gemüt*, his "feeling," and this is what makes the *Gemütlichkeit* for which Vienna is famous and for which no word exists in any other language. This semantic lack has occurred, probably, for the simple reason that no one else has such a feeling and clearly has no need of a word for it.

Vienna is the capital of the country in which no one passes anyone else without saying *"Gruss Gott*—greet God," or just *"S'Gott,"* whether they are complete strangers or old friends. And although Vienna has grown too large for everyone to greet everyone else, a low *S'Gott* can still be heard as strangers pass in the quieter streets and in the outlying districts. The temptation to speak to his fellow man is still alive in the heart of every Viennese, and he will, without a moment's hesitation, interrupt a conversation or tell a stranger exactly how to feed his dog. A Viennese will tell a man where to park or criticize a passing motorist, although he himself may very well not know how to drive. He will tell the shopkeeper in the doorway exactly what he thinks of the day, the weather, and the politics, and, if the fancy takes him and the young lady is really pretty, he will tell her so in passing. He usually interrupts his journey with little purchases, *Zuckerl*, sweets, for a passing child and some for the old dray horse at the corner. Life is leisurely, and the other men and women he passes on the street, being also Viennese, understand and share his urge for communication and respond accordingly.

Everyone who has ever been to Vienna has tried to explain the charm of the Viennese and of the city, from the poorest student to the guests at the Congress of Vienna, who dragged out their negotiations in order to prolong their stay, but in a way, each has failed. The charm of Vienna cannot really be described in words, and so I rely on anecdotes, on memories, and on the recipes of the food that so typifies the Viennese way of life.

It has been a pleasure for me to relive my memories and assemble my recipes of Vienna. Many of them may be different from those which have appeared in previous Austrian cookbooks. I must warn the reader there are exactly as many ways of preparing *Salzburger Nockerln* as there are people in Salzburg and, in many cases, as many ways of doing a Viennese specialty as there are Viennese.

Besides the Viennese, I want to thank Mr. Earle MacAusland, whose understanding, sympathy, and generosity throughout this project have been without limit.

LILLIAN LANGSETH-CHRISTENSEN

NEW MILFORD, CONNECTICUT

1958

Foreword to the Revised Edition

THE MEMORIES of which I wrote in the first edition of the *Old Vienna Cookbook* all related to the Vienna of the 1920s, when I went there to study design with Josef Hoffmann.

In fact, the Vienna I truly knew was the postwar one. The city was impoverished, her citizens longed for the past and wondered at having to adjust to the demands of the republic. In their hearts the Viennese still mourned Franz Josef and the loss of the pomp and beauty of his court.

The life the Viennese slowly reestablished was based upon their own memories of the good and glamourous years between the turn of the century and 1914, when happiness hinged on good food and good wine, on Strauss waltzes, on outings to the lovely countryside along the Danube, and on suppers at the Sacher after the opera.

Like all things, the niceties of life did return, but haltingly. Boiled beef eventually reappeared, for example. But we were living in the past, when messages were still delivered by hand and one could anticipate an ice in the afternoon at Demel's.

Times, of course, have changed in Vienna. That city, however, looks very much the same, her food is still fine, and the Viennese are as endearingly unpredictable as ever. I take this opportunity to thank Mrs. Jean MacAusland, publisher of GOURMET, for allowing me to meander back among my memories and in so doing experience them once again.

LILLIAN LANGSETH-CHRISTENSEN
LUNZ AM SEE, AUSTRIA
1982

Vorspeisen

V IENNESE CHILDREN were brought up to a rumbling accompaniment of admonitions that started with "Sit straight!" and went on to cover punctuality, orderliness, silence, and walking with toes pointing outward. But the leitmotif of their entire upbringing and the hardest of all orders to understand and to obey was, "Don't spoil your appetite—*Du sollst deinen Appetit nicht verderben!*" This order was thundered so often and so sternly that it sounded like a latter-day commandment.

It was doubly difficult for children to learn not to spoil their appetites, because their parents condemned as extremely harmful all the sweets which they really wanted to eat, while all the things they didn't want to eat anyway, such as *Spinat* (an even less popular word than spinach) and farina pudding, were the rewards for which their parents expected them to keep their appetites intact. But when they had grown up and had made the happy discovery that they were keeping their appetites unspoiled for better things than farina and spinach, they appreciated the wisdom of the admonition; and they, in turn, drummed the same old lesson into their own children. As a result, all Viennese sat up straight at table and kept unspoiled that most precious possession—their *guten Appetit*.

The fine point at which the Viennese were no longer spoiling their appetites and were, in fact, correctly gratifying them was established geographically and horologically. Anything eaten anywhere *except* in the dining room, no matter how tempting or nourishing, was frowned upon. Anything eaten before the appointed dinner hour was considered a definite spoiling of the appetite. Everything that was eaten *in* the dining room, after one sat down at table—with clocklike punctuality and very straight,

15

of course—was smiled upon as legitimate and proper dining, the very thing for which the appetite had been so carefully protected and preserved. Under these conditions, the announcement of dinner was always greeted with the greatest pleasure, unless for some unthinkable reason it was late, in which case there were frowns and an audible "*Endlich*—at last!" when the dining-room doors were opened. No one lingered; they leapt to their feet and began a light and elegant stampede to the dining room and to the long-awaited *Vorspeise*.

The first course, the *Vorgericht* or *Vorspeise*, had to be more a chef-d'oeuvre than an hors-d'oeuvre; it was approached with accumulated appetite and curiosity and an eye unblurred by *apéritif* or Sherry. It was supposed to take the first edge off the *Appetit*, but at the same time it was to increase rather than to diminish it, to stimulate rather than to satisfy. Goose liver pâté studded with toasted almonds or a mushroom soufflé over a tart of dilled crayfish was supposed only to increase the appetite for the soup, the roast, and the dessert to follow. They were *bei Tisch*, at table, at last. It was the moment for which they had waited, the moment for which they had conserved their appetites, and even the heartiest *Vorspeise* was only a prelude to that which was to follow.

The *Vorspeisen* were often egg dishes, but they could be of meat or fruit, fish or vegetable—there was no inflexible rule. These dishes were more substantial than appetizers but less substantial than the course that used to be called a side dish. A *Vorspeise* could be a small cheese pudding or an artichoke bottom filled with a purée of chestnuts; it could be oysters or caviar. It could be simple or elaborate, hot or cold, but it was rarely omitted and never neglected. It showed the hostess' imagination and the cook's ability; it was the test of both skill and creativeness.

The *Vorspeise* has changed very little from the days of the Empire, although Vienna has had its first cocktail party and the Viennese *Haus-herr*, head of the house, now owns a "Bar" from which he serves rather sweet Martinis and Manhattans. Eating lightly in the drawing room is no longer frowned upon, and the Viennese, who were brought up to preserve their appetites so carefully, must, in self-protection, eat little salty "bakeries" to accompany their cocktails.

None of this foreign activity takes away from the *Wiener Vorspeisen*. They have been cut into smaller portions and sometimes they actually find their way into the living room, but mostly they continue as first courses at table. They are still approached with an appetite, which even the most conservative Viennese must admit is rather stimulated than spoiled by the *ausländische Getränke* that are sometimes served in, of all places, the formal salon. What's more, the guests no longer sit quite so straight at table, and, to the horror of the cook, they are not nearly so punctual in reaching the dining room as was once the reliable custom when dinner was announced with the striking of the clock.

Endive Salad with Cheese — *Endiviensalat mit Käse*

ARRANGE 6 HEADS of cleaned endive, quartered, on 6 salad plates, allowing 1/2 head per serving. Cut 1 pound Emmenthal cheese into pencil-thin strips and cut the strips the same length as the endive. Divide the cheese sticks equally among the plates.

To 3/4 cup mayonnaise, add 1/2 cup stiffly whipped cream, measured after whipping, 2 tablespoons lemon juice, 1 tablespoon mild mustard, the grated rind of 1 lemon, and salt to taste. Mask the endive and cheese generously with this mayonnaise.

Garnish each plate at the last moment with a few slices of apple, peeled and cut paper-thin.

Cheese Toast I — *Käsebrötchen 1*

TRIM THE crusts from 6 slices of 2-day-old bread and dip the slices quickly, one at a time, in 1 cup white wine. Mix 1/2 cup grated Parmesan with 1 beaten egg and add salt to taste. Cover the bread with the cheese mixture, dot it with butter, and toast it in a moderate oven (350° F.) until it is golden brown.

Cheese Toast II — *Käsebrötchen 2*

TRIM THE crusts from 6 slices of rye bread and brown the bread lightly on both sides in 1/4 cup butter. Blend 2 tablespoons brown mustard with 1/4 cup beer and add 1 cup grated sharp Cheddar cheese. Spread the cheese mixture on the bread and broil the bread under moderate heat until the cheese is melted and very hot.

Fondue Südtirol   *South Tyrolean Fondue*

ALTHOUGH THIS recipe is called a fondue, it is really a soufflé.

Stir 1 1/2 cups cream into 3 tablespoons flour and cook the mixture over low heat, stirring, until it thickens. Add 2 cups freshly grated Parmesan, stir well, and take the pan from the heat. Cool the mixture and add 6 egg yolks and salt and pepper to taste. Fold in 6 stiffly beaten egg whites and pour the mixture into a buttered baking dish. Bake it in a hot oven (400° F.) for 35 minutes, or until it is puffed and golden. Serve at once.

Käsepfannkuchen   *Cheese Pancakes with Shrimps*

INTO A MIXING bowl sift 3/4 cup flour with 1/4 teaspoon salt. Stir in 1/2 cup cream and 3/4 cup lukewarm milk, 2 egg yolks, and 1 tablespoon melted butter. Beat the mixture to a smooth batter and let it stand for 1/2 hour. Add 1/2 cup grated Parmesan and 1/2 teaspoon onion juice and let the batter stand for 1/2 hour more. Add 1/2 cup cold cooked chopped shrimps and salt and pepper to taste and fold in 2 stiffly beaten egg whites.

Make small pancakes on a hot buttered griddle. Roll them up at once, sprinkle them with grated Parmesan, and keep them hot. Sprinkle the pancakes with more cheese and brown them under the broiler. Garnish them with fried onions and serve with cheese sauce.

Käsesauce   *Cheese Sauce*

IN THE TOP of a double boiler, over gently boiling water, cook 2 cups milk with 2 whole eggs, 2 tablespoons flour, and a pinch of nutmeg, stirring, until the sauce thickens. Add 1 cup grated sharp white Cheddar cheese and continue to stir until the cheese melts. Keep the sauce warm and, just before serving, fold in 1 cup salted heavy cream, stiffly whipped. Reheat the sauce for a minute.

Käsepudding   *Cheese Pudding*

IN A SAUCEPAN, over low heat, stir 1/2 cup sifted flour into 1/4 cup melted butter and gradually add 1 cup scalded milk. Cook the mixture, stirring constantly, until it seems dry and leaves the sides of the pan. Cool the

mixture and add 4 egg yolks, 3/4 cup Parmesan, 1/2 teaspoon salt, and a pinch of nutmeg. Fold in 4 stiffly beaten egg whites, pour the batter into a well-buttered pudding mold, cover the mold tightly, and steam the pudding in a kettle of boiling water, covered, for 40 minutes. The water should reach no more than halfway up the sides of the mold. Add boiling water, if necessary, to keep the same level during the cooking. Unmold the pudding and serve it with cheese sauce.

Cheese Soufflé in Tomatoes   *Käseauflauf in Paradeis*

IN THE TOP of a double boiler, stir together 1/4 cup sifted flour and 1/2 cup heavy cream, stir in 3 egg yolks and 1/4 cup melted butter, and season to taste with salt, pepper, and nutmeg. Cook the mixture over boiling water, stirring constantly, until it is smooth. Take the pan from the heat and add 1 cup grated Parmesan, 1 tablespoon finely chopped parsley, 1 teaspoon onion juice, and 3 egg yolks. Fold in 6 stiffly beaten egg whites and with the mixture fill 8 large tomatoes that have been hollowed out, drained, and seasoned with salt and pepper. Arrange the tomatoes in an ovenproof dish, sprinkle them with grated Parmesan, and add 1/2 cup water and

1 tablespoon butter to the pan. Bake the tomatoes in a moderately hot oven (375° F.) for 10 minutes, increase the heat to 400°, and bake for 15 minutes.

Käsetörtchen auf Spinat   *Cheese Tarts with Spinach*

SIFT 1 CUP flour onto a pastry board, make a well in the center, and add 1/3 cup butter, 3 tablespoons cold water, and 1/2 teaspoon each of sugar and salt. Stir the mixture well and gradually work the flour into the ingredients in the center, to make a smooth dough. Chill the dough for 2 hours, roll it out, and cut 6 rounds with a 4-inch fluted cookie cutter. Arrange the rounds in well-buttered muffin tins and cool them for 1 hour. In the top of a double boiler, combine 1 cup grated Parmesan, 4 eggs, 2 tablespoons flour, and salt, pepper, and nutmeg to taste. Stir the mixture until it is smooth, add 3/4 cup cold milk, and cook it over boiling water, stirring constantly with a whisk, until it is smooth and thick. Fill the pastry shells three-fourths full with the mixture and bake the tarts in a moderately hot oven (375° F.) for 15 minutes. Sprinkle the tarts lightly with paprika and bake them until they are puffed and brown, about 10 minutes more. Arrange the hot tarts around a shallow platter of puréed spinach and garnish the center with a star of quartered hard-cooked eggs.

Kloster-Auflauf   *Convent Pudding*

BREAK 1/2 CUP macaroni into small pieces and cook it in salted water until it is just tender. Drain the macaroni and rinse it in cold water. Scald 1 cup each of milk and cream and pour the liquid over 1 cup dried bread crumbs. Reserve one-third of the crumb mixture and combine the rest with the macaroni, 1 green pepper and 1 pimiento, both finely chopped, 3 well-beaten eggs, 2/3 cup grated Parmesan, 1/4 cup melted butter, 1 tablespoon minced parsley, 1 teaspoon onion juice, and salt to taste. Pour the mixture into a deep ovenproof baking dish and top it with the reserved crumbs. Bake the pudding in a moderate oven (350° F.) for about 1 hour, or until it is done. Serve it with tomato sauce.

Hard-Cooked Eggs   *Hartgekochte Eier*

To HARD-COOK eggs for stuffing, with the yolks set in the centers of the
eggs, start with eggs at room temperature. Bring the water to a rapid boil,
dip a perforated spoon into the water, place an egg on it, lower the egg
slowly into the water, and boil for 12 minutes. Or start the eggs in cold
water, bring the water to a simmer, stirring, and simmer, stirring frequently, for 12 minutes. Place the eggs at once under running cold water
and leave them there until they are cool. Shell the eggs and leave them in
cold water until they are needed.

To make halved eggs stand more securely, cut a thin slice from the
underside of each white. Stuffed eggs can be nested in lettuce leaves,
chopped aspic, chopped parsley, or on a bed of mayonnaise.

Stuffed Eggs   *Gefüllte Eier*

Eggs Stuffed with Red Caviar   *Kaviar Eier*

HALVE 6 HARD-COOKED eggs crosswise. Rice the yolks and add 1 1/2 teaspoons minced onion, 1 1/2 tablespoons red caviar, 2 tablespoons mayonnaise, 1 tablespoon sour cream, and salt, if the caviar is unsalted. Fill the
egg whites with the mixture and cover each little mound with caviar. Pipe
little dots of mayonnaise around the mounds, on the egg whites, if desired.
(Picture, page 114.)

Stuffed Eggs with Shrimps   *Indische Eier*

HALVE 6 HARD-COOKED eggs lengthwise. Rice the yolks and mix them with
4 tablespoons butter, creamed, 4 teaspoons mayonnaise, 2 teaspoons minced
onion, and 1 teaspoon each of curry powder and salt. Stand a cold cooked
shrimp, curve up, in each of the egg whites. Pile the mixture on either
side of each shrimp, leaving half of it exposed, and flank the shrimps
with a few capers on each side.

Eggs Stuffed with Sardines   *Portugiesische Eier*

HALVE 6 HARD-COOKED eggs lengthwise. Mash together 1 small can skinless sardines, drained, with 1 tablespoon brown mustard, 1 teaspoon each
of thick mayonnaise, minced onion, and grated lemon rind, 1/2 teaspoon

lemon juice, and salt and pepper to taste. Add the mashed egg yolks and mix well. Fill the egg whites with the mixture and decorate each egg with a sprig of parsley and half of a thin lemon slice.

Spanische Eier   *Stuffed Eggs with Sliced Olives*

STUFF EGGS as for Russian stuffed eggs and decorate each egg with a slice of olive or almonds. *(Picture, page 114.)*

Norwegische Eier   *Eggs Stuffed with Smoked Salmon*

COOK 6 SMALL eggs for just 10 minutes. Cool them under cold running water and shell them. Cut a slice from the thin side of the white of each egg and carefully scoop out the yolk. Rice the yolks and mix them with 1/4 pound smoked salmon, minced, and enough whipped cream to bind the mixture. Add salt if necessary. Grate the rind of 1/2 lemon over the mixture and fill the eggs. Lay the eggs on a platter on lettuce leaves, with the open sides down, so that they appear to be whole. Grind fresh black pepper over them generously and garnish the platter with capers and slices of lemon.

Or halve 6 hard-cooked eggs lengthwise. Rice the yolks, mix them with the salmon, whipped cream, and lemon rind and stuff the whites. Cut six small rounds of smoked salmon. Lay a round on each stuffed egg and dot the salmon with capers.

Sardelleneier   *Stuffed Eggs with Anchovies*

HALVE 6 HARD-COOKED eggs lengthwise. Rice the yolks and mix them with about 2 tablespoons anchovy paste. Use more or less, depending on the mildness of the paste. Add 2 tablespoons mayonnaise and 1 tablespoon each of butter, creamed, and sour cream. Fill the egg whites with the mixture. Sprinkle the stuffed eggs with chopped cashew nuts or almonds or curl an anchovy filet on each egg and beside it insert slivers of toasted cashews or almonds.

Gefüllte Eier mit Räucherlachs   *Stuffed Eggs with Salmon*

HALVE 6 HARD-COOKED eggs lengthwise. Rice the yolks and combine them with 2 tablespoons mayonnaise, the grated rind of 1/2 lemon, 1 teaspoon lemon juice, 1 tablespoon freshly grated horseradish, 1/2 teaspoon scraped onion, a grating of black pepper, and salt to taste. Use only enough mayonnaise to obtain a stiff paste. Refill the egg whites with the mixture, smoothing it level with the flat of the egg. Arrange the stuffed eggs on a bed of lettuce. Cut smoked salmon, thinly sliced, into small pieces, about 1 1/2 inches square, and form the squares into little cornucopias. Just before serving, fill each little cornucopia with 1/2 teaspoon fresh caviar and lay one on each stuffed egg. Garnish with lemon wedges.

Eggs Stuffed with Goose Liver Pâté — *Gänselebereier*

HALVE 6 HARD-COOKED eggs, crosswise or lengthwise. Rice the yolks and mix them with 4 ounces goose liver pâté or liver paste, 2 teaspoons minced onion, and 1 1/2 tablespoons mayonnaise. Add salt to taste—pâtés differ in mildness. If the pâté contains a truffle, put a thin sliver on each egg, and a tiny tuft of parsley.

Eggs Stuffed with Crab Meat Mimosa — *Mimoseneier*

HALVE 6 HARD-COOKED eggs, crosswise or lengthwise. Rice 3 yolks into 1/2 cup mayonnaise and add 1 teaspoon minced onion, and salt to taste. Blend the mixture until it is smooth and add 1 cup crab meat, cleaned and picked over. Fill the egg whites and rice the remaining yolks over the filling. *(Picture, page 114.)*

Stuffed Eggs with Caviar Stripes — *Gefüllte Eier mit Kaviarstreifen*

HALVE 6 HARD-COOKED eggs lengthwise and rice the yolks. Combine the yolks with 1 tablespoon grated onion, the grated rind of 1/2 lemon, 3 tablespoons mayonnaise, and salt to taste. Add just enough more mayonnaise to make a soft paste. Refill the egg whites loosely with the mixture, smoothing it level with the flat of the egg. Lay two strips of red caviar diagonally across each egg and pipe a strip of the remaining yolk mixture between the two strips of caviar. Serve with lemon wedges.

Russian Stuffed Eggs — *Russische Eier*

HALVE 6 HARD-COOKED eggs, crosswise or lengthwise, and rice the yolks. Combine them with 2 tablespoons mayonnaise, 1 tablespoon brown mustard, 3 tablespoons sweet pickle relish, drained, 1 1/2 teaspoons minced onion, and 1/2 teaspoon each of dry mustard and salt. Mix all together with a fork, correct the seasoning, and fill the whites with the mixture, using the fork so that the stuffing is not smoothed over. Dust the stuffed eggs with paprika and decorate them with capers and parsley.

Gefüllte Eier mit Spargel *Stuffed Eggs with Asparagus*

HALVE 6 HARD-COOKED eggs lengthwise and rice the yolks. Combine the yolks with 2 tablespoons mayonnaise, the grated rind of 1 lemon, salt to taste, and a pinch of dry mustard. Add just enough more mayonnaise to make a thick paste. Refill the egg whites with the mixture, smoothing it level with the flat of the egg. Boil 6 small green asparagus spears in salted water until they are tender but not soft and marinate them in tart French dressing while they are cooling. Drain them well. Lay 1 asparagus spear down the center of each egg and put a little band of red pimiento across the center of the asparagus.

Kreneier *Eggs with Horseradish Cream*

HALVE 6 HARD-COOKED eggs lengthwise, remove the yolks, and fill each half with 1 tablespoon smoked trout purée. Fold 3/4 cup freshly grated

horseradish into 1 cup whipped cream and add the grated rind of 2 lemons and salt to taste. Mound the cream on a platter, sprinkle it with 3 table-spoons chopped chives, and arrange the eggs around it. Rice the egg yolks over the trout.

Garlic Stuffed Eggs   *Eier mit Knoblauch*

HALVE 6 HARD-COOKED eggs crosswise and cut a slice off the ends so that they can stand. Rice the yolks and mix them with 1/4 cup butter, creamed, 2 tablespoons each of mayonnaise and minced chives, 1 tablespoon minced parsley, 2 small garlic cloves, crushed, and salt and pepper to taste. Refill the egg whites and sprinkle the eggs with minced chives.

Cobenzl Eggs   *Cobenzleier*

SIMMER 6 EGGS in water below the boiling point for 15 minutes, without turning them, so that the yolk sets on one side. Peel them and cut a slice from each egg on the side where the white is thinnest. Scoop out the yolks with a small spoon and rice them. Add 1 1/2 tablespoons mayonnaise salted to taste, 1/4 onion, finely minced, and about 1/3 cup liver paste. Mix these to a smooth cream. Add more salt and onion if necessary; the mixture should not be bland. Fill the eggs and lay them in a circle, cut side down, on a bed of shredded lettuce. Lay a small thin slice of tomato on each egg and pipe rosettes of the egg-yolk mixture onto the tomato slices. Sprinkle the rosettes with finely chopped onion. Fill the egg circle with diced aspic that has been tinted pink with tomato paste. Sprinkle the aspic with finely chopped chives.

Cucumber Ring   *Gurkenring*

BLANCH IN BOILING salted water 4 large unpeeled cucumbers, 4 stalks celery, and 1 small onion, all sliced, with 3 sprigs each of parsley and dill. Drain the mixture well and purée it in batches in a food processor or in a blender. In a small bowl let 2 tablespoons unflavored gelatin soften for 10 minutes in 1/2 cup white wine. In a saucepan bring 1 1/2 cups chicken broth to a boil, remove the pan from the heat, and stir the gelatin mixture, stirring. Stir until the gelatin mixture is completely dissolved and add it to the cucumber purée. Pour the mixture into a rinsed 6-cup ring mold and chill the mold for at least 4 hours. Unmold the ring onto a chilled platter lined with lettuce and fill the center of it with crab meat or shrimp salad.

Serve the filled cucumber ring as a light luncheon entrée and accompany it with thinly sliced buttered dark bread.

*A*alsalat   *Eel Salad*

BOIL 1 POUND potatoes in salted water until they are medium soft, peel them, and slice them while they are hot. Sprinkle them with 1/2 cup olive oil and let them cool. Sprinkle the potatoes with salt and pepper only after they are cold and add the grated rind and juice of 1/2 lemon and 1/2 cup heavy sour cream. Turn the potatoes carefully with a wooden spoon and add more lemon juice to taste. Skin 1/2 pound smoked eel, cut it into 1/2-inch chunks, and discard the spine. Mix the eel slices with the potatoes, and add 1/4 cup chopped dill pickle. Serve the salad with thin slices of black bread. The amount of eel in the salad may be increased, if desired.

*G*arnierter *A*al   *Eel and Apple Salad*

DICE 1 APPLE, peeled and cored, 1 dill pickle, drained, and 2 hard-cooked eggs. Bind the mixture with 1/2 cup mayonnaise to which 1 teaspoon chopped dill has been added and add salt and pepper to taste. Mound the salad in the center of a shallow salad bowl and surround it with a border of chopped white-wine aspic and lettuce leaves. Cover the salad with pieces of smoked eel, skinned and boned. Have a pepper mill at table and serve lemon wedges.

*A*al mit *S*pargel   *Eel and Asparagus*

SALT 2 POUNDS hot steamed asparagus lightly. While it is still warm, sprinkle it with 1/2 teaspoon sugar, 1 tablespoon lemon juice, and pepper to taste. Pour over the asparagus 2 tablespoons each of tarragon vinegar and olive oil and marinate it until it is cool. Chill it. Arrange it on a serving platter and cover it with slices of smoked eel, with skin and spine removed.

Combine 1/2 cup tart mayonnaise and 1/2 cup salted whipped cream and add 1 teaspoon finely chopped dill. Just before serving, grate 2 tablespoons fresh horseradish and add it. Serve the sauce separately.

Smoked Eel Platter — *Aalplatte Victoria*

COMBINE 1/2 CUP each of cooked small green peas, cooked cauliflower flowerets, finely diced celery, and beans, cut across diagonally into 1/4-inch pieces to form small diamond shapes. Bind the vegetables with 1/2 cup mayonnaise mixed with the juice and grated rind of 1/2 lemon and 2 tablespoons chopped dill. Chill the salad.

Place a lemon basket in the center of a large platter. Divide the vegetable salad into four parts and arrange it to resemble 4 petals radiating from the lemon. Slice 4 hard-cooked eggs. Use 16 or 20 of the large uniform center slices. Lay 4 or 5 slices in each of the four spaces between the salad sections and place 1/4 to 1/2 teaspoon black capers decoratively on each slice.

Surround the salad "flower" with a ring of smoked-salmon rolls and decorate the rim of the platter with thin lemon slices, sprinkled alternately with minced parsley and paprika. Fill the lemon baskets with sprigs of fresh dill or parsley. Fill any empty spaces on the platter with thin slices of dill pickle. Skin half a smoked eel and cut 2-inch strips of eel away from the bones. Lay the pieces, about 24 in all, across the 4 sections of salad. Serve with a pepper mill and fresh water cress at each end of the platter.

Smoked Salmon Rolls — *Lachsrollen*

COMBINE A 3-OUNCE package cream cheese with 2 tablespoons drained horseradish and spread 4 slices smoked salmon with the cheese. Roll up the salmon slices. The rolls may be cut into 3/4-inch pieces. Insert a small sprig of dill or parsley into each roll and chill them.

Smoked Salmon Cornucopias — *Geräucherte Lachstüten*

A NOTE before an old Viennese recipe says "One may in a dish not recognize that she very much with the hands in contact has come." There follows a recipe for plain smoked salmon slices served with lemon wedges and capers. In a regretful postscript, there is a recipe for rolling up triangles of sliced smoked salmon to form little cornucopias and filling half of these with a mixture of freshly grated horseradish and salted whipped cream and the other half with fresh caviar.

Gefüllte Gurken   *Cucumber Cups with Salmon*

PEEL 3 CUCUMBERS, using a fluted knife, if possible, to leave stripes of green rind. Cut the cucumbers in 3/4-inch slices and hollow out each slice with a round potato cutter, to make little cups. Blanch the cucumber cups for a few seconds in boiling salted water, drain them well, and sprinkle them with 1/4 cup French dressing.

Combine 3/4 cup shredded salmon with 1 hard-cooked egg, riced, the grated zest and juice of half a lemon, and a generous grinding of black pepper. Add salt if necessary. Drain the cucumber cups and fill each with a mound of the ground salmon. At serving time, sprinkle the salmon with freshly grated horseradish and insert in each cup a little sprig of parsley. Makes about 30 cups.

Krabben in der Haube   *Crab Meat under Cheese*

SAUTÉ 1/4 CUP finely chopped onion in 1 tablespoon butter for 1 minute. Dust the onion with 2 tablespoons flour and cook, stirring constantly, for 2 minutes more, but do not let it turn brown. Add 2 cups heavy cream and salt and pepper to taste and cook the mixture until it is reduced to a smooth sauce. Sauté 1 pound crab meat, in chunks, in 2 tablespoons butter until it is golden. Add the crab meat to the cream with the grated rind of 1 lemon, 1/2 teaspoon dry mustard, and 1 teaspoon each of finely chopped chives and parsley, and correct the seasoning. Cook only until the crab meat is heated through. Divide the mixture over small toast rounds sautéed lightly in butter, for individual service, or pour it over a bed of sautéed toast. Fold 2 egg whites, beaten stiff, into 1/2 cup thick mayonnaise mixed with 1/2 cup grated Parmesan and cover the crab meat with the mixture. Dust it lightly with paprika and brown it under the broiler. Watch carefully—the mixture will brown in less than 1 minute. Serve at once, decorated with parsley.

Crayfish or Shrimp Salad $\mathcal{K}$*rebssalat*

BLANCH A medium celery root in boiling water for a minute and peel it. Boil the root in salted water to cover for 1/2 hour or more, until it is just tender. Cut the root into cubes and marinate the cubes for 1/2 hour in a mild vinaigrette sauce. Drain and chill them.

In a kettle combine 3 cups water, 1 cup white wine, 1 onion, sliced, 1 stalk of celery, 1 bay leaf, 1 teaspoon caraway seeds, a sprig of thyme, 1/2 teaspoon pepper, and 1 teaspoon salt. Simmer this court bouillon for 30 minutes. Wash 1 pound crayfish well and remove the intestinal vein at the tail. Boil the crayfish in the court bouillon for about 20 minutes. Remove the meat from the tails and pour 1/4 cup tarragon vinegar over it, tossing the warm meat so that it will absorb the vinegar. Chill the crayfish meat.

Beat together 1 uncooked egg yolk and the yolks of 2 hard-cooked eggs. Add 1 1/2 tablespoons tarragon vinegar, 1 teaspoon each of sugar and salt, 1/2 teaspoon each of Dijon mustard and white pepper, and a pinch of cayenne pepper and beat well. Beat in 1/4 cup olive oil, drop by drop, and 1 egg yolk. Slowly beat in 3/4 cup salad oil, in a steady stream. Add 1 1/2 teaspoons tomato ketchup and 1 teaspoon each of minced fresh chervil, tarragon, and dill. Add more salt and pepper to taste and chill the sauce.

Combine the crayfish meat and celery root and add 1 1/2 cups cubed melon, using cantaloupe or firm-fleshed melon. Arrange the salad on lettuce leaves on individual serving plates. Fold 1/2 cup cream, stiffly whipped, into the sauce and pour about 1/4 cup dressing over each portion.

Shrimps may be substituted for the crayfish. Shell and devein 1 pound shrimps and cook them in boiling salted water with 1/4 teaspoon caraway seeds for about 4 minutes. Drain them, cut them in half, shake them in tarragon vinegar, and chill.

Hummersoufflés Maria   *Individual Lobster Soufflés*

CHOP FINELY the meat of a 2-pound boiled lobster. Reserve any coral.

Melt 1/3 cup butter, stir in 2/3 cup flour, and cook the *roux,* stirring constantly, until it starts to turn golden. Gradually add 1 cup warm milk and simmer the mixture for 10 minutes. Stir the sauce and add the lobster coral, if there is any. Add 1/2 teaspoon minced shallot, salt and pepper to taste, and a pinch of cayenne. Take the sauce from the heat, cool it slightly, beat in 3 egg yolks, and add the chopped lobster meat. Add 3 truffles, poached in Madeira, peeled, and chopped, and 2 ounces brandy. Beat 5 egg whites stiff and add 3 tablespoons whipped cream. Fold the egg whites into the lobster mixture. Fill 6 individual buttered soufflé molds and set them in a shallow pan of water. Bake the soufflés in a moderately hot oven (375° F.) for 15 to 20 minutes, or until they are puffed and golden. Serve at once.

Helgoländer Hummersalat   *Lobster Salad Heligoland*

BOIL TWO 2 1/2-pound lobsters in a generous amount of salted water for about 15 minutes. Let the lobsters cool in the cooking liquid and remove the meat and coral. Combine 4 cups diced lobster meat, including the coral, with 2 cups cold boiled diced potatoes, 2 cups cooked diced artichoke bottoms, and 1 cup finely chopped dill pickle. The potatoes should be firm and rather crisp.

Sprinkle the salad with a dressing made by combining 1/4 cup white wine, 6 tablespoons olive oil, 3 tablespoons vinegar, 1 teaspoon salt, and 1/4 teaspoon white pepper. Stir the salad gently and chill it for 1 hour.

Combine 1 1/2 cups mayonnaise with 1/4 cup tarragon, finely chopped, 2 tablespoons ketchup, and 1/2 teaspoon each of dry mustard and salt. Drain the salad and bind it with the mayonnaise.

Mound the lobster salad in a high pyramid on a serving platter and sprinkle it generously with finely chopped truffles. Decorate the top with 4 cold boiled crayfish, arranged vertically, or with a ring of cold shrimps, and surround the salad with cucumbers filled with horseradish cream. Serves 12.

Cucumber Cups with Horseradish Cream   *Gurken mit Kren*

STRIPE 6 UNIFORM cucumbers lengthwise, using a fluted knife to make clear dark and light green bands, cut the cucumbers crosswise into uniform 2-inch lengths, and hollow out the pieces with a melon ball cutter, to make little cups. Combine 1 cup heavy cream, whipped, 1/2 cup finely grated fresh horseradish, 1/4 cup blanched ground almonds, and salt to taste. Salt the cucumber cups and mound them high with the horseradish cream. Serve at once. The horseradish darkens the cream.

Fried Oysters and Coleslaw   *Austern mit Krautsalat*

CUT OFF the top of a large white cabbage, to make a "lid," and hollow out the cabbage, leaving a thin shell. Chop the leaves that were removed very fine and combine them with 1 cup mayonnaise, 1 small onion, chopped fine, 2 tablespoons chopped gherkins, 2 tablespoons small capers, 1 tablespoon mustard, and salt and pepper to taste. Stuff the hollow cabbage with the salad and chill it.

Drain 1 pint oysters well and pat them dry. Dip the oysters first into 1/2 cup flour mixed with 1/2 teaspoon salt, then in 1 egg beaten with 1/4 cup milk and a little pepper, then in 2/3 cup dry bread crumbs. Fry them in deep hot fat (375° F.) for 1 minute and drain them well. Arrange the hot oysters around the cold cabbage and serve immediately.

Oysters with Herb Butter   *Austern mit Kräuterbutter*

MIX 1/3 CUP soft butter with 1 tablespoon each of minced parsley, chervil, and chives, 1 finely minced shallot, and 1/4 teaspoon salt. Form the butter into a short thick roll, wrap it in wax paper, and chill it.

Allow 3 to 4 oysters per person. Shuck the oysters and wash and dry the deep shells. Spread these with soft butter, lay an oyster in each, and cover it with a thick layer of dried bread crumbs and freshly grated Swiss cheese combined in equal amounts. Add a pinch of cayenne to each oyster and salt to taste. Sprinkle the oysters with lemon juice, lay a very thin slice of the cold herb butter on each, and cook them under the broiler until the butter has melted and the crumbs are browned. Serve at once.

Austern nach Tartaren Art   *Oysters with Herbs*

POACH 2 DOZEN oysters for 1 minute in lightly salted simmering water and drain them. Wash and dry the deep shells and lay 1 drained oyster in each half shell. Sprinkle with salt and pepper to taste. Combine 4 shallots, finely chopped, 1/4 cup each of chopped capers, finely chopped dill pickle, and caviar, and 1 teaspoon each of parsley, chervil, tarragon, and chives, all finely minced. Cover each oyster with 2 teaspoons of this mixture. Pipe 1 small rosette of lemon mayonnaise onto each oyster and serve chilled, with rye-bread rounds lightly sautéed in butter.

Austern mit Estragon   *Oysters with Tarragon*

POACH 2 DOZEN oysters in their own juice for 3 minutes, or until the edges curl. Drain the oysters and trim them. Wash and dry the deep shells. Mince 6 sprigs of tarragon, 4 sprigs of parsley, 2 sprigs of rosemary and 1 sprig of orégano and add 3 shallots, very finely chopped, the grated rind of 1 lemon, and salt to taste. Divide the herb mixture among the 24 oyster shells. Return the oysters to the shells and decorate each oyster with 2 crossed tarragon leaves dipped in cool but still liquid tarragon aspic to make them adhere. Chill the oysters for 15 minutes. Pour tarragon aspic over each oyster and chill them.

Kamm-Muscheln in Senfsauce   *Scallops in Mustard Sauce*

SIMMER 1 1/2 CUPS small bay scallops in salted water until they are opaque and tender, about 5 minutes, and drain them well. As soon as they are cool, sprinkle them with the juice of 1/2 lemon and 1 tablespoon tarragon vinegar and place them in the refrigerator. Turn them a few times and let them marinate at least 1 hour.

Whip 3/4 cup cream with 1/2 teaspoon salt until it is half whipped. Stir in good brown mustard, Düsseldorf or Dijon, to taste and add 1/2 cup finely diced celery root, which has been peeled, cooked, and chilled. Correct the seasoning and add the scallops and the grated rind of 2 lemons and additional lemon juice to taste. Sprinkle with chopped parsley and decorate with lemon wedges.

Marinated Shrimp Cocktail  *Inselkrebse*

MARINATE 2 POUNDS shelled cooked shrimps in 3/4 cup vodka or gin for 1 hour, turning them several times. Drain them well. Combine 2/3 cup thick mayonnaise, 1/3 cup whipped cream, and 2 tablespoons lemon juice and add 2 tablespoons tomato ketchup, 1 teaspoon Worcestershire sauce, the grated rind of 1 lemon, and salt and pepper to taste. Pour the sauce over the drained shrimps and chill them. Serve in individual iced glasses, lined with lettuce leaves.

Shrimps Flambé *Krebse Flambé*

SHELL AND devein 2 pounds shrimps, without removing the tails. Sauté the shrimps in 1/2 cup salt butter, until they turn pink and most of the butter is absorbed, about 5 minutes. Add salt and pepper to taste. Add 1 cup warm rum, light it, and let it burn until the flame dies down. Serve the shrimps at once with cocktail picks. Or serve them in a parsley rice ring, as a *Vorspeise*. In this case, remove the tails when the shrimps are shelled.

Shrimps Sigurd  *Krebse Sigurd*

SHELL AND devein 1 pound shrimps and cook them for 4 minutes in salted water to which 1/2 teaspoon caraway seeds has been added. Drain them well and place them in a bowl. Sprinkle 1/4 cup tarragon vinegar over the shrimps while they are warm and turn them several times while they are cooling. Combine 1 large minced onion, 1/4 cup minced parsley, the grated rind of 1 lemon, and the juice of 1/2 lemon. Pour the mixture over the cool shrimps, stir them, and chill them.

Clean 1 pound mushrooms, but do not wash them unless it is necessary.

Cut the stems off even with the caps and slice the caps across as thinly as possible. Slice the good part of the stems across and discard the woody ends. Lay the sliced mushrooms in a wide bowl and pour over them 1/2 cup each of tarragon vinegar and olive oil seasoned with 1 teaspoon salt and 1 crushed garlic clove. Marinate the mushrooms at room temperature, turning them frequently with a wooden spoon, until they turn dark.

Cut 3 hard-cooked eggs into quarters and sprinkle the eggs with 2 tablespoons each of tarragon vinegar and olive oil. Grind black pepper over the eggs and let them marinate. When ready to serve, toss the shrimps and mushrooms together until they are well mixed and add the eggs and 1/2 cup mayonnaise to which 1/4 cup each of minced parsley and chives have been added. Stir the mixture carefully so that the eggs do not break and serve it chilled, as an hors-d'oeuvre or salad.

Verlorene Eier Farneser Art

*Poached Eggs in
Chicken Liver Rings*

SAUTÉ 6 CHICKEN livers in butter with 2 tablespoons chopped onion until they are brown, add salt and pepper to taste, and let them cool. Sauté 6 mushrooms, chopped, in butter with 2 tablespoons chopped onion until they are lightly browned and let them cool. Put the cool livers, onions, and mushrooms through the food chopper with 1 slice stale white bread and bind the mixture with 2 tablespoons butter that has been creamed with 1 egg yolk. Season the mixture to taste with salt, pepper, and a little cayenne and chill it for at least 2 hours. Stir the cold mixture and add an egg yolk, if necessary, to make it pliable. Fill a pastry bag, fitted with a large fluted tube, and pipe 6 rings of the mixture onto a buttered baking sheet. Bake them in a slow oven (300° F.) for 5 to 10 minutes, or until they are hot, but have not begun to run. With a spatula lift them onto a serving platter and lay 1 hot poached egg, drained and trimmed, in each ring. Coat 3 of the eggs with béarnaise sauce and 3 with tomato sauce.

Poached Eggs with Chicken Livers   *Verlorene Eier Erzbischof*

SAUTÉ 6 CHICKEN livers in butter with 2 tablespoons chopped onion until they are brown. Crush them with a fork and add 2 tablespoons Sherry and salt to taste. Divide the liver mixture among 6 hot puff-paste shells and sprinkle it with 2 tomatoes, peeled, seeded, and diced. Lay 1 hot poached egg, drained and trimmed, in each shell. Serve with béarnaise sauce or mask each egg with 2 tablespoons of the sauce and decorate with a truffle slice.

Chicken Liver Ragout   *Hühnerleberragout*

CUT 1/4 POUND calf's liver into slivers and sauté them in 1/2 cup butter with 14 whole chicken livers, 6 chicken hearts, chopped, and 12 small ham wedges. Sauté the meat only long enough to brown the livers, but leave them pink inside. Sprinkle the meat with 1/2 cup chopped parsley and salt to taste, take it from the heat, and add 1/2 cup button mushrooms, cooked in butter, and 3/4 cup each of cauliflower flowerets and green peas, both cooked in salted water and drained. Add browned butter, if necessary, and serve the mixture in a ring of buttered noodles.

Small Chicken Pancakes   *Kleine Hühnerpfannkuchen Julia*

BEAT 1 EGG into 1 cup milk and beat in 1/2 cup flour and 1/4 teaspoon salt. Bake the pancakes on a lightly buttered Swedish pancake pan, called a *plättar* pan, which has seven 3-inch depressions. Turn the pancakes once. Makes twenty-four 3-inch pancakes.

Soak 2 cooked breasts of chicken overnight in 1 cup Sherry, drain them, and mince them. Sauté 6 mushrooms, finely chopped, in 2 tablespoons butter for 5 minutes, add the minced chicken, and cook the mixture for 3 minutes. Dust it with 1 tablespoon flour, and add salt and pepper to taste. Cook the mixture, stirring, until it is a creamy paste. Pour off any butter that the flour does not absorb. Spread 1 tablespoon of the filling on each 3-inch pancake. Roll up the pancakes. Lay 4 in each of 6 individual baking dishes. Pour 4 tablespoons sauce around each serving of pancakes, sprinkle each with 1 teaspoon grated Parmesan, and brown the pancakes in a hot oven (400° F.).

To make the sauce, melt 3 tablespoons butter, blend in 3 tablespoons flour, and gradually add 1 1/4 cups strained chicken stock and salt and pepper to taste. Simmer the sauce for 15 minutes. Stir in 4 tablespoons Sherry, or to taste. You may brown the pancakes and serve the sauce separately.

Kartoffelpfannkuchen   *Small Potato Pancakes*

IN A FOOD processor blend 1 1/3 cups tightly packed riced cooked potatoes, 2 eggs, 1 egg white, and 3 tablespoons *crème fraîche* or heavy cream. Add 2 tablespoons flour mixed with 1/2 teaspoon each of double-acting baking powder and salt. Add 1/2 cup hot milk and process for a few seconds until the batter is smooth.

Heat a griddle or wide skillet over medium heat until a drop of water sizzles on its surface, brush it lightly with butter, and drop small rounds of the batter, about 1 1/8 inches in diameter, onto the griddle. Turn the pancakes with a spatula as soon as bubbles show on their surface. Brown the second side for less than a minute and transfer the pancakes to a sheet of wax paper. There will be about 120 pancakes. Reheat the pancakes in the top of a double boiler over simmering water.

Melt 1 cup butter, stir in 1 large onion, minced, and 1/2 cup tightly packed chopped parsley, and salt to taste. Heat the sauce until it is hot but not sizzling and serve it with the pancakes.

The pancakes can be frozen and reheated in the top of a double boiler, covered, over simmering water or wrap them in foil and heat them in a slow oven (300° F.).

Serve the pancakes as an accompaniment to roast or broiled meats or with poultry or game dishes. The pancakes can also be served as a light luncheon dish, with a tossed green salad.

Goose Liver "Porcupines" with Apples **Gänseleber Igel mit Äpfeln**

CHILL 12 OUNCES *pâté de foie gras* with truffles. Brown 1/2 cup slivered almonds with about 2 teaspoons salted butter in a very slow oven (200° F.), shaking them frequently. Sprinkle them with 1/4 teaspoon salt and drain them on absorbent paper. Remove both ends of the *foie gras* can and push out the pâté. Slice it 1/2 inch thick with a hot knife and stick the slices with the slivered almonds. Peel apples and slice them 1/2 inch thick. Use only the 4 or 5 center slices. Trim the slices into even rounds with a cookie cutter and cut out the core. Sauté the apple slices gently in butter until they are golden and just tender. Apples differ in consistency and some cook much faster than others. Transfer the hot apple slices with a spatula to a hot serving platter and lay a slice of goose liver on each. Serve the "porcupines" at once with dry Sherry.

Herring in Sour Cream **Herringe in Sahne**

DIVIDE 6 MATJES herring filets, cut into diagonal pieces, among 6 individual casseroles or crocks. Add 1 tart apple, peeled, quartered, and sliced, to each portion and 1/2 medium onion, sliced and divided into rings. Depending on the size of the casseroles, whip 2 cups of sour cream with 1/4 cup heavy cream until smooth and pour the cream over the herring, apple, and onion combinations. Top each casserole with 3 slices of dill pickle, a wedge of tomato, a slice of hard-boiled egg, and a large sprig of dill. Chill the casseroles, covered, until ready to serve and serve them with hot peeled steamed potatoes and thickly sliced buttered pumpernickel bread. Accompany the herring with cold beer. *(Picture, page 115.)*

Small Ham Croquettes **Kleine Krusteln von Schinken**

COMBINE 1/2 CUP each of ham and cooked artichoke bottoms, both finely diced, and 3/4 cup finely diced mushrooms and add just enough thick béchamel sauce to bind the mixture. Season it to taste with salt and pepper. Chill it and shape it into small croquettes, using about 2 tablespoonfuls for each. Roll the croquettes in fine bread crumbs, dip them in 2 eggs beaten with 2 tablespoons milk, roll them again in bread crumbs, and fry them in deep hot fat (375° F.) until they are brown, about 5 minutes. Serve them with hot onion sauce or with cold shallot mayonnaise.

Schinkenroulade   *Ham Roll*

HEAT A BAKING sheet in a hot oven (400° F.).

Beat 5 egg whites stiff, add 1/2 teaspoon salt and 1/4 teaspoon sugar, and continue to beat until the whites are very stiff. Sprinkle 1 1/2 teaspoons finely minced parsley over the egg whites. Beat 4 egg yolks light and creamy and fold them gently into the whites. Sprinkle 1/2 cup flour over the mixture, a little at a time, and fold it in gently until it is incorporated. With a spatula, spread the batter 1/2 inch thick, in a rectangle about 11 by 15 inches, on a piece of wax paper. Sprinkle the batter with 1 tablespoon grated Parmesan. Lay the hot baking sheet beside the wax paper, slip the paper onto the sheet, and return it to the oven. Bake the batter for 8 to 10 minutes, or until it is golden and the sponge roll comes away from the wax paper easily. Invert the sponge roll on a towel sprinkled with flour. Carefully peel off the wax paper, roll up the sponge roll in the towel,

and let it cool. Put 1/2 pound ham through the food chopper and combine it thoroughly with 1/2 cup creamed butter, 1 teaspoon prepared brown mustard, 1/2 teaspoon dry mustard, salt and pepper to taste, and 1/2 cup thick white sauce. Add 2 shallots, finely minced, 1 tablespoon Port, 2 tablespoons brandy, and 2 1/2 ounces liver paste. Correct the seasoning with salt. Unroll the cooled sponge roll and spread it evenly with the ham filling. Roll it up, wrap it in wax paper, and chill it. At serving time, trim the ends of the roll, lay it on a platter, and spread it with a mixture of one 3-ounce package of cream cheese, 2 teaspoons anchovy paste, and 2 tablespoons sour cream. Sprinkle the roll with a hard-cooked egg, riced, and decorate the platter with parsley. Serve the roll in 1/2-inch slices.

Cold Meat Platter — *Feiner kalter Aufschnitt*

CUT 6 VERY thin slices each of Prague ham, smoked tongue, roast veal, and roast pork and arrange them on a very large flat platter. On these arrange 6 slices of rare filet of beef, 6 paper-thin slices each of Italian salami and Bologna or *mortadella* sausage, and 6 slices of *Sülze,* cut 1/2 inch thick. Dot each slice of *Sülze* with 1 teaspoon minced onion. In the center of the platter pile shaved curls of fresh horseradish and surround the horseradish with finely cut radish roses.

Chop finely 3 hard-cooked eggs and bind them with mayonnaise mixed with a little brown mustard. Cut 6 paper-thin slices of Westphalian ham, roll the slices into cornucopias and, with a teaspoon, fill them with the egg salad. Arrange the cornucopias around the radish ring alternately with 6 rosettes of cold butter. Combine butter and cream cheese in equal amounts, flavor with anchovy paste to taste, and pipe the mixture around the platter. Set into this border slices of dill pickle and sweet gherkins. If desired, arrange on the meat 6 small mounds of jellied meat aspic, diced. Accompany the platter with a basket of pumpernickel, rye bread, and other dark breads, sliced.

Jellied Pigs' Knuckles — *Sülze*

PUT 4 TO 6 well-washed pigs' knuckles in a large kettle with 6 cups water. Add 2 teaspoons salt, 1 onion, 8 peppercorns, 1/2 bay leaf, 2 sprigs of thyme, 2 cloves of garlic, and 1/2 cup vinegar. Simmer the knuckles, uncovered, for about 2 hours, adding more water if it boils away to less than half the original quantity. The knuckles are done when the bones pull out of the meat easily. Take the knuckles from the broth and cut the meat into strips or cubes. Sprinkle the meat with 2 tablespoons chopped parsley and with freshly ground pepper. Strain the broth, simmer it 1/2 hour longer, and let it cool. Skim off all the fat, return the meat to the broth, and simmer it for 15 minutes. Correct the seasoning and add a pinch of sugar. Soften 1 envelope of gelatin in 1/4 cup water, remove the broth from the heat, and dissolve the gelatin in it.

Spoon the meat into an enamel bread pan, arrange on it 1/2 cup each of chopped dill pickle and diced tongue, 3 whole hard-cooked eggs, and 1 tablespoon capers, and pour in the broth. Chill the *Sülze* until it is set, unmold it, and serve it thinly sliced. Top each slice with a little finely chopped onion and pass vinegar separately or serve vinaigrette sauce.

Krapferln mit Sardellenbutter
Profiteroles with Anchovy Butter

MAKE *pâte à choux*—cream-puff paste *(page 329)*—and cool the paste. Shape it into rounds the size of walnuts and bake them on a buttered baking sheet in a hot oven (450° F.) for 12 to 15 minutes, until they are puffed. Reduce the heat to moderate (350° F.) and bake the puffs for about 10 minutes longer, or until they are golden. Let the puffs cool. Slit them at the bottom and fill them with anchovy paste beaten with cream cheese and finely chopped stuffed olives.

Toska-Törtchen
Chicken and Cheese Soufflé Tarts

BAKE TART shells using the dough for *Toska Törtchen*. Fill each hot shell with 2 tablespoons chicken hash, sprinkle the hash with chopped pimientos, and cover with the mixture for cheese soufflé I, using half the recipe. Pile the soufflé mixture high on the tarts and bake them in a moderately hot oven (375° F.) for 10 minutes, or until they are puffed and brown.

Dough for Toska-Törtchen

CUT 2/3 CUP butter into 2 1/4 cups flour until it is evenly distributed. Make a well in the center of the flour and put in 2 egg yolks and 2 ounces

Cognac. Stir the ingredients with salt to taste until they are roughly mixed and sprinkle over the mixture enough cold white wine, about 3 tablespoons, so that it can be worked into a smooth dough. Roll out the dough 3/16 inch thick and line very small buttered timbale or muffin tins or little boat-shaped molds. Prick the dough with a fork and fill the shells with cherry pits (the Viennese always find a use for everything) or dried peas. Bake the tart shells in a moderately hot oven (375° F.) until they are light brown and loosen easily from the tins, about 15 minutes. Cool them carefully. Store the tart shells in a cool dry place. Yield 30 to 35 shells.

If the shells are to be baked again after they are filled, it is important to take them from the oven when they are very pale and not to unmold them but to leave them in the tins and fill them at once.

Pastry-Boat Dough   *Schiffchen*

KNEAD A GENEROUS 1/2 cup butter in ice water until it has the consistency of soft dough and is free of lumps. Squeeze the washed butter to extract any pockets of water and chill it in the refrigerator until it is firm.

Sift 2 cups flour onto a pastry board, make a well in the center, and into it put the butter, 3 tablespoons cold water, the grated rind of 1/2 lemon, and a pinch of salt. Work the ingredients into a rough dough, sprinkle over it 1 more tablespoon cold water, and continue to work it until it is smooth. Let the dough rest at least 1 hour. Roll out the dough 1/6 inch thick and cut it into rounds to fill small buttered tart molds or ovals to fill boat-shaped molds. Trim the edges. Fill the shells with dried beans or raw rice and bake them in a moderately hot oven (375° F.) for 15 minutes, or until they are golden and lift easily from the molds.

Curry Boats   *Indische Schiffchen*

COMBINE 3 COOKED artichoke bottoms, chopped, and 1/2 cup each of cold cooked rice, tiny melon balls, and curry mayonnaise. Fill baked *Schiffchen*.

Onion and Red Caviar Boats   *Russische Schiffchen*

LIGHTLY MIX equal quantities riced egg white, riced egg yolk, tiny pearl onions, and caviar. Bind the mixture with lemon mayonnaise. Fill baked *Schiffchen* and sprinkle them with grated lemon rind.

Schiffchen Gräfin Landi   *Pastry Boats with Onion Soufflé*

BAKE LITTLE boat-shaped pastry shells, using puff pastry or the dough for
Toska Törtchen. Fill the shells with a mixture of half liver paste and half
minced ham. Pile high onto the little tarts the mixture for onion soufflé—
using half the amount of the recipe. Dust the *Schiffchen* lightly with
paprika and bake them in a moderately hot oven (375° F.) for about
8 minutes, or until the soufflés are puffed and brown.

Schiffchen Admirals Art   *Pastry Boats with Shrimps*

BAKE LITTLE boat-shaped pastry shells, using puff pastry or the dough
for *Toska Törtchen,* each large enough to hold 1 shrimp. Lay 1 cooked
shrimp in each baked shell and cover it with 1/2 teaspoon each of capers,
onions, and parsley, all finely chopped. Pile high onto the little tarts any
mixture for shrimp soufflé. Make only a small amount of the mixture. Bake
the *Schiffchen* in a moderately hot oven (375° F.) for about 8 minutes,
or until the soufflés are puffed and brown.

Baumgartenkastanien   *Artichokes with Chestnut Purée*

PEEL 24 LARGE chestnuts. Poach the chestnuts in beef stock to cover
for 15 minutes, or until they are soft, with 1 small onion, sliced, 1 stalk of
celery, chopped, and a *bouquet garni.* Drain the hot chestnuts thoroughly
and rub them through a sieve, with the onion and celery, into a small
saucepan. Add 2 tablespoons melted butter. Cook the chestnuts over low
heat, stirring, for a minute and add salt and pepper to taste.

Brown 2 tablespoons butter, stir in 3 tablespoons flour, and cook the
roux, stirring, until it is golden. Add the stock in which the chestnuts cooked
and more stock, if necessary, to make 1 cup in all. Bring the sauce to a
boil, stirring, and simmer it for 10 minutes. Strain the sauce and add just
enough of it to the puréed chestnuts to make a paste that can be piped
without spreading. Simmer the chestnut paste, stirring constantly, for 3
minutes.

Remove the chokes and center leaves of 6 freshly cooked artichoke
bottoms whose leaves have been cut down to 1 inch. With a pastry bag,
pipe the chestnut paste in a spiral onto each artichoke and pour over the

artichokes a little melted meat glaze. Bake them in a moderately hot oven (375° F.) for 5 minutes. Serve with brown sauce made with Sherry.

Artichoke Bottoms with Egg Salad   *Gefüllte Artischockenboden*

FILL COLD cooked artichoke bottoms with chopped hard-cooked eggs bound with lemon mayonnaise. Sprinkle with capers.

Filled Artichoke Leaves   *Gefüllte Artischockenblätter*

REMOVE THE leaves of 2 cooked artichokes and reserve the best large leaves. Remove the chokes, trim off any stem, and mash the 2 artichoke bottoms with 2 tablespoons tarragon vinegar and 1 tablespoon olive oil. Add 1 hard-cooked egg, riced, 1 tablespoon chopped capers, and salt and pepper to taste. Chill the mixture and cut each reserved artichoke leaf off squarely, 2 inches from the base. Lay 1 tablespoon of the chilled mixture on the base of each leaf and sprinkle with chopped parsley. Arrange the filled leaves in a circle on a round platter. Serve very cold.

43

Artischockenboden mit Krebsen   *Artichoke Bottoms with Shrimps*

PEEL AND devein 12 shrimps, boil them in salted water for 4 minutes, drain them and sprinkle them with 1/4 cup tarragon vinegar while they are hot. Let them cool and chill them. Lay the shrimps on 12 chilled artichoke bottoms. Combine 1 finely riced hard-cooked egg and 1 tablespoon each of onion and capers, both minced, and bind the mixture with just enough mayonnaise to hold it. Fill the artichoke bottoms with this mixture. Spread shrimps and filling with thick mayonnaise, about 1 cup in all, to which the finely grated rind of 1 lemon has been added and top each artichoke with 1/2 teaspoon black caviar.

Sprinkle the mayonnaise with 3 peeled and chopped truffles, if preferred. The capers should then be omitted.

Gebackener Spargel   *Deep-Fried Asparagus*

WASH AND trim thick green asparagus spears and cut them 4 inches long. Tie the spears together and set them upright in a deep saucepan in 1 inch of boiling water. Cover the saucepan and steam the asparagus for 10 minutes. Take it from the water, dry it well, and let it cool to lukewarm. Roll the spears in flour, dip them in 2 eggs beaten with 1/2 teaspoon salt, and roll them in 1 cup dry bread crumbs mixed with 2 tablespoons grated Parmesan.

Lower the breaded spears carefully into deep hot fat (375° F.), fry them until they are uniformly brown, and drain them. Fry only 6 or 8 at a time and keep the cooked spears hot in a slow oven (300° F.).

Make a thick hollandaise sauce of 2 egg yolks and 2/3 cup butter and the juice and grated rind of 1/2 lemon. Add salt and pepper to taste and 1/4 cup each of parsley and ham, both finely chopped. Serve at once, with the hot fried asparagus spears.

Kernweiche Eierspargelring   *Asparagus Ring with Eggs Mollet*

CHOP ENOUGH asparagus, the tender green part only, to make 3 cups. Bring 3 cups water to a boil, add 1/2 teaspoon each of salt and sugar, and drop in the asparagus. Let the water return to a boil, reduce the heat, and simmer the asparagus until it is soft, about 15 minutes. Press the asparagus through a sieve or purée it in a blender. Reduce the water in which it boiled by half.

Cream 5 tablespoons butter and gradually add 4 egg yolks, 4 tablespoons grated Parmesan, 1/2 cup flour, and the juice of 1/2 lemon. Add 4 tablespoons cream, 4 tablespoons of the asparagus water, and the puréed asparagus. Season the mixture with salt and pepper to taste and a pinch of paprika and fold in 4 stiffly beaten egg whites. Pour the mixture into a well-buttered ring mold, cover it securely, and steam it for 1 hour in a covered kettle in boiling water reaching halfway up the sides of the mold. Replace the water in the kettle with more boiling water as it evaporates, to keep the level constant.

Cook 8 to 10 very fresh eggs in simmering water for 4 minutes and plunge them immediately into a bowl of cold water. Peel them carefully under the cold water and return them to warm water until they are needed. As they should not overboil, nor stay in the cold water too long, it is best to cook only a few at one time.

Unmold the asparagus ring onto a large round platter and fill the center with the eggs. Sprinkle them with 6 slices tongue cut into fine julienne. Surround the ring with tart shells mounded high with thick hollandaise sauce dusted with finely minced truffles.

Asparagus with Horseradish Mayonnaise   *Spargel mit Kren Mayonnersauce*

ARRANGE 2 POUNDS cold steamed asparagus, well drained, on a serving plate with 2 strips of pimiento laid across it to simulate the red tapes with which asparagus is usually tied into bunches. Surround the asparagus with 1 cup diced aspic and garnish it with parsley. Serve it with horseradish mayonnaise.

Ham and Asparagus   *Schinkenspargel*

CREAM 4 TABLESPOONS butter and with it just barely bind 1/2 pound Westphalian ham, sliced and cut into 1/4-inch squares. Pile the mixture high on six 3-inch rounds of white bread that have been toasted and buttered. You may also use Italian *prosciutto*. In that case, do not mix ham and butter but spread 1 tablespoon creamed butter on each toast round, mounding it towards the center. Dip the buttered side of the rounds into the chopped *prosciutto*. It will cling in a light mound to the butter.

Arrange 2 pounds hot steamed asparagus on a serving platter and surround it with the ham rounds. Sauté 1 1/2 cups dry bread crumbs in 1/4 pound butter until they are golden and pour the brown crumbs over the asparagus stalks. Sprinkle the grated rind of 1 orange over the crumbs and serve. Pass more brown butter in a sauceboat.

Spargel auf Malteser Art   *Asparagus Maltese*

ARRANGE 2 POUNDS hot steamed asparagus on a serving platter. Fill half orange shells with Maltese sauce, sprinkle the sauce with chopped toasted hazelnuts, and arrange the shells around the asparagus.

Spargelrollen   *Asparagus Pastry Roll*

SIFT 4 CUPS flour onto a pastry board, make a well in the center, and into it put 1 teaspoon salt, 1/4 teaspoon sugar, 1 egg, and 1 1/4 cups softened butter. Stir the ingredients in the center and incorporate enough flour to make a dough that can be worked with the hands. Gradually add 1/2 cup ice water and continue to work the dough until it is smooth. Chill the dough in the refrigerator. Cook about 20 stalks of asparagus in salted water to cover for about 8 minutes, or until it is nearly tender. Do not overcook the asparagus, as it will be baked later. Drain and cool the asparagus completely. Cut off the asparagus stalks 3 or 4 inches from the tips, discarding the stalk bottoms.

Divide the dough into 4 parts. On a floured pastry board roll one part of the dough into a strip 1/4 inch thick and about 4 by 16 inches. Sprinkle the rolled dough with 1 tablespoon grated Parmesan and 1/4 teaspoon salt. Lay 4 or 5 asparagus spears end to end along one long edge of the strip, roll up the dough lengthwise, and trim all surplus dough from the ends of the roll. Paint the seam of the finished roll with egg white and press the dough together to seal it. Lay the roll on a buttered baking sheet, seam-side down. Prick the roll with a fork, paint it generously with 1 egg yolk beaten with 1 teaspoon water, and sprinkle it generously with grated Parmesan. Make similar rolls with the rest of the dough and asparagus. Bake the rolls in a moderate oven (350° F.) for 20 minutes, or until they are brown. Serve at once, cutting a 4-inch piece for each serving.

Asparagus Salad *Spargelvorspeise*

CHILL 18 STEAMED asparagus spears, and cut them into 1/2-inch lengths. Use only the tender green part of the asparagus and add more stalks if less than 5 inches of the asparagus are usable. Combine the asparagus with 1 cup diced ham, 1/2 cup cold cooked rice, and 1 cup diced fresh pineapple. Add salt and pepper to taste and bind the salad with 3/4 cup thick mayonnaise to which 1 teaspoon lemon juice, the grated rind of 1/2 lemon, and 1 teaspoon brandy have been added. Mound the salad on a bed of Boston lettuce and sprinkle it with 3 tablespoons slivered orange rind and 1/4 cup chopped parsley.

Salmon and Asparagus *Lachsspargel*

CHOP 6 SLICES smoked salmon. Toast six 3-inch rounds of white bread and spread 1 tablespoon creamed butter on each round. Mound the chopped salmon on the buttered rounds.

Arrange 2 pounds hot steamed asparagus on a serving platter and surround it with the salmon rounds. Sauté 1 1/2 cups dry bread crumbs in 1/4 pound butter until they are golden and pour the brown crumbs over the asparagus heads. Quickly grate the rind of 1 lemon over the crumbs and serve. Pass more brown butter in a sauceboat.

Broccoli Roll *Spargelkohlroulade*

IN A SAUCEPAN melt 1/2 cup butter, add 1 small onion, chopped, and stir it over low heat until the onion is transparent. Add 3/4 cup flour and stir until the flour is golden. Remove the saucepan from the heat and add 1 cup warm milk, stirring until the mixture is smooth. Return the pan to the stove and simmer the sauce, stirring constantly, until it thickens. Cool the sauce for 5 minutes and beat in 4 egg yolks. Add 1 1/2 cups puréed cooked broccoli and salt and pepper to taste. Fold in 4 stiffly beaten egg whites and 1/2 cup grated Parmesan.

Butter a jelly-roll pan, add 1/2 cup bread crumbs, and shake the pan so that the crumbs adhere evenly. Pour the broccoli mixture into the pan and spread it to a 1/2-inch depth.

Bake the broccoli roll in a moderate oven (350° F.) for 12 minutes, or until it starts to shrink from the sides of the pan. Spread it with the following light ham filling: Mix 1 pound cooked ham, finely ground, with 3 egg yolks, 1 cup heavy sour cream, 1/4 cup chopped pistachio nuts, and salt to taste. If the mixture is too thick to spread, add more sour cream. Roll it up immediately, return the broccoli roll to a slow oven (300° F.) for 5 minutes, and slice it. Serves 12.

Blumenkohlpudding   *Cauliflower Pudding*

CREAM 2/3 cup butter with 4 egg yolks and 1/2 teaspoon salt. Add 4 slices white bread, free of crust, and soaked in 1/3 cup cream or milk, and 5 stiffly beaten egg whites. Spread a pudding mold with 1 1/2 tablespoons butter and coat it with 3 tablespoons dry bread crumbs. Arrange the separated flowerets of 1 large cooked cauliflower in the mold and spread the egg mixture over them. Cover the mold and set it in a kettle of boiling water. The water should reach halfway up the mold. Steam the pudding for 1 hour. Unmold it and sprinkle it with browned bread crumbs. Serve it with brown butter mixed with chopped parsley.

Mushrooms with Eggs   *Schwämme mit Ei*

COMBINE 1/2 CUP water, 1/4 cup butter, 1 tablespoon lemon juice, and 1/2 teaspoon salt, add 1 pound small mushrooms, and cook them for 3 minutes. Add 1 onion and 2 tablespoons parsley, both finely chopped, and cook the mushrooms for 3 minutes more. Add 1/2 cup heavy sour cream or heavy cream, off the heat, and cook until it is very hot, but do not let it boil.

Divide the mushrooms and sauce among 6 slices of buttered toast and lay 1 trimmed poached or fried egg on each slice. Sprinkle each portion with 1 teaspoon chopped chives and serve at once.

Marinated Mushrooms   *Marinierte Champignons*

CLEAN, BUT do not wash, 1 pound medium-sized firm white mushrooms. Cut the woody ends off the stems and slice the mushrooms across thinly, stems and all. In a saucepan bring to a boil 3 cups water with the juice of 1/2 lemon. Add the mushrooms, immediately reduce the heat, and simmer them for 3 minutes. Drain them well and place them in an earthenware bowl. In a saucepan heat 3/4 cup tarragon vinegar with 1/4 cup olive oil, 1 crushed garlic clove, 1 teaspoon salt, 3 peppercorns, 1/4 teaspoon thyme, a pinch of coriander, and 1 bay leaf. Bring the marinade to a boil and immediately pour it over the sliced mushrooms. Cool and chill them. Serve them very cold, sprinkled with 1/4 cup chopped parsley. Evenly sized button mushrooms, unsliced, may be used instead of the sliced ones.

Mushroom Onion Tart   *Champignonpastete*

REMOVE THE STEMS from 1 pound mushrooms. Slice the caps very fine and chop the stems. Slice 1 pound small white onions fine and separate the slices into rings. Sauté the onions in 2 tablespoons butter until they are transparent but not brown. Take the onions out of the pan. Add 3 tablespoons butter to the pan, sauté the mushrooms for 6 minutes, and season them with salt and pepper. Line 2 pie plates with the dough for open tarts and divide the onions and mushrooms between them. Beat 2 1/2 cups heavy cream with 2 1/2 tablespoons flour, 5 eggs, and 1 teaspoon each of paprika and salt. Pour the mixture over the filling and bake the tarts in a moderately hot oven (375° F.) for 15 minutes. Reduce the temperature to moderate (350° F.) and bake them 35 to 40 minutes more, or until they are puffed and brown. Turn off the heat and leave the tarts in the oven for 10 minutes. Sprinkle one tart with 1 teaspoon paprika and the other with 2 tablespoons chopped parsley.

Champignonauflauf Rudolfina   Mushroom Soufflé Rudolfina

CLEAN AND slice 1 pound mushrooms. Sauté 1 onion, minced, in 1/3 cup butter until it is puffed and golden. Add the mushrooms, the juice of 1/2 lemon, and salt and white pepper to taste, and cook the mixture, covered, over low heat for 6 minutes. Add 1/2 cup heavy cream stirred with 2 tablespoons flour and cook the mushrooms, stirring constantly, for 3 minutes. Transfer the mushrooms to a buttered soufflé dish and keep them hot.

Melt 3 tablespoons butter, blend in 5 tablespoons flour, and cook the *roux*, stirring, for 3 minutes. Gradually add 1 cup warm milk and cook the sauce, stirring, until it is smooth and thick. Take it from the heat and add 4 egg yolks, 1/2 cup grated Parmesan, 3 tablespoons minced parsley, and salt to taste. Fold in 5 stiffly beaten egg whites. Spread the soufflé mixture over the mushrooms and place the dish in a pan of hot water. Bake the soufflé in a moderately hot oven (375° F.) for 40 minutes, or until it is puffed and brown. Serve it at once.

Champignonauflauf mit Krebsen   Mushroom Soufflé over Dilled Shrimps

FIT A DEEP baking dish with rich pie dough, line it with wax paper, and fill it with raw rice or beans. Bake it until it is half done. Discard the rice or beans. Arrange in the half-baked shell 1 pound shelled and deveined shrimps and sprinkle over them 1/4 cup chopped dill and 1/2 teaspoon salt.

Clean 3/4 pound mushrooms, add them to 2/3 cup boiling water with the juice of 1/2 lemon, 3 tablespoons butter, 1/2 teaspoon salt, a *bouquet garni*, and salt and pepper to taste. Cook the mushrooms for 3 minutes and remove the *bouquet garni*. Drain the mushrooms and reserve the liquid. Mince the mushrooms.

Melt 3 tablespoons butter and blend in 3 tablespoons flour. Gradually add the liquor from the mushrooms, stirring, and just enough milk to make a thick sauce, about 1 cup liquid in all. Add the minced mushrooms,

1 small onion, minced, 1 teaspoon chopped parsley, and 5 egg yolks, lightly beaten. Fold in 5 stiffly beaten egg whites. Pour the soufflé mixture over the shrimps in the prepared pastry shell and bake the soufflé in a moderately hot oven (375° F.) for 35 minutes for a soft soufflé and 45 minutes for a dry one. Serve from the baking dish, with hollandaise sauce.

Mushrooms Filled with Mushroom Soufflé   *Champignonauflauf Albertina*

CLEAN, BUT do not peel, 24 large mushrooms. Remove the stems and chop them finely. Sauté the chopped stems and 1 onion, chopped, in 3 tablespoons butter. Melt 2 tablespoons butter, blend in 2 tablespoons flour, and cook the *roux* for a few minutes, stirring. Gradually add 1 cup chicken stock, and cook the sauce for 5 minutes, stirring, until it thickens. Add the sautéed mushroom stems and let the sauce cool. Add 4 well-beaten egg yolks, 1/2 teaspoon lemon juice, and 3 sprigs of parsley, chopped, and fold in 4 egg whites, beaten very stiff. Brush the mushroom caps with butter, pile them high with the soufflé mixture, and arrange them on a buttered baking sheet. Dust them with 1/2 cup grated Parmesan and bake them in a moderate oven (350° F.) until the soufflés are puffed and brown, about 15 minutes. Garnish with parsley and serve at once.

Mushrooms with Onion Soufflé   *Zwiebelchampignon Soufflé*

SAUTÉ 1 ONION, chopped, in 2 tablespoons butter until it is puffed and golden, add 1/2 pound firm white mushrooms, sliced, the juice of 1/2 lemon, and salt and pepper to taste. Cook the mushrooms, covered, for 5 minutes. Stir 1/4 cup cream into 1 tablespoon flour and add it to the mushrooms. Cook them 1 minute longer. Divide the mushrooms among 6 individual buttered soufflé molds.

Melt 3 tablespoons butter, blend in 5 tablespoons flour, and cook the *roux*, stirring, for a few minutes. Gradually add 3/4 cup warm milk and salt and pepper to taste and simmer the mixture for 5 minutes. Take it from the heat and stir in 3 egg yolks and 1/2 cup finely chopped onion. Add 1 tablespoon minced chives and fold in 3 stiffly beaten egg whites.

Divide the mixture among the molds and bake them in a hot oven (400° F.) for 15 minutes, or until they are puffed and brown. If baked in a single large mold, increase the cooking time to 35 to 45 minutes.

Gefüllte Schwämme   *Stuffed Mushrooms*

REMOVE THE STEMS of 24 uniform mushrooms. Discard the woody ends and chop the stems fine. Wash the caps and dry them. Sauté 1 onion, chopped fine, in 1/4 cup butter until it is puffed, add the chopped mushroom stems, and sauté the mixture until the onion is golden. Add 1 1/2 cups chicken livers and cook them until they are just pink inside. Mash the livers with a fork, off the heat, mixing all the ingredients well. Add salt to taste and stuff the mushroom caps with the filling. Bake the stuffed mushroom caps in a lightly buttered baking dish in a moderately hot oven (375° F.) for 15 minutes. Sprinkle them with 2 tablespoons chopped parsley or riced egg yolk.

Eier mit Champignonfülle   *Mushroom Eggs*

HALVE 6 HARD-COOKED eggs crosswise and remove the yolks. Cut a slice from the bottom of each egg white so the whites will stand upright. Sauté 1/4 pound mushrooms, chopped, in butter. Mix them with the yolks, and fill the egg whites. Stand the filled eggs in a lightly buttered ovenproof dish and surround them with 6 large mushrooms, sliced and sautéed in butter.

Add 2 tablespoons butter to the pan in which the mushrooms were cooked, blend in 1 1/2 tablespoons flour, and cook the *roux* for about 5 minutes without letting it brown, stirring constantly. Blend in gradually 1 cup heavy cream, to make a medium thick sauce. Pour the sauce over the stuffed eggs and sliced mushrooms and sprinkle them with grated Parmesan. Brown the topping under the broiler. Serve the eggs immediately, with a green salad sprinkled with the egg yolks, riced.

Champignons mit Spinat   *Mushrooms Stuffed with Spinach*

REMOVE THE STEMS of 16 large mushrooms and chop them finely. Sauté them in 2 tablespoons butter with 1 small onion, chopped, and 2 tablespoons chopped parsley. Combine 3/4 cup well-washed and cooked spinach, squeezed dry and chopped, with the sautéed mushroom stems. Add 2 tablespoons dry bread crumbs, 1 egg yolk, and salt and pepper to taste and combine the mixture well. Sprinkle the outside of the mushroom caps with the juice of half a lemon, salt them lightly, and fill the insides with the spinach mixture mounding it evenly. With a pastry brush, brush the mushrooms, the outsides as well as the filling, with melted butter and bake the mushrooms in a gratin dish in a moderately hot oven (350° F.) for 10 minutes, or until they are lightly golden on the sides.

Serve the stuffed mushrooms as an hors d'oeuvre, as a first course, or as an accompaniment to stuffed filet of beef *(page 181)*. *(Picture, page 274.)*

Mushrooms Stuffed with Peas *Champignons mit Erbsen*

BOIL 2 CUPS green peas in salted water until they are very soft, drain them well, and purée them in a blender or a sieve. Season the purée with salt and pepper to taste and a pinch of sugar.

Remove the stems from 24 large uniform mushrooms and chop them. Sauté them with 1 tablespoon chopped shallots in 2 tablespoons butter until they are golden. Add them to the pea purée, correct the seasoning, and add 2 tablespoons Madeira. Brush the mushroom caps with melted butter and fill them with the pea purée, heaping it high. Sprinkle the filling generously with grated Parmesan, pour a little melted butter over each mushroom cap, and brown them on a buttered baking sheet in a moderately hot oven (375° F.). Serves 12.

Gefüllte Champignons Paradeis

REMOVE THE STEMS of 18 large mushrooms and put them through the food chopper with 1/2 pound cold cooked veal. Cook the mixture in 3 tablespoons butter with 2 tablespoons Madeira and 1/2 teaspoon Worcestershire sauce for 6 minutes. Add 1 tablespoon grated onion, 1 shallot, chopped, just enough heavy cream to bind the mixture, and salt and pepper to taste. Stuff the mushroom caps with this filling. Bake them in a buttered baking dish in a moderate oven (350° F.) for 15 minutes. Cool the stuffed mushrooms and chill them.

Soften 1 envelope of gelatin in 1/4 cup cold water for 5 minutes and dissolve it in 1/2 cup boiling consommé, off the heat. Let the mixture cool. Add 1/2 cup thick mayonnaise, 2 tablespoons tomato ketchup, and salt and pepper to taste. Coat the mushrooms with this cool but still soft tomato-mayonnaise jelly and chill them. Decorate each coated mushroom with a sprig of parsley and arrange them on a round serving platter with a mound of chopped aspic in the center. Garnish the platter with 3 tomatoes, peeled and sliced, and with small sweet pickles cut into fans.

Spinatauflauf

IN 1/2 CUP boiling water, cook 1 pound spinach until it is soft. Drain it and reserve the water. Purée the spinach in a food processor or in a blender and add 1/4 cup finely chopped onions. Melt 3 tablespoons butter and blend in 4 tablespoons flour without letting the *roux* brown. Gradually stir in 1/2 cup bouillon and 1/2 cup of the spinach water. Bring the sauce to a boil and cook it for 1 minute. Take the pan from the heat and stir in 4 well-beaten egg yolks. Cook the sauce over low heat, stirring constantly, for 2 minutes, and let it cool. Add the spinach purée and salt to taste and fold in 5 egg whites, beaten stiff. Pour the batter into a buttered soufflé dish, sprinkle it with 1 teaspoon grated Parmesan, and bake the soufflé in a moderately hot oven (375° F.) for 45 minutes. Serve the soufflé with mushroom sauce.

Spinatsoufflé Prager Art

POUR A LAYER of the mixture for spinach soufflé into a buttered soufflé dish. Add a layer of the mixture for ham soufflé and pour in a top layer of the spinach soufflé mixture. Bake as usual and serve with mushroom sauce.

Spinach and Cheese Soufflé — *Spinatsoufflé Landeck*

POUR A LAYER of the mixture for spinach soufflé into a buttered baking dish. Add a layer of the mixture for cheese soufflé and pour in a top layer of the spinach soufflé mixture. Bake as usual.

Spinach Soufflé Modena — *Spinatsoufflé Modena Art*

ARRANGE A CELERY root, cooked and sliced, in a buttered dish. Over it spread a mixture of 1 cup minced ham and 1 small onion, chopped. Pour in the mixture for spinach soufflé. Bake as usual.

Spinach Roll — *Spinatroulade*

WASH 2 POUNDS spinach and cook it, covered, in only the water that clings to the leaves, until it is reduced and soft. Stir it frequently with a wooden spoon. Press the spinach out thoroughly and put it through a sieve or food chopper.

Sauté 1 onion, chopped, in 1/4 cup butter until it is puffed and add 1/2 cup flour. Reduce the heat, stir in 1/2 cup milk, and cook the mixture 3 minutes longer. Take the pan from the heat and add 4 egg yolks, 1/4 cup grated Parmesan, and the very dry spinach purée. Fold in 4 stiffly beaten egg whites. Spread the mixture 3/4 inch deep in a heavily buttered and lightly crumbed jelly-roll pan and bake it in a moderately hot oven (375° F.) until it tests done with a straw and shrinks from the sides of the pan. Spread the surface evenly with chicken filling, such as the one for soup pancakes, and roll up the *roulade* quickly. Return the *roulade* to the oven for 5 minutes. Pour over it 1/2 cup browned butter, dust it with 1 riced hard-cooked egg, and serve it with mushroom sauce.

Spinach Tart — *Spinatkuchen Andrea*

WASH 1 POUND spinach and cook it, covered, in the water that clings to the leaves, until it is wilted. Drain it well and purée it in a food processor

to make a fine purée. Stir 2 tablespoons flour into 1 cup cream and beat
in 3 eggs. Add the spinach purée and salt and pepper.

Cut 4 tablespoons vegetable shortening and 4 tablespoons butter into
2 cups flour mixed with 1/4 cup grated Parmesan, until the mixture resembles coarse meal. Moisten it with 4 to 6 tablespoons cold white wine,
add 1/4 teaspoon salt, and work the ingredients into a smooth dough.
Roll the dough out 1/8 inch thick and line a square cake pan with it.
Cook 4 slices bacon until they are transparent. Drain the bacon and dice
it. Spread the bacon in the tart shell. Add the spinach mixture and bake
the tart in a moderately hot oven (375° F.) until it is brown and puffed,
about 40 minutes. Arrange on the cooked tart cutouts of the pastry, baked
separately, and 3 hard-cooked eggs, sliced.

Tomaten auf überraschende Art   *Tomato Surprise*

FILL 6 VERY small tomatoes, peeled, hollowed out, and drained, with
1 cup sharp French dressing and chill them for 1 hour. Pour out the dressing and fill them with shrimp salad. Serve the tomatoes with paper-thin
lemon slices and garnish the platter with fresh water cress.

Gefüllte Tomatenviertel   *Stuffed Tomato Quarters*

SOFTEN 1 ENVELOPE of gelatin in 1/4 cup Sherry and dissolve it, off the
heat, in 1/2 cup hot consommé. Add 1/4 cup more Sherry. Cool the mixture
and stir it into 1 1/2 cups goose liver purée before the gelatin begins to set.
Divide the mixture among 6 medium tomatoes, peeled, hollowed out,
drained, and chilled. Chill the stuffed tomatoes until the filling is firm. To
serve, cut them into quarters with a very sharp knife and garnish the sides
of each quarter with a slice of truffle. On a platter of diced aspic, re-form
the tomatoes, arranging the quarters by fours, like the petals of a half-open
flower. Set a sprig of parsley in the center of each tomato.

Gemüse in Backteig   *Fritter Batter for Vegetables*

BEAT 3 EGG yolks, add 1 teaspoon salt, 1 tablespoon olive oil, and 2 1/3
cups flat tepid beer. Beat in well 2 2/3 cups flour. Let the batter rest

for 30 minutes. Fold in 3 stiffly beaten egg whites. Add more beer if the batter is too thick. Dip prepared vegetables into the batter and fry them in deep hot fat (375° F.) until they are golden. Drain them and serve at once, with an appropriate sauce.

Brussels Sprouts Fritters   Kohlsprossen in Backteig

DIP COOKED well-drained Brussels sprouts in the batter and fry them in deep hot fat (380° F.) until they are golden. Drain them and serve with mayonnaise seasoned with 1 tablespoon each of onion and capers, both chopped, and chilled.

Celery Root Fritters   Selleriescheiben in Backteig

COOK SLICES of celery root in salted water acidulated with lemon juice until they are tender and drain them well. Dip the slices into the batter and fry them in deep hot fat (380° F.) until they are golden. Drain them and serve with a tart tomato sauce.

Cauliflower Fritters   Karfiol in Backteig

DIP WELL-DRAINED cooked cauliflower, broken into flowerets, into a thick white sauce and roll the flowerets in chopped ham. Dip them carefully into the batter and fry them in deep hot fat (380° F.) until they are golden. Serve with tartare sauce.

Fried Mushrooms   Gebackene Champignons Hotel Schloss Dürnstein

WIPE 1 POUND small mushrooms and cut the stems even with the heads. Dredge them with seasoned flour, dip them in beaten egg, and roll them in dry bread crumbs. Fry the mushrooms in deep hot fat (375° F.) until they are golden, about 3 minutes. Drain the mushrooms well on a double layer of paper towels. Serve the mushrooms while they are still warm with lemon wedges and tartare sauce.

Or dip them in fritter batter and fry them, 5 or 6 at a time, in deep hot fat (375° F.) for about 4 minutes, or until they are golden. With a slotted spoon transfer the mushrooms to a warm ovenproof platter and set the platter in a warm oven (200° F.). Just before serving, dust the mushrooms with chopped parsley, and serve them as hot as possible, with

lemon wedges. Serve the following sauce separately:

Combine 1/2 onion, chopped very fine, 2 tablespoons capers, chopped fine, 3 tablespoons drained sweet pickle relish, 1/2 teaspoon dry mustard, the grated zest and juice of half a lemon, and 2 tablespoons dill pickle, finely chopped, with 3/4 cup mayonnaise. Add salt to taste and chill the sauce. Add a little cream if the sauce is too thick. The hot mushrooms are dipped in this ice-cold sauce.

For *Gabelfrühstück*, or second breakfast at eleven, allow 2 or 3 mushrooms for each serving. *(Picture, page 117.)*

Kalte Platten   *Cold Platters*

THE VIENNESE like to arrange elaborate Russian or Swedish platters of cold fish, salads, eggs, and meat, and serve them as a first course. Usually, in the center, there is a mound of salad coated with mayonnaise or, if the platter is a *feine Platte,* there are petal-like scoops of goose liver pâté arranged to simulate a tempting flower. Lines of diced aspic usually separate the various foods and serve to introduce any flavor that may be needed, such as tarragon, Sherry, or onion. No one helps himself to all of anything, so that everyone ends with a little of everything.

Russian Platter — *Russische Platte*

MOUND 3 CUPS Russian salad in the center of a large platter. Surround the salad with a ring of Russian stuffed eggs and fill the spaces between the eggs with chopped aspic. Circle the eggs with a row of alternating sardines and asparagus spears, fanning outward, and around these place a row of ham rolls—sliced ham rolled up evenly and cut into 1 1/2-inch lengths. Border the platter with small tomatoes, peeled, hollowed out, and filled with sharp chive mayonnaise. If there is room, add cooked chilled artichoke bottoms with 1 tablespoon mayonnaise in each. Garnish the platter with sprigs of parsley.

Swedish Platter — *Schwedische Platte*

A SCHWEDISCHE PLATTE differs from *Russische Platte* only in that the salad in the center is a fish salad, such as herring salad, and the eggs should be stuffed with shrimps. The row of ham rolls is replaced by rolls of smoked salmon, and sprigs of dill are used instead of parsley. Fill the tomatoes with tuna-fish salad and the artichoke bottoms with herring roe bound with mayonnaise. Dill and sweet pickles should garnish the platter.

Bird's Nest Salad — *Vogelnest*

BIRD'S NEST salads are very popular in Vienna, and the ingredients vary, depending on the season and the occasion. Only the arrangement of ingredients and the egg yolk in the center remain the same. The salad usually appears on a flat round crystal plate or shallow bowl and the ingredients are arranged in wedges, like sections of a pie. Each wedge may be different, but the main ingredient usually repeats in two opposite sections and the less important ingredients occur only once.

For a herring salad, for instance, there would be 3 wedges of chopped herring, 2 wedges of chopped beets, 1 wedge of chopped onions, 1 of chopped anchovies, 1 of capers, 1 of chopped egg white, and 1 of riced egg yolk. Chopped beets must never adjoin chopped egg white or chopped onions, as the red color runs into the white. Some of the wedges may be separated with lines of chopped parsley or chives. A raw egg yolk stands in the center of the whole arrangement. The salad is so pretty that one hesitates to stir it all together. The mixture usually takes on the color of the chopped beets. It is served with thin sliced buttered black bread and each guest spreads the salad on the bread. The egg yolk, the natural juices of the herring, anchovies, and onions, and the marinade of the beets serve to bind the salad. Chop the type of herring filet that is packed in red wine and use the beets, marinated, as in *Rote Beeten,* beet salad. Apples, chopped dill pickle, sweet pickle, and other smoked fishes are often substituted for or added to the ingredients.

Brionisalat   Celery Root Salad with Anchovies

BOIL 3 LARGE celery roots in salted water to cover until they are soft, about 25 to 30 minutes. Peel and slice them while they are hot, and marinate them for 3 hours in a mixture of 1/2 cup each of olive oil and tarragon vinegar, 1/2 teaspoon salt, and 1/4 teaspoon pepper. Turn the celery slices over carefully in the marinade every hour. Drain the slices well and bind them with 1/2 cup mayonnaise mixed with 1/2 teaspoon dry mustard and 1/2 to 3/4 teaspoon anchovy paste. Handle the salad carefully with wooden spoons so that the slices are not broken. Add a little more mayonnaise, if necessary.

Arrange the celery root on a flat platter and surround it with rolled anchovy filets. Rice 1 hard-cooked egg yolk over the celery root and sprinkle it with 1 teaspoon each of chopped parsley and chervil. Stir 2 riced hard-cooked egg yolks into 1/2 cup mayonnaise, add 1 teaspoon scraped onion, and salt and pepper to taste. Pipe large rosettes of the mixture through a fluted tube to garnish the platter and decorate it with sprigs of curly parsley.

Salat von grünen Bohnen   Green Bean Salad

PARBOIL 1 POUND French-cut green beans in salted water and let them cool. Pour over them 1 cup boiling tarragon vinegar diluted with 1 cup boiling water. Add 4 whole cloves, 1 tablespoon chopped tarragon, and salt and pepper to taste. Let the beans cool and marinate them for 3 hours in the refrigerator. Drain them. Serve them with a dressing of 2 tablespoons oil and 4 tablespoons vinegar mixed with 1/2 tablespoon dry mustard and salt and pepper to taste. Sprinkle the salad with chopped parsley.

White Salad — Weisser Salat

CUT 3 HEADS of endive crosswise in 1/4-inch slices. Add 4 pale hearts of Boston lettuce, 1 heart of chicory, separated and broken, the white part of 1 cooked leek, sliced crosswise, 3 small onions, sliced paper-thin and divided into rings, and the slivered whites of 3 hard-cooked eggs. Bind the salad with 1/2 cup pale mayonnaise mixed with 3 tablespoons whipped cream. Serve it with an open mushroom or lobster tart.

Fried Elder Blossoms — Gebackene Holunderblüten

STIR 1/2 CUP white wine into 7/8 cup flour and add 1 egg and 1/2 teaspoon each of oil and salt. Mix the batter thoroughly and set it aside for 10 minutes. Wash 6 large clusters of elder blossoms in cold water and dry them carefully. Remove all the coarse stems and dust the clusters lightly with flour. Beat the batter well and dip the clusters into it. Let the excess batter drip off and fry the clusters until they are brown in vegetable shortening 1 inch deep. Turn them once. Serve them hot, with tartare sauce.

Fresh Figs as a First Course — Frische Feigen

SERVE CHILLED fresh figs as a first course with roughly ground black pepper and salt.

SERVE CHILLED ripe figs with slices of prosciutto ham, and a wedge of lime.

SERVE CHILLED fresh or ripe figs with mild smoked salmon, roughly ground black pepper, and a wedge of lemon.

SERVE CHILLED fresh figs with slivered toasted almonds and slivers of cold cooked duck.

SERVE CHILLED fresh figs marinated in Port for 3 hours, drained, and dusted with sugar.

SERVE CHILLED fresh figs with riced salted cream cheese.

SERVE CHILLED fresh figs with paper-thin slices of salami or any hard Italian sausage.

Indische Melone
Melon Balls with Orange Sauce

WITH A MELON ball cutter, cut balls from cantaloupes and from casaba and Spanish melons, if they are available. Allow approximately 12 small melon balls for each serving. To serve 6, cut 72 melon balls and chill them for at least 1 hour. Combine 1 cup orange juice, strained, 3/4 cup melted red currant jelly, 1/4 cup kirsch, 1/4 cup minced chutney, and 2 teaspoons Dijon mustard. Add salt and pepper to taste and chill the sauce. Drain the melon balls and serve them in tall glasses. Pour the cold sauce over them. Garnish the glasses with parsley and a thin lemon slice.

Oranges with
Avocado Dressing   *Mandarinen mit Avocadobirnen*

PEEL 6 LARGE oranges and remove all the pith. Slice the oranges evenly across and remove the seeds. Keep the slices from each orange together. Place the peel of one orange in a small saucepan with cold water to cover and simmer the peel until it is soft. Drain the peel, scrape off the loosened white pith with a spoon, and shred the scraped zest.

Peel 3 small avocados and mash them gently, so as not to discolor them. Add the juice of 2 limes, 3 tablespoons Dijon mustard, and enough mayonnaise to make a creamy dressing. On lettuce leaves on individual plates, reassemble the slices from each orange, to simulate whole oranges. Pour the dressing over the oranges and garnish them with the shredded orange rind and sprigs of parsley.

Open Sandwiches   *Offene Butterbrötchen*

LAY SMALL open sandwiches on a platter and arrange chopped aspic around the sandwiches and bordering the platter. Garnish it with lemon wedges and sprigs of parsley.

Meat and Poultry

ON A THIN slice of buttered pumpernickel, spread scraped raw beef, add an onion ring, sliced thick, and in it drop a raw egg yolk. Decorate the sandwich with capers and parsley.

ON A THIN slice of buttered black bread, spread a layer of freshly grated horseradish and add a thin slice of cold rare roast beef and a wedge of tomato.

ON A THIN slice of buttered pumpernickel, lay a slice of rare roast beef and add a slice of tomato, cut in half and laid with the curved edges touching. Garnish with curls of fresh horseradish.

ON A THIN slice of buttered black bread, lay 3 slices of rare filet of beef. Grind black pepper over the meat and garnish with parsley.

ON A THIN slice of buttered pumpernickel, lay a thin slice of rare roast beef and in the center set a mound of well-drained potato salad sprinkled with chopped chives and capers.

ON A THIN slice of buttered brown bread, lay a slice of cold roast beef and then a warm trimmed fried egg.

ON A THIN slice of buttered rye bread, lay a thin slice of cold roast lamb and in the center set a mound of well-drained cucumber salad sprinkled with chopped chives.

ON A THIN slice of buttered rye bread, lay a paper-thin slice of cold roast pork. Spread it with a mixture of apples, capers, onions, and parsley, all minced, bound with thick mayonnaise.

ON A THIN slice of buttered rye bread, lay a thin slice of cold roast pork and a thin slice of apple in which capers have been substituted for the apple seeds. Garnish with lettuce.

ON A THIN slice of buttered pumpernickel lay a paper-thin slice of ham. Cut and fan out 1 small gherkin and lay it on one edge of the sandwich.

CHOP WESTPHALIAN ham and press a layer of it onto a well-buttered slice of dark bread. Add a little mound of egg that has been scrambled with chopped chives and parsley.

ON A THIN slice of buttered rye bread, lay a slice of ham and add a mound of scrambled egg sprinkled with chopped chives.

ON A THIN slice of buttered rye bread, lay a thin slice of tongue and 2 well-drained steamed asparagus spears marinated in salad marinade. Add a rosette of thick mayonnaise.

ON A THIN slice of buttered white bread, spread liver paste. Sprinkle it with chopped scallions and add a thin slice of aspic cut the size of the bread.

AT ONE END of a thin slice of buttered black bread, lay 2 slices hard-cooked egg, cut lengthwise. Cover the rest of the bread with 2 rounded spoons of liver paste and garnish the sandwich with parsley.

On a slice of buttered toast, spread liver paste. Sprinkle over it 1 slice of crisp cooked bacon, crumbled, and 1 teaspoon chopped mushroom.

On a thin slice of buttered brown bread, lay thin slices of cold roast duck and, crosswise, a thin slice of unpeeled apple. In the curve of the apple slice, mound a little shredded red cabbage that has been marinated in salad marinade.

Fish

Spread buttered white bread with anchovy butter and arrange on it slices of hard-cooked egg. Put a rolled anchovy filet on each egg slice and decorate the sandwich with parsley.

On buttered bread, lay anchovy filets interwoven with thin strips of smoked salmon. Put a small caper in each space in the latticework.

On a thin slice of buttered black bread, lay well-drained cod roe, a wedge of lemon, and a sprig of parsley.

On a thin slice of buttered dark bread, arrange scrambled eggs and on them lay pieces of smoked eel.

On a thin slice of buttered pumpernickel, lay filets of Bismarck or *matjes* herring or smoked eel. Add thin onion rings and grate fresh pepper over the sandwich.

On a thin round slice of buttered pumpernickel, lay a slice of mild smoked salmon. Pipe a little circle of salted whipped cream in the center and fill the circle with horseradish. Serve with lemon wedges.

On a thin slice of buttered black bread, lay a slice of smoked salmon and spread it with a mixture of grated horseradish and capers, onion, and parsley, all minced, bound with salted sour cream.

Combine 2 parts chopped hard-cooked egg with 1 part each of diced smoked salmon and caviar and bind the mixture with lemon mayonnaise. Spread it on thin slices of buttered brown bread and garnish with chopped parsley.

ON A THIN slice of buttered pumpernickel, lay a sardine and pipe mustard butter around it.

COVER A SLICE of buttered pumpernickel with tiny pink cooked shrimps, in a scale pattern.

ON A THIN slice of buttered pumpernickel, lay a slice of smoked sturgeon and a paper-thin slice of lemon, cut in half. Garnish 2 corners of the sandwich with chopped chives bound with mayonnaise and sprinkle with capers.

Cheese

ON THIN slices of buttered black bread, lay thin slices of Swiss cheese, cut in triangles, and pipe lines of mustard on the cheese. On the cheese triangle, arrange a smaller triangle of chopped pimientos.

ON THIN slices of buttered rye, pumpernickel, or whole-wheat bread, lay slices of Swiss, Gouda, or Emmenthal cheese. Decorate the sandwiches with lines of piped mustard, slices of pickle, and aspic.

SPREAD THIN slices of buttered dark bread with Gorgonzola, Camembert, or Brie cheese and sprinkle the cheese with chopped chives, toasted almonds, or parsley.

Vegetables and Salads

SPREAD A THIN slice of buttered pumpernickel with a mixture of equal parts of chopped apple and onion and diced crisp bacon bound with a little mayonnaise.

ON A THIN slice of buttered dark bread lay cold cooked marinated asparagus spears and pipe lemon mayonnaise down the spears.

ON A THIN slice of buttered rye bread, spread a layer of shredded lettuce and add a thin slice of orange, peeled and seeded. Sprinkle with salt, pepper, and paprika, to taste.

ON A THIN slice of buttered pumpernickel, lay thin uniform slices of marinated mushrooms and sprinkle them with chopped chives.

ON A THIN slice of black bread, spread thick mayonnaise and a layer of highly seasoned chopped cooked green peas. Sprinkle the sandwich with chopped mint.

ON A THIN slice of buttered dark bread, lay a slice of tomato and a trimmed fried egg. Sprinkle the sandwich with chopped sautéed onion.

COVER A THIN slice of bread with slices of tomato and sprinkle the tomato with riced hard-cooked egg and chopped chives.

CUT OUT the center of a slice of tomato, peeled and drained. Lay the tomato slice on a round slice of pumpernickel and in it lay 1 shrimp. Mask with thick lemon mayonnaise mixed with relish —3 parts mayonnaise to 1 part relish.

ON A THIN slice of buttered black bread, lay thin slices of tomato, peeled and seeded. Fill the little sections of the tomato slices with onions and chives, both chopped, and with hard-cooked egg.

BIND CHOPPED water cress with lemon mayonnaise and spread it on a thin slice of buttered black or Russian bread. Add a thin slice of tomato and a smaller slice of dill pickle.

ON A THIN round slice of buttered black or rye bread, lay a slice of tomato, a round slice of cheese, a slice of cucumber, and a slice of hard-cooked egg, in a pyramid. Top the pyramid with a rolled anchovy filet, an olive slice, or half a radish.

VARIOUS KINDS of salads are used to make open sandwiches. Drain the salads well and spread them on thin slices of buttered white or rye bread. Use vegetable salad and sprinkle it with chopped parsley. Or use egg salad sprinkled with chopped chives or chicken salad sprinkled with chopped pimiento. Tuna fish salad should be sprinkled with chopped capers and salmon salad with riced hard-cooked egg and parsley. Bind lobster or shrimp salad with lemon mayonnaise and sprinkle it with lobster coral or with chopped dill.

BEAT 1/2 CUP softened butter with 1/2 teaspoon salt and at the last minute add 1/2 cup grated horseradish. Spread 24 thin 1 1/2-inch round slices of white bread with the mixture. Peel tomatoes and, from the outside walls of the tomatoes, cut solid discs 1 1/2 inches in diameter. Four or five discs can be cut from a small tomato. Drain the discs and lay one on each slice

68

of bread. Set a mound of freshly grated horseradish in the center of each tomato disc, pinching it so that it will adhere in a rosette.

Pumpernickel with Cheese and Nuts — *Pumpernickel mit Käse und Nüssen*

CRUSH 1/2 POUND Roquefort cheese with 1/2 cup creamed butter and add 1/4 cup mixed chopped fresh herbs. If possible, use chervil, tarragon, dill, chives, and a little rosemary. Add just enough Sherry to bind the mixture and salt and pepper to taste. Mound the cheese on 2-inch rounds of pumpernickel and sprinkle it with chopped almonds, toasted and salted. Set a sprig of parsley in each mound.

Black Bread Fingers — *Belegtes Schwarzbrot*

STIR 2 EGG yolks with 1 tablespoon olive oil and 1 tablespoon French mustard until the mixture is smooth. Gradually add 1 onion, grated, 10 anchovies, minced, and 2 hard-cooked eggs, riced. Add the grated rind of 1 lemon and season to taste with lemon juice and roughly ground black pepper. Spread the mixture on black-bread, or pumpernickel, fingers and sprinkle with chopped chives.

Sandwich Loaf — *Jourbrot*

A JOURBROT is traditionally made from a loaf of the long narrow *Kasten-brot,* sliced lengthwise. The slices are filled with salty pâtés and other fillings, and the reshaped loaf is iced and decorated with piped rosettes of anchovy cream and with nuts and radishes as elaborately as a *Torte.*

Kastenbrot is not obtainable here in food shops, but *Jourbrot* can be made from any firm white bread. These fillings are sufficient for 12 slices measuring 7 inches long by 3 inches wide by 1/2 inch thick. Use day-old bread, free of crusts. Lay 3 slices end to end on a tray or on a long board, butter them, and spread them generously with calf's liver paste. The layers of filling should be as thick as the bread. Cover with 3 more slices of bread, set end to end, butter them, and chill.

Mix 4 hard-cooked eggs that have been pressed through a ricer with 1/4 cup soft butter, 2 white onions, chopped fine, 2 tablespoons chopped chives,

4 tablespoons mayonnaise, and salt and pepper to taste. Spread the second layer of bread with this mixture.

Cover with 3 more slices of bread, butter them, and chill again. Mix 12 chopped olives with 1/2 pound softened cream cheese and spread the third bread layer with this mixture. Cover with the remaining 3 slices of bread and chill.

Whip 1 pound softened cream cheese with 2 ounces anchovy paste. Spread the loaf thickly with this anchovy cream and press 1 cup toasted salted almonds, chopped, on the four sides. Decorate the top with rosettes of anchovy cream piped through a pastry tube and with a dozen rolled anchovy filets. Sprinkle with unpeeled chopped radishes. Garnish the platter with parsley.

The *Jourbrot* should be about 4 inches high. When it is thoroughly chilled, it can be cut into 1/4-inch slices—about 80—which should then be eaten with a fork. The fillings may be varied to include smoked salmon, ham, chicken, and the like.

Gefüllte Brötchen   *Stuffed Rolls*

HOLLOW OUT from both ends hard rolls or a long narrow loaf of French bread—cut into 2 or 3 pieces—to make tubes of bread crust. Spread the inside of these tubes thickly with anchovy butter. Mix the anchovy butter in the proportion of 1 tablespoon anchovy paste to 1/2 cup butter. Chill the buttered bread tubes for 1/2 hour. Cream 3/4 cup butter and add 3/4 cup each of finely ground ham, with its fat, finely ground cooked veal, and finely ground smoked tongue. Stir well, add 2 hard-cooked eggs, riced, 3 slices bacon, cooked, drained, and crumbled, 1 dill pickle, chopped, and 1/4 cup chopped pistachio nuts, and last of all stir in 5 skinless sardines, boned and mashed. Salt the mixture, if necessary, and fill the bread tubes, packing them solidly and tightly. Wrap the filled bread in wax paper and chill it until the filling is hardened. Cut the bread across diagonally in 1/4-inch slices and serve the slices, along with salty "bakeries," as an accompaniment to cocktails.

Suppen und Suppeneinlagen

ONTRARY TO custom in all other countries, where each man tries to emulate the man above or, if possible, the man at the top, the Austrians make every effort to copy the man below. The Emperor, dressed in his Tyrolese peasant's hat and his *Jankerl,* his jacket, felt a greater understanding for his people than he possibly could feel in his state uniform. Countesses were prouder of their dirndls and aprons than of their Paris gowns, and everyone tried to speak as much like a *Fiakerkutscher,* or carriage driver, as he possibly could. None of this simplicity was affectation. It stemmed from an effortless and sincere democracy and had its roots in mutual respect.

This attitude extended to the love of soups, the peasants' daily fare. In the ascent up the social scale, the soups became thinner, emptier, and more elegant, and the sound that accompanied their consumption gradually faded away. By the time the *Almanach de Gotha* had been reached, the soups were refined bisques and bouillons with decorative rather than hardy garnishes floating in them, but they were *never* omitted from the daily menu. (To start a meal without soup—*unglaublich,* unbelievable! That could happen only in America!)

A girl preparing for her wedding did not worry as much about her blankets and linens as she worried about her soup tureen, her large generous soup plates, and her enormous soup spoons. A girl who was assembling such a trousseau was of course so perfectly brought up that she would know how to describe a magnificent curve through the air with her new soup spoon that ended with the spoon's tip facing straight into her mouth and her hand well out near the wineglasses. There would be a final upward tilt—and the fact that she was a lady would be obvious to all. She did this soundlessly, after a good fourteen years of Fräulein's saying *"Nicht Schlürfen"* twice each day. Besides her soup tureen, the hopeful bride needed bouillon *Tassen,* or cups; these enabled her to serve hot bouillon with the meat course, some thirty minutes and two courses after having started dinner with a thick soup in her soup plates.

The Viennese not only serve their soups from large tureens, they eat them from large plates with large spoons and frequently pass their plates for second helpings. Soup for six in Vienna does not mean preparing a quart of soup. It means preparing at least six large cupfuls for the guests and one for the tureen, so that the hostess does not have to tilt the hot tureen to get the last ladleful nor scrape the bottom.

The soups were never dull: they originated with the peasants, who put everything into them that they had on hand and who added great chunks of bread as they ate.

The *Einlage,* the inlay (a word which is less reminiscent of the dentist in German than in English), was all important. The steaming soup tureen came to the table accompanied by hot soup plates with pretty "inlays" arranged in them: Mounds of slivered pancakes or warm rice and salted cream cheese, for instance, were piled in the plates and covered with parsley. Some inlays were so pretty that it seemed a shame to ladle strong bouillon over them. Other inlays were "layed in" after the soup, and still others made a lovely nest in the bottom of the tureen—only to have the hot soup poured over them. A light pancake for each plate could be cut into quarter-inch strips, or a dumpling could be as large as a baseball. There could be a whole little chicken or a squab in the soup. There was plenty of room—the plates were large and deep and the rims were so wide that whole arrays of bones could be piled on them.

Some homes and all restaurants served up their soup in a silver-handled mug that came in standing in the hot soup plate. The waiter placed the plate and underplate before the guest and carefully decanted the soup from the metal mug. Every eye was riveted on the ritual, every breath was held. Sometimes the inlay just came out with the soup, but usually there was a happy plop at the end, when, in the wake of the soup, first green peas and finally a lovely large *Knödel* came to light. A final flourish, and the mug was gone. Everyone ate with that fine abandon of enjoying himself while he might and disregarded the two or three courses that, according to the amount of flat silver, were inevitably going to follow.

Consommé Supreme — *Feinste Kraftbrühe*

IN A VERY large kettle lay 2 stewing chickens, cut into pieces, 6 pounds boiling beef—brisket, neck, or shin—and 1 shank of lamb which has previously been half broiled or half roasted and cut in half. Add 1 cup parsley, or 4 parsley roots, scraped, 4 carrots, scraped and sliced, 3 turnips, peeled and sliced, and 1 celery root, peeled and sliced. Chop the white part only of 3 leeks and add them to the kettle with 2 onions, each stuck with 2 cloves, and gently sautéed in butter until they are golden. Add 3 tablespoons salt, 6 peppercorns, and cold water to cover—there should be 6 to 7 quarts. Cover the kettle and cook the stock slowly for 4 hours, removing the scum that rises to the top when the soup comes to a boil. Add 1 cup cold water every hour. Strain the bouillon, add salt to taste, and let it cool. Carefully lift off the fat and return the bouillon to the kettle, pouring it through a fine, wet cloth.

Stir 3 pounds lean ground beef with 6 egg whites, lightly beaten, and 1 cup cold water and add 2 cups chopped vegetables. Use 1 carrot, scraped, 2 stalks of celery, 1 small onion, the white part of 2 leeks, 8 parsley stems, scraped, and 1/2 small turnip. (The vegetables may be omitted at this time, in which case increase the quantity of vegetables cooked in the original bouillon.) The consommé may be frozen or the recipe halved.

Stir the mixture into the bouillon and bring it slowly to a boil, stirring. Let it simmer undisturbed for 2 hours, then strain it through a fine wet cloth and add 1/2 to 1 cup Cognac to taste. Add salt to taste and serve the consommé clear or with various garnishes. Serves 24.

Beef Soup or Stock — *Wiener Rindsuppe*

WIPE 2 1/2 POUNDS brisket, neck, or shin of beef. Place the meat in a large kettle, add 2 quarts cold water, and bring the water very slowly to a boil. Do not remove the scum that forms on the surface unless the soup is made in larger quantity. Wash 2 pounds soup bones, boil them for 3 minutes, and rinse them in cold water. Combine 1 tomato, 1 turnip, 3 mushrooms, 3 carrots, 3 stalks of celery, 1/2 peeled celery root, 1 large onion, and the white part of 3 leeks, all sliced, a quarter head of cauli-flower, coarsely chopped, and 2 chopped parsley roots, or 6 sprigs of parsley. Slowly sauté all the vegetables in 1/4 cup butter until they are coated and golden. Add the bones and vegetables to the soup and bring it to a boil, covered, then add 1 clove, 3 peppercorns, a sprig of thyme, a grating of nutmeg, and 1 teaspoon salt. The soup should cook, covered, very slowly, for about 1 1/2 to 2 hours. Skim off any large eyes of fat that come to the surface and add 1/2 cup cold water 2 or 3 times during the cooking. Remove the meat, carefully strain the stock, and use it as a base for other soups or sauces or to make a strong *Kraftbrühe,* or consommé.

If the soup meat is to be eaten, as for *Rindfleisch,* follow the same directions, but place the meat in boiling water instead of in cold water, to seal in the juices. The soup will be less flavorful but the meat more so.

This *Wiener Rindsuppe* is made with a large quantity of meat and bones in proportion to the water used. As a result, it simmers for a shorter time than most stocks and the scum is not removed. The water can be increased to 4 quarts and the scum can be removed after the soup comes to a boil. The stock should then simmer for 4 hours and 1/2 cup cold water should be added each hour.

Brühe   *Unbrowned Beef Stock or Bouillon*

WITH A DAMP cloth, wipe 2 pounds lean round of beef and cut the meat into cubes. Place the meat and 2 pounds marrowbone, sawed in 2-inch lengths, in a kettle with 3 quarts cold water and soak meat and bones for 30 minutes. Place the kettle over heat and bring the water just to the boiling point, but do not let it boil. Skim the surface thoroughly and simmer the stock for 3 hours. Add 1 tablespoon salt, and 1/3 cup each of diced carrot and turnip, 1 onion, chopped, and 2 celery stalks, diced, and cook the stock 1 hour longer. Pour it through a fine strainer and cool it quickly. Remove the layer of fat from the surface. Use this stock, or bouillon, as it is as a base for soups or clarify it for consommé.

The bouillon or stock becomes a consommé when it is recooked with additional meat and clarifed. A double consommé (doppelte Kraftbrühe) *is obtained by doubling the quantity of meat used.*

Kraftbrühe oder Consommé   *Beef Consommé*

PREPARE A BEEF bouillon, or stock, as in the previous recipe, but add 1 stewing chicken. It is not necessary to increase the quantity of cold water.

Simmer the stock for 2 to 3 hours. Let it cool, chill it, and carefully remove all the fat from the surface. Strain it through a fine sieve and measure 2 quarts into a kettle. Mix 1 onion, 1 carrot, 3 mushrooms, and 1 leek, all chopped, with 2 lightly beaten egg whites and 1 pound lean beef, chopped. Add 1 teaspoon salt, 1 peppercorn, 1 clove, and 1 cup cold water, and let the mixture stand for 20 minutes. Stir the mixture into the cold stock and bring it to a slow boil, stirring gently. Cover the kettle and simmer the stock for 1 hour. Strain it through a fine wet cloth. Serve this consommé clear or with a garnish or use it for any of the recipes that call for a strong consommé base.

Glace de Viande or
Meat Extract or Glaze

Getrocknete Fleischessenz

MAKE A strong beef stock, as in the recipe above for *Brühe,* basing the quantities on 4 pounds beef. Instead of taking it from the heat after 5 hours, however, simmer it for 6 to 7 hours. Cool the stock, chill it, and remove the layer of fat that forms on the surface and any remaining specks. Reheat the stock and strain it through a double thickness of cheesecloth into a shallow pan. Reduce it over moderate heat to about half its quantity. Cool

it again and if any fat should form on the surface, remove it carefully.
Place the pan in a larger pan of water and cook the stock until it is further
reduced. At this point there should be about 1/2 cup of essence, which
will be a dark paste. Store the essence in a cool place overnight and cut
it into 1/4-inch dice. Dry the dice in a cool place and store them, wrapped
in wax paper, in the refrigerator.

This *glace,* or extract, colors and flavors soups and sauces, and it is
spread on some meat dishes. Melt it in hot soup—and consider yourself
successful when you boil 4 pounds of beef down to a little less than half
a cup of *Getrocknete Fleischessenz.* Meat extract or meat glaze can also
be bought in specialty shops.

Karamel   *Caramel Coloring for Soup*

BOIL 1 CUP granulated sugar in an iron pan with 6 tablespoons water until
it is dark brown. Add 6 more tablespoons water and continue to simmer
the syrup until it is like thin dark molasses. Store it in a corked bottle.
Use a few drops in any soup when a darker color is desired.

Klarifizieren   *Clarifying*

DIRECTIONS FOR making clear strong consommés by clarifying stock are
given after the beef, game, chicken, and fish stock recipes. Here, however,
are the general rules.

Cool the strained stock or bouillon and then chill it. It is better to
allow enough time for chilling, because the fat can be removed more easily
when it is cold. With a sharp knife, loosen the edges of the hardened fat
from the container and lift it off. Remove any remaining particles of fat
with a piece of cheesecloth wrung out in hot water.

The cold soup is returned to a kettle and lean ground beef, chicken, or
fish mixed with lightly beaten egg white is stirred into it. Chopped vegetables may be added at this time, but they are not necessary if the original
bouillon was cooked with vegetables. The stock is slowly stirred as it comes
slowly to a boil. The kettle should be covered and the stock left to simmer
undisturbed for 30 minutes. The scum should then be removed and the
stock poured through a cloth which has previously been wrung out in cold
water. Allow 1 egg white, lightly beaten, for every quart of soup.

Simple Clarifying

SOUPS MAY be clarified with lightly beaten egg white only. For each quart of stock, use the white and shell of 1 egg. Beat the egg white slightly and add 2 teaspoons cold water and the crushed eggshell. Add the mixture to the cold stock. Stir the stock constantly until it comes to a boil. Take it off the heat and let it stand undisturbed for 20 minutes. Strain it through a fine strainer lined with 2 thicknesses of cheesecloth.

Jellied Consommé — Kalte Geleésuppe

To MAKE a jellied soup, use any clear consommé as the foundation. Heat 4 cups of the clear consommé to boiling. Soften 1 envelope of gelatin in just enough cold water to cover. Take the consommé from the heat and add the softened gelatin, stirring until it is dissolved. Cool the consommé and chill it. Before serving, stir the jellied soup. It should not be too stiffly jellied. Garnishes are added just before serving.

If one looks over Viennese menus for a single month, it becomes quite obvious that the Resis and Annas in every Viennese kitchen cooked a very mighty meat stock every Monday. Boiled beef, which contributed to the stock while cooking in it, appeared with alternating sauces and garnishes each week, and the clear soups distilled from the stock came to table filled, in succession, with Leberknödel, Einlauf, Nudeln, Pfannkuchen, Erbsen, *and* Eierstich, *as regularly as clockwork. When Herr Hofrat sat down to* Leberknödel, *he could say to himself with confidence,* "Aha! Heute ist Donnerstag—*it's Thursday.*"

Consommé Elizabeth — Kraftbrühe Elisabeth

BRING 6 CUPS beef consommé to a boil, add the white part of 3 leeks, cut in 1/4-inch slices, and simmer the consommé until the leeks are almost soft, about 12 minutes. Add 3/4 cup of the thinnest noodles and cook 8 minutes more. Add 3 cooked artichoke bottoms, diced, and simmer the soup for 10 minutes. Season it to taste and serve with grated Parmesan.

Polnische Zitronensuppe *Polish Lemon Soup*

STIR 2 TABLESPOONS butter into 2 cups hot rice, cooked in salted water to the medium soft, or *al dente*, stage, and stir the buttered rice into 6 cups simmering beef consommé. Whip 3/4 cup heavy cream with 1/4 teaspoon salt until it is stiff and gently fold in 2 egg yolks beaten with 1 tablespoon lemon juice and the grated rind of 1 lemon. Garnish each serving of the soup with a generous topping of this whipped cream and with 3 paper-thin slices of lemon.

Kraftbrühe alte Art *Consommé with Liver Pâté Croutons*

TOAST IN THE oven 1 1/2-inch rounds of bread and spread each with 2 teaspoons goose liver pâté mixed with 1 teaspoon finely minced onion. Dust the rounds with minced parsley and drop them into strong consommé after it is served.

Kalte Kraftbrühe mit Trauben *Jellied Consommé
with Grapes*

To 6 CUPS cold half-jellied consommé add 2 cups chilled seedless green grapes and 1/2 cup each of finely diced ham and mixed finely minced fresh herbs—parsley, chives, chervil, and tarragon.

Arme Leute *Consommé with Potatoes and Croutons*

FOR 6 CUPS strong hot consommé, pass separately 3/4 cup grated Parmesan and 1 1/2 cups each of diced hot boiled potatoes and toasted dried bread cubes cut the same size as the potatoes. The bread cubes may be tossed with a little garlic butter—1 crushed garlic clove mixed with 3 tablespoons melted butter—before they are toasted.

Kraftbrühe mit Pfannkuchen *Consommé with Pancake Strips*

MAKE *Frittaten Nudeln oder Pfannkuchen,* soup noodles or pancakes, adding 1 tablespoon minced parsley to the batter. Add the pancake strips to boiling beef consommé and cook them until they are hot. The soup should be full of pancake strips; they are not just a garnish but an ingredient of the soup. Sprinkle the soup with 1/2 cup chopped parsley. *(Picture, page 123.)*

Consommé with Filled Pancake — Karlsbader Suppe

HEAT 6 CUPS clear beef consommé until it is very hot, but not boiling. Serve it in heated soup plates, each garnished with a small rolled-up soup pancake filled with tongue or ham mousse. Float in each plate 3 lozenges cut out of thinly sliced cooked celery root or boiled turnip. Sprinkle 1/2 cup chopped chervil over the garnished soup.

Farina Soup — Griess-Suppe

MELT 2 TABLESPOONS butter, add 1 cup farina, and stir the mixture until it is yellow. Pour in 1 cup boiling beef bouillon and stir the mixture until it is smooth. Stir it into 5 cups simmering beef bouillon and continue to simmer the soup for 15 minutes, without stirring. Sprinkle with 1/4 cup chopped parsley and serve at once.

Bouillon with Egg — Bouillon mit Ei

AT LUNCHEON in Vienna, it was considered especially elegant to serve clear bouillon in cups and to pass separately the egg yolk that should have been stirred into it. The yolks were placed in half eggshells, which were set into a deep dish of salt in order to stand upright. For each cup of clear bouillon, carefully separate an egg yolk from the white. Trim half the shell with small sharp scissors, return the yolk to the shell, dust it with paprika, and set the shells securely into a deep dish of fine salt. Each person stirs an egg yolk into his bouillon.

German Consommé — Deutsche Kraftbrühe

COOK 6 TABLESPOONS tapioca in 6 cups strong beef consommé until it is soft. Add 3 crushed juniper berries and cook the soup 10 minutes longer.

Strain the soup, add 1 cup of cooked, finely shredded red cabbage, 2 skinned beef frankfurters cut in thin slices, and salt and pepper to taste. When serving, add 1 teaspoon freshly grated horseradish to each plate of soup at the last moment.

Braune Kalbsbrühe *Brown Veal Stock*

WITH A damp cloth, wipe clean 5 pounds knuckle or shank of veal. Cut the meat from the bones in small pieces, then crack the bones. Place the bones and two-thirds of the meat in a kettle and cover them with 4 quarts cold water. Let them stand for 30 minutes. In a skillet, render a small amount of fat cut from meat. In it brown the remaining meat cubes well. Add them to the mixture in the kettle. In the same fat, brown 1 onion, sliced, and add it to the kettle with 1 stalk of celery, sliced, 1 tablespoon salt, 1/2 teaspoon peppercorns, and 1 blade of mace. Heat the water gradually to the boiling point, skimming often, and simmer the stock 4 to 5 hours. Strain it through cheesecloth. Use it as a base for soup requiring brown veal stock.

White Veal Stock   *Weisse Kalbsbrühe*

HAVE THE butcher chop 2 pounds veal bones medium fine, place them in boiling water for 3 minutes, and rinse them in cold water. Put them in a kettle with 2 quarts cold water and 1 pound veal, cut into chunks. Bring the water slowly to a boil, add 2 onions, 2 leeks, and 2 carrots, all sliced, 1 small turnip, peeled and sliced, 3 stalks of celery or 1/2 peeled and sliced celery root, 1 sprig of thyme, 1/2 bay leaf, 2 peppercorns, 2 cloves, and 1 teaspoon salt. Simmer the stock gently, covered, for 2 hours. Strain it and let it cool. Remove the fat that rises to the surface and store the stock, tightly covered, in the refrigerator. Use it for recipes that call for veal stock.

Veal Consommé   *Klären von Kalbsknochenbrühe*

CHOP 1 ONION, 1 leek, 1 carrot, and 3 stalks of celery. Place them in a kettle with 3 sprigs of parsley or 1 parsley root, 1 sprig or 1/2 teaspoon each of thyme, chervil, and tarragon, 2 peppercorns, a squeeze of lemon juice, and 1/2 pound ground lean beef mixed with 1/4 cup cold water and let the mixture stand for 20 minutes. Add 2 egg whites, lightly beaten, 1 crushed eggshell, and then 2 quarts cold veal stock and bring the liquid very slowly to a boil, stirring constantly. As soon as the stock boils, lower the heat and let it simmer, uncovered, for 30 minutes, without stirring. Strain it through a cloth and add salt to taste. After the clarified veal stock, or consommé, is cold, refrigerate it until needed.

Veal Dumpling Soup with Herbs   *Kalbsknödelsuppe mit Kräutern*

BROWN 1/2 POUND cubed veal with 3 sprigs of parsley, chopped, 3 shallots or 1 onion, chopped, and 1/4 pound chopped mushrooms in 3 tablespoons butter. Add 2 tablespoons veal stock and continue to cook the meat, adding small quantities of stock, until it is tender. Add salt to taste and put the meat and vegetables twice through the medium blade of the food mill. Cream 6 tablespoons butter with 3 eggs, beat the mixture until it is light and foamy, and add the purée. Add salt and pepper to taste. Turn the mixture into a small buttered mold and cover the mold. Set it in kettle of boiling water, cover the kettle, and steam the mixture for about 45 minutes, or until it is set. The water should reach halfway up the mold. Unmold and slice the veal garnish and serve it in 6 cups clear veal consommé to which 1/4 cup finely minced mixed fresh herbs—parsley, chervil, tarragon, and chives—has been added.

Hühnerbouillon   *Chicken Stock or Bouillon*

PLACE A 4 1/2- to 5-pound fowl in a large kettle with some extra chicken wings and 8 cups cold water. Bring the water to a boil, very slowly, and skim off any scum that rises to the top. Add the white part of 2 leeks, sliced, 1 turnip, peeled and sliced, 4 stalks of celery with the leaves, 1 onion stuck with 4 cloves, 6 sprigs of parsley, 2 sprigs of thyme, 1 bay leaf, 3 peppercorns, and 2 teaspoons salt. Simmer the stock, covered, for 3 hours, adding 1/2 cup cold water each hour. Strain it. Cool it slowly, then chill it. Take the solid layer of fat carefully from the top.

Hühnerconsommé   *Chicken Consommé*

FOLLOW THE directions for *Hühner Bouillon*. Return the stock to the kettle and stir in 1/2 pound ground raw chicken meat mixed with 2 lightly beaten egg whites. Bring the stock very slowly to a boil, stirring slowly. Simmer the stock for 1/2 hour and strain it through a cloth wrung out in cold water. Serve the consommé with garnishes or use when a clear chicken consommé is required.

Grossherzoginsuppe   *Grand Duchess Soup*

ADD 3/4 CUP white chicken meat cut in strips and 3/4 cup tongue cut in strips to 6 cups chicken consommé in which 3 chopped truffles have been heated for 15 minutes. Add 1 chicken dumpling to each serving.

Kolumbinensuppe   *Chicken Consommé with Pigeon Eggs*

SIMMER 6 CUPS chicken consommé with 1/2 cup each of carrot balls and turnip balls until the vegetables are soft. Use the smallest vegetable cutter or cut the vegetables into small dice. Add pieces of squab, previously poached for 1 hour in salted water to cover, and float in each serving 1 poached pigeon egg. Lacking these—foreseeably—poach the smallest pullet eggs obtainable. Trim the poached eggs neatly. Sprinkle the soup with chopped parsley.

Chicken Soup with Curry   *Hühnersuppe mit Curry*

IN A LARGE kettle melt 1/2 cup butter, add one 3-pound frying chicken, cut in pieces, 1 pound veal bones, and 4 onions, chopped. Sauté the mixture until the chicken is lightly browned and the onions are golden. Add 5 teaspooons curry powder and stir well. Add 1 carrot, diced, 1 turnip, peeled and sliced, the white part of 1 leek, and 1 celery stalk, chopped. Sprinkle the vegetables with 1/4 cup flour and add 2 quarts chicken stock, stirring. Season the soup with salt and pepper to taste and simmer it for 2 hours. Remove the chicken and strain the soup into a saucepan. Add 1/2 cup warm white wine or to taste and 1 cup cooked rice. Cut the white meat of the chicken into small pieces and add it to the soup. Heat the soup well and at the last moment sprinkle each serving generously with ground coconut sautéed in butter until it is brown and crisp. This soup may also be served cold.

Squab Soup   *Taubensuppe*

MELT 4 TABLESPOONS butter in a kettle, add 3 squabs, sprinkled with salt and pepper, 1/4 pound ham, chopped, and 2 onions, chopped, and sauté them until they are golden brown. Blend in 4 tablespoons flour— more may be needed if more butter is used—and 1 tablespoon paprika and add 2 quarts veal stock. Cook the soup gently for 45 minutes. Remove the squabs to a warm place and strain the soup. Correct the seasoning with salt and stir in 1 cup heavy cream mixed with 2 well-beaten egg yolks. Cook the soup for a few minutes longer, being careful that it does not boil or it will curdle. Carve off the 6 breasts, or suprêmes, of the squabs, each in one piece, and remove the skin. Garnish each serving with a suprême and with 2 or 3 cooked cauliflower flowerets.

Squab chickens may be substituted for squabs. In this case, garnish the soup with cooked broccoli flowerets instead of with cauliflower.

Taube in Suppe   Squab in Soup

BRING 3 1/2 CUPS water to a boil with 1 stalk of celery, sliced, 1 carrot, scraped and sliced, 3 sprigs of parsley, and 1 teaspoon salt. Add 1 squab, cleaned, with its chopped giblets. Simmer the squab, covered, until it is tender, about 3/4 hour. Take out the squab and keep it warm.

Strain the soup and return it to the heat. Stir 2 tablespoons fast-cooking farina into the boiling soup, and cook, stirring constantly, for about 3 minutes. Remove the soup from the heat and let it cool very slightly. Beat 1 egg well and stir it very gradually into the soup. There should be no traces of egg white visible in the soup. If it is not smooth, strain it. Correct the seasoning, return the hot skinned squab to the soup, and serve it at once, sprinkled with 1 teaspoon chopped parsley. Serves 1.

Hühner in Spinatsuppe   Spinach Soup Leopold

IN A KETTLE place two 2-pound broilers with 4 stalks of celery, 2 carrots, 1 onion, 3 sprigs of parsley, a sprig each of chervil and tarragon, 1/4 bay leaf, 2 peppercorns, and 2 quarts water. Cover the kettle and bring the water slowly to a boil. Add 1 teaspoon salt and cook the chickens until they are tender, about 40 minutes. Skin the chickens, quarter them, and keep them hot. Strain 5 cups of the stock.

Wash 2 pounds spinach, free it of all coarse stems, and cook it in the water that clings to the leaves for about 2 minutes, or until it is soft. Drain it well and put it through a food chopper or sieve. Melt 2 table-spoons butter, blend in 2 tablespoons flour, and gradually add to the *roux* 1 cup of the warm chicken stock, stirring constantly. Cook the mixture, stirring, until it thickens. Add 4 cups chicken stock, the puréed spinach, and salt to taste. Beat 2 egg yolks into 1/2 cup warm heavy cream and stir them into the soup just before serving. Put a piece of chicken in each soup plate and pour in the hot spinach soup. Serve with cheese triangles made of Cheddar cheese stick dough II.

Hühnerrahmsuppe   Cream of Chicken Base

IN A SAUCEPAN, melt 3 tablespoons butter, stir in 1/3 cup flour, and cook the *roux* over low heat, stirring constantly, until it starts to turn golden.

Add 6 cups strained chicken stock and cook, stirring with a wire whisk, until the soup is smooth. Add 1 carrot, scraped and chopped, 1 onion, sliced, the white part of 1 leek, sliced, 1 stalk of celery with its leaves, chopped, and 1 parsley root, scraped, or 3 sprigs of parsley. Simmer the soup for 30 minutes, add salt and pepper to taste, and strain it. Use in any recipe that calls for a cream of chicken base.

Cream of Chicken Soup   *Geflügelrahmsuppe*

RETURN STRAINED cream of chicken base to the kettle and simmer it for 5 minutes. Beat 2 egg yolks into 1 cup heavy cream, reduce the heat so that the soup is just below the boiling point, and stir in the egg yolk mixture. Stir the soup until it is smooth and add warm milk, if the soup is too thick, and salt and white pepper to taste. Garnish with chicken dumplings or toasted bread croutons.

Cream of Chicken Soup Variations

Cream of Chicken Soup with Caraway   *Rahmsuppe Brahms*

ADD 1 TEASPOON caraway seeds to 6 cups cold chicken stock and bring it to a boil. Add the stock to the *roux*, as in cream of chicken base, and simmer the soup for 30 minutes. Strain the soup, garnish it with 1/2 cup each of carrot, turnip, and potato balls, cut from vegetables with the smallest cutter, and cook until tender.

Rahmsuppe Schlossfrauen Art
Cream of Chicken Soup
with Chestnuts

COOK PEELED chestnuts in salted milk and purée enough to make 1 cup. Add the hot purée to 5 cups hot cream of chicken soup. Thin with warm cream, if necessary.

Schöne Suppe
Cream of Chicken Soup Imperial

BRING 6 CUPS cream of chicken base to a boil. Arrange in each soup cup 2 cooked green asparagus tips and 2 small cooked shrimps and sprinkle them with 1 teaspoon riced hard-cooked egg, and a little chopped parsley. Pour the hot soup over the garnish and sprinkle it with finely chopped truffles.

Lothringer Hühnersuppe
Cream of Chicken Soup Lorraine

CUT 6 ROUNDS of any pastry dough to fit small muffin pans and fit them into the pans. Mix 1/2 cup each of ground blanched almonds and grated Cheddar cheese and divide this mixture among the lined pans. Beat 2 eggs with 1 teaspoon flour and 1/4 teaspoon salt, add 1 cup cream, and strain this custard over the cheese and almond mixture. Bake the custard tarts in a moderately hot oven (375° F.) for about 25 minutes. Add one warm pastry to each serving of cream of chicken soup and sprinkle with chopped parsley.

Wildbrühe
Game Stock or Bouillon

THE GAME stocks used as a base for various game soups are prepared in the same way as beef bouillon, but the meat and bones of venison, hare, or other game are used instead of beef. Chickens are replaced by game birds—pheasant, partridge, or grouse—and carcasses of game birds should also be added. All meat, bones, birds, and carcasses must always be browned in butter or fat as a first step in making game stock. Crushed juniper berries and sprigs of basil and rosemary are usually added to the seasonings.

In a large kettle, brown 2 pounds venison, 1 1/2 pounds venison bones, cracked, and 2 partridges in 1/2 cup butter. Add 4 quarts water, cover the kettle, and bring the water to a boil very slowly. Remove the scum and add 2 teaspoons salt. Sauté an onion stuck with 3 cloves in butter and add it with 2 carrots, scraped and sliced, 1 turnip, peeled and sliced, the white part of 3 leeks, sliced, 1 bunch parsley stems, 1 bay leaf, 6 sprigs each of parsley, thyme, basil, and rosemary, 6 bruised peppercorns, and 6 crushed juniper berries. Simmer the stock, covered, for 2 hours. Strain it and add salt to taste.

Game Consommé   *Wildconsommé*

GAME BOUILLON is clarified to make game consommé in the same manner as beef bouillon, but with ground lean venison or game meat mixed with egg whites or with the carcasses of game birds, chopped and mixed with egg whites, instead of with beef.

Carefully lift the layer of hardened fat from the top and turn the cold stock or bouillon into a kettle. Stir 1 pound lean venison, ground, with 2 lightly beaten egg whites and 2 cups finely chopped roots— 1 carrot, 1 onion, the white part of 2 leeks, and 8 parsley stems. Stir the mixture into the game stock. Stir it slowly until it boils. Cover the kettle and simmer the stock for 1 hour. Strain the game consommé through a wet cloth and serve it with garnishes or use it in recipes that call for a game consommé base.

Pheasant Soup   *Schönbrunnersuppe*

ROAST 2 PHEASANT, uncovered, in a moderate oven (375° F.) for 50 minutes to 1 hour, basting them frequently with 1/2 cup melted butter. Cut off the breasts and reserve them.

Simmer the pheasant carcasses for 1 hour in 3 quarts strong brown stock with 2 stalks of celery, 3 sprigs of parsley, 1 teaspoon thyme, and a bay leaf. Strain the pheasant stock.

In a large saucepan, melt 1/2 cup butter, stir in gradually 1 cup flour, and cook the *roux* over low heat, stirring, until it is golden. Add the strained pheasant stock and simmer the mixture gently for 1/2 hour. Beat 4 egg yolks lightly and add 2 cups cream and a little of the hot soup. Return the mixture to the pan and reheat it with 1 cup dry Sherry, the pheasant breasts, diced, the juice of half a lemon, a dash of cayenne, and salt to taste. Serves 12.

Fischbrühe *Fish Stock*

COMBINE 2 POUNDS assorted white fish, cut into pieces, with 1 pound fish heads and bones, 6 cups cold water, 1 cup white wine, 2 sliced leeks, 1 sliced onion, 2 small celery stalks, peeled and sliced, 6 sprigs of parsley or 2 parsley roots, scraped, 1/2 bay leaf, a sprig of thyme, 1 clove, and 1 teaspoon salt. Bring the water to a boil and simmer the fish for half an hour. Pour the stock through a fine sieve, let it cool, and store it in the refrigerator in a tightly covered container.

Fischkraftbrühe *Fish Consommé*

CHOP 1/2 POUND white fish, preferably pike, or purée it in a food processor. Stir in 1 egg white and add 1 onion, finely chopped, the white part of 1 leek, finely chopped, and 1 parsley root, scraped. If parsley root is not available, use 2 tablespoons chopped parsley. Stir in 1 cup white wine and then stir the mixture into 2 quarts fish stock. Stir the stock over high heat until it comes to a boil and reduce the heat. Cover the stock and simmer it for 45 minutes, without stirring. Strain the stock through a fine cloth and add salt and white pepper to taste. Use this fish consommé as a base for fish soups.

Oyster Soup — *Nordseeausternsuppe*

MELT 3 TABLESPOONS butter in a saucepan, stir in 1/2 cup flour, and cook the *roux,* stirring constantly, until it starts to turn golden. Add 6 cups fish stock, and cook, stirring, until the soup is smooth. Simmer it for 20 minutes, stirring occasionally. Season it with 1/2 teaspoon lemon juice, a pinch of cayenne, and salt and pepper. Mix 2 egg yolks with 1 cup cream and a little of the hot liquid, stir the eggs into the soup, and cook, but do not boil it, for 3 minutes. Remove the soup to a warm place. Just before serving, poach 18 freshly opened oysters in Champagne to cover until the edges curl. Add them and the Champagne to the soup and heat it to just below the boiling point. Serve it at once, sprinkled with chopped parsley.

Eel Soup — *Aalsuppe*

PLACE IN A large kettle 1 stewing chicken, 2 pounds beef, cubed, 2 pounds beef and veal bones, chopped, and, if possible, 1 calf's foot. Cover the ingredients with cold water, cover the kettle, and bring the water slowly to a boil. Remove any scum from the surface, add 1 teaspoon salt, and simmer the stock for 4 hours, adding a ladleful of cold water, about 1/2 cup, once each hour.

In a second kettle place the white part of 3 leeks, chopped, 1 celery root, peeled and chopped, 2 cups freshly shelled peas, 3 carrots, scraped and diced, 3 stalks of celery, diced, 2 parsley roots, scraped, or 1/2 cup chopped parsley, and 6 mushrooms, chopped. Add beef stock just to cover and cook the vegetables slowly until they are soft, about 1/2 hour. Cook 1 quart raspberries and 1 quart currants with 1/2 cup sugar in water to cover until the berries are soft. Drain them well and press them through a sieve. Set the berry purée aside.

Strain the meat stock, rinse out the kettle, return 8 cups of the strained stock to it and place it over low heat. Stir in 4 tablespoons butter into which 4 tablespoons flour have been worked. Stir the soup until the butter is dissolved and add the vegetables with their broth and the berry purée.

Cut into 2-inch lengths 1 large or 2 small eels, which have been cooked in fish stock or salted water for 25 minutes. Draw off the skin and add the pieces to the soup.

Simmer 6 small pears, quartered and cored, and 6 plums, quartered and stoned, in water to cover, only long enough to soften them. Do not cook them until they fall apart.

Melt 1/2 cup currant jelly in 1/4 cup wine vinegar, add 1/2 cup hot Sherry, 6 freshly chopped sprigs each of thyme, marjoram, tarragon, and mint, and salt and pepper to taste. Add this mixture to the soup. The soup should be sweet-sour and the warm Sherry should be added to taste.

Serve the soup in large soup plates with pieces of eel in each plate. Add pieces of pear and plum to each serving and garnish each with 2 *Mehlklösse,* or flour dumplings.

Krebssuppe   *Crayfish Soup*

WASH 20 CRAYFISH well and remove the intestinal vein from under the tail. Poach them in boiling salted water with several sprigs of fresh dill for 10 to 15 minutes, depending on their size, or until they are bright red. Drain them and break the meat out of the claws and tails.

Dry the empty shells in the oven for a short time and pound them in a mortar until they are broken up as finely as possible. Melt 1/2 cup butter over simmering water, add the pulverized shells, and cook for 10 minutes without letting the butter boil. Remove the mixture from the heat, blend in 1/4 cup flour, and add 2 quarts rich fish consommé. Simmer the soup gently over direct heat for 30 minutes. Strain it through a fine sieve and season with salt and pepper. At serving time bring the soup to the boiling point and finish it with 1/4 cup cream and 2 tablespoons each of butter and Sherry. Garnish it with the crayfish meat and generous spoon- fuls of freshly cooked green peas, white asparagus heads, and cauliflower flowerets and with several small mushroom dumplings and chicken dumplings.

Russische Krebssuppe   *Cold Russian Crayfish Soup*

WASH 30 CRAYFISH well and remove the intestinal vein from under the tail. Poach them in boiling salted water with several sprigs of fresh dill for 10 to 15 minutes, depending on their size, or until they are bright red.

Drain them and break the meat out of the claws and tails. Remove the gall sack and crush the bodies and empty shells in a mortar with 1 cup beef stock. Transfer the mixture to a kettle, add 3 cups beef stock and 3 sprigs of dill, and simmer the mixture, covered, for 1 hour. Cool it, remove the fat, and strain the stock. Cook 10 beets, scrubbed, in salted water until they are soft, about 20 minutes. Peel them while they are hot and chop them roughly in a china or enamel bowl. Do not use a wooden bowl, so that none of the red juice will be lost. Drain off the juice and continue to chop the beets until they are finely minced and all the remaining juice can be pressed out of them. Add the red beet juice to 2 cups sour cream and add 1 cup heavy cream, 1/2 cup Madeira, and Worchestershire sauce to taste. Add the cooled and strained beef stock and salt and pepper to taste. Chill the soup for at least 2 hours and add the claws and tails of the crayfish. Stir well and serve with buttered black bread fingers dusted with chopped dill.

Merano Fish Soup — *Meraner Fischsuppe*

IN A LARGE kettle sauté 1 carrot, scraped and chopped, 2 celery stalks, diced, 2 onions, chopped, and the white part of 1 leek, chopped, in 1/2 cup olive oil until the onions are puffed and golden. Add 2 cups white wine and 3 cups water or fish stock to the vegetables and 1 pound of any white fish and season with 6 sprigs of chopped parsley, 1 garlic clove, and salt and pepper to taste. Simmer the soup about 15 minutes, until the fish is opaque and the vegetables are nearly tender. Add 1/2 pound shrimps, shelled and deveined, 1 cup scallops, 1 cup rice, only half cooked or *al dente,* and 1 teaspoon mild mustard stirred smooth with 2 tablespoons of the hot fish soup. Cook the soup about 5 minutes more, or until the shrimps are done. Stir in threads of saffron until the soup is pale yellow and add salt and pepper to taste. Serve the soup sprinkled generously with chopped chives.

Lobster Soup — *Hummersuppe*

SPLIT A SMALL live lobster down the back and discard the intestinal vein. In a skillet melt 1/4 cup butter and sauté the lobster until the shell is red, turning it constantly with a spoon. Add 1 cup dry white wine, 3 tablespoons chopped dill, 1 tablespoon caraway seeds, 1 tablespoon chopped parsley, and 1 teaspoon finely chopped chives. Cook the lobster gently for 15 minutes and let it cool in the sauce. Melt 1/4 cup butter in a saucepan and stir 1/3 cup flour. Cook this *roux,* stirring, until it begins to turn golden. Add gradually 2 quarts fish stock, stirring constantly, and cook, stirring, until the soup is smooth. Simmer it for 5 minutes.

Cut the cooled lobster tail into sections and crack the claws. Crush the rest of the lobster shell in a mortar, and add it to the soup, together with the sauce from the cooked lobster. Simmer the soup for 45 minutes and strain it through a fine sieve. Steep 1 teaspoon saffron threads in hot fish stock and strain it into the soup. Season with salt and pepper. Mix 2 egg yolks with 1/2 cup cream, stir the yolks into the soup, and cook it for 3 minutes, but do not let it boil. Garnish the soup with the reserved lobster claws and tail sections and sprinkle it with finely chopped fresh dill.

Gemüsebouillon

Vegetable Bouillon

IN A KETTLE sauté 2 onions, chopped, in 2 tablespoons butter. When they are puffed and golden add the white part of 2 leeks, chopped, 1 medium-sized celery root, peeled and sliced, 2 carrots, scraped and sliced, 1/8 head

of cabbage, roughly chopped, 1 small cauliflower, separated into flowerets, and 1 turnip, sliced. Season the vegetables with 1 teaspoon salt and 1/2 teaspoon each of chopped thyme, rosemary, and basil, and add 2 quarts cold water. Cook the bouillon slowly for 30 minutes. Strain the bouillon and add salt and pepper to taste, and a grating of nutmeg. This bouillon, or stock, can be used as a base for sauces and soups, or it can be pressed through a rough sieve and served as a purée of vegetable soup, in which case it is better when 3 small potatoes, peeled and sliced, are added to the vegetables.

Artichoke Soup — *Artischockensuppe*

REMOVE THE hard outer leaves of 6 artichokes, trim the stems, and with a sharp knife cut off the leaves about 1/2 inch from the base. Cut out the center chokes and rub the cut parts with lemon juice. Melt 1/4 cup butter in a saucepan, add the white part of 2 leeks, sliced, 1/2 head lettuce, shredded, and the juice of 1/2 lemon, and cook the vegetables for 2 minutes. Add 2 quarts chicken stock. Bring the liquid to a boil, add the artichoke leaves, and simmer for 25 minutes. Add 1 cup shelled green peas and cook 20 minutes longer. Purée the soup in a food processor and season it with salt and pepper.

Melt 4 tablespoons butter in a saucepan, stir in 4 tablespoons flour, and cook the *roux*, stirring constantly, until it starts to turn golden. Gradually add 1 cup chicken stock, stirring. Add the soup and cook it, stirring, until it is smooth. Remove it from heat and add 1/3 cup heavy cream.

Mix together 1 hard-cooked egg, riced, 1 small onion, chopped, 2 tablespoons chopped parsley, 2 tablespoons capers, and 1 tablespoon grated lemon rind. Fill the 6 cooked artichokes with the mixture and garnish with a slice of lemon cut paper thin. Reheat the soup and add 1 filled artichoke to each serving.

Balkan Chlodnik — *Balkanische Chlodnik*

IN A LARGE kettle boil 1 bunch well-scrubbed beets with 1 pound well-washed beet leaves in 6 cups salted water until they are soft. Chop the cooked beets and leaves fine in a wooden bowl and return them to the soup with all the juices in the bowl. Add, off the heat, 1/2 pound cold boiled shrimps, chopped, 3 hard-cooked eggs, riced, 1 cucumber, seeded and chopped, 1 thinly sliced lemon, 1/4 cup finely chopped dill, and 3 tablespoons chopped chives. Add 4 cups sour cream, 2 cups beer, and salt and pepper to taste and stir well. Chill the soup, garnish it with cold cooked shrimps, and serve it with an ice cube in each soup plate. Serves 12.

Balkanische Suppe — Balkan Soup

COVER A 3-pound chicken in a kettle with cold water, add 1 teaspoon salt, and bring the water to a boil. Add 1 onion, 1 leek, 1 carrot, 4 sprigs of parsley, and a pinch of ground mace. Cook the chicken, covered, until it is tender, about 1 hour, adding more water if necessary. Strain the chicken stock, cool it, and skim off the fat. There should be about 6 cups.

Melt 1/4 cup butter in a large saucepan and add 1 finely chopped onion, 1 seeded chopped green pepper, 1/4 cup finely chopped ham, the diced white meat of the chicken, and 1 teaspoon sweet paprika. Cook the mixture 10 minutes, stirring constantly. Add 1 cup tomatoes, peeled, seeded, and chopped, 2 tablespoons rice, 1 teaspoon salt, and white pepper to taste and cook, stirring, until the rice is coated with butter. Add the chicken stock to the saucepan and simmer the soup until the rice is soft, about 30 minutes. Rice 1 hard-cooked egg over the soup and serve it at once, dusted with 1/2 cup chopped parsley.

Westfälische Bohnensuppe — Westphalian White Bean Soup

SOAK 2 CUPS dried white beans in 4 cups water overnight. Drain the beans and cook them with 1 onion in 3 cups water until they are soft, about 1 hour. Press the beans through a sieve while they are still hot, with the water in which they were boiled. Stir the bean purée into 4 cups simmering beef stock and boil the soup for 3 minutes. Season to taste with salt and pepper and add 1 tablespoon vinegar or the juice of 1/2 lemon. Garnish the soup with 1/2 cup each of baby Lima beans, carrot balls, and potato balls, all cooked, and 1/4 cup finely chopped chives. Cut the carrot and potato balls with the smallest melon cutter and cook them in salted water for 10 to 15 minutes, depending on their size. Stir 4 ounces white wine into the soup before the garnishes are added, if desired.

Polish Beet Soup   *Polnische rote Rübensuppe*

COOK 3/4 POUND peeled, diced beets in 6 cups strong beef stock until
they are tender. Purée the soup in a processor and add the juice of 3 raw
beets which have been grated and pressed out to obtain all the juices.
Add 1/2 cup red wine, 1/4 pound lean diced ham, and 2 skinned diced
beef frankfurters. Beat 1/2 cup sour cream with the juice and the grated
rind of 1/2 lemon, 1 tablespoon finely minced dill, and 1 teaspoon sugar.
Add salt and pepper to the soup to taste and beat in the sour cream, or
serve it on top of the soup, dusted with minced fresh dill.

White Cheese Soup   *Weisse Käsesuppe*

IN A kettle cook 2 chopped onions and 1 cup chopped leek, the white
part only, in 3 tablespoons butter until the vegetables are soft. Blend in
3 tablespoons flour and cook, stirring constantly, until the mixture is golden.
Gradually stir in 5 cups warm water and 1/2 teaspoon salt and cook for
15 minutes. Crush two 3-ounce packages of warm cream cheese with salt
and white pepper to taste and beat in 1 cup yoghurt. Add 2 eggs and beat
the mixture until it is smooth. Keep the soup just below the boil and slowly
stir in the cheese mixture. Add more salt and pepper, if necessary, and
cook the soup, stirring, for 5 minutes. Add 1/4 cup finely chopped chives.

Iced Cucumber Yoghurt Soup   *Tarador*

MIX 4 MINCED garlic cloves with 1 teaspoon salt and 2 tablespoons olive
oil and stir the mixture into 2 cups yoghurt. Add 1 cucumber, seeded and
chopped, the juice and grated rind of 1/2 lemon, and 2 cups cold water
and stir well. Add 1/4 cup chopped parsley, 1/2 cup chopped walnuts,
and salt and pepper to taste and chill the soup. Serve an ice cube in each
cup. A smaller amount of garlic may be used or it may be omitted.

Goulash Soup   *Gulyássuppe Hotel Bristol*

IN A KETTLE or Dutch oven, brown 1 onion, minced, in 1 tablespoon butter
and 1 tablespoon bacon fat. Stir in 2 teaspoons sweet paprika and

add 3 pounds brisket of beef, cut in medium chunks, and 1/4 pound calf's liver. Brown the meat on all sides and dust it with a little flour. Add 1 cup white wine and salt to taste. Cover the pan and cook the meat gently for about 1 hour. Remove the liver, mince it, and return it to the kettle with 1 green pepper, seeded and chopped. Cook the *Gulyássuppe* for an hour or so longer, until the meat is tender. Boil 1 pound potatoes, peeled and quartered, in salted water to cover until they are barely tender. Add the potatoes to the *Gulyássuppe* with enough of the cooking water to make a medium thick soup. Add more paprika and salt to taste and cook all together for a few minutes longer.

Serve the meat and soup in soup plates and pass separately, as garnish for the soup, *Spätzle* dressed with melted butter. *(Picture, page 122.)*

Gulyássuppe   *Goulash Soup*

SAUTÉ 1/2 POUND chopped onions with 1/4 pound finely diced bacon, until the onions are puffed and golden. Add 3 tablespoons vinegar, 1 teaspoon each of paprika and caraway seeds, a pinch of marjoram, and 1 garlic clove, crushed, and stir for 5 minutes. Paprika becomes bitter if it is cooked too long. Add 6 cups beef stock, 1 pound finely cubed soup meat, 1 teaspoon salt, and 3 large tomatoes, peeled, seeded, and diced. Simmer the soup for 20 minutes. Add 3/4 pound peeled and diced potatoes and add more beef stock, if necessary. Continue to cook the soup until the meat and potatoes are soft. Stir 1/4 cup flour into 3/4 cup water and stir the mixture slowly into the soup. Continue to cook the soup until it is thickened. Cut 3 peeled cooked beef frankfurters into 1/4-inch slices and add them to the soup with a squeeze of lemon juice.

Bulgarische Hammelsuppe   *Bulgarian Lamb Soup*

IN A LARGE kettle combine 1/2 pound shoulder of lamb, free of all fat and cut into medium dice, and 6 cups cold water. Bring the water to a boil and add 1 teaspoon salt. Cook the meat until it is nearly soft, about 20 minutes, and add 3 peeled tomatoes and 3 green peppers, all seeded and chopped, 1 large onion, chopped, and 2 tablespoons rice. Cook 15 minutes longer. In a saucepan melt 2 tablespoons butter and blend in 2 tablespoons flour. Add slowly 1 cup of the lamb broth, strained, and cook the mixture, stirring constantly, until it thickens. Gradually stir it into the boiling soup and cook for 5 minutes. Beat 2 egg yolks into 1/4 cup yoghurt and add the juice and grated rind of 1/2 lemon. Reduce the heat so that the soup does not boil and add the yoghurt mixture and salt and pepper to taste. Sprinkle the soup with finely chopped parsley.

Lentil Soup with Red Wine   *Linsensuppe mit Rotwein*

SOAK 2 CUPS washed lentils in 1 quart water for 12 hours. In a large kettle sauté 2 onions, chopped, and 6 slices of bacon, diced, in 2 table-spoons butter until the onions are puffed and golden. Stir in the lentils with the water in which they soaked, 4 cups beef stock, and 1 cup red wine. Add 1 ham bone, 1 carrot, sliced, 2 stalks of celery, diced, 1 bay leaf, and 1 pinch each of thyme and marjoram. Cover the kettle and simmer the soup for 45 minutes. Add 2 peeled potatoes, diced, and 1/2 cup red wine and cook the soup until the potatoes have disintegrated, about 45 minutes. Remove the bone and bay leaf and purée the soup in a processor. Add 1 tablespoon tarragon vinegar and salt and pepper to taste. Reheat the soup and add 4 peeled hot beef frankfurters cut into 1/4-inch slices. Sprinkle the soup with 1/4 cup chervil, finely minced, and serve separately about 1 cup croutons, to be added to the soup at the last moment.

Mushroom Soup   *Schwämmerlsuppe*

LIGHTLY BROWN 1 pound mushrooms, chopped, and 2 onions, chopped, in 1/2 cup butter. Add 1 cup beef stock and cook the mushrooms slowly for 20 minutes. Stir 1 cup light brown sauce (see Sauces) into the mush-rooms and continue cooking, stirring constantly, until the mixture is well heated but not boiling. In a large kettle heat 6 cups clear brown veal stock and season the soup to taste with salt and pepper and a few grains of cayenne pepper. Slowly add warm Madeira to taste, using from 1/4 to 3/4 cup. Stir the mushroom mixture into the soup and heat it to boiling. Garnish each soup plate with 1/2 cup diced tongue and 1 teaspoon snipped chives, sprinkled over 1 chicken dumpling. The tongue and chives may be incorporated in the chicken dumplings before they are cooked, if preferred.

Erbsensuppe mit Schweinefüssen

*Country Pea Soup
with Pigs' Knuckles*

SOAK 2 CUPS dried green peas in cold water overnight and drain them. Boil 2 pigs' knuckles with 1 tablespoon salt in water to cover for 15 minutes. Drain them well and rinse them in cold water. Place them in a large kettle with the drained peas, 1 onion, 1 carrot, and 3 stalks of celery, all chopped, and 1 teaspoon salt. Add 2 quarts cold water. Simmer the soup slowly, covered, until the peas are soft, about 2 hours. Remove the pigs' knuckles, purée the soup in a processor, and season it to taste. Cut the meat from the bones, return it to the soup, and serve at once. The peasants eat this soup as it is, unstrained.

Kartoffelsuppe mit Käse

Potato Soup with Cheese

PEEL AND DICE 8 medium-sized potatoes and 1 onion and cook the vegetables in 6 cups salted water for 10 minutes. In a saucepan melt 2 tablespoons butter, blend in 2 tablespoons flour, slowly add 1 cup of the hot potato water and cook, stirring constantly, until the mixture is smooth.

98

Return the mixture to the pan containing the potatoes. Add 1 teaspoon each of dill, mint, parsley, chervil, and chives, all chopped, and salt and pepper to taste and cook the soup until the potatoes are soft, stirring. Crush one 8-ounce package of warm cream cheese with salt and pepper to taste. Rice it through a coarse sieve into 6 hot soup plates and sprinkle each portion with 1 tablespoon chopped parsley. Pour the hot potato soup over the cheese and serve at once.

Potato Soup *Kartoffelsuppe*

PEEL AND DICE 6 large potatoes and cook them until they are soft in 6 cups salted water or beef stock. Add 3 stalks of celery and 2 carrots, chopped. Brown 1 chopped onion in 2 tablespoons butter, blend in 2 tablespoons flour, and cook the mixture 1 minute. Add gradually 1 cup of the potato soup and continue to cook, stirring constantly, until the mixture is smooth. Combine it with the rest of the potato soup and simmer the soup 20 minutes. Add 1 crushed garlic clove, a pinch each of crushed caraway seeds and marjoram, and salt and white pepper to taste. Purée the soup in a processor and add more stock, if it is too thick. Serve with a dusting of grated lemon rind and finely minced raw mushrooms and minced chives, or break crisp cooked bacon into the soup.

Sauerkraut Soup *Sauerkrautsuppe*

SIMMER 1 POUND sauerkraut in 3 cups beef stock for 1/2 hour. Sauté 2 large chopped onions with 3 slices of diced bacon until they are golden. Stir in 1 teaspoon paprika and add 3 cups beef stock, 1/4 cup puréed tomatoes or 1 tablespoon tomato paste, 1/2 teaspoon caraway seeds, and salt to taste. Stir the sauerkraut with its stock into the soup kettle and add 2 potatoes that have been peeled, grated, soaked in cold water, and pressed out. Continue to boil the soup for 1/2 hour. Before serving, add enough more stock to have 6 cups in all, 1/4 pound lean diced ham, and 2 beef frankfurters, skinned and sliced. Cook the soup long enough to heat the meat through.

Tomatensuppe   *Basic Tomato Soup*

BAKE 2 POUNDS tomatoes, quartered, in a lightly buttered, covered casserole in a slow oven (300° F.) for 40 minutes, or until they are softened. In a large kettle sauté 1 onion, chopped, in 3 tablespoons butter until the onion is puffed and transparent, add 3/4 cup diced ham and 1 turnip, peeled and sliced, and stir well. Dust 2 tablespoons flour over the mixture and stir it until the flour is absorbed. Add 6 cups boiling beef stock to the kettle with 1 garlic clove, 1/2 teaspoon minced rosemary, and a sprig each of basil, thyme, and parsley. Cover the kettle and let the soup come slowly to a boil. Add the tomatoes and simmer the soup for 30 minutes. Purée it in a processor and add salt, pepper, and sugar to taste.

Kalte Paradeissuppe   *Paradise Soup*

PURÉE 2 1/2 pounds chopped red ripe tomatoes and strain them through a sieve. There should be 3 1/2 cups of purée. Chill it thoroughly. When ready to serve, add 2 ice cubes, 1 tablespoon sugar, 2 teaspoons salt, 1/2 teaspoon onion juice, and the juice and grated rind of 1/2 lemon and stir well. Add 1/2 cup sour cream and beat the soup until it is smooth. Cut 8 slices cold boiled ham into thin julienne strips and add them.

With a large French cutter scoop out an equal number of balls from a cantaloupe, a casaba melon, and from large cucumbers. Salt the melon and cucumber balls and grind a little pepper over them. Mound the seasoned melon and cucumber balls and sprinkle them with minced parsley and mint. Pour the chilled soup around the garnish. *(Picture, page 120.)*

Kalte Tomatensuppe mit Wein   *Iced Tomato Soup with Wine*

CUT UP 2 pounds tomatoes, slice 1/2 pound onions, and cook the vegetables in 4 cups beef consommé with 1 teaspoon sugar until very thick. Purée the soup in a processor, correct the seasoning, and chill it. Chop 1 cucumber, seeded, very fine and chill it. Make a paste of 1/2 teaspoon each of salt and paprika, 1/4 teaspoon freshly ground black pepper, and 1 egg yolk. Crush 2 garlic cloves and add them to the paste. Beat in 2 to 3 tablespoons olive oil, drop by drop, as in mayonnaise, until you have a very thick cream. Chill it.

When serving, pour 1 cup chilled white wine into the soup, add the chopped cucumber and stir in the cream mixture. Put an ice cube in each soup plate and pour the soup over it. Cover the top of soup with chopped parsley.

Cheese Tomato Soup — *Tomatensuppe mit Käse*

COOK 2 POUNDS ripe seeded tomatoes in 6 cups boiling water until they are soft. Remove the tomatoes, purée them in a processor, and return the tomato purée with 1/2 cup rice to the water in the kettle. Add salt and pepper to taste. In a saucepan melt 2 tablespoons butter, blend in 2 tablespoons flour, and slowly add 1 cup of the hot tomato broth. Cook the mixture, stirring constantly, for 5 minutes, then gradually stir it into the hot soup. Add 1 tablespoon minced mint leaves and simmer the soup until the rice is soft. Crush one 3-ounce package warm cream cheese with salt and white pepper to taste and press the cheese through a coarse sieve into the soup.

Sprinkle the soup with 2 tablespoons chopped parsley and serve it at once.

Monks' Soup — *Kapuzinersuppe*

SAUTÉ 1 MEDIUM onion, sliced, in 2 tablespoons butter until it is soft and transparent, and add 4 cups chicken stock, 1/2 teaspoon salt, a pinch of freshly ground black pepper, and 2 teaspoons flour blended into a paste with 3 tablespoons cold water. Cook the soup, stirring constantly, until it boils. Carefully wash 2 pounds spinach and cook it without additional water until it is soft. The spinach must be stirred frequently until it wilts. Purée the spinach in a blender or put it through the finest blade of the food chopper, with its own liquid. Add the spinach and 1 cup heavy cream and cook the soup until it is heated.

Prepare 6 large *profiteroles* the size of lemons, one for each soup plate. Fill the hot *profiteroles* with 3 tablespoons each of a mixture of 1 hard-cooked egg, riced, 1/2 cup diced cooked chicken, and 1/4 cup diced cooked ham, and enough stiff lemon mayonnaise to bind. The soup and *profiteroles* should be hot. The salad in the *profiteroles* should be cold but not chilled.

Tiroler Gemüsesuppe
Tirolese Vegetable Soup

SLICE 2 SCRAPED carrots, 1/2 head cauliflower, 3 celery stalks, 1 garlic clove, 6 mushrooms, 1 small celery root, and the white part of 2 leeks. There should be 4 cups of sliced vegetables in all. In a heavy saucepan, simmer 1 onion, and 2 slices bacon, all diced, in 1/2 cup butter. Add the vegetables and cook them, stirring, until they are coated and wilted. Add 2 tomatoes, peeled, seeded, and chopped, and 2 tablespoons tomato paste and cook for 5 minutes. Add 2 quarts beef stock and cook the soup for 2 hours. Half an hour before serving, add 1/4 cup rice and 1/2 cup macaroni broken into very short lengths. In a small saucepan boil 1/2 cup dried white beans in water for 1 1/2 hours. Add the beans with the water in which they cooked, 1/2 cup chopped parsley, and salt and pepper to taste. Serve with 1/2 cup grated Parmesan.

Kalte Brunnenkressesuppe
Cold Water Cress Soup

BRING 3 CUPS beef stock, or beef consommé, to a boil and add 4 medium potatoes, peeled and sliced, and 1 large onion, chopped. Cook the potatoes until they completely disintegrate, about 1/2 hour, stirring to obtain a smooth creamy liquid. If the potatoes are still lumpy, purée them and keep them hot. Clean 1 large, or 2 small, bunches of water cress and remove the heavy stems. Reserve the nicest sprigs to garnish the soup plates. Chop the water cress very finely and sauté it in 4 tablespoons butter for about 5 minutes. Add the sautéed water cress to the potato stock and simmer the soup for about 10 minutes. Take it from the heat and stir in the yolk of 1 egg beaten into 1 cup heavy cream. Chill the soup thoroughly and add 2 tablespoons Moselle wine. Garnish with water cress. Serve separately thin slices of apple, cored and peeled, made into thin open sandwiches and cut into fingers. The apple should be cut at the last moment and sprinkled with lemon juice.

Cream of Vegetable Soup   *Gemüserahmsuppe*

ASPARAGUS, BROCCOLI, Brussels sprouts, cauliflower, spinach, and the like are appropriate for creamed soups. Cook the vegetable in salted water until it is just tender. Set aside a few cooked tips, sprouts, or flowerets for garnish. Strain the cooking water.

Melt 1/4 cup butter in a saucepan, blend in 1/3 cup flour, and cook the *roux,* stirring constantly, until it is well blended and golden. Do not let it brown. Add gradually 6 cups liquid—use up to 3 cups of the strained vegetable cooking water plus enough chicken, veal, or beef stock to make 6 cups in all. (For a cream of cauliflower soup, for instance, the salted water in which the cauliflower cooked would be used with chicken stock.) Cook the soup, stirring constantly, until it is smooth. Add the cooked vegetable, except the bits reserved for garnish, and simmer the soup for 30 minutes. Purée the soup in a processor. Stir in 1 cup cream beaten with 2 egg yolks. Return the soup to the heat for a few minutes, but do not let it reach the boiling point. Add salt and pepper to taste and swirl in a little piece of butter just before serving. Cream of vegetable soups should be thinned with warm milk. Garnish with the reserved vegetable: asparagus tips for cream of asparagus soup, cauliflower flowerets for cream of cauliflower soup, and so on.

In some cases it is not necessary to precook the vegetable in water. It can simply be simmered for 30 minutes in the soup and then pressed through a sieve. In this case the chicken or meat stock is increased to 2 quarts.

Cream of Vegetable Soup Variations

Spargelkohlsuppe Toska   Cream of Broccoli Soup Tosca

COOK 1 POUND broccoli and make cream of broccoli soup as for cream of vegetable soup, above. Garnish each serving with a lemon basket filled with curls of salted whipped cream and circle the basket with cooked broccoli heads. Serve the soup hot or chilled.

Karfiolpüreesuppe Liane   Cream of Cauliflower Soup

COOK 2 MEDIUM heads of cauliflower and make cream of cauliflower soup as in cream of vegetable soup. Thin it with 1 cup hot milk and garnish with ham, cut in strips, and bread croutons, fried in onion butter. Or chill cream of cauliflower soup and garnish it with strips of ham, strips of raw mushroom, and diced raw cauliflower.

Or thin cream of cauliflower soup with hot milk and serve it with cauliflower flowerets surrounding 1 chicken dumpling in each soup plate.

Kohlsprossensuppe   Cream of Brussels Sprout Soup

COOK 1 POUND Brussels sprouts. Retain 12 to 18 Brussels sprouts as garnish. Make cream of Brussels sprouts soup as in cream of vegetable soup. Garnish it with the Brussels sprouts and browned chopped chestnuts.

Erbsensuppe   Cream of Green Pea Soup

COOK AND purée 4 cups shelled peas. Melt 1/4 cup butter, blend in 1/4 cup flour, and cook the *roux*, stirring constantly, until it starts to turn golden. Add a little of the liquid in which the peas cooked and 6 cups hot chicken stock, stirring constantly. Cook the soup, stirring, until it is smooth. Add 1 onion, sliced, 2 lettuce leaves, 1 sprig of parsley, and salt to taste. Simmer the soup for 20 minutes. Purée the soup in a processor, add the pea purée, and correct the seasoning. Stir in 1 cup cream beaten with 2 egg yolks and reheat the soup, but do not let it boil.

Erbsensuppe Rigoletto   Cream of Green Pea Soup Rigoletto

SIMMER 6 CUPS cream of green pea soup with 1 cup spinach leaves, washed, dried, and chopped, for 10 minutes. Serve separately slices of toast spread with any cheese soufflé mixture, dusted with grated Parmesan, and baked in the oven until they are puffed and golden.

Cream of Green Pea Soup with Mushroom Soufflés — *Erbsensuppe Felicitas*

INTO 1/2 CUP thick béchamel sauce, beat 2 egg yolks and 1/2 cup finely minced, cooked ham and season with freshly ground black pepper. Fold in 2 egg whites, beaten stiff but not dry, and blend well. Wash, dry, and stem large perfect mushrooms and fill the caps with the ham soufflé mixture. Sprinkle the little soufflés with grated Parmesan and bake them in a moderately hot oven (375° F.) for about 12 minutes. Add one mushroom soufflé to each serving of hot cream of green pea soup and serve at once.

Beer Soup — *Biersuppe*

SIMMER 3 CUPS beer for 3 minutes, take it from the heat, and stir in 3/4 cup sugar and 3 egg yolks beaten into 3 cups milk. Return the soup to the heat, but do not let it come to a boil. Beat it until it is smooth and foamy and serve it at once.

Cold Fruit Soups — *Kaltschalen und Suppen*

KALTSCHALE, TRANSLATED, means "cold cup," and it is probably a forerunner of the fruit-juice appetizer. These cold fruit soups are served in soup plates or bouillon cups and are garnished and treated in every way as any cold summer soup would be.

Cold Lemon Soup — *Kalte Zitronensuppe*

GRATE THE rind of 4 lemons over 1/2 cup sugar and squeeze their juice over the sugar. Beat 5 egg yolks with 1 cup light white wine and 1 cup water in the top of a double boiler, over simmering water, until the eggs start to thicken. Gradually add the lemon juice and sugar mixture, beating constantly. Continue to beat until the mixture is smooth and thick and has tripled in volume. Take it from the heat and beat it until it is cold. Serve it with a dusting of ground cloves.

The Viennese advise adding sugar to taste. Chill the soup until it is needed.

Kalte Weinsuppe   Cold Wine Soup

To 5 CUPS rich beef consommé add 1 cup dry white wine and chill the soup. Garnish each serving with a thin slice of orange and sprinkle the soup with finely chopped parsley. Serve very cold, with salty orange macaroons.

Pfirsichkaltschale   Cold Peach Cup

SCALD 8 LARGE peaches and peel them. Cut the peaches in half. Remove the stones but retain them. Cut 3 of the peaches in thin slices, sprinkle them with lemon juice and sugar, and place the sugared slices on ice. Press the 5 remaining peaches through a sieve or purée in a blender and add the juice and grated rind of 1 lemon and 1 quart white wine. Add cold syrup made by boiling 1 1/2 cups sugar in 2 cups water to the thread stage. Crack the peach stones, extract the almonds, draw off their skins, and sliver them. Serve the soup garnished with the peach slices and the slivered almonds. Add peach brandy to taste and serve very cold.

Erdbeerkaltschale   Strawberry Cold Cup

HULL 1 POUND strawberries, retain the best ones, and prepare the soup as for cold peach cup. Garnish it with the whole strawberries and lace it with maraschino.

Himbeer oder Aprikosenkaltschale   Raspberry or Apricot Cold Cup

HIMBEERKALTSCHALE and *Aprikosenkaltschale* are both prepared as *Pfirsichkaltschale* is. Use apricot brandy for the apricot soup and maraschino for the raspberry soup.

Apple Soup   Apfelsuppe

SIMMER 4 LARGE sour apples, peeled, cored, and sliced, in 6 cups water
with 3/4 cup sugar, the peel of 1 lemon, and 1 piece of cinnamon stick
for 5 minutes. Add 7 tablespoons rice and simmer for 30 minutes longer,
or until the rice is soft. Purée the soup in a processor, return it to the heat,
and simmer it for 5 more minutes with 3 tablespoons raisins, sugar and
lemon juice to taste, and 1/2 cup dry white wine, or more to taste. Serve
the soup hot or cold, with zwieback.

Suppen Einlagen
Soup Garnishes

Almond Dumplings   Mandelklösse

SIMMER 1 1/3 CUPS dry bread crumbs in 1 cup milk with 4 tablespoons
butter. Cool the mixture slightly and stir in 2 egg yolks, 1 tablespoon flour,
1 tablespoon grated Parmesan, and salt and pepper to taste. Add 1/4 cup
finely chopped—but not ground—blanched almonds. Fold in 2 stiffly
beaten egg whites and form the mixture into small dumplings. Simmer
them gently in soup for 5 to 6 minutes.

Chicken Dumplings   Hühnerknödel

MINCE THE raw breast meat of 1 broiler and pound it with a meat or
ice mallet until it is fine. Bring 2 tablespoons butter to a boil in 1/2 cup
water, add 1/2 cup flour, all at once, and stir the mixture until it forms
a smooth paste and loosens from the sides of the saucepan. Take the
paste from the heat, stir the chicken meat into it, and add 2 tablespoons
butter, 1/2 tablespoon farina, 1 teaspoon chopped parsley, 1 teaspoon salt,
1/2 teaspoon grated onion, and pepper to taste. Stir in 1 egg and, after
it is incorporated, add 2 egg yolks. Stir the mixture into a perfectly smooth
paste. Form it into walnut-size dumplings and simmer them in salted
water for 5 to 8 minutes. Add a little farina if the first dumpling seems too

soft. Take the dumplings from the water with a slotted spoon and add them to any of the soups, as directed.

Käseknöderln   *Cheese Dumplings*

CREAM 3 TABLESPOONS butter in a warm bowl and stir in 1/2 cup grated Swiss cheese, 2 tablespoons flour, 1 egg yolk, 1 tablespoon minced parsley, and salt and pepper to taste. With floured hands, form the dough into small balls and drop them into gently boiling soup. Let the soup boil until the cheese dumplings rise to the surface and serve at once.

Griessknödel   *Farina Dumplings*

MIX 2 TABLESPOONS chopped parsley with 1 cup farina. Add 2 tablespoons hot melted butter. Beat about 8 tablespoons boiling beef bouillon into 1 egg and stir just enough of this liquid into the farina mixture to bind it so that it can be shaped into dumplings. Make 12 dumplings, lower them carefully into simmering beef bouillon, and cook them, covered, for 1/2 hour. *(Picture, page 123.)*

Light Farina Dumplings   *Griessnockerln*

STIR 1/2 CUP farina and 1/2 teaspoon salt into 1/4 cup butter that has been creamed with 2 eggs. Set the mixture aside for 15 minutes. Make a trial finger-shaped dumpling and lower it carefully into simmering beef bouillon. If it falls apart, add 1 tablespoon farina to the mixture; if it seems too solid, add 1 tablespoon milk. The dumplings should swell and rise to the surface. Shape the rest of the mixture into finger-shaped dumplings with slightly pointed ends. Lower them into the simmering soup with a slotted spoon and simmer them until they rise to the surface.

Light Finger Dumplings   *Leichte Nockerln*

MELT 1/4 CUP butter over medium heat, stir in 3/4 cup flour, and cook, stirring, until the mixture forms a smooth paste. Add salt and 2/3 cup cold water all at once and stir the paste until it is smooth. Take it from the heat and immediately stir in 2 small eggs until they are absorbed. When the mixture is cold, lower scoops of it with a slotted spoon into simmering beef bouillon and cook the dumplings for 20 minutes. Make a test dumpling and, if it falls apart, stir 2 tablespoons flour into the mixture. Dust the dumplings with 1/4 cup parsley, chopped, and serve.

Flour Dumplings   *Mehlknödel*

CREAM 4 TABLESPOONS butter, gradually add 2 egg yolks, 1/2 teaspoon salt, and, alternately, 1 1/2 cups flour and 1/2 cup milk. Fold in 2 stiffly beaten egg whites and form the mixture into dumplings the size of small walnuts. Lower them gently into boiling salted water and cook them, covered, for 6 minutes, or until they are done. Test one dumpling by cutting it in half. If the center is moist and dark, the dumplings will need another minute. Skim them from the water. Serve in clear soups.

Fish Dumplings   *Fishklösse*

SOAK 2 SLICES of stale bread in water and press out all the moisture. Sauté 1 small onion, finely chopped, in 1 tablespoon butter for 5 minutes without letting it brown. Add the bread and cook for 5 minutes longer. Take the pan from the heat and add 1 cup ground fresh halibut or cod, 1 egg yolk, 1 whole egg, a pinch of powdered thyme, and salt and pepper to taste, and stir well. Shape the mixture into small dumplings, roll them in flour, and simmer them gently in a shallow pan of court bouillon or salted water for 8 minutes. Remove them carefully with a skimmer and serve as a garnish for fish soups or as a garnish for fish dishes.

Schinkenknöderln   Ham Dumplings

CREAM 4 TABLESPOONS butter and add 2 egg yolks and 1/2 cup ground ham. Stir in 2 tablespoons cream and 1 1/3 cups dry bread crumbs. Stir the mixture well and add salt and pepper to taste. Fold in 2 stiffly beaten egg whites and form the mixture into small dumplings. Simmer them for 5 to 6 minutes in soup, or in salted water. Minced onion or parsley may be added to taste.

Leberknödel   Liver Dumplings

MIX 1 CUP minced or ground raw calf's liver with 1 cup dry bread crumbs and add 1/4 cup melted butter, 2 egg yolks, 1 grated onion, 1 teaspoon salt, and 1/2 teaspoon pepper. Fold in 2 stiffly beaten egg whites. Form 18 round dumplings and boil them gently in clear soup for 5 to 6 minutes or cook them in salted water and add them to soup just before serving. The cooked dumplings may be dusted with chopped parsley or 1/4 cup finely chopped parsley may be added to the dumpling batter.

Champignonschöberln   Mushroom Dumplings

SOAK 6 LARGE slices of white bread in water and press out all the moisture. Stir the bread with 1 teaspoon grated onion, to make a smooth paste, and gradually stir in 3 egg yolks. Add 12 medium mushrooms, finely chopped, 2 tablespoons chopped parsley, and enough dry bread crumbs to make a thick paste, about 2 to 3 tablespoons. Add salt and pepper to taste and fold in 3 stiffly beaten egg whites. Spread the mixture about 3/4 inch deep in a buttered pie pan and bake it in a moderately hot oven

(375° F.) for 20 minutes, or until it is puffed and lightly browned. Cut the mushroom "pudding" into dumpling-sized rounds and serve them in hot soup or pass them separately, to be added to the soup.

Emperor's Garnish — Kaisernockerln

BEAT 3 EGG yolks light and creamy. Stir in 1 tablespoon flour and 1 cup milk and salt and pepper to taste. Pour the mixture into a shallow heat-proof dish and place it in a pan of boiling water. Let the water boil until the mixture is firm and set. Cut out little scoops with a teaspoon and add them to any clear consommé or bouillon, or serve them in cream of tomato or cream of green pea soup.

Soup Noodles or Pancakes — Frittaten Nudeln oder Pfannkuchen

BEAT 2 EGGS, 1 cup flour, and 1/2 teaspoon salt into 1 cup milk until the batter is smooth. Butter an omelet pan lightly and pour enough of the batter into the pan to make a thin pancake. Tilt the pan to spread the batter thinly and evenly. When the pancake is light brown, turn it with a spatula and brown the other side. Roll up the baked pancakes and cut the rolls across into 1/4-inch noodles. Drop the noodles into soup. Or fill the pancakes with an appropriate filling and roll them up. Serve the rolled pancakes in hot soup. A little grated cheese or finely minced herbs may be mixed with the batter. Makes about 12 pancakes.

Chicken Hash Filling — Hühnerhachéefülle

SAUTÉ 1/4 cup finely chopped onion in 2 tablespoons butter until it is golden and add 1 cup finely ground cooked chicken, 1 teaspoon finely chopped parsley, and salt and pepper to taste. Sauté the chicken, stirring constantly, for 2 minutes, add 2 tablespoons heavy cream, and continue to cook for 2 minutes. Take the pan from the heat and add 1 egg yolk. Stir well and add a second egg yolk only if the mixture is too dry. Divide the chicken hash among 6 hot pancakes and fold them in from both sides. Roll up the folded pancakes, so that the filling cannot run out, and place one in each soup plate.

Spinatomelette   *Spinach Omelet Strips*

CREAM 1 1/2 tablespoons butter, add 2 egg yolks, 1 1/2 tablespoons flour, salt to taste, and 2 stiffly beaten egg whites. Melt 2 tablespoons butter in an omelet pan, pour in two-thirds of the batter, and cook it over medium heat until it starts to brown slightly. Mix the remaining batter with 1/3 cup spinach, cooked, minced, and pressed dry, and pour it over the half-cooked omelet in the pan. Finish cooking the omelet until it is well browned, roll it up, and cut the roll across, into narrow strips. Add the spinach omelet strips to hot consommé and sprinkle with freshly grated cheese.

Goldscheiben Suppe   *Gold Piece Soup*

PREPARE SOUP pancakes as for *Frittaten Nudeln oder Pfannkuchen* (page 111), adding 2 tablespoons minced parsley and salt to taste to the batter. Let the cooked pancakes cool slightly on a rack or on a double layer of paper towels and cut them into gold-piece-sized rounds with a 1-inch round cutter or with a knife. Cut rounds of the same size from cooked carrot slices and from 6 slices of Bologna sausage or 3 slices of cooked ham. (Make sure that all the rounds are cut to the same thickness.) Add the pancake, carrot, and meat rounds to 8 cups of simmering beef bouillon and continue to cook the soup until the garnishes are heated through thoroughly.

Pass toasted croutons, cut to the same size, as an accompaniment if desired.

Käseeierstichwürfel   *Cheese Custard Diamonds*

IN A HEATPROOF bowl beat 2 eggs with 1/4 cup grated Parmesan, 3 tablespoons cream, and 1/4 teaspoon salt. Add 2/3 cup hot milk, stirring constantly. Cover the bowl and place it in a deep pan of simmering water that extends three-quarters of the way up the sides of the bowl. Bring the water to a rapid boil. Reduce the heat and let the water simmer for 25 to 30 minutes, or until the cheese custard is firm. Invert the custard onto a pastry board, carefully cut it into 1/2-inch slices, and cut the slices into diamond shapes. Serve the cheese custard diamonds in clear soups or in cream of pea soup. *(Picture, page 123.)*

Assorted Stuffed Eggs   *(recipes, pages 21, 22, and 23)*

Herring in Sour Cream   *(recipe, page 37)*

Cauliflower Polonaise

(recipe, page 270)

Fried Mushrooms Hotel Schloss Dürnstein   *(recipe, page 57)*

Green Bean Salad

(recipe, page 357)

Steamed Asparagus Vinaigrette

(recipe, page 265)

Paradise Soup

(recipe, page 100)

Herring Salad   (recipe, page 367)

Goulash Soup Hotel Bristol

(recipe, page 95)

Consommé with Farina Dumplings, Pancake Strips,
and Cheese Custard Diamonds

(recipes, pages 108, 111, and 112)

Hot Fish Mousse Hotel Schloss Dürnstein

(recipe, page 145)

Shrimps with Rice and Peas   *(recipe, page 174)*

Whole Smoked Trout

(recipe, page 138)

Blue Carp Hotel Bristol   *(recipe, page 138)*

127

Ham Garnish

Schinkeneinlage

PUT 2 SMALL onions through the food chopper with 1/2 pound cooked ham and add 3 egg yolks lightly beaten and salt to taste. Stir the mixture into 6 cups cool strong chicken stock and heat the soup, but do not let it boil. Add large pieces of hot cooked chicken and sprinkle the soup with chopped parsley.

Baked Chicken Toasts

Gebackene Hühnerbrötchen

PUT THROUGH the finest blade of the food mill enough raw chicken meat to make 1/2 cup, stir in 1 egg white and 1/2 teaspoon salt, and grind the mixture a second time, or purée it in a processor. Put the mixture into a bowl over a larger bowl of ice and stir it with a wooden spoon until it is cold. Gradually stir in 1/2 cup heavy cream, and chill the chicken paste.

Toast on one side 6 bread rounds, cut with a 2-inch cookie cutter, and lay on each toasted side 1 large thin slice of onion. Lay a thin slice of

St. Stephen's Cathedral

cucumber over the onion and mound chilled chicken paste onto the cucumber. Sprinkle the 6 rounds with 1/2 cup grated Parmesan and dust the Parmesan with paprika to taste. Dot each round with a piece of butter and bake the rounds in a moderate oven (350° F.) for 15 minutes, or until the cheese is browned.

Serve 1 toast round in each plate of soup or pass them separately, to be put in the soup after it is served. Serve with mushroom or chicken soup.

Suppenmakronen   *Salty Orange Macaroons*

STIR 1/4 CUP grated blanched almonds and 1 tablespoon bread crumbs into 1 well-beaten egg yolk mixed with 1 tablespoon orange juice. Add 1/2 teaspoon each of grated orange rind and salt. Fold in 2 stiffly beaten egg whites and drop the mixture by teaspoons onto a baking sheet covered with brown paper. Bake the macaroons in a slow oven (300° F.) for 20 minutes. Float 3 to 4 macaroons on each plate of soup or pass them separately to be dropped into the soup after it is served.

Fische und Fastentiere

A<small>T ONE TIME</small>, the Austrian Empire owned a few precious miles of seaboard and, with it, a gallant little navy that was commanded by handsome officers in perfectly beautiful uniforms. To a people who view everything in the diminutive in any case, the fact that the sea, the shore, and the navy were small made them all the more endearing.

The Viennese loved their Adriatic—das Adriatische Meer, die Adria. It was their link with the great seaways to the east and the west, their way to the Orient and the Occident. Even though they had access to a relatively small sea, it was all real salt water. It had tides and whirlpools and it was notoriously treacherous; it could brew monumental storms, and the Viennese regarded it as utterly romantic.

When they went down to the Adria, they rarely got into it. But they sat in the sun on seaside terraces next to it and traveled over it in small steamers on lovely excursions to the islands. From the Adriatic, they could sail into the great Mediterranean, and from that larger sea to the Atlantic or the Indian Ocean, and so to the Pacific. It was all a long way round, and few of them took such a journey; but the important thing was that they had their sea and, with it, their own salt-water fish and shellfish.

All that is a dream of the past. The empire of the Hapsburgs lost its arm to the sea, and found itself suddenly without its lovely little navy and lovely little fishes. Much that the Viennese longed to eat became "Import," coming either from the North Sea or, bitterest of all, from their own beloved Adria.

The Rhine supplied them with salmon, the North Sea with oysters, but in order to eat native fishes, they had to turn to their own rivers, lakes, and ponds. A city bereft of its sea was forced to eat trout and carp, many of them actually pets. A kind fate left them their two greatest delicacies, their crayfish and the trout from their icy mountain streams.

An Austrian fisherman's gear usually includes a neat little watertight wooden keg, shaped something like a fish, which hangs over his shoulder on a leather strap. There is a door on the top side, and when he catches a trout, he lowers it gently into the keg with some water from its native stream so that it remains alive until he brings it home. There it is dropped into a simmering stock and, by virtue of its complete freshness, turns a magnificent blue.

Any Austrian inn or hotel that is near a stream, especially those in the Tyrol, has a wire enclosure in the stream to hold the trout that the fishermen bring in their kegs. The waters that rush through the wire are as cold and the food as good as any trout could wish. When a guest orders a trout, a kitchen-fisherman equipped with a net selects a fish, and the guest is served a blue trout within minutes. Someone finds time, during this rapid process, to weigh the fish so that it can be presented to the guest with a toothpick in its mouth holding a card with its weight—and, *ergo,* its price. No guest has ever minded this mercenary note: the blue trout is more delicate than any other fish and well worth the cost. Restaurants and hotels that are not near streams, in fact even those in cities, have basins and reservoirs for their live fish, at the bottom of which there is usually a carp, who, like the dollar bill one finds displayed in so many American establishments, has grown up with the restaurant, and no one would have the heart to kill it.

The Viennese call shellfish *Fastentiere,* fasting animals, although an elaborate *Languste* is hardly a proper Lenten dish. They eat shellfish as often as they can import them, and consider anything of this kind a great delicacy, especially if it comes from their beautiful lost Dalmatian coast or Istrian peninsula. Cold *Langusten* rear their spiky heads from most buffet tables and feasts of crayfish, cooked in beer with dill and served in steaming kettles, are an impatiently awaited annual event. Some of Vienna's fish and fasting animals differ somewhat from ours; in such cases, appropriate substitutions have been made in the recipes.

Methods of Cooking Fish

Boiling

PLACE THE FISH in a suitable kettle with a generous amount of cold salted water, court bouillon, or fish stock. Bring the liquid to a boil quickly and skim the scum from the top. Reduce the heat and simmer the fish until it is done. "Boiled" fish are really "simmered." Always place a large whole fish in cold water then bring the liquid to a boil, in order to keep the skin from puckering. However, a piece of fish that has a cut surface should go into water already boiling so that the cut surface will be sealed immediately. Cook small fish or pieces of fish that will require less than 30 minutes, cooking time in a prepared court bouillon. Large fish may simply be placed in salted water with the vegetables, herbs, and spices of a court bouillon, and the stock will cook with the fish.

Poaching

FILETS OF fish and small fish are poached: that is, they are cooked in just enough liquid to cover them. Lay the fish in a buttered open pan and add fish stock, mushroom stock, or white wine, as the recipe requires, and salt and pepper. Cook the fish in a moderate oven (350° F.) until it is done, basting it from time to time with the *fond,* pan juices, or with additional stock. The cooked fish is removed from the pan and the reduced *fond* is used to make the sauce.

Blaukochen

COOKING A FISH so that it turns blue can only be done if the fish is alive until a moment before it is immersed in boiling water and vinegar. In Austria, trout, carp, eel, and tench are most often prepared in this way. The fish is cleaned with a single stroke, the surface of the skin is not handled, and the smaller trout are dropped immediately into boiling water, salted and acidulated. Boiling vinegar is poured over the large fish before they go into the boiling water. Fish prepared in this way turn brilliant blue.

Braising and Steaming

THESE METHODS are suitable for large fish or large sections of fish. The stock usually consists of half stock and half white or red wine. The fish is covered only to two-thirds its depth in the stock, and strips of lard or bacon slices are laid over it. The kettle is covered and placed in a moderate oven (350° F.), and the fish is basted frequently. When the stock has reduced, the cover is removed so that the fish can glaze during the last few minutes of cooking. The fish is removed from the pan and kept hot, and the reduced stock is used as a base for the sauce.

Deep-Fat Frying

THIS METHOD of preparation is only used for small fish or small pieces of fish. The skin of a small fish has to be lightly cut two or three times crosswise on each side. The fish is dipped in milk and flour or in egg and bread crumbs. It is fried in deep hot butter or oil until it is golden. The pieces must always be small enough so that the time required to gild the coating will be enough to cook the piece of fish through. The fat must always be deep enough so that the fish swims in it, and it has to be hotter for the smaller pieces than for the larger ones.

Sautéing

SMALL FISH filets or pieces are dredged with flour and sautéed on both sides in butter. They are served immediately, with lemon wedges, and the remaining butter is poured over them. They should be served very hot.

Broiling

BROILING OR grilling of fish is suitable for small and medium fish, but the large ones must be cut into steaks in order to be broiled. Fish that are fatty can be broiled without additional butter; lean fish have to be brushed with butter before and after they are turned. Large fish must be crosscut to allow the heat to penetrate more deeply and they must be turned. Fish are broiled with various herbs and seasonings.

Basic Fish Preparations

Fischsud I   *Court Bouillon I, with White Wine*

SAUTÉ 3 SMALL carrots, 3 stalks of celery, and 1 large onion, all finely chopped, in 6 tablespoons butter until the onion is puffed and transparent.

Add 4 cups each of water and white wine and 2 1/2 pounds fish trimmings, preferably from haddock, halibut, salmon, or cod. Add 4 sprigs of parsley, 2 sprigs of thyme, 4 peppercorns, 2 cloves, 1 bay leaf, and 2 teaspoons salt. Simmer the liquid for 1 hour. Strain it and use it as required. Makes about 6 cups.

Court Bouillon II — *Fischsud II*

PLACE 3 SMALL carrots, 3 stalks of celery, and 1 large onion, all finely chopped, in 7 cups water acidulated with 1/2 cup vinegar and the juice of 1 lemon. Add 2 1/2 pounds fish trimmings, preferably from haddock, halibut, salmon, or cod, and 4 sprigs of parsley, 2 sprigs of thyme, 4 peppercorns, 2 cloves, 1 bay leaf, and 2 teaspoons salt. Simmer the liquid for 1 hour. Strain it and use it as required. Makes about 6 cups.

Court Bouillon for Lobster — *Kochsud für Hummer*

SIMMER 8 CARROTS and 8 onions, both sliced, 1/2 bunch of parsley or 4 parsley roots, 3 sprigs of thyme, 3 bay leaves, and 2/3 cup salt in 6 quarts water and 1 1/4 cups vinegar for 20 minutes. Add 12 peppercorns and simmer the liquid for 10 minutes longer. Strain the liquid and use it for cooking lobsters.

Fish Fumet — *Fischfumet*

FISH FUMET is a more concentrated court bouillon.

Sauté, covered, 1 pound fish bones and trimmings, chopped, 1 small onion, chopped, 6 sprigs of parsley, and 6 peppercorns in 1/4 cup butter for 10 minutes. Add 2 cups water, 1 1/2 cups white wine, and 1/4 teaspoon salt. Simmer the liquid for 30 minutes. Strain the *fumet* and use it as required. Makes 1 quart white fish *fumet*.

Make red fish *fumet* with red wine instead of white.

Fish Aspic — *Fischaspik*

To 1 QUART white fish *fumet* add 1/2 pound of any white fish, finely chopped, the white part of 1 leek, chopped, 3 sprigs of parsley, and 1 egg white and crushed egg shell. Bring to a boil, stirring constantly, and simmer, uncovered, for 20 minutes. Strain the stock through a fine sieve. Soften

1 1/2 tablespoons gelatin in 1/2 cup white wine and stir it into the hot stock. For molds or glazing, use the aspic as soon as it is cool but before it starts to set. Pour it into a jelly-roll pan, and chill it until it is firm. Roll up the sheet of aspic and cut it into narrow strips. Cut the strips into small regular dice.

Make red fish aspic with red fish *fumet*.

Fischgelée *Fish Glaze*

REDUCE WELL-STRAINED white fish *fumet* by simmering it until it becomes thick and gelatinous. Strain it and use it as required.

Fischfond *Fish Fond*

FOND IS the remaining juice of all poached, steamed, or baked fish. If the *fond* is to be part of the sauce, it is usually augmented by fish stock or wine. It is used to baste the fish during the cooking, then it is strained, reduced, and used as a basis for the sauce. It can be thickened with *roux* or white sauce, and made more interesting with the addition of capers, anchovies, or mushrooms.

White Wine Marinade   *Weissweinmarinade*

SAUTÉ 1 SMALL carrot, 1 small onion, the white part of 1 leek, and 3 shallots, all finely chopped, in 1 tablespoon olive oil with 3 sprigs of parsley, 1 sprig of thyme, 3 peppercorns, and 1 clove of garlic, 1/2 bay leaf, and 1 clove. Add 5 1/4 cups white wine and 3/4 cup tarragon vinegar and simmer the marinade for 40 minutes. Use the marinade hot or cold, as directed.

Red Wine Marinade   *Rotweinmarinade*

PREPARE A MARINADE as above, but use 6 cups red wine instead of the white wine and omit the vinegar.

Eel in Beer   *Aal in Bier*

ALL GERMAN dictionaries and cookbook indexes start with eels, because of their spelling rather than their popularity.

Cut 3 pounds eel into 2-inch lengths. Salt the pieces well and let them rest in a colander for 1 hour. Pour boiling water over them and, after they have drained, pour cold water over them and draw off the skin. Simmer the eel in beer to cover with 2 onions, sliced, 1 lemon, sliced, 2 teaspoons salt, 9 peppercorns, and 1 bay leaf for 20 minutes, or until the eel is tender. Remove the eel and keep it hot. Strain the beer and thicken it with 2 tablespoons butter kneaded with 1 tablespoon flour. Add to the beer sauce 1 teaspoon sugar, salt to taste, and the onion, puréed in a blender. Return the pieces of eel to the sauce, bring it to a boil, and add 1 cup hot potato balls and 3 tablespoons chopped parsley.

Sea Bass in White Wine   *Seefisch Aadalbert*

SEASON A 3-POUND sea bass with salt and pepper and place it in a well-buttered baking dish with 2 cups white wine and 1/4 cup mushroom essence. Cover it with buttered paper and poach it in a moderate oven (350° F.) for 15 to 18 minutes.

Melt 2 tablespoons butter in a saucepan, stir in 2 tablespoons flour, and cook the *roux* over low heat, stirring constantly, for a few minutes. Gradually add 1 cup warm fish, veal, or chicken stock, and cook the sauce for 10 minutes, stirring constantly. Lift the bass carefully onto a hot serving platter and add the *fond,* or pan juices, to the sauce. Take the sauce from the heat and beat in 2 egg yolks beaten with 1 tablespoon hot water, 1 tablespoon butter, and 1/2 teaspoon lemon juice. Add to the sauce salt and pepper to taste and 3/4 cup small shrimps, simmered for 3 minutes in salted water and drained. Garnish the bass with lemon wedges and parsley. Serve the sauce separately.

Geräucherte Forelle *Whole Smoked Trout*

BRINE A 5- TO 6-pound brook trout with rough salt in an earthenware container for about 36 hours. Hot-smoke it at about 150° F. in a portable electric smoke-box, according to the manufacturer's directions. If the smoking is started in the morning the trout should be ready to serve hot from the smoke-box in the evening, or after about 8 hours.

Lift the trout onto a heated platter, cut the skin at head and tail, and remove it carefully. Surround the trout with hot steamed potatoes rolled in melted butter and minced parsley. Whip 1 cup heavy cream until stiff, fold in 1/2 cup freshly grated or well drained bottled horseradish, and put 1/2 cup cold lingonberry sauce in the center. Stir the whipped cream and lingonberry sauce together before passing them with the hot trout and potatoes. *(Picture, page 126.)*

Karpfen Blau Hotel Bristol *Blue Carp*

PEEL OR SCRAPE and cut into a julienne 1/2 medium celery root, 4 carrots, 2 onions, and 2 leeks. Combine half of each of the vegetables in a large fish kettle and add 1/2 cup white wine, 1/4 cup wine vinegar, 1 bay leaf, 1 tablespoon salt, 1 teaspoon white peppercorns, and 1 teaspoon each of chopped parsley and thyme. Add 10 cups water and boil the mixture, uncovered, for 30 minutes. Add a 4- to 4 1/2-pound carp, cleaned, but with head and tail intact, reduce the heat, and simmer, covered, for 30 minutes longer.

Boil the remaining vegetables separately in salted water until they are just tender. Peel 2 pounds potatoes, cut them into ovals, and boil them in salted water until tender.

Drain the carp, transfer it to a napkin-lined fish platter, and garnish it with the potatoes, well drained. Cover the fish lightly with the julienne vegetables, all well drained, and 2 thinly sliced lemons.

Melt 1/4 pound butter, without letting it brown, and serve it separately in a sauceboat. The Sirk, in the Hotel Bristol, serves blue carp with cucumber salad as a fish course or, traditionally, as a main course on Christmas. *(Picture, page 127.)*

Gypsy Carp   *Zigeunerkarpfen*

SPLIT A 3-POUND carp in half lengthwise. Sprinkle the cut sides with 3/4 teaspoon salt and let them rest for 1/2 hour. Melt 1/2 cup butter in a large baking dish or casserole and line the bottom evenly with 1 1/2 pounds potatoes, parboiled, peeled, and thinly sliced. Lay the carp on the potatoes, cut side down, and cover it with 6 rashers of bacon. Spread 3 large onions, thinly sliced, over the bacon. Dust the fish with pepper and paprika and sprinkle it with 1/2 teaspoon each of dried thyme, marjoram, and dill, or, better, use fresh herbs if they are available. Pour 1 cup sour cream over the fish and bake it in a hot oven (400° F.) for 12 minutes. Add 1 cup cream and bake the fish 6 minutes longer. Cover the fish with a mixture of 3 large green peppers, seeded, scalded, and cut in fine julienne, and 2/3 cup chopped pimiento. Sprinkle the fish with 1 hard-cooked egg, riced, 1/4 cup chopped parsley and the grated rind of 1 lemon.

Hungarian Carp   *Ungarischer Karpfen*

SAUTÉ A 3-POUND carp, whole or cut into 6 serving pieces, in 1/2 cup butter for 3 minutes on each side. Remove the carp and sauté 6 large onions, thinly sliced and separated into rings, in the butter in the pan until they are puffed and transparent. Stir in 2 teaspoons paprika and sauté the onions until they are golden. Add 2 cups each of beef stock and heavy cream and simmer for 5 minutes, stirring constantly. Add salt and pepper to taste and return the carp to the pan. Simmer it, covered, for 10 to 15 minutes, or until it is done. Serve the carp in the sauce with boiled potatoes. If preferred, strain the sauce before adding the carp.

Kalter Karpfen   *Cold Carp with Walnuts*

SAUTÉ 6 ONIONS, sliced and separated into rings, in 1/4 cup olive oil until they are soft and lightly browned. Add 1/2 cup walnuts, roughly ground, 1/2 cup chopped parsley, and salt and pepper to taste. Stir the mixture well and stuff it into a well-salted 4- to 6-pound carp. Sew or skewer the opening securely, and roast the carp on a rack in a moderately hot oven (375° F.), basting it with 1/4 cup each of olive oil and white wine mixed with 1 teaspoon salt, for about 1 hour or until the carp is browned and done. Although it may be served hot with lemon wedges and browned butter, it is usually eaten cold with lemon mayonnaise seasoned with chopped parsley.

Kabeljaupudding   *Cod Pudding*

BRING TO a boil, 1 1/2 cups rice in 2 cups cold salted water, add 3 cups milk, and simmer the rice until it is medium soft, about 15 minutes. Stir in 1/4 cup each of butter and chopped parsley, salt and pepper to taste, and a pinch of sugar. When the rice is cool, add 2 cups cooked cod, finely chopped, and 2 well-beaten egg yolks. Fold in 2 stiffly beaten egg whites and correct the seasoning. Pour the mixture into a well-buttered and crumbed baking dish, cover it with crumbs, and bake it in a moderately hot oven (375° F.) for 1 hour, or until the crumbs are golden. If this pudding is made with salt cod, soak it overnight and reduce the salt.

Kabeljau mit Kartoffeln Anna   *Cod Baked with Potatoes*

SIMMER 3 POUNDS cod in salted water for 20 minutes. Remove the skin and bones and let it cool. Line a well-buttered baking dish with 2 overlapping layers of thinly sliced peeled potatoes, soaked in cold water for 5 minutes and dried. Use about 4 potatoes. Sprinkle them with 2 tablespoons chopped onions and add 1/4 cup melted butter. Pile in the cod and sprinkle it with salt and pepper to taste. Make an overlapping border all around of potato slices so that when the pudding is unmolded it will show an unbroken surface of potatoes. Cover the cod with more potato slices and pour 1/4 cup melted butter over them. Bake the pudding in a moderately hot oven (375° F.) until the potatoes are golden, about 45 minutes.

Cold Cod *Kalter Kabeljau*

SIMMER A 3-POUND piece of cod in court bouillon to cover for 30 minutes. Remove the fish, drain it, and cool it. Soften 1 envelope of gelatin in 1/2 cup cold water and dissolve it in 1/2 cup boiling water, off the heat. Let it cool, add 1/2 cup mayonnaise, and fold in 1/2 cup heavy cream, whipped. Mask the fish with the gelatin mixture and chill it.

Fill 6 chilled cooked artichoke bottoms with 2 cups green peas, cooked and mixed with 2/3 cup lemon mayonnaise. Arrange the fish on a platter and surround it with the stuffed artichoke bottoms, 6 hard-cooked eggs, sliced, and sprigs of parsley. Pipe decorations onto the fish with a mixture of 1/2 cup butter and 2 teaspoons anchovy paste. Garnish the dish with chopped parsley and lemon slices and serve very cold.

Frogs' Legs *Froschkeulen*

MARINATE 18 MEDIUM frogs' legs or 24 small ones for 3 hours in 3/4 cup olive oil with 1 onion, chopped, 1/2 cup chopped parsley, the juice and grated rind of 2 lemons, and 2 teaspoons each of salt, dry mustard, and chopped basil. Drain them well and broil them close to the heat for 4 to 6 minutes on each side, depending on their size. Heat the marinade and beat in 1/2 cup butter with 2 cloves of garlic, crushed. Pour the sauce over the frogs' legs and serve at once.

Froschkeulen Grün-Rot   *Frogs' Legs with Peppers*

SAUTÉ 18 MEDIUM or 24 small frogs' legs in 1/2 cup butter until they are gilded and opaque, about 3 to 6 minutes. Season them with salt, pepper, and cayenne and add 1/2 cup white wine. Continue to cook for 5 minutes, turning the frogs' legs once, and add 1 green pepper, seeded and diced, 1/4 cup each of onions, pimiento, and parsley, all chopped, and cook for 10 minutes longer. Correct the seasoning and serve the frogs' legs dusted with 1 riced hard-cooked egg and 2 tablespoons chopped parsley.

Gefüllter Schellfisch   *Stuffed Haddock*

STUFF A 4-pound haddock with a mixture of 1/2 cup milk, 3/4 cup dry bread crumbs, 1 egg, 24 anchovies, chopped, and 2 tablespoons each of chopped parsley, capers, and shallots. Sew up the stuffed fish, rub it with a mixture of 1 tablespoon each of salt and vinegar, and let it rest for 30 minutes. Place the fish in a buttered baking dish, paint it with 1 beaten egg white, and dust it with 1/2 cup bread crumbs and the grated rind of 1/2 lemon. Bake the haddock in a moderate oven (350° F.) for 30 minutes, basting it 3 times with melted butter. Garnish it with parsley and lemon wedges. Serve it with boiled new potatoes and horseradish cream.

Fischmus mit Dillsauce   *Smoked Trout Mousse*
                                                    with Dill Sauce

IN A FOOD processor with the steel blade purée the meat of 3 smoked trout, free of skin and bones, to a smooth paste. Add the grated rind of 1 lemon, 2 tablespoons lemon juice, and 1/4 cup *crème fraîche* and process until smooth. Season to taste with salt and freshly ground white pepper. Fold 1 egg white, beaten stiff, and 2/3 cup heavy cream, whipped, into the mixture and spoon it into a rinsed mold. Chill the mold for 4 hours and serve the mousse with a sauce of 1/2 cup sour cream whipped with 1/2 cup thick mayonnaise and 3 tablespoons finely cut dill.

Cold Halibut Mousse Atlantic   Kaltes Fischmus Atlantic

PLACE A FISH mold on a bed of cracked ice and coat the bottom and sides with a thin layer of cool but still liquid fish aspic. Outline the fins, tail, and eye with thin strips of black olives. Sprinkle some liquid aspic over each piece of olive to set the decorations, chill the mold, and when the aspic is firm pour in aspic to cover by 1/2 inch. Soften 1 tablespoon unflavored gelatin in 1/4 cup dry white wine, heat 1 cup dry white wine to boiling, and add the gelatin mixture to the wine, stirring, until the gelatin is dissolved. Add the gelatin mixture to 1 1/2 cups well packed halibut flakes and fold in 1/2 cup heavy cream whipped until stiff. Season the mousse with salt and white pepper and spoon it carefully into the mold, leaving a 1/2-inch border between the mousse and the sides of the mold. Chill the mousse, covered, until it is set. Fill the border between the mousse and the sides of the mold with liquid fish aspic and chill the mousse until it is firm. Unmold the mousse onto a cold platter.

German Perch   Barsch auf deutsche Art

IT'S NICE that the word *Art,* which appears here, occurs so often in this book, even though what *"auf Art"* means is "in the manner of."

Marinate three 1-pound perch with the juice of 1 lemon, 1 onion, sliced, and a *bouquet garni* for 1 hour. Dip them in 3 egg yolks beaten with 1 teaspoon water and then in 3 tablespoons grated Parmesan. Sauté the perch in butter, turning them once, until they are golden, about 15 to 20 minutes. Serve them with lemon wedges and fried parsley.

Perch Filets Vinaigrette   Barschfilets Vinaigrette

POACH 12 FILETS of perch in fish stock to cover for 12 minutes, or until they are done. Let them cool and chill them in the stock.

Combine 2/3 cup olive oil, 1/3 cup vinegar, 1 onion and 1 hard-cooked egg, both finely chopped, 1 tablespoon chopped capers, 2 teaspoons chopped parsley, 1 teaspoon each of chopped chervil and grated lemon rind, and salt and pepper to taste.

Drain the perch filets well and arrange them on a serving platter with a border of chopped fish aspic. Garnish with lemon wedges and parsley sprigs. Pile 2 tablespoons of the vinaigrette mixture on each filet and pour over the fish the remaining sauce.

Hechtkotelette   *Pike Cutlets*

IN A MORTAR, pound to a paste 3 pounds pike, skinned and boned, with 4 egg whites and salt and pepper to taste. Place the paste over ice and gradually stir in 2 cups heavy cream. Add 2 tablespoons each of finely chopped parsley and chives and form the paste into 6 cutlets. Dip the cutlets into 1 cup seasoned flour, then into 2 beaten eggs, and coat them with 1 1/2 cups bread crumbs. Sauté the cutlets in butter until they are golden, about 12 minutes, turning them once.

Peel and hollow out 6 firm ripe tomatoes and warm them in a slow oven (300° F.) for 5 minutes. Arrange the hot pike cutlets on a platter. Place 1 tablespoon béarnaise sauce, *Béarnersauce,* in each tomato and fill them with white wine potato salad. Surround the cutlets with the warm tomatoes. Garnish with sprigs of parsley and serve immediately.

Hechtpastete Ottilie   *Deep Dish Pike Pie*

SPLIT 2 MEDIUM-SIZED pike and remove the skin and bones. Cut the flesh of 1 fish into 1 1/2 inch cubes, dust them with salt and pepper, and sprinkle them with 1/4 cup chopped parsley and the juice of 1 lemon. Cover the fish and set it aside for at least 1 hour. Soak 6 slices white bread in water and press it until it is completely dry. Stir the bread in 1/2 cup butter over low heat for 5 minutes. Mince the second pike very fine, and combine it with 2 whole eggs and 2 egg yolks, 6 anchovies, finely chopped, the cooled bread, and 4 tablespoons grated Parmesan cheese. Fill a well-buttered pudding dish with alternate layers of the minced fish and the pieces of pike. Cover the dish with a thick layer of rich pie crust and decorate the outside edge with a fluted border of crust. Cut a hole in the center and bake the pie in a moderately hot oven (375° F.) for 50 minutes. If the crust starts to brown too soon, reduce the heat to moderate

(350° F.) or cover the crust with a piece of buttered brown paper. Just before serving, pour 2 cups hot caper sauce through the hole in the crust and return the pie to the oven for 10 minutes.

Hot Fish Mousse   *Fischmus Hotel Schloss Dürnstein*

PURÉE 1 3/4 POUNDS of pike and/or trout, free of skin and bones, in a food processor with the steel blade until it is a paste. Add, one by one, 3 egg whites and process until they are fully incorporated. Add 4 anchovy filets, drained, and 3 ounces raw bone marrow and process until smooth. Add salt and pepper, a sliver of garlic, and a pinch of cayenne. With the motor running, add, little by little, 3 cups heavy cream. Chill.

Make a strong stock of the heads, bones, and fish trimmings and reduce it over high heat to 1 1/2 cups. Stir 1/2 cup cornstarch into a little cold stock, add it to the simmering stock, and stir until thick. Chill it and process it with the fish mixture. Beat in 4 eggs, correct the seasoning, and chill again. Pour into 8 to 10 *dariole* molds, cover with foil, and transfer to a baking pan. Fill the baking pan with water halfway up the sides of the pan. Bake in a moderate oven (350° F.) for 1 hour. Serve with white butter sauce. Garnish with puff-paste *fleurons. (Picture, page 124.)*

Pike in Sour Cream   *Hecht Smetana*

CUT A 4-POUND pike into 2-inch lengths, and lay them in a well-buttered baking dish with 3 onions, sliced, 3 sprigs each of parsley, dill, and thyme, 1/2 bay leaf, 3 peppercorns, and 1 teaspoon salt. Pour 1/2 cup melted butter over the pike, cover the dish, and bake it in a moderately hot oven (375° F.) for 15 minutes. Add 1 cup warm sour cream and cook the pike approximately 5 minutes longer, or until it is tender and opaque. Remove the fish and keep it warm. Purée the sauce in a processor and bind it, over very low heat, with 2 tablespoons butter kneaded with 1 tablespoon flour. Add enough sour cream to obtain 2 cups of sauce and add 1/4 cup drained capers. Stir the sauce until it is just under boiling and pour it over the pike. Serve it with boiled potatoes dusted with crushed crisp bacon.

*In these recipes, pompano has been substituted for the European plaice,
or* Scholle, *a fish unavailable in this country.*

Scholle mit Sardellen   *Pompanos with Anchovies*

WASH AND dry three 2-pound pompanos. Lay them in a pan and pour
1/2 cup lemon juice over them, making sure that some of it reaches the
inside of the fish. Cream 1 1/2 cups butter with 3 tablespoons anchovy
paste and add 12 anchovy filets, crushed in a mortar. Spread the fish
completely with the anchovy butter and fill the cavities with it. Let the
fish stand in the refrigerator for 8 to 9 hours. Bake the fish in a moderately
hot oven (375° F.) until they are brown, about 45 minutes, basting frequently with 3/4 cup white wine mixed with the juice of 1 lemon and with
the pan juices. The butter melts and runs off the fish and it is important
to baste them heavily with it to achieve a very brown crisp skin. Carefully
remove the fish to a hot serving platter and add 1/4 cup white wine to
the liquid in the pan. Stir it over low heat and add 2 to 3 tablespoons heavy
cream, or just enough to bind the sauce. Pour it into a sauceboat.

Cut scored cucumbers crosswise into six 2-inch lengths. Hollow out
the pieces to make little cups and marinate them in French dressing. Fill
the cups with a mixture of 1/2 cup cream, whipped stiff with a pinch of
salt, and 3 tablespoons each of freshly grated horseradish and ground

blanched almonds. Surround the fish with the cucumber cups. Serve with parsley potato balls.

Pompanos with Walnuts — *Scholle mit Nüssen*

FOLLOW THE recipe for cold carp with walnuts, *kalter Karpfen,* using three 1 3/4-pound pompanos instead of 1 carp. Reduce the cooking time to 30 minutes, or until the pompanos are browned and done. Combine 1/2 cup melted butter, 3 tablespoons each of chopped parsley and brown bread crumbs, and 1/2 teaspoon grated lemon rind, salt the sauce to taste, and heat it thoroughly. Pour the sauce over the fish and serve it with parsley potato balls.

Salmon Steaks with Onions and Leeks — *Lachsschnitten alte Art*

WIPE 6 SALMON steaks with a damp cloth, salt them, and let them rest for 30 minutes. Poach them gently in court bouillon to cover until they are tender and opaque, about 10 to 12 minutes. Sauté 3/4 cup each of chopped onions, parsley, and the white part of leeks, in 1/4 cup butter until the onion and leeks are puffed and golden. Drain the salmon slices well and arrange them on a heated serving platter. Cover the salmon with the hot onion and leek mixture, garnish with sprigs of parsley and with lemon slices, and serve at once, with hollandaise sauce.

Salmon with Anchovy Sauce — *Warmer Lachs mit Sardellen*

PLACE A 3- TO 4-pound center piece of salmon in 3 cups water and 1/2 cup vinegar, with 1 carrot and 1 onion, both chopped, 2 sprigs each of thyme and parsley, 1 bay leaf, 1 curl of lemon peel, diced, and salt and pepper to taste. Simmer the salmon for 30 minutes, or until it is opaque and tender. Drain the fish, transfer it to a platter, and peel off the skin. Glaze the salmon with 1/4 cup butter, set aside, and keep it warm. Add the skin to the stock and cook it, uncovered, until the liquid is reduced to 2 cups. Add 1 cup red wine, 1 small onion, minced, 4 mushrooms, sliced, 3 sprigs each of parsley and thyme, 6 peppercorns, 1 clove garlic, 1 bay leaf, and 1/2 teaspoon each of allspice and salt, and simmer for 1/2 hour.

Strain the mixture and add 1/2 cup brown sauce. Just before serving the sauce, stir in 2 tablespoons each of butter and anchovy paste. Serve the salmon with the sauce, boiled parsley potatoes, and cucumbers.

Lachsbeignets   *Salmon Fritots*

PUT 2 CUPS cold poached salmon through the food chopper and add 1/4 cup Sherry and 1 teaspoon salt. Form the mixture into balls the size of small plums.

Combine 2 cups sifted flour and 2/3 cup beer, add 1 tablespoon melted butter, and fold into the batter 1 stiffly beaten egg white.

Dip the salmon balls in thick lobster sauce, roll them in fine cracker crumbs, and dip them in the beer batter. Fry the salmon balls in deep hot fat (380° F.) until they are golden brown. Drain them on absorbent paper and serve them with hot lobster sauce thinned with Sherry to taste.

Hummersauce   *Lobster Sauce*

FINELY FLAKE or grind 1 cup cooked lobster meat and simmer it in 1/4 cup heavy cream until it is heated thoroughly. Blend 2 tablespoons melted butter and 2 tablespoons flour, add 1/2 cup warm milk, and heat gently, stirring until it thickens. Season the sauce with 1/4 teaspoon salt and a dash of paprika. Combine with the lobster mixture and 2 tablespoons Sherry. Serves 4.

Lachsmus Frederika   *Hot Salmon Mousse*

PUT 1 POUND raw salmon, free from bones and skin, through the finest blade of a food chopper. Gradually add 3 egg whites, working them into the salmon thoroughly.

Melt 2 tablespoons butter, add 2 tablespoons flour, and slowly add 2 cups milk. Cook, stirring constantly, until the mixture is smooth. Add 3 well-beaten egg yolks, stirring, without letting the sauce boil. Cool the white sauce and add it to the fish, add salt and pepper to taste, and chill the mixture for at least 1 hour.

Fold 1/2 cup heavy cream, whipped, into the fish mixture. Pour it into a buttered mold, and cover it with buttered paper. Put the mold in a pan containing about an inch of hot water and bake it in a moderate oven (350° F.) for 30 minutes, or until it is firm. Unmold the fish and serve it immediately with lobster sauce.

Spring Rhine Salmon in Aspic  Frühlings-Rheinlachs

REMOVE THE head from a salmon, wrap the fish in cheesecloth, and poach it in equal parts of fish stock and Champagne to cover for about 12 minutes per pound. Let the salmon cool in the stock. Lift it out very carefully, cut away the cheesecloth, and let the salmon drain well. Pour a layer of cool but still liquid fish aspic 1/4 inch deep onto a long fish platter, let the aspic set, and lay the salmon on it. Carefully remove the skin on the upper side of the fish, leaving a 2-inch border of skin all around. Cut the border of skin into scallops with kitchen scissors so that a panel of salmon-pink meat is exposed, surrounded by a scalloped edge of dark skin. Decorate the center of the panel with tulips cut from hard-cooked egg white. Add tarragon leaves and stems cut from parsley stalks. Dip the flowers, leaves, and stems into liquid aspic before applying them to the salmon. Chill the entire platter for 15 minutes. Glaze the flower panel and the rest of the salmon with 3 or 4 coats of aspic, painting the first coat on very carefully in order not to disturb the decoration. Pour the following coats on carefully, being sure that the sides of the salmon are also well glazed. Chill the fish platter after each coating of aspic and keep the remaining aspic from solidifying by setting it in warm water. Surround the salmon with chopped aspic. Lay overlapping slices of cucumber on its tail, like scales.

Halve 4 hard-cooked eggs and fill them with the riced yolks mixed with enough creamed butter to bind and with 2 tablespoons caviar. Arrange the eggs around the salmon. Place 8 to 10 small salmon mousses, glazed with aspic, between the stuffed eggs and top each with a slice of truffle. Garnish the platter with notched lemon halves and parsley. Serve the salmon very cold, with lemon mayonnaise in a separate bowl.

Small Salmon Mousses Kleinlachsmus

MASH 2 CUPS ground cooked salmon and purée it in a processor. Soften 1 envelope of gelatin in 3 tablespoons cold water and dissolve it over hot water. To 1/2 cup béchamel sauce add the dissolved gelatin and 1/2 teaspoon each of dry mustard and salt. Work the sauce into the salmon and add 1 cup whipped cream. Divide the mixture among small individual molds and chill them until they are firm. Unmold the mousses, glaze them with liquid fish aspic, and chill them.

Lachscreme   *Cold Salmon Mousse*

PLACE 1 POUND fresh salmon, sliced, in a saucepan with 2 cups light white wine, cover the pan, and simmer the fish in the wine until it flakes easily, about 12 minutes. Drain the fish well and pound it in a mortar to a fine paste or put it through the finest blade of the food chopper twice. Heat 1 tablespoon butter in a saucepan with 1 tablespoon finely chopped onion until the butter bubbles. Add 1 tablespoon flour and stir over low heat for a few minutes, taking care not to brown the butter. Take the pan from the heat and stir in 1/2 cup warm milk. Return the sauce to low heat and cook it very slowly for a few minutes. Add a pinch of cayenne and 1/2 teaspoon anchovy paste and stir the sauce into the salmon paste. Season to taste with salt and pepper, bearing in mind that whipped cream will be added, so that the mixture becomes blander. Add 1 tablespoon fresh dill and 1/4 cup pistachio nuts, both finely chopped, and chill the mixture.

Soften 1 envelope of gelatin in 1/2 cup cold water. To 1/2 cup strong chicken stock add 1/3 cup Sherry and bring the stock just to a boil. Remove the stock from the heat, stir in the dissolved gelatin, and cool the aspic.

Set a 1-quart fish mold in a bed of cracked ice. Coat the bottom and sides with a layer of cool, but still liquid, aspic and let it set. Lay a round slice of truffle in the mold as an eye and a line of crescent-shaped truffle slices to show the spine of the fish. Black olives may be substituted for the truffle. Pour in a second layer of aspic and continue to paint the sides of the mold until it has a coating of at least 1/8 inch. Chill the rest of the aspic in a shallow pan in the refrigerator until it sets.

Whip 1 cup heavy cream with a pinch of salt. Fold it carefully into the salmon paste, correct the seasoning, and blend the mixture until it is smooth. Turn it into the mold and chill the mousse for at least 2 hours.

Unmold the salmon mousse onto a large platter, surround it with sliced hard-cooked eggs, water cress, and cold boiled shrimps, and decorate the platter with chopped aspic. Serve fresh herb mayonnaise separately.

Halibut will do well in these recipes as a substitute for turbot, which is not readily available in the United States.

Halibut or Turbot with Peaches   *Steinbutt Suzon*

POACH 6 FILETS of halibut or turbot, covered, with 3/4 cup each of red wine and fish stock for 15 minutes. Drain the filets thoroughly. Draw off their skins and keep them hot on a heated platter. Reduce the liquid in the pan to 3/4 cup. Thicken it with 1 tablespoon *beurre manié*—equal parts butter and flour kneaded together—add 1/2 cup cream, bring the sauce to a boil, and let it boil for a few seconds.

Surround the hot halibut or turbot filets with 6 peaches, peeled, halved, and heated for 10 minutes in their own juice with 1/4 cup sugar and a little water, if necessary. Pour the sauce over the fish and serve at once.

Halibut or Turbot
with Green Butter   *Steinbutt mit grüner Butter*

CREAM 1 CUP butter with 3 hard-cooked egg yolks, riced. Blend in 1 table-spoon each of anchovy paste and olive oil. Add 1 shallot, blanched and

chopped, and 1/2 clove of garlic, crushed. Blanch 9 young spinach leaves, with the stems removed, with 6 sprigs each of water cress, parsley, tarragon, and chervil. Drain them well, plunge them into cold water, and dry them with a soft towel. Pound them in a mortar with 1 gherkin, chopped, and 1 teaspoon chopped capers to a smooth purée and add it to the butter mixture. Add salt and pepper to taste and chill the green butter well.

Wipe a 3-pound slice of halibut or turbot with a damp cloth and place it in a shallow buttered pan. Add 1 onion, sliced, 3 shallots, chopped, and a *bouquet garni*. Add enough white wine to cover and salt and pepper to taste. Poach the fish very gently for 30 minutes, or until it is opaque and tender. Drain it well and arrange it on a platter. Garnish with hard-cooked egg and chopped chives and serve the fish very hot, with a slice of cold green butter on each serving.

Seezunge Remy   *Filets of Sole with Tomatoes*

POACH 6 LARGE filets of sole with 1/4 cup each of carrots, onions, and celery, all finely diced, in a buttered pan with 1/2 cup fish stock and 2 ounces brandy until they are tender, about 8 to 10 minutes. Remove the filets carefully to a hot serving platter. Purée the sauce until smooth, add salt and pepper to taste, and beat in 2 tablespoons butter over low heat. Surround the filets with tomato slices, sautéed in butter for 5 minutes, and 1 cup hot cooked button mushrooms. Pour the sauce over the fish and serve with duchess potatoes.

Seezunge Elisabeth   *Artichokes Stuffed with Filets of Sole*

SIMMER 6 ARTICHOKES in salted water until they are tender, about 45 minutes, trim the leaves down to within 1 inch of the base, and remove the center leaves and chokes. Salt 6 filets of sole, roll them up, and tie them with string. Poach them in a buttered pan with 1/2 cup each of white wine and water for 6 minutes, turning them once. Drain the rolled filets and set them upright in the artichokes. Pull out more leaves, if necessary, so that the rolled filets just fill the artichokes. Remove the strings.

Sauté 1 tablespoon finely chopped onion over low heat in 2 table-spoons butter for 2 minutes. Stir in 1/4 cup flour and cook, stirring, until the flour just starts to turn golden. Gradually add 2 cups milk and 1 cup of the broth in which the fish poached and salt and pepper to taste. Simmer the sauce, stirring frequently, for 30 minutes. To half the sauce add 1/4 cup chopped chives. Pour the chived sauce into the centers of the rolled filets and into any spaces around the fish. Set the 6 artichokes in a baking pan, pour over them the remainder of the sauce, and sprinkle each artichoke with 2 tablespoons Parmesan. Bake them in a moderate oven (350° F.) for 10 to 15 minutes, or until the cheese is brown and the artichokes and fish are hot.

Lemon Sole in White Wine Hollandaise   *Seezunge mit holländischer Sauce*

IN A SHALLOW pan place 3/4 cup halved white seedless grapes, 3 tomatoes, peeled, seeded and chopped, 3 shallots, chopped, and 3 sprigs of parsley, chopped. Over this lay 6 filets of sole and cover with 3 cups dry white wine. Simmer the fish very gently for about 10 to 12 minutes, or until they are cooked. Remove the filets very carefully to a hot serving dish and keep them hot. Strain the sauce, pressing the tomatoes and grapes through the sieve, and season it lightly with salt and pepper. Stir the tomato-and-grape sauce very gently into hollandaise sauce. Pour the sauce over the sole and garnish the fish with a small bunch of seedless grapes and with parsley or grape leaves. Serve at once.

Filets of Sole and Asparagus   *Seezunge und Spargel*

SIMMER 8 FILETS of sole in white wine to cover, with 1/2 teaspoon salt to 2 cups wine, until they are opaque, about 8 to 10 minutes. Lift them carefully onto a heatproof platter and keep them warm. Cook two 1-pound lobsters in salted water for 15 minutes and keep them warm.

Melt 4 tablespoons butter, blend in 2 tablespoons flour over low heat, and cook the *roux,* stirring, for a few minutes. Gradually add 1 cup cream and 1/2 cup white veal stock and cook the sauce, stirring constantly, for 6 minutes. Add 5 tablespoons of the strained white wine in which the sole was cooked, 1/4 cup Sherry, and salt and pepper to taste. Pour the sauce over the filets and bake them in a moderate oven (350° F.) for about 5 minutes.

Garnish the ends of the platter with the claw and tail meat of the lobster. Surround the entire platter with warm crescents of puff paste made with a dusting of salt and Parmesan at the last "turn." Or make crescents of short pie dough.

Drain 2 pounds hot cooked asparagus well. Lay half the stalks diagonally, an inch apart, across the dish and then lay the remaining stalks in the other direction, making a diamond-shaped latticework of green asparagus over the white fish sauce. Garnish the platter with parsley and serve at once. Serves 8.

Seezunge auf Wiener Art   *Viennese Filets of Sole*

SEASON 8 FILETS of sole with salt and pepper and mince 2 of the filets fine. Sauté 1 medium onion, chopped, for 3 minutes, add 1/2 cup mushrooms, finely chopped, and sauté 3 minutes longer. Remove the pan from the heat and add 1 tablespoon finely chopped parsley, 1/4 teaspoon salt, and the minced filets. Boil 1/2 cup water with 1 teaspoon butter and stir in 2 1/2 tablespoons flour and 1/4 teaspoon salt until the mixture forms a smooth paste. Take it from the heat and stir in the minced sole mixture. Coat the 6 filets with the mixture on the side that will roll inward naturally, roll them up, tie them, and set them close together in a buttered pan. Pour 1/4 cup melted butter and 2 tablespoons lemon juice over the filets and bake them in a hot oven (400° F.) for 15 minutes, or until they are done. Remove them to a hot serving dish and keep them warm. Add 2 tablespoons flour to the juices in the baking pan and cook them, stirring constantly, for 1 minute. Add 1 cup fish or veal stock, 1/2 cup mushrooms, finely sliced, and 1 teaspoon mushroom essence, and simmer the sauce for 5 minutes. Reduce the heat and add slowly 1 egg yolk beaten with 1 tablespoon lemon juice. Do not let the sauce boil. Beat in 2 teaspoons butter, one at a time, and add 6 hot cooked crayfish tails or shrimps. Pour this sauce over the fish filets, sprinkle them with chopped parsley, and serve at once.

Seezunge Sylvia   *Filets of Sole with*
Shrimps and Vegetables

SPRINKLE 6 FILETS of sole with salt and with 2 tablespoons lemon juice and let them rest for 15 minutes. Place them in a well-buttered baking dish with 1/2 cup white wine, 1/2 bay leaf, and salt and pepper to taste. Cover the fish with buttered paper and cook them in a moderate oven

(350° F.) for 10 to 12 minutes, or until they are tender. (Flounder may be substituted for sole; in this case, the cooking time must be increased by at least 5 minutes.) Remove the filets carefully to an ovenproof serving dish and cover them with 1/2 cup each of chopped cooked mushrooms, shrimps, carrots, and green peas.

Stir 3 tablespoons flour into 2 tablespoons melted butter and gradually add the strained wine in which the filets cooked and enough of the liquor in which the mushrooms cooked to make 1 1/4 cups in all. Simmer the sauce, stirring constantly, for 6 minutes. Add 1/4 cup heavy cream, and, at the last moment, remove the pan from the heat and swirl in 1/2 tablespoon butter. Pour the sauce over the hot fish, glaze it for 1 minute in the oven, and serve it garnished with lemon and parsley.

Filets of Sole with Artichoke Bottoms — *Seezunge mit Artischocken*

MARINATE 6 FILETS of sole in 1/4 cup olive oil and the juice of 2 lemons with 1 small onion, chopped, and salt and pepper to taste for 1 hour. Drain and dry them well, dredge them with flour, and sauté them in butter until they are golden, turning them once. Sauté 8 or 9 cooked artichoke bottoms in 3 tablespoons butter in a covered pan with salt to taste for 5 minutes and cut them into thin strips. Grate the rind of 1/2 lemon over them and mound them in the center of a hot serving platter. Surround the artichokes with the filets. Heat 1 cup *espagnole* sauce with 2 tablespoons each of mushroom essence and Madeira, but do not let the sauce boil. Beat in 2 teaspoons meat glaze, 1 tablespoon butter, and the juice of 1/2 lemon and add 1 tablespoon chopped parsley. Serve the sauce separately.

Filets of Sole in Tomatoes with Caviar — *Seezunge auf russische Art*

GENTLY FLATTEN 6 thin filets of sole and trim off the tapering ends. Wrap the filets around well-buttered wooden sticks, about the thickness of a heavy pencil, and tie them with string. Poach the rolled filets in salted fish stock to cover with the juice of 1 lemon until the fish is opaque and done, about 8 to 10 minutes. Take the rolls from the water carefully, let them cool, and chill them.

Hollow out 6 peeled tomatoes, each large enough to hold a rolled

filet. Put 1 teaspoon salad marinade in each tomato and let them marinate for at least 30 minutes. Place 1 tablespoon diced fish aspic in each tomato. Remove the strings and wooden sticks from the rolled filets and put a filet in each tomato. Fill the cavities left by the wooden sticks with caviar and surround the stuffed tomatoes with diced fish aspic and water cress. Serve with Russian sauce.

Blaue Forelle
Blue Trout

THE SUCCESS of blue trout depends on leaving undisturbed the natural film that covers the scales. Handling disturbs this film; the fish should be touched as little as possible and only with wet hands on a wet surface.

The trout should come into the kitchen or to the campfire alive. Kill the fish and split and clean each with a single stroke. Pour warm vinegar over the trout, allowing 1/4 cup for 2 fish. Plunge them immediately into a kettle of simmering salted water, in which 2 cloves, 2 peppercorns, 1 small onion, and 1 bay leaf have simmered for 10 minutes. Simmer the trout for 12 to 15 minutes, depending on their size. Drain them and serve at once with new potatoes. True blue trout and potatoes are served hot enough, on hot plates, so that they can be eaten with portions of cold fresh butter, but they may also be served with hot clarified butter, salted to taste. Allow 1 trout per serving. This recipe is for 2 trout. They may also be served cold, with lemon mayonnaise.

Smoked Trout *Geräucherte*

REMOVE THE HEADS, tails, fins, and skin on 3 smoked trout. Bone the trout, arrange the filets on plates, and cover them with the skins to keep them moist. Garnish each plate with 1 small tomato and water cress sprigs. Whip 2/3 cup heavy cream until stiff, fold in 1/2 cup freshly grated horseradish or well-drained bottled horseradish. Remove the skins, divide the cream among the plates, and serve with hot toast.

Trout in Batter *Forelle im Teig*

SIFT 1 CUP flour with 1/2 teaspoon salt, make a well in the center, and break 2 eggs into it. Blend the flour and eggs well and gradually stir in 1 cup milk, 2 tablespoons heavy cream, and 1 tablespoon melted butter. Dip 6 cleaned and salted trout in the pancake batter and sauté them in 3/4 cup butter until they are golden, turning them once. Keep them hot in a slow oven (300° F.). Sauté 1/4 cup chopped hazelnuts in the butter until they are lightly browned. Add 1 cup seedless grapes or peeled and seeded green grapes and heat them thoroughly, shaking the pan to mix them well. Add salt and pepper to taste and stir in 2 tablespoons butter.

Arrange the crisp trout on a heated serving platter, pour over them the hot grape and nut sauce, and serve at once.

Trout with Port *Forelle im Portwein*

SAUTÉ 1/2 POUND mushrooms, chopped, 2 shallots, finely chopped, and 1 tablespoon chopped parsley in 1/2 cup butter until the mixture thickens. Add 1 cup thick *velouté* sauce or white sauce and keep it warm. Filet 6 trout, dust them with pepper and salt, and sauté them in 1/4 cup butter for 8 minutes. Place 6 of the filets in a shallow ovenproof dish and spread them with the mushroom mixture. Cover them with the 6 remaining filets and keep them warm in the oven. In the top of a double boiler, stir 1/2 cup butter and 1 cup heavy cream over gently boiling water until the mixture is thoroughly blended. Add slowly 1/2 cup Port and cook, stirring, until the sauce is smooth and slightly thickened. Pour the hot sauce over the trout and serve it immediately.

Kalte Forelle *Cold Stuffed Trout*

IN A SHALLOW pan, poach 6 cleaned trout for 15 to 20 minutes in salted water to cover, with 1 carrot and 1/2 onion, both sliced, 1 bay leaf, and 3 peppercorns. Remove the cooked trout from the water and let them cool. Remove the skins carefully, leaving the heads and tails intact. Skin and slice enough large tomatoes to cover the serving platter that will hold the fish. Fill the cavities of the trout with fresh caviar and lay the fish on the tomatoes. Lay a line of finely chopped tarragon along the center of each trout. Lay a line of finely riced hard-cooked egg yolk and a line of finely riced hard-cooked egg white on either side of the chopped tarragon. Decorate the platter with parsley and place a circle of lettuce leaves at each end. Fill 6 small hollowed-out tomatoes with a sauce made by mixing 1 1/4 cups thick mayonnaise with 4 shallots, finely minced, 3 tablespoons dill, chopped, and salt and pepper to taste. Place the tomatoes on the lettuce beds. Serve each guest a trout and a tomato and pass Melba toast made by sprinkling thin slices of 2-day-old bread with salt and browning them in a very slow oven (250° F.).

Kalte Forelle mit Bohnen *Cold Trout with Beans*

PREPARE 6 FRESHLY caught trout as for blue trout and let them cool.

If fresh-killed trout are not available, use ordinary trout. To enough salted water to cover the fish add 1/2 cup vinegar, 1 medium onion, 2 peppercorns, 2 cloves, and 1 bay leaf and simmer the mixture for 10 minutes. Add the fish and simmer them for 12 to 18 minutes, depending on their size. Drain the trout well and remove the skins, leaving the heads and tails intact. Let them cool and chill them.

Reduce the cooking liquid over high heat for 15 minutes. Soften 1 envelope of gelatin in 1/4 cup cold water and strain 1 cup of the cooking liquid into the gelatin. Stir the gelatin until it is dissolved and add the juice of 1/2 lemon and salt to taste. Pour the aspic onto a dish so that it will be 1/2 inch deep. Cool the aspic and chill it until it is firm.

Cut 1 pound green beans crosswise into 1/8-inch pieces and cook them in well-salted water to cover until they are just tender. They should still be crisp. Drain the beans and chill them. To 1 cup mayonnaise add the grated rind of 1 lemon, a pinch of dry mustard, and salt to taste. Add enough mayonnaise to the beans to bind them.

To serve, arrange the trout, spaced well apart, on a large chilled platter. Cut the aspic into 1/2-inch cubes and surround the trout with the aspic cubes. Decorate the ends of the platter with lemon wedges. Cover each trout with a layer of the bean salad and spread 3 pimientos, chopped fine, over the salad. Border the platter with bands of hard-cooked egg yolk and hard-cooked egg white, riced separately. Thin the remaining mayonnaise with cream and serve it separately.

Lemon Trout   *Zitronenforelle*

IN A SAUCEPAN combine 2/3 cup each of white wine and olive oil and 1/3 cup tarragon vinegar. Add 1 onion, thinly sliced, 2 shallots, sliced, 4 sprigs of parsley, 1/2 bay leaf, 1 teaspoon salt, 1/2 teaspoon thyme, and 3 peppercorns and boil the marinade for 15 minutes. Strain it and let it cool.

Lay 6 trout, warmed to room temperature, in an oiled roasting pan. Pour the cooled marinade over the trout and add water just to cover. Cover the fish with oiled paper and simmer them very gently in a moderately hot oven (375° F.) for 15 minutes. For large trout, increase the cooking time. Let the trout cool in the liquid, then lift them carefully from the pan and remove the skin, leaving the heads and tails intact. Lay the trout on a serving platter, 1 1/2 inches apart. Coat the fish heavily with lemon mayonnaise, leaving the heads and tails exposed, and arrange grated horseradish down the center of each trout. Use 2 tablespoons of it for each fish. Surround the trout and border the platter with finely minced chicken aspic and garnish the platter with parsley and thinly sliced lemons.

Kalte Bachforelle 1   *Cold Brook Trout*

SIMMER 2 CARROTS, 1 onion, and 1 stalk of celery, all chopped, in 1 quart white wine for 10 minutes. Add 6 sprigs of parsley, 1 clove of garlic, crushed, 1 teaspoon salt, and 3 peppercorns, and simmer 20 minutes longer. Strain the stock and pour it over 6 cleaned brook trout. Add enough water to cover and simmer the trout gently for 15 minutes, or longer if they are large. Cool the fish in the stock and chill them.

Cook separately 1 cup small cauliflower flowerets and 3/4 cup each of peas, green beans, small Lima beans, chopped carrots, and turnips in salted water until they are just tender and chill them. Combine the drained cold vegetables and pour over them 3 tablespoons French dressing.

Arrange the trout on a platter, pile 2 cups of vegetable salad at each end, garnish the platter with lemon wedges and parsley, and pour over the fish a little of the stock.

Pound 9 raw spinach leaves with 2 tablespoons each of chopped chives, chervil, and parsley. Combine the mashed greens with 1 cup of mayonnaise and add salt and white pepper to taste. Serve this green mayonnaise separately.

Kalte Bachforelle 2   *Cold Brook Trout with Cucumber Salad*

SIMMER 6 TROUT in 2 quarts salted water with 2 onions, sliced, 2 carrots, sliced, and 1/2 bay leaf, about 15 to 20 minutes. Remove the trout, cool, and chill them. Remove the skins carefully, leaving the fish whole, with head and tail intact. Stuff each trout with cucumber salad. Slice thinly 6 tomatoes, peeled and drained, arrange the slices in a serving dish, and lay the stuffed trout on them. Serve the trout with a sauce made by combining 1/2 cup heavy cream, whipped, 6 sprigs of fresh dill, finely chopped, or 1 tablespoon dried dill, and 1/2 teaspoon dry mustard. Add salt to taste and at the last moment add 1/3 cup horseradish, freshly grated. Decorate with parsley and lemon wedges.

Lachsforelle mit Paradeis   *Salmon Trout on Tomato Mousse*

STEAM 1 POUND tomatoes, peeled, seeded, and drained, with 1/2 cup butter and 1/2 teaspoon salt until they are soft. Press them through a sieve and add 3 tablespoons white sauce and 2 envelopes of gelatin softened in 1/2 cup tomato juice. Stir the mixture until it is cold. Season it well with salt, pepper, and cayenne and chill until it just starts to set. Carefully fold in half as much whipped cream as the quantity of the tomato mousse. Pour the mousse into a fish mold that will exactly hold a 3-pound salmon trout.

Poach the trout in half white wine and half fish stock to cover for 20 to 30 minutes, or until it is done. Cool it in the stock and draw off the skin carefully after it is cold, leaving head and tail intact. Heat 1 cup strained fish stock to boiling and dissolve in it 1 envelope of gelatin softened in 1/4 cup cold white wine. Glaze the salmon trout with this aspic. Lay on it a design of scalded tarragon leaves and small rounds cut from egg white and tomatoes and glaze it again with aspic. Unmold the tomato mousse on an oval platter and lay the glazed fish on the mousse. Garnish the platter with crisp water cress and lemon wedges and serve mayonnaise separately. Serve the fish very cold.

Fish Pudding   *Fischpudding*

RESERVE THE skin and trimmings of 3 pounds halibut, sole, or flounder —use a combination of any two—and put the fileted fish twice through the finest blade of the food chopper. Pour off any juices. Put the fish again through the food chopper with 1 cup butter.

Combine 1/4 cup flour, 4 egg yolks, 2 teaspoons salt, 1/4 teaspoon pepper, and 1/2 teaspoon each of finely chopped chervil and dill with 2/3 cup heavy cream. Add the cream mixture to the ground fish and work the mixture until it is smooth. Fold in 3/4 cup cream, whipped stiff, and 4 egg whites, beaten stiff.

Turn the pudding into a 3-quart fluted tube mold, generously buttered and lightly dusted with fine dry bread crumbs. Cover the mold securely and put in on a rack in a kettle with hot water that reaches halfway up the sides of the mold. Cover the kettle and steam the pudding for 1 1/2 hours, adding more hot water as necessary. Unmold the pudding on a large warm serving platter and garnish the platter with small boiled potato balls, rolled in melted butter and in finely chopped parsley. Pass lobster sauce separately. Serve the pudding with a salad of diced cucumbers dressed with French dressing or sour cream.

Fischpudding Conrad   *Fish Pudding Conrad*

SCRAPE ENOUGH raw haddock with a knife to make 2 tightly packed cups, put it through the food chopper 3 times with 1 cup cold butter, and pound it in a mortar until it is entirely smooth. Stir 1/4 cup flour into 4 egg yolks and add gradually 1 1/2 cups heavy cream, 2 teaspoons each of salt and sugar, and 1/2 teaspoon white pepper. All the ingredients should be cold. Add this mixture very gradually to the fish, 1 tablespoon at a time, pounding the fish constantly. Add salt and white pepper to taste. Fold in 5 egg whites beaten so stiff that they do not move when the bowl is inverted. Pour the mixture into a very well-buttered ring mold dusted with 3 tablespoons bread crumbs. Cover the mold and steam it in a covered kettle of boiling water for 1 1/2 hours. Add boiling water to the kettle from time to time so that it maintains a level halfway up the mold.

Unmold the pudding carefully on a serving platter. Fill the center with cooked shrimps bound with a little dill or mushroom sauce and surround the ring with parsley potato balls. Serve more dill or mushroom sauce separately.

Fish Soufflé   *Osloer Fischauflauf*

BOIL 1/2 ONION, 1/2 carrot, 1/2 stalk of celery, sliced, 4 peppercorns, 1 bay
leaf, and 1/2 teaspoon salt in 2 cups water with 1 tablespoon vinegar for
5 minutes. Add 1 1/2 pounds flounder or other white fish. Simmer the
fish until it is tender and take it from the broth. Reduce the broth to
1 cup and strain it. Cool the fish and put it through the food chopper.
There should be 1 1/2 cups, packed firmly. Blend 4 tablespoons flour with
3 tablespoons butter over low heat and gradually add the cup of fish broth.
Beat 4 egg yolks until they thicken and add them carefully. Cook the
sauce over low heat, stirring constantly, for about 2 minutes, but do not
let it boil. Let it cool. Add the ground fish and 1 tablespoon fresh
dill, finely chopped. Beat 5 egg whites with 1/8 teaspoon salt until they
are very stiff. Fold the whites into the fish mixture and turn it into an
ungreased baking dish. Place the dish in a pan of hot water and bake
the soufflé in a moderately hot oven (375° F.) for 1 hour. Serve it at once
with dill sauce and cucumber salad.

Fish Goulash I   *Fisch Paprika*

SALT 3 POUNDS pike or pickerel well and let it rest for 2 hours. Lay the
fish in a roasting pan, on a bed of 2 onions, 1 carrot, 1 turnip, and 1/2
celery root, all finely chopped. Add 6 sprigs of parsley, 4 cloves, 3 peppercorns, 1 bay leaf, and 1/2 teaspoon salt. Beat 1/2 cup olive oil with 2 teaspoons paprika, 1 teaspoon lemon juice, and 1/2 teaspoon pepper and pour
it over the fish. Add 1/2 cup white wine. Poach the fish, covered, in a
moderately hot oven (375° F.) for 15 minutes, or until it is done. Take
out the fish. Stir 1 cup sour cream with 1 tablespoon flour, add it to the
pan, and cook it for 5 minutes over direct heat. Add salt and paprika
to taste. Strain the sauce over the fish. Serve it with boiled potatoes.

Fish Goulash II   *Halászlé*

SAUTÉ 2 ONIONS and 2 carrots, both sliced, in 1/2 cup butter until the
onions are golden. Stir in 1 tablespoon each of paprika and tomato paste.
Boil 1 pound flounder in 3 cups salted water for 10 minutes. Add the
sautéed vegetables and pan juices to the fish and simmer it, covered, for

1 hour. Press this sauce through a sieve into a shallow casserole, add 3 medium potatoes, peeled and quartered, and simmer them for 10 minutes. Add 3 pounds fish—carp, pike, pickerel, or any combination of fish— cleaned and cut into pieces, 3 tomatoes, peeled, seeded, and chopped, and 1/2 cup water. Simmer the fish for 12 to 18 minutes, or until it is opaque and tender. Add salt, pepper, and paprika to taste, and sprinkle the goulash with 1/2 cup finely chopped green pepper.

Wiener Fischfilets　　　　　　　*Vienna Fish Filets with Sour Cream*

WASH, DRY, and salt 6 filets of any white fish—haddock, flounder, or sole. Lay 2 filets in a buttered casserole and sprinkle them with the juice of 1/2 lemon. Cover them with 1/2 cup salted sour cream, whipped, topped with 2 slices crisp crumbled bacon, 1/4 cup diced cucumber, and 1 teaspoon capers. Add 2 more filets, mask them with 1/2 cup sour cream, whipped with 1 tablespoon brown mustard, and add bacon, cucumber, and capers, as above. Add the 2 remaining filets, mask them with 1/2 cup plain salted sour cream, and add bacon, cucumbers, and capers as before. Sprinkle the fish with 1/4 cup grated Parmesan and bake it in a moderately hot oven (375° F.) for about 20 minutes, or until the filets are done.

Fastentiere
Shellfish

Krabben Ida　　　　　　　*Crab Meat in Potato Cheese Ring*

MELT 3 TABLESPOONS butter in the top of a double boiler over boiling water, blend in 3 tablespoons flour, and stir until the flour is transparent. Gradually stir in 1 1/2 cups heavy cream. Cook the sauce for 15 minutes and add salt and paprika to taste. Add 1 1/2 pounds picked-over crab meat and cook for 15 minutes longer.

Rice 6 medium-sized boiled potatoes while they are hot, add 3 tablespoons each of sour cream and cream cheese, and stir the mixture to a paste. Add salt and pepper to taste. Through a pastry bag fitted with a

1/2-inch fluted tube pipe a thick border of the potato mixture around the edge of an ovenproof dish. If the mixture is too mealy to pipe smoothly, add more cream cheese. Pile the crab meat into the potato ring, sprinkle it with 1/4 cup grated Parmesan, and bake it in a hot oven (400° F.) for 6 minutes, or until the cheese is lightly browned.

Crab Soufflé
with Shrimps and Cucumbers   *Dänischer Auflauf*

IN A DEEP ovenproof dish lay 1 pound cooked shrimps. Cover the shrimps with 2 large cucumbers, thinly sliced and blanched. Blend 3 tablespoons flour into 3 tablespoons melted butter and gradually add 1 cup hot milk. Cook the sauce, stirring constantly, until it comes to a boil and thickens. Cool the sauce and fold in 4 egg yolks, beaten until they are thick and lemon colored. Fold in 1/2 cup thick mayonnaise seasoned with 1/4 teaspoon salt, 1/8 teaspoon dry mustard, a sprinkling of pepper, and a small dash of cayenne. Fold in 1 pound flaked cooked crab meat. Beat 4 egg whites until they will stand in peaks and fold them into the mixture. Pile it lightly over the shrimps and cucumbers and dust it with paprika. Bake the soufflé in a hot oven (400° F.) until it is puffed and brown, about 45 minutes. Serve it immediately.

Cold Crayfish Mousse   *Lukullische Krebse*

SIMMER 36 LIVE crayfish in half highly seasoned fish stock and half Champagne to cover, until they turn brilliant red. Cool them in the stock. Reserve 3 whole crayfish. Break open the remaining shells and remove the tail meat. Pound the shells in a mortar with 1/2 cup butter. Dry the pounded shells in a slow oven (250° F.) until they are brittle, about 18 minutes. Add 2 cups thick béchamel sauce and press the mixture through a fine sieve.

Soften 3 envelopes of gelatin in 1/2 cup white wine. Bring 1 cup of the broth in which the crayfish cooked to a boil. Dissolve the softened gelatin in it, off the heat, and add it to the strained béchamel sauce. Chill the sauce and fold in 2 cups heavy cream, whipped, and add salt and pepper to taste.

Turn the mousse into a wide oiled mold with a flat bottom. Chill it for 3 hours. Unmold the mousse onto a cold crystal platter and decorate the top with the crayfish tail meat and with truffle slices. In the center, arrange the 3 whole crayfish, tails up. Secure them with wooden picks. Surround the platter with water cress or parsley. Serve the mousse on iced plates and accompany it with Champagne.

Krebse vom Rost   *Broiled Shrimps or Crayfish*

SPLIT AND clean, but do not shell, 36 crayfish tails or halve 36 shelled and deveined shrimps lengthwise. Marinate the shellfish in the refrigerator for 3 hours in 1 cup olive oil and the juice and grated rind of 3 lemons with 1 cup chopped onion, 1/2 cup chopped parsley, 2 cloves of garlic, crushed, and 2 teaspoons each of salt, dry mustard, basil, rosemary, and tarragon. Broil the split crayfish tails or the shrimps, undrained, 3 inches from the heat for 6 to 8 minutes. Heat the remaining marinade and beat in 3 tablespoons butter. Pour a little over the crayfish or shrimps and serve at once.

Krebse auf polnische Art   *Crayfish with Sour Cream*

IN A KETTLE, sauté 1 carrot and 1 onion, both chopped, in 2 tablespoons butter until the onions are golden. Add 2 shallots, finely chopped, an herb bouquet, made of 1 stalk of celery, 2 sprigs of parsley, a sprig each of thyme and chervil, and half a bay leaf, 2 cups white wine, 1 1/2 cups fish stock, 2 ounces brandy, and salt and pepper to taste. Simmer the mixture for 10 minutes. Add 36 cleaned crayfish and simmer them, covered, for 15 minutes. Take out the crayfish and keep them hot. Reduce the stock by half, remove the herb bouquet, and add 1 cup heavy sour cream. Reduce the heat and stir in 1/2 cup soft white bread crumbs and salt, pepper, and cayenne to taste. Add 2 tablespoons chopped fennel or dill, and beat in 1 tablespoon butter. Pour the sour cream sauce over the crayfish and serve it at once.

Hummer Prinz Heinrich   *Lobster Ragout*

SPLIT THREE 1 1/2-pound lobsters and cut the claws and tails into 2 or 3 pieces each. Sauté 2 onions and 2 leeks, both chopped, in 2 tablespoons

butter for 5 minutes. Add the lobster pieces and steam them, covered, for 5 minutes. Add 3 cups fish stock, 1 cup rice, a pinch of saffron thread or powdered saffron, and salt, pepper, and cayenne to taste. Simmer the lobster and rice over very low heat, stirring frequently, until the rice is just tender, about 15 to 20 minutes. Add more hot fish stock, if necessary. Sprinkle with chopped parsley.

Lobster with Tarragon
Hummer mit Estragon

SPLIT SIX 1-pound lobsters lengthwise with a sharp knife, inserting the knife at the tip of the back. Reserve the coral, if there is any, and the tomalley. Detach the claws and tails, cut each across once, and sauté the pieces in 1 cup olive oil until the meat is just opaque and the shells start to turn red. Pour off half the oil, add salt and pepper to taste, 1/4 cup finely chopped onions, and 2 cloves of garlic, crushed, and sauté the mixture, covered, for 5 minutes. Add 3/4 cup warm brandy and flame it. When the flame dies down, add 6 tomatoes, peeled, seeded, and chopped, 2 tablespoons tomato purée, 6 long sprigs of tarragon, and 1 sprig each of thyme and marjoram. Pour 3 cups white wine over the lobster and cook it, covered, in a moderate oven (350° F.) for 25 minutes.

Take out the lobster pieces, the herb sprigs, and the crushed garlic, reduce the sauce slightly, and press it through a sieve. Add the tomalley and coral and cook the sauce for 9 minutes longer. Add salt and pepper to taste and beat in 1 tablespoon butter. Return the lobster to the sauce with 3 tablespoons each of freshly chopped tarragon and parsley.

Hummer auf indische Art   *Curried Lobster with Rice*

BOIL TWO 2-pound lobsters for 20 to 25 minutes. Split them and drain them well. Take out all the meat and cut it into large pieces. Reserve the coral, if there is any, and the tomalley. Sauté 2 large onions, chopped, in 1/2 cup butter until they are golden. Add 2 tablespoons curry powder and stir until it is dissolved. Add 2 tablespoons tomato purée and sprinkle 2 tablespoons flour over the sauce. Stir it until it is smooth. Add 1 cup each of white wine and fish stock and all the lobster meat and heat it in the sauce for 10 minutes.

Sauté 1 onion, finely chopped, in 1/4 cup butter, add 1 1/4 cups rice, and sauté the rice until it is coated with butter and transparent. Add 2 1/2 cups chicken stock and cook the rice, covered, in a moderate oven (350° F.) for 20 minutes. Add 1/2 cup toasted slivered almonds, 1/4 cup white raisins, and salt and pepper to taste. Press the rice into a buttered ring mold and bake it in the oven for 6 minutes. Unmold the Turkish rice ring carefully onto a hot platter and fill it with the curried lobster. Sprinkle the lobster with 1/4 cup chopped parsley.

Hummer unter Blätterteig Gregor   *Lobster in Puff Pastry Gregor*

PLUNGE TWO 2-pound lobsters into a large kettle of boiling water to which 2 onions, 1/2 cup vinegar, a few sprigs of parsley, and salt to taste have been added, and boil them for 20 minutes. Strain the broth. Cut the lobster tail meat into even crosswise slices. Remove the claw meat without breaking it. Remove the meat from the body shells and reserve any coral or tomalley. Keep the meat warm in a little of the strained broth.

In the top of a double boiler melt 1/2 cup butter, stir in 1 cup flour, and cook the *roux* slowly for a few minutes but do not let it take on color.

Gradually add 4 cups of the strained lobster broth, stirring constantly until the sauce reaches a boil, and cook the sauce over gently boiling water for 1 hour. Strain the sauce, and add the coral and the tomalley, 1 cup cooked artichoke bottoms, quartered, 1/2 cup Sherry, and salt, pepper, and lemon juice to taste. Add the tail meat. If the sauce is too thick, add 1/2 cup hot cream.

Arrange the meat and sauce on a large flat serving platter and cover it with a trellis of the following herbed puff pastry: Follow the directions for ordinary puff paste, making 3 turns and sprinkling the dough with 1 tablespoon mixed parsley, dill, and tarragon, all finely minced, each time it is rolled out. After chilling the dough for the last time, roll it out 1/4 inch thick, cut it into 1/4-inch strips, using a fluted pastry wheel, and twist each pair of strips together to make long double strands.

Measure the serving platter. On a wet baking sheet, lay twisted strips of puff paste in a rectangle or oval as large as the outside edge of the lobster platter. Lay diagonal strips across the rectangle or oval to make a latticework of paste. Press down well at all joints and bake the puff paste in a very hot oven (450° F.) for 10 minutes. Reduce the heat to moderate (350° F.) and continue baking the puff paste until it is brown. Cool the puff paste, loosen it carefully from the baking sheet, and slide it onto the lobster platter. Place the claw meat in the openings of the trellis, and decorate the other openings with parsley. Decorate the ends of the platter with puff-paste crescents.

Lobster with Two Sauces   *Hummer Dagmar*

SPLIT THREE 1 1/2-pound boiled lobsters lengthwise, remove the meat, and slice the tail and claw meat. Reserve the shells, unbroken. Sauté 4 tomatoes, peeled, drained, and chopped, with 1 cup chopped mushrooms in 1/4 cup butter for 5 minutes. Drain the mixture well and fill the lobster shells with it. Keep the shells warm.

Make a rich hollandaise sauce, using 6 egg yolks and 1 cup butter. Flavor half the sauce with 2 teaspoons mustard, the other half with enough paprika to make it pink. Pour the mustard hollandaise into the shells over the mushrooms and tomatoes, cover it with the sliced lobster meat, and mask the lobster with the paprika-flavored hollandaise. Glaze the filled shells under the broiler for 1 minute. Serve garnished with parsley sprigs.

*H*ummersauce   *Lobster in Dill Sauce*

SAUTÉ THE warm meat, cut into large chunks, of a 2-pound boiled lobster in 1/2 cup butter for 5 minutes, stirring it several times. Add 1 cup white wine and simmer the lobster very gently for 5 minutes more. Simmer 6 to 8 sprays of dill or 2 tablespoons dried dill in 2 cups fish or lobster stock until the liquid is reduced to 3/4 cup. Strain the stock and add it to the lobster with 1 tablespoon very finely minced fresh dill or 1/2 tablespoon dried dill. Add salt and pepper to taste and thicken the sauce with about 1/2 cup heavy cream or with fish *velouté*. Add the lobster, stir the mixture well, and simmer it for 5 minutes longer. Add a little cream just before serving. Serves 2.

*H*ummersalat in *A*spik   *Lobster Salad in Aspic*

HEAT 4 CUPS clear meat stock to boiling, take it from the heat, and add 4 envelopes of gelatin softened in 1 cup white wine. Stir the gelatin until it is dissolved. Let the aspic cool and pour it into a rinsed cylinder mold. Chill it until the aspic sets around the edges and pour off the still liquid aspic from the center. Make a line of red pimiento, cut into thin strips, around the mold about halfway up, dipping the pimiento into the aspic before putting it in place. Stand a circle of cold cooked asparagus stalks around the entire mold, with the heads down, keeping them as close together as possible and filling any spaces between them with additional aspic.

Combine 1 pound cold cooked lobster meat, 3 tomatoes, peeled, seeded, and chopped, 1 apple and 1 truffle, both chopped, 1/2 cup mayonnaise, 1/2 cup of the aspic and salt and pepper to taste. Fill the center of the mold with this salad and pour in the remaining aspic. Chill the mold for at least 2 hours. Unmold it in the center of a platter, surround it with crisp water cress, and serve it with lemon mayonnaise.

*H*ummermus 1   *Cold Lobster Mousse I*

RESERVE THE claw meat of two 2-pound cooked lobsters. Chop the rest of the meat, add 1/4 cup cold butter, and purée the mixture until it is smooth. Melt 2 tablespoons butter, blend in 3 tablespoons flour, and gradually add 3/4 cup milk to make a smooth sauce. Add it to the lobster paste. Soften 2 envelopes of gelatin in 1/2 cup cold chicken consommé and dissolve it in 1 cup boiling chicken consommé, off the heat. Cool the aspic and add 3/4 of it to the lobster mixture with salt and pepper to taste. Stir the mixture over ice until it is thoroughly chilled and add 1 cup heavy cream, whipped. Chop the reserved claw meat and add it with any coral the lobsters may have had. Turn the mixture into an oiled mold, preferably in the shape of a lobster, and chill it for at least 2 hours. Unmold the mousse and glaze it with the remaining aspic. Set truffle cutouts along the back of the lobster, chill it until the aspic sets, and glaze it again. Chill it. Serve with shallot mayonnaise.

Cold Lobster Mousse II   *Hummermus 2*

PURÉE 2 CUPS cold cooked lobster meat with 1/2 cup creamed butter and 1 teaspoon salt in a processor until smooth. Melt 2 tablespoons butter, blend in 3 tablespoons flour, and gradually add 3/4 cup fish or meat stock. Cook this white sauce over low heat, stirring constantly, until it thickens and combine it with the lobster paste. Add 1 tablespoon brandy, 1 teaspoon tomato purée, 1/4 teaspoon paprika, and salt and pepper to taste. Beat the mixture until it is light.

Soften 3 envelopes of gelatin in 1 cup white wine and dissolve it in 3 cups boiling fish or meat stock, off the heat. Let the aspic cool. Pour the cool aspic into a rinsed mold and chill it until the edges start to set. Pour off the liquid aspic in the center, leaving a thin coating on the mold. Add 1/2 cup aspic to the lobster mousse, correct the seasoning, and pour the mousse into the mold. Chill it for 2 hours. Pour the remaining aspic into a shallow pan, chill it until it is set, and dice it. Unmold the mousse on a serving platter and surround it with the diced aspic. Serve it with mayonnaise flavored with finely minced dill.

Scallops with Grapes   *Seemuscheln Georg*

SAUTÉ 2 CUPS scallops in 2 tablespoons butter for 10 minutes. Sauté 2 onions, chopped, in 2 tablespoons butter until they are golden, add 1 tablespoon flour, and stir the mixture over low heat for 1 minute. Add 1 cup of the liquor in which the scallops cooked or white stock and cook the

sauce, stirring constantly, until it is smooth. Season to taste with salt, pepper, and cayenne, and add the scallops. Reduce the heat and add 1 cup warm white seedless grapes, 1 tablespoon chopped parsley, 1/4 clove of garlic, crushed, and 2 egg yolks beaten with 1/2 cup warm cream. Turn the mixture into a large heatproof baking dish, spread it with 1 cup dry bread crumbs, and pour over it 1/4 cup melted butter. Brown the crumbs in a hot oven (400° F.) for 6 minutes. Garnish the dish with parsley.

Cocktail von Scampi

Shrimp Cocktail

SIMMER 24 SHELLED and deveined shrimps in salted water with 1/2 teaspoon caraway seeds for 5 minutes, or until they are opaque and pink. Drain the shrimps well and pour 1/4 cup tarragon vinegar over them while they are hot. Turn the shrimps every 10 minutes until they are cold. Divide them among 6 cocktail glasses and pour over them a sauce of 6 tablespoons mayonnaise, 1 tablespoon each of ketchup, brandy, and kirsch, a dash of Worcestershire sauce, and salt, pepper, and cayenne to taste. Garnish each glass with a sprig of parsley and serve cold.

Shrimps with Melon Balls   *Scampi Adria*

PREPARE 24 SHRIMPS as for *Cocktail von Scampi* and fill a large hollowed-out melon shell with the shrimps and the meat of the melon cut into balls. Stir the juice and grated rind of 1 lemon into 1 cup thick mayonnaise, add 1/4 cup tomato ketchup, a dash each of Worcestershire sauce and Angostura bitters, and salt, pepper, and sugar to taste. Add 1/4 cucumber, peeled and chopped, and pour the sauce over the shrimps in the melon. Serve surrounded with water cress and pass chutney separately.

Shrimps in Melon Shell   *Krebs in Melone*

COOK 1 POUND shelled and deveined shrimps in 2 quarts boiling salted water until they are pink and opaque, about 4 minutes. Drain them thoroughly, pour over them 1/4 cup tarragon vinegar, and chill. Cut a lid from the top of a large cantaloupe, cutting carefully with a sharp knife held at an angle, so the lid will fit back on when the melon is filled. Remove the seeds and fibrous membrane from the cantaloupe, and chill. Combine 1/3 cup thick mayonnaise, 1/4 cup tarragon vinegar, 1 onion, chopped fine, 1 tablespoon each of brown mustard, ketchup, and apricot marmalade, 1 teaspoon each of parsley and tarragon leaves, finely chopped, and salt to taste. Pour this sauce over the shrimps, fill the melon with the mixture, and replace the lid. Chill the melon. Bring the whole melon to the table, packed in enough ice to support it firmly. To serve, remove the lid and serve shrimps and a melon wedge for each portion.

Marinated Shrimps   *Marinierte Krebse*

SIMMER 2 1/2 POUNDS shelled and deveined shrimps in water to cover with 1 tablespoon pickling spices and salt for 2 minutes, or until they turn pink and opaque. Drain the shrimps well and arrange them in a shallow earthenware or glass dish. Cover the shrimps with 3 bay leaves and 3 Bermuda onions, sliced very thin and separated into rings. Pour over a dressing made of 1 cup each of oil and vinegar, the juice and grated rind of 2 lemons and 2 limes, and 1 tablespoon each of sugar, celery seed, and chopped dill. Add 1/4 cup Cognac and 1/2 teaspoon each of ground cinnamon, ground cloves, and peppercorns. Refrigerate for 24 hours.

*K*rebssalat mit gefüllten *E*iern   *Shrimp Salad with Stuffed Eggs*

HARD-COOK 8 EGGS, cut a slice from the wide end of each egg, and remove the yolk with a small spoon. Rice 4 egg yolks, and reserve them. Rice 2 egg yolks, add 3 tablespoons caviar, and fill as many of the egg whites as possible with the mixture. Rice the 2 remaining egg yolks and add 2 tablespoons anchovy paste, 1 tablespoon mayonnaise, and 1/2 cup chopped ham. Fill the remaining egg whites with the ham mixture.

Wash 1 1/2 cups button mushrooms and remove the stems. Simmer 1 cup tarragon vinegar with 1 teaspoon salt, 1 bay leaf, and 1 clove of garlic for 5 minutes, add the mushrooms and 3 whole cloves, and simmer for 6 minutes longer. Let the mushrooms stand in the liquor until they are needed.

Combine the 4 reserved riced egg yolks with 2 tablespoons each of tarragon vinegar and mild French mustard. Stir in 1/4 cup olive oil and add to the dressing 1 tablespoon chopped capers, 1 shallot, minced, a pinch of sugar, and salt and pepper to taste.

Drain the mushrooms and sprinkle them with 1 tablespoon minced parsley. Combine them with 1 pound cold cooked shrimps and pour over them enough dressing to coat them. Line a salad platter with lettuce leaves and arrange the eggs in a ring, cut ends down. Fill the ring with the mushroom and shrimp salad and pour the remaining egg-yolk dressing over it.

*S*campi *R*eis und *E*rbsen   *Shrimps with Rice and Peas*

IN A KETTLE boil 1 3/4 cups long-grain rice in salted boiling water for 11 minutes. Drain it in a colander and set the colander over boiling water. Steam the rice, covered, for 15 minutes, or until tender. Combine the rice with 2 cups cooked peas, 1/4 cup toasted slivered almonds, and 1/3 cup melted butter. Press the rice mixture into a buttered ring mold, cover the mold, and keep it warm in a slow oven.

Simmer 1 1/2 pounds large shelled and deveined shrimps in salted water for 3 minutes and drain them well.

Melt 1/4 cup butter, blend in 5 tablespoons flour, and stir over low heat until the *roux* starts to turn golden. Add 3 cups chicken stock gradually and stir the sauce until it is smooth. Simmer the sauce over low heat for 15 minutes and stir in 1 tablespoon tomato paste blended with 1/4 cup brandy. Add the peel of 1/2 orange, finely slivered, and salt and pepper to taste. Unmold the rice, fill the center with the shrimps and sauce, and sprinkle with 1/4 cup toasted shaved almonds. *(Picture, page 125.)*

Fried Shrimp Risotto   *Scampi Reis*

SAUTÉ 1/4 CUP chopped onions in 1/4 cup butter until they are golden. Add 1 cup rice and stir well until the rice is coated and transparent. Simmer the rice in a double boiler with 2 cups fish stock and 1 herb bouquet until the rice is just tender, adding fish stock if necessary. Remove the bouquet, season the rice well with salt and pepper to taste, and dry it in a moderate oven (350° F.) for 5 minutes. Cut 12 shelled and deveined shrimps in half lengthwise, dip them in 1 cup flour seasoned with 1 teaspoon salt, then in 1 cup milk, and again in flour. Fry the shrimps in deep hot fat (375° F.) for about 3 minutes, or until they are golden, drain them well, and add them to the hot rice. Serve the risotto sprinkled with grated Parmesan to taste.

Skewered Shrimps and Bacon   *Krebse am Speiss*

SHELL AND devein 2 pounds large shrimps, wash them, and dry them with a towel. Marinate them in a shallow dish for 2 to 3 hours in 1/2 cup each of brandy and tarragon vinegar. Wrap each shrimp in 1/3 slice of bacon. Thread them on 6 skewers and broil them about 3 inches from the heat for 5 to 6 minutes, or until the bacon is crisp and brown, turning the skewers once. Keep the skewers warm in a chafing dish. Pour 1/2 cup warm brandy over them and flame it. Serve with tart lemon-and-tarragon mayonnaise.

Christmas Shrimp   *Weihnachts Krebse*

SAUTÉ 1 CUP chopped onion in 1/2 cup butter in a large skillet over medium heat until it is golden. Blend in 3 teaspoons Madras curry powder. Add 2 pounds shelled and deveined shrimps, and cook them for 2 minutes, or until they are opaque and pink. Pour the shrimps into a hot serving dish and add 1/2 cup each of seeded and finely chopped green pepper and chopped pimiento, and salt to taste. Stir the mixture well, cover it, and keep it warm. Before serving, add 1/2 cup chopped chutney and the separately riced yolks and whites of 2 hard-cooked eggs, stir the mixture once, sprinkle it with 1/2 cup chopped parsley, and serve.

Krebse mit Mandeln   Shrimps with Almonds

SAUTÉ 2 CARROTS, 2 onions, and 3 shallots, all chopped very fine, 4 sprigs of parsley, 1/2 bay leaf, and a pinch of dried thyme in 5 tablespoons butter until the vegetables are tender. Add 5 tablespoons olive oil and 2 pounds shrimps, shelled and deveined. Cook the shrimps until they are pink and opaque, about 2 minutes. Add 2 cups white wine, 6 tomatoes, peeled, seeded and chopped, and 1/8 teaspoon saffron powder. Cover the mixture and cook it gently for 10 minutes. Salt it to taste. Remove the shrimps, keep them warm, and strain the sauce. Add 1 cup cream and 3/4 cup blanched chopped almonds and reheat the sauce. Return the shrimps to the sauce and heat it thoroughly. Serve the shrimps with rice.

Krebse mit Cognac   Shrimps and Brandy

SHELL AND devein 2 pounds shrimps, leaving the tails intact. Place them in a pan over medium heat, with 1/2 cup butter, 1 teaspoon chopped dill, and 1 teaspoon each of chopped green and red sweet bell peppers. Sauté the shrimps until they turn pink, 2 to 3 minutes. Remove the shrimps.

Add 1 cup washed rice to the butter in the pan and cook it gently, stirring constantly, for 5 minutes. Add 4 medium tomatoes, peeled and chopped, and 1 large onion, chopped, and cook, stirring, for another 5 minutes. Add 1/2 cup white wine and 4 ounces brandy and cook, stirring, 5 minutes more. Transfer the rice mixture to a double boiler, add 2 cups bouillon, and cook it over boiling water until the rice is medium soft. Add the shrimps, salt and pepper to taste, and more brandy, if desired. Cook until the shrimps are thoroughly heated and serve at once.

Meat

Fleischspeisen

I T HAS BEEN said of the Viennese that they eat so much veal because there is not room enough in Austria to let all the calves grow into cows. Thanks to this lack of bovine *Lebensraum,* the Viennese can eat his beloved *Wienerschnitzel* and his *Kalbsgulyás* to his heart's content, forgetting, of course, that if he ate less veal he would need room for fewer cows, since every tender calf has a large and hungry mother with a bell around her neck, grazing on one of Austria's green meadows. And of course, pasturage has to be found somehow for the calves that do grow up and supply the strange and varied cuts of beef that go into beef roasts and the famous boiled beef dishes.

Austria, like all countries in which meat is not plentiful, has devised more ways of cutting and preparing meat than the countries where meat is more abundant. A Viennese housewife will learn fifty ways of preparing a filet of beef, though she has a chance to prepare it only once a year, while a more fortunate housewife in some other country, who serves beef once a week, may always broil it in exactly the same way. The Viennese appreciate their meat, they treat it tenderly, and if they cannot afford something they want, they prepare something else to taste like it. There are many old recipes for making beef taste like venison, for turning ground meat into a *falscher Hasenbraten*—a fake saddle of hare. And they have ways of marinating pork to taste like wild boar, a delicacy brought in from Hungary under the double eagle of the Austro-Hungarian Empire.

The Viennese eat very little lamb and mutton, in spite of the fact that these meats come into lavish use farther down the Danube, in the Balkan countries, from which many dishes came to Vienna. The Viennese enjoy

177

pork in two distinct and ever popular ways: fresh and smoked. There are many more cuts of smoked pork to choose from than are generally available in this country. Smoked spareribs and smoked pigs' knuckles with sauerkraut may sound like peasant fare, but the elegant Viennese take great pleasure in a sturdy meal, and pork and pork sausages are dear to the hearts of all.

No one driving or walking through Austria can escape an intimate acquaintance with her meat-on-the-hoof. Cars come to a standstill while a placid cow crosses a narrow bridge, and no one would want to upset a herd on its way to be milked. Barefoot children confidently hold up the stream of progress while they drive the sheep home to the barn, and many a cow takes her leisurely way down the middle of the road with her calf wobbling behind her while traffic waits. The rural Austrian scene, though changed, still includes the old woman driving a pig before her, with a piece of string tied to its hind leg, and children herding across the grass a brace of sheep or goats who nibble more slowly but just as efficiently as any mower.

The Viennese lady, or her cook, goes to market and prods and peers at the meat before she chooses just the cut she wants. Her butcher is her friend and also the source of much gossip and information. He bows her in and out of his shop and cuts her meat exactly to her order. He lards, he bones, he trims, and he rolls. He adds meat for the dog and chops bones for soup stock. He is an intimate, in that he knows the dates of family anniversaries and celebrations and he is the receiver of confidences. His shop has anything from a magnificent golden bull's head to a lowly sausage over its door, and the butcher's boy sweeps up the sawdust on the floor and replaces it every few hours, between deliveries.

When the meat comes to the kitchen, carried in a crocheted shopping bag or delivered by the butcher's boy, it is not just another piece of meat. It has often been saved for, it is happily anticipated, and it has been individually selected. It will be pounded and prepared with loving care, and, if all things have gone right, the chances are good that it will be breaded into the *Wienerschnitzel* that everyone loves so well.

Boiled Beef

Rindfleisch Hotel Bristol

COMBINE 1 POUND short ribs of beef, 2 onions, 2 carrots, and 1 stalk of celery, all sliced, 3 sprigs of parsley, 5 peppercorns, 1/2 teaspoon salt, and 4 quarts water. Bring the liquid to a boil, skim off the scum, and simmer the stock for 1 hour. Bring the stock to a boil, plunge in a 3-pound piece of top round of beef and 1/2 beef marrow bone. Skim the stock again after it returns to a boil. Reduce the heat and simmer the beef, covered, leaving just enough space for steam to escape, for 2 to 2 1/2 hours. Slice the marrow and serve the meat very hot with it and the vegetables. Serve caper, tomato, or horseradish sauce separately.

Boiled Beef in Beer

Rindfleisch in Bier

POUND A well-trimmed 4-pound piece of beef, rump or flank, with a wooden mallet and rub it well with salt and black pepper. Lay it in a deep casserole on a bed of 6 slices of bacon, and spread 2 onions, 2 carrots, and 2 turnips, all chopped, 6 peppercorns and 6 juniper berries, 2 bay leaves, and 3 curls of lemon rind, over and around the meat. Add just enough beer to cover and simmer the meat, covered, for 2 1/2 hours. Drain off the reduced broth and keep the meat hot. Brown 2 tablespoons butter, blend in 3 tablespoons flour, and cook the *roux* over very low heat, stirring, until it is brown and smooth. Gradually add 2 cups of broth from the meat and simmer the sauce over very low heat for 20 minutes. Add salt and pepper to taste and pour the sauce over the beef. Serve from the casserole.

Sauerbraten

Sauerbraten

COVER 1/2 POUND larding pork, cut into 1/2-inch strips, with a mixture of 1 large onion, finely minced, 1 tablespoon salt, 1/2 tablespoon pepper, 1 teaspoon grated lemon rind, and 1/2 teaspoon allspice. Cut deep incisions in a 4- to 5-pound piece of top round of beef, press a piece of larding pork into each incision, packing in as much of the onion mixture as possible, and rub the remaining onion mixture into the meat. Roll the meat, tie it into a round, and put it in a deep bowl. Make a marinade of 3 onions and half a lemon, both sliced, 12 peppercorns, 6 cloves, 1 bay leaf, 2 cups vinegar, and 1 cup water. Bring the marinade to a boil. Pour the hot marinade over the meat. Marinate the meat in a cool place for 3 days, turning it once a day.

Place the meat in a roasting pan, mix 1 tablespoon sugar into the marinade, and pour it over the meat. Cover the pan and cook the meat in a moderate oven (350° F.) for 3 hours, or until it is very tender, basting frequently. Transfer the meat to a heated platter and remove the strings.

Strain the gravy and skim off the fat. Add 2 tablespoons flour mixed to a paste with 1/2 cup cold water and 4 pfeffernusse, crumbled, and simmer the gravy in the roasting pan on top of the stove, stirring in all the brown bits, for 5 minutes. Pour half the sauce over the meat and serve the rest in a sauceboat. Serve the *Sauerbraten* with potato dumplings and hot prunes stewed with lemon rind and cloves.

Rostbraten Schöne Gärtnerin   *Garden Beef Platter*

ROAST A HEAVY 5-rib roast. Follow roasting directions for rare roast beef, approximately 15 minutes per pound in a moderate oven (325° F.). Cool the roast and chill it. Cut the meat carefully from the ribs in one piece. Trim the 2 ends to expose the rare meat and cut away the outer brown crust, leaving a layer of white fat on the surface of the meat.

Set the cold meat crosswise on a large rectangular flat platter, and at the back of the platter, so that the foreground is left empty. Pour 2 to 3 cups cool but still liquid beef aspic around the meat to a depth of 1/4 inch over the entire platter and chill it until the aspic is set. Thinly cut the first 6 to 9 slices of the beef and lay them, overlapping slightly, in front of the meat across the width of the platter, on top of the aspic.

Glaze the top and sides of the meat with aspic, leaving only the face of the meat unglazed. Arrange a large bouquet of vegetables, cut in the form of flowers, on top of the meat, securing it with picks and skewers. Use carrots, beets, turnips, radishes, or parsnips and garnish the bouquet with sprigs of parsley.

In the 2 corners at the back of the platter, arrange 2 small nests of Boston lettuce and fill them with freshly grated horseradish, mounded to resemble small cauliflowers, or with small marinated cauliflowers. Lay diagonal lines of cold parsley potatoes, pickled beets, small cold cooked carrots and cooked green asparagus spears from the beef to the edges of the platter. Glaze the vegetables with aspic and lay cold marinated fluted mushrooms along the front of the platter. Fill any empty spaces with diced aspic. Serve cold béarnaise sauce separately.

Stuffed Filet of Beef   *Edler Lungenbraten*

TRIM THE thin end from a heavy filet of beef, leaving a 3 1/2- to 4-pound piece. Make a deep cut lengthwise and spread the meat out on wax paper on a wooden board. Cover it with wax paper and pound it with a wooden mallet into an oblong 3/4 inch thick. Season it well with salt and pepper. Combine 1 1/2 cups chopped mushrooms and 1 cup each of chopped onions and parsley sautéed together with 1/4 cup butter until golden with 1/3 cup bread crumbs, 1 egg yolk, and 1/2 cup calf's liver paste and spread the mixture evenly on the meat in a thin layer, leaving a 1-inch border. Add salt and pepper to taste. Beginning with a long side, roll up the filet and tie it with kitchen string at 2-inch intervals. On the top of the stove brown the filet in 1/4 cup butter and roast it in a very hot oven (450° F.), basting it with melted butter, about 20 to 25 minutes, until it is brown on the outside but still rare within. Slice the filled filet just before serving it. Accompany it with Madeira sauce and spinach-stuffed mushrooms.

Filet of Beef in Crust   *Filet in Kruste*

SPRINKLE A 5-POUND filet of beef with 1 teaspoon dry English mustard, tie larding pork over it, and roast it for 25 minutes in a hot oven (400° F.). Let the filet cool. Remove the larding pork. Skim the pan juices.

In 2 tablespoons butter sauté for 5 minutes 1/2 pound mushrooms and 1/4 pound cooked ham, both finely chopped, and half a small clove of garlic, crushed. Add 1/3 cup Sherry and 4 chicken livers, sautéed and chopped, 1 tablespoon each of tomato purée and meat extract, and 3 shallots, finely chopped. Mix well and remove the pan from the heat.

Roll out a sheet of puff paste large enough to enclose the filet. Lay the cold filet in the center of the puff paste and pile the ham and mushroom mixture on and around it. Carefully wrap the filet in the puff paste, turning in the ends, and press all the seams together firmly. Lay the filet seam side down on a baking sheet and paint the puff paste with egg white. Cut decorative shapes from puff paste—leaves, circles, or strips to form braids. Paint the cutouts with egg white and affix them to the top of the wrapped filet. Bake it in a hot oven (425° F.) for 25 to 30 minutes, or until the pastry is golden.

To the reserved pan juices add 1/2 cup each of beef stock and Sherry and 1 tablespoon chopped tarragon and heat the sauce for 5 minutes. Arrange the filet on a serving platter and carefully slice it. Keep the crust intact around each slice. Serves 8.

Kaltes Filet Dürnstein   *Cold Filet of Beef in Crust*

ROAST A FILET of beef as for filet Wellington, let it cool, and chill it.

Sauté 1 pound chicken livers in 2 to 3 tablespoons butter until they are tender. Mash the livers and let them cool. In the butter in the pan sauté 1/2 pound mushrooms, minced, until they are soft and let them cool. In the same pan sauté 1 onion, minced, until it is transparent and let it cool. Combine the livers, mushrooms, and onions with 1/4 pound ground cooked ham and 2 1/2 ounces liver paste. Add salt and pepper and chill the mixture. Spread the filet evenly with the liver mixture and chill it again, covered.

Roll out pie dough, chilled overnight, and wrap the filet completely. Seal edges and decorate with 8 or 9 heart shapes. Prick the dough, paint it with an egg yolk beaten with 1 teaspoon water, and bake the filet in a moderately hot oven (375° F.) for 20 minutes, or until the pastry is golden. Cool the filet slowly and chill it. Transfer the filet carefully to a serving platter and garnish the platter with horseradish cream rosettes, water cress, and spiced sweet cherries. Serves 8.

Wiener Rostbraten mit Zwiebel   *Rib Steak with Onions*

THE CUT of beef used for the *Wiener Rostbraten* is a slice of the standing rib roast that is also called a rib steak. The slice is cut 1/2 inch thick and must be trimmed of all fat. Pound the steak well, season it with salt and pepper to taste, and sprinkle it very lightly with flour. Heat a heavy skillet over high heat and add 2 tablespoons butter. Add the rib steak at once and sauté it on one side for about a minute. Add 3/4 cup very thin onion rings and another 2 tablespoons butter and continue to cook the steak about 3 minutes, or until it is brown. Turn the steak and cook it only long enough on the other side to seal in the juices. Invert the steak on a very hot plate, pour the onions and butter over it, and serve it at once. *Wiener Rostbraten* is sometimes served with crumbled bacon and chopped parsley sprinkled over the onions. Serves 1.

Sliced Steak with Marsala Sauce *Dünner Rostbraten*

BROWN 2 ONIONS, finely chopped, in 1/4 cup butter, and add to the pan 6 thin slices of sirloin steak. Sauté the steaks for 1 minute on each side. Pile the meat to the side of the skillet and add 3 tablespoons each of mushrooms and parsley, both finely chopped, 1 tablespoon each of Worcestershire sauce and Marsala, and 1/4 cup more butter. Bring the sauce to the boil. Combine the steaks with the sauce and add salt and pepper to taste.

Filets Flamed with Brandy *Filet Constanze*

RUB 6 THICK slices of beef filet with a cut clove of garlic and sprinkle them with coarse salt and freshly ground pepper. Rub a skillet with butter, and, when the pan is sizzling hot, sauté the steaks over high heat until they are brown on both sides. Add 2 tablespoons butter and 2 ounces warm brandy. Flame the brandy and cook for half a minute longer after the flame dies down. Serve the filets on hot plates with the sauce from the skillet poured over them. Garnish the plates with water cress.

Broiled Steak on Apples *Filet mit Äpfeln*

RUB SIX 1 1/2-inch slices of filet of beef well with salt and pepper and let them stand at room temperature for 1 hour.

Rice 1 pound hot potatoes, cooked and peeled, and stir in 2 well-beaten egg yolks and 2 tablespoons ground horseradish. Add salt and pepper to taste and shape the potatoes into 6 cakes the same size as the filets. Place them on a buttered baking sheet and brown them in a moderate oven (350° F.), turning them once. Remove and keep them warm.

Melt 2 tablespoons butter in a skillet and add 6 mushrooms, peeled, and 2 cooking apples, peeled, cored, and sliced. Sauté them until they are tender, but not soft.

Broil the filets, 3 inches below the heat, until they are done, turning them once. The filets take about 7 minutes on each side, for rare.

Arrange the hot potato cakes on a warm platter, top each with a slice of apple, and cover each slice with a filet. Garnish with a mushroom, and pour over the butter from the skillet.

Lendenschnitten   *Sautéed Tournedos*

SAUTÉ 6 TOURNEDOS, cut about 1 inch thick, in 1/4 cup butter in a heavy skillet over medium heat. As soon as the meat is brown, about 4 to 5 minutes, turn it and sauté it 5 minutes more. Allow 10 minutes in all for rare *tournedos* and 15 minutes in all for medium rare. Arrange the *tournedos* on round croutons cut the size of the meat and pour the pan juices over them. Or serve them on rice or potato croquettes. Serve them with herb butter or Madeira sauce, or as the recipes below suggest.

Lendenschnitten Grossgasthofs Art   *Tournedos Béarnaise*

SAUTÉ 6 TOURNEDOS, remove them to a hot platter, and add 1/2 cup white wine to the pan juices. Let the liquid boil up once, add salt and pepper to taste, and pour it over the meat on a hot platter. Place a hot cooked artichoke bottom filled with 2 tablespoons béarnaise sauce beside each tournedos. Serve with braised celery and Teutonia potatoes.

Lendenschnitten Metternich   *Tournedos with Rice Molds*

IN THE TOP of a double boiler, combine 1 1/2 cups rice, 2 1/2 cups water, 3 tomatoes, peeled, seeded, and chopped, 2 truffles, chopped, 1 tablespoon butter, and 1 teaspoon salt and cook the rice, covered, over simmering water until it is tender but not soft. Drain it well and press it into 6 small buttered cup molds. Stand the molds in an inch of hot water to keep them hot.

Sauté 6 *tournedos,* remove them from the pan, and keep them hot. In another pan, sauté 1/2 pound finely sliced mushrooms in 2 tablespoons butter and add them to the juices in the skillet. Stir in 1 teaspoon *glace de viande,* or meat extract, and add 1/4 cup heavy cream and

1 tablespoon butter. Cook the sauce over low heat, stirring, for a few minutes and gradually add 1/2 cup beef stock.

Arrange the *tournedos* on a hot platter on 6 round croutons cut the size of the meat. Unmold the rice mounds between the *tournedos*. Pour the sauce over the meat.

Tournedos with Shrimps   *Lendenschnitten Aïda*

SAUTÉ 6 PEELED and deveined shrimps, chopped, with 1 tablespoon each of chopped mushrooms and parsley in 2 tablespoons butter for 3 minutes. Add salt and pepper to taste. Sauté 6 *tournedos* for 3 minutes on each side. Pile the mixture on the *tournedos* and arrange them on croutons cut the size of the *tournedos*. Stir about 1/4 cup butter with 3/4 cup dry bread crumbs and 1/4 cup grated Parmesan over low heat until the butter bubbles. Use enough butter so that the crumbs can be spread. Spread the hot crumbs over the shrimp mixture and bake the *tournedos* in a hot oven (400° F.) for about 6 minutes, or until the crumbs are browned and crusted. Serve with Madeira sauce.

Tournedos with Onion Purée   *Lendenschnitten auf Aschenbrödel Art*

ARRANGE 6 SAUTÉED *tournedos* on 6 large cooked artichoke bottoms, each filled with 3 tablespoons onion purée mixed with 1 teaspoon finely chopped truffles.

Tournedos with Chestnuts   *Lendenschnitten auf Schlossfrauen Art*

ARRANGE ON a platter 6 *Lendenschnitten auf Aschenbrödel Art, tournedos* with onion purée, and garnish the platter with 12 hot glazed chestnuts and 1 1/2 cups browned potato balls. Serve with Madeira sauce.

Filets Mignons
with Stuffed Mushrooms   *Filets Mignons Nesselrode*

LIGHTLY POUND 6 thick filets mignons and season them with 1 teaspoon salt and 1/2 teaspoon pepper.

Sauté 6 very large mushroom caps for 4 minutes on each side in 2 tablespoons butter with 1 teaspoon salt and a pinch of white pepper. Keep the mushrooms hot. In the same skillet, sauté the 6 filets mignons for 6 minutes on each side, adding a little more butter, if necessary. Arrange them on a hot platter on 6 croutons cut the size of the meat. Fill the mushroom caps with about 1 3/4 cups chestnut purée salted to taste and lay one on each filet mignon.

To the juices in the pan add 1/2 cup each of hot consommé and *sauce demi-glace* and warm Sherry and salt to taste. Pour the sauce around the meat.

Filets Mignons Adalbert   *Filets Mignons with Chestnuts*

MELT 1 TABLESPOON butter, blend in 1 tablespoon flour, and cook the *roux* over low heat for a few minutes. Gradually add 1 cup beef stock and simmer for 3 minutes, stirring, to make a thin brown sauce. Add 1 cup warm Marsala, correct the seasoning, and add 3 dozen hot cooked drained chestnuts. Keep the sauce hot.

Dip 6 individual filets mignons in 5 tablespoons melted butter and broil them 3 inches from the heat, turning them only once. The cooking time depends on the thickness of the filets; broil them approximately 5 to 9 minutes to a side for rare. Place each filet on a crouton and garnish with fresh water cress. Serve immediately, with the hot chestnut and Marsala sauce.

Wienersaft Gulyás   *Viennese Goulash*

CRUSH TOGETHER 2 teaspoons dried marjoram, 1 teaspoon each of caraway seeds and grated lemon rind, and 1 clove of garlic and add the mixture to 1 1/2 cups hot beef stock. In a large kettle sauté 2 pounds onions, sliced, in 2/3 cup lard, stirring until the onions are golden. Add 1 tablespoon sweet Hungarian paprika and stir 5 minutes. Add half the stock with 1/2 tablespoon vinegar and 2 pounds beef, rump or round, trimmed and cut into even chunks. Stir in 2 tomatoes, peeled, seeded, and chopped, 1 red pepper, seeded and diced, and 1 tablespoon tomato paste. Cover the kettle tightly and simmer the goulash, adding as little of the stock as possible, until the meat is tender, about 1 1/4 to 1 1/2 hours. Add the remaining stock and enough water to cover, season to taste, and sift 1/4 cup flour over the mixture. Cover, bring to a rapid boil, immediately reduce heat, and simmer 15 minutes. For a thinner sauce, omit the flour.

Serve the goulash with *Spätzle,* noodles, or boiled potatoes. In Hungary, slivered green peppers are sprinkled on this *gulyás.* It may also be garnished with pieces of red pepper.

WITH A SILVER spoon, scrape a 2-pound slice of top round of beef. It should be at room temperature. Hold the meat on a wooden board with one hand and scrape away from you with the other. As the scraped beef is cupped in the spoon, form it into a mound. Turn the slice several times, to get the meat from both sides. Only a net of sinews and fat should remain. Cover the scraped beef and chill it, but only for a few minutes, as it turns dark very quickly.

Mound the beef in 2 rounds on a platter, flatten them, and make a depression in the center of each.. Drop 1 raw perfect egg yolk into each depression. Surround the beef with small mounds of garnishes: 1/4 cup onions, 2 tablespoons capers, 12 thin slices dill pickle, 8 anchovy filets, and a medium bunch of chives, all finely chopped, and 1 small bunch red radishes. Add little piles of caraway seed, paprika, chopped parsley, salt, and black pepper. At table, mix the beef and garnishes, using them to taste. Serve with buttered black bread or rye bread. The anchovies are a popular garnish, but they tend to obscure the flavor of the meat.

Beefsteak tartare may be served as a main dish. Arrange 1 mound of beef for each portion. Properly scraped, a 1-pound slice of beef should make 2 very generous servings. Or use chopped beef, about 1/2 pound per person. Put 1 egg yolk in each mound. Set the circles of beef around a mound made of wedges of onion, finely chopped, herb mustard, and capers, with chopped chives and parsley. *(Picture, page 275.)*

CUT 6 THICK slices of cold rare roast beef from a 4-rib roast. Remove the dark upper section and use only the rare center.

Peel, hollow, and drain 6 large tomatoes and fill them with the following onion-and-wine-sauce: In the top of a double boiler, over hot but not boiling water, cook 3 beaten egg yolks combined with 1/4 cup white wine, stirring constantly, until the mixture thickens. Stir in 1/2 cup butter, cut in small pieces, and add 1 small onion, minced, and salt and pepper to taste. Cool the sauce and fold in 1/2 cup cream, stiffly whipped. Chill the filled tomatoes.

Arrange the tomatoes on a large platter and alternate them with the slices of beef. Add a heavy layer of caviar as thick as the beef to each beef slice and garnish the platter with water cress.

Lammrücken Helena   *Roast Saddle of Lamb*

RUB A SADDLE of lamb with salt and pepper and roast it in a hot oven (400° F.) for 35 minutes. Remove the saddle and drain off the fat from the pan. Return the lamb to the pan and cover it with a mixture of 1 cup buttered bread crumbs, 1/2 cup chopped capers, and 1/4 cup chopped chives. Roast the lamb in a moderate oven (350° F.) for 15 minutes to the pound, or until the top is crusty and brown.

Remove the saddle carefully from the pan, arrange it on a large heated platter, and keep it warm. Pour off the excess fat from the pan and add 1/4 cup *sauce demi-glace*. Bring the mixture to a boil, scraping the brown bits from the pan. Slowly add as much hot brown stock as needed to make 1 cup thin sauce. Season it to taste and serve it very hot, with the crusty lamb. To serve, slice the saddle of lamb from the bone in thin strips lengthwise, not crosswise.

Lammschlegel Parkstrasse   *Leg of Lamb with Garlic and Thyme*

MIX 4 TABLESPOONS soft butter to a paste with 4 cloves of garlic, crushed, and 1/2 teaspoon thyme. With a sharp knife, make several incisions in a 6-pound leg of lamb and insert the paste in the pockets. Rub the meat with salt. Lay the meat on 6 sliced onions in a roasting pan and roast it in a moderate oven (350° F.), allowing 25 minutes per pound and basting it occasionally with 1/4 cup melted butter and 2 cups stock. Remove the lamb from the pan and keep it warm. Skim the fat from the pan juices and add to them 1/2 cup dry bread crumbs, the grated rind of 1 lemon, 2 tablespoons vinegar, 1 bay leaf, and a pinch of nutmeg, and heat the mixture on top of the stove, stirring well. Add 1 cup sour cream and

heat the sauce thoroughly, but do not let it boil. Correct the seasoning and strain the sauce. Serve the lamb garnished with parsley and serve the sauce separately.

Gedünstete Lammkeule

Leg of Lamb with Onions

BROWN A 6-POUND leg of lamb on all sides in 1/4 cup butter and season it well with salt and pepper. Place it in a casserole with 1 cup each of water and white wine, 3 carrots, finely sliced, 1 bay leaf, and 1/2 teaspoon caraway seeds. Simmer the lamb, covered, for 30 minutes. Skim the fat from the pan and add 6 small white onions, sliced, and 4 tomatoes, peeled, seeded, and diced. Simmer the lamb until it is almost tender, about 1 1/4 hours, adding water to keep the lamb three-quarters covered. Add 36 small white onions, dust with 2 tablespoons flour, and simmer the lamb until the onions are tender and the meat is done. Add salt and pepper to taste and add 1 hot cooked cauliflower, divided into flowerets. Sprinkle the dish with 2 tablespoons chopped parsley and 1 tablespoon chopped dill.

Melanzani Lammfleisch
Lamb with Eggplant

CUT A BONED rolled leg of lamb into slices 1/2 inch thick. Dust the slices generously with salt and pepper and 1/2 cup each of dill and parsley, both chopped. Cut an eggplant into slices 1/4 inch thick, peel them, and salt them. Place slices of eggplant between the slices of lamb and trim them to the same size as the lamb. Secure the slices with skewers or string and put the re-formed leg of lamb into a casserole on 6 slices of bacon. Pour over it 1/2 cup olive oil and roast it in a moderate oven (350° F.) until it is almost tender, about 1 1/4 hours, basting it frequently with tomato juice. Sprinkle the meat with 3/4 cup grated Parmesan or grated Swiss cheese and cook it for about 15 minutes longer.

Lammsrippchen mit Käseauflauf
Lamb Chops with Cheese Soufflé

PREPARE THE following soufflé mixture: Melt 4 tablespoons butter in a saucepan, blend in 4 tablespoons flour, and to the *roux* add gradually, off the heat, 1 cup warmed milk. Return the sauce to the heat and cook, stirring constantly, until it is thick. Add 1/4 cup each of Cheddar cheese and Parmesan, both grated, 3 shallots, very finely chopped, and salt and pepper to taste. Stir in the cheese until it is well blended, remove from the heat, and add the yolks of 4 beaten eggs. Mix well and let the mixture cool.

Broil lightly 6 lamb chops, boned and trimmed of fat, until they are just brown on both sides. They should be rare. Sprinkle them with salt and pepper to taste, drain the chops, and arrange them in the bottom of a deep ovenproof dish. Fold the whites of 6 eggs, beaten stiff, into the cooled soufflé mixture, and pour the soufflé over the chops. Sprinkle with 4 tablespoons grated Parmesan, and bake the soufflé in a moderately hot oven (375° F.) for 30 minutes. Serve immediately.

Lamm nach Schloss Art
Broiled Lamb Chops

LET 2 CUPS long-grain rice soak in cold water to cover for 2 hours and drain it well. Bring a kettle of salted water to a boil, add the rice, and boil it for exactly 15 minutes. Drain the rice well in a colander, set the colander over boiling water, and steam the rice, covered, for 15 minutes, or until it is tender. To the hot rice add 2 cups cooked and well drained small green peas, 3 tablespoons grated Parmesan cheese, and 3 to 4 tablespoons butter. Combine the mixture well.

Starting at the stem end, peel 6 large cooking apples about 1/4 way down. Core the apples carefully, without cutting all the way through, and hollow them out to be filled. Sauté 1 large onion, chopped, in 3 tablespoons butter until it is soft, add 8 chicken livers, and sauté them until they are browned on the outside but still pink within. Mash the livers with a fork, add 1/2 cup toasted bread crumbs, and season the mixture with salt, pepper, and a pinch of cinnamon. Fill the apples with the mixture and arrange them in a baking dish. Pour over 2 cups apple cider and bake the filled apples in a moderate oven (350° F.), basting them frequently, for 45 minutes.

Broil 6 double loin lamb chops about 16 to 18 minutes in all, until they are browned on both sides. Arrange the chops on a heated platter, surround them with the rice, and garnish the platter with the apples. Serve at once with a slice of cold herb butter on each chop. If preferred, the broiler pan may be deglazed with the cider remaining in the baking dish. Add salt to taste and serve the sauce separately.

Lamb Casserole   *Balkanisches Lamm*

SOAK 2 DOZEN prunes for at least 6 hours, or until they are well puffed. Cut 4 pounds shoulder of lamb into 3-inch squares and dredge them in well-seasoned flour. In a heavy skillet, sauté 3 onions, coarsely chopped, in 3 tablespoons butter until they begin to color. Add the meat and brown it well on all sides. Add 1/4 teaspoon each of allspice, cinnamon, and nutmeg and 3 cups white stock. Add more stock, if necessary, to cover the meat. Stir the mixture and simmer it, covered, for 1 1/4 hours. Add the soaked prunes, pitted, and continue to simmer until the prunes are tender, about 15 minutes. Correct the seasoning. Serve with saffron rice.

Saddle of Veal with Paprika Sauce   *Kalbsrücken Metternich*

ROAST A 6- TO 8-pound saddle of veal in a slow oven (300° F.) for 25 minutes per pound, or until it is tender, basting it frequently with butter.

In a saucepan melt 2/3 cup butter over low heat, blend in 2/3 cup flour and 1 tablespoon paprika, and stir in gradually 1 cup hot veal or beef stock and 1 cup hot milk, strained, in which 1 chopped onion has been boiled until it is soft. The stock and milk should be hotter than the *roux* when they are added. Allow the sauce to simmer over low heat for 20 minutes, stirring. Add salt to taste.

Carefully remove the meat from the bones of the cooked saddle. Cover the bones with a layer of the thick paprika sauce. Cut the meat across in even slices, 1/2 inch thick, and put 1 slice of peeled truffle between each 2 slices. Replace the meat slices on the bones in their original form, securing the first and last with skewers. Beat 4 egg yolks into the remaining sauce, thin it with hot cream, if necessary, and add 1 teaspoon paprika. Cover the saddle evenly with sauce and sprinkle it with 3/4 cup freshly grated Parmesan. Carefully pour 3/4 cup melted butter over the cheese and sprinkle the saddle with 3/4 cup dry bread crumbs. It is important that cheese, butter, and crumbs form a thick coating on the meat. Return the meat to the oven and bake it for about 15 minutes more, or until the cheese and crumbs form a crust. Thin the remaining sauce with hot cream and pass it separately. Serve the veal with baked tomatoes stuffed with mushrooms and rice.

Kalbsrücken mit Estragonbutter — *Roast Rack of Veal with Tarragon Butter*

RUB A 5- to 7-pound rack of veal with salt, pepper, and 1/4 cup butter. Roast the veal in a moderate oven (325° F.) for 30 minutes per pound, basting it frequently with a mixture of 1/2 cup each of melted butter and white wine and 1/4 cup chopped tarragon. Remove the veal to a warm serving platter and surround it with large roasted potatoes hollowed out and filled with green peas. Garnish the platter with water cress. Skim the fat from the pan juices and add enough brown veal stock to make 2 cups. Reduce the sauce quickly to 1 1/2 cups and add salt and pepper to taste. Serve it separately. Just before serving, pipe onto the meat through a pastry bag fitted with a fluted tube a decorative design of cold tarragon butter. Chill the butter well. It must be very cold when it is piped onto the roast.

Roast Rolled Loin of Veal
with Mushrooms   *Kalbsbraten Othmar*

RUB WITH salt and 1/2 cup butter a 6-pound loin of veal, boned and rolled.
Place it in a roasting pan with a *bouquet garni* composed of 1 stalk of
celery, 3 sprigs of parsley, a sprig of thyme and chervil, and a bay leaf.
Add 3/4 cup stock and roast the veal in a moderate oven (350° F.) for
30 minutes per pound, basting frequently with the pan juices. Lay 4 slices
bacon over the roast and return it to the oven for 15 minutes longer, or
until the bacon is golden and crisp. Add 1 cup sour cream and continue
to roast the veal, basting frequently, until the meat is tender. The meat
should be well done.

Arrange the roast on a heated platter. Strain the pan gravy into a
saucepan and remove all the fat. Add 1/2 pound sautéed mushrooms,
1 cup sweet cream, and 1/2 cup strong cold beef stock. Taste for seasoning, bring the sauce to a boil, and serve it from a large sauceboat.

Loin of Veal
with Stuffed Mushrooms   *Kalbsbraten nach Botschafter Art*

HAVE A 5-POUND loin of veal rolled with 2 kidneys. Cover it with 6 slices
of larding pork and lay it in a roasting pan on a bed of 5 leaves of lettuce,
2 carrots, chopped, and 2 onions, sliced. Season it with salt and pepper.
Add 3 cups veal or chicken stock and roast the meat in a moderate oven
(350° F.) for 1 1/2 hours. Remove the veal. Simmer the liquid until it
is reduced to 1 1/2 cups. Remove the larding pork from the veal and roll
the meat in 4 beaten eggs, then in 2 cups dry bread crumbs, and finally
in 1 cup grated Parmesan. Return the meat to the pan and pour over it
1/2 cup melted butter. Roast in a moderate oven (350° F.) until the top
is brown. Remove the veal and strain the liquid in the roasting pan.

Chop finely 12 mushroom stems, 1 onion, and 1/2 cup blanched
almonds and sauté the mixture lightly in about 3 tablespoons butter until
the onions are puffed but not brown. Remove it from the heat and add
1 cup browned bread crumbs. Sauté 12 large mushroom caps in about
2 tablespoons butter for 5 minutes. Stuff the caps with the mixture, piling
it high and heat them in the oven for 5 minutes. Season 6 halved tomatoes
with salt and pepper, broil them, and keep hot. Melt 2 tablespoons butter,
blend in 2 tablespoons flour, and cook the *roux* until it is golden brown.
Gradually add the strained liquid from the roasting pan and cook the
sauce, stirring constantly, until it is smooth and thick. Add 1 tablespoon

each of finely chopped chervil, parsley, and chives. Arrange the veal on a heated platter and surround it with the stuffed mushrooms and broiled tomatoes. Serve the sauce separately.

Kalbsbraten Theresia   *Noisettes of Veal with Pâté*

SELECT 2 OR 3 noisettes of veal, or 2 boned veal loins. If loins are used, roll and shape them into 2 cylinders and tie them with rows of string, knotting each string separately so that the meat may be cut into small round slices. Cover the bottom of a roasting pan with slices of larding pork and cover these with a layer of carrots and onions, both sliced. Lay the veal on the vegetables and add a sprig of parsley. Place the veal in a very hot oven (425° F.), add 2 cups stock, and roast the meat until it is brown. Add 3 cups more stock and 1 cup light white wine, and cover the meat with buttered paper. Reduce the heat to moderate (325° F.) and continue cooking it, basting it frequently until it is done, about 2 hours in all. Remove the meat from the roasting pan, boil the stock until it is reduced by half, and strain it. Remove the fat.

Untie the meat and carefully cut it crosswise in even 1/2-inch slices. Lay a slice of hot *Leberparfait* between each 2 slices of veal, reconstructing the loin shapes, and lay an overlapping line of very thin lemon slices along the ridges of the roasts. Dust the meat very generously with 1 cup roasted slivered almonds and 1/2 bunch of fried parsley, return it to the oven for 5 minutes, and serve it immediately. Serve the hot stock in a separate sauceboat. Serves 12.

Leberparfait   *Calf's Liver Pâté*

SAUTÉ 1 CHOPPED onion in 2 tablespoons butter until the onion is golden, and add 2 pounds sliced calf's liver, 4 chicken livers, and 2 ounces Sherry. Cook the mixture, covered, for 10 minutes. Drain the livers, reserving the pan juices, and put them through the finest blade of the food chopper with 2 slices of crisp bacon. Mix in the reserved pan juices, 1 tablespoon soft butter, 2 slices of bread, soaked in milk and pressed dry, 2 eggs, and salt, pepper, and grated lemon rind to taste. Press the pâté into a long narrow buttered mold of approximately the same diameter as the veal slices. Cover the mold and steam the pâté in a kettle of boiling water for 45 minutes.

Cool the pâté slightly before slicing it.

*Cold Loin of Veal
with Caper Sauce* $\mathcal{K}$*altes* $\mathcal{K}$*albfleisch mit* $\mathcal{K}$*apernsauce*

WIPE A 4- TO 6-pound piece of loin of veal with a damp cloth and place
it in a roasting pan with 2 onions, 2 stalks of celery, and 1 carrot, all sliced,
1 clove of garlic, chopped, and 1 cup flaked tuna fish, well drained. Rub
the top of the roast generously with 2 tablespoons butter and sprinkle it
with salt and pepper. Roast it in a hot oven (400° F.) for 30 minutes,
until it is browned. Add 1 cup each of white wine and veal stock and
cover the pan. Reduce the heat to moderate (325° F.) and roast the
veal for 2 hours longer, basting it every 20 minutes with the liquid in
the pan and adding more stock as necessary. The meat should be well
done.

Let the veal cool in the broth, drain it well, and chill it. Strain the
pan juices through a very fine sieve and add 2 tablespoons of the strained
liquid to 1 cup mayonnaise. Coat the chilled meat with the mayonnaise.
Slice the coated meat and arrange the slices in a chilled low serving dish.
Pour over them the remaining strained sauce, cover with 1 cup well-
drained small capers, and chill.

Roast Veal with Princess Sauce $\mathcal{K}$*albsbraten* $\mathcal{P}$*rinzessinen* $\mathcal{A}$*rt*

LINE A ROASTING pan with 3 slices of larding pork and put a rolled veal
roast, weighing about 6 pounds, in the pan. Spread the top of the roast
with 4 tablespoons butter and add 1 onion and half a carrot, both sliced,
and 1 teaspoon salt. Roast the meat in a hot oven (425° F.) until it is
well browned on all sides, basting it frequently. Add 2 cups stock, reduce
the heat to moderate (350° F.), and continue roasting the meat for 1 1/2
hours, or until it is done, basting from time to time. Remove the strings
and brush the top of the rolled roast with 1 well-beaten egg. Sprinkle
the roast with 1 cup bread crumbs and 1/4 cup Parmesan and return it
to the oven for 15 minutes, or until the top is golden. Serve the roast
with princess sauce.

Princess Sauce $\mathcal{P}$*rinzessinensauce*

IN A COVERED skillet, over low heat, sauté 1 onion, finely chopped, in
2 tablespoons butter for 6 minutes, or until the onion is golden. Blend in
1 1/2 teaspoons flour and cook for 3 minutes longer. Add 4 tomatoes,

peeled, seeded, and chopped, 1/2 teaspoon each of sugar and beef extract, and 1/4 teaspoon each of salt and pepper. Cook the sauce over low heat for 15 minutes, stirring, and strain it. Stir in 1 tablespoon butter and bring the sauce to a boil. Remove the pan from the heat and add the yolks of 2 eggs beaten with 1 cup cream.

Kalbsnuss   Veal "Nut" or Noix de Veau

THE KALBSNUSS, noix, *or "nut," is the tender piece of meat that lies along the inner side of the calf's hind leg. It is cut from the bone in one piece lengthwise and weighs from 2 to 4 pounds. It is often larded before it is roasted and it may also be braised. Americans may have to substitute 2 to 4 pounds of boneless veal cut from the leg in a single cylindrically-shaped piece.*

Kalbsnuss Dagobert   Roast Veal with Pea Purée

LARD A 2-POUND *noix de veau,* or another boneless solid piece of veal cut from the leg, and sprinkle it with salt. Lay it in a roasting pan on a bed of 4 stalks of celery, 2 onions, and 1 carrot, all chopped, and roast it in a moderate oven (350° F.) for 1 1/2 hours, or until the meat is tender,

basting it frequently with 1/4 cup melted butter and 1/2 cup veal or beef stock. Remove the veal and keep it hot.

Strain the pan juices. Add 1 cup béchamel sauce and cook the sauce over low heat, stirring, until it is smooth. Add 2 egg yolks beaten with 1/2 cup cream and a dash of lemon juice, and salt and pepper to taste. Stir the sauce well and heat it for another few minutes, but do not let it come to a boil.

With a pastry tube, pipe a wide border of duchess potatoes onto the edge of the platter. Fill the platter with a pea purée, using 3 pounds shelled peas. Slice the veal thinly and lay the slices, alternating with thin slices of smoked tongue, on the pea purée. Use 1/8-inch-thick slices, trimmed to fit the veal slices, and heat them in simmering bouillon. Pour the sauce over the veal and sprinkle it with 1/2 cup each of bread crumbs and grated Parmesan. Pour over 1/4 cup melted butter. Paint the potato border with an egg yolk beaten with 1 tablespoon water and brown lightly under the broiler.

Serve at once. Serve the sauce separately.

Roast Veal on Sauerkraut   *Kalbsnuss Elsasser Art*

ROAST A *noix de veau* as for *Kalbsnuss Dagobert,* but do not make the sauce. Slice the veal thinly. On a platter lay a bed of 2 pounds sauerkraut cooked with 1/2 teaspoon caraway seed. Lay the veal slices on the sauerkraut alternating them with slices of boiled ham, cut the same size as the veal and heated in stock. Pipe a border of duchess potatoes around the platter, paint it with an egg yolk beaten with 1 tablespoon water, and brown it lightly under the broiler. Serve separately the pan juices, strained and thickened with *beurre manié*—equal parts of butter and flour kneaded together—or serve brown sauce.

Veal Cutlets   *Kalbsschnitzel*

FOR VIENNESE *veal cutlets, large slices are cut crosswise from the thickest part of the calf's leg. Each slice is about 1/2 inch thick and weighs about 1 1/2 pounds. It is trimmed and the bone removed, then it is cut into serving pieces—from 3 to 4, usually. These pieces are pounded as thin as the recipe requires. One such flattened piece is enough for 1 serving.*

Wienerschnitzel Hotel Goldener Hirsch
Viennese Veal Cutlets

TRIM 2 VEAL cutlets—each about 1/2 inch thick and weighing 1 1/2 pounds—remove the bones, and cut the meat into 6 serving pieces. Cut the pieces across the grain of the meat, leaving the little "nut" which is divided from the rest of the cutlet by a thin skin, in a single piece. Pound each piece thin, until it is as large as 6 inches by 8 inches. Dip first in 1/2 cup seasoned flour, then in 2 beaten eggs, and then in 1 cup dry sieved bread crumbs. Sauté over medium heat, a few at a time, in 2 skillets with 3/4 cup butter or oil in each for not more than 8 minutes, until they are golden brown on both sides. Keep the cooked schnitzel hot in a very slow oven (250° F.) until all are done. Serve the *Wienerschnitzel* with lemon slices and parsleyed potatoes. *(Picture, page 281.)*

Schnitzel Modena
Veal Cutlets with Noodles

CUT 3 POUNDS veal cutlets into 6 to 8 serving portions and pound them very thin. Chill the meat well and dip it into 2 eggs beaten with 2 tablespoons water and then into 1 1/2 cups fine white bread crumbs mixed with 3/4 cup grated Swiss cheese. Season the cutlets with salt and pepper and sauté them slowly in butter until they are golden brown on both sides, about 5 minutes in all. Remove the cutlets and keep them hot. Add to the pan 2 cups brown sauce, 4 slices cooked ham, cut into fine julienne, and 2 pimientos, chopped, and heat the sauce. Stir 1/2 cup each of butter and grated Swiss cheese into 4 cups hot broad noodles. Mound the hot noodles in the center of a hot platter, surround them with the cutlets, and pour the brown sauce over the noodles.

Paprikaschnitzel
Paprika Veal Cutlets

SAUTÉ 4 SLICES of bacon, chopped, and 2 onions, thinly sliced, in 1/2 cup butter until they are golden. Stir in 1 teaspoon paprika. Cut 3 pounds veal cutlets into 6 to 8 serving portions and pound them until they are thin. Dip only one side in seasoned flour. Sauté them quickly in the hot butter, until they are lightly browned on both sides. Remove the cutlets and keep them warm. Discard the bacon, deglaze the skillet with 2 cups stock, and stir in 1 cup sour cream and 1 teaspoon paprika, or more, to taste. Return the cutlets to the pan and cook them over low heat for about 20 minutes, or until they are tender. Correct the seasoning. Serve with broad noodles.

Sautéed Veal Cutlets   *Naturschnitzel*

TRIM 2 VEAL cutlets—each about 1/2 inch thick and weighing 1 1/2 pounds —remove the bones, and cut the meat into 6 serving pieces. Cut the pieces across the grain of the meat, leaving the little "nut," which is divided from the rest of the cutlet by a skin, in a single piece. Pound each piece lightly: the pieces should be thicker than *Wienerschnitzel* or *scaloppine*. Sprinkle the 6 cutlets with salt and dredge them lightly in sifted flour. Sauté them in a large skillet in 4 tablespoons butter for 10 minutes, until they are brown on both sides. Keep the sautéed cutlets hot in a very slow oven (250° F.) until all are done.

Make the following sauce: To the juices in the skillet add 1/2 cup beef or veal stock, 2 tablespoons butter, the juice of 1/2 lemon, and 1/2 teaspoon *glace de viande,* or meat extract. Bring the sauce to a boil and pour it over the cutlets. Garnish the platter with lemon wedges and parsley. *Naturschnitzel* are best prepared for a small number of people and served at once, without being kept hot in the oven.

Gypsy Cutlets   *Zigeuner Schnitzel*

SAUTÉ 6 VEAL cutlets as for *Naturschnitzel* but do not make the sauce. Serve them on a platter with alternating slices of lightly sautéed ham, cut the size of the veal slices. Serve with *Zigeuner-Sauce,* gypsy sauce.

Russian Veal Cutlets   *Russisches Schnitzel*

SAUTÉ 1/2 POUND sliced mushrooms in 2 tablespoons butter until they are lightly browned, stir in 1 tablespoon flour, and cook for 3 minutes, stirring constantly. Gradually add 2 cups sour cream, stir well, and cook the mushrooms over low heat for 3 minutes longer. Remove the pan from the fire and add 1/2 cup slivered dill pickle. Sauté 1/2 cup tomatoes, peeled, seeded, and chopped, in 1 tablespoon butter for 3 minutes and add them to the sauce. Add warm sour cream, if needed. Sauté 6 veal cutlets as for *Naturschnitzel* but do not make the sauce. Pour the mushroom-tomato sauce over the cutlets and lay 1 thick slice of tomato, peeled, on each schnitzel. Place 1 tablespoon black caviar on each tomato slice. Serve with lemon wedges.

Bismarck Schnitzel — *Veal Cutlets with Tomato Sauce and Egg*

SAUTÉ 6 LARGE or 12 small veal cutlets as for *Naturschnitzel* but do not make the sauce. Pour over the cutlets 1 1/2 cups tomato sauce and garnish each with 1 poached pullet egg (Bismarck had plovers' eggs). Garnish each egg with 1 large truffle slice and 2 tablespoons chopped cooked mushrooms.

Schnitzel Holstein — *Veal Cutlets with Fried Eggs*

SAUTÉ 6 VEAL cutlets as for *Naturschnitzel* and make the sauce. Place 1 well-trimmed fried egg on each schnitzel and cross 2 anchovy filets over the eggs. Garnish the platter with lettuce cups filled with capers and sliced dill pickles.

Holsteinisches Schnitzel anderer Art — *Veal Cutlets with Caviar*

PREPARE *Schnitzel Holstein,* but do not use the lettuce-cup garnish. Instead, garnish the platter with 6 small hot puff-paste shells filled with cold caviar and alternate the shells with 6 rolled slices of smoked salmon and 6 sardines.

Esterhazy Schnitzel — *Veal Cutlets in Sour Cream*

PREPARE 6 VEAL cutlets as for *Naturschnitzel* and sauté them quickly on both sides in 3 tablespoons butter until they are browned. Add 2 teaspoons paprika, stir well, and add half a carrot, half an onion, half a parboiled turnip, and 4 mushrooms, all cut into fine julienne. Stir in 1 cup sour cream. Simmer, covered, for 10 minutes, or until the meat and vegetables are tender. Add salt, pepper, and paprika to taste and serve with buttered *Spätzle.*

Badische Schnitzel — *Veal Cutlets with Noodles*

SAUTÉ 6 LARGE or 12 small veal cutlets as for *Naturschnitzel* but do not make the sauce. Keep them hot in a very slow oven (250° F.). To the

butter left in the skillet add 2/3 cup each of stock and sour cream, and
1/2 teaspoon meat extract. Add salt and pepper to taste and bring the
sauce to a boil, stirring constantly. Mound 3 cups hot broad noodles in
the center of a heated platter and pour over 1/4 cup brown butter. Lay
the cutlets around the noodles, pour over the sour cream sauce, and
garnish with chopped parsley.

Veal Cutlets with Sour Cream and Lemon   *Kaiserschnitzel*

SAUTÉ 6 VEAL cutlets as for *Naturschnitzel* but do not make the sauce.
Keep the cutlets hot. Add 1 cup warm sour cream to the skillet in which
the meat was sautéed and cook over low heat, stirring, until the sour
cream is golden. Add just enough lemon juice to thin the sauce to the
desired consistency, and salt and pepper to taste. Add the finely slivered
rind of 1 lemon and pour the sauce over the hot schnitzel.

Veal Cutlets with Shrimps   *Schnitzel Oskar*

SAUTÉ 6 VEAL cutlets as for *Naturschnitzel* and make the sauce. Serve
them on a bed of 2 cups thick tomato purée, surrounded by 18 steamed
asparagus tips arranged alternately with 18 small cooked shrimps. Garnish
with 1/8 cup finely chopped tarragon and serve with béarnaise sauce.

Veal Goulash I   *Kalbsgulyás 1*

CUT INTO small pieces 1 1/2 to 2 pounds shoulder or leg of veal, boned.
Brown the veal and 10 whole small white onions in 6 tablespoons butter.
Sprinkle 2 tablespoons flour over the meat and blend it in. Add 1 cup
hot stock, 2 tablespoons tomato purée, salt and pepper to taste, and 6
sprigs of parsley. Cook the veal for 30 minutes, and add 1 pound mushrooms, thinly sliced, and 1 cup dry white wine. Cook the veal for 30 minutes longer. Discard the parsley and correct the seasoning.

Veal Goulash II   *Kalbsgulyás 2*

MELT 3 TABLESPOONS butter in a heavy casserole, and stir in 1 tablespoon sweet Hungarian paprika. Do not let the paprika brown. Add 1

pound onions, thinly sliced, and 3 pounds shoulder or leg of veal, cut into 1 1/2 inch cubes, and sauté it over low heat for 3 minutes, or until it is brown, shaking the casserole from time to time. Add 1 cup boiling beef stock and simmer the veal for 45 minutes, covered, shaking the pan occasionally and adding more stock as needed. Add 3 tomatoes, peeled and sliced, and simmer the *gulyás* for 15 minutes longer. Add 1/2 teaspoon crushed caraway seeds and correct the seasoning. Serve with *Spätzle* or buttered broad noodles mixed with bread crumbs.

Kalbsrippen nach Nathalia
Veal Chops with Mushrooms and Tomatoes

SELECT 6 VEAL rib chops with large surfaces and score the edges to keep them from curling. Pound them lightly and sprinkle them with salt and pepper to taste. Brown the chops lightly on one side, cooking them all on the same side so that the bones form a uniform pattern. Lay them, cooked side up, on a buttered baking sheet.

Beat into 2 cups hot mashed potatoes 1 tablespoon butter and 1 egg, add salt and pepper to taste, and turn the potatoes into a pastry bag fitted with a star tube. Pipe a border of potatoes around the edge of each chop. Sauté 1/4 pound mushrooms, finely sliced, in 1 tablespoon butter for 5 minutes, and divide them over the chops, filling the centers of the potato borders. Cover each layer of mushrooms with a 1/4-inch slice of peeled tomato, and lay a very thin slice of goose liver pâté on each tomato slice.

Melt 2 tablespoons butter in a saucepan, stir in 2 tablespoons flour, and add 2/3 cup warm milk. Simmer the mixture for 5 minutes, stirring constantly. Remove the pan from the heat and beat in 1 egg yolk, 1/2 teaspoon tomato paste, and salt and pepper to taste. Pour the sauce over the centers of the veal chops. Bake the chops in a moderately hot oven (375° F.) for 10 minutes, add 1/2 cup grated Parmesan, and bake for 5 minutes longer, or until the cheese is browned, in a hot oven (400° F.). Garnish the chops with parsley.

Kalbsrippen mit Nüssen
Veal Chops with Walnuts

SPRINKLE 6 THICK veal chops with salt and pepper and score the edges to keep the chops from curling. Sauté them in 6 tablespoons butter until

they are brown on both sides. Reduce the heat, cover the pan, and cook the chops until they are done.

In the top of a double boiler over hot water, heat 5 tablespoons liver pâté, 1/2 cup heavy cream, 4 tablespoons Sherry, and 1/3 cup walnuts and 3 pickled walnuts, all crushed, and salt and pepper to taste. Add more cream, if necessary. The sauce should be thick, however.

To serve, arrange the chops on a heated platter, pour over the hot sauce, and surround the chops with small boiled onions.

Veal Chops with Banana Fritters   Kalbskoteletten mit Bananen

SAUTÉ 6 THICK veal chops in 1/2 cup butter for 5 minutes, turning them once. Do not allow the butter to brown. Remove the chops and keep them warm. Add 3 tablespoons flour to the butter in the pan, blend it in thoroughly, and add 3/4 pound small whole mushrooms and 1 large onion and 1 tablespoon parsley, both chopped. Stir in 1 1/2 cups stock and simmer the sauce until it is smooth, stirring constantly. Return the chops to the pan and cook them over low heat for 20 minutes, or until they are done, turning them frequently. The chops should not brown. Add salt and pepper to taste. Beat 3 egg yolks with 1 cup cream. Remove the chops from the pan, take the pan from the heat, and add the egg yolks to the sauce, stirring well. Return the pan to the heat, but do not allow the sauce to boil. Accompany the veal chops with banana fritters.

Banana Fritters   Bananenbeignets

SIFT 1 1/2 CUPS flour into a bowl. Make a well in the center, add 1 cup water and 2 teaspoons oil, and gradually work in the flour. Fold in 2 egg whites, beaten stiff. Peel and quarter 6 bananas. Dip them into the batter and sauté them gently in 6 tablespoons butter until they are brown. Carefully remove the bananas with a spatula to a hot platter, and sprinkle them with 1 tablespoon rum. Serve the fritters with the veal chops.

Veal Chops with Orange Sauce   Kalbskoteletten Malta

SAUTÉ 6 VEAL chops in 6 tablespoons butter until they are brown on both sides. Cover the pan and continue to cook, over very low heat, until the chops are tender, turning them once. Remove the chops to a heated oven-proof platter and keep them hot.

Sauté 2 oranges, peeled, seeded, and sliced, in the same skillet for 5 minutes, and add 1/2 cup orange juice. Blend in 1 tablespoon meat extract and cook the mixture until it boils. Add salt and pepper to taste.

Lay the hot orange slices on the veal chops, pour over the orange sauce from the skillet, and sprinkle generously with 1/4 cup chopped parsley.

Kalbsbraten Excelsior   *Veal Steak Excelsior*

MAKE POCKETS in 2 thick veal steaks, weighing 1 1/2 pounds each, and stuff each steak with a duck liver, browned in butter and sliced. Skewer the openings and brown the veal steaks on both sides in 1/4 cup butter. Add 1/2 cup beef stock and cook the steaks, turning once, for 30 minutes, or until they are done. Remove the steaks to a heated platter and deglaze the skillet with 1/2 cup Madeira and 2 tablespoons meat glaze. Pour this sauce over the veal steaks and garnish with water cress.

Bake 6 parboiled artichoke bottoms in a pan with 3/4 cup beef stock for 10 minutes, fill them with béarnaise sauce, and sprinkle them with fresh tarragon, finely chopped. Serve with the veal steaks.

Egerländerschinken   *Ham with Orange Sauce*

BOIL AN 8- to 10-pound precooked ham in water to cover for 1 hour. Remove the rind, leaving a collar, and score the fat in a diamond pattern. Press 1/2 cup firmly packed dark brown sugar over the top of the ham and bake the ham in a moderate oven (350° F.), basting it frequently with a mixture of 1 cup each of orange juice, Sherry, and water, for 1 hour. Turn off the oven and let the baked ham stand in the oven for 20 to 30 minutes to "toast."

In a heavy skillet brown 2 tablespoons powdered sugar and pour over it 4 ounces warm Curaçao. Ignite the spirit and, when the flame dies out, add to the mixture the juice of 2 oranges, the slivered rind of the oranges, and salt to taste.

Just before the ham is served, strain 1 cup of the pan juices, skim off the fat, and add the juices to the orange sauce. Heat the sauce and correct the seasoning. Serve the ham with German cucumber salad. *(Picture, page 283.)*

Christmas Ham *Weihnachtsschinken*

BOIL A 10- TO 12-pound ham and trim off the brown rind, leaving a cuff around the bone.

Bring 2 cups stock to a boil and dissolve in it, off the heat, 2 envelopes of gelatin softened in 2/3 cup tomato juice. Let the aspic cool and chill it in a shallow baking pan until it is set.

Cut from the ham a 1/2-pound wedge, trim off the fat, and put the meat through the finest blade of the food chopper with 3 to 4 ounces goose liver paste, 1/2 pound butter, 1/2 cup thick béchamel sauce, and 2 tablespoons each of brandy and Madeira. Add 2 shallots, finely minced, 1/2 teaspoon thyme, pepper to taste, and salt if needed, and chill the mousse.

Cut 24 slices cold boiled ham, not too thin. Roll them into cornucopias and, using a pastry bag, fill them with the ham mousse. Garnish the opening of each cornucopia with a slice of stuffed green olive.

Arrange the ham on a ham rack at one end of a very large platter and decorate it with a bunch of green grapes and leaves, held in place with wooden picks. Surround it with parsley and arrange the cornucopias in front of it. Skin about 2 dozen tomatoes graduated in size. Cut a slice from the top of each and hollow them out. Fill them with tangerine sauce. Replace the tops and place on each a round slice of truffle. Border the platter with the

tomatoes, placing the largest one at the end opposite the ham, the rest curving away from it in descending order of size. Chop the sheet of pink aspic and fill any spaces around the cornucopias and tomatoes with chopped aspic. Serves 12.

Schinken in Aspik   *Glazed Ham Imperial*

BOIL A 10- to 12-pound ham and trim off the brown rind, leaving a saw-toothed cuff around the bone.

Bring 4 cups white stock to a boil and dissolve in it, off the heat, 3 envelopes of gelatin softened in 1 cup Sherry. Let the aspic cool. Chill half of it in a shallow baking pan until it is set.

Cut a large section from the ham, leaving a curved hollow. Trim the fat from the meat and put it through the finest blade of the food chopper. Stir in 2 teaspoons prepared mustard, a little cayenne, and 2 tablespoons Sherry. Fold in 1 cup heavy cream, whipped, and chill the mixture. Cut 12 uniform slices of cold boiled ham, not too thin. Roll them into cornucopias and, using a pastry bag, fill them with the ham mousse. Decorate each cornucopia with half a glazed cherry or a tiny tomato. Arrange the ham on a platter and arrange the cornucopias decoratively in the cutout hollow. Glaze the entire surface of the ham and the cornucopias with cool but still liquid aspic. Chop the chilled aspic and surround the ham with it. Fill the spaces between the cornucopias with chopped aspic. Arrange a large bunch of parsley at the bone end of the ham and put a paper ruff on the bone. Add 2 cups sour cherries to Cumberland sauce and serve the sauce separately.

Gefüllter Pragerschinken   *Stuffed Prague Ham*

HAVE THE butcher bone an 8- to 10-pound precooked ham and cut a hollow through the entire ham. (Use the meat removed for ground-ham dishes.) Fill the hollow with a mixture of 1 pound mushrooms, chopped fine and browned in butter, 1 cup dry whole-wheat or rye bread crumbs, 2 1/2 ounces goose-liver paste, 1/2 cup blanched almonds, slivered, and 1 onion, minced. Add Sherry to taste. The stuffing should be very firm.

Trim off any rind and all excess fat and bind the ham with a strip of cloth, securing the filling but leaving most of the surface of the ham exposed. Bake the ham in a moderately hot oven (375° F.) for 45 minutes, basting it occasionally with Sherry. Serve it surrounded with fresh pineapple rings filled with *marrons glacés* and accompany it with potato balls mixed with tiny glazed onions. The ham may be served hot or cold.

Ham with Almonds  *Mandelschinken*

BAKE A TRIMMED 8- to 10-pound precooked ham in a moderately hot oven (375° F.) for 1 hour. Cut the center section into slices 1/2 inch thick. Rub each slice with a cut garlic clove, dip the slices in beaten egg, and roll them in blanched slivered almonds until they are well coated. Pound the almond slivers firmly into the ham. Sauté the ham slices very carefully in butter until the almonds are brown. As they are done, transfer them with a spatula to the center of a wide ovenproof dish and keep them hot. Border the dish with a ring of uniform cold peeled tomatoes stuffed with pink potato salad. Follow any potato salad recipe, adding enough tomato paste to tint it pink. Sprinkle the stuffed tomatoes with chopped parsley.

Ham Slices with Sherry Sauce *Schinkenschnitten*

SIMMER 2 SLICES of precooked ham, each 1 1/2 inches thick and free of fat, in water to cover with 1 tablespoon honey for about 30 minutes, and let them cool in the water. Drain them.

Simmer together 1 1/2 cups each of sugar and Sherry until the syrup thickens, about 20 minutes. In a skillet, melt a little of the ham fat and brown the drained ham slices lightly on both sides. Remove the ham slices to a heated serving platter. Add 1 cup ground unsweetened pineapple, heated, and 1/2 cup raisins to the Sherry syrup and pour this sauce over the ham slices. Garnish the platter with fresh water cress. Serve with German cucumber salad I and cooked new potatoes rolled in butter and in finely chopped chives.

Ham Pockets  *Schinkentaschen*

SIFT 2 CUPS sifted flour with 1/4 teaspoon salt onto a pastry board. Make a well in the center of the flour and in it put 1 cup butter, 1/2 pound cream cheese, and 1 egg yolk. Work the center ingredients into the flour to make a smooth dough. Chill the dough for 1 hour.

Sauté 2 medium onions, finely chopped, in 1 tablespoon butter. Remove the pan from the heat and mix the onions well with 1/2 pound ham, chopped, 2 tablespoons sweet pickle relish, 2 teaspoons each of salt and prepared mustard, 1 teaspoon paprika, and 1/2 teaspoon pepper.

Roll the dough out 1/8 inch thick on a lightly floured board, cut it into 2-inch squares, and on each square place a teaspoon of filling. Pinch the corners of the squares together over the filling and press together the edges of the dough to seal them. Bake the ham pockets on an unbuttered baking sheet in a moderate oven (350° F.) for 15 minutes, or until the pastry is nicely browned. Serve hot. Makes about 6 dozen.

Schinkenmus   Cold Ham Mousse

SOFTEN 2 ENVELOPES gelatin in 1/2 cup Sherry and off the heat stir it into 1 cup boiling bouillon. Melt 3 tablespoons butter over low heat, stir in 3 tablespoons flour, and add 1 cup milk, stirring, until the sauce is thick. Grind 1 1/2 pounds cooked ham or ham scraps in the food processor until fine, add 1 dill pickle, roughly chopped and patted dry, 1 pimiento, and 1/2 cup pistachio nuts. Process until the pickle is diced. Combine the ham mixture, the gelatin, and the white sauce and pour the mixture into an oiled ring mold. Chill the mousse, covered, for at least 6 hours. Unmold the mousse onto a platter, fill the center with diced Sherry aspic, and serve with Cumberland sauce.

Schinkenauflauf   Ham Soufflé

MELT 3 TABLESPOONS butter and blend in 3 tablespoons flour. Cook the *roux* for a few minutes, stirring, until it is golden. Gradually stir in 1 cup warm milk. Cook the sauce, stirring constantly, until it is smooth and thick. Stir in 4 lightly beaten egg yolks, off the heat, and cook the sauce over low heat for 2 minutes longer, stirring, but do not allow it to boil. Combine 1/2 pound cooked ham, chopped, with 1 tablespoon each of green pepper, pimiento, and onion, all chopped, and 1/2 teaspoon each of salt and prepared mustard. Add the ham mixture to the sauce and fold in 5 egg whites, beaten stiff. Turn the soufflé mixture into an unbuttered soufflé dish. Place the dish in a pan of hot water and bake in a moderately hot oven (375° F.) for 1 hour, or until it is puffed and golden.

Ham Fritots — *Schinkenkrapfen*

MIX TOGETHER 2 cups ground cooked ham, 3 small gherkins, chopped fine, 1 teaspoon brown mustard, 1/2 teaspoon curry powder, and salt and pepper to taste. Shape this mixture into small balls and roll them in grated Parmesan. Dip the ham balls in a batter made by blending 1 1/2 cups flour, 3/4 cup each of beer and water, 1 teaspoon salt, and 2 egg whites, stiffly beaten. Fry the *fritots* in deep hot fat (375° F.) until they are golden. Drain them well and serve them at once with mustard cream sauce.

Roast Fresh Ham — *Schweinebraten*

SCORE DEEPLY the skin of a fresh ham, or leg of pork, in two directions, in a diamond pattern. Rub the meat well with a cut clove of garlic, salt, pepper, and 1 teaspoon crushed caraway seeds. Lay it, skin side down, on a bed of 4 onions and 2 carrots, all sliced, 1 bay leaf, and 3 cloves in a roasting pan and add 1/2 cup water. Roast it, uncovered, for 1 hour in a moderate oven (350° F.), basting it frequently with the pan juices and 1/2 cup white wine. Turn the meat skin side up and roast it for 2 hours longer, or for 25 minutes per pound. Baste it frequently, to make the skin crisp and brown. Add more white wine, if necessary. Take the meat from the pan and keep it hot.

Strain the juices and skim off the fat. Stir in 2 tablespoons flour mixed with 2 tablespoons water and cook the sauce over direct heat until it is smooth. Add 1/2 cup white wine and salt and pepper to taste. Just before serving, reduce the heat and stir in 1 cup heavy sour cream. Serve the roast fresh ham with sauerkraut, potato dumplings, and cold compote of apple quarters cooked with cloves and cinnamon.

Fresh Ham with Raisin Pudding — *Schweinebraten mit Rosinenpudding*

REMOVE THE skin from a fresh ham, or leg of pork, and rub the meat well with salt and pepper. Marinate it for 24 hours, turning it frequently, in

1/2 bottle of white wine and 1/2 cup olive oil with 6 bay leaves, 3 cloves, and 3 peppercorns. Transfer the meat with its marinade to a roasting pan and roast it in a moderate oven (350° F.) for approximately 25 minutes per pound, basting it frequently with the marinade. Remove the meat and keep it hot. Strain the pan juices, and skim the fat. Stir 2 table-spoons flour mixed with 2 tablespoons water into the liquid and simmer the sauce over low heat until it is thickened and smooth. Add 1 cup drained hot stewed prunes. Reheat the meat in the sauce and serve with raisin pudding.

Rosinenpudding   *Raisin Pudding for Ham*

MAKE CREAM-PUFF PASTE *(page 430)*, but use 1 1/3 cups milk, 1/2 cup butter, 1 cup flour, 5 egg yolks, and 1/4 cup sugar. Add the grated rind of 1 lemon and 1 cup raisins, steeped in brandy and drained. Fold in 5 egg whites, stiffly beaten. Butter a pudding mold well, dust it with 1/4 cup dry bread crumbs, pour in the batter, and cover. Place it in a kettle of boiling water. The water should reach two-thirds of the way up the mold. Cover the kettle and steam the pudding for 1 1/2 hours. Add more hot water, if necessary, to keep the water at the same level. Unmold the pudding on a hot platter. Serve it with roast fresh ham or with baked ham and apple-sauce.

Spanferkel   *Roast Suckling Pig*

WASH AND dry a suckling pig, weighing about 12 pounds dressed. Rub the cavity with salt and 1 teaspoon caraway seeds. Make the follow-ing stuffing: Sauté 2 pounds sauerkraut for 10 minutes with 1/2 cup butter, 1 onion, chopped, and 1/2 teaspoon caraway seeds, and add 2 apples, peeled, cored, and chopped.

Stuff the suckling pig loosely, secure it with large skewers, and lace the opening with heavy twine. Truss the forelegs and hind legs forward, and close under the body.

Lay the pig on a rack, or across two wooden spoons, in a large pan. Cover the ears and tail with little envelopes of buttered brown paper and place a wooden plug in the mouth. Soak the rind from a 1/2-pound piece of unsliced bacon in 1 1/2 cups beer and place it near the stove. Roast the suckling pig in a moderate oven (350° F.) for 4 to 5 hours, depending on its size, or until it is golden brown, rubbing it every 10 minutes with the beer-soaked bacon. Uncover the ears and tail, replace the wooden plug with a small apple, and serve the pig on a bed of water cress.

Pour all superfluous fat from the roasting pan and stir in 3 tablespoons flour and 2 cups hot strong stock. Stir the gravy over low heat until it comes to a boil, strain it, and serve it with the suckling pig. Accompany the pig with potato dumplings.

Peasants' Feast

SIMMER 3 POUNDS well-drained sauerkraut in 4 cups beer with 1 teaspoon caraway seeds for 3 hours. When the sauerkraut has cooked for 1 hour, boil in a kettle of water a 2-pound smoked loin of pork, or Canadian bacon, for 1 hour. Add it to the sauerkraut and simmer, covered, 1 hour more. Roast a 3 3/4-pound fresh pork loin in a hot oven (450° F.) for 1 1/2 hours. At the same time boil 1 1/2 pounds corned pork, *Selchfleisch*. Prepare 2 1/2 pounds assorted sausages. Mound the sauerkraut on a platter, arrange the roast pork loin, cut into chops, on top of it, and surround the chops with the smoked pork and corned pork, sliced. Arrange the sausages and 1/2 pound thick bacon, fried, over the pork. *(Picture, page 279.)*

Sauerkraut Goulash   *Szekely Gulyás*

IN A CASSEROLE, brown 1 onion, chopped, in 2 tablespoons bacon fat. Add 2 pounds drained sauerkraut, reserving the juice, and 1/2 teaspoon caraway seeds, and sauté it for a few minutes, stirring well to coat it with fat. Add the reserved sauerkraut juice (about 1 cup), cover the casserole, and cook the sauerkraut until it is tender, about 1 1/2 to 2 hours, adding water if necessary. The sauerkraut should cook longer than the meat.

In another pan, sauté 1 onion, chopped, in 3 tablespoons bacon fat until it is puffed and golden. Add 3/4 pound each of shoulder of pork and shoulder of beef, cut in large pieces, 2 teaspoons paprika, and the grated rind of half a lemon, and brown the meat on all sides. Add 1/2 cup white wine and cook the meat, covered, until it is tender, about 1 1/2 hours, adding 1/2 cup strong stock when the wine has cooked away.

Sprinkle the meat with seasoned flour and add it to the cooked sauerkraut. Stir together 1 cup sour cream and 1/4 cup milk, add salt to taste, and stir the mixture into the goulash. Correct the seasoning and serve the goulash very hot, accompanied with boiled new potatoes.

Jungfernbraten   *Pork Tenderloin with Cream*

LARD 3 TENDERLOINS of pork, each weighing 1 1/2 pounds, with 3/4 cup larding pork cut in strips. Brown the tenderloins in 1/2 cup butter with 1 onion and 1 carrot, both chopped, in a hot oven (400° F.) for 10 minutes. Reduce the heat to moderate (350° F.), add 1 cup brown stock, the juice and grated rind of 1 lemon, 3 sprigs of thyme, 1 bay leaf, and salt and pepper to taste. Braise the meat, covered, until it is tender, about 30 to 40 minutes. Take out the meat and keep it hot. Strain the pan juices. Stir 1 cup heavy cream into 1/4 cup flour and stir the cream into the strained pan juices. Heat the sauce over direct heat but do not let it boil. Add 1/4 cup capers. Slice the tenderloins and pour the sauce over them. Sprinkle them with 2 tablespoons chopped parsley. Serve with noodles and lingonberries.

Schweinskoteletten mit gebackenen Äpfeln   *Pork Chops with Baked Apples*

SPRINKLE 6 THICK pork chops with salt and pepper and brown them on both sides in 3 tablespoons butter. Add 1/2 cup brown stock and 1 small onion, chopped, and braise the chops, covered, in a moderate oven (350° F.) until they are tender, about 40 minutes. Baste them frequently and add more stock, if necessary. Remove the chops to a platter, strain the pan juices, and skim off the fat. Stir in 1/2 cup heavy cream. Add salt and pepper to taste and reheat the sauce. Surround the chops with 6 baked apples. Border the platter with mashed potatoes and sprinkle them with 3 tablespoons chopped chives. Pour the sauce over the chops.

Gebackene Äpfel   *Baked Apples*

COMBINE 1 CUP each of sugar and water and 1/4 cup orange marmalade and cook the syrup until it spins a thread, or a candy thermometer registers 230° F. Pour the syrup over 6 apples, peeled and cored, and bake them in a moderate oven (350° F.) for 15 to 20 minutes, or until they are soft, basting them frequently. Fill the hot apples with 1 cup raspberries, crushed and sweetened to taste with confectioners' sugar.

Pork Chops with Apricots — *Schweinskoteletten mit Aprikosen*

SOAK 1 CUP dried apricots overnight in 1 cup apple cider or white wine. Purée them in a food processor and add to the purée the liquid in which the fruit soaked. Brown 6 pork chops, dredged in seasoned flour, on both sides in butter. Arrange the chops in a casserole, pour over them 1/2 cup warm water or stock, and coat them with the apricot purée. Cover the casserole and bake the chops in a moderate oven (350° F.) for 30 minutes. Correct the seasoning and sprinkle over them 1/4 cup brown sugar. Bake the chops for 10 minutes longer, or until they are well done and evenly glazed.

Viennese Stew — *Wienereintopf*

CUT 2 POUNDS shoulder of pork into 1 1/2-inch cubes and season them well with salt and pepper. Sauté 3 white onions, sliced, in 6 tablespoons butter until they are golden and drain the onions, reserving the butter. Slice 3 peeled potatoes into 1/4 inch rounds, cut 2 carrots into julienne, and chop enough white cabbage to make 1 cup. Arrange half the potato slices in the bottom of a buttered ovenproof casserole. Cover the potatoes with alternate layers of the meat, the onions, and the carrots and cabbage, sprinkling each layer with salt, pepper, and caraway seeds. Make a top layer of potato slices, sprinkle with salt, pepper, and caraway seeds, and pour over the reserved butter. Cover the mixture with light stock and bake the stew, covered tightly, in a moderately hot oven (375° F.) for 1 1/2 hours. Remove the casserole cover shortly before the stew is done to allow the potato topping to brown. Serve the stew from the casserole.

Rinderzunge mit Gemüse   Beef Tongue Platter Lydia

SOAK 2 SMOKED beef tongues in cold water overnight. Put them in a large
kettle with as much water as possible, and add 2 onions, each stuck with
3 cloves, and 2 bay leaves. Simmer the tongues for about 3 1/2 to 4 hours,
or until a pin can be moved easily in and out of the tip. Remove the skins,
trim the roots, and drain the tongues well. Arrange one tongue on a large
platter and cut only a few slices. Slice the second tongue completely and
arrange the slices on the platter. Arrange around the tongue tart shells
filled with green pea purée, mounds of cooked asparagus sprinkled with
orange rind, and potato-almond-and-truffle croquettes and garnish the
platter with carrot roses and sprigs of parsley. Serves 12.

Serve Maltese sauce separately. Make the following sauce also and
serve it separately. Sauté 1 onion, finely chopped, in 1 tablespoon butter
until it is lightly browned. Dust with 1 tablespoon flour and cook the
mixture a minute or two. Stir in gradually 1/4 cup red wine and add
2 cups of the broth, strained, in which the tongues cooked, 1 cup beef
stock, and 1 tablespoon tomato paste. Cook the sauce, stirring, until it is
smooth, and simmer it until it is reduced by half. Strain it and add
Madeira to taste and chopped thyme, and correct the seasoning.

Rinderzunge Europa   Beef Tongue Fritters

SIFT 1 1/3 CUPS flour with 1/2 teaspoon salt and stir in 3/4 cup light
beer and 1 tablespoon olive oil. Pour over the batter a little melted butter
or oil and chill it.

Soak a 3 1/2-pound mild smoked beef tongue in cold water for 1 hour
and scald it for 15 minutes in boiling water to cover. Transfer the tongue
to cold water again and add an herb bouquet of 3 sprigs each of parsley,
chervil, and thyme, 1 bay leaf, and 3 peppercorns. Simmer the tongue,
covered, for 3 1/2 hours. Remove the skin, trim the root, and cut the
tongue into slices 1/2 inch thick. Lay them in a shallow dish and marinate
them for 3 hours under a layer of 3 onions, finely chopped, and 1/2 cup
chopped parsley with the juice and grated rind of 2 lemons.

Fold 3 stiffly beaten egg whites into the batter. Wipe the slices of
tongue, draw them through the batter, and fry them in deep hot fat
(375° F.) for 5 minutes, or until they are brown. Drain the slices. Garnish

the serving platter with lemon wedges and parsley. Serve separately tomato sauce to which 1 cup, or more to taste, of the onion marinade may be added.

Beef Tongue in Aspic   *Zunge in Aspik*

COOK 2 POUNDS apples, peeled, cored, and quartered, in 1 cup water with 1/2 cup sugar and the rind and juice of 1 lemon until they are tender. Cool the fruit. Heat 1 cup stock from a boilĕd smoked beef tongue with 1 cup strong chicken stock and 1/2 cup white Port. Dissolve in the hot liquid 2 envelopes of gelatin softened in 1/2 cup Port. Add salt to taste and let the aspic cool.

Arrange slices of cold boiled tongue around a large platter, pile the apples in the center, and pour the cool but still liquid aspic over all. Chill the platter until the aspic is firm. Serve with raisin sauce.

Beef Tongue with Oranges   *Rinderzunge mit Orangen*

SOAK A 3- TO 4-pound smoked beef tongue in water to cover for 12 hours. Drain the meat, cover it with fresh cold water, and boil for 10

minutes. Reduce the heat and simmer the tongue for 3 hours, or until it is tender. Remove the skin, trim the root, and drain the tongue.

Make the following sweet-and-sour brown sauce: Melt 2 tablespoons butter, blend in 2 tablespoons flour, and cook the *roux* until it is brown. Gradually add 1 cup stock from the tongue, strained. Remove the brown sauce from the fire, add a mixture of 1/4 cup each of sugar, browned, and vinegar, 1/2 cup each of raisins and walnuts, chopped, and the grated rind of 1 orange. Slice the tongue and border the platter with 5 oranges, peeled, sliced, and tossed in 1/2 cup olive oil seasoned with 1 teaspoon paprika and 1/2 teaspoon salt. Serve the sauce in a sauceboat.

Kalbshirn Alfons   *Calf's Brains*

SOAK 3 CALF's brains in cold water for 3 hours. Remove the skin. Place them in water to cover with 1/4 cup vinegar, 1 onion, 1 teaspoon salt, and 3 peppercorns. Simmer the brains for 9 minutes and cool them in the broth. Lay them on 3/4 cup ham, cut in fine julienne, and add 1/2 cup white wine, the juice of 1 lemon, and chicken stock to just cover. Lay 3 slices of lean bacon on the brains and simmer them, covered, for 15 minutes. Drain the brains well and cut them into slices 1/2 inch thick. Pour over them 1/2 cup browned butter. Serve them with tomato sauce.

Nieren Lelia   *Lamb Kidneys with Mustard Sauce*

PLUNGE INTO boiling water 12 lamb kidneys, drain them immediately and remove the thin skin and tough center. Slice them thinly. Sauté the kidneys in 1/4 cup butter over high heat for about 5 minutes and add 3 tablespoons prepared brown mustard, 3/4 cup beef stock, 1 large onion, diced and browned, and 1 teaspoon caraway seeds. Sprinkle the mixture with 2 tablespoons flour and add 1 tablespoon lemon juice. Correct the seasoning with salt and stir thoroughly. Serve the kidneys with rice.

Nieren in Weisswein   *Lamb Kidneys in White Wine*

PREPARE AND slice 10 lamb kidneys as for *Nieren Lelia*. Sprinkle the slices with salt and pepper. Sauté the kidneys in 1/2 cup butter over high heat, shaking the pan, for 2 minutes. Add 6 large mushrooms, sliced very fine, and 1 tablespoon each of shallots and parsley, both chopped, and continue to sauté for 3 minutes longer. Sprinkle the mixture with 2 tablespoons flour and cook it until it has browned. Add 3/4 cup white wine and bring the liquid just to a boil. Season the kidneys to taste, stir them well, and serve them at once, sprinkled with parsley.

Veal Kidneys in Pimiento Sauce   *Kalbsnieren Baden-Baden*

SPLIT 6 VEAL kidneys in half, remove the tough center, and slice them fine. Lightly brown 1/3 cup butter in a skillet and add the kidneys with 1 1/2 teaspoons salt and 1/2 teaspoon pepper. Sauté them for 3 minutes and add 1/2 cup Sherry, 1 cup finely sliced mushrooms, and 6 tablespoons finely chopped pimiento. Simmer the kidneys, covered, for 6 minutes, reduce the heat, and add 3 egg yolks beaten into 1 1/4 cups heavy cream. Cook, stirring, until the sauce is smooth, but do not let it boil. Correct the seasoning. Serve the kidneys with wedges of puff pastry.

Calf's Liver Dumplings   *Leberknödel*

SOAK 2 SLICES of white bread, free of crusts, in 1/2 cup milk. Squeeze out the milk and mash the bread.

Sauté 1/2 cup parsley, 1 large onion, and 1 stalk of celery, all chopped very fine, in 2 tablespoons butter until the onions are golden. Mix well and cool the mixture. Salt to taste 2 1/2 pounds ground calf's liver and add 2 tablespoons flour. Combine the liver, the bread, and the cooked parsley mixture. Stir in 5 beaten egg yolks and fold in 5 egg whites, beaten stiff. Shape one egg-sized dumpling and simmer it in salted water for 10 minutes. If it separates, add more flour to the remaining mixture. Shape and cook the remaining dumplings. Pour 2 tablespoons browned butter over the dumplings and serve them with sauerkraut and onion sauce.

Skewered Liver   *Leber am Spiess*

CUT 1 1/2 POUNDS calf's liver into long strips. Wrap a small strip of bacon around each piece of liver and thread the meat onto skewers, alternating it with tomato cubes and whole mushrooms. Lay the skewers in a pan and broil the meat under high heat, turning it to brown all sides and basting frequently with 1/4 cup melted butter. Remove the skewers to a heated platter. Add to the pan juices a squeeze of lemon juice, 2 teaspoons flour, and 1 cup beef stock and reheat the sauce. Sprinkle the liver with freshly chopped dill. Serve it with rice and green beans.

Kalbsleber mit Äpfeln   *Slivered Calf's Liver*

CUT 2 POUNDS thinly sliced calf's liver into slivers, trimming it and removing all veins. In a skillet, melt 5 tablespoons butter until it is sizzling, add 1 onion, chopped, and the liver. Stir with a wooden spoon until the liver is no longer red, about 3 minutes. Sprinkle the liver with 1 1/2 tablespoons flour and stir until it is absorbed. Add to the skillet 3 tablespoons each of dry white wine and bouillon and bring to a rapid boil. Remove the skillet from the heat and stir in 3 to 4 tablespoons *crème fraîche* until the sauce is smooth. Season with salt and pepper and serve at once with fried apple slices and individual rounds of Viennese fried potatoes.

Kalbsbries Imperial   *Sweetbreads with Paprika Sauce*

SOAK 3 PAIRS of sweetbreads in cold water for 1/2 hour. Cover them with boiling water, add 1 teaspoon salt and 2 tablespoons vinegar, and simmer for 15 minutes. Plunge the sweetbreads into cold water and trim the tubes and membranes. Press the sweetbreads lightly under a cloth. Make small incisions and stud the sweetbreads with little wedges of tongue. Use about 2 thick slices.

Sauté the sweetbreads in 5 tablespoons butter for 10 minutes, or until they are golden. Cut them in half lengthwise and fill each half with 1 tablespoon goose liver pâté. Arrange in a shallow copper pan 3 cups cooked rice mixed with 3 tablespoons butter, 2 tablespoons chopped parsley, and salt to taste, and lay the sweetbreads on the rice. Cover with 1 1/2 cups paprika sauce and sprinkle with 3 tablespoons Parmesan. Bake the sweetbreads in a hot oven (400° F.) for 6 minutes, or until the cheese is browned. Surround the rice with green peas and decorate the pan with sprigs of parsley. Serve from the pan.

Poultry

Geflügel

F OR SOME reason, the Austrian chickens and geese took longer than feathered creatures in other countries to adapt themselves to the change from the beautiful horse-drawn monarchy to the gas-fumed, mechanized, and motorcycled postwar republic. When American hens had finally learned, the hard way, that they could not cross the road in front of an automobile without disaster, Austrian fowl were still pecking about the country highways. The irate farmer and the be-goggled and be-dustered American motorist haggling together over the cost of a priceless hen was already a thing of the past when the Viennese who drove around Austria were still confronted with undecided chickens fleeing down the middle of the road or frantically crossing and recrossing the road with terrified and heart-rending squawks.

Besides these hazards of the highway, they had also to endure the disconcerting experience of being viciously hissed at by geese in narrow village streets and on the open roads. Great ganders were apt to charge with spread wings and unmistakable hatred and, if the car was small enough, they might even attack the passengers. Mother geese with wedges of ugly goslings monopolized the puddles in the streets and the sight of an "Indian," a turkey, stopped traffic completely.

The smiling children might wave and throw bouquets of cornflowers at the passing cars, but as long as the geese hissed and charged, the motorist could never feel really at home. He knew that if he harmed a feather on a single goose, the pitchforks would come out; after all, the goose represented not only a source of eggs and goslings, it meant Christmas dinner, warm featherbeds, and a delicious liver.

The Viennese take great pride in their fat and tender *Poularden,* brought in from Steiermark and comparable only to the French *poularde de Bresse*. Their own famous *Backhendl*, breaded chicken, and the paprika chicken they learned of from the Hungarians appear on every restaurant menu and in every home, and no one seems to lose pleasure in them. Since the birds are fresh killed and sautéed in country butter, there is nothing we can do to emulate their flavor. The Indian, which the Viennese believe came to them directly from India, is of course an American Indian. Turkeys are scarce and highly appreciated, and if Vienna had a special day set aside for Thanksgiving, there would hardly be enough Indians to go around.

When the Viennese sit down to a dinner of duck, *Ente,* someone is sure to say, *"Ente gut, alles gut,"* a mild pun of "All's well that ends well," but when they sit down to a dinner of roast goose, the alliterative and awesome proverb is *"Eine gut gebratene Gans ist eine gute Gabe Gottes* —a well-roasted goose is a good gift from God." To which gift is added the pleasure of goose fat on black bread for days to come.

The Viennese are carefully brought up with an eye to *Tischmanieren,* table manners, but these may differ considerably from those acceptable in this country. Their approach to the eating of poultry is very frank: They may pick up the bones in their fingers and a healthy crunch can often be heard when a knuckle is eaten by a dinner guest.

The hungry American who says he could eat an ox has a more realistic counterpart in Vienna, who says he feels so hungry he could eat a goose and often does so. Real proof of prowess is to eat a whole goose at a single sitting, right up to, but not including—as the saying goes—the beak or *Schnabel*. An ugly word, and better said than eaten.

Anyone who has been sick in Vienna knows that the worst is over when the Herr Doktor orders a squab boiled in soup. Later there may be a breast of chicken, a slice of pale pink Prague ham, or a little scraped beef, but the squab in soup represents the quickest way to regain lost strength and the first step to recovery. After that, the restored Viennese can again eat his squab stuffed, roasted, and garnished as he pleases.

Roast Chicken   *Pikante Poularde*

WASH AND dry a fine plump 6-pound roasting chicken. Rub the inside
with 3 tablespoons butter and salt and pepper. Truss the fowl and place
it in a roasting pan. Add 1 carrot and 2 onions, all sliced, 2 tablespoons
butter, 1/2 cup white wine, and 1/4 cup water to the pan. Cover the
chicken with buttered paper and roast it in a moderate oven (325° F.)
for 1 1/2 hours. Remove the paper and continue roasting the chicken,
basting it occasionally, until it is tender, about 30 minutes.

Sauté 1 cup chopped mushrooms, the chicken liver and heart, chopped,
2 tablespoons chopped pimiento, 1/4 cup blanched almonds, and 2 onions,
chopped fine, in butter until the mixture is golden and hot. Add it to
3 cups freshly cooked hot rice and keep the rice warm.

Remove the roasted chicken to a carving platter and keep it warm.
Skim all but 1 tablespoon of fat from the roasting pan. Over direct heat,
blend into the juices 1 tablespoon flour and add 1 teaspoon tomato paste
and a pinch of thyme. Gradually add 1 cup chicken stock and cook the
sauce, stirring constantly, until it is smooth. Bring it just to a boil, add
2 tablespoons Sherry and salt to taste, and strain it.

Carve the chicken and arrange the slices in the center of a large
heated platter. Surround the chicken with the rice and garnish the rice
with 4 tomatoes, peeled, seeded, and chopped, and sautéed gently in
butter with 1/4 cup raisins. Surround the platter with 4 peeled apples,
cut in quarters and sautéed in butter, and 4 bananas, halved and browned
in butter. Serve the sauce separately.

Roast Capon with Chestnuts   *Kapaune mit Kastanien*

WASH AND dry a 5- to 6-pound capon and rub it inside and out with a
mixture of salt and pepper.

With a sharp knife slit the shells of 16 chestnuts on the flat side
and roast them in a hot oven (400° F.) for 5 minutes. While the chestnuts are hot, remove the shells and the inner skins with a sharp knife.
Chop the chestnuts and combine them with 4 cups bread crumbs, 6 sprigs
of parsley, chopped, and 1 clove of garlic, crushed.

Sauté the capon liver in 2 tablespoons butter with 2 onions, chopped,
until they are golden. Mash the liver with a fork and add salt and pepper
and a pinch of nutmeg. Combine the liver and the chestnut mixtures.

Stuff the capon with this filling and secure the opening with a skewer. Cover the bird with buttered brown paper and roast it in a moderate oven (325° F.) for about 2 hours, or until it is golden brown and tender.

In a small saucepan, simmer the wing tips, the heart, and the giblets in cold water to cover with 1 onion, 3 celery leaves, and 1/2 teaspoon each of salt and pepper for 1 hour. Strain the stock and correct the seasoning. Chop the giblets.

Remove the paper from the capon during the last 1/2 hour of roasting and baste the bird thoroughly with melted butter. Five minutes before removing the bird from the oven, brush it with 1 egg yolk, diluted in water, so that it will brown. Remove the roasted capon to a platter and keep it warm.

Pour off all but about 1 tablespoon of the fat in the roasting pan, blend in 1 tablespoon flour, and stir in 1 1/2 cups of the giblet stock. Scrape the bottom and sides of the pan to get all the brown particles. Add the chopped giblets and simmer the sauce for 5 minutes. Serve it separately. Garnish the capon with bunches of water cress.

Kapaune am Spiess   *Spit-Roasted Stuffed Capon*

WASH, DRY, and salt a 5- to 6-pound capon. Combine 1/2 pound mushrooms, 6 shallots, 6 dried mushrooms, and 1/4 cup fresh parsley, all finely chopped, 3 slices of bacon cut in small dice, and the chopped giblets. Combine 1/2 cup each of beef stock and white wine, add the mushroom mixture, and simmer it until all the moisture is absorbed. Add salt and pepper to taste and bind the stuffing with 2 egg yolks. Rub the cavity of the bird with 2 tablespoons butter, fill it with the mushroom mixture, and skewer the opening. Truss the bird. Place it on a rotisserie spit and roast it for 2 hours at high heat, until it is golden and crisp. Or roast the bird in a moderate oven (325° F.), basting it frequently with melted butter. Serve the capon with a mixed fruit compote and a salad.

Schöne Poularde   *A Beautiful Chicken*

WASH, DRY, salt, and truss a 5- to 6-pound roasting chicken and place it in a deep kettle. Pour over it 1/2 cup warm brandy and set the spirit aflame. When the flame dies down, pour over the chicken 3 cups chicken stock, and add 1 carrot, 2 onions, and 2 stalks of celery, all cut in pieces. Simmer the chicken, covered, until it is a little more than half cooked, about 75 minutes. Remove the chicken and keep it warm.

Strain the stock and reduce it somewhat. Add 1 cup red wine and reduce the liquid until there are only 2 cups. Melt 2 tablespoons butter, blend in 2 tablespoons flour, and cook the *roux,* stirring, until it is brown. Stir in the chicken stock and wine, add 1 teaspoon tomato paste, and season the sauce to taste.

Remove the skin from the chicken. Spread the chicken with 1/2 cup liver paste and sprinkle it with salt and pepper. Roll out pie dough into a sheet large enough to enclose the chicken. Spread on the dough 1/4 pound button mushrooms, chopped and sautéed in butter. Wrap the dough around the chicken and press the seams firmly. Paint the top of the dough with 1 egg yolk beaten with 1 tablespoon water. Cut a vent in the dough and bake the chicken in a buttered roasting pan in a hot oven (400° F.) for 30 minutes, or until the crust is golden brown.

Halve 6 hard-cooked eggs and mash the yolks with 1/2 cup liver paste. Add salt and pepper to taste. Press the mixture into the egg whites through a pastry bag fitted with a fluted tube. Place the "beautiful chicken" on a platter. Arrange the warm stuffed eggs around it and garnish the platter with water cress. Serve the hot sauce separately.

Chicken with Prunes and Raisins   *Hühner nach Balkan Art*

WASH, DRY and truss 2 broilers, weighing about 3 pounds each, and tie thick strips of bacon over their breasts. Salt them and put them in a casserole with 4 carrots, scraped and diced, 1 large onion, grated, a grinding of black pepper, and 1/4 cup butter. Bake the chickens, covered, in a moderate oven (325° F.) for 1 hour, or until they are tender, basting them frequently with melted butter.

Cook 1 cup rice in salted water until it is tender but not soft. In another pan, simmer 12 dried prunes in water to cover with the juice of 1 lemon until they are soft. Add 1/2 cup raisins and cook the mixture until they are puffed. Drain the fruit and stone it. Melt 3 tablespoons butter, blend in 3 tablespoons flour, and gradually add 1 cup milk. Add paprika to taste and simmer the sauce for 6 minutes, stirring. Garnish the chickens with the rice and prunes and raisins and pour the paprika sauce over them.

Huhn in Champagner   Chicken in Champagne

LIGHTLY BROWN 2 onions, sliced fine, and 1 carrot, chopped, in 1/2 cup butter. Add 3 broilers, weighing about 3 pounds each, cut in half, 3 sprigs of parsley, 1 bay leaf, and a pinch of thyme, and sauté the chicken until it is light brown on both sides. Transfer the chicken to a baking dish and pour over it 2 cups Champagne. Bake the chicken, covered, in a moderate oven (325° F.) until it is tender, about 1 hour. Remove the birds and keep them warm on a warm platter. Discard the parsley sprigs and the bay leaf, add 2 cups cream to the sauce in the pan and cook it on top of the stove, stirring constantly, for 1 minute. Pour some of the sauce over the chicken and serve the remainder separately. Garnish the platter with cold stewed peaches. Accompany the chicken with hot cooked rice.

Kronjuwelenhühner   Crown Jewel Chickens

CUT INTO quarters 3 broilers, weighing about 3 pounds each. Put the pieces in a casserole and add 1/2 cup butter, cut in pieces. Bake the chicken, covered, in a moderate oven (325° F.) until it is partly tender, about 45 minutes. Add 18 small uniform new potatoes and 9 artichoke bottoms, sliced. Add salt and pepper to taste. Bake the chicken 15 minutes longer, shaking the casserole frequently. Add 1 cup red wine, the juice and grated rind of 1 lemon, a pinch of thyme, and 1 bay leaf. Correct the seasoning and bake the chicken until it is tender, about 10 minutes longer. Remove the bay leaf and dust the chicken with parsley.

Huhn mit Gurken   Chicken with Curry Sauce and Cucumbers

COMBINE 1 1/2 cups rice, parboiled in salted water for 10 minutes and drained, and 6 chicken livers, chopped and sautéed in butter. Stuff a 6-pound roasting chicken with this filling. Skewer the opening, truss the bird, and wrap it in 6 slices of bacon. Lay the bird in a deep casserole, brown it lightly in 1/2 cup butter, and pour over it 4 cups chicken stock.

Braise the chicken, covered, in a moderate oven (350° F.) until most of the stock is absorbed and the chicken tender, about 1 1/2 hours, or until the juices run clear when tested with a fork. Remove the chicken.

Strain the juices in the casserole and add 3 egg yolks beaten in 3/4 cup light cream with 1 tablespoon curry powder. Heat the sauce thoroughly, but do not let it boil, and pour it over the chicken.

Sauté 6 cucumbers, peeled and cubed, in 1/4 cup butter for a few minutes. Add 3/4 cup cream and simmer the cucumber until it is tender. Add salt to taste. Surround the chicken with the cucumbers and sprinkle it with 1/2 cup chopped parsley.

Chicken with Grapes   *Huhn mit Trauben*

WASH AND dry a plump 6-pound roasting chicken and rub the cavity with salt and pepper. Stuff the bird with 1 medium onion, peeled and halved, and 1/4 cup butter. Rub the outside with 1/4 cup butter. Truss the bird, place it in a roasting pan, and pour over it 1 1/2 cups each of white wine and water. Braise the chicken in a moderate oven (350° F.) for 1 1/2

225

hours, or until it is tender, turning and basting it every 15 minutes. Remove the chicken to a hot serving platter and keep it warm.

Strain the juices in the roasting pan into a small saucepan. Add 1 cup chicken stock and reduce the liquid to 1 1/2 cups. Add 3/4 cup heavy cream, 1/4 cup very finely chopped parsley, and 1 1/2 pounds seedless grapes. Heat the sauce thoroughly. Pour it over the chicken and serve at once.

Junge Hühnchen mit Trauben
Squab Chickens Stuffed with Grapes

WASH AND DRY 6 squab chickens, weighing about 1 pound each, and rub them with salt and pepper. Place them in a roasting pan, pour 1/2 cup melted butter over them, and roast them in a very hot oven (425° F.), basting them frequently, for 20 minutes. Remove the birds and fill each one with 1/3 cup seedless grapes. Secure the openings with skewers and roast the birds in a moderately hot oven (375° F.) for 30 to 35 minutes longer. Keep the birds warm on a platter.

Skim off the fat, to the juices in the roasting pan add 1 cup chicken stock, and reduce the liquid over high heat by about half. Correct the seasoning with salt and pepper. Pour a little of the pan sauce over the chickens and serve the remainder separately.

Accompany the birds with duchess potatoes and a salad of green peas garnished with chopped mint.

Petersilienhuhn
Chicken under Parsley

TRUSS A 4-POUND chicken and brown it in a deep casserole in a moderately hot oven (375° F.) until it is light golden, basting it frequently with butter. Pour over it 2 tablespoons chicken glaze, or chicken stock reduced from 1 cup to 1/4 cup, and 1 cup white wine. Cover the casserole tightly and braise the chicken in the oven until it is tender, about 50 minutes.

Parboil 24 small white onions in salted water to cover and sauté them in butter until they are golden. Add them to the chicken in the casserole for the last 10 minutes of cooking. Disjoint the chicken. Fry 4 to 5 bunches clean dry parsley in deep oil and bury the pieces completely under mounds of the fried parsley. There must be so much parsley that each portion can be buried more than an inch deep under fried parsley sprigs. The natural juices from the chicken and the butter from the drained parsley make the sauce. Serve with cauliflower accompanied with hollandaise sauce.

Chicken with Paprika Sauce *Paprikahuhn Hotel Bristol*

IN A SAUCEPAN, place the necks, wing tips and giblets of 3 broilers, weighing about 3 pounds each, and add 1 onion, 1 teaspoon salt, and 3 cups water. Simmer the giblets for about 1 hour.

Cut the broilers in quarters and salt the pieces. In a large skillet, sauté 1 cup chopped onion in 1/2 cup butter until it is puffed but not brown. Stir in 1 tablespoon paprika. Add the chicken and cook it, covered, for 20 minutes, turning the pieces several times. Add 3 cups warm sour cream and bake the chicken in a moderately hot oven (375° F.) for 20 minutes. Add 1 cup tomatoes, peeled, seeded, diced, and drained. Cook the chicken, covered, about 15 to 20 minutes longer, or until it is tender. Transfer the chicken to a deep platter and keep it hot.

Strain the giblet stock and reduce it over high heat to 1 cup. Stir 2 tablespoons flour with 1/2 cup sour cream until the mixture is smooth. Stir in 1/4 cup hot giblet stock and add the mixture to the juices in the skillet. Cook the sauce on top of the stove for 5 minutes, stirring constantly. Add the remaining stock, paprika, and salt to taste. Pour the sauce over the chicken and sprinkle it with sautéed julienne strips of green and red pepper. *(Picture, page 282.)*

Chicken with Fruit Sauce *Hühner in Obstsauce*

CUT INTO quarters 3 broilers, weighing 2 1/2 to 3 pounds each, season them with salt and pepper, and sprinkle them with 1 cup flour mixed with 1/4 teaspoon poultry seasoning. Heat together 1/2 cup butter and 1/4 pound suet in a large skillet and brown the chicken on both sides.

Reduce 1 cup chicken stock to 1/4 cup and add the juice of 4 large oranges, 1/2 cup seedless raisins, 15 almonds, blanched and halved, 2 tablespoons butter, 1 tablespoon orange chutney, 1 teaspoon ground cinnamon, and 1/4 teaspoon each of ground cloves and ground ginger. Simmer the fruit sauce over low heat until it is thoroughly blended. Add the browned chicken and cook it slowly, uncovered, for about 45 minutes, or until it is tender. Add 1 cup chicken stock to the sauce if it becomes too thick.

Königin der Hühner   *Queen of Chickens*

CUT INTO quarters 3 broilers, weighing about 3 pounds each, remove the skin, and dry the pieces well. Rub them with a mixture of 1/2 cup flour, 4 teaspoons curry powder, and 1 teaspoon salt. Simmer the giblets and wing tips in 2 cups water to make a stock. Clarify 1 cup butter and sauté the chicken in it for 5 minutes. Add 1 cup Sherry and 3 slices cooked ham, chopped fine. Simmer the chicken and ham, covered, for 15 minutes, adding the strained giblet stock to the chicken as the sauce reduces. Chop the giblets, add them to the sauce, and cook the chicken for 30 minutes longer. Finish the sauce with 1 cup warm cream and cook it for a few minutes longer.

Lay a poached egg on each serving of chicken and garnish with a slice of truffle and a sprig of parsley.

Hühner mit Brunnenkresse   *Poached Chicken*
                                               with Water Cress Sauce

WIPE WITH a damp cloth 3 broilers, weighing about 3 pounds each. Place the birds in a large kettle with 1 carrot, sliced, 1 onion, 1 stalk of celery, 3 sprigs of parsley, 1/2 teaspoon salt, 3 peppercorns, a sprig of thyme, and a bay leaf and add chicken stock barely to cover. Poach the chickens gently for 45 minutes. Cut them in half, remove the skin, and keep them warm.

Wash 2 large bunches of water cress and reserve 10 to 12 small sprigs. Simmer the remaining water cress in 1 1/2 cups water for about 25 minutes, or until it is soft. Press it through a fine sieve twice or purée it in the blender, to make 1 cup purée. Add to the purée salt and pepper to taste, 2 egg yolks beaten with the strained juice of 1/2 lemon, and 1 teaspoon sugar and place the mixture in the top of a double boiler. Cook the sauce over boiling water, stirring constantly, until it thickens. Correct the seasoning. Pour the hot sauce over the chickens and garnish the platter with the reserved water cress.

Mimosenhühner   *Chicken Mimosa*

CUT INTO quarters 3 broilers, weighing 3 pounds each, and simmer them in salted water to cover until they are tender, about 30 to 40 minutes.

Simmer 2 onions, quartered, 2 carrots, sliced, 1/2 bay leaf, a pinch of mace, 3 peppercorns, and salt to taste in 3 cups milk for 20 minutes. Strain the milk.

In a saucepan melt 1/2 cup butter, stir in 1/2 cup flour, and cook the *roux* for a few minutes without letting the flour take color. Gradually add the strained milk, stirring with a wire whisk. Sauté the chicken livers until they are just pink inside and rice them into the sauce. Cook it, stirring frequently, until it is smooth and creamy. Strain it through a fine sieve and add 4 hard-cooked egg whites, chopped. Correct the seasoning and keep the sauce warm.

Remove the skin from the chicken, arrange it on a serving platter, and surround it with cooked rice. Pour the sauce over the chicken and rice 4 hard-cooked egg yolks over it. Garnish the platter with sprigs of parsley.

Chicken in Spinach   *Huhn in Spinat*

HALVE 3 BROILERS, weighing about 3 pounds each, and put them in boiling salted water to cover with 3 small onions and 3 stalks of celery. Simmer the chicken until it is tender, about 40 minutes.

Cook the necks, wing tips, and giblets separately in salted water to cover for 30 minutes. Strain the giblet stock and chop the giblets. Strain the stock in which the chicken cooked. Combine the chicken and the giblet stocks and reduce the combined stock to about 3 cups. Melt 3 tablespoons butter, blend in 3 tablespoons flour, and cook the *roux* until it is golden. Gradually add the reduced stock, stirring constantly until the sauce is smooth.

Wash 2 pounds young spinach and remove the large stems. Cook the spinach, covered, in only the water that clings to the leaves, until it is wilted.

Beat 2 egg yolks into 1 cup cream and stir the cream slowly into the sauce. Add salt and pepper to taste. Heat the sauce but do not let it boil. Arrange alternate layers of chicken and spinach in a serving dish and pour the hot sauce over them.

Breast of Chicken with
Duchess Potato Mound   *Hühner auf dressierten Kartoffeln*

POACH 3 PLUMP 3-pound chickens, with the giblets, in salted water to cover until they are tender, about 40 minutes. Remove the giblets when they are done. Remove the skin from the cooked chickens and cut off the two breasts, or suprêmes. Each suprême may be cut in half, if they are large. Put the dark meat through the food chopper with the giblets. Reduce the stock to about 3 cups and strain it.

In a skillet, sauté the suprêmes in 1/2 cup butter, with salt and pepper to taste, until they are golden, but do not let them brown. Remove them. Blend 2 tablespoons flour with the butter in the skillet. Gradually stir in about 1 1/2 cups of the strained chicken stock, or enough to make a smooth sauce. Add the ground chicken and giblets and cook the sauce until it is thick. Season it with salt and pepper and stir in, off the heat, 1 beaten egg. Spread the chicken mixture in a buttered ovenproof serving dish.

Press duchess potatoes through a pastry bag into a pyramid on top of the chicken mixture. Arrange the suprêmes around the potatoes. Heat the chicken and potatoes thoroughly in a moderately hot oven (375° F.).

Melt 2 tablespoons butter, stir in gradually 2 tablespoons flour, and cook the *roux* gently over low heat until it is golden, stirring. Stir in slowly 1 cup strained chicken stock and cook the sauce until it is smooth and thick. Remove it from the heat and stir in 1 egg yolk beaten in 1/2 cup heavy cream. Serve the sauce separately. Garnish the serving dish with cooked broccoli flowerets or with cooked artichoke bottoms filled with cooked asparagus tips. Serves 12.

Paprikahühnchen   *Squab Chickens with Paprika Sauce*

WASH, DRY, and sprinkle with salt 6 plump squab chickens or Rock Cornish game hens, weighing about 1 pound each. Render 8 slices bacon, diced, in a large skillet or casserole, add 2 onions, grated, and stir in 2 tablespoons sweet Hungarian paprika. Heat the fat to sizzling again and in it sauté the birds, turning them frequently, until the fat is absorbed and the birds are lightly browned. Add 2 cups chicken stock, cover the pan, and simmer the birds for about 25 minutes. Turn them several times with two spoons, being careful not to pierce the skins. Add more hot chicken stock if necessary. Crush the birds' livers, add them to the sauce, cover the skillet, and steam all for 10 minutes longer. The birds should be cooked for 45 to 60 minutes in all, depending on their size. Stir in 1 1/2 cups sour cream— more, if more sauce is desired—and heat the sauce thoroughly. Adjust the seasoning with paprika and salt to taste.

Arrange the birds in a circle on a round platter and pile buttered broad noodles in the center. Sprinkle the birds with paprika, pour a little of the sauce around them, and serve the remainder separately. Serves 8.

Squab Chickens with Egg Sauce   *Junge Hühnchen mit Eiersauce*

SIMMER 6 SQUAB chickens or Rock Cornish game hens, each weighing 1 pound, in beef stock to cover until they are tender, about 30 minutes. Remove the skin and keep the chickens hot. Strain 1 cup of the cooking stock and add 1 tablespoon tarragon vinegar, or more, to taste. The mixture should be slightly tart. In the top of a double boiler over simmering water, beat 6 egg yolks creamy. Gradually beat in the vinegar and stock mixture and then as much of 1 cup of heavy cream as necessary to make a thick creamy sauce. Add salt to taste and 1/2 cup finely chopped chives. Pour the sauce over the hot chickens and cover them with paper-thin lemon slices dusted with minced parsley. Serve at once.

Roast Squabs   *Gebratene Tauben*

SAUTÉ 1 LARGE onion, chopped, in 1/2 cup butter for 10 minutes, or until it is transparent. Add 3 chicken livers and 6 squab livers and sauté them for about 5 minutes, turning them once. Mash the livers with a fork. Add 1/4 pound mushrooms, chopped fine, and enough dry bread crumbs to make sufficient stuffing for 6 squabs. Stir the stuffing well and add salt and pepper to taste. Wash and dry 6 squabs and stuff them with the mixture. Secure the openings with skewers. Cover the breast of each bird with a slice of bacon. Place the birds in a roasting pan, add 1/2 cup salted butter, and roast the birds in a hot oven (400° F.) for 45 minutes, basting them frequently with the pan juices.

Squabs in Casserole   *Tauben Sophia*

ARRANGE IN a casserole a layer of 3/4 cup each of grated onions and chopped mushrooms and 1/2 cup chopped parsley. Halve 6 squabs, add them, and season well with salt and pepper. Cover them with another layer of 3/4 cup each of onions and mushrooms and 1/2 cup parsley and

cover the vegetables with a layer of bacon slices. On the bacon lay the 6 livers. Add 1 1/2 cups white wine and simmer the birds, covered, until they are tender, about 50 minutes. Remove the livers and rice them through a sieve. Add 3 egg yolks and the juice of 1/2 lemon. Drain the juices from the casserole. Add the riced livers to these pan juices and enough hot sour cream to bind the mixture. Season it well with salt and pepper and pour it back over the squabs. Serve from the casserole.

Hühner nach Talleyrand Chicken Talleyrand

WIPE WITH a damp cloth 3 broilers, weighing 2 1/2 to 3 pounds each, and place them in 6 cups chicken stock, adding water, if necessary, to barely cover. Simmer the chickens for 10 minutes. Skim the stock and add a *bouquet garni* of a stalk of celery, 4 sprigs of parsley, a sprig of thyme and chervil, and a bay leaf. Cook the chickens for 25 minutes longer, or until they are tender. Remove them and keep them warm. Strain the stock.

In a saucepan, melt 3 tablespoons butter, blend in 3 tablespoons flour, and cook the *roux,* stirring, until it is golden. Gradually add 1 1/2 cups strained chicken stock, and cook the sauce, stirring constantly, until it is smooth and thick. Add 1 1/4 cups Madeira and reheat the sauce. Cut the chickens into serving pieces, add the pieces to the sauce, and heat them in it for 5 minutes.

Peel, core, and halve 16 small apples. Sprinkle the apples with 1/2 cup sugar and bake them on a buttered baking sheet in a hot oven (400° F.) for 10 minutes. Arrange the hot apples in a circle on a warm platter, alternating them with uniform rounds of cranberry jelly. Arrange the chicken pieces in the center and pour over them some of the sauce. Lay a round of smoked tongue, cut with a biscuit cutter, on each piece of chicken and place a slice of olive on each round of tongue. Serve the remaining sauce separately.

Or arrange hot spiced crab apples in a pyramid in the center of a platter. Decorate the apples with a few green leaves. Arrange the chicken pieces and tongue around the pyramid.

Spiced Crab Apples   *Gewürzte Holzäpfel*

COMBINE 1 1/2 cups sugar, 1/2 cup each of vinegar and water, the juice and grated rind of 1 lemon, 1/2 teaspoon each of ground clove and cinnamon, 1/2 tablespoon whole cloves, tied in a bag, and 1/2 cup grenadine. Simmer the syrup until it spins a light thread, or registers 225° F. on a candy thermometer. Remove the clove bag and add a few drops of red coloring, if desired. Cut out the blossom ends of 36 crab apples, but leave the stems. Polish the apples. Pile them in a deep baking dish, pour the hot syrup over them, and bake them in a moderate oven (350° F.), basting often, until they are tender but not soft, about 10 minutes. Serve hot or cold, with meat or poultry.

Broiled Chicken with
Cold Cucumber Cream Sauce   *Hühner mit Gurkensauce*

MIX 5 TABLESPOONS grated horseradish, 1 1/4 teaspoons each of brown mustard, tarragon vinegar, and confectioners' sugar, and 1 cucumber, peeled and minced. Fold in 1 1/4 cups cream, lightly beaten, and chill.

Split 3 broilers, weighing about 3 pounds each, and wipe them with a damp cloth. Season the halves with salt and pepper and broil them for 15 minutes on each side, about 5 inches from the heat. Baste them frequently with butter. Serve the broilers hot, with the chilled cucumber sauce.

Wiener Backhendl Hotel Schloss Dürnstein   *Viennese Fried Chicken*

WASH AND PAT dry 3 broilers, each weighing about 3 pounds, bring them to room temperature, and remove their skins. Sift together onto a wide plate or platter 3 cups flour with 2 teaspoons salt and in a bowl beat 4 eggs with 2 tablespoons oil. Have ready 3 cups bread crumbs on another wide plate or platter. Quarter the broilers and dip as many pieces as can be fried at one time into the flour mixture, then into the egg mixture, and finally into the crumbs. The pieces should be evenly coated. Shake off any loose crumbs.

In a deep fryer, heat shortening, 2 inches deep, to 370° F. Fry the dark meat chicken pieces for 10 to 12 minutes, turning them only once and touching them as little as possible with the fork. Transfer the pieces to a roasting pan and pour over them 1/4 cup melted butter. Put the pan in a slow oven (250° F.). Reheat the oil to 370° F. and fry the remaining chicken pieces until they are brown, about 8 to 10 minutes in all. As the pieces are completed, add them to the pan in the oven and pour hot melted butter over them. When the last pieces have been fried, bake all the chicken for 10 minutes longer.

Arrange the chicken on a large platter and garnish it with fried parsley. Accompany it with new peas, new potatoes, and cucumber salad. The chicken may also be eaten cold, with potato salad.

Geröstete Petersilie   *Fried Parsley*

WASH PARSLEY and dry it well. Drop the sprigs into deep hot fat (375° F.) and fry them for a few seconds. Drain the fried parsley on absorbent paper, salt it, and serve at once.

Zopf   *Creamed Chicken or Turkey in Pastry Braid*

SOFTEN 1 cup butter, add 2 cups flour, sifted, 1/2 cup sour cream, and a pinch of salt. Work these quickly into a smooth dough and let it rest for 1/2 hour in a cool place.

Divide the dough into 3 parts. Form each into a long sausagelike roll. Place the rolls side by side on a lightly buttered baking sheet and braid them loosely. Join the two ends of the braid to make a circle. Cover the top of the circle with wax paper and bake it in a moderate oven (350° F.)

for 1 hour. Remove the wax paper and paint the top of the braid with beaten egg. Return it to the oven for 15 minutes. Slide it onto a platter.

Heat 3 cups cooked chicken or turkey, cut into large pieces, with 2 cups cream sauce. Add 1 cup hot cooked green peas and salt and pepper to taste. Fill the pastry braid with the mixture and dust it with paprika.

Chicken Rounds   *Pikante Hühnerkugeln*

IN THE TOP of a double boiler, over boiling water, melt 3/4 cup butter and add 1 1/4 cups flour, stirring the mixture until it is smooth. Add 1 cup milk and cook the mixture, stirring constantly, until it is a thick paste. Add the chopped meat of a 2-pound poached chicken, 1/2 cup grated Parmesan, and 2 egg yolks, lightly beaten. Pour the mixture onto a cold surface and let it set. Cut out rounds with a cutter, dip them in seasoned beaten egg and then seasoned bread crumbs and fry the rounds in deep hot fat (375° F.) until they are golden, about 6 minutes.

Chicken and Almond Fritots   *Hühnerkrapfen*

COMBINE 1 1/2 cups chicken stock, 1/4 cup butter, and 1/2 teaspoon salt and bring the mixture to a boil. When it is boiling, add 1 cup flour, all at once, stirring vigorously until the mixture leaves the sides of the pan. Remove the pan from the heat and cool the mixture for 2 or 3 minutes. Add 4 eggs, one at a time, beating vigorously after each addition. Add 1 cup ground cooked chicken, 1/2 cup finely slivered blanched almonds, 1/2 small onion, minced, and salt and pepper to taste. Shape the mixture into balls with floured hands. Fry the balls in deep hot fat (375° F.) for 3 minutes, then raise the temperature to 390° F. and continue to cook the *fritots* until they are golden. Drain them on absorbent paper. Serve the *fritots* hot, with mayonnaise seasoned with finely chopped parsley.

Glazed Chicken with Apples   *Kalte Hühner Rada*

SLICE THE white meat of 2 freshly roasted chickens. Place the dark meat, skin, and bones in a kettle. Add 4 cups each of water and chicken stock and 1 cup brown sauce. Simmer the mixture until it is reduced by half. Strain the stock and add 1/4 cup finely chopped parsley and 1/4 teaspoon each of salt and pepper. There should be at least 4 cups of liquid. Soften 2 envelopes of gelatin in 1/2 cup Sherry and dissolve it in the hot stock. Cool the aspic. Pour 1 cup liquid aspic into a shallow pan and chill it until it is set. Chill the remaining aspic until it is partly set.

Peel, core, and halve crosswise 6 uniform apples. Arrange the halves, round side up, on a buttered baking sheet, sprinkle them with confectioners' sugar, and bake them in a hot oven (400° F.) until they are tender but not soft. Let them cool.

Arrange the slices of chicken in a ring around a chilled oval platter. Pour the partly thickened aspic over the chicken slices and chill the platter again until the aspic sets.

To serve, fill the center of the platter with the cold cooked apples. Garnish the chicken with 1/4 cup each of cold ham, tongue, and gherkins, all cut in julienne. Surround it with the remaining aspic, diced. Garnish the platter with sprigs of water cress. Serve very cold.

Schlossberghühnchen in Aspik   Squab Chickens in Aspic

IN A KETTLE, put 3 squab chickens, weighing about 3/4 pound each, or 3 Rock Cornish game hens, weighing about 1 pound each, 1 onion and 1/2 lemon, both sliced, 2 bay leaves, 6 peppercorns, 1/2 teaspoon salt, and 1 cup white wine and add water to cover. Poach the birds for 30 to 40 minutes, or until they are tender. Remove the skins from the birds, rub them with cut lemon to bleach them, and let them cool. Reduce the stock to about 5 1/2 cups and add up to 3/4 cup white wine, salt to taste, and 1 tablespoon tarragon vinegar. Strain the stock and clarify it with 2 egg whites. Soften 3 envelopes of gelatin in 3/4 cup white wine and dissolve the gelatin in the hot clarified stock. Let the aspic cool.

Halve 3 hard-cooked pullet eggs, rice the yolks, and mix with the mashed sautéed chicken livers. Fill the whites and re-form the eggs. Stuff each chicken with an egg. Oil 3 molds. Pour a 1/4-inch layer of cool but still liquid aspic into each mold and chill them. Put a stuffed chicken into each mold and fill the molds with aspic. Chill them until the aspic is firm. Unmold the chickens, which should be encased in aspic. Surround them with mounds of cauliflower flowerets and asparagus stalks, all cooked and chilled, and with slices of cucumber, mounds of potato salad with chives, and hollowed-out tomato halves filled with chive mayonnaise. Cut the molds in half and serve each guest half a bird.

Capon in Aspic
with Asparagus   *Kapaune auf Wiener Art mit Spargel*

SELECT TWO 5- to 5 1/2-pound capons, truss one of them, and rub them both with lemon juice. Roast the capons, covered, in a moderately slow oven (325° F.) for 2 hours, with 1 cup water, 4 tablespoons butter, and a *bouquet garni* made of 1 stalk celery, 1 sprig parsley, a bay leaf, and a pinch of thyme. Baste the birds often and add more water as needed. Remove the birds and let them cool. Strain the pan juices.

Combine the wing tips, necks, and giblets of the birds with salted water to cover and simmer them for about 1 1/2 hours, to make a strong stock. Strain the stock and add the strained pan juices. There should be about 5 cups of liquid. Let the stock cool and skim the fat from the top. Heat the stock and stir in 1 egg white, lightly beaten. Bring the stock to a boil, stirring constantly, cover the pan, and let the stock boil for 2 minutes. Remove the pan from the heat and let the stock stand in a warm place for 20 minutes, without stirring it. Return the stock to a boil and remove 1/2 cup of it to make white *chaud-froid* sauce. Soften 5 envelopes gelatin in 1 cup Sherry, remove the remaining stock from the heat, and add the gelatin mixture to it. Let the aspic cool, pour 2 cups of it into a shallow pan, and chill it to set in a thin sheet. Reserve the remaining 4 1/2 cups of stock to glaze the molds and capon.

Cut the meat from the untrussed bird, put it through the finest blade of the food chopper with 1 pound chicken livers, sautéed, 1 onion, chopped and browned, and the giblets, and add 1/2 cup dry Sherry, the grated rind of 1 lemon, and salt and pepper to taste. Add 1 cup of the *chaud-froid* sauce, 4 tablespoons butter, 3 sprigs of parsley, chopped, and a few drops of lemon juice. Correct the seasoning and chill.

Rinse 18 small timbale molds with cold water and coat the sides of the molds with a thin layer of aspic, as follows: Fill the molds with cool but still-liquid chicken aspic, place them in a pan of ice, and watch them carefully. There will not be enough liquid aspic to fill all the molds at one time. Fill as many as possible and, when the aspic sets on the chilled sides of the molds, pour the still-liquid center aspic into the remaining molds. Lay a pimiento cutout in each coated mold, chill the aspic until it sets firmly, and add 1/2 teaspoon white *chaud-froid* sauce to make a light background for the cutout. Fill the molds with the chicken capon and chill them again.

Skin the remaining capon and decorate it with pimiento cutouts affixed with aspic. With a pastry brush, paint the bird with layers of aspic, letting each layer set before applying the next.

Arrange the glazed bird at one end of a very large platter. Chop the thin sheet of aspic and garnish the platter with chopped aspic and parsley. Arrange in front of the bird small bunches of cold cooked asparagus that has been marinated in French dressing and simulate a red ribbon over each bunch with a band of pimiento. Unmold the timbales around the garnished platter. Serves 12.

Ente mit Ananas und Orangen   *Duck with Pineapple and Oranges*

WASH AND dry a 5- to 6-pound duckling. Season with salt and place a peeled orange in the cavity. Reserve the orange skin. Truss the duck. Roast it in a very hot oven (450° F.) for 15 minutes, lower the temperature to moderate (350° F.) and cook the duck for 1 to 1 1/2 hours longer, or until it is tender and brown.

Scrape the white pulp from the orange skin, scald the skin, and cut it into julienne. Halve 3 oranges, cut out the half segments, and reserve them. Scrape the shells and fill them with pineapple sherbet. Chill the filled shells in the freezer.

Remove the duck to a serving platter and keep it warm. Pour off all but 2 tablespoons fat from the roasting pan. Over direct heat, blend in 2 tablespoons flour, and cook the *roux* until it is golden brown. Add 3/4 cup brown stock and 1/2 cup dry white wine and cook the sauce, stirring constantly, until it is smooth. Add the orange segments and a small peeled pineapple, thinly sliced, and heat thoroughly.

Sprinkle the sherbet-filled orange shells with chopped mint. Surround the duck with them and with the pineapple slices, skimmed from the sauce. Serve the remaining sauce separately.

Obstgartenente   *Duck with Fruit*

WASH AND dry two 5-pound ducks and truss them. Roast them in a hot oven (400° F.) for 1 1/2 hours, or until the juices run clear when tested

with a fork. Simmer the wing tips, necks, and giblets in water to cover
for about 1 hour, before roasting the ducks, and baste them frequently
with this stock.

Remove the ducks from the oven and keep them hot. Pour off all but
2 tablespoons of the fat from the pan and add 1 cup each of chicken stock,
Curaçao, and orange juice. Reduce the liquid to 2 1/2 cups and strain it.
Add 1/4 cup each of grated orange rind and bitter orange marmalade.
Correct the seasoning and add 2 cups mixed sliced fruit: pineapple, grapes,
peaches, orange, and grapefruit. Simmer the fruit sauce for 2 minutes and
pour it around the ducks. *(Picture, page 284.)*

Serbian Duck   *Serbische Ente*

STUFF TWO 4-pound ducks with 2 onions, halved, and 2 apples, cored
and quartered, for each bird. Roast the ducks in a very hot oven (450° F.)
for 20 minutes, pour off all the fat, reduce the heat to moderate (325° F.),
and roast the ducks, pouring off the fat as it accumulates, for 45 minutes
longer. Roast the ducks for another 15 minutes, basting frequently with
3/4 cup orange juice.

Half cook about 3/4 cup rice in chicken consommé and spread it in
a large buttered casserole. Spread on the rice a layer of thin onion rings,
a layer of potato, thinly sliced, and finally a layer of thin green pepper
rings, seeded. Add salt and pepper to taste. Arrange the ducks in the
casserole and bake them in a moderate oven (350° F.) for 1/2 hour,
basting them frequently with butter.

Cold Duck Bristol   *Bristol-Ente*

TRUSS AND salt 3 ducks, weighing about 5 pounds each. Prick the skin
with a fork and roast the birds in a moderate oven (325° F.) for about
2 hours, or until tender. Cool them. Cut the breasts from the 3 ducks,
cut the remaining meat and skin from 1 duck, and discard the carcass.

Sauté 2 tablespoons chopped onion in 1 tablespoon butter until it is
transparent, remove it from the pan, and drain it well. Add 1 1/2 tablespoons butter to the pan and sauté 1 pound mushrooms, coarsely chopped,
until they are soft. Drain the sautéed mushrooms. Add to the pan 2 pounds
chicken livers and the 3 duck livers and sauté them in the butter until

they are tender, adding more butter if necessary. Drain the livers. Squeeze 2 oranges, reserving the juice. Scrape the white pulp from the inside of the orange rinds. Combine the duck meat cut from the carcass, the skin from the 6 breasts, the chicken and duck livers, the mushrooms and onions, 2 1/2 ounces liver paste, the 2 orange rinds, and 2 tablespoons chopped parsley. Put the mixture through the finest blade of the food chopper twice, to obtain a smooth paste. Moisten the paste with equal parts of orange juice and Sherry. Adjust the seasoning with salt and pepper and add more Sherry to taste. The paste should not be too dry, but it must be stiff enough to hold its shape. Peel and slice 3 truffles. Cut heart or diamond shapes out of the largest slices. Chop the smaller slices and scraps and add them to the paste.

Slice the 6 breasts to make 12 thin slices of duck and spread the slices smoothly with the paste. Fill the 4 cavities from which the duck breasts were removed with the remaining paste, building up the filling generously to cover the breast bones. Decorate the re-formed duck breasts and the sliced breasts with the truffle cutouts and chill the 2 birds and the breasts. Skim the fat from the juices in the roasting pan and add enough bouillon to make 3 cups liquid. Reheat the liquid, add enough *glace de viande,* or extract, to color it golden, about 1/2 teaspoon, and Sherry to taste, and bring the mixture to a boil. Soften 2 envelopes of gelatin in 1/2 cup water. Remove the roasting pan from the heat and dissolve the softened gelatin in the liquid, stirring. Let the aspic cool and thicken somewhat. Paint the two ducks and the slices of duck breast masked with paste with a layer of the cool aspic. Use a pastry brush and keep the aspic warm enough to flow but not to run off the birds. Paint the ducks with several layers of aspic, until they are heavily coated. Decorate each with an attelet threaded with 2 roses cut from cooked beets. Place them on serving platters and surround them with the glazed breasts. Pour the remaining aspic in a thin layer around the ducks and let it set. Hollow out half oranges, pink the edges, and fill the halves with lingonberries. Set the oranges between the glazed breasts. Serve a spoonful of the paste from the re-formed birds with each slice of breast meat. Serves 12.

Perlhühner Smetana   *Guinea Hens in Sour Cream*

CLEAN 2 GUINEA hens, weighing about 2 pounds each. Put the birds in a roasting pan with 3/4 cup butter and 1 onion, sliced, and roast them in a moderate oven (350° F.) for 45 minutes per pound. Baste frequently with melted butter. Pour over them 1/2 cup warm sour cream and add a pinch of powdered juniper berries. Roast them, basting with additional cream, for 20 minutes longer, or until they are tender. Remove the skin and place the birds on a warm platter. Strain the sauce.

Simmer 1/2 pound button mushrooms in water to cover with a squeeze of lemon juice and 1/4 teaspoon salt until they are tender. Drain the mushrooms and add them to the sauce. Add warm sour cream to the sauce, if necessary. Carve the birds and pour the sauce over them. Serve with buttered noodles, lingonberries, and Brussels sprouts sprinkled with bread crumbs browned in butter.

Roast Guinea Hens with Water Cress   *Perlhühner mit Kresse*

CLEAN 3 GUINEA hens, weighing about 2 pounds each, season them with salt, and tie thick bacon slices over their breasts. Simmer the wing tips and giblets in salted water for 1 1/2 hours. Strain the stock.

Rub the birds thoroughly with 3/4 cup butter and roast them in an open pan in a hot oven (400° F.) for 1/2 hour, basting them frequently. Add a little of the strained giblet stock and roast the birds in a moderate oven (350° F.) for 3/4 hour, or until they are tender. Remove the birds and keep them warm. Add 2 tablespoons flour to the fat in the pan and stir the *roux* until it is golden. Add 1 1/2 cups of the giblet stock, stirring constantly. Add 1/2 cup melted currant jelly and correct the seasoning. Keep the sauce warm. Sauté 1 cup bread crumbs in 4 table-spoons butter. Remove the bacon and skin from the birds, carve them, and arrange them on a serving platter around a bunch of crisp water cress. Pour a little sauce over the birds and sprinkle them with the crumbs. Rice the livers from the giblet stock into the remaining sauce and serve it separately.

Guinea Hens with Sauerkraut   *Perlhühner mit Sauerkraut*

CLEAN 2 GUINEA hens, weighing about 2 pounds each, season them with salt and pepper, and marinate them for 8 hours in 1/2 bottle of white wine. Turn them frequently. Drain and dry the birds. Lard the thickest part of each thigh with 3 strips of larding pork and tie slices of larding pork over the breasts. Truss the birds and roast them in a moderate oven (325° F.) for 1 1/4 to 1 1/2 hours, until they are tender and brown. Baste them with 1/4 cup butter until they start to take on color, remove the larding strips, then baste them frequently with sour cream, using about 2 cups in all.

Simmer 2 pounds sauerkraut in water to cover with 1 tablespoon caraway seeds for 1 hour. Drain it, reserving the cooking liquor. Melt 2 tablespoons butter, blend in 2 tablespoons flour, and cook the *roux* slowly over low heat, stirring, until it browns. Add 1/2 cup of the sauerkraut liquor. Stir the sauce until it is smooth, strain it over the sauerkraut, and stir it in. Arrange the sauerkraut on a platter. Remove the slices of larding pork and carve the guinea hens. Lay the pieces on the sauerkraut.

Strain the juices in the roasting pan, add 1/2 cup salted heavy cream, half whipped, and pour the sauce over the birds. Serve them with a compote of stewed apples and plums.

Perlhühner oder Fasan mit Ananas

*Guinea Hens
or Pheasant
with Pineapple*

CLEAN 3 PLUMP young birds, weighing about 2 pounds each, salt them moderately, and truss them. Tie a thin slice of salt pork over the breast of each bird. Melt 1 generous cup butter in a deep casserole and add the birds. Roast them in a moderate oven (350° F.) for 1/2 hour, basting them frequently with the butter. Remove the salt pork and roast the birds until the breasts are brown and the meat is tender, about 1 hour longer.

Heat 12 slices of fresh pineapple in 1 cup pineapple juice and 1 1/2 cups white wine. Remove the birds and cover them with foil to keep them hot. Drain half the fat from the casserole and add 3/4 cup strong brown stock and the hot pineapple juice and white wine. Cook the sauce rapidly over direct heat until it is reduced by one-half and add salt to taste.

Arrange the warm pineapple slices in the wine sauce in the casserole, carve the birds, and return them to the sauce. Serve from the casserole and serve frozen horseradish cream separately. Or unmold frozen horseradish cream on a platter and arrange the carved birds and pineapple slices around the cream on a bed of parsley. Serve the wine sauce separately.

Roast Goose with Potato and Onion Stuffing $\qquad$ *Gefüllte Gans*

COOK 8 LARGE peeled potatoes in boiling salted water to cover for 25 minutes. Drain them and dry them out well by shaking the pan over the heat until all the moisture has evaporated. Rice them. Cook 1 pound small peeled white onions in boiling salted water for 10 minutes. Drain them and add them to the riced potatoes. Add 1/4 cup cream, 2 table-spoons butter, 1 teaspoon minced sage, and salt and pepper to taste. The mixture should be very dry.

Wash and dry a 10-pound goose. Rub the goose inside and out with salt and pepper and stuff it with the potato mixture. Sew up the opening. Turn the skin of the neck backward and secure it with a small skewer. Twist the wings back and skewer the thighs. Prick the bird well with a fork. Place it on a rack in a roasting pan, add 1 cup hot water, and roast it in a moderately hot oven (375° F.) for 20 to 25 minutes per pound, or until it is brown and almost cooked, basting it frequently.

Simmer the giblets and neck in water to cover with 1 small onion, a few celery leaves, 1/2 teaspoon salt, and pepper to taste for 1 hour. Add the liver and cook for 30 minutes longer. Strain the stock and chop the giblets and liver fine.

Combine 1 cup Port and 2 teaspoons brown mustard and add salt to taste. Remove the cooked goose from the oven and pour the Port into it through the neck opening, saturating the stuffing. Return the goose to the oven for 10 minutes longer. Transfer it to a platter, remove the skewers and threads, and keep it warm.

Skim most of the fat from the roasting pan and stir in 3 tablespoons flour. Gradually add the giblet stock and a little water, if necessary, to make 2 1/2 cups liquid in all, stirring constantly and scraping the brown bits from the bottom and sides of the pan. Add the chopped giblets and simmer the sauce for 5 minutes. Serve it separately. Accompany the roast goose with roasted apples and green peas.

Christmas Goose
with Apple Stuffing $\qquad$ *Gebratene Gans mit Äpfeln*

SOAK 18 TO 20 PRUNES overnight in Port to cover. Simmer them in the Port for 20 minutes, or until the stones can be easily removed. Stone the prunes and add 8 apples, peeled, cored, and quartered, and sugar to taste.

Wash and dry a 10- to 12-pound goose and rub the cavity with 1 tablespoon salt. Stuff the goose with the apple mixture and sew up the opening. Rub the bird with 1 tablespoon salt, turn the skin of the neck backward, and secure it with a small skewer. Twist the wings back and truss the thighs. Prick the bird well with a fork and place it on a rack in a roasting pan. Spread 1 tablespoon butter over the breast, add 1 cup boiling water, and roast the goose in a moderately hot oven (375° F.), allowing 20 to 25 minutes per pound, basting it frequently. Turn the goose until it is light brown on all sides. Remove the threads and skewers and transfer the goose to a large serving platter. Keep it warm.

Simmer the heart and the gizzard in cold water to cover with 1 onion and salt to taste for 2 hours. Strain the stock and chop the heart and the gizzard. Sauté the liver in butter and chop it. Pour off all but 1/4 cup of the fat in the roasting pan and add 3 tablespoons flour. Cook the sauce over low heat, stirring, for 5 minutes. Gradually add 2 1/2 cups giblet stock and cook the sauce 5 minutes longer. Add the chopped giblets. Serve the sauce separately.

Garnish the goose with twelve 3-inch-round toasted bread croutes onto which seasoned carrot purée has been piped through a pastry bag fitted with a plain tip. Sprinkle the purée with 1/4 cup minced fresh mint. If desired, accompany the goose with sliced cucumbers sautéed in butter and with molded chestnut purée. Surround the chestnut mold with cinnamon sticks and with cooked peach halves. *(Picture, page 285.)*

Gebratene Gans mit Stachelbeeren

Roast Goose with Gooseberry Stuffing

CLEAN 3 CUPS gooseberries and combine them with 1/2 cup each of sugar and butter and enough water to cover. Bring the gooseberries to a boil, drain them, and force them through a sieve. Add 2 tablespoons grated orange rind. Prepare a goose, stuff it with the mixture, and roast it, as for roast goose with apple stuffing.

Sauce für gebratene Gans

Sauce for Roast Goose

IN THE TOP of a double boiler, combine 1 cup Port, 1/4 cup brown mustard, the juice and grated rind of 2 lemons, and a pinch of cayenne pepper. Cook the sauce over boiling water until it is thoroughly heated. Serve it with roast goose.

Bulgarian Goose with Rice Stuffing — Gans auf bulgarische Art

SAUTÉ 1 ONION, chopped, in 2 tablespoons butter until it is puffed and transparent. Add 1 cup rice and the heart, liver, and gizzard of the goose, all finely chopped, and sauté the mixture until all is coated with butter. Add 1 cup hot water. Simmer the rice until it is just tender but not soft, adding more hot water when necessary. Add 1/2 cup each of chopped parsley and raisins, 1 teaspoon each of sugar and caraway seeds, and salt and pepper to taste.

Wash and dry a 10-pound goose. Rub the goose inside and out with salt and stuff it with the rice mixture. Pour 1/2 cup chicken stock over the stuffing in the goose and sew the opening. Rub the goose with fat. Turn the skin of the neck backward and secure it with a skewer. Twist the wings back and skewer the thighs. Sprinkle the bird with paprika and prick it well with a fork. Place it on a rack in a roasting pan, add 1 cup water, and roast the bird in a moderately hot oven (375° F.) for 20 to 25 minutes per pound. Baste it with 1 more cup of water. Serve with stewed apples and red cabbage.

Roast Goose with Cucumber Salad — Pester Gans

SALT THE cavity of a 10-pound goose. Lay fresh marjoram leaves on 1 or 2 rolls and stuff the goose with the rolls, to soak up some of the fat. Sew up and skewer the goose and roast it as for roast goose with apple stuffing, basting it every 10 minutes for the first 45 minutes, then rubbing it with bacon rind every 15 minutes. Serve with the following salad.

Slice 4 cucumbers thinly, sprinkle them with 1 tablespoon salt, shake them well, and weight them with a plate. Let them stand for 15 minutes, to draw out the moisture. Drain them well, salt them again moderately, let them stand for 15 minutes longer, and drain them again. Pour over them 3/4 cup white wine vinegar and dust them with sweet paprika. Let rest for 4 hours. Add 2 tablespoons chopped dill and sour cream to bind.

Roast Turkey with Turkish Stuffing — Indian mit türkischer Fülle

COMBINE THE neck and gizzard of the turkey, 1 carrot, 1 onion, sliced, 1 clove of garlic, 1/2 bay leaf, 1/2 teaspoon salt, and 4 peppercorns and add 4 cups water. Simmer the mixture for 1 hour, or until the liquid is reduced by half. Skim and strain the giblet stock.

Sauté 1 onion, finely chopped, in 6 tablespoons butter until it is golden. Add 1/2 cup blanched slivered almonds and cook the mixture for 3 minutes. Add 1 cup rice and cook for 5 minutes longer. Add the warm stock and 1/2 cup currants. Simmer the rice mixture, covered, until all the stock is absorbed. Sauté the turkey heart and liver, both chopped, in 1 tablespoon butter for a few minutes and add 1 teaspoon chopped dill and 4 teaspoons tomato paste. Add this mixture to the rice.

Wash and dry a 10-pound turkey and rub the body cavity well with salt. Fill the body and neck cavities loosely with the rice stuffing and sew up the openings or secure them with skewers. Truss and place breast up in a roasting pan. Spread it with softened butter, dip a cloth in melted butter, and lay it over the bird. Roast the turkey in a moderate oven (325° F.) for about 25 minutes per pound, basting it every half hour with the pan juices and a little stock, if necessary. Remove the cloth 1/2 hour before the turkey is done.

Indian auf Teufels Art   *Deviled Turkey*

COAT 6 COLD roast turkey slices heavily with about 1/2 cup brown mustard. Dust salt and a pinch of cayenne over the mustard and broil the turkey slices until they are hot. In a saucepan, combine 1 cup vinegar, 1/2 cup brown sauce, 6 shallots or 2 onions, chopped, 1/4 cup tomato paste, 1 tablespoon butter, 1 teaspoon meat extract, 1/4 teaspoon powdered clove, 2 bay leaves, and 1 clove of garlic, crushed. Simmer the sauce for 10 minutes and strain it. Pour it over the turkey slices.

Game and Game Birds

Wildbret und -geflügel

BOYS SEEMED to stay younger longer in Vienna than anywhere else, possibly because their parents kept them in short trousers and caps until they had distinct shadows on their upper lips. Then suddenly they grew mustaches and turned into men of dignity and distinction overnight. Many of them were "Herr Doktors" when they graduated and, in no time at all, they owned otter- or caracul-trimmed fur-lined black winter coats; youth, such as it had been, was over. They dressed conservatively and became completely ageless until their mustaches turned white, a time that they sometimes delayed with the help of the Herr Friseur, the barber.

It was always surprising to see these respected pillars of Viennese society bring out their skates and perform figure eights and pirouettes all over the Viennese skating rinks, or to watch them play excellent tennis when the rinks reverted back to courts. They all skied with a passion, climbed mountains, and "faltbooted" on the Danube; they raced cars and rode superbly in the Concours Hippique, the horseshow. They followed *Fussball* madly, rode across the plains of Hungary after wild boar, and proved, under their wing collars and Prince Albert coats, to be excellent sportsmen. They had only to put on their *Lederhosen,* their leather pants, to be splendid shots.

Every erudite Herr Doktor or Professor maintained an Argus or Hektor or even a Liesel, somewhere out in the country, a loyal dog who spent the year waiting for his or her master to come out from Vienna to shoot. These gentlemen owned or leased game preserves or they knew a game warden. Sometimes they had a cousin who had a *Jagdschloss,* a hunting seat, or at least a chalet or *Hütte* from which the *Gemse,* the chamois, and the

247

Auerhahn, the heath cock, could be stalked. Whatever it was he hunted, Herr Hofrat or Herr Direktor always came back to Vienna with a feather or a beard for his hat. If his *Wild* was neither feathered nor bearded, it could at least be relied upon to be toothed, and in that case Herr Hofrat had its best tooth set in a little silver frame and pinned to the back of his hunting hat from Habig.

After enjoying their sport, the Herr Direktors returned to their homes in Vienna and to their Prince Alberts and their dignified pursuit of life. While they worked in their *Bureaus* and sat at important meetings, their game was hanging and aging to perfection in the country. At exactly the right moment, Herr Direktor's properly prepared and perfectly aged game would follow him to Vienna, because the fruits of the chase always ended on the table. The peasant counted on a hare for his *Hasenpfeffer* no less seriously than Herr Direktor counted on the *Rehrücken,* the venison, and the pheasant for his dinner parties. The fields, forests, and streams of Austria gave up their game for sport but also for table.

As soon as the game arrived, it was put into a marinade, and, if it was big enough, guests were invited to share the pleasure of eating it. In spite of the fact that game was once more available in Austria than in most countries, all game remained a delicacy and everyone looked forward to the racks of venison and the saddles of hare that would follow the gentlemen home after their hunting trips.

The Viennese were always ready to try new combinations, new marinades, and new methods, but at heart they preferred juniper berries and sour cream to everything else that they could combine with game. They always ate *Preisselbeeren,* lingonberries, as a garnish, and usually accompanied the meat with red cabbage and flour dumplings. They saved their best and their second-best bottles of red wine, the first to drink with their game, the second to marinate and then cook it in and they often threw in a little of their oldest brandy. They always larded game and, with practice, they could produce beautiful geometric patterns with the larding strips. A braid of lard would run along the spine of a saddle of venison to protect it from too much heat and a hare would look a little like a porcupine with beautiful double rows of larding. Every little trimming and scrap of meat was saved to go into the game ragout or pie that traditionally marked the end of the season.

Game birds were equally popular in Vienna and were wisely prepared according to their age. If Herr Hofrat had the misfortune to come home with a scrawny old pheasant, it went into a soup pot and ended up producing a soup, a little pâté, and part of the stuffing for a younger and a better bird. If the arrival of young and plump pheasant followed his return home, the cook carefully wrapped the birds in larding pork, larded their legs in triple rows, and did everything possible to keep them moist and tender. Saturated in sour cream, or basted constantly with butter, they always came to the table fit for a Viennese.

Jugged Hare  *Hasenpfeffer*

CLEAN 2 HARES, reserving the livers and blood. Remove the saddles and reserve them for roasting. Disjoint the front and back legs and place them in a deep casserole with the meat from the neck and shoulders. Add 4 onions, sliced, 4 shallots, chopped, 4 sprigs of parsley, 2 cloves of garlic, crushed, half a bay leaf, 1 teaspoon salt, and 1/4 teaspoon each of thyme, rosemary, and pepper. Add enough red Bordeaux wine to cover and 1/2 cup wine vinegar. Cover the casserole and let the meat marinate at room temperature for 24 hours.

Drain the meat well, pat it dry and dredge it with flour. Put it in a large skillet with 12 small peeled onions, 1/2 pound lean bacon, diced, and 2 tablespoons butter. Sauté the mixture until the onions are golden, stirring in 2 tablespoons flour. Transfer meat and onions to the marinade in the casserole and add 1/2 cup strong beef stock and 2 tablespoons brandy. Cover the casserole and simmer the meat for 1 1/2 hours. Add 1/4 cup each of kirsch and melted currant jelly and the reserved livers and blood. Simmer the *Hasenpfeffer* for 15 minutes more and correct the seasoning. Serve from the casserole and accompany with noodles, dumplings, or *Spätzle*. Serves 8.

Warm sour cream may be added to the sauce 15 minutes before serving.

Roast Hare with
Sour Cream Sauce  *Hasenbraten mit Rahmsauce*

LARD A SADDLE of hare well with strips of larding pork, rub it with 1 teaspoon salt and 1/2 teaspoon paprika, and sprinkle it generously with flour. Brown the hare on all sides in 1/2 cup butter in a roasting pan. Pour over it 1 cup hot sour cream and add to the pan 1/2 cup strong beef stock,

1/4 cup vinegar, 1 bay leaf, 4 crushed juniper berries, and 1/2 teaspoon.
thyme. Roast the meat in a moderately hot oven (375° F.) for about
1 hour, or until it is tender. The roasting time will vary somewhat, depending on the age of the hare. The meat should be pink and juicy. Baste
the meat frequently and add more sour cream if necessary. Transfer the
meat to a platter and keep it hot. Strain the pan juices and add the juice
of 1/2 lemon, 2 tablespoons small capers, a pinch of sugar, and enough
hot sour cream to make 2 cups of sauce. Stir in 1 tablespoon butter kneaded
with 2 teaspoons flour and bring the sauce to a boil. Serve it separately.

Rehrücken Smetana   *Saddle of Venison Smetana*

POUR OVER a well-aged saddle of venison the juice of 1 lemon and 1/2
cup olive oil and let the meat marinate for 3 hours. Lard the venison in
even rows with strips of larding pork 2 inches long. For a small saddle,
2 rows of larding on each side of the top will be enough. Let the ends
of the strips project in 8 rows.

Crush 1 teaspoon juniper berries with 1 teaspoon salt and rub the
mixture into the meat. Lay the venison, larded side down, in a roasting
pan, add 1 onion, sliced and separated into rings, a 3-inch curl of lemon
peel, and 1/2 cup vinegar, and pour 1/2 cup simmering melted butter over
the meat. Roast the venison for 15 minutes in a moderate oven (350° F.),
pour over it 1 cup hot sour cream, and roast it for 45 minutes more,
basting it frequently. Add 1/2 cup more hot sour cream during the roasting.
Turn the venison, dust it with 2 tablespoons flour, and continue to roast
the meat, basting, until it is brown and the lard is crisped. Allow 20 minutes per pound for medium rare.

Transfer the venison to a serving platter, pour over it 1/4 cup hot
melted butter, and keep the meat hot. Strain the pan juices, correct the
seasoning, and stir in enough hot *crème fraîche* to make 1 1/2 cups sauce.
Pour over the meat 1/2 cup of sauce and serve the remaining sauce separately. Accompany the venison with red cabbage and dumplings.

Rehrücken Andreas   *Saddle of Venison Andreas*

MARINATE A WELL-AGED full-length saddle of venison for 24 hours in
1 bottle red wine with 1 cup Calvados, 2 ounces brandy, 3 bay leaves,

6 juniper berries, 4 peppercorns, and 3 sprigs each of tarragon and dill. Drain it well. Lard it in 2 double rows with strips of larding pork and lay a braid of larding pork strips along the spine. Strain the marinade. Roast the saddle in a very hot oven (500° F.) for 5 minutes, reduce the heat to 450° F., and roast it for 1 hour, basting every 6 minutes with 1/2 cup melted butter and the pan juices. Reduce the heat to hot (400° F.) and roast the saddle until it is done to taste, about 30 minutes longer, basting every 10 minutes.

Place the saddle on a hot platter and keep it hot. Pour off all but 1/2 cup of the pan juices. Place the pan over low heat and add 1 cup of the strained marinade, 1/2 cup red wine, and 2 cups warm sour cream into which 1 tablespoon flour has been stirred. Cook, stirring constantly, until the sauce is smooth and add salt to taste. Serve it separately. Simmer 24 mushroom caps in salted water to cover with 2 tablespoons butter and the juice of 1/2 lemon until they are tender, about 10 minutes. Drain them and fill them with liver paste. Lay on each mushroom a walnut half sautéed in butter and brush with meat glaze. Accompany with potato dumplings, red cabbage with apples, and stewed lingonberries sprinkled with slivered orange rind.

Saddle of Venison with Port Wine   *Rehrücken Rudolf*

MARINATE AND lard a saddle of venison as for *Rehrücken Andreas* and lay it on a bed of 3 carrots and 3 onions, all sliced. Add 1/2 cup butter and roast the venison in a very hot oven (500° F.) for 10 minutes. Reduce the heat to hot (400° F.) and roast for 2 hours, or until the meat is done, basting it every 10 minutes with the pan juices and warm Port, using 1 to 1 1/2 cups Port in all. Remove the saddle and keep it hot. Skim the fat from the pan and add 1 cup melted currant jelly and 1 tablespoon sugar mixed with 1/4 teaspoon each of ground cinnamon and cloves. Add salt and pepper to taste and cook the sauce 5 minutes longer. Serve with the venison.

Leg of Venison in Red Wine   *Rehschlegel in Rotwein*

CUT LARDING pork into 3-inch strips and sprinkle the strips with tarragon, parsley, and onion, all finely minced. Lard a well-aged leg of venison generously with the seasoned strips. Dust the venison with 2 tablespoons flour and, in a large kettle, brown it on all sides in 1/4 cup lard over high heat. Add 2 carrots and 2 onions, both sliced, 2 celery stalks, 3 sprigs of parsley, a slice of lemon, 2 bay leaves, 1 teaspoon salt, 6 peppercorns, 6 cloves, and 1/2 teaspoon thyme. Pour in 1 bottle red wine, cover the kettle tightly, and braise the venison in a moderate oven (350° F.) about 2 hours, or until it is tender, depending on the size and age of the meat. Turn it once after the first hour. Transfer the meat to a platter and keep it hot. Strain the juices in the kettle, correct the seasoning, and serve the sauce separately. Serve also cold game sauce. Serves 8.

Rehpfeffer   *Stewed Venison*

MARINATE 4 TO 5 pounds scraps and small cuts of venison in 1 1/2 cups red wine and 1 cup each of vinegar and water with 1 onion stuck with 3 cloves, 1 carrot, sliced, 3 sprigs of tarragon, 6 juniper berries, and 1 tablespoon salt for 3 days in summer and 5 days in winter. Drain the meat well. Sauté it in 3 tablespoons butter with 1/4 cup diced bacon until it is browned. Add enough liquid to half cover the meat, using half marinade and half strong beef stock and simmer it, covered, for 1/2 hour.

Brown 3 tablespoons butter over low heat, stir in 6 tablespoons flour, and gradually add 1/4 cup warm red wine, stirring. Whisk the sauce until it is smooth and gradually add 1/2 cup each of marinade and beef stock, stirring constantly. Add the sauce to the *Rehpfeffer* and add salt and pepper to taste and 1 teaspoon sugar. Simmer the stew, covered, for 1 1/2 hours. If possible add 1 cup venison blood at the last and reheat the stew without boiling. Serve with potato dumplings and glazed onions.

Rehrücken Hotel Goldener Hirsch   *Saddle of Venison*

REMOVE THE 2 *loins* from a saddle of venison. Brown the bones in half butter and oil, deglaze the pan with water, and reserve the cooking liquid. Marinate the loins in 1 cup light brandy, 1/2 cup olive oil, the juice of 2 lemons, 1 onion and 1 carrot, both sliced, 4 shallots, 3 sprigs of parsley and thyme, 4 peppercorns and 4 cloves, turning them frequently, for 12 hours. Remove the loins, pat them dry, and salt them. Strain the marinade and reserve 1 cup of it.

Lay 3 thin slices of bacon in a roasting pan, scatter 1 onion, thinly sliced, over the slices, and add 1/4 cup each of butter and oil and the loins. Set the pan in a very hot oven (450° F.), reduce the heat to moderate (350° F.), and roast the loins, turning them frequently, for about 15 minutes per pound, or until they are browned on the outside but still rare within.

Transfer the loins to a platter and keep them warm. Strain the pan juices into the marinade and add the cooking liquid from the bones and 1 cup dry red wine. Reduce the sauce over high heat and add 2 tablespoons each of cream and currant jelly. Correct the seasoning, pour a little of the sauce over the loins, and serve the remaining sauce separately. Serve each guest 4 thin slices of the venison and sliced button mushrooms, sautéed in butter, *Dukaten Kartoffeln*—potatoes thickly sliced, cut into rounds the size of ducats and browned in butter—and red cabbage balls made by compressing into balls 1/4-cup portions of steamed red cabbage. *(Picture, page 280.)*

Fruit Garnish for Game — Obstbeilage zu Wild

IN THE TOP of a double boiler over boiling water stir 1/2 teaspoon each of cinnamon and ground cloves with 2 tablespoons sugar and 1 1/2 glasses each of Port and red currant jelly until the jelly is melted. Pour the hot sauce over 4 cups hulled strawberries, pitted black cherries, or well-drained stewed peach halves. Serve with any game dish.

Partridge in Casserole — Rebhühner mit Kraut

CLEAN 6 PARTRIDGE and truss them. Tie strips of bacon over the breasts and season the birds with salt to taste. In a saucepan melt 6 tablespoons butter, brown the partridge, and transfer them to a casserole. Add 2 cups mushrooms, sliced, 1 cup carrots and 1 turnip, both diced, and 1 cup stock. Cover the casserole and place it in a hot oven (400° F.) for 60 to 70 minutes, or until the birds are done.

Stir 2 tablespoons flour into the butter in the pan in which the birds were browned, and gradually add 1/2 cup stock and 1 teaspoon meat glaze. Cook, stirring constantly, until the sauce thickens. Add 1/2 cup

Port. Skim the fat from the casserole, remove the bacon and trussing strings, and pour the sauce over the birds. Serve the partridge with sauerkraut.

Rebhühner mit Schinken   *Partridge with Ham*

WRAP THE breasts of 6 plump partridge with 2 slices of bacon each. Truss the partridge and rub them well with 3 tablespoons butter. Roast them in a moderate oven (350° F.), covered, for 40 minutes. Remove the bacon and strings.

Arrange 6 slices of ham, cut 1/4 inch thick, in the bottom of a casserole, and lay 1 carrot and 1 onion, both finely sliced, over the ham. Lay the partridge on this bed, pour over 2 cups stock, and cover all with 1 cabbage, cut into wedges and parboiled for 15 minutes. Cover the casserole and bake in a moderately hot oven (375° F.) for 30 minutes. Drain off the stock, adding extra stock, if necessary, to make 2 cups.

Melt 3 tablespoons butter in a saucepan, blend in 3 tablespoons flour, and cook the *roux* gently for a few minutes. Blend in carefully the 2 cups stock and cook until very hot, stirring constantly to make a light brown gravy. Correct the seasoning and pour the sauce over the birds. Serve hot with browned potatoes and lingonberries.

*Partridge
with Chestnuts*

Brüsseler Rebhühner mit Kastanien

SALT AND PEPPER 6 partridge and truss them. Tie larding pork or bacon over their breasts and roast in a preheated moderate oven (350° F.) for 40 minutes, on a bed of 1/2 cup each of chopped onions and carrots with 1 cup game or beef stock. Baste them every 5 minutes with melted butter, using 1/2 cup butter in all. Remove the larding pork or bacon and roast in a preheated very hot oven (425° F.) for 20 minutes longer, or until they are golden, basting every 10 minutes. Remove them and keep them hot in a casserole. Strain and skim the pan juices. Add 1/2 cup each of game or beef stock and Madeira and simmer the sauce for 15 minutes. Combine 1 pound Brussels sprouts, cooked in salted water and drained, and 18 large cooked chestnuts. Sprinkle them with 2 tablespoons sugar and glaze them in 1/4 cup butter, shaking the pan until the sprouts and chestnuts are glossy. Remove the strings from the partridge, add the sprouts and chestnuts to the casserole, and pour over all the hot sauce. Serve the birds from the casserole.

Viennese Partridge

Wiener Rebhühner

WRAP 6 SMALL cleaned and salted partridge in 6 large cabbage leaves and tie them securely with string. Lay them in a casserole with 3 cups finely chopped onions and 3/4 cup butter. Add 2 teaspoons salt and 1/4 teaspoon pepper and roast them, covered, for 45 minutes in a moderately hot oven (375° F.). Pour over the birds 1 cup sour cream beaten with 2 tablespoons flour and cook them 15 to 20 minutes longer, or until they are tender. Remove the string and serve the birds from the casserole.

Chukar Partridge

Chukar Rebhühner

CLEAN 6 PLUMP chukar partridge and rub inside and out with 1/3 cup brandy. Mix together 3/4 loaf of stale white bread, ground, the grated rind and juice of 1 lemon, 1/3 cup melted butter, 1 well-beaten egg, and salt and pepper to taste. Blend the stuffing thoroughly, divide it into 6 portions, and fill the cavities. Rub the birds well with butter, place them in a casserole, and sprinkle them with 1/3 cup Sherry.

Place the giblets, reserving the livers, in 1 1/2 cups salted water and simmer them until they are tender. Add 3/4 cup giblet stock to the casserole, reserving the rest, and add the reserved livers, and 1/3 cup celery, chopped. Cover the casserole and cook the birds in a moderately slow oven (325° F.) for 2 1/4 hours, basting frequently, and adding 1/3 cup Sherry after the first hour. Just before serving, add the remaining giblet stock, 1/3 cup Sherry, 1 1/2 tablespoons sour cream, and 2 teaspoons red currant jelly. Sauté 1 cup button mushrooms in butter. Add them to the casserole, deglaze the skillet with 1/4 cup water, and add this liquid. Heat the casserole and serve.

Fasan in Orangen   Mandarin Oranges with Pheasant Mousse

SELECT 16 MANDARIN oranges or any small oranges. Cut 1/4-inch slice from the top of each orange and scoop out the pulp with a pointed spoon.

Simmer the pheasant giblets in salted water to cover for about an hour, to make a stock. Remove the giblets and reduce the stock to half its original quantity.

Tie strips of bacon or larding pork over the breasts of 3 pheasants and roast them in a moderate oven (350° F.) for about 50 minutes, or until they are tender. Remove the larding pork or bacon, cool the pheasant, and chill them. Carefully slice the breast meat from the cold birds, to make 8 to 12 slices in all. Cut the rest of the meat from the carcasses and put it through the food chopper with a little of the bacon or larding pork. Salt the ground meat to taste, add about 2 tablespoons very heavy mayonnaise, and 1 egg yolk, and mix the ingredients into a very stiff paste. Bring the reduced giblet broth to a boil. Add bouillon, if necessary, to obtain 2 cups of liquid. Soften 2 envelopes of gelatin in 1/3 cup water and dissolve it in the hot liquid, off the heat, stirring. Pour the aspic 1/4 inch deep into a flat dish and chill it until it is firm.

Whip 1/2 cup cream stiff, salt it lightly, and fold it gently into the pheasant paste. Use more whipped cream to bind the mousse, if necessary. Add salt and more mayonnaise, if the mousse is too dry. Fill half the mandarin oranges with mousse and place a spiced mushroom on each. Fill the remaining oranges with thick Cumberland sauce. Arrange the slices of pheasant breast on peeled orange slices around the edge of a chilled serving platter and place the stuffed mandarin oranges in the center. Surround the oranges with parsley. Dice the aspic into 1/4-inch cubes and mound the cubes between the pheasant breasts. Serves 8.

*Roast Pheasant
with Hubertus Sauce*   *Gebratener Fasan Hubertus*

SALT AND truss 2 pheasant and tie larding pork over the breasts. Pour over the birds a little hot melted butter and roast them, uncovered, in a moderate oven (350° F.). Baste them every 5 minutes with melted butter, using at least 1 cup in all, and adding more, if necessary. Remove the larding pork after 50 minutes and roast the birds, basting, for 10 minutes more, or 20 minutes for large birds. Reserve the pheasant livers. Simmer the other giblets, the necks, the wing tips, and 2 onion slices in 2 cups salted water for about 40 minutes. Strain the stock.

In a small saucepan sauté 4 chopped shallots in 2 tablespoons butter until they are golden. Add the pheasant livers, chopped, and 2 tablespoons flour and cook the mixture, stirring, until the flour is browned. Remove the pan from the heat, stir in 1 cup of the strained stock, and cook the sauce over low heat for 20 minutes.

In a saucepan reduce by half 1/2 cup vinegar seasoned with 8 crushed peppercorns. Add 1/2 ounce unsweetened chocolate, grated, 1/2 cup Port, 1/4 cup melted red currant jelly, the remaining giblet stock, and the shallot sauce. Heat the sauce and correct the seasoning. Strain the sauce and serve it separately. Remove the trussing strings, arrange the pheasant on a serving platter, and garnish the platter with water cress and with mushrooms sautéed in a little butter.

Roast pheasant may also be served with a bread sauce. In this case, make the shallot sauce but do not add to it the chocolate-Port-jelly mixture. Serve the bread sauce as a second sauce.

Roast Pheasant with Apples   *Fasan mit Äpfeln*

CORE 4 LARGE red apples without cutting through to the bottoms and enlarge the hollows. Put 1/2 teaspoon butter in each apple and bake the apples, uncovered, with 1 cup white wine in a moderate oven (325° F.) until they are tender but still firm.

Rinse the cavities of 2 pheasant with Sherry. Put 2 tablespoons liver paste in each bird. Salt the birds, truss them, and bind larding pork over their breasts. Roast them as for roast pheasant with Hubertus sauce. Add 1/2 cup Sherry to the pan juices, reduce the liquid, and thicken it with 1 tablespoon butter kneaded with 1 tablespoon flour.

Remove the trussing strings, arrange the pheasant on a hot serving platter, and garnish the platter with the apples and with bunches of water cress. Fill the warm apples with 1 cup cranberry sauce mixed with 1 tablespoon each of chopped orange rind and fresh grated horseradish, and 2 teaspoons French mustard. This filling should be cool.

Gebratener Fasan mit Trauben   Roast Pheasant with Grapes

SEASON AND truss 2 large or 3 small pheasant and tie strips of bacon over the breasts. Sauté the pheasant in a roasting pan in 1/2 cup melted butter, over direct heat, until they are golden. Transfer them to a platter and stir the pan juices together. Force 3/4 pound white grapes through a sieve and add the pulp and juice. Return the birds to the pan, pour over them 4 ounces warm brandy, and set it aflame. When the flame dies down, roast the birds in a moderate oven (350° F.) for 50 minutes, or until they are done. Baste the birds every 5 minutes with the pan juices and 1 cup stock. Remove the bacon during the last 15 minutes of cooking and add 1/2 pound white grapes, peeled and seeded. Brown 1 cup bread crumbs in 6 tablespoons butter. Sprinkle the pheasant with the crumbs and rice 2 hard-cooked egg yolks over them. Stir 1/2 cup heavy cream into the sauce and pour the sauce and the grapes around the pheasant. *(Picture, page 287.)*

Fasan mit Champignons   Pheasant with Mushrooms

SPRINKLE 3 PHEASANT with salt and truss them. Tie larding pork over the breasts. Cut off the stems of 2 pounds uniform small mushrooms and sauté the caps in 1/2 cup butter until they are coated. Add 3 onions, chopped, and salt and pepper to taste. Stuff the birds with the mushrooms and skewer the openings. Cover the pheasant with buttered paper and roast them, uncovered, in a moderately hot oven (375° F.) for 45 minutes, basting every 10 minutes with melted butter, using 1 cup in all. Remove the paper and larding pork and roast the pheasant 20 to 25 minutes longer, until they are brown, basting every 10 minutes.

Simmer the wing tips, necks, and giblets in 3 cups salted water for 45 minutes with 1/2 bay leaf and 3 juniper berries and strain the stock. Sauté 8 shallots, finely chopped, in 3 tablespoons butter until they are golden, add the pheasant livers and 3 chicken livers, and sauté them for

3 minutes. Dust with 3 tablespoons flour, crush the livers, and gradually stir in the strained giblet stock. Remove the pheasant to a hot platter and add the remaining pan juices to the sauce. Surround the birds with wild rice.

Pheasant with Mushrooms and Sour Cream   *Fasan Smetana*

TRUSS 3 PHEASANT and tie bacon strips over their breasts. Rub them with 1 cup butter and salt and pepper. Put them in a casserole with 6 juniper berries, lightly crushed, and roast them, uncovered, in a slow oven (300° F.) for 35 minutes. Cover the casserole and cook them 30 minutes longer, or until they are tender. Baste the pheasant every 5 minutes with melted butter, using 1 cup in all.

Simmer 1 pound button mushrooms in 1 cup water with 3 tablespoons butter, the juice of 1/2 lemon, 1/2 teaspoon salt, and a *bouquet garni*. Let the mushrooms stand in the liquor. Discard the bacon strips 10 minutes before the pheasant are done and add to the casserole 1 1/2 cups warm sour cream and the mushrooms, drained.

Pheasant with Raisins   *Chinesischer Fasan mit Rosinen*

MARINATE 3 SMALL pheasant in dry red wine to cover, with 6 shallots, chopped, 3 cloves of garlic, minced, 6 peppercorns and 6 juniper berries, all crushed, 3 cloves, 1 bay leaf, and 1 sprig each of thyme, parsley, tarragon, and basil, all chopped. Cover the container and chill the birds for 3 to 9 days, as desired, turning them once each day.

Remove the pheasant, dry them well, and bone them, leaving the skin intact. Fill the cavities with 1/3 cup each of bread crumbs and liver paste mixed with 1/4 cup almonds, blanched and slivered. Add 1/4 peeled apple to each bird's stuffing. Sew up the birds and truss them with kitchen string. Sauté the birds in 1/2 cup butter until they are golden and flame them with 1 cup warm Cognac. Add 2 cups Sherry and 1 cup red wine. Braise the birds, covered, in a moderate oven (350° F.) about 60 minutes, or until they are tender. (These birds can also be prepared without boning, in which case they should be braised on a rack.) Remove the birds, strain the stock, and thicken it with 1 tablespoon cornstarch dissolved in 1/4 cup cold water. Stir the sauce well and add 1 cup seeded raisins which have been plumped in Port.

Wachteln nach Feinschmecker Art   *Quail with Sauerkraut*

RUB 12 QUAIL generously with salted butter. Sauté 1/2 cup each of onions and tender white celery stalks, all finely chopped, in 1/4 cup butter until the onions are golden, add 2 cups dry bread crumbs, and cook over low heat, stirring constantly, until the crumbs are puffed and lightly browned. Add 1/4 cup finely chopped walnuts, cool the stuffing for 5 minutes, and add 1 well-beaten egg, and salt and pepper to taste. Fill the quail with the stuffing, tie a large slice of salt pork over the breast of each bird, and truss the birds. Roast the quail in a large roasting pan with 1 cup white wine in a moderate oven (350° F.) for 20 minutes, basting every 5 minutes.

Fill a large shallow casserole with 6 cups drained sauerkraut cooked with 1 teaspoon caraway seeds and salt and pepper to taste. Peel and core 6 apples and cut them into 8 wedges each. Simmer them in water or cider to cover with 1/2 cup sugar for 10 minutes, or until they are half tender. Drain them well, mound them in the center of the sauerkraut, and sprinkle them with 1/4 cup sugar. Discard the salt pork and arrange the birds on the sauerkraut around the apples. Pour 1 tablespoon melted butter over each quail and place the casserole in a hot oven (400° F.) for 10 minutes, or until the apples are lightly browned and the quail are golden.

Heat the juices remaining in the roasting pan, add 3 tablespoons flour stirred with 1/2 cup water, and cook over low heat until the sauce thickens. Add 1 cup sour cream gradually and stir until the sauce is hot and smooth, but do not let it boil. Paint the quail once more with hot butter and serve with the sauce.

Quail with Cherries   *Wachteln mit Kirschen*

TRUSS 8 QUAIL and rub the birds with a little salt. In a large skillet, in 1/2 cup butter, brown the quail carefully over medium heat for 15 to 20 minutes, turning and basting them constantly. Cover the pan and roast the quail in a moderate oven (350° F.) for 8 to 10 minutes. Remove the birds and keep them hot. Pour any remaining butter out of the pan. Add 1/2 cup warm brandy, flame it, and deglaze the pan, scraping all the brown crustiness from the sides and bottom. Add 1/2 cup each of melted currant jelly and warm Port, and the rind of half an orange, slivered. Return the quail to the pan. Cook the quail for 5 to 10 minutes, depending on their size, and add the juice of 1/2 lemon and salt and pepper to taste. Remove the trussing strings. Just before serving, add 1 cup preserved pitted Bing cherries that have been heated in their own juice with 1/2 teaspoon each of cinnamon and powdered cloves. Add enough of the juice to make about 1 1/2 cups sauce.

Serve the quail with buttered wild rice. Serves 4. *(Picture, page 286.)*

Quail with Pineapple   *Wachteln mit Ananas*

STUFF 8 QUAIL with 1 drained pineapple chunk and 1 tablespoon of liver paste each. Sew or skewer the openings, salt the quail, and truss them. In a large skillet, in 1/2 cup butter, brown the quail carefully for 15 to 20 minutes, basting and turning them constantly. Transfer the quail to a buttered pan and roast them, covered, in a moderate oven (350° F.) for 8 to 10 minutes. Add 1 cup white Port to the juices in the skillet, reduce the liquid slightly, and add 1/4 cup each of pineapple juice and strong chicken stock. Reduce the sauce to 1 cup.

Spread a platter with a bed of bread crumbs, sautéed in butter, arrange water cress in the center, and set the quail around the water cress. Serve the sauce separately. Serves 4.

Quail in Tart Shells   *Liebhaber-Wachteln*

MAKE *pâté à foncer ordinaire*, plain tart paste, without sugar, line 6 fluted tartlet pans, and bake the shells until they are golden. Remove them from the pans and paint the rims with 1 egg yolk beaten with 1 teaspoon water. Return the shells to a moderately hot oven (375° F.) for 8 to 10 minutes, until the edges are brown and glazed.

Mix 1 1/2 cups liver paste with 2 tablespoons each of chopped shallots and Sherry and fold in 1 1/2 cups salted whipped cream. Pipe the mixture into the tart shells, leaving a small space in the center.

Roast 6 trussed and salted quail, larding pork tied over the breasts, in a hot oven (400° F.) with 1/2 cup butter, basting every 5 minutes with the melted butter. Remove the larding pork after 15 minutes and continue to roast the birds, still basting, until they are golden and tender. Place a quail in each tart shell and sprinkle the breasts of the birds with finely minced tongue or Prague ham. Garnish the tart shells with minced parsley. Serve with individual dishes of cooked cauliflower surrounded by shoestring potatoes. Serve the tarts as a first course or light luncheon entrée.

Sonntagswachteln   *Poached Quail in Green Pea Ring*

SAUTÉ 12 TRUSSED and salted quail in 1/2 cup butter until they are golden, turning and basting them constantly. Add 3 cloves, 3 peppercorns, 1 carrot and 1 onion, both chopped, the grated rind of 1 lemon, 2 teaspoons salt, and water to cover. Simmer the birds for 10 to 15 minutes, or until they are tender. Remove them and keep them hot. Skim the stock, reduce it slightly, and strain it. Brown 3 tablespoons butter, stir in 3 tablespoons flour, and cook the *roux* over low heat, stirring, until it is brown. Gradually stir in 3 cups of the quail stock, and add 1/2 pound small button mushrooms. Simmer the sauce 10 minutes, stirring constantly, and add 1 cauliflower, cooked in salted water and divided into flowerets. Remove the strings and return the quail to the sauce and add salt and pepper to taste. Serve the birds in the center of a green pea pudding cooked in a large ring mold.

Vegetables

Gemüse

As Viennese children grow up, they accumu-
late a fund of practical and impractical
knowledge that the average American child would never need. They learn,
among other things, to use suitable quotations from Goethe's dramas for
every occasion and how to play the piano "four hands." Girls learn how
to curtsy and boys learn how to kiss the hand. But the knowledge that
stands them in the best stead is the recognition of edible and inedible
mushrooms.

Parents who know their children to be well versed in this lore can
trust them to go out into the woods and fields to gather dinner without
poisoning the entire family. Every Viennese brings home sinister looking
fungi and obscure herbs from an *Ausflug,* an outing, or from a stay in
the country. There is never any danger, since, as children, they all learned
what to take and what to leave. In the suburbs, they run out into their
gardens after rainstorms to gather bright mushrooms for an omelet or
soufflé. They gather seeds and berries, shoots and grasses, and interrupt
their walking trips to pick green edibles along the way.

The Viennese love their greens, and almost the nicest thing about
their cuisine is the fact that they do not accompany their meat course with
plain boiled vegetables. Almost every vegetable recipe is planned as a
separate vegetable course; a mushroom soufflé or a spinach pudding, for
example, may precede the meat or be served as a main course. While in
America we sometimes do serve corn and asparagus as separate courses,
the Viennese treat all their vegetables with respect. They prepare yellow
wax beans, for instance, as though they were dealing with asparagus and
serve them in the same way.

It is much more work for the cook to turn a vegetable into a tart, a purée surrounded with puff-pastry crescents, or a light pudding, but it also gives the diner much more pleasure to be served a baked tomato or a stuffed mushroom rather than a plain boiled carrot. Of course, the Viennese menu includes many plain vegetables, but the Viennese designate them as *à l'anglaise,* or in the English style, and reserve this method of preparation for vegetables so young and tender that it would be wrong to treat them in any other way. They simmer young green peas with a spring onion and sugar, but they turn old hard green peas into a pea pudding and old carrots into a light purée.

The Viennese cook will prepare little baskets of puff pastry or of fried potatoes; she will hollow out large tomatoes, mushrooms, or artichokes and fill them with green peas or vegetable purées. Spinach is sieved and re-sieved to a green-velvet consistency and always ornamented with hard-cooked eggs or little cheese bakeries. Cauliflowers come to the table topped with crumbs or ham, capers or cheese; they are baked in sour cream or served under dill sauce. Asparagus gets the most elaborate treatment of all, from buttered crumbs to Maltese sauce. The Viennese manage to eat all their greens and everything that is good for them, but they eat this food at its best, prepared in the most interesting way possible and given the same importance as any other part of the meal.

When the Viennese do serve vegetables with meat, it is as a garnish. Meat almost always appears this way, on a garnished platter, rather than accompanied with vegetables in separate dishes.

These rules change when the meat is boiled. The Viennese traditionally accompany *Rindfleisch,* boiled beef, with cold cucumber and beet salads. If there is a hot vegetable, however, it is boiled, but it is usually a dish like a mushroom ragout, a cross between a vegetable and a sauce for the dumplings. Even sauerkraut, which is boiled, is often covered with apples and baked.

A Viennese dinner might start with a soup and go on to stuffed mushrooms, meat, potatoes or rice, and dessert. On another occasion, dinner might consist only of the soup, asparagus pudding, and dessert, and everyone would be just as happy. By making vegetables interesting and often cooking them with small quantities of meat, the Viennese hardly realize that they are not having meat on their tables two or three times each day. And small Viennese children love their spinach pudding. They do not know that across the Atlantic plain boiled chopped spinach is the classic culinary bugbear of their contemporaries.

Artichoke Bottoms   *Artischockenböden*

REMOVE THE stems from 12 small artichokes, trim the bottoms neatly with
a sharp knife, and rub the exposed cut surface of the vegetable with lemon
juice to prevent discoloration. With a very sharp knife trim the leaves so
that only about 1/2 inch of the green is left around the artichokes. Combine 6 cups water, 2 teaspoons salt, and the juice of 1 large lemon or 3
tablespoons vinegar. Bring the water to a boil, add the artichokes, and
cook them from 30 to 45 minutes, or until they are tender. Drain them
upside down. Remove the center choke.

Stuffed Artichokes Anna   *Kalte Artischocken Anna*

FILL COLD cooked artichoke bottoms with a mixture of cooked tiny green
peas, carrots cut in cubes, and pearl onions, all marinated in French dressing.
Spread a smooth layer of lemon mayonnaise on a crystal serving dish
and arrange the stuffed artichokes on it.

Artichokes Stuffed with Rice   *Mailänderartischocken*

CUT THE leaves of 6 artichokes down to 1 1/2 inches. Simmer them in
salted water with the juice of 1 lemon until the inside leaves pull out easily.
Remove the chokes with a melon cutter and cook the artichokes 10 minutes longer, about 30 to 40 minutes in all. Drain them. Lay 1 onion slice,
sautéed in butter, in each artichoke, and cover it with 1/2 teaspoon chopped
filberts, 1/2 cup hot risotto, and 1 teaspoon Parmesan. Bake the stuffed
artichoke in a hot oven (400° F.) until the cheese is browned.

Steamed Asparagus Vinaigrette   *Spargel Vinaigrette*

STEAM 2 POUNDS green or white asparagus, peeled and trimmed, in an
asparagus steamer with 2 cups salted water. If a steamer is not available,
tie the asparagus into a tight bunch and stand it in 2 inches of simmering
salted water in the lower section of a small double boiler. Invert the top of
the double boiler over the asparagus heads. Do not lift the top or the steam
will escape. Steam young stalks 12 to 20 minutes. Drain and cool. Arrange

the stalks on a platter and put 1 strip each of riced hard-cooked egg white, minced parsley, and riced hard-cooked egg yolk across the middle of the bunch. Serve with vinaigrette sauce *(page 394)*. *(Picture, page 119.)*

Spargel Holstein
Asparagus Holstein

STEAM 2 POUNDS asparagus until it is just tender and drain it well. Arrange it in 6 equal portions in a shallow baking dish. Place 1 fried egg on each of the 6 asparagus portions and pour over 3 tablespoons browned butter. Sprinkle the portions with 1/2 cup grated Parmesan and broil them under moderate heat for 10 minutes, or until the cheese is golden brown. Serve as an accompaniment for veal or minute steaks. If *Spargel Holstein* is to be served as a luncheon dish, lay each portion on a slice of sautéed ham.

Spargel mit Zitronenschale
Asparagus with Lemon Crumbs

STEAM 2 POUNDS asparagus until it is just tender and drain it well. Sauté gently 1/2 cup bread crumbs in 1/2 cup melted butter for about 5 minutes, or until they are golden. Add the grated rind of 2 lemons and salt and pepper to taste. Scatter the mixture over the hot asparagus stalks and pour over them browned butter.

Spargel mit Haselnüssen
Asparagus with Hazelnuts

STEAM 3 POUNDS asparagus until it is just tender, but firm enough so that the tips will not break apart. Cut off the green tips. Reserve the rest of the asparagus stalks for another use. Sauté the tips in 1/4 cup butter with 1/2 cup chopped hazelnuts for about 3 minutes. Sauté 1 cup sliced mushrooms in butter until they are tender but not brown and add them with 1/4 cup minced parsley and the grated rind of 1/2 lemon.

Spargel im Aspik
Asparagus in Aspic

FILL A DEEP, straight-sided mold with white wine aspic. The aspic should be showing the first signs of setting. Chill the mold for 15 minutes. Pour off the aspic that is still liquid and keep it at room temperature. The coating of aspic left on the mold should be 3/16 inch thich. Brush pimiento strips with liquid aspic and ring the inside of the mold with them, halfway up the sides, to simulate a ribbon. Hold the strips in place with wooden picks. Chill the mold until the strips adhere and remove the picks. Chill a bunch of cooked asparagus stalks, trimmed to the same length, and stand them in the mold, heads down. Pour in enough liquid aspic to fill the mold and cover the asparagus completely. Chill the mold in the refrigerator until the aspic sets. Unmold the asparagus onto a serving platter and surround the mold with a wreath of water cress. Serve with mayonnaise.

Viennese Green Beans   *Wienerbohnen*

SIMMER 2 POUNDS French-cut green beans in salted water for about 15 minutes, or until they are just tender, and drain them. Sauté 1 onion, chopped, with 2 tablespoons each of chopped dill and parsley and 1 tablespoon chopped savory in 5 tablespoons butter until the onion is puffed but not brown. Blend in 5 tablespoons flour and cook the *roux* over low heat, stirring, until it is smooth. Add just enough beef stock to make a medium thin sauce, about 2 cups. Add the beans and salt, pepper, and sugar to taste. Cook the mixture until the beans are hot and add the juice of 1/2 lemon and 1/2 cup warm heavy cream just before serving.

Green Beans with Liver   *Grüne Bohnen*

SIMMER 2 POUNDS French-cut green beans in salted water for about 15 minutes, or until they are just tender, and drain them. Sauté gently 2 slices calf's liver and 1 thinly sliced onion, separated into rings, in 1/4 cup butter for about 6 minutes, or until the liver is browned. Cut the liver into small dice and sprinkle the dice with salt to taste. Simmer 3 apples, peeled, cored, and sliced, with 1 tablespoon sugar in apple juice or water to cover for about 10 minutes, or until the apples are tender but not soft, and drain them. Stir 2 tablespoons melted butter into the green beans and mound them on a round serving plate. Pour over them the liver dice and onions and sprinkle generously with chopped parsley. Surround the mounded green beans with the apples.

Ungarisches Bohnengulyás   *Hungarian Bean Goulash*

SOAK 1 POUND small dried white beans in water to cover overnight. Drain the beans and put them in a large kettle with 1 cup diced cooked ham, 2 onions, chopped, 1 tablespoon flour, 1 teaspoon paprika, and 1 clove of garlic, crushed. Add hot water or stock to a depth 1 inch above the mixture. Simmer the beans gently for 2 to 3 hours, or until they are tender. Add 2 tablespoons tomato paste, 1/2 teaspoon rosemary, and salt to taste. Sprinkle 1 cooked potato, finely diced, over the stew a few minutes before serving. Serve as a main dish.

Spargelbohnen   *Wax Beans*

THESE ARE also called *Wachsbohnen*. Tie together 6 bundles of wax beans, 12 to 14 in each, and simmer them in salted water until they are tender but not too soft, about 10 to 15 minutes. Drain them well and discard the strings. They may then be served in any way that asparagus is served. The most popular way is to align the beans on a platter and pour over them 3/4 cup bread crumbs browned in 1/2 cup salted butter.

Kohlsprossen   *Brussels Sprouts*

CLEAN 1 QUART small Brussels sprouts, discarding the wilted leaves. Simmer them in salted water to cover for about 10 minutes, or until they are tender. Drain them well and season them highly with freshly ground black pepper and salt to taste. Arrange the hot seasoned sprouts in a warm dish, pour over them 1/4 cup browned butter, and grate the rind of 1 lemon over them. Sprinkle them with the juice of the lemon and garnish the dish with 1/4 cup chopped parsley mixed with 2 hard-cooked egg whites, riced.

Gedämpfte Kohlsprossen   *Braised Brussels Sprouts*

CLEAN 1 QUART compact Brussels sprouts and arrange them in a shallow buttered baking dish. Heat 3/4 cup stock with half a garlic clove, crushed, and pour it over the sprouts. Cover the dish and bake in a slow oven

(300° F.) for 30 minutes, or until the sprouts are tender. Sprinkle them with 4 slices crisp bacon, crumbled, and 1 teaspoon chopped chervil.

*Brussels Sprouts
with Ham and Mushrooms*   *Gebackene Kohlsprossen*

SIMMER 1 POUND Brussels sprouts in salted water for about 20 minutes, or until they are tender, and drain them. Chop enough lean cooked ham to make 1 cup and slice 1/2 pound mushrooms. Place half the Brussels sprouts in a well-buttered casserole and cover them with alternate layers of the ham, the mushrooms, and the remaining Brussels sprouts, finishing with a layer of ham. Beat 2 egg yolks into 3/4 cup heavy cream, add 1/4 cup grated Parmesan, and pour the sauce over the casserole. Sprinkle with 2 tablespoons grated Parmesan and bake the Brussels sprouts in a hot oven (400° F.) for 10 to 15 minutes.

Red Cabbage with Apples   *Rotkraut mit Äpfeln*

SHRED A LARGE red cabbage and sprinkle it with salt and freshly ground pepper to taste. In an enamel saucepan, melt 2 tablespoons lard, add the cabbage, and sprinkle it with 1/2 cup tarragon vinegar. With a wooden spoon, stir and press down the cabbage. Cook it over low heat, without adding more liquid, if possible. Add 1/2 cup red wine, if necessary.

Dissolve 3 tablespoons sugar in 3 tablespoons water and cook the syrup until it is brown. Add the caramel to the cabbage and cover the pan. Simmer the cabbage for 1 1/2 hours. Add 2 tart apples, peeled, cored, and thinly sliced, 1/2 cup red wine, 2 tablespoons red currant jelly, and 1/2 teaspoon each of powdered cloves and caraway seeds. Simmer the cabbage for 20 minutes more, drain it, and serve it at once.

Carrot Purée   *Püree aus gelben Rüben*

SIMMER 3 CUPS diced carrots in salted water to cover with 1 tablespoon butter, 1 teaspoon sugar, and 3 sprigs of parsley, stirring, for 15 minutes. Dust with 1 tablespoon flour and cook until very soft, about 30 minutes in all. Remove the parsley, drain them well, and purée them through a processor. Add salt, pepper and sugar to taste. Press the purée through a

pastry tube onto croutes and sprinkle it with finely minced mint. Serve as a garnish with roast goose or meat. *(Picture, page 285.)*

Karotten mit Kräutern   *Carrots with Herbs*

SCRAPE 24 VERY young carrots and simmer them in beef stock to cover until they are tender and the stock is reduced, about 8 minutes. Lay the carrots in a shallow pan and add 3 tablespoons butter and 1 tablespoon each of parsley, chives, tarragon, and chervil, all chopped. Shake the pan over low heat to coat the carrots with butter and herbs and add just enough of the remaining stock to moisten them lightly. Add salt, pepper, and sugar to taste.

Polnischer Blumenkohl   *Cauliflower Polonaise*

SIMMER A VERY large cauliflower in salted water to cover for about 20 minutes, or until it is just tender. Do not overcook. Drain it well and arrange it in a heated serving dish just large enough to hold it. Sprinkle it with 2 teaspoons lemon juice. Crush 6 Holland rusks, brown the crumbs lightly in 1/2 cup butter, and pour the crumbs over the cauliflower, letting them dribble down the sides of the head. Sprinkle 1/3 pound sliced cooked ham cut into fine julienne strips over the crumbs and around the edge of the dish. Top the ham with the sieved white of 1 hard-cooked egg, top the white with the sieved yolk of 1 hard-cooked egg, and sprinkle 2 table-spoons finely chopped parsley over the top. Sprinkle the garnished cauli-flower with the grated rind of 1 large lemon and pour 1/4 cup hot brown butter over the head. Serve the dish immediately, with additional hot brown butter, if desired. *(Picture, page 116.)*

Cauliflower with Ham　　　　　　　　　*Blumenkohl mit Schinken*

SIMMER 2 MEDIUM-SIZED heads of cauliflower in salted water until they are half cooked, about 10 to 15 minutes. Drain them well and separate them into flowerets.

Grind enough cold boiled ham to make 2 1/2 cups. Butter an oven-proof dish and fill it with alternate layers of hot cauliflower and ground ham. Press the ham into the spaces between the flowerets. Sprinkle the layers with grated Parmesan as you fill the dish, using about 1/2 cup.

Beat 2 egg yolks into 1 1/2 cups sour cream and add 2 tablespoons finely chopped onion, 1 tablespoon chopped parsley, 1 teaspoon paprika, and 1/2 teaspoon salt, if the ham is very mild. Beat the mixture well and pour it over the ham and cauliflower, making sure it penetrates the whole mixture. Spread the casserole with 1/4 cup grated Parmesan, dot it with butter, and bake it in a moderately hot oven (375° F.) for 20 minutes, or until the top is browned. Accompany the casserole with a green salad.

Cauliflower with Green Pea Sauce　　　　*Blumenkohl mit Erbsensauce*

RUB 2 CUPS cooked peas through a sieve twice. Add 2 tablespoons butter and 1/4 cup cream to make a smooth purée and add 1 cup hot milk. Season the sauce to taste and pour it over 1 large cooked cauliflower. Sprinkle the cauliflower with 1/2 cup buttered bread crumbs.

Kastanien zu schälen   *To Peel Chestnuts*

WITH A SHARP knife, cut a cross on the flat sides of 2 pounds chestnuts.
Heat them in a moderate oven (350° F.) for 10 minutes, or until the
shells curl back. Peel them while they are hot and simmer them in water
to cover for 3 to 6 minutes. Remove the brown inner skins.

Kastanienpüree   *Chestnut Purée*

PEEL 2 POUNDS chestnuts as described above and simmer them in beef
stock to cover with 1/2 tablespoon each of butter and sugar until they
are very soft and fall apart, about 30 minutes. Rice the hot chestnuts,
add salt and pepper, and, if necessary, beat in a little beef stock and butter.

Kastanien als Gemüse   *Whole Chestnuts*

PEEL 2 POUNDS chestnuts as described above and simmer them in beef
stock to cover with 1/2 tablespoon each of butter and sugar until they
are tender, about 18 to 20 minutes. Drain them. Brown 2 tablespoons
butter with 2 tablespoons sugar, sprinkle the mixture with 1 tablespoon
flour, and add 1/2 cup beef stock. Add the drained chestnuts and shake
them over low heat until they are coated. Add salt and pepper to taste
and, depending on the mealiness of the chestnuts, add beef stock if necessary to make them moist and glossy. Serve the chestnuts plain, as a vegetable, or add 1/2 cup raisins simmered in beef stock until they are puffed.

Glasierte Kastanien   *Glazed Chestnuts*

PEEL 1 POUND chestnuts as described above and simmer them in milk to
cover with 1 tablespoon each of butter and sugar until they are just
tender, about 18 to 20 minutes. Drain them. Brown 3 tablespoons butter
with 1/4 cup sugar and add 2 teaspoons arrowroot stirred into 3 tablespoons beef stock. For a deeper color add 1/2 to 1 teaspoon meat glaze
to the sugar. Add the drained chestnuts and shake them over low heat
until they are coated, glossy, and brown. Serve the chestnuts as a garnish
for meat or add them to red cabbage or Brussels sprouts.

Detail of a Gate outside The Hofbu

Stuffed Filet of Beef with Mushrooms
Stuffed with Spinach

(recipes, pages 181 and 52)

Garnished Beefsteak Tartare

(recipe, page 187)

Boiled Beef Hotel Bristol

(recipe, page 179)

Boiled Beef in Beer   *(recipe, page 179)*

Grilled Sausages with Sauerkraut

(recipe, page 296)

Peasants' Feast

(recipe, page 211)

Saddle of Venison
Hotel Goldener Hirsch

(recipe, page 252)

Wienerschnitzel
Hotel Goldener Hirsch

(recipe, page 198)

Chicken with Paprika Sauce
Hotel Bristol

(recipe, page 227)

Ham with Orange Sauce
and German Cucumber Salad I

(recipe, pages 204 and 348)

Duck with Fruit

(recipe, page 238)

Christmas Goose with Apple Stuffing   (recipe, page 243)

285

Quail with Cherries

(recipe, page 261)

Roast Pheasant with Grapes

(recipe, page 258)

Molded Chestnut Purée   *Gelierte Kastanienpüree*

SOFTEN 2 ENVELOPES of gelatin in 1/2 cup consommé and dissolve the
softened gelatin in 1/2 cup hot heavy cream, off the heat. Add the gelatin
mixture to 3 cups chestnut purée. Spoon the purée into a mold rinsed out
in cold water, adding about 1 cup whole chestnuts. Lay the whole chestnuts near the sides of the mold so that they will show when the purée is
unmolded. Let the purée set until it is firm. Unmold it on a crystal dish
and surround it with spiced peaches and whole chestnuts.

Chestnuts with Prunes   *Kastanien mit Pflaumen*

COOK 1 POUND chestnuts as for *Kastanien als Gemüse,* or whole chestnuts,
and add 1/4 cup raisins puffed in beef stock. Simmer 1/2 pound prunes,
soaked in water overnight, with a curl of lemon peel and 2 tablespoons
sugar for 8 minutes. Drain the prunes and remove the pits. Combine the
prunes and the chestnuts and serve hot.

Garnished
Chestnut Purée   *Kastanien mit Äpfeln oder Kohlsprossen*

PEEL 2 POUNDS chestnuts as described above and cook the peeled nuts
in water to cover until they are soft, about 30 minutes. Rice them and
add 1/2 cup each of milk and brown stock and salt to taste. Add more
stock, if necessary, to make a smooth thick purée that will hold its shape.
Press the purée into a shallow platter and cover it with stewed sliced apples
or turn it into a serving dish and cover it with 1 pound cooked Brussels
sprouts.

Stuffed Cucumbers   *Gefüllte Gurken*

MIX 3 HARD-COOKED eggs, riced, with 1/3 cup each of bread crumbs,
grated Parmesan, and chopped almonds. Add salt, pepper and sugar to
taste and a pinch of powdered cloves and bind the filling with 2 beaten
egg yolks. Peel, cut in half lengthwise, and seed 3 large cucumbers.
Blanch them in salted water, drain them, and fill them with the egg
mixture. Lay the stuffed cucumbers in a shallow pan with 3 tablespoons

atue of Johann Strauss in Stadtpark

onny Jaques

butter and bake them in a moderate oven (350° F.) until they are tender, about 10 to 15 minutes. Brown 1/2 cup butter and add 3 tablespoons chopped chives. Pour the sauce over the cucumbers.

Gedämpfte Gurken 1   Braised Cucumbers I

PEEL 4 LARGE or 6 small cucumbers, seed them, and cut them into strips. Blanch the strips in salted water. Drain them well and cook them, covered, in 1/4 cup butter until they are tender. Add 1 teaspoon meat glaze and salt and freshly ground pepper to taste and shake them well with their juice. Dust them with finely chopped dill, chives, or parsley.

Gedämpfte Gurken 2   Braised Cucumbers II

COOK CUCUMBERS cut into strips as for braised cucumbers I. When they are tender, dust them with 2 teaspoons flour and add 1/4 cup each of white wine, beef stock, and vinegar. Stir them until the sauce is smooth and season them with salt, pepper, and sugar, mixed with a pinch of powdered cloves and cinnamon.

Linsenpüree   Lentil Purée

SOAK 2 CUPS lentils overnight, simmer them in salted water until they are soft, about 2 hours, and press them with 4 small hot boiled potatoes, peeled, through a sieve, or purée them through a food mill. Add 6 table-spoons butter, salt to taste, and enough heavy cream to make a light purée. Top the lentil purée with crisp crumbled bacon, chopped chives, sliced frankfurters or diced Bologna.

Eierpflanze   Baked Eggplant

CUT 1 LARGE eggplant, peeled, into 1/4-inch slices, parboil the slices for 6 minutes, and drain and dry them. Dredge the slices with flour and sauté them in 1/2 cup olive oil combined with 1 clove of garlic, crushed, until they are lightly browned. Lay the slices in a buttered baking dish, insert a slice of tomato between the eggplant slices, and sprinkle with salt and pepper and 1/2 cup grated Swiss cheese. Sauté 2 onions, finely chopped, in the oil in which the eggplant was sautéed, and spread the onions over the eggplant and tomato. Sprinkle another 1/2 cup grated Swiss cheese over the onions, dot with butter, and bake the casserole in a moderately hot oven (375° F.) for 30 minutes.

Skewered Mushrooms *Schwämmerln am Spiess*

CLEAN 2 POUNDS medium-sized mushroom caps and season them with salt and pepper to taste and a pinch of nutmeg. Thread the mushrooms on 6 skewers, roll each skewer in seasoned olive oil, and broil the mushrooms for 10 minutes, turning them frequently. Lay the skewers in a warm shallow ovenproof pan, pour over them 1/2 cup warmed brandy, and flame the spirit. Serve as soon as the flame dies down.

Mushrooms with Rice and Almonds *Mandelreis mit Schwämmen*

CLEAN 3/4 POUND mushrooms, put them in a saucepan with 1/2 cup water, the juice of half a lemon, and 3 tablespoons butter, and cook for 5 minutes. Sauté 1 onion, chopped, in 1/2 cup butter, until it is golden. Add 1 cup rice and cook, stirring constantly, until it is well coated with butter and transparent. Add 2 cups stock, 1 cinnamon stick, and 1 bay leaf, cover the skillet, and bake in a moderately hot oven (375° F.) for 15 minutes. Add the prepared mushrooms and 24 almonds, blanched and chopped, stir the rice well, and continue to bake it until the rice has reached the *al dente* stage. Add the mushroom liquor if it is too dry. Remove the bay leaf and cinnamon stick. Serve with grated Parmesan, if desired.

Mushrooms in Hollandaise *Holländische Champignons*

REMOVE THE stems from 1 pound mushrooms and sauté the caps in 3/4 cup melted butter for 5 minutes over high heat, stirring constantly. Drain the mushrooms well and keep them hot. Pour the butter in which the mushrooms cooked into the top of a double boiler and place it over hot water. Do not allow the water to come to a boil. Add 3 egg yolks and stir with a wire whisk until they are light, gradually adding 1/4 cup butter, bit by bit, and stirring constantly as the sauce thickens. When the sauce is thickened, remove the pan from the heat and continue beating. Add 2 teaspoons lemon juice, the grated rind of 1 lemon, and a pinch each of white pepper and salt. Pour this mushroom-hollandaise over the mushrooms and sprinkle them with 1/4 cup finely chopped chives.

Glasierte Zwiebeln   *Glazed Onions*

PEEL 2 POUNDS small white onions, simmer them in salted water for 10 minutes, and drain them well. Sauté them in 1/3 cup butter until they are golden and sprinkle them with 3 tablespoons sugar. Shake the pan until they are glossy. Serve with *Rehpfeffer,* venison stew, and lamb roasts.

Gebackene Zwiebeln   *Baked Onions*

PARBOIL 6 LARGE onions, peeled, in salted water for 15 minutes and drain them well. Carefully scoop out the centers, leaving a 1/2-inch-thick shell, and chop the centers finely. Sauté 1/2 cup chicken livers in 1 tablespoon butter until they are just browned, crush them with a fork, and combine them with the chopped onion and the riced yolk of 1 hard-cooked egg. Pack the onion shells with this stuffing and place them close together in a buttered baking dish.

Combine any remaining stuffing with 3/4 cup cream, 1 tablespoon brandy, and salt and pepper to taste, and pour over the onions. Bake the onions in a moderate oven (350° F.) for about 15 minutes, or until they are tender, dust them with 2 tablespoons chopped parsley, and serve with roast or fricasseed chicken.

Zwiebeln mit Haselnüssen   *Baked Onions with Hazelnuts*

PARBOIL 6 LARGE onions, peeled, in salted water for 10 minutes and drain them well. Carefully scoop out the centers, leaving a 1/2-inch-thick shell, chop the centers finely, and combine them with 1/2 cup buttered bread crumbs and 1/4 cup hazelnuts, chopped. Pack the onion shells with this stuffing and place them close together in a buttered baking dish. Blend 2 tablespoons flour into 2 tablespoons melted butter and cook the *roux* over low heat for a few minutes. Do not let it brown. Add slowly, off the heat, 1 cup milk and simmer the sauce for 6 minutes. Add 1/4 cup hazelnuts, chopped, 2 tablespoons Cognac, and salt to taste, and pour the sauce over the onions. Bake the onions in a moderate oven (350° F.) for 35 minutes. Before serving, sprinkle them with 2 tablespoons parsley and 1 tablespoon chives, all chopped.

Onion and Walnut Soufflé   *Zwiebelauflauf*

MELT 3 TABLESPOONS butter and blend in well 1/4 cup flour. Gradually add to the *roux* 1 cup milk and simmer the sauce for 6 minutes, stirring. Boil 8 to 10 white onions, chopped, for 15 minutes in 1 cup milk with 1/2 teaspoon salt. Add the onions with the milk in which they cooked, 1/2 cup chopped walnuts, and pepper to taste. Simmer the mixture for 3 minutes longer, remove it from the heat, and stir in 5 beaten egg yolks, 1 tablespoon chopped parsley, and salt to taste. Fold in 5 egg whites, beaten stiff. Bake the soufflé in an unbuttered baking dish, set in a pan of hot water, in a moderate oven (350° F.) for 45 minutes, or until it is puffed and golden.

Onion Purée   *Zwiebelpüree*

SAUTÉ 1 POUND sliced onions in 1/2 cup butter until they are golden. Combine them and their butter with 1 cup rice and add 2 cups chicken or beef stock. Steam the rice, covered, until it is soft, about 30 minutes. Add salt, pepper, and sugar to taste, and force the mixture through a sieve or purée it in a blender. Add just enough heavy cream to make a light purée.

Green Peas   *Grüne Erbsen*

SHELL 3 POUNDS green peas and wash the shells. Simmer the shells in salted water to cover for 20 minutes. Discard the shells and cook the peas in the same water, uncovered, until they are almost tender, about 8 to

10 minutes. Pour off most of the water, leaving enough to not quite cover the peas, and add 2 teaspoons each of butter and sugar. Sprinkle over the peas 2 teaspoons flour and cook them 5 minutes longer. Add salt and pepper to taste, and a little warm cream, if desired.

Erbsenpüree   Pea Purée

COMBINE 6 CUPS shelled green peas, a sprig of parsley, 1 tablespoon sugar, and 1 generous teaspoon butter in a little simmering water. Cover the peas with half a head of Boston lettuce and cook them until they are soft. Discard the lettuce and drain the peas. Put them through a food mill and add 3 tablespoons cream, 2 tablespoons butter, and salt and pepper to taste. This purée may be used in various ways as a garnish.

To serve the purée as a vegetable, mound it into a serving dish and decorate it with triangular croutons or triangles of cheese pastry. Sprinkle the peas with 1/2 cup chopped onion browned in 2 tablespoons butter.

Erbsenpastete mit Krebsen   Green Pea and Shrimp Tart

MAKE *Pastetenteig,* pie dough, doubling the quantity, and bake 1 large pie shell and 6 small tart shells. Shell and cook 4 pounds green peas in lightly salted water until they are tender. Drain and purée them in a blender. To 2 1/2 cups of the purée, add 2 tablespoons each of cream and melted butter, 1 teaspoon grated onion, and salt and pepper to taste. Fill the pie shell with the hot purée. Fill the tart shells with hot cooked shrimps, mask them with *Aurorensauce,* shrimp hollandaise sauce, and arrange them on the purée.

Erbsen mit Schinken   Green Peas with Ham

SIMMER 3 POUNDS green peas in 2 cups salted water until the peas are tender. Drain them well and combine them with 1 cup ham and 3 tablespoons onion, all chopped. Pour over them 1 cup warm cream, add salt and pepper to taste, and mix well. Pour the mixture into a well-buttered casserole, sprinkle it with 1/4 cup grated Parmesan, and brown the top under the broiler.

Green Pea Pudding   *Grüne Erbsenpudding*

SAUTÉ 4 CUPS green peas in 1/4 cup butter for a few minutes and add salt to taste. Moisten the peas with 1 1/2 cups hot bouillon, add a pinch each of sugar, cinnamon, and allspice, and cook them until they are tender. Drain the peas, reserving the liquid, and purée them in a blender. Add 1 tablespoon flour and 3 crushed macaroons to 1/4 cup melted butter. Moisten with a little of the reserved liquid, keeping the mixture very stiff and dry, and add the pea purée and 3 well-beaten egg yolks. Fold in 3 stiffly beaten egg whites and pour the mixture into a buttered baking dish or ring mold. Place the dish in a pan of hot water and bake the pudding in a moderately hot oven (375° F.) for 60 minutes.

Baked Lettuce   *Kopfsalat*

CLEAN AND trim 2 heads of romaine lettuce, cut off the bitter stems, and divide each head lengthwise into 3 portions. Blanch the lettuce for 1/2 minute in boiling salted water and drain it. Combine 1 onion and 1 carrot, cut into dice, 1/2 cup diced ham, and a mixture of 3 peppercorns, crushed, 1/2 teaspoon each of basil, thyme, and salt, and 1 bay leaf, and spread the mixture in a buttered pan. Lay over it neatly the 6 lettuce portions, cover each portion with a piece of salt pork or bacon, and add 2 cups reduced beef consommé. Bake the *Kopfsalat* in a slow oven (275° F.) for 45 minutes, basting it with the consommé at least 4 times. Discard the salt pork or bacon before serving.

Sauerkraut   *Sauerkraut*

SAUTÉ 1 ONION, chopped, in 3 tablespoons butter until it is golden. Blend in 3 tablespoons flour and cook the mixture, stirring constantly, for a minute. Add 1/2 cup beef stock, 1 tablespoon sugar, and salt and pepper to taste. Stir the sauce until it is smooth. Add 3 cups sauerkraut, cooked and drained, and simmer the mixture, uncovered, for 1/2 hour. Stir it frequently and add a little more beef stock, if necessary. Serve the sauerkraut with grilled sausages. *(Picture, page 278.)*

Apfelkraut   *Apple Sauerkraut*

COMBINE 2 POUNDS cooked sauerkraut with its juice, 3 apples, peeled, cored, and sliced, 3 tablespoons sugar, 1 tablespoon vinegar, 1 teaspoon caraway seeds, and salt and pepper to taste. Simmer the mixture for 20 to 25 minutes, or until the apples are just tender. Lay the sauerkraut in a shallow baking dish, arrange the apple slices in rows across the top, and sprinkle the apples with 2 tablespoons sugar. Brown under the broiler.

Spinatpudding   *Spinach Pudding*

CREAM 1/2 CUP soft butter with 8 egg yolks and stir in 1 1/2 cups puréed spinach and 1/4 cup chopped parsley. Soak 4 slices of white bread, with crusts, in milk and press them out very well. Add the bread to the spinach with 3/4 cup sour cream and salt and pepper to taste. Fold in 8 egg whites, beaten very stiff, and dust over the whites 1 3/4 cups dry bread crumbs while folding them in. Pour the batter into a well-buttered pudding mold and put the covered mold in a kettle with enough water to reach halfway up the mold. Cover the kettle and steam the pudding for 1 to 1 1/4 hours, replenishing with more boiling water if necessary. Unmold the pudding carefully on a platter. Surround it with cooked artichoke bottoms filled with mounded *mousseline* sauce. Serve cheese bakeries and ham separately.

Spinach Soufflé Caroline   *Spinatauflauf Karoline*

MELT 1/2 CUP butter, stir in 1/4 cup flour over low heat without letting it brown, and add about 1/4 cup warm milk very gradually, until the mixture leaves the sides of the pan and forms a ball. Cool the mixture and add 8 egg yolks, one at a time, 1 1/2 cups finely chopped spinach, and salt and pepper to taste. Fold in 8 stiffly beaten egg whites. Pour the mixture into an unbuttered soufflé dish, stand the dish in a pan of water, and bake the soufflé in a moderately hot oven (375° F.) for 45 minutes, or until it is puffed and lightly browned. Serve it with brown butter sauce. The Viennese like to pour this soufflé mixture over chopped meat, cooked fish, or vegetables, and then bake it as directed.

Baked Tomatoes   *Gebackene Paradeis*

HALVE 6 FIRM ripe tomatoes of uniform size and place them, cut side up, in a well-buttered baking dish. Add pepper generously and press 1 rolled anchovy filet into each tomato. Combine 2 tablespoons each of shallots and parsley, all chopped, with 2 tablespoons butter, and spread this mixture on the cut sides of the tomatoes. Bake the tomatoes in a hot oven (400° F.) for 8 minutes, or until they are tender.

Tomatoes Stuffed with Rice   *Serbische Tomaten*

SAUTÉ 1 CHOPPED onion in 2 tablespoons butter until it is golden, add 1/2 cup rice, and stir it until it is lightly browned. Add 2 cups water or beef stock, 1 cup diced cooked beef, a pinch of saffron, and salt and pepper to taste, and cook the rice, covered, over low heat, stirring frequently, until it is medium soft. Scoop out the pulp of 6 large tomatoes and drain the shells. Add the tomato pulp to the rice with 1 teaspoon finely minced basil, 1/2 teaspoon thyme, and a pinch of sweet marjoram. Sprinkle the tomatoes with salt and pepper, pack them with the rice, and place them in a baking dish with 1/2 cup water. Dust the tops with 6 table-spoons grated Parmesan, dot with butter, and bake the tomatoes in a moderately hot oven (375° F.) for 20 minutes. Sprinkle them with chopped parsley.

Gemüsepudding Lukullus   Molded Vegetable Pudding

CREAM 1/2 CUP butter, add 6 egg yolks, and beat the mixture until it is light and creamy. Add 3/4 cup parboiled chopped spinach, from which all liquid has been pressed before measuring. Add 1/2 cup parboiled finely chopped green asparagus, also pressed dry, and 1/4 cup minced raw mush-rooms. Soak 6 slices of bread in cream until the bread is thoroughly moist, press out all moisture, and add the bread to the vegetables with 1/2 cup dry bread crumbs, 2 tablespoons each of finely chopped parsley and grated Parmesan, and salt and pepper to taste. Beat 6 egg whites very stiff with a pinch of salt and fold them in. Pour the mixture into a generously buttered pudding mold and cover the mold tightly. Put the mold in a kettle with enough boiling water to reach halfway up its sides, cover the kettle, and steam the pudding for 1 to 1 1/4 hours. Add more boiling water, if necessary. Unmold the pudding and surround it with large mushroom caps sautéed in butter and filled with thick *mousseline* sauce. Pipe a rosette of *mousseline* sauce on the top of the pudding.

Zuchetti mit Dill   Zucchini with Dill

CUT 6 ZUCCHINI, each weighing 1/2 pound, into 1/4-inch slices. Melt 1/2 cup butter in a saucepan and sauté the slices, covered, over slow heat with 1 tablespoon chopped dill, 1 teaspoon dill seed, and salt and pepper to taste for about 8 minutes, or until the zucchini are tender and trans-parent. Watch carefully, as the slices should not fall apart. Cover the zucchini with 1 cup sour cream beaten with 1 tablespoon lemon juice, 1 teaspoon each of sugar and paprika, and salt to taste. Heat the mixture, but do not let it boil, and serve it with a sprinkling of dill and paprika.

*Dumplings, Noodles,
Potatoes, and Rice*

Teigwaren,
Kartoffeln und Reis

HERE IS a story, at least in Vienna, that when God was naming all the animals He was asked (and no one in Vienna knows by whom) why He called the giraffe a giraffe. The answer was: "Because it looks so exactly like one." This story may explain why a *Knödel* is called a *Knödel*. It looks so very like one. The reason why they find less favor in English-speaking countries than in Vienna is that they are called "dumplings," a word which in no way expresses the round, slippery substantiality, the characteristic solidity, the indigestibility of a good provincial *Knödel*, or the pleasurable foamy inflation of a light one.

The only other situation in which the word *"Knödel"* appears happily and expressively occurs when a tenor is making his debut in Vienna. If he sings with that crowded adenoidal quality that only one word can truly express, every Viennese in the audience turns to his neighbor and says, *"Er knödelt."* This makes for a very disconcerting hum from the auditorium and usually condemns the tenor to an early retirement.

A *Knödel,* culinary not vocal, may be as large or even larger than a baseball, or as small as a walnut. It may be filled with toasted bread cubes or chopped parsley; a dessert *Knödel* may be filled with a plum, an apricot, or a little bunch of cherries. The *Knödel* is first cousin to the *Spätzle* and *Nockerl*, and, if diminutive, may be called a *Knöderl*. Dumplings may sink or swim in soup or they may substitute for potatoes with the meat or poultry. Boiled beef, veal roast, pork roast, venison, and hare almost always come to table with their own characteristic dumplings: potato dumplings for game, flour dumplings for veal. Ham and liver dumplings serve as a meal, and a very sturdy one, in themselves.

To prepare a dumpling according to Viennese directions is utterly frustrating. The amount of flour necessary depends on the mealiness of the potatoes, the number of eggs needed depends on the amount of flour, and the rest of the ingredients invariably depend upon the size of the eggs. The dumplings must be simmered in salted water until they are "done," and who but a Viennese cook, born with the instinct, knows when a *Knödel* is done? The moment a foreign body is inserted to test for doneness, the dumpling splits open. Sometimes when they are done, they rise to the surface of the liquid in which they are simmering, but sometimes they linger in the middle waters and neither rise nor sink. If the dumpling is not perfectly cooked through, it shows a telltale dark center when it is cut open. *Tsh, tsh, eine Schande,* a shame. The secret of the successful dumpling is the "test" dumpling to which even the best cooks resort. Make one dumpling, simmer it, and open it. If all is well, proceed; if all isn't well, make another test after adding a little more flour.

Most Viennese make their own noodle dough, a simple formula of flour, water, salt, and an egg. It is almost the first thing a mother teaches her daughter to make, at a time roughly corresponding to the mud-pie stage in other countries. The noodles are cut with little wheels and are left spread out on a table to dry. They may be as fine as "angel's hair" or as wide as ribbons; they may be used to garnish soup or mixed with ham, nuts, mushrooms, or cheese as a main course.

The Viennese eat a great deal of rice, although not as much as the Italians, whose beautiful *risottos* provide the inspiration for many of Vienna's rice dishes. Nevertheless, the Viennese will staunchly defend his *Risi-Pisi* as his very own. The various kinds of pasta are used less than would be expected, considering that Austria borders on Italy. *Stopferl* are named for the little potato "stuffers," fed to geese to bring about an enlargement of the liver. The custom is deplored for geese, but very much enjoyed by the Viennese who add butter and bread crumbs.

The Viennese cook beats flour and water together in proportions that would make dependable library paste in America, but in Vienna, for some unknown reason, the combination makes wonderful *Teigwaren,* or dough products. When you plead for the recipe, the Viennese cook will tell you, "How do I *know* how much flour and water I use? *Ich hab' es in der Hand, nicht im Köpferl*—I have the knowledge in my hand, not in my head."

The recipes in this chapter call for exact quantities, but remember that even the finest Viennese cook resorts to the "test" dumpling.

Flour Dumplings   *Semmelknödel*

STIR 2 WELL-BEATEN eggs into 3/4 cup milk and mix with 3 cups sifted
flour. Add salt to taste and 1 cup bread cubes, sautéed until crisp in
6 tablespoons butter. Shape the dough into dumplings the size of base-
balls, boil them in salted water for 15 minutes, and drain them. Slice the
dumplings and serve them with browned butter.

Cheese Dumplings   *Topfenknödel*

MIX 1 3/4 CUPS sieved cottage cheese with 1/2 cup butter and 4 egg
yolks until smooth. Add 1 1/4 cups dry bread crumbs, 1/2 cup sugar, and
a pinch each of cinnamon and salt. Using 2 tablespoons, shape the dough
into small dumplings and drop one into lightly salted simmering water.
If the dumpling is too light, add more bread crumbs; if it is too hard,
add a little cream. Simmer the dumplings for 7 to 9 minutes, or until
they test done. Remove them immediately with a slotted spoon. These
sweet dumplings may be served as a dessert or as a main luncheon course
with hot brown butter.

Potato Dumplings   *Erdäpfelknödel*

TO 1 1/2 POUNDS potatoes, boiled, peeled, and riced, add when cool about
1 1/2 cups flour, 1/2 teaspoon salt, and 1 beaten egg. With the hands,
work the mixture into a dough, adding more flour if the dough is too
moist. Shape it into dumplings the size of golf balls, drop them into a
large kettle of simmering salted water, and simmer them until they rise
to the surface. Skim the dumplings from the water, drain them well and
split them in half with two forks. Arrange them on a hot platter. Pour
over them 1/4 cup hot browned butter and sprinkle them with 1/2 cup
fine bread crumbs browned in butter.

Filled Potato Dumplings   *Gefüllte Erdäpfelknödel*

ON A PASTRY board, rice 6 large potatoes, boiled and peeled. Make a
well in the center and put in 1 egg, well beaten with 1 teaspoon salt

and 1/4 teaspoon sugar. Gradually sprinkle over 1 cup sifted flour, work the ingredients into a soft smooth dough, adding more flour gradually. The amount of flour required depends on the mealiness of the potatoes. It will be approximately 1 1/2 to 2 1/2 cups.

In 1/2 cup butter sauté 1 cup bread crumbs with 1 large onion, chopped, and salt and sugar to taste until the crumbs are brown. Roll out one-half the potato dough, spread it with the crumb mixture, and roll it up. Cut the roll in 1 1/2-inch lengths. Roll out the second half of dough as thinly as possible. Cut it into squares and wrap each section of rolled dough in one of the squares. With floured hands, shape the dumplings so that no seams are left.

Lower the dumplings carefully into simmering salted water and let them simmer 1 minute after they rise to the top. Drain them well and pour over them the browned butter in which the crumbs were sautéed, adding more browned butter if necessary.

Käseklösschen mit Spinat   *Cheese Gnocchi with Spinach*

BRING TO a boil 4 cups milk, 1/4 cup butter, and 1/2 teaspoon salt. Add 1 1/2 cups farina and cook the mixture over low heat, stirring constantly, for 20 minutes. Remove it from the heat, let it cool slightly and stir in 3 egg yolks and 1 cup each of grated Emmenthal cheese and chopped cooked spinach. Let the mixture rest for 2 hours. Cut it into oval shapes and lay them in a well-buttered shallow baking pan. Dust the *gnocchi* with 1/2 cup grated Emmenthal and pour over 1/2 cup melted butter and salt, pepper, and nutmeg to taste. Bake the *gnocchi* in a moderate oven (350° F.) for 20 minutes.

Käsenockerl   *Cheese Gnocchi*

BRING TO a boil 1 cup water, 6 tablespoons butter, and 1 teaspoon each of salt and finely minced parsley. Add 1 cup sifted flour all at once and beat the batter with a wooden spoon until it is glossy and leaves the sides of the pan. Remove it from the heat and gradually add 4 small or 3 large eggs beaten with 1/3 cup each of grated Emmenthal and Swiss cheese. Beat the mixture until it is smooth and pipe it through a pastry bag fitted with a plain 1/2-inch tube into a saucepan filled with simmering salted water. As the *Nockerln* come out of the tube, cut them with a wet knife into 1- to 2-inch lengths and simmer them, covered, for 5 minutes. Shake the pan once or twice and remove them with a slotted spoon. Drain the *Nockerln* well and put them into a buttered shallow baking dish. Melt 4 tablespoons butter, stir in 1/3 cup flour, and cook the *roux* over low heat. Do not let it brown. Gradually stir in 1 1/4 cups warm milk mixed with 3/4 cup water in which the *Nockerln* simmered. Season with salt and pepper. Stir the sauce until it is smooth and simmer it, covered, for 15 to 20 minutes. Pour the sauce over the *Nockerln*, dust them with 1/4 cup grated Parmesan, and dot with 2 tablespoons butter. Brown the *Nockerln* under the broiler for about 15 minutes.

Spätzle

MIX TOGETHER well 1 1/2 cups sifted flour, 1 beaten egg, 3/4 cup water, and 1/2 teaspoon salt. If the egg is large, use a little less water to make a soft dough that will not flow and is stiff enough so that it will not run off a spoon. Let the batter stand for 30 minutes. Scoop up a generous amount of the dough with a wooden spoon. With a knife cut off small slices of the dough and drop them directly from the spoon into a large kettle of boiling salted water. The *Spätzle* will rise to the surface when they are cooked. Drain them well in a colander and transfer them to a deep heated serving dish. Pour 1/4 cup melted butter over them and, if desired, stir in 1/4 cup warmed sour cream. Shake the *Spätzle* well.

Ferenz Spätzle

FOLLOW THE recipe for *Spätzle,* only add less water to make a drier dough. Shape the dough into little "sausages" with floured hands and cut them into 1-inch lengths. Cook the *Spätzle* as directed.

For more Knödel *recipes, and a Viennese never seems to have enough, turn back to soup garnishes.*

Nudelteig 1 *Noodles I*

SIFT 2 CUPS sifted flour onto a pastry board, make a well in the center, and place in it 1 egg beaten with 2 tablespoons warm water and 1/4 teaspoon salt. Work the flour into the egg, adding gradually about 1/4 to 1/2 cup warm water until the dough is stiff and smooth. Divide the dough into 2 equal pieces, roll out each piece as thinly as possible, and let the pieces dry for 30 minutes to 1 hour. With a noodle cutter, cut the dough into thin soup noodles and medium or heavy ribbon noodles. Boil the thin noodles in salted water for 6 to 10 minutes, the ribbon noodles for 10 to 15 minutes, or until all are tender.

Drain them well and rinse them in cold water before using them for any of the following recipes.

Nudelteig 2 *Noodles II*

SIFT 2 CUPS sifted flour onto a pastry board, make a well in the center, and place in it 2 eggs, well beaten, 1/2 teaspoon melted butter, 1/4 teaspoon salt, and 2 tablespoons water. With the hands work the dough until it is stiff and divide it into 6 equal parts. Roll out each part as thinly as possible and let it rest for 15 minutes. Cut the dough into ribbon noodles 1/2 inch wide and spread them out to dry.

Gradually drop the noodles into a kettle of boiling water with 1 tablespoon salt and boil them for 12 minutes. Drain them and use them as the recipes require.

Nudelring *Noodle Ring*

FOLLOW THE recipe for noodles I, cutting the dough into thin noodles, and boil the noodles in salted water for 6 minutes. Drain them and sauté them in 3 tablespoons butter and 1/2 teaspoon salt for 3 minutes. Press the noodles tightly into a buttered ring mold and smooth the top evenly. Set the mold in a pan, add enough hot water to reach halfway up the mold, and bake the noodles in a very slow oven (200° F.) for 12 minutes. Let the ring cool slightly and unmold it onto a hot platter. Fill it with meat or vegetables, pour over a little melted butter, and sprinkle with chopped parsley or grated cheese.

Green Noodles   *Grüner Nudelteig*

PREPARE NOODLE dough II and add 1 cup spinach purée. Roll, rest, and
cut the dough according to the recipe and cook the green noodles as
directed. Drain them, shake them with 2 tablespoons each of butter and
finely minced parsley, and serve them with veal or chicken or as a separate course with mushroom or cheese sauce.

Nut Noodles   *Nussnudeln*

SAUTÉ 4 CUPS hot boiled ribbon noodles, made as for noodles I, in 3 tablespoons butter until they are glossy, turning them carefully. Combine 1/2
cup each of grated walnuts, grated Parmesan, and browned bread crumbs,
stir them into the noodles, and pour over 1/4 cup browned butter.

Noodles with Mushrooms   *Cortina Nudeln*

FOLLOW THE recipe for noodles II and sauté the noodles in 3 tablespoons butter with 1/2 cup each of chopped onions, mushrooms, and
peeled and seeded tomatoes, and 1/2 teaspoon salt, for 5 minutes. Place

the noodles in a well-buttered baking dish, stir in 1/4 cup grated Parmesan, and bury 6 small peeled tomatoes among the noodles. Spread the top with 3 tablespoons each of bread crumbs and grated Parmesan and bake the noodles in a moderately hot oven (375° F.) for 15 to 20 minutes, or until the top is brown.

Schinkenfleckerln   *Ham with Noodle Squares*

ON A BOARD break 3/4 pound medium noodles into little squares. Boil the noodle bits in lightly salted water for 10 minutes and drain them well. The amount of salt will depend on the saltiness of the ham. Pour over the noodles 1 cup cold water and drain them again. Combine the cooked noodle bits with 2 1/2 cups finely ground ham and 1 cup finely diced Swiss cheese. In a baking dish, cream 1/4 cup butter and spread it on the sides and bottom of the dish. Turn the ham and noodle mixture into the dish and pour over it 1 cup cream mixed with 3 well-beaten eggs and salt, if needed. Sprinkle 2 tablespoons melted butter over the top and bake the mixture in a moderate oven (350° F.) for 1 hour, or until the top is well browned. Serve the casserole with tomato salad.

Kartoffelpfannkuchen   *Potato Pancakes*

SOAK 6 PEELED medium-size potatoes in cold water for 10 minutes and grate them with 1 onion as quickly as possible. Press all the moisture out of the potatoes and add 2 whole eggs, well beaten, 2 tablespoons flour, 1/2 teaspoon salt, and 1 pinch of sugar. Stir in 2 to 3 tablespoons heavy cream or sour cream and continue to stir the mixture for 3 minutes. Fry small pancakes of the mixture in shallow hot fat (375° F.) until they are brown and the edges are crisp. Serve the pancakes with applesauce or as an accompaniment to meat.

Kartoffelpfannkuchen mit Birnen   *Potato Pancake with Pears*

COVER THE bottom of a heavily buttered roasting pan with 3 pears, peeled, cored, and thinly sliced. Peel 4 large boiled potatoes, rice them while they are hot, and combine them with 1 egg, well beaten, 3/4 cup sifted flour, and 1 cup strained cottage cheese. Cover the pears with the mixture and pour over 2 tablespoons melted butter. Bake the pancake in a moderately hot oven (375° F.) for 20 minutes, or until it is golden.

Viennese Fried Potatoes — Geröstete Kartoffeln

BOIL 6 POTATOES in their skins until just tender, peel them, and slice them. In a skillet, sauté 1 onion, chopped, in 4 tablespoons butter until golden, add the potato slices, and cook the potatoes, turning them once, for about 12 minutes. Add 1 teaspoon caraway seeds and salt to taste and cook the potatoes, covered, over moderate heat, turning them carefully once, for 10 minutes longer. Sprinkle the fried potatoes with finely chopped parsley and serve immediately.

Duchess Potatoes — Herzoginnenkartoffeln

BOIL 2 1/2 POUNDS potatoes, peeled and cut into halves, in salted water for about 20 minutes, or until they are tender. Drain them, dry them by shaking the pan over the heat, and rice them. Beat together lightly 2 egg yolks and 1 whole egg and add them to the potatoes. Mix in 1/4 cup melted butter and 1/4 teaspoon each of salt and pepper, and beat the mixture until it is well blended.

Duchess potatoes are commonly used to garnish hot serving dishes. The mixture is piped through a pastry tube in an attractive design and the dish is browned in the oven or under the broiler.

Teutonia Potatoes — Kartoffeln Teutonia

RICE 6 MEDIUM-SIZED hot boiled potatoes and stir in 1 tablespoon butter, 1 egg, 1/4 teaspoon pepper, and 1/2 teaspoon salt. Add 1/2 cup each of toasted chopped hazelnuts and parsley and 1/2 teaspoon chopped rosemary. Shape the mixture first into balls and then into pyramids. Brush the pyramids with 2 eggs beaten with 2 tablespoons water and bake them on a buttered baking sheet in a moderately hot oven (375° F.) until they are golden, about 15 minutes.

Gräfinnenkartoffeln   *Potato Balls*

MAKE THE mixture for duchess potatoes and form it into balls 1 1/2 inches
in diameter. Dip the balls first into 2 tablespoons olive oil mixed with
2 egg whites and then in 3/4 cup seasoned dry bread crumbs. Lower them
gently into deep hot fat (375° F.), fry them until they are puffed and
brown, and drain them. Pile the balls in a mound and garnish them with
sprigs of parsley and browned slivered almonds.

Königliche Kartoffeln   *Potatoes with Orange Rind*

DRY 1 POUND peeled boiled potatoes by shaking the pan over low heat
and rice them. Add to them 2 tablespoons each of softened butter and
heavy cream, 1 tablespoon grated orange rind, a pinch of sugar, and salt
and pepper to taste. Add 2 egg yolks, one at a time, beating briskly after
each addition. Shape the potato mixture into walnut-size balls and dip
them first into 1 beaten egg and then in a mixture of 3/4 cup each of
seasoned dry bread crumbs and grated Parmesan. Lower them gently into
deep hot fat (375° F.) and fry them until they are puffed and brown.

Kaiserliche Kartoffeln   *Potatoes with Chestnuts*

FOLLOW THE recipe for potatoes with orange rind, but halve the rind,
and press 1 hot salted boiled chestnut into the center of each uncooked
potato ball. Dip the potato balls first into 2 beaten eggs and then in
1 1/2 cups seasoned dry bread crumbs, and fry them as directed.

Kartoffelkroketten   *Potato-Almond Croquettes*

FOLLOW THE recipe for potatoes with orange rind. Halve the orange rind,
add 3 scallions, finely chopped, and shape the potatoes into croquettes.
Dip the croquettes first into 1 beaten egg and then in 1 1/2 cups finely
chopped salted almonds and fry them as directed.

Potato Baskets

Gefüllte Kartoffeln

PARBOIL 6 MEDIUM-SIZED uniform peeled potatoes in salted water for 10 minutes. Drain them and roast them with meat or poultry. The oven temperature will depend on the roast. Or roast them separately with 1/2 cup butter in a moderately hot oven (375° F.) for 20 minutes, increase the temperature to hot (400° F.), and roast them for 10 minutes longer. Baste them every 10 minutes. With a ball cutter, scoop a hollow out of the flat side of each potato and fill it with green peas or with purée of green peas, mounded high or piped through a pastry bag. Other puréed vegetables may be used.

New Potatoes

Kartoffeln in der Schale

COOK 3 POUNDS small new potatoes of uniform size in their jackets in simmering salted water for about 15 minutes, or until they are just tender. In a skillet, in 1/2 cup butter, sauté 1 onion, finely chopped, until it is golden. Add the potatoes, 3 tablespoons sugar, and salt and pepper to taste. Stir the mixture well and sauté it until the sugar is browned and the potatoes are glossy. Sprinkle with 2 tablespoons chopped chives.

Garlic Potatoes

Kartoffeln mit Knoblauch

PARBOIL 18 SMALL new potatoes, covered, in salted water for 5 minutes and drain them. Sauté the potatoes in 1/4 cup melted butter until they are golden and tender, tossing them often to cook evenly. Arrange the potatoes with their butter in a hot serving dish. Combine 2 garlic cloves, crushed, 1/2 cup finely chopped parsley, and 2 teaspoons coarse ground salt, and sprinkle the mixture over the potatoes.

Paprika Potatoes

Paprika-Kartoffeln

SAUTÉ 3 SLICES bacon until they are crisp, drain them, and crumble them. Pour off all but 3 tablespoons fat in the pan, and in it sauté 1 cup chopped onions until they are golden. Add 2 teaspoons paprika and 1 teaspoon salt, and stir the mixture for 1 minute. Remove it from the heat, mix in 1 1/2 cups sour cream and 3 cups diced cooked potatoes, and simmer for about 15 minutes, or until the potatoes are soft but not mushy. Sprinkle the potatoes with paprika and the bacon and garnish them with parsley.

Erdäpfel mit Käse und Brunnenkresse

Potatoes with Cheese and Water Cress

CRUSH 3/4 POUND cream cheese, warmed to room temperature, and beat in, drop by drop, enough tarragon vinegar to give it the consistency of mayonnaise. Add salt and pepper to taste and a dash of onion juice. Mask 12 to 18 new potatoes, boiled and peeled, with the sauce and sprinkle it with 1 bunch water cress, stemmed and chopped.

Kartoffelauflauf mit Zunge

Potato Soufflé with Tongue

To 3 POUNDS warm potatoes, boiled, peeled, and riced, add 2 tablespoons butter and let them cool. Add 6 egg yolks and 1/4 cup heavy cream and mix in 1/2 cup cold tongue, cubed, 3 large shallots, finely chopped, and salt and pepper to taste. Fold in 6 egg whites, beaten stiff, pour the mixture into a buttered baking dish, and bake it in a moderately hot oven (375° F.) for about 40 minutes, or until it is brown.

Gebackene Kartoffeln

Potatoes and Onions

LINE A WELL-BUTTERED casserole with 1 cup crushed zwieback crumbs. Combine 6 potatoes and 2 large onions, all peeled and sliced, 1 table-spoon chopped parsley, 1/2 teaspoon salt, and pepper to taste. Arrange the mixture in the casserole and pour over 1 cup sour cream mixed with 1/2 cup grated Parmesan. Top with 1 cup zwieback crumbs mixed with 2 tablespoons grated Parmesan, and bake the potatoes in a moderately hot oven (375° F.) for 45 minutes, or until they are tender.

Kartoffelring

Cheese Potato Ring

RICE 6 MEDIUM-SIZE potatoes, boiled and peeled, beat in 3 tablespoons butter and 1/4 cup cream, and add salt and pepper to taste.

Sprinkle a heavily-buttered ring mold with 1/2 cup each of bread crumbs and grated Parmesan and press in the mashed potatoes. Cover with paper and bake the potatoes in a hot oven (400° F.) for 20 minutes. Unmold onto a serving platter and fill the center of the potato ring with green peas, Brussels sprouts, or any fresh vegetables coated with 1/4 cup browned butter.

Potatoes Anna with Cheese   *Kartoffelkäsekuchen 1*

SOAK 8 LARGE potatoes, peeled and thinly sliced, in cold water for 5 minutes and dry them. In a large buttered soufflé dish, arrange a layer of overlapping slices of potato over the entire bottom and sides. Sprinkle the potatoes with 3 tablespoons grated Parmesan, salt to taste, and 1 tablespoon butter. Cover the bottom and sides of the dish with another layer of potato slices. Continue arranging potato layers in this manner, sprinkling each layer with Parmesan, salt, and butter until all the potatoes are used and the dish is full. Bake the potatoes in a hot oven (400° F.) for about 45 minutes. Reduce the heat to 350° F., bake them for about 20 minutes more, or until the potatoes are golden brown, and invert them onto a heated round platter.

Potatoes with Cheese and Onion   *Kartoffelkäsekuchen 2*

To 1 1/4 POUNDS potatoes, boiled, peeled, and riced, add 2 tablespoons flour, salt and pepper to taste, and enough hot milk so that the potatoes obtain the consistency of a thick paste. Spread them in a well-buttered shallow baking dish and cover the top with 1/2 cup sour cream beaten with 1 egg. Sprinkle 1/2 cup grated Swiss cheese over the cream and cover the surface with 6 slices crisp bacon, sautéed and crumbled. Lay 3 sliced onions, separated into rings, over the bacon, and bake the potatoes in a moderately hot oven (375° F.) for 20 minutes, or until browned.

Cheese Potato Slices   *Käsekartoffelschnitten*

COMBINE 3 EGG yolks and 1/4 pound grated Emmenthal cheese with 1/2 cup creamed butter, add salt and pepper to taste, and chill the mixture.

Cut 4 large uniform potatoes, boiled and peeled, into 1/2-inch slices, lay the slices on a buttered baking sheet, and cover each slice with a thick layer of the cheese mixture. Bake the potatoes in a hot oven (400° F.) for about 10 minutes, or until they are golden, and sprinkle them with paprika. If preferred, raw potato slices may be baked at 350° F. until almost tender, then spread with the cheese mixture and baked 15 minutes longer. For a heavier dish, lay a slice of crisply sautéed bacon between the potato and the cheese.

Kartoffeln nach Prager Art *Potato Casserole*

RICE 8 POTATOES, boiled and peeled, and combine two-thirds of the potatoes with 1/2 cup finely chopped ham. Sauté 1/4 cup finely chopped onions in 1/4 cup butter for 5 minutes, taking care it does not brown, add 1/2 teaspoon each of salt and pepper, and stir it into the potatoes and ham. Add 3 egg yolks, lightly beaten, and pile the mixture into a buttered baking dish.

Combine 1/4 cup parsley, chopped, and 1/2 cup cream with the remaining one-third of the potatoes. Add salt and pepper to taste, fold in 3 stiffly beaten egg whites, and spread the mixture over the potatoes in the baking dish. Sprinkle the top first with 1/4 cup bread crumbs and then with 1 tablespoon melted butter. Bake the potatoes in a moderately hot oven (375° F.) for about 30 minutes, or until they are puffed and golden.

Potatoes with Sour Cream Dressing — Warmer Kartoffelsalat

IN A SAUCEPAN, heat 1/3 cup vinegar until it is hot but not boiling. Slowly add the beaten yolks of two eggs and cook the mixture over low heat until it thickens. Remove it from the heat, cool it slightly, and fold in 1 cup warm sour cream, 1/2 cup chopped parsley, 1/4 cup minced white onion, 2 teaspoons fine sugar, 1 teaspoon prepared mustard, and 1/4 teaspoon each of salt and white pepper. Pour the dressing over 6 medium-size old potatoes, boiled, peeled, and cut in crosswise slices, mix gently, and garnish them with sliced hard-cooked eggs and sprigs of parsley.

Chilled Molded Potatoes — Kaltes Kartoffelmus

BOIL 6 MEDIUM-SIZE potatoes, peeled and cut into halves, in salted water with 1 bay leaf and a stalk of celery for about 20 minutes, or until they are tender. Drain them and rice them. Add to them 4 tablespoons melted butter, 1 beaten egg, and 1/2 teaspoon prepared mustard, and beat the potatoes until they are light and fluffy. Fold in 3 tablespoons minced onion, 1 tablespoon finely chopped parsley, and 2 teaspoons onion juice and stir the mixture lightly until all the ingredients are well blended. Pile the potato mixture into individual custard cups and chill them. Unmold them onto lettuce leaves and garnish them with sliced hard-cooked eggs and sprigs of parsley. Serve with French dressing.

Mushroom Rice — Meraner Reis

SAUTÉ 1 1/2 CUPS rice in 1/4 cup butter with 2 tablespoons chopped onion until it is transparent and glazed. Add 2 cups beef stock and simmer the rice, stirring frequently. As the rice absorbs the liquid, stir in 1 more cup stock. Cook the rice, stirring, until it is tender but not soft, remove it from the heat, and add 1/2 cup sour cream, 3 egg yolks, 1/4 cup grated Parmesan, salt and pepper to taste, and 3 stiffly beaten egg whites. Pour one-third of the rice into a buttered baking dish and cover with 1/4 pound mushrooms, chopped and sautéed in butter with 2 tablespoons chopped parsley, and 1 teaspoon lemon juice. Add one-third of the rice and cover with a layer of tomatoes, peeled and sliced. Add the remaining rice. Sprinkle with 1/2 cup grated Parmesan and dot with 2 tablespoons butter. Bake in a moderately hot oven (375° F.) until browned, about 15 minutes.

Grüner Reis   Green Rice

IN THE TOP of a double boiler, over boiling water, cook 1 cup washed rice, 2 cups hot water, and 1 teaspoon salt, covered, for 20 minutes. Do not remove the cover during the cooking.

Beat 2 eggs well with 1 1/2 cups milk and 1/4 cup olive oil. Stir in gently with a fork the cooked rice, 2 cups grated Cheddar cheese, 1 cup finely chopped parsley, 2 stalks celery, finely diced, 1 medium-size white onion, chopped, 3/4 teaspoon sage, and salt and pepper to taste. Pour the rice into a 9-inch buttered ring mold or baking dish and bake it in a moderately slow oven (325° F.) for 25 minutes.

Risi-Pisi   Rice and Peas

IN THE TOP of a double boiler, over boiling water, steam 1 1/4 cups rice with 2 cups stock or salted water for 30 minutes, or until all the stock is absorbed. Combine the rice well with 1 cup cooked peas, 2 tablespoons butter, salt to taste, and a pinch of sugar, and cook the mixture over simmering water for 2 minutes. Serve with *Wiener Backhendl.*

Reis Montgelas   Rice with Artichoke Bottoms

SAUTÉ 1 TABLESPOON minced shallots in 1/4 cup butter until they are puffed and add 1 1/2 cups rice. Stir the rice until it is transparent and add 2 cups chicken stock. Cook, stirring frequently, and add 1 cup chicken stock as the liquid is absorbed. Cook to the *al dente* or semi-soft stage, about 20 minutes. Add salt to taste and stir in 1 cup chopped artichoke bottoms, cooked in salted water and sautéed in butter. Add 1 teaspoon each of finely minced chervil and dill and sprinkle with grated Parmesan.

Rice with Melon Balls   *Persischer Reis mit Melonen*

SOAK 1 1/2 CUPS Patna rice in lukewarm water for 2 hours, changing the water when necessary to keep it lukewarm. Drain the rice, pour it into a large kettle of boiling salted water, and boil it 15 minutes. Drain the rice well, cool it, and spread it out on a cloth until it is thoroughly dry. Place the rice in a shallow casserole, dot it with 2 tablespoons butter, and bake it in a moderate oven (350° F.) for 10 minutes. Serve the hot rice mixed with 1 cup cold melon balls, 1/2 cup each of chopped pineapple and walnuts, the juice from the pineapple and melon, 2 tablespoons melted butter, and salt to taste. Serve with meat or poultry.

Rice with Peppers   *Rot-grüner Pfeffer-Reis*

BRING TO a boil 1 1/2 cups rice and 4 cups water, reduce the heat, and simmer the rice for 15 minutes. Stir in 1/3 cup butter and steam the rice, covered, in a moderately hot oven (375° F.) for 10 to 15 minutes. Sauté 1 onion, 1 pimiento, and 1 small green pepper, all chopped, in 5 tablespoons butter until the onion is golden and pour all over the rice. Add salt to taste and 1/4 cup finely chopped parsley and stir the rice.

Saffron Rice   *Safranreis*

WASH 1 1/2 CUPS rice thoroughly in several waters, drain it, and place it in a heavy saucepan with 4 1/2 cups cold water and 1 teaspoon each of salt and lemon juice. Add a generous pinch of saffron shreds, stir the rice well, and bring it to a boil over high heat. When the water foams to the top of the saucepan, cover it, reduce the heat, and simmer the rice for about 15 minutes, stirring every 5 minutes, until the water is absorbed and the rice is tender and yellow. Add more saffron shreds during the cooking if a deeper yellow color is desired.

Indischer Reis-Pilaff
Indian Rice

SIMMER 3 POUNDS veal shoulder, cut in serving pieces, in 4 cups salted water, covered, for 40 minutes. Add 12 small white onions and cook 20 minutes longer. Strain the stock and keep the veal and onions warm.

Sauté 1 1/2 cups washed rice in 1/4 cup butter for 3 minutes. Add 3 cups of the warm veal stock, 2 white onions, sliced, a 1-inch-long cinnamon stick, and 4 cloves. Simmer the rice, covered, over low heat until it is tender and the stock has been absorbed. Discard the cinnamon stick and cloves, fluff the rice with a fork, and add 1/2 cup blanched and slivered almonds and 1/2 cup raisins sautéed lightly in 1/4 cup melted butter. Pile the rice into a buttered ring mold and heat it in a slow oven (300° F.) for 15 minutes. Unmold the ring onto a heated platter, fill it with the veal and onions, and sprinkle them with 2 sieved hard-cooked egg yolks and paprika.

Dolomiten Reis
Rice with Turmeric

RUB 1 1/2 cups rice between 2 towels and sauté it in 1/4 cup butter with 3 chicken livers, minced, and 1 onion, finely diced, until the rice is transparent. Add 2 1/2 cups strong chicken stock, 1 teaspoon powdered turmeric, dissolved in 1/4 cup stock, and 1/4 teaspoon each salt and sugar. Lay a kitchen towel over the skillet, put on the lid securely, and steam the rice over medium heat for 15 minutes. Stir the rice well and steam it 5 to 10 minutes longer. Stir in 1/4 cup freshly grated Parmesan and 1 tablespoon butter. Serve the rice with meat dishes or with zucchini and salad.

Reis mit Trauben
Brown Rice with Grapes

SAUTÉ 2 SMALL onions, finely chopped, in 3/4 cup butter, add 1 cup brown rice, and cook it until it is well coated with the butter. Add 2 cups stock and a *bouquet garni* and bake the rice, covered, for 20 minutes in a moderately hot oven (375° F.), adding more stock if necessary. Add 1 cup warm seedless grapes, 1/2 cup pine nuts, and salt and pepper to taste. With a fork, stir the rice well, return it to the oven until the grapes are hot, and stir it again.

Eierspeisen

D AS EI, the egg. Unless we actually eat an ox, we have nothing so short or so simple in American culinary language as an *Ei*, which is pronounced "i," as in "I like eggs." This rather egocentric relationship of the *Ei* and I makes for a very personal approach to its preparing and eating.

One must admit, after hearing the very loud noise the hen makes when she lays it (which the Viennese call *ein Spektakel*), the noise the cook makes when she prepares it, and the sighs and contented murmurs of the guest who eats it, that a single egg starts an unusual number of sound waves on their way around the world.

The egg prepared with loving care, to be eaten as an egg and not as a part of anything else, is respected and cherished. If boiled, it comes in a lovely little china or silver egg cup and sometimes even has a little hand-crocheted hat, a sort of egg cozy to keep it warm. There are special spoons for eating boiled eggs, and no one finishes his egg without a last look into the shell to see that every bit has been eaten. An egg is an egg in Vienna and not to be treated lightly. It is always timed by an hour-glass rather than by a clock, which just might be inaccurate. If the egg is shirred or fried, it is called *ein Spiegelei,* a mirror egg. Right there, in comparing it to a mirror in which he can see himself reflected, the diner makes the fried egg a delicacy. When the egg is poached, it is called rather sadly *ein verlorenes Ei,* a lost egg. It is not clear whether this has to do with the little edges lost in trimming the egg, or just the fact that the egg temporarily disappears in a whirlpool of water. An *oeuf mollet* is *ein kernweiches Ei,* an egg with a soft kernel and, when eggs are scrambled, they become *Rühreier,* stirred eggs, often stirred with

317

chives, truffles, cheese, or anything else that strikes the Viennese fancy. There are special porcelain dishes for every kind of egg, and no one would decline a second breakfast or a light supper of eggs.

All this solicitude applies to the individual beautiful egg, the laying hen's daily masterpiece. After the war, the dinner guest who brought his hostess a single egg found his gift enthusiastically appreciated. Another Viennese might walk miles into the country to bring back just one fresh egg. But the moment eggs are considered en masse in Vienna, and not individually, they become a means to an end and are ruthlessly handled. A cook may beat fourteen, even eighteen eggs into a *Torte* without hesitation, but when she is interrupted to prepare one "lost egg" for her mistress' *Gabelfrühstück,* she will follow the maid to the dining room door to see that it arrives safely and intact.

The Viennese kitchen is full of *Nockerln,* puddings, *beignets,* and *Aufläufe,* surprise omelets, and various puffs all made of eggs beaten separately. Sauces are finished with yolks and cream, and pastry and bread are egg-washed and yolk-painted. Meringues—called *Spanischer Wind,* Spanish wind—use up all the whites remaining from the egg yolk sauces. The Viennese have no angel cake but they have *Busserln,* little kisses that also take care of any leftover egg whites. Hard-cooked egg yolks are riced and crushed into dressings and mayonnaises and even go into some of the bakeries and *Torten.* Many Viennese claim their *Linzertorte* as the best, because they hard-cook the yolks that go into it.

The Viennese do not limit themselves almost entirely to the egg of the hen, as we do. They have the opportunity of tasting the eggs of other barnyard fowl, and they consider the *Kiebitz Ei,* the plover's egg, a particular delicacy and go to great lengths to produce it.

Like poultry and meat in Austria, eggs do not come from a distant and impersonal source. The Viennese who stays at a small country inn will order himself a *Spiegelei* for his second breakfast and find the waitress uninterested and lackadaisical. Suddenly she will brighten and say, "Of course, *Mein Herr.*" She has heard the reassuring and unmistakable *Spektakel* from the barnyard that announces the laying of a brand new egg and the possibility of filling the order.

Some Methods of Cooking Eggs

Coddled. Lower eggs into rapidly boiling water, immediately turn off the heat, cover the pot, and leave the eggs in the water for 10 minutes. Serve at once.

Poached—round. In a deep saucepan, stir rapidly boiling water briskly in one direction and break a single egg directly into it. Each quart of water should contain 1 tablespoon each of vinegar and salt. Skim the egg from the water with a slotted spoon when it is set.

Poached—flat. Break eggs into a saucer and slide them into a shallow pan of simmering water, about 2 inches deep. Each quart should contain 1 tablespoon each of vinegar and salt. Remove the eggs with a slotted spoon after about 4 minutes.

Baked. Place butter or cream in individual ramekins or cocottes, heat them in the oven, and break an egg carefully into each dish, leaving the yolk intact. Season with salt and pepper. Stand the cocottes in a pan of hot water and bake the eggs in a moderately hot oven (375° F.) from 6 to 8 minutes.

Shirred. Break one or more eggs into a shirred-egg dish in which butter has been melted, keeping the yolks intact. Add salt and pepper. Bake the eggs to desired doneness, about 4 minutes, or cook them over direct heat.

Eggs Mollet. Boil small eggs for just 5 minutes, large eggs for 6. Plunge them in cold water at once and peel them carefully. The white is sufficiently set to hold the soft yolk. Use them as you would poached eggs. Chill them for aspics or keep warm in warm salted water, to serve immediately.

Deep-Fried Poached Eggs   *Eier Eleonore*

DIP 6 COLD poached eggs into 2 beaten eggs, roll them carefully in 1 1/2 cups dry salted bread crumbs, and fry them in hot deep fat (375° F.) for 1 minute, or until they are brown. Serve them with the meat of 6 lobster claws, sautéed in butter. Serve with tomato sauce.

Aschenbrödeleier   *Poached Eggs in Baked Potatoes*

HALVE 3 LARGE baked potatoes lengthwise and scoop out the meat. Mix
it with 6 hot cooked shrimps, chopped, 3 tablespoons butter, and salt to
taste. Refill the potato shells and place 1 hot poached egg deep in the
center of each potato half. Lay 1 anchovy filet over each egg and sprinkle
the eggs and potatoes with 1/2 cup grated Parmesan. Bake them in a hot
oven (400° F.) until the cheese is brown.

Eier, heiss und kalt   *Poached Eggs on Baked Tomatoes*

CUT 3 LARGE tomatoes in half and bake them with 1/4 cup olive oil in
a moderately hot oven (375° F.) in a covered casserole for 10 minutes,
or until they are hot but not too soft. Scoop a little of the meat from each
tomato half and place 1 tablespoon crushed sardine or tuna salad in each.
Season well with salt and pepper as the egg and the tomato are bland.
Serve with béarnaise sauce.

Grüne Eier   *Green Eggs*

SOFTEN 2 ENVELOPES of gelatin in 1/2 cup Sherry. Bring 1 1/2 cups beef
stock to a boil and dissolve the gelatin in it, off the heat. Let the aspic
cool. Dip 6 neatly trimmed cold poached eggs into the liquid aspic and
turn them in 2 cups finely minced parsley, to coat them completely. Chill
the green eggs until the aspic is set. Pour the remaining aspic into a
shallow dish and chill it.

Peel and partially hollow out 6 large tomatoes and chill them well.
Arrange the tomatoes on a large platter, place 1 tablespoon liver paste
in the bottom of each tomato, and put a green egg on top of the paste.
Garnish the center of the platter with stars cut from the aspic and sprinkle
them with finely chopped black olives.

Husareneier   *Poached Eggs and Mushrooms in Tomatoes*

SAUTÉ 6 LARGE mushrooms, sliced, with 3/4 cup ham, cut in julienne,
in 3 tablespoons butter until they are transparent. Halve 6 large tomatoes,

hollow the halves out, put 1/2 teaspoon butter in each, and bake them for 10 minutes. Fill them with the mushroom mixture and lay 1 hot poached egg, poached so that it is round, not flat, on each. Serve the tomatoes with hollandaise sauce.

Poached Eggs in Mushrooms   *Verlorene Eier Pepita*

SAUTÉ 6 VERY large mushroom caps in 2 tablespoons butter for 2 to 3 minutes on each side. Sauté the stems, chopped, with 2 chopped chicken livers and 2 chopped shallots in 3 tablespoons butter until they are brown. Add salt and fill the caps with the mixture. Cover each with a hot poached egg and dust the eggs with 2 tablespoons finely chopped tarragon. Serve with tarragon butter.

Poached Eggs on Artichoke Bottoms   *Verlorene Eier Cavour*

PLACE 6 WELL-TRIMMED poached eggs on 6 hot cooked artichoke bottoms and put them into 6 individual egg dishes or cocottes, or 1 large one. Cover each egg with the mixture for cheese soufflé, using half the amount of the recipe, and bake in a moderately hot oven (375° F.) for 9 to 12 minutes, or until the soufflé is puffed and browned. Bake a few minutes longer if a large dish is used.

Poached Eggs on Noodles   *Verlorene Eier Karoly*

ARRANGE 3 CUPS of very fine soup noodles, cooked in salted water and well drained, on a hot serving platter, and pour over them 3 tablespoons hot melted butter. Arrange 6 poached eggs on the noodles and dust them with paprika and 1/4 cup grated Parmesan. Serve with paprika sauce.

Poached Eggs with Lobster   *Verlorene Eier mit Hummerragout*

HALVE 3 TOMATOES and squeeze out the seeds. Bake the halves in a buttered pan in a moderately hot oven (375° F.) for 10 to 15 minutes. Arrange them on a hot serving platter and place 1 hot poached egg, poached so that it is round, not flat, on each tomato. Surround them with 2 1/2 cups cooked lobster heated in 1 1/2 cups cream sauce flavored with 2 teaspoons chopped dill.

Holländische Kernweiche Eier   *Eggs Mollet with Asparagus*

ARRANGE 2 POUNDS steamed asparagus on a serving platter and mask it with 2 cups hollandaise sauce. Lay 6 eggs *mollet* on the sauce and sprinkle them with 1 cup julienne of cold tongue and 2 tablespoons chopped parsley.

Spiegeleier auf Lothringer Art   *Shirred Eggs Lorraine*

LAY 6 SLICES of bread in a buttered ovenproof dish and cover each with a slice of bacon, grilled, and a thin slice of Swiss cheese. Break 6 eggs over the cheese and pour 1/4 cup cream around the yolks. Bake the eggs in a moderately hot oven (375° F.) until they are set.

Spiegeleier auf Tartaren Art   *Shirred Eggs Tartare*

MIX 2/3 CUP finely scraped or ground raw beef with 2 tablespoons butter and spread the mixture over the bottom of an ovenproof dish. Sprinkle the meat with 2 tablespoons finely chopped onion, and salt and pepper to taste. Break 6 eggs over the mixture, sprinkle them with 1/4 cup sour cream, and bake in a moderately hot oven (375° F.) until they are set. Sprinkle with 2 tablespoons finely chopped parsley.

Eier Tante Emma   *Shirred Eggs with Crumbs*

MIX TOGETHER 1/4 cup each of creamed butter, dry bread crumbs, and mixed chopped herbs—parsley, chives, chervil, and tarragon. Stir in 4 egg yolks and add salt and pepper to taste. Press the mixture around the edges of 6 buttered shirred-egg dishes, or cocottes, and break an egg into each. Place the cocottes in a pan of hot water and bake the eggs in a moderately hot oven (375° F.) for 8 to 10 minutes, or until they are set. Lay anchovy filets in a cross on each egg. Serve very hot.

Shirred Eggs with Duchess Potatoes   *Eier Duchesse*

Mix DUCHESS potatoes with finely chopped chives to taste and pipe them with a pastry bag fitted with a fluted tube around 6 individual buttered shirred-egg dishes. Pour 2 tablespoons heavy cream into each dish and break an egg into each ring. Bake the eggs in a moderately hot oven (375° F.) until the whites are set. Sprinkle them with a little freshly grated horseradish.

Baked Eggs with Hollandaise   *Bismarck-Eier*

Mix 1/4 POUND cooked ham, chopped fine, with 3/4 cup grated Parmesan. Butter 6 custard cups well, break 1 egg into each, sprinkle them with salt and pepper, and cover them with the ham and cheese mixture. Set the cups in a pan of boiling water and bake the eggs in a moderately hot oven (375° F.) for 8 to 10 minutes. Turn out the eggs on plates and mask them with hollandaise sauce.

First-Course Scrambled Eggs   *Rühreier als Vorspeise*

While the Viennese use eggs heedlessly in their cookery, they approach with respect and tenderness eggs served singly, or in twos and threes. The daughter of the house will often excuse herself from the table to scramble the eggs to her parents' liking.

Scrambled Eggs I   *Rühreier 1*

BEAT 3 EGGS with 2 tablespoons cream and salt to taste. Melt 3 tablespoons sweet butter in an omelet pan over low heat and add the eggs as soon as the butter is melted. Cook them, stirring slowly with a wooden spoon, being careful that flaky masses of the egg are stirred from the bottom of the pan before they become too firm. The eggs should be light and flaky and they should not cook long enough to become hard or dry. Serve at once. Serves 2.

Rühreier 2 *Scrambled Eggs* II

MELT 2 TABLESPOONS butter in an omelet pan and add 4 eggs, beaten with salt and white pepper. Cook them over low heat, stirring constantly with a wooden spoon, until they are lightly set and stir in gradually 2 tablespoons each of butter and heavy cream. The eggs should be creamy rather than flaky. Serve at once.

Rühreier mit Speck *Scrambled Eggs with Bacon*

SAUTÉ 3 SLICES lean bacon, diced, until it is transparent. Drain the dice and add them with 2 tablespoons grated Parmesan to scrambled eggs I, while the eggs are cooking. Scatter over the cooked eggs 1/2 cup tomatoes, peeled, chopped, and sautéed in butter for 1 minute. Serves 2.

Rühreier Ursula *Scrambled Eggs with Asparagus and Shrimps*

SAUTÉ 12 COOKED asparagus tips and 12 small cooked shrimps in butter. Drain them. Cook scrambled eggs I, using shrimp butter, instead of plain butter. Add the drained asparagus and shrimps when the eggs are half cooked. Serve the eggs on a hot platter surrounded by toast rounds, each spread with anchovy butter and covered with a thin slice of tomato, peeled and seeded. Serves 4.

Scrambled Eggs with Herbs — Rühreier mit Kräutern

SPRINKLE 1 TABLESPOON each of chopped parsley and chives, and 1/2 minced shallot over scrambled eggs I when they are half cooked and continue cooking as usual.

Scrambled Eggs with Chicken Livers — Rühreier Meyerbeer

MIX 1 TABLESPOON tomato paste into scrambled eggs I while they are cooking. Serve the eggs around 6 chicken livers, sautéed with 1 tablespoon chopped onion and bound with 1/4 cup Madeira sauce. Serves 3.

Scrambled Eggs and Smoked Salmon Sandwiches — Lachsbrot mit Rühreier

TRIM THE crust from 6 large slices of pumpernickel bread and spread them evenly with butter. Lay a thick slice of smoked salmon on each slice of bread and trim the edges, and season the salmon generously with freshly ground black pepper. Beat 4 eggs with 2 tablespoons heavy cream and salt to taste and scramble them in butter over low heat. Divide the scrambled eggs among the 6 sandwiches, mounding them in the center of each, sprinkle the eggs with chives, finely minced, and decorate with parsley and lemon slices. Serve the sandwiches immediately.

Scrambled Eggs with Chicken Livers and Green Beans — Esterhazy-Eier

SNAP OFF the ends of 1 pound tender young green beans, but leave the beans whole. Cook them in boiling salted water until they are tender. Drain them and keep them hot. Sauté 12 slices of bacon until they are transparent and drain them. Thread the bacon alternately with 1 cup chicken livers on 6 short wooden skewers and sauté the livers for 3 minutes in 2 tablespoons butter, turning them 3 times. Pour over the livers 1 cup hot consommé, season to taste, and cook gently until the livers are done, about 5 minutes. Beat well 6 eggs with 3 tablespoons cream but not until they are frothy. Add salt and white pepper to taste. Scramble the eggs to a soft consistency. Arrange the livers in the center of a warm platter and surround them with mounds of the beans and the scrambled eggs. Pour over them the sauce from the pan in which the livers were cooked. Sprinkle with finely chopped parsley and serve at once.

Bulgarische Eier   *Eggs and Potatoes*

SAUTÉ 3 MEDIUM-SIZED potatoes, peeled and sliced, in butter until they are tender and lightly browned. Add 6 hard-cooked eggs, sliced, 1/4 cup chopped parsley, and salt to taste. Grind black pepper over the eggs and add 1/2 cup grated Emmenthal, Swiss or Parmesan cheese. Stir the mixture carefully and add 1/4 cup heavy cream. Serve hot, with a cold lettuce salad.

Parma Eier   *Eggs Parmesan*

STIR 6 EGG yolks with 6 tablespoons grated Parmesan and 2 1/2 tablespoons each of heavy cream and melted butter until they are light. Add salt to taste and a pinch of cayenne. Fold in 6 stiffly beaten egg whites. Divide the soufflé mixture among 6 custard cups and dust each with a teaspoon of grated Parmesan. Bake for 8 to 10 minutes in a moderate oven (350° F.).

Gefüllte Eier   *Stuffed Eggs*

Recipes for a variety of stuffed eggs may be found in the chapter on Vorspeisen, *or first-course dishes.*

Cheese

Käse

"Aber geh'!" says the Viennese, and he says it often and with conviction; when necessary he even says *"Aber geh'! Geh'! Geh'!"* It means "But go!" and the implication is "Go on and tell that to someone else, because I know it is unheard of —absolutely *unerhört*—and what is unheard of in Vienna naturally doesn't exist."

When a Viennese is told there are people who eat meat for breakfast, lunch, and dinner, he says *"Aber geh'!"* finally and emphatically. He cannot believe that such wealth and madness exist.

To a people who combine a scarcity of meat with a scarcity of money and a full complement of fasting days, days of abstinence, and forty days of Lent each year, cheese becomes a necessity; and in its way, the preparation, recognition, and appreciation of cheese becomes an art. There are cheese shops and wonderful cheese smells on Vienna's streets, and no *Kaffeehaus* would be complete without black bread and a good Swiss cheese for the patron who needs a little extra sustenance to help him on his way to another *Kaffeehaus* down the street.

In a country where cheese is eaten as a main dish, as dessert, or as a *Vorspeise,* or first course, it cannot always take the form of plain sliced cheese. The peasant may eat his bread and cheese while he herds the goats that give the milk from which the cheese is made, the Viennese bakes and cooks cheese dishes and cheese bakeries, and knows a new cheese dish for every day of Lent, if not for every day of the year. He eats cheese baked with vegetables and cheese combined with fruit. He bakes pastries in which cheese takes the place of butter, and eats puddings and soufflés in which cheese is combined with everything from tomatoes, spinach, rice,

and crayfish to pears and potatoes. No Viennese would choose to eat
meat three times a day if it would mean having to sacrifice his beloved
Käsepfannkuchen or *Florentiner Pudding.*

The Austrian cheeses are good and plentiful, and resemble on the
whole the famous cheeses made across her borders in Switzerland and
Germany. Most common are the Emmenthal type of cheeses—called
Emmental by the Swiss and Gruyère by everyone else—and those which
resemble the German *Limburger Käse.* There are Austrian cheeses that
resemble Edam, and from Hungary comes the Liptauer cheese. Cream
cheeses, often called *Gervais,* and *Topfen,* cottage cheese, are made
on every farm in every province. There are goat cheeses and wonderful
rural cheeses that can be eaten only in the valley or on the mountainside
where they were made, and that never reach the commercial markets.

Cooking and baking with *Topfen* and cream cheese are common to all
parts of Austria, although the Hungarians probably taught the Viennese
to love *Palatchinken* and *Strudel* filled with cottage cheese beaten with
egg yolks, sugar, and raisins. The *garnierter Liptauer Käse* is a combination of mild soft cheeses, served in the center of an elaborate ring of
condiments and garnishes. Everyone mixes his own Liptauer, or a host
who stirs it all together will first serve the guest who doesn't want the caraway seeds before he incorporates them. The usual Liptauer is served with
butter curls, paprika and caraway-seed mounds, various mustards, chopped
chives, and other herbs. Other additions are capers, anchovies, and anything that strikes the fancy of the creator of the platter. The Liptauer
turns pink from the addition of the paprika, and a large and elaborate
Liptauer platter will keep a supper party perfectly happy for hours.

The Viennese, who look across their borders with nostalgia and
curiosity, observe the cheeses of Germany, Italy, and Switzerland, the
Sbrinz and Walliser, the Parmesan and Gorgonzola, which they cannot
imitate, and see such cheese splendors on every side that they are led
to invent Austrian dishes to accommodate them and to import the cheeses
they do not make themselves.

Pâte à Choux or
Cream-Puff Paste with Cheese   *Brandteig*

IN A SMALL saucepan, bring to a boil 3/4 cup water and 1/4 cup milk, and add 1/3 cup butter and 1/2 teaspoon salt. When the butter is melted, add 1 cup flour all at once and stir with a wooden spoon until all the flour is absorbed and the mixture leaves the sides of the pan and forms a ball. Remove the mixture from the heat and let it cool slightly. Beat in 4 large or 5 small eggs, one at a time, stirring in each egg thoroughly before adding the next one. Add 1/2 cup each of grated Swiss and Parmesan. Divide the dough into 12 even rounds and place them 3 inches apart on a buttered baking sheet. If necessary, dip two spoons into egg white to facilitate handling of the dough. Bake the rounds of dough in a hot oven (400° F.) for 10 minutes. Reduce the temperature to moderately hot (375° F.) and continue to bake the puffs for 20 minutes, or until they are puffed and golden. Do not open the oven door for the first 15 minutes.

Filled Baked Puffs   *Gefüllte Windbeutel*

MAKE CREAM-PUFF PASTE as described above and bake the puffs. Let them cool slightly. Make a small slit on the underside of each puff and pipe into it through a pastry bag any appropriate filling. Serve the puffs warm or cold, garnished with parsley and accompanied with a green salad. Makes 12. To use filled puffs as a soup garnish, divide the dough into 24 rounds, bake and fill them, and drop them into hot bouillon.

Cheese Filling I   *Creme zum Füllen 1*

COMBINE 3 EGG yolks, 1 cup heavy cream, 3 tablespoons flour, 2 tablespoons butter, and 2/3 cup grated Swiss cheese or Cheddar cheese, and cook the mixture over low heat, or in the top of a double boiler over boiling water, until it is smooth and the cheese is melted. Use the mixture to fill baked puffs or other pastries.

Cheese Filling II   *Creme zum Füllen 2*

IN A SMALL saucepan, over low heat, melt 2 tablespoons butter, add 2 tablespoons flour, and cook the *roux,* stirring constantly, until it is well blended. Do not let it brown. Gradually add 1 cup hot milk and continue to stir the mixture until it thickens. Add 1/2 cup grated Swiss or Cheddar cheese and stir the sauce with a whisk until the cheese is melted. Remove the sauce from the heat, cool it slightly, and stir in 1 egg yolk, 1/4 cup sour cream, and salt to taste. Use the mixture to fill baked puffs.

Creme zum Füllen 3 — Cheese Filling III

COMBINE 2 CUPS whipped cream, 1/2 cup grated Swiss or Cheddar cheese, 1 egg yolk, and salt to taste. Use the mixture to fill baked puffs.

Überraschungskrapfen — Ham and Cheese Balls

BRING TO a boil 1 cup water, 1/3 cup butter, 1/2 teaspoon salt, and a pinch each of pepper and nutmeg. Stir in well, off the heat, 1 generous cup flour, cook the mixture over low heat for 3 minutes, stirring constantly, and cool it for 6 minutes. Add 4 egg yolks, one at a time, 1 cup diced Emmenthal or Cheddar cheese, 2/3 cup diced ham, and 1/4 cup slivered almonds. Roll the mixture into balls, dust them with flour, and fry them in deep hot fat (375° F.) for 4 minutes, or until they are brown and puffed.

Käsering — Cheese Ring

PREPARE THE mixture for ham and cheese balls but omit the ham and almonds. Shape the mixture in a ring on a buttered baking sheet, paint it with 1 beaten egg yolk, and cover it with 1/2 cup finely slivered Swiss cheese. Bake the ring in a very hot oven (425° F.) for 40 minutes.

Camembertkrapfen — Camembert Rounds

SCRAPE 1 CAMEMBERT cheese, press the cheese through a sieve with 2 tablespoons butter, and stir in 3 egg yolks and salt and pepper to taste. Spread the mixture 1/3 inch deep in a baking pan and chill it until it is firm. Cut the mixture into 1-inch rounds, sprinkle them with grated Swiss cheese, and dip them first in beaten egg and then in bread crumbs. Dip the

rounds again in beaten egg and bread crumbs and sauté them on both sides in 3 tablespoons butter until they are golden. Serve them with salad or as a dessert.

Cheese Fritters — *Käsekrapfen*

COMBINE 1 1/3 cups bread crumbs with 1 cup grated Parmesan, add a generous 1/2 cup butter, 2 egg yolks, and salt and paprika to taste, and work all the ingredients into a smooth paste. Shape the mixture into flat rounds, dip them first into beaten egg and then in dry bread crumbs, and fry them in deep hot fat (370° F.) until they are golden.

Cheese Beignets — *Käsekrapfen Talleyrand*

BRING TO a boil 1 cup milk and a generous 1/2 cup butter, add 2 cups flour all at once, and stir the mixture until it leaves the sides of the pan. Let it cool and add 7 eggs, one at a time, stirring in each egg thoroughly

before adding the next one. Add 1 1/4 cups diced Swiss cheese and salt,
paprika, and pepper to taste. Using 2 tablespoons, form the mixture into
walnut-size rounds, drop a few at a time into deep hot fat (375° F.),
and fry them until they are golden. Serve the *beignets* with tomato sauce,
or make them smaller and serve them on picks with cocktails.

Käsetaschen   *Cheese Canapés*

WORK INTO a smooth dough 1/2 cup softened butter, one 3-ounce package
cream cheese, and 1 cup flour. Roll out the dough 1/4 inch thick, chill it
for 30 minutes, and cut it into 2-inch rounds. Place a sliver of Cheddar
cheese on half of each round, fold over the other half, and press it down
well. Bake the rounds on a buttered baking sheet in a moderately hot
oven (375° F.) for 10 minutes, or until the cheese is golden. Serve them
at once.

Käseleckerbissen   *Cheese Wedges*

COMBINE THOROUGHLY into a paste 2 1/4 cups grated Swiss cheese, 1/2 cup
each of creamed butter and chopped ham, 4 egg yolks, 1 teaspoon dry
mustard, and salt to taste. Spread the mixture 1/4 inch thick on very thin
slices of white bread and cover with a second slice. Press down the sandwiches well, trim off the crusts, and cut each sandwich into 6 or 8 wedges.
Dip the wedges first into 2 well-beaten eggs and then in 1 cup dry bread
crumbs. Fry the cheese wedges, a few at a time, in deep hot fat (375° F.)
until they are golden. While they are still hot, roll them in 1 cup grated
Parmesan.

Westfälische Käseschnitten   *Cream Cheese and*
                                                Radishes on Pumpernickel

RICE ONE 8-ounce package cream cheese with 1/4 cup softened butter,
stir in just enough sour or sweet cream to make a smooth paste, and add
1/4 teaspoon crushed caraway seeds and salt and paprika to taste. Pipe
the mixture through a pastry bag fitted with a fluted tube around the
edges of 6 round slices of buttered pumpernickel. Fill the centers with
1/2 cup radishes and 1/4 cup spring onions, both finely chopped and bound

with thick mayonnaise, seasoned to taste with salt. Sprinkle the tops with chopped chives.

Molded Russian Cheese   Russischer Käse

PRESS 1 CAMEMBERT cheese, 1/4 pound Roquefort cheese, and one 3-ounce package of cream cheese through a sieve and work the cheeses into a very smooth paste with 1/4 pound sharp Cheddar cheese and 1/2 cup Edam cheese, both ground. Add 1 cup grated Swiss cheese and work in a quantity of butter that is one-fourth the quantity of the cheese. Add salt and pepper to taste and press the paste into an earthenware or enameled mold. Chill the paste until it is hard, unmold it onto a serving platter, and surround it with butter balls, radishes, and black and rye bread. The proportions and combinations of cheeses may be varied according to taste.

Filled Camembert   Gefüllter Camembertkäse

CAREFULLY CUT out the center of a Camembert cheese, leaving the bottom and a 1/4-inch edge intact. Mix the cheese with 1/2 cup creamed butter and add salt and paprika to taste. Whip 1/2 cup cream until it is stiff, fold it into the cheese, and pipe the mixture through a pastry bag into the cheese shell. The cheese shell may be lined with 1/4 cup each of cold seedless grapes and toasted slivered almonds. Place the filled Camembert on a round wooden platter and surround it with triangles of buttered black bread and red radish roses.

Garnished Liptauer Cheese   Garnierter Liptauer Käse

GARNIERTER LIPTAUER KÄSE is a general name for a dish in which several cheeses are combined and the mixture elaborately garnished. The name is not that of any one cheese used in the dish, but refers to the combination, however much it may vary.

Combine well equal parts of Liederkranz cheese, Camembert cheese, skinned, and cream-type cottage cheese. Place the cheese mixture in the center of a large platter and surround it with little mounds of paprika, minced onion, caraway seeds, caviar, butter balls, chopped capers, chopped chives, German mustard, sprigs of parsley, black pepper, and thin slices of rye and black bread. Each guest mixes his own combination, or the host mixes everything, with the exception of the bread and butter. Serve with beer.

Camembertsülze   *Camembert in Aspic*

BRING TO a boil 3 1/2 cups clarified beef stock, remove it from the heat, and add 2 envelopes of gelatin softened in 1/2 cup Sherry. Stir until the gelatin is dissolved, add salt to taste, and let the aspic cool. Pour the aspic into 6 to 9 individual rinsed molds, filling them to the top. Place them in the refrigerator and, as soon as the edges start to set, pour off the liquid centers, leaving the molds lined with an even coat of aspic. Keep the poured-off aspic liquid over warm water and chill the lined molds for 15 minutes. Fill them three-quarters full with a mixture of 1 Camembert cheese, skinned, sieved with 1/2 cup softened butter and seasoned sharply with salt and paprika. Cover the molds with a layer of aspic and chill them. Unmold each aspic onto a round slice of pumpernickel bread and serve them with red radishes and thin mayonnaise flavored with onion juice to taste.

Edamer Käse   *Filled Edam Cheese*

SCOOP OUT a 1-pound Edam cheese and grind the cheese in the food chopper. Add 1 cup softened butter, 1/4 cup brandy, 1/2 teaspoon each of powdered celery seed and dry mustard, and salt to taste. Beat the mixture until it is well blended. Refill the red shell of the cheese, mounding the mixture high.

Käsepudding   *Cheese Pudding*

IN A SAUCEPAN, melt 1/4 cup butter and cool it. Add 1/4 cup sifted flour and stir the *roux* until it is smooth. Gradually add 1 cup milk and stir

the sauce over low heat until it is hot and smooth. Do not let it boil. Cool it slightly and add 3 egg yolks, one at a time, and stir in each yolk thoroughly before adding the next. Add 3/4 cup grated Parmesan and salt and pepper to taste and fold in 3 stiffly beaten egg whites. Pour the pudding into a well-buttered pudding mold, cover it, and place in a kettle of boiling water. The water should cover two-thirds of the mold. Cover the kettle and steam the pudding for 50 minutes, adding more boiling water if necessary. To unmold the pudding, run a knife around the upper edges of the mold and invert it onto a warm platter. Serve it with a green salad and sliced dill pickles. It may also be served with a tomato sauce, as a first course, or with a cheese sauce, as a last course.

Cheese Soufflé   *Käseauflauf 1*

MELT 3 TABLESPOONS butter, blend in 3 tablespoons flour, and cook the *roux*, stirring, until the flour is transparent. Gradually add 1 cup milk and cook the sauce for 1 minute. Add 1/2 cup each of grated Parmesan and grated Cheddar cheese, cook the sauce, stirring, until the cheese is melted, and cool it slightly. Beat in 5 egg yolks, one at a time, and add salt and pepper to taste. Beat 6 egg whites stiff but not dry. They are stiff enough when the bowl can be tilted without the egg whites moving from the bottom. Fold the whites into the cheese mixture and pour it into an unbuttered baking dish or soufflé mold.

Stand the dish in a pan of hot water and bake the soufflé in a moderately hot oven (375° F.) for 45 to 55 minutes, or until it is puffed and lightly browned. Do not open the oven door for the first 30 minutes. Serve the soufflé at once, with chive sauce, if desired.

Käseauflauf 2   *Cheese Custard with Meringue*

COMBINE 1 CUP thick sour cream with 1/2 cup freshly grated Parmesan or Swiss cheese, 1/4 teaspoon paprika, and salt to taste. Beat 3 egg yolks until they are light and add them to the cheese mixture. Pour the mixture into a well-buttered baking dish or soufflé mold, stand the dish in a pan of hot water, and bake the custard in a moderately hot oven (375° F.) for 20 minutes. Beat 3 egg whites with 1/2 teaspoon salt until they are stiff and fold in 1/2 cup finely chopped walnuts and 2 tablespoons grated Parmesan. Remove the custard from the oven, quickly pile the stiff egg-white mixture onto the top, and return it to the oven for 6 to 8 minutes, or until the meringue is browned. Or brown the meringue under the broiler.

Kleine Käseaufläufe   *Small Cheese Soufflés*

DRY 3/4 CUP bread crumbs in a slow oven (250° F.) for 15 minutes, shaking them every 5 minutes. Over low heat, warm 1 1/2 cups heavy cream with 2 tablespoons butter, add the bread crumbs, and continue to stir the mixture until it thickens. Let the mixture cool. Stir in 6 egg yolks, 1 cup grated Parmesan or 1/2 cup each of grated Parmesan and grated Swiss cheese, and salt and pepper to taste, and fold in 6 stiffly beaten egg whites. Pile the mixture into 6 small buttered baking dishes or soufflé molds, bake the soufflés in a moderate oven (350° F.) for 15 to 20 minutes, or until they are puffed and golden brown, and serve them at once.

Cheese Pancakes   *Käsepfannkuchen*

BEAT THOROUGHLY 1 cup heavy cream with 4 eggs and 2/3 cup flour
and add 3/4 cup grated Parmesan or Swiss cheese and salt to taste. Sauté
small pancakes of the batter in a buttered skillet and serve them very hot
with browned butter.

Filled Cheese Pancakes   *Gefüllte Käsepfannkuchen*

SPREAD CHEESE pancakes with cheese filling I and roll them up. Fold
over the ends, secure them with a pick, and dip the pancakes first into
beaten egg then in bread crumbs. Sauté the pancakes in butter, turning
them once, until they are golden, remove the pick, and serve them very hot.

Swiss Pancakes   *Schweizer Pfannkuchen*

MELT 1/4 CUP butter in the top of a double boiler over boiling water,
stir in 1/2 cup flour, and cook the *roux* for 5 minutes. Gradually add 2 1/4
cups milk and stir the sauce with a whisk until it is smooth and thick.
Add 1 3/4 cups finely diced Swiss cheese, continue cooking the sauce until
the cheese is melted, and add salt, pepper, and paprika to taste. Remove
the mixture from the heat and beat in 2 egg yolks. Pour it 1/2 inch deep
into an oiled baking pan and let it cool. Cut the mixture into 24 rectangles.
    Stir 1 1/2 cups milk and 1 cup water into 1 1/2 cups flour sifted with 1
teaspoon salt, beat in 2 eggs, and let the batter stand for 1 hour. Make
twenty-four 6-inch pancakes. Wrap 1 pancake around each cheese rectangle and dip them first into beaten egg and then in salted bread crumbs.
Fry the breaded pancakes in deep hot fat (375° F.) for about 6 minutes,
or until they are brown. Serve the pancakes with spinach or tomato purée
and a salad as a main dish.

Cheese Cream Slices   *Käseschaumschnitten*

ADD 6 EGG yolks and 1/2 teaspoon each of salt and paprika to 1/2 cup
creamed butter and beat the mixture until it is foamy. Fold in 6 stiffly
beaten egg whites and sprinkle the batter with 1 1/2 cups grated Swiss

cheese and 2/3 cup flour sifted with 1 teaspoon baking powder. Pour the batter 1/2 inch deep into a buttered and floured pan and bake in a moderate oven (350° F.) for 35 minutes, or until it tests done. Cool the cake, cut it into 2- by 4-inch pieces, and split them across.

Cream 1/2 cup butter with 1 1/2 cups grated Parmesen, season sharply with salt, pepper, and paprika to taste, and fold in 3/4 cup cream, whipped. Fill the split cakes generously with the cheese cream, pipe a rosette of the cream on each slice, and put a toasted almond in each rosette.

Bayrische Käsecreme   *Cheese Bavarian Cream*

BRING TO a boil 1 1/2 cups milk, remove it from the heat, and stir in 3 envelopes of gelatin softened in 3/4 cup cold milk. Let the mixture cool. Combine into a soft paste two 8-ounce packages cream cheese, riced, and 1 cup sour cream, and add it to the gelatin mixture with salt and pepper to taste and a grating of nutmeg. Chill the mixture for 10 minutes, add 1/4 pound grated Parmesan, and fold in 2 cups heavy cream, whipped. Correct the seasoning, pour the cream into a 3-quart mold rinsed in cold water, and chill it for 3 hours. Unmold the cream onto a serving platter and decorate it with cucumber slices and parsley.

Käsemus   *Cold Cheese Mousse*

MELT 1/4 CUP butter, stir in 1/2 cup flour, and cook the *roux* over low heat, stirring constantly, for 3 minutes. Add 1 1/4 cups milk and stir the sauce with a whisk until it is smooth and thick. Remove it from the heat and add 2 envelopes of gelatin softened in 1/2 cup chicken stock. Stir the sauce until the gelatin is dissolved and beat in 4 egg yolks, 2/3 cup grated Parmesan or Swiss cheese, 1/2 small onion, minced, 1 teaspoon dry mustard, and salt, pepper, and paprika to taste. Cool the mixture and fold in 4 stiffly beaten egg whites and 1/4 cup whipped cream. Dust a lightly oiled 2-quart mold with 1/4 cup chopped chives and pour in the cheese mixture carefully so that the chives remain on the lining of the mold. Chill the mousse for 3 hours and serve it surrounded with water cress with French dressing.

Cheddar Cheese Sticks I   *Käsestangen 1*

WORK INTO a smooth dough 2 1/4 cups flour, 1 1/4 cups sharp Cheddar
cheese, grated, 1 cup softened butter, and salt and paprika to taste. Chill
the dough for 1/2 hour and roll it out 1/4 inch thick on a floured board.
Paint the surface with 1 egg beaten with 1 teaspoon water, dust with
1/2 cup grated Parmesan, and cut the dough into 1 1/4-inch squares.
Bake the squares on an unbuttered baking sheet in a moderate oven
(350° F.) for about 15 minutes, or until they are golden. Serve hot.

Cheddar Cheese Sticks II
and Cheddar Cheese Pigs   *Käsestangen 2*

SIFT TOGETHER 1 cup sifted flour, 1/2 teaspoon salt, and 1/4 teaspoon
paprika and toss with 1/2 cup grated Parmesan and 1/3 cup grated sharp
Cheddar cheese. Cut in 1/2 cup butter and work in 1 tablespoon heavy
cream to make a smooth dough. Chill the dough for 1 hour and roll it
out on a lightly floured board into a rectangle about 1/8 inch thick. With
a floured pastry wheel cut strips 1/2 inch wide and 8 to 10 inches long.
Paint the sticks with an egg yolk beaten with 1 teaspoon water and sprinkle
them with freshly ground salt and caraway seeds. Bake the sticks on an
unbuttered baking sheet in a moderately slow oven (325° F.) for 12 minutes, and serve them warm. Makes about 4 dozen. The Viennese sometimes cut this dough in the shape of little pigs. *(Picture, page 483.)*

Cheese Sticks   *Käsebatons*

ROLL OUT the dough for Cheddar cheese sticks I into pencil-thin rolls,
paint them with 1 egg beaten with 1 teaspoon water, and sprinkle them
with poppy seeds. Cut the rolls into 3-inch lengths and bake them on
an unbuttered baking sheet in a moderate oven (350° F.) for about 15
minutes, or until they are golden. *(Picture, page 483.)*

Filled Cheese Sticks   *Gefüllte Käsestangen*

ROLL OUT the dough for Cheddar cheese sticks I as thinly as possible and
cut it into strips 1 inch wide and 4 inches long or circles. Bake them on

an unbuttered baking sheet in a moderate oven (350° F.) for about 15 minutes, or until they are golden. Sandwich the pastries together with cheese filling I and serve them warm with soup. *(Picture, page 483.)*

Parmesan Käsestangen   *Parmesan Cheese Sticks*

WORK INTO a smooth dough 1 cup each of grated Parmesan and flour, 1/4 cup butter, 7 tablespoons sour cream, and salt and paprika to taste. Chill the dough for 1/2 hour and roll it out 3/16 inch thick on a floured board. Cut the dough into strips 1/2 inch wide and 9 inches long, and twist the strips into spirals. Bake the cheese sticks on an unbuttered baking sheet in a moderate oven (350° F.) for 15 minutes, or until they are golden. Serve them hot.

Parmesanbiskuit   *Cheese Strips*

CREAM 1/4 CUP butter with 3 egg yolks, add 6 tablespoons each of grated Parmesan and flour and salt, pepper, and nutmeg to taste. Fold in 6 stiffly beaten egg whites and pipe the mixture through a pastry bag in thick strips onto a buttered baking sheet. Sprinkle the strips with salt and grated Parmesan to taste and bake them in a hot oven (400° F.) for 20 minutes, or until they are puffed and brown. Cut the strips diagonally into 2-inch lengths and serve them hot.

Käserolle   *Cheese Roll*

BEAT 6 EGGS in the top of a double boiler over low heat until they are thick and foamy. Remove the pan from the heat and continue to beat the eggs until they are cool. Fold in 1 cup each of sifted flour and grated Parmesan or Swiss cheese and 1/2 teaspoon salt. Line a baking sheet with heavy buttered and floured paper and spread it with the batter, about 1/4 inch thick. Bake the pastry in a moderate oven (350° F.) for 20 minutes.

Cream 3/4 cup butter with 2 cups grated Cheddar cheese and mix in thoroughly 1/4 cup each of finely chopped almonds and chives. Turn the baked pastry out at once onto a pastry board, spread it with this filling, roll it up, and wrap it in wax paper. Chill thoroughly and slice.

Cheese Palmiers 𝒦*äseschweinsohren*

SIFT 2 CUPS flour with 1 teaspoon salt. Cut in 5 tablespoons butter or lard and work in 8 tablespoons ice water mixed with 3 tablespoons iced kirsch. Work the dough until it is smooth and chill it well. Roll the dough into an 8- by 12-inch rectangle on a lightly floured pastry board and let it rest, loosely covered, in a cool place.

Work 2 sticks cold butter with 1/3 cup flour. Spread it over two-thirds, or 7 by 7 inches, of the dough. Fold the unbuttered third, or 4- by 8-inch piece, over half the butter and fold the last third over it to make three layers of dough and two layers of butter.

Give the dough a half turn and roll it out again into an 8- by 12-inch rectangle. Fold it again and repeat the turning, rolling, and folding 5 more times, chilling the dough in the freezer for 20 minutes between each turn.

After the last rest, roll the dough out on a pastry board, lightly dusted with grated Parmesan cheese, to an 8-inch-wide strip, about 30 inches long. Brush an egg wash down the center of the strip and fold the strip in four lengthwise, making a double fold from each side to the center. Sprinkle each fold with grated Parmesan cheese, flatten with a rolling pin, and make sure the two folds to the center are pressed down on the egg wash.

Cut the flattened roll into 1/3-inch-thick slices and lay them 1 1/2 inches apart, cut side down, on a baking sheet lined with parchment paper.

Sprinkle them with more Parmesan and bake them in a hot oven (425° F.) for about 9 minutes. Turn the palmiers with a spatula, or pancake turner, and bake them about 10 minutes longer, until they are golden. Remove them at once and serve them with cocktails, soup, or salad.

Mandelkäsebiskuits   *Almond Cheese Cookies*

SIFT 2 CUPS flour onto a pastry board and sprinkle it with 1/2 cup grated Parmesan. Beat 2 eggs with 1/2 teaspoon salt. Make a well in the center of the flour and pour all but 3 tablespoons of the beaten egg into it. Cover the flour with 1/2 cup thinly sliced cold butter. Cut in the butter and work the mixture quickly with the hands into a smooth dough. Chill it for at least 2 hours. On a lightly floured board roll it out 1/8 inch thick. Cut out cookies with a fluted cookie cutter and place them on an unbuttered baking sheet. Paint them with the reserved egg mixed with 1 teaspoon water. Dust them with salt and caraway seeds and 1/2 cup slivered blanched almonds and bake them in a moderately hot oven (375° F.) for 15 minutes, or until they are golden. They will darken slightly after being taken from the oven.

Käse Algeriennes   *Cheese Shells*

WORK INTO a smooth paste 1/2 pound Roquefort cheese, 2 tablespoons creamed butter, and a little cayenne to taste. Whip 1/2 cup heavy cream until it is stiff, add salt to taste, and fold in the cream. Pipe the mixture through a pastry bag fitted wih a fluted tube into very small baked short pastry shells or endive leaves. Dust with a little paprika.

Roquefort Schaumtorte   *Roquefort Tart*

CREAM 1 1/2 CUPS Roquefort cheese with one 3-ounce package cream cheese, 1/4 cup butter, and 2 tablespoons Sherry. Press the mixture through a sieve and beat it until it is light and foamy. Add salt and paprika to taste and fold in 1 cup cream, whipped. Using a pastry bag, pipe the cheese into a baked cooled 9-inch tart shell of pie dough. Sprinkle the tart with chopped chives.

Salate

I<small>F THE</small> V<small>IENNESE</small> did not love his fellow man so well, the interest that he takes in the other fellow's affairs might appear to be vulgar curiosity. Actually, everyone has his nose, so to speak, in everyone else's business, and what goes on next door is always twice as interesting as what goes on at home. The entire city of Vienna is an unbroken chain of concern, not only for everyone else's activities, but for everything that happens beyond the Austrian frontiers in that mysterious place, the *Ausland*. A friend who suddenly appears on the street with the top of his hat crushed in is not a friend gone mad but only a Viennese who has read somewhere that in America absolutely everybody is wearing the pork pie hat.

So it is with salads. To the Viennese the other salad, like the other pasture, is always greener, and anything done in the *Ausland* must be better than what is done in the *Inland*. A Viennese hostess will present her guests with individually arranged salads, odd combinations of food under a rosette of mayonnaise, in the happy illusion that this method is the last word from America, or she will toss various greens in a wooden bowl because it is so terribly chic to try to do things as only the French can do them.

The beautiful Viennese salads really lie halfway between arranged salads and tossed salads, and they are usually served from crystal salad platters or bowls. Many of them stem from a period when fresh vegetables were scarce in winter and the root vegetables had to be used, lightened by an occasional green salad the cook cuts from a sunny window box with a snip just before dinner. Lentils and dried beans and peas form a group known as the *Hülsenfrüchte*, the pod fruits, and the combinations and varieties of these salads are endless. Lentils combined with diced potatoes, celery root, and dill pickle clearly represent a winter salad recipe. Beets, onions, apples, or dried mushrooms appear in wonderful combinations with rice and smoked fish for fall salads, and only the summer salads contain water cress, Bibb lettuce, chicory, or endive.

Almost everything that goes into the typical Viennese salad is first marinated in *Salatmarinade*, salad marinade, and the combined salad bound with a second and heavier dressing just before it is served. A lobster salad in Vienna tastes unlike other lobster salads because the lobster meat is marinated in a tart tarragon vinegar dressing, and drained before it is bound with a thick lemon mayonnaise. The subtle carry-over of flavors from the marinade enhances the salad and enriches it. The mayonnaise that binds the salad is used in rather small quantities, as the lobster has already been saturated with the marinade. Some people use mayonnaise only to mask a salad, and others prefer to pass it separately, serving the salad with the marinade only.

Viennese salads fall into three groups and are eaten at three entirely different stages of the meal. Those most frequently served are the rather tart and simple salads that serve as a garnish for the meat and fish course. The cucumber salad that accompanies so many breaded meat and fish dishes, the beet salad without which the Viennese could not eat his boiled beef, and the light green salad, prepared at the last moment to go with the *Wiener Schnitzel*, all belong in this group. Potato salad stands alone. Its unique importance can best be judged from a scene in the fourth act of *Faust;* everyone knows that the soldiers' chorus at the Viennese Opera House sings lustily *"Wir wollen keinen Kartoffelsalat"* instead of *"Gloire immortelle de nos aïeux, sois nous fidèle mourons comme eux."*

The second group of salads includes almost all the rest. These are served as a separate course, either as a *Vorspeise,* or first course, with which most of them are interchangeable, or as a salad course between the poultry and the compote or between the meat and the dessert.

The last group comprises the enormous salads—not only a course, but a meal in themselves. These are the buffet and late-supper party salads. But most important, they are the Sunday-night salads that make Sunday evening in Vienna a high instead of a low spot in the week: informal supper without servants but with a salad into which practically everything has gone.

Bacon Salad *Specksalat*

DICE 6 SLICES of bacon and cook them. To the hot bacon fat in the pan, add half as much vinegar, about 3 tablespoons. Into this stir 1/2 teaspoon each of sugar and salt and grind over it a little fresh pepper. Pour the warm dressing over a large bowl of crisp cold salad greens and quartered lettuce hearts. Sprinkle the salad with the crisp diced bacon. Boston, romaine, and iceberg lettuce, combined with water cress, chicory, and a few spinach leaves, make an excellent combination for this salad, but the Viennese also serve the bacon dressing over hearts of Boston lettuce alone.

Cabbage Salad I *Krautsalat 1*

SHRED 1 HEAD of white cabbage and soak the shreds in ice water for 2 hours. Drain them well and press them out until they are quite dry. Bind the salad with thick mayonnaise, flavored with just enough ketchup to tint it pink. Add 1/2 cup chopped walnuts, the grated rind of 1 orange, the orange sections, free of pith and membranes, and salt and pepper to taste. Grate a little fresh horseradish over the cabbage salad, if it is available.

Cabbage Salad II *Krautsalat 2*

SHRED 1 MEDIUM head of white cabbage very fine. Parboil the cabbage in salted water for 3 minutes and drain it well. Add 1 tablespoon caraway seeds and salt to taste and grind black pepper over it. Add 1/3 cup tarragon vinegar and 1/2 teaspoon sugar and let the cabbage cool. To the cool cabbage, add more salt and sugar to taste and 3 tablespoons olive oil.

Cook 1 celery root, if available, in salted water until it is soft, about 30 minutes. Cool, peel, and slice it. Arrange the celery root slices and shredded cabbage in layers in a deep bowl. If the salad is too dry, add a little vinegar and oil. Dust it with paprika. Serve with venison or game birds.

Warm Cabbage Salad *Warmer Krautsalat*

REMOVE THE outer leaves from 1 small head each of red and white cabbage, cut the heads into wedges, and remove the cores. Shred the cabbages separately into 2 pans and scald each in boiling water for 1 minute. Drain well and press out all the moisture. Boil 3 new potatoes until they are just tender and peel and slice them while they are still hot. Combine the potatoes and the cabbage in a large bowl.

Combine 1/4 cup each of red wine vinegar and olive oil, 1/4 teaspoon salt, and a pinch of pepper. Stir the mixture well and add 1/2 cup chopped onion and 1/4 cup chopped parsley. Pour the dressing over the salad and serve it while it is warm.

Selleriesalat   *Celery Salad*

DISCARD THE tough outside stalks of 3 medium bunches of celery. Cut the inside stalks, but not the hearts, into 2-inch lengths and slice the lengths into strips. Combine the strips, the 3 celery hearts and roots, and some of the tenderest yellow leaves and cover them with ice water. Chill the celery until the strips curl.

Whip 1 cup mayonnaise with 1/3 cup heavy cream until it is smooth and add 2 tablespoons lemon juice, the grated rind of 1 lemon, 2 to 3 teaspoons brown mustard, and salt and pepper to taste. Whip the dressing until it is light. Drain the celery well. Arrange the strips on a platter and pour the dressing over them. Chop the 3 roots fine and sprinkle them over the strips. Garnish the platter with the 3 inside hearts and the tender yellow leaves.

Celery and Egg Salad

Frou-Frou Salat

To A PEOPLE who called all candies bonbons and all poodles Koko, Gigi, or Pompom, the name Frou-Frou naturally brought great delight. It came from the city where the cancan was born. . . .

Cut enough celery—the inside stalks and heart—into julienne to make 2 cups. Combine it in a large bowl with 1 cup cooked beans and 3 hard-cooked egg whites, all cut into julienne, 4 heads of endive, cut into the same length julienne, and 4 radishes, cut into the longest strips possible. Surround the salad with a ring of escarole leaves. Sprinkle it with salt and pepper to taste and pour over it 1/2 to 3/4 cup salad marinade. Sprinkle with chopped chervil.

I Know Everything Salad

Ich Weiss Alles

COMBINE 4 HARD-COOKED egg yolks, riced, 6 anchovy filets, finely minced, 1 teaspoon dry mustard, 2 tablespoons tarragon vinegar, 1/4 cup olive oil, and salt and pepper to taste and stir until the dressing is smooth. Chop the inside stalks, the hearts, and the roots of 2 bunches of celery and add 6 cooked artichoke bottoms and 1 cooked beet, all chopped, 2 heads of Boston lettuce, torn into pieces, and 4 diced truffles. Arrange the salad in a large bowl, pour the dressing over it, and sprinkle it with 2 tablespoons each of chopped chervil and chopped chives. Border the salad with a ring of sliced cooked beets and garnish it with Bibb lettuce or water cress.

Turkish Cucumber Salad I

Türkischer Gurkensalat 1

SPRINKLE 4 LARGE cucumbers, thinly sliced, with 2 teaspoons salt and arrange them in a large bowl. Weight the slices with a small plate for 1 hour, to press out the moisture. Press down the plate, invert the bowl, and shake out all the moisture.

Crush 1 large clove of garlic, press it through a sieve with 3/4 cup cottage cheese (3/4 cup cream may be added to the garlic in place of the cheese), and add about 1/4 cup sour cream, or enough to make a thick dressing. Add the dressing to the cucumbers and salt and pepper to taste. Border the bowl with a ring of lettuce leaves, chill the salad, and at serving time mix with it 1/2 cup chopped ice.

Türkischer Gurkensalat 2   *Turkish Cucumber Salad II*

MAKE THE following dressing: Combine 1 crushed clove of garlic with 1/4 cup ground hazelnuts, and add 1/2 cup fresh white bread crumbs and the juice of 1/2 lemon. Pound the mixture in a mortar or crush it with a wooden spoon until it is smooth and add just enough cream to make a thick dressing. Prepare 4 cucumbers as for *Türkischer Gurkensalat I*. Combine the dressing with the cucumbers, add salt and pepper to taste, and chill the salad.

Deutscher Gurkensalat 1   *German Cucumber Salad I*

SCORE 4 UNPEELED cucumbers lengthwise with a silver fork. Slice the cucumbers very thin, shake them with 1 teaspoon salt in a small bowl, and let them stand 1/2 hour, covered.

Bring to a boil 1/2 cup tarragon vinegar, 1/4 cup water, and 1 teaspoon sugar and let the dressing cool. Drain the cucumbers well, add the cooled dressing, and sprinkle generously with freshly ground black pepper. Serve the salad cold. *(Picture, page 283.)*

Deutscher Gurkensalat 2   *German Cucumber Salad II*

SPRINKLE 4 CUCUMBERS, peeled and thinly sliced, with 1 tablespoon salt and let them stand for 3 hours. Drain them thoroughly, season with salt and pepper to taste, and add 1 cup sour cream beaten with the juice of 1/2 lemon. Sprinkle the salad with 1/4 cup chopped chives and chill it.

Deutscher Gurkensalat 3   *German Cucumber Salad III*

SPRINKLE 4 CUCUMBERS, peeled and thinly sliced, with 1 tablespoon salt and let them stand for 3 hours. Drain the cucumbers thoroughly and mix them well with 1 cup sour cream and the juice of 1/2 lemon. Add the grated rind of 1 lemon, 2 tablespoons each of capers and freshly ground horseradish, 1 tablespoon minced onion, and salt and pepper to taste. Sprinkle the salad with 2 tablespoons finely chopped parsley and the riced yolk of 1 hard-cooked egg. Serve it very cold.

Dandelion Salad   *Löwenzahnsalat*

WASH AND pat dry 1 pound small tender dandelion leaves, remove the
large stems, and chill the greens until they are crisp. Place the leaves in a
large salad bowl and sprinkle over them 2 tablespoons chopped tarragon
and 1 tablespoon chopped chervil. Add 6 tablespoons salad dressing I and
toss the salad until every green leaf glistens.

Endive with Swiss Cheese   *Endiviensalat mit Käse*

CUT EACH of 4 chilled heads of endive lengthwise into 6 strips. Cut Swiss
cheese into strips as long as the endive and about 1/4 inch thick. Lay the
cheese strips on a platter and the endive strips over them, so that the
cheese strips are hidden. Arrange the chilled sections of 3 oranges, free of
pith and seeds, on the endive.

Combine 1 teaspoon paprika, 1/2 teaspoon each of salt and sugar,
1/4 teaspoon each of pepper and dry English mustard, and 2 tablespoons
vinegar. Stir in 1/2 cup olive oil and add 1 tablespoon chopped onion.
Serve the dressing separately.

Endive and Lentil Salad   *Österreichischer Endiviensalat*

CUT 10 CRISP cold endive hearts into strips lengthwise and divide them
among 6 salad plates. Pour over the endive 3/4 cup paprika dressing I
mixed with 1 teaspoon each of chives, chervil, and parsley, all chopped.
Add the following warm lentil purée: Boil 1/3 cup lentils, soaked in cold
water overnight, in salted water until they are very soft, about 30 minutes.
Drain them well and purée them in a blender. Stir the purée to a
smooth paste with 1/2 tablespoon heavy cream and add salt and pepper
to taste.

Leek Salad   *Lauchsalat*

COOK THE white parts of 12 to 18 tender young leeks in salted water for
15 to 20 minutes, or until they are soft. Allow 2 to 3 leeks for each serving.
Drain the leeks well and marinate them for an hour or more in vinaigrette

sauce I. Cut cold cooked chicken or lamb into strips the same length as the leeks. Arrange the leeks and meat strips on a platter, pour over them vinaigrette sauce I, and sprinkle the salad with 1/4 cup finely chopped chives. Chill it well.

Schwämmerl Salat   *Mushroom Salad*

BOIL NEW potatoes until they are just tender, peel them while they are still hot, and cut them in 1/4-inch slices. Let the slices cool and, with a cutter, cut them into 1-inch rounds. There should be 1 1/2 cups potato rounds.

Slice very thinly 3/4 pound mushrooms, washed and trimmed, and add 2 radishes, trimmed and chopped fine, 1 tablespoon chopped chervil, and the potato rounds.

Combine 1/2 teaspoon salt and 1/8 teaspoon each of dry mustard and pepper with 1/3 cup tarragon vinegar and gradually beat in 1/3 cup olive oil. Pour the dressing over the salad and chill it.

Exzelsior   *Mushroom, Potato, and Truffle Salad*

WIPE 3/4 POUND clean white mushrooms with a soft towel. Do not wash them. Cut the stalks even with the caps. Slice the mushrooms and sprinkle them with 1/3 cup each of tarragon vinegar and olive oil and 1 table-spoon lemon juice. Marinate the mushrooms for about 1 hour, or until they are darkened, turning them in the marinade with a wooden spoon every 15 minutes.

Boil 9 small new potatoes in salted water until they are just tender and peel and slice them thinly while they are still hot. Sprinkle the warm potatoes with 1/4 cup tarragon vinegar and let them cool.

Combine the mushrooms and potatoes in a deep crystal bowl and add 1/2 cup each of finely diced celery and finely chopped onion, 1/4 cup each of chopped parsley and chopped chives, and 5 truffles, peeled and thinly sliced.

To 3 cooked sliced artichoke bottoms add a dressing made of 1/4 cup each of tarragon vinegar and olive oil, 2 tablespoons lemon juice, 1 teaspoon salt, and 1/2 teaspoon pepper. Pour over the salad the artichoke slices in the dressing and garnish the bowl with sprigs of parsley.

Onion Salad

Zwiebelsalat

SLICE 6 LARGE onions across into 1/4-inch slices and sauté the slices in 3 tablespoons butter over low heat until they are golden. Turn them and sauté until both sides are done. Chill the cooked onion slices and arrange them on a bed of Boston lettuce and romaine, both broken into pieces. Combine 1/2 cup salad dressing II with 1 teaspoon each of finely chopped chervil and parsley, and 1/2 teaspoon chopped dill. Pour this dressing over the salad and toss it. Serve with thin buttered bread dried in a very slow oven (250° F.).

Green Pea Salad

Erbsensalat

BIND 3 CUPS cold cooked green peas with 1/4 cup salad marinade I and 1/4 cup mayonnaise, or more, to taste. Add 2 tablespoons chopped mint.

Portuguese Salad

Portugiesischer Salat

THE VIENNESE combine equal quantities of mushrooms, potatoes, and tomatoes, all marinated separately, add ripe olives, and call the salad *portugiesischer Salat*.

Combine 1 1/2 cups each of marinated mushrooms, white wine potato salad, and sliced tomatoes marinated in salad marinade. Sprinkle the salad generously with chopped ripe olives.

Frühlings-Radieschensalat   *Spring Radish and Cucumber Salad*

HALVE 2 CUCUMBERS lengthwise and remove the seeds. If the skins are very tough, peel them. Slice the cucumbers very thin, sprinkle them with 1 teaspoon salt, and chill them, covered. Combine 1 cup sour cream, 2 tablespoons tarragon vinegar, 1 teaspoon celery seed, and a little freshly ground pepper. Drain the cucumbers well and add 2 bunches of radishes, thinly sliced, and the dressing. Adjust the seasoning, heap the mixture in the center of a tomato aspic ring, and dust it with a little ground pepper.

Helenensalat   *Spinach and Water Cress Salad*

WASH AND pat dry 1 pound spinach, remove all the large stems, and tear the leaves into pieces. Wash and pat dry 1 bunch of water cress and remove all the stems. Chill all the greens until they are crisp.

Combine 1 clove of garlic, crushed, 1/2 teaspoon each of salt and grated lemon rind, 1/4 teaspoon each of paprika and pepper, and 2 tablespoons tarragon vinegar. Add gradually 1/2 cup olive oil, beating constantly, and beat in 2 tablespoons sour cream. Mix the well-chilled spinach and water cress in a large bowl. Pour over the sour cream dressing, toss the salad well, and crumble 6 slices cooked crisp bacon over it.

By a very circuitous route, which is the usual Viennese way, a tomato is a Paradeis-apfel, *or just a* Paradeis, *for short. It seems that Adam and Eve, so often pictured under an apple tree, really stood in front of a tomato vine, and Eve tempted Adam with a tomato, the true apple of paradise. Somewhere along the way, for no reason at all, the "i" and the "e" were reversed: A tomato is still* ein Paradeis, *but paradise is* das Paradies, *and, in Vienna at least, man's downfall is symbolized by a large and glossy tomato.*

Aïda Salat   *Tomato, Artichoke, and Endive Salad*

COMBINE 4 PEELED sliced tomatoes, 6 cooked artichoke bottoms, diced, 6 large stalks of endive, cut crosswise into 1/4-inch slices, and 1 small green pepper, seeded and cut into thin strips. Add 1/2 cup paprika dressing I seasoned with 1 teaspoon Dijon or Dusseldorf mustard. Surround the salad with lettuce leaves and sprinkle it with 3 hard-cooked egg whites, riced, and 2 tablespoons pimiento, cut in fine julienne.

Tomato and Green Bean Salad   *Paradeis mit Bohnen*

IN A SALAD BOWL, combine 6 tomatoes, peeled and sliced, 2 cups cold cooked green beans, 1 head of lettuce, cleaned and broken into pieces, and 1/4 cup chopped parsley. Rice 2 hard-cooked egg yolks over the mixture.

Heat 1/2 cup heavy cream in the top of a double boiler over hot water and add 4 tablespoons olive oil, 2 tablespoons each of Dijon mustard, white vinegar, and tarragon vinegar, and salt and pepper to taste. Cook the sauce, stirring constantly, until it thickens. Pour the warm sauce over the salad and toss it gently. Sprinkle it with 1 cup toasted bread cubes.

Stuffed Tomato Salad   *Gefüllte Tomaten*

PEEL AND hollow out 6 tomatoes. Mix 1/4 cup vinegar, 1/2 teaspoon salt, 1/8 teaspoon pepper, and 1/4 teaspoon paprika, and add 1/4 cup olive oil. With this marinade, drench the inside of the tomatoes. Bind 1 cooked and peeled celery root, cut in julienne, with 1/2 cup mayonnaise and add salt and pepper to taste. Stuff the tomatoes with the mixture. Bind 2 cucumbers, thinly sliced and drained, with 1/2 cup mayonnaise stirred with 3 tablespoons cream and 1 tablespoon anchovy paste. Chill the stuffed tomatoes and the cucumbers. Line a salad bowl with lettuce leaves, pile the cucumbers in the center, surround them with the stuffed tomatoes, and garnish each tomato with a sprig of parsley.

Truffle and Avocado Salad   *Millionärsalat*

IT WAS easier for a Viennese to become a millionaire (in Kronen) than for an American (in dollars), and as soon as he becomes a millionaire, he eats a salad that contains those greatest proofs of affluence—the *Alligatorbirne* and the truffle.

Simmer 2 to 3 peeled truffles in 1/2 cup aged Madeira until the wine is reduced by half. Reserve the wine. Let the truffles cool and slice them fine. Add them to 2 large or 3 small avocados, peeled and sliced. Make a bed of broken crisp inner leaves and hearts of Boston lettuce in a crystal salad bowl and lay the truffles and avocados on it. Sprinkle them with 1/2 cup slivered toasted almonds. Just before serving, beat 3/4 cup lemon mayonnaise with the 1/4 cup reduced Madeira and pour it over the salad.

Wiener Salat   *Viennese Salad*

COMBINE 1 CUP well-drained cucumber slices with 6 hearts of Boston lettuce, quartered, and 1 cup finely diced celery, using only the white inner stalks and the white celery root. Add 3 medium-sized hot boiled potatoes, peeled and sliced, 3 warm hard-cooked eggs, sliced, and salt and freshly ground pepper to taste. Pour over the salad 1 cup salad marinade and add 1/4 cup chopped chives. Stir the salad carefully, while it is warm, using 2 wooden spoons, and serve it at once.

Water Cress and Apple Salad — *Brunnenkresse mit Äpfeln*

WASH, DRAIN, and dry thoroughly 2 bunches of water cress. Arrange 3 thinly sliced apples in a salad bowl and scatter the cress over them. Combine 4 tablespoons olive oil, 2 tablespoons vinegar, 1/2 teaspoon sugar, salt and pepper to taste, and 1 teaspoon finely minced chervil. Pour this dressing over the salad and sprinkle it with 1/2 cup dry bread crumbs browned in butter. Toss the salad before serving.

Water Cress and Mushroom Salad — *Brunnenkresse mit Schwämmerln*

MARINATE FOR 1 hour 1 cup thinly sliced mushrooms in 1/2 cup olive oil and 1/4 cup wine vinegar beaten with 2 teaspoons heavy cream, 1/2 teaspoon each of salt and sugar, and 1/4 teaspoon freshly ground black pepper.

Combine the mushrooms and marinade with 1 onion and 1 peeled and cored tart apple, both sliced fine, and 2 bunches of cleaned water cress. Sprinkle the salad with 1 teaspoon each of chopped chervil and chives.

Water Cress and Ham Salad — *Schinken mit Brunnenkresse*

ARRANGE 1 HEAD of lettuce and 1 bunch of water cress in a salad bowl. Pile in the center 1 cup diced ham mixed with 3 hard-cooked egg whites, chopped. Over this sprinkle the riced yolks and 2 tablespoons chopped parsley. Combine 6 tablespoons olive oil, 3 tablespoons tarragon vinegar, 1 shallot, chopped, and 1/2 teaspoon each of dry mustard and salt. Pour this dressing over the salad and mix it well.

Water Cress and Onion Salad — *Brunnenkresse mit Zwiebeln*

WASH, DRY, and stem 2 bunches of water cress, wrap them loosely in foil, and chill them for 30 minutes. Slice 9 to 12 small peeled white onions paper thin and separate the slices into rings. There should be about 2 cups of onion rings. Lay the onions in a wooden salad bowl and cover them with the cress. Mix 4 tablespoons tarragon vinegar, 1/2 teaspoon salt, and 1/4 teaspoon each of pepper and dry mustard. Add 1/2 cup olive oil. Pour this dressing over the cress and onions and mix the salad well.

Wienerschnitzel Salat

ON 6 CHILLED salad plates, arrange small beds of Bibb lettuce mixed with a few crisp raw spinach leaves. Slice as thin as possible 6 small tomatoes, peeled, and fan one out around each lettuce bed. Slice 6 large white mushrooms paper thin and fan one out around each tomato. On each lettuce bed, arrange 3 fingers of cold breaded veal cutlet. Top the veal with thin lemon slices. Prepare a dressing of 3 tablespoons lemon vinegar, 1/4 cup oil, 1 tablespoon Dijon mustard, and 3 hard-cooked egg yolks, riced. Add salt and pepper to taste and divide the dressing among the salads.

Alexandra Salat mit Artischocken

TRIM THE outside leaves of 6 small cooked artichokes down to 1 inch, remove the center leaves and chokes, and trim the stems so that the artichokes stand upright. Chill the artichokes. Scrape the tender meat from the ends of the center leaves and add it to 8 hard-cooked eggs, diced, and 8 filets of anchovy, chopped, bound with 3/4 cup thick lemon mayonnaise. Fill the artichoke bottoms with the egg and anchovy mixture. Top each artichoke with a paper-thin slice of lemon.

Artischocken Vinaigrette

ARRANGE THE best leaves of 2 cooked artichokes around a salad bowl. Combine the 2 bottoms, chopped, the chopped whites and riced yolks of 2 hard-cooked eggs, 1 onion, chopped fine, and 2 tablespoons each of chopped capers and parsley. Stir the mixture carefully and pile it in the center of the bowl. Mix 1/2 cup olive oil, 1/4 cup tarragon vinegar, 1 teaspoon each of salt and paprika, and 1/2 teaspoon each of black pepper, dry English mustard, tarragon, and chervil and pour the dressing over the salad. Sprinkle the salad with 2 tablespoons chopped parsley.

Neapler Salat

CUT 2 POUNDS cold cooked asparagus stalks 3 inches from the top. Arrange the short green tips in 6 even stacks on lettuce leaves. Arrange on the asparagus 1 cup Swiss cheese, cut in julienne. Cover with 3 tomatoes, peeled and thinly sliced. Pour over the salad 6 tablespoons salad dressing II to which 1 clove of garlic, crushed, has been added.

Beet Salad   *Rote Beete*

COOK 8 TO 10 BEETS in salted water until they are tender, about 20 to 30 minutes. Do not cut off the leaves or roots and do not pierce the beets with a fork to test them. There should be no bleeding. Draw the skins off the hot beets and cut off the leaves and roots. Cut the beets crosswise into very thin slices, retaining all the juice. Simmer 1/2 cup each of tarragon vinegar and water with 1/4 teaspoon caraway seeds, 3 cloves, 2 peppercorns, 1/2 bay leaf, and salt to taste for 9 minutes. Strain the hot marinade over the warm beets and their juice. Add about 6 whole cloves or 2 tablespoons horseradish. Let the salad cool and chill it.

Green Bean Salad   *Salat aus grünen Bohnen*

COOK 2 POUNDS French-cut green beans until they are just tender and drain them. Marinate the warm beans in 1/2 cup each of vinegar and olive oil with 1/2 teaspoon salt and 1/4 teaspoon pepper for about 1 hour and chill them.

Peel and slice thin 1 bunch of freshly cooked beets and let them cool. Reserve the water in which they cooked. Boil together for 5 minutes 1/2 cup each of vinegar and beet water with 4 cloves. Lay the beets in a shallow dish and pour the hot marinade over them. Let them cool and chill them.

Arrange the leaves of 2 heads of lettuce in a large salad bowl. Mound the beans in the center. Drain the beets and arrange them around the beans. Pour over the lettuce any dressing left from the beans. *(Picture, page 118.)*

Green Bean and Shrimp Salad   *Marschallinsalat*

TRIM THE ENDS from 1 pound thin young green beans and cook the beans until crisp, for about 12 minutes. Drain well, divide them among 6 salad plates, and chill, covered. Add 3 cooked shrimp to each portion. Divide

6 raw mushrooms and 3 sautéed chicken livers, all sliced paper thin, among the plates as garnish and serve with mustard dressing.

Schminkbohnensalat mit Zwiebel   *Kidney Bean and Onion Salad*

Cook 2 cups kidney beans, soaked overnight, in salted water to cover for 45 minutes, or until they are crisp and tender, but not soft. Drain them. Marinate them in 2/3 cup tarragon vinegar for 12 hours, turning them carefully several times. Add 1/3 cup olive oil, 1 onion thinly sliced and separated into rings, 1/2 teaspoon dry English mustard, and salt and pepper to taste. Turn the beans again and add 2 tablespoons chopped parsley and 1/2 teaspoon chervil. Arrange the salad in a bowl and chill it. Just before serving, cover the salad with thinly sliced onion rings and sprinkle it with 2 tablespoons chopped parsley.

Salat der Könige   *Wax Bean Salad*

Beat 2 eggs until they are light and foamy and add 1/4 cup milk, 2 tablespoons finely chopped chives, and salt to taste. In a buttered skillet cook the eggs over moderate heat until they are scrambled. Cover 6 slices of boiled ham with the eggs, roll up the slices, and place them, seam side down, around the sides of a salad bowl lined with lettuce. Have ready 3 large tomatoes, peeled and sliced thin.

Cut 1 pound yellow wax beans into 1/4-inch pieces. Cook the beans in salted water to cover with 2 teaspoons chopped savory for 10 minutes and drain them at once. They should be crisp. Bind them with 1 cup well-salted mayonnaise, add 1 teaspoon chopped savory, and mound the salad on the lettuce leaves in the bowl. Sprinkle the salad with 3 radishes, finely chopped, and arrange the tomato slices over it.

Salat Pompadour   *White Bean Salad*

Soak 2 cups dried white beans in cold water overnight, drain them and cook them in salted water to cover about 45 minutes, or until they are crisp and tender, but not soft. Drain and chill them. Add to the beans 4 hard-cooked egg whites, sliced, 2 cups diced cooked potatoes, marinated in 1/4 cup each of tarragon vinegar and white wine, and 1 cold cooked cauliflower, separated into flowerets. Bind the salad with mayonnaise seasoned with salt and brown mustard to taste. Border the bowl with a ring of crisp lettuce leaves.

Turn of the Century Salad   *Jahrhundert-Ende*

WAX BEANS are called *Spargelbohnen* in Vienna, which means "asparagus beans," and they are handled very much as asparagus is handled. Trim the beans and tie them in even bunches with cord. Steam them or simmer them in salted water until they are just tender but still crisp and yellow. Chill the beans. Serve them whole, as asparagus is served. Do not cut them as green beans would be.

Arrange approximately 1 pound cooked long yellow wax beans in a neat pile in the center of a large crystal salad platter, with 1 bunch of cold cooked green asparagus spears of the same size and length as the beans on one side and a similar bunch of endive cut into narrow strips on the other side. Surround the yellow, green, and white piles with alternating mounds of cold cooked green peas, bound with mayonnaise seasoned with finely chopped mint, well-drained beet salad, cut in julienne, and cooked artichoke bottoms, marinated in herb dressing.

Decorate· the salad platter with lettuce leaves and parsley sprigs, and pour French dressing over the wax beans, asparagus, and endive. Across the piles arrange 3 bands of riced hard-cooked egg white alternating with 2 bands of riced hard-cooked egg yolk.

Brüssler Salat   Brussels Sprouts Salad

MARINATE 2 1/4 CUPS cold cooked Brussels sprouts in salad dressing III for at least 2 hours. Prepare 2 1/4 cups white wine potato salad and 3/4 cup chopped cooked chestnuts.

Lay the yellow leaves of 2 heads of chicory on a salad platter and mound the chestnuts in the center. Arrange around the chestnuts alternate mounds of potato salad and Brussels sprouts, using three mounds of each.

Sprinkle over the platter 1/2 cup chopped onions and 1/4 cup mixed parsley, chervil, and chives, all chopped. Serve with vinaigrette sauce I.

Karfiol mit Paradeis   Cauliflower and Tomato Salad

SEPARATE A COOKED cauliflower into small flowerets and drain them. Peel and scoop out 6 large tomatoes. Combine 1 1/2 cups cooked green peas, 1/2 cup thick mayonnaise, 6 shallots, finely chopped, and salt and pepper to taste. Stuff the tomatoes with this mixture. Place the flowerets on lettuce leaves in the center of a platter, arrange the tomatoes around them, and chill the salad. Combine 3 tablespoons vinegar, 1 teaspoon celery seed, 1/4 teaspoon salt, and 1/8 teaspoon pepper and beat in gradually 6 tablespoons olive oil. Pour this dressing over the cauliflower and sprinkle it with 2 tablespoons chopped dill.

Blumenkohl Vinaigrette   Cauliflower Vinaigrette

COOK 1 CAULIFLOWER in boiling water to cover with 1/2 cup milk, 1 slice white bread, and 3 teaspoons salt until it is just tender. Rinse it in cold water, drain, and chill it. Mix 1 teaspoon salt, 1/4 teaspoon pepper, and 1/8 teaspoon dry mustard. Add gradually 3 tablespoons vinegar, stirring constantly, and 6 tablespoons oil. Add 1 hard-cooked egg, riced, 1 tablespoon each of chopped capers and parsley, and 1 tablespoon minced onion and mix well. Pour the dressing over the chilled cauliflower.

German Cauliflower Salad   *Deutscher Karfiolsalat*

SEPARATE 1 LARGE cauliflower, cooked, drained, and chilled, into flowerets and arrange them on a bed of lettuce leaves. Sauté 6 slices of bacon until they are golden and crisp and drain them well. Add 1/4 cup vinegar and salt and pepper to taste to the bacon fat in the pan and pour this warm dressing over the cauliflower. Sprinkle the crumbled bacon and 3 table-spoons chopped parsley over the salad.

Turkish Cauliflower Salad   *Türkischer Blumenkohlsalat*

DIVIDE 1 LARGE cauliflower into flowerets, cook them in salted water until they are just tender, and cool them. Pour over them in a large bowl the hazelnut and garlic sauce as in *Türkischer Gurkensalat 2* (Turkish cucumber salad 11). Chill the salad before serving.

Celery Root and Potato Salad   *Adlon Salat*

COOK 1 LARGE or 2 small celery roots in salted water to cover for 30 to 40 minutes, or until they are tender, and peel them while they are hot. Cut the root into 1/3-inch slices and the slices into thick julienne. Marinate the warm julienne in 1/2 cup tarragon vinegar for 1/2 hour. Add 3 large cooked potatoes, peeled and cut in the same size julienne. Add 1/4 cup vinegar and marinate the mixture for 1/2 hour more. Add 3 tart apples, peeled and cut in the same size julienne. Bind the salad with 1/2 cup thin mayonnaise and add salt and pepper to taste. Pile the salad in a salad bowl and surround it with the crinkled inside leaves of chicory. Drain 1/2 cup beet salad of all liquid and cut it in fine julienne. Scatter the beets over the salad at the last moment so the color will not spread.

Grinzing Salad   *Grinzinger Salat*

IN SEPARATE bowls soak 1 cup each of lentils and dried white beans in cold water for 14 hours, adding more water if it is absorbed. Drain both lentils and white beans. Cook the lentils in salted water to cover for 15 minutes and let them cool in the cooking water. Cook the white beans in salted

water to cover for 45 minutes and let them cool in the water. Both the
lentils and beans should be soft but not at all mushy. Drain them well.

Cook 1 celery root and 2 potatoes in water to cover until they are
tender, and cool, peel, and dice them. Combine the lentils, white beans,
potatoes, and celery root and add 1 onion, finely diced, 2 tablespoons small
capers, 1/2 cup tarragon vinegar, and salt and freshly ground pepper to
taste. Stir the ingredients carefully, using a wooden spoon to avoid breaking
the vegetables. Add 8 slices of Bologna, cut into small squares, 1 dill
pickle, diced, 3 anchovies, chopped, and 1/4 cup wine herring, drained
and chopped.

Combine 2 egg yolk with the juice of 1/2 lemon and 1/2 tablespoon
brown mustard. Beat in 1 cup olive oil, drop by drop, to make a stiff
brown mayonnaise. Stir the mayonnaise into the salad and let it rest for
at least 2 hours. Press the salad down firmly in the bowl and invert it on
a serving platter. Garnish the mound with sliced cucumbers, sliced dill
pickles, and onion rings. Surround it with piles of kidney bean and onion
salad and white bean salad and with more pickles. The salad may be stored
in the refrigerator for several days.

Italienischer Salat   *Italian Salad*

COMBINE 1 CUP each of cooked sliced potatoes and cooked sliced celery
root. Add to them 2 cups dried white beans, soaked overnight and cooked
in salted water to cover about 45 minutes, or until they are crisp and
tender, but not soft. Marinate the salad in paprika dressing II, using
only enough dressing to moisten, for 1 hour. Bind the salad with mayonnaise and add salt and pepper to taste. Arrange it in the center of a
crystal salad bowl, border it with a ring of crisp lettuce leaves, and cover
the salad with alternating slices of hard-cooked egg and cervelat. Garnish
the salad with 1/2 cup tiny pearl onions, drained and mixed with 3 tablespoons chopped chives.

Linsensalat   *Lentil Salad*

SOAK 1 POUND lentils in cold water overnight and drain them. Cook them
for 8 minutes with 1 bay leaf, 1 onion stuck with 3 cloves, and 1 teaspoon
salt. The cooked beans should still be as crisp as almonds. Drain them well

and remove the bay leaf and onion. Combine 1/4 teaspoon each of salt and pepper, 1/2 teaspoon each of dry mustard and paprika, and 3 shallots and 2 sweet pickles, all finely chopped. Add 1/4 cup tarragon vinegar and 1/2 cup olive oil, stir the dressing well, and pour it over the cooked lentils. Chill the salad. Sprinkle it with 1 tablespoon chopped parsley and 1 teaspoon chopped chervil.

Potato Salad with Egg Yolk — *Kartoffelsalat mit Eigelb*

BOIL 9 NEW potatoes until they are just tender. Peel and dice them while they are still hot, add salt and pepper to taste, and sprinkle the potatoes with 2 tablespoons finely chopped onions.

Mix together the grated rind of 1 lemon, 1 teaspoon salt, 1/4 teaspoon pepper, and 1/8 teaspoon dry mustard with 1 1/2 tablespoons each of tarragon vinegar and lemon juice. Gradually add 6 tablespoons olive oil, stirring constantly.

Pile the salad in a large bowl and add the dressing. Sprinkle with 1/4 cup chopped chives and decorate with riced hard-cooked egg yolks.

German Potato Salad — *Deutscher Kartoffelsalat*

SLICE 8 BOILED potatoes while they are still hot and place them in a bowl in alternate layers with 1 onion, sliced very thin. Sprinkle the hot potatoes with 1 teaspoon salt and 1/4 teaspoon pepper and pour 1 1/2 cups mild vinegar over them. Let them marinate for several hours, turning them several times. When the potatoes have absorbed most of the vinegar, drain them and fold in carefully 1/2 cup mayonnaise blended with 1/2 cup heavy cream. Sprinkle the salad with dill.

Potato Salad with Green Pea Sauce — *Kartoffelsalat mit Erbsensauce*

STEAM 18 TO 24 NEW potatoes, in their skins, until they are just tender but not too soft. Peel them while they are still hot and slice them into a salad bowl. Moisten them at once with 3 tablespoons tarragon vinegar and 2 tablespoons meat stock. Add 1/4 cup finely chopped onion and salt and pepper to taste. Marinate the salad for 1 hour. Add 1/4 cup salad dressing III and 1 teaspoon each of chopped tarragon, parsley, and chervil. Thin 3/4 cup purée of cooked green peas with 1/4 cup each of cream and salad dressing III, add thick mayonnaise to taste, and correct the seasoning. Pour the purée of pea sauce over the potato salad.

Feinschmeckersalat   *Potato and Tongue Salad*

COOK 4 OR 5 LARGE potatoes in salted water until they are medium soft, peel them, and cut them into strips. Sprinkle over the warm potato strips 1/4 cup white wine, 2 tablespoons tarragon vinegar, and 1 teaspoon salt. Cut 1/4 pound cold sliced tongue into strips, combine the potatoes and tongue, and let them marinate for 1/2 hour. Bind them with 3/4 cup mayonnaise seasoned with 2 teaspoons each of minced parsley and tarragon.

Just before serving the salad, peel, core, and dice 2 apples. Bind the apple dice with 1/4 cup thin mayonnaise, arrange them in a mound in the center of a serving platter, and mound the potato and tongue salad over them, covering them completely. With a cutter, cut rounds from a sheet of beef aspic 1/4 inch thick. Surround the salad with alternating aspic rounds and rounds cut from cold liver paste and decorate the platter with parsley. Serve with thin buttered black bread.

Potato and Water Cress Salad   *Kresshändlerin Salat*

BOIL 6 NEW potatoes until they are just tender, peel them while they are
still hot, and slice them. Salt the potatoes lightly. Sprinkle them with 2
tablespoons finely chopped shallots and pour over them 1 cup white vinegar, heated with a pinch of pepper. Let the potato slices absorb the vinegar,
tossing them carefully several times. When they are thoroughly moistened,
toss them with 2 bunches of washed, dried, and chilled water cress, from
which the large stems have been removed. Add enough olive oil, spoonful
by spoonful, to coat the potatoes and the water cress. Garnish the salad
with 2 hard-cooked eggs, sliced, and 1/4 cup chopped parsley.

White Wine Potato Salad   *Weisswein Kartoffelsalat*

COOK 10 POTATOES in their jackets until they are tender and peel them
while they are hot. Slice them into a warmed bowl and season them with
1 1/2 teaspoons salt and 1/2 teaspoon white pepper.

    Combine 3/4 cup white wine, 1/2 cup olive oil, and 1/4 cup tarragon
vinegar and pour the marinade over the sliced potatoes. Turn them lightly
with a wooden spoon until they have absorbed the marinade.

    Stir in gently 1/2 cup each of minced shallots and chopped fresh parsley.
Transfer the salad to a wooden salad bowl that has been rubbed with
a clove of garlic and let it stand at room temperature for 2 to 3 hours.
Garnish the salad with chopped parsley and with scallions, cut in pieces.

Black and White Salad   *Schwarz-weisser Salat*

A VIENNESE recipe that begins "take equal quantities of potatoes and
truffles" has rarely been read beyond the first sentence. Actually, the salad
is made with 6 large boiled potatoes, peeled and sliced, and 6 small truffles,
peeled and cut into short matchsticks. Pour over the potatoes and truffles
white-wine dressing with chopped onions, salt, and white pepper, as in
white-wine potato salad, and let them marinate for 3 hours. Bind the salad,
mixing it very carefully with a wooden spoon, with 1/2 cup mayonnaise
combined with 3 tablespoons heavy cream, 1 tablespoon mild brown
mustard, and salt and pepper to taste. Decorate the salad with uniform
slices of potato on which truffle cutouts are laid—painting the lily.

Arme Leute   *Poor People Salad*

COMBINE EQUAL quantities of cold boiled potatoes, sliced, cold cooked cauliflower, broken into flowerets, and cold cooked baby Lima beans. Bind the
salad with salad marinade and sprinkle it generously with chopped parsley.

Andalusischer Salat   *Rice, Onion, and Tomato Salad*

CRUSH 3 SMALL cloves of garlic in 3/4 cup paprika dressing II and let it
stand for 1 hour. Combine 6 small white onions, thinly sliced, and separated
into rings, with 4 tomatoes, peeled and sliced, and 1 small red pepper,
seeded and thinly sliced. Add 3 cups cold cooked rice and 1/2 cup finely
chopped parsley. Pour the dressing over the salad.

Paradeis mit Reissalat   *Rice and Tomato Salad*

MARINATE 4 TOMATOES, peeled and thinly sliced, in 1/2 cup vinegar with
1/2 teaspoon salt and 1/4 teaspoon pepper. Rinse in cold water 1 cup rice,
cooked until it is just tender, and chill it. When it is cold, add 1/2 cup
mayonnaise and 1 tablespoon Dijon mustard. Line a salad bowl with
the leaves of a head of lettuce. Pile the rice in the bowl, sprinkle it with
2 tablespoons chopped parsley, and surround it with tomato slices.

Zuchettisalat   *Cold Zucchini Salad*

SAUTÉ 6 MEDIUM zucchini, cut into 1/4-inch slices, for 2 minutes in 1/2 cup
olive oil, heated with 1 tablespoon scraped onion. Sprinkle the zucchini
with salt and freshly ground pepper and cook it until it is tender. Watch it
carefully; it should not be too soft. Drain the zucchini and chill it. Add
1/4 cup tarragon vinegar and 1 tablespoon sugar to the oil in the skillet
and bring the dressing to a boil. Cool the dressing. Sprinkle the zucchini
with 1 tablespoon each of chopped parsley and fresh basil and pour the
dressing over the salad.

Herring Salad   *Heringesalat*

PREPARE 1/2 CUP each of finely chopped anchovies, herring, boiled beets, capers, and onions and 1/2 cup diced boiled potatoes. Rice separately the yolks and whites of 2 hard-cooked eggs. Arrange these foods in pie-shaped wedges on a platter. Garnish the platter with parsley.

Combine 1 teaspoon sugar, 3/4 teaspoon salt, 3/4 teaspoon English mustard, 1/2 teaspoon paprika, and 1/8 teaspoon pepper. Stir in 3 tablespoons tarragon vinegar and 1/3 cup olive oil. Just before serving, pour this dressing over the salad and mix it well. Serve the salad with thin buttered black or rye bread. *(Picture, page 121.)*

Russian Salad   *Russischer Salat*

THE VIENNESE fill a Russian salad with absolutely everything they can think of. Even if they use very small quantities of all the ingredients, it is still a very large salad, and it is often served as a main course at Sunday-night or late-supper parties.

The first ingredient is a cold boiled lobster, the tail meat cut in slices and the claw meat diced. Combine 1 cup each of the lobster meat, marinated in 3 tablespoons tarragon vinegar, and white-wine potato salad. Add 1/2 cup each of cold cooked carrot and parsnips, cut in julienne, and cooked French-cut green beans. All the vegetables should be drained and marinated in salad dressing I before they are added to the salad. Add 1 dill pickle, chopped, 1/2 cup German cucumber salad I, drained, and 1 cup white dried beans that have been soaked in water for 12 hours, cooked in salted water for 9 minutes, or until they are tender but still crisp, and well drained. Pick them over and remove any loosened skins that have curled away from the beans. Add 3/4 cup each of diced cold boiled ham and tongue and 1/4 cup each of chopped anchovy filets and capers. The quantity of anchovies may be increased, to taste. Bind the salad with mayonnaise and add any remaining marinades from the various ingredients. Mound the salad high on a crystal platter. Sprinkle it generously with riced hard-cooked eggs and chopped chives, parsley, dill, and chervil.

Surround the salad with 24 uniform slices of sausage, such as Bologna, and arrange 24 marinated mushroom caps on the overlapping sausage slices.

Hummersalat   *Lobster Salad*

COMBINE 1 CUP cold boiled diced lobster meat and 1/2 cup sliced cold
white meat of chicken. Add 1/2 cup each of shredded romaine lettuce, the
crisp inside leaves only, and raw sliced mushrooms, and 1/2 cup finely
chopped mixed fresh herbs: chervil, chives, dill, tarragon, and parsley,
with a little rosemary.

Mix 1/4 cup tarragon vinegar, 1/4 cup olive oil, 1 teaspoon salt, and
1/4 teaspoon white pepper. Pour the dressing over the salad and toss it
well. Chill the salad and toss it several times while it is chilling. Just before
serving, pour 1/2 cup thick rémoulade sauce over the salad.

Hummersalat Auguste Viktoria   *Lobster, Grapefruit,*
and Asparagus Salad

COMBINE 2 CUPS cold cooked lobster meat and 1 pound cold cooked
asparagus, both cut in pieces, with the chilled sections of 2 grapefruit.
Reserve any grapefruit juice. Arrange the salad on lettuce leaves in a salad
bowl. Combine 1 1/2 cups mayonnaise, 2 hard-cooked egg yolks, riced, 2
hard-cooked egg whites, chopped, 1 small onion, chopped fine, 1/4 cup
finely chopped parsley, 1/4 cup sweet pickle relish, drained, 2 tablespoons
chopped capers, 1 scant teaspoon salt, 1/4 teaspoon pepper, and the grapefruit juice. Pour the dressing over the salad and garnish it with parsley.

Gottlicher Salat   *Shrimp Salad*

SIMMER 36 SMALL shelled and deveined shrimps in salted water to cover
with 1/2 teaspoon caraway seeds for 5 minutes, or until they turn pink and
opaque. Drain them well and place them, still hot, in a deep bowl with
1/4 cup tarragon vinegar. Stir and turn them several times while they cool,
to saturate all the shrimps with vinegar. Chill the shrimps.

Cut 6 cooked artichoke bottoms and 1 small cooked and peeled celery
root into strips and marinate the warm strips in 1/4 cup tarragon vinegar,
turning them as they cool. Chill the mixture.

Combine the shrimps and the artichoke and celery root strips with just
enough mayonnaise to bind, adding all the remaining vinegar. Place the
salad in a bowl, surround it with lettuce leaves, and sprinkle it with
1 teaspoon chopped dill.

Roast Beef Salad   *Nordsee Salat*

To 1 CUP cubed cold rare roast beef add 1 cup tomatoes, peeled, seeded, chopped, and drained, 1/2 cup chopped dill pickle, 3 hard-cooked eggs, quartered, and 1 onion, chopped. Combine 1 teaspoon salt, 1/4 teaspoon pepper, 1/2 cup olive oil, and 1/3 cup tarragon vinegar. Pour this dressing over the salad, stir it carefully, and chill it. Sprinkle it with 1/4 cup chopped chives and a grinding of rough black pepper.

Cheese Salad   *Käsesalat*

COMBINE 2 CUPS each of chopped celery and cold cooked chopped beets and bind them with 1/2 cup mayonnaise. Add salt and pepper to taste. Arrange lettuce leaves in a large bowl, pile the vegetables in the center, and sprinkle them with 1 1/2 cups coarsely grated Swiss cheese. Garnish the salad with 2 hard-cooked eggs, sliced, and decorate each egg slice with a rolled anchovy. Serve additional mayonnaise with the salad.

Bristol Salat   *Chicken, Apple, and Asparagus Salad*

COMBINE 1 CUP each of diced cooked chicken meat and peeled diced apples and 1 large dill pickle, chopped. Add 3 peeled truffles, chopped, and 18 cooked green asparagus stalks. Thin 1/2 cup mayonnaise with 2 tablespoons sour cream, add 1 teaspoon Dijon or Düsseldorf mustard, and fold this dressing into the salad. Surround it with lettuce leaves and sprinkle it with 1 tablespoon finely chopped parsley.

Hühnersalat mit Ei   *Chicken and Egg Salad*

MARINATE 2 CUPS cold diced chicken for 2 hours in 1/4 cup tarragon vinegar mixed with 1 small onion, chopped fine, 1 tablespoon small capers, 1 teaspoon Dijon mustard, and salt and pepper to taste. Add 1/2 cup mayonnaise and 1/4 cup sour cream and stir the mixture well. Pile it in the center of a salad bowl lined with lettuce leaves. Sprinkle the top with 1 teaspoon each of chopped parsley and dill. Surround the mound with 1 tomato, peeled and sliced, and 4 hard-cooked eggs, sliced. Crumble 6 slices of crisp warm bacon over the salad.

Türkischer Salat   *Turkish Chicken Salad*

BIND 3 CUPS diced cold cooked chicken and 3 cucumbers, diced and well drained, with 1 cup mayonnaise to which 1 tablespoon lemon juice and 1/2 teaspoon minced dill have been added. Add salt and pepper to taste. Pile the salad in the center of a platter and surround it with leaves of Boston lettuce. Sprinkle the salad with the riced yolks of 3 hard-cooked eggs and 1/2 cup finely chopped walnuts and garnish it with 6 sprigs of parsley and 1/4 cup white raisins.

Ägyptischer Salat   *Chicken Liver, Artichoke, and Mushroom Salad*

PRESS 6 COLD cooked chicken livers through a coarse sieve. Add 6 cooked artichoke bottoms, chopped, 6 large raw mushrooms, chopped, 1 cup each of cold cooked green peas and rice, 1/2 cup diced ham, and 1/4 cup finely chopped pimiento. Bind the salad with 3/4 cup paprika dressing II. Mound it in the center of a salad bowl and surround it with the small inside leaves of 3 heads of Boston lettuce. Include lettuce leaves with each serving of salad.

Egg and Chicken Liver Salad · Römischer Salat

SAUTÉ 1 ONION, chopped fine, in 4 tablespoons butter until it is puffed. Add 1/2 pound chicken livers and cook them until they are no longer pink inside. Tear 1 large head of romaine and 2 of Boston lettuce into pieces and put them in a large salad bowl. Combine 1 cup mayonnaise, the juice of 1 lemon, 3 hard-cooked egg whites, chopped, and salt and pepper to taste. Pour this dressing over the lettuce. Press the warm cooked chicken livers and onions through a coarse sieve onto the lettuce and sprinkle with the 3 hard-cooked egg yolks, riced, and salt and freshly ground black pepper to taste. Garnish the salad with 1/4 cup chopped parsley.

Cold Poached Egg Salad · Kalter Eiersalat

TRIM 6 COLD poached eggs. Lay them on 6 cooked chilled artichoke bottoms and sprinkle them with freshly ground black pepper. Line a large shallow platter with lettuce leaves, arrange the egg-filled artichokes in a circle, and lay 1 bunch cold cooked asparagus in the center.

Combine 1/2 onion, 1 bunch chives, 2 tablespoons parsley, and 1 teaspoon chervil, all chopped. Mix these with 1/2 cup each of mayonnaise and sour cream and add salt and pepper to taste. Pour this dressing over the eggs, artichokes, and asparagus and garnish the salad with sprigs of parsley.

Asparagus and Poached Egg Salad · Spargelsalat Holstein

ON EACH individual plate arrange 6 to 9 stalks of cold cooked asparagus and on the asparagus lay a cold trimmed poached egg. Pour vinaigrette sauce I over each portion and sprinkle the eggs with chopped tarragon and parsley.

Adam-und-Eva Salat   *Adam and Eve Salad*

COMBINE 1 1/2 CUPS green grapes, peeled and seeded, the sections of 4 grapefruit, free of pith and seeds, 1/3 cup blanched and slivered almonds, and 2 young white celery hearts, cut into julienne.

Add 6 tablespoons whipped cream and 1 tablespoon grated orange rind to 1 cup mayonnaise. In a large bowl, arrange crisp leaves from 1 head each of Boston lettuce and romaine. Bind the fruit mixture with 1/4 cup of the cream dressing and pile the fruit into the center of the bowl. Chill the salad. Serve the remaining dressing separately.

Apfelsalat   *Apple Salad*

CHOP 1/4 CUP anchovies and 1/2 cup herring filets and add 4 shallots, 3 small dill pickles, and 3 thick slices Bologna sausage, all chopped. Chop a quantity of tart apples equal to the amount of all the other ingredients combined and add the chopped apples. Bind the salad with salad marinade and add salt and freshly ground pepper to taste. The quantity of anchovies and herring may be increased, to taste. The Viennese use as much as 1/2 pound anchovies and omit the milder herring entirely.

Martini Salat   *Apple and Grape Salad*

MIX TOGETHER 1 1/2 cups diced, peeled apples, 3/4 cup diced celery, and 6 tablespoons chopped walnuts and bind them with 6 tablespoons mayonnaise. Remove the tops of 6 fine large oranges, scoop out the pulp, and fill the shells with the mixture. Mix the orange pulp with sections of 3 more oranges and 1 1/2 cups seedless grapes and bind the fruit with 1/2 cup paprika dressing II. Line a platter with crisp Boston lettuce leaves. Pile the orange-and-grape salad in the center and surround it with the stuffed oranges. Chill the salad and garnish it with sprigs of mint.

Delikater Salat   *Fruit Salad*

DRAIN WELL the sections of 3 oranges, free of pith and seeds, and combine them with an equal quantity of drained pineapple dice and 3 tomatoes, peeled, sliced, and seeded. Discard the outer leaves of 3 heads of Boston lettuce, quarter the heads, and add the fruit to the lettuce quarters in a large bowl. Chill the salad. Stir 2 tablespoons lemon juice, the grated rind of half a lemon, and salt to taste into 3/4 cup heavy cream. Pour the dressing over the salad.

Fresh Fruit with Mint Dressing   *Fruchtsalat Leonore*

COMBINE 1 1/2 CUPS pink and green melon balls, cut from a cantaloupe and a honeydew melon, with 2 cups grapefruit sections and 1 1/2 cups orange sections, free of pith and seeds, and chill the fruit. Place the 2 half honeydew melon shells in a large salad bowl and fill them with the chilled fruit. Stir 1/2 cup vinegar with 2 tablespoons finely chopped mint, 1 teaspoon minced onion, 1 1/2 teaspoons salt, and 1/4 teaspoon pepper, and add 1 cup olive oil. Pour this dressing on the fruit, sprinkle it with 1 tablespoon each of finely slivered grapefruit and orange rind, and decorate it with sprigs of mint. Surround the melon shells with lettuce leaves. Serve the salad very cold.

Grapefruit and Cherry Salad   *Alexandra Salat mit Kirschen*

SPREAD OPEN a large head of Boston lettuce and cut out the center so as to leave a hollow. Fill the head with 2 cups grapefruit sections marinated in salad dressing III and dusted with 1 teaspoon paprika. Surround the filled lettuce head with a border of 3 cups stoned cherries sprinkled with 1/2 cup chopped walnuts. Serve the salad with salad dressing III.

Melon with Grapes and Chicken   *Melonen mit Trauben und Hühnchen*

PEEL 2 CANTALOUPE melons and cut them into wedges. Slice the white meat of 1 cold cooked chicken and arrange the slices on a platter with the melon wedges and 1 pound seedless white grapes, skinned. Red grapes may be used, halved and seeded. Mix together 1 cup mayonnaise, 1/2 cup cream, and 2 tablespoons chopped chutney. Set the dressing aside. Mix 2 tablespoons apricot jam, or to taste, with a little cream until it is smooth and add it to the dressing. Pour the dressing over the salad. Serve the salad chilled and garnished with parsley.

Melonen mit Reissalat   *Melon and Rice Salad*

CUT EACH of 2 large cantaloupes into thirds, remove the melon pulp, and reserve the shells. Dice the fruit and set it aside to drain.

Mix together 3 tablespoons chutney, 2 tablespoons vinegar, and 1 teaspoon salt and pour the mixture over the melon dice. Add 1 cup sour cream mixed with 1/2 cup mayonnaise and stir in 1 1/2 cups cold cooked rice. Correct the seasoning and arrange the mixture in the melon shells. Serve the shells on crisp lettuce leaves.

Orangen- und Endiviensalat   *Orange and Endive Salad*

SEPARATE 4 ORANGES into sections and free the sections of pith and seeds, reserving any juice. Chill the oranges. Discard the outside leaves from 8 heads of endive and slice the endive into rounds. Cut 1 pound Swiss cheese and 6 slices of Bologna sausage into rounds the same size as the endive.

Beat together 2 teaspoons each of sugar and Dijon mustard, 1 1/2 teaspoon salt, 1 teaspoon paprika, 3/4 cup olive oil, 1/2 cup tarragon vinegar, and 1/4 cup orange juice. Chill the dressing.

Mix the endive and the cheese and sausage rounds with the oranges. At serving time, pour the dressing over the salad.

Diplomatensalat   *Diplomat Salad*

COMBINE 3 CUPS finely diced pineapple with 1 1/2 cups each of chopped celery and diced apples. Sprinkle the mixture with the juice of 1/2 lemon and bind it at once with tart mayonnaise. Add salt to taste and mound the salad in the center of a crystal salad bowl. Surround the base of the salad with marinated beets, prepared as for beet salad and cut with a cookie cutter, and lay half walnuts on the beets. Garnish the mounded salad with more beet slices.

Sauces

Saucen

THE VIENNESE have always been careful of their pronunciation of the foreign words they use. They have earnestly learned to say "Visky and Zoda," they go on "Vikents" to the country and take along a "Zandvitch" for the road. In view of this commendable effort, it is regrettable that, although they have retained the French spelling as well as the French inspiration for their basic sauces, they pronounce them *"Sossen."*

Viennese refer to the basic sauces as the classic sauces, *Die klassischen Saucen,* and give most of them the French names they should rightly have. At heart a genealogically inclined people, they are apt to draw up a pedigree for their sauces as they would for their dogs or even for themselves. In this way, they know which sauce is the child and which the mother. Although the Viennese classic sauces resemble the French sauces, their use differs considerably.

The Viennese use a great many mushroom sauces with meat, many different horseradish and caper sauces, many cucumber, spinach, and tomato sauces with fish, eggs, poultry, and meat. In Vienna it is possible to eat boiled beef for half the year without repeating the sauce. The man who insists on caper sauce with his beef respects the man who can eat it only with horseradish sauce, and both of them tolerate the man who wants a different sauce each time. Preferences in this matter are so accepted that a hostess who plans to serve boiled beef will prepare as many as three or four different sauces to please her guests. This procedure seems entirely proper to her.

There are gooseberry sauces, rosehip and hazelnut sauces for meat, and poultry, and even for fish. There are paprika sauces for almost everything, but for Vienna's two specialties—the *Wienerschnitzel* and the *Wiener Backhendl*—there is never a sauce.

Wonderful sauces have found their way up the Danube to become part of Viennese cooking under the names *Zigeuner,* or gypsy, Hungarian, Balkan, Turkish, and *Teufel,* the devil. Polish sauces have added their flavor and variety to Viennese cuisine. Many combine dried fruits, nuts, spice, cake crumbs, and oranges. The orange-flavored hollandaise, Maltese sauce, is served often in Vienna, as is *Chaudeau* sauce in which the egg yolks are beaten with white wine and sugar to enhance a dry cake or a pudding.

All good Viennese try to pour just enough sauce over the food on their plates, but if they miscalculate they happily have a little more sauce for the pudding and a little more pudding for the sauce until—*Aber Nein!*—the pudding and the sauce are all gone.

Braune Grundsauce oder spanische Sauce 1

Brown Sauce or Sauce Espagnole

MELT 1/4 CUP butter in a small heavy saucepan. Add 2 tablespoons diced fat salt or pork, 1 carrot, 1 stalk of celery, and 1 onion, all chopped, and sauté the vegetables just until they start to turn golden, shaking the pan to cook them evenly. Blend in 1/4 cup flour, and cook, stirring, until it takes on a rich brown color. Add 2 cups hot brown stock, stirring constantly. Cook the sauce until it starts to thicken. Add 1 cup more hot stock, 2 sprigs of parsley, and 1/2 bay leaf. Cook the sauce very slowly over low heat for 1 hour, stirring occasionally and skimming off any excess fat. Add 1/4 cup Sherry and strain the sauce. Add 1/4 cup tomato purée and 1 cup more hot stock and correct the seasoning. Cook the sauce slowly for 30 minutes longer, skimming the surface if necessary. Strain the sauce and cool it, stirring occasionally.

Spanische Sauce 2

Simple Brown Sauce

SAUTÉ 2 TABLESPOONS each of ham, onion, carrot, and celery, all finely chopped, in 2 tablespoons butter for a few minutes. Blend in 4 teaspoons flour and stir well for 3 minutes. Add 2 cups beef stock, 1 teaspoon salt, 3 peppercorns, and a *bouquet garni*. Simmer the sauce for 15 minutes longer and strain it. Use the sauce for meats or as a base for other sauces. Makes 2 cups.

Gypsy Sauce — Zigeuner Sauce

To 1 CUP brown sauce, add 3 tablespoons white wine and 2 teaspoons thick tomato purée. Sauté 3 tablespoons each of slivered mushrooms and tongue in 1 tablespoon butter for about 3 minutes, or until the mushrooms are lightly browned. Bring the sauce to a boil and add the tongue and mushrooms. Serve with meat.

Périgord Sauce — Perigorder Sauce

COOK 2 CUPS brown sauce for 30 minutes, to reduce it to 1 cup. Add 2 tablespoons truffle liquor and 2 truffles, peeled and chopped. Reheat the sauce and add 1/4 cup Madeira. Bring the sauce to the boiling point, but do not let it boil. Gradually add, bit by bit, 2 tablespoons butter, stirring so that the butter melts without cooking. Serve at once.

Polish Sauce — Polnische Sauce

SIMMER 2 CUPS beef stock with half a bay leaf, 1 sprig of thyme, and 2 cloves. Stir 1 tablespoon flour blended with 1 tablespoon tarragon vinegar into 1/2 cup white wine and add 2/3 cup stale gingerbread or gingersnap crumbs. Stir the mixture gradually into the sauce and cook it until it is smooth. Strain the sauce and add 1 tablespoon sugar, the juice of 1/2 lemon, and 1/4 cup each of raisins, slivered blanched almonds, and chopped parsley. Reheat the sauce and add salt and pepper to taste.

Mushroom Sauce — Champignonsauce

SAUTÉ 1/2 POUND mushrooms, finely sliced, in 3 tablespoons butter until they are very lightly browned, add 1 tablespoon minced onion, and cook 1 minute longer. Melt 1/4 cup butter, blend in 6 tablespoons flour, and cook the *roux,* stirring, until it browns. Stirring constantly, add 2 cups brown beef stock. Simmer the sauce over low heat for 20 minutes, stir it well, and add the mushrooms. Reheat the sauce. Add salt and pepper to taste. Thin the sauce with warm cream and reduce the heat to below a simmer. Add 3 tablespoons chopped parsley just before serving.

Trüffelsauce   *Truffle Sauce*

To 1 CUP brown sauce, add 1 tablespoon tomato purée and 3 tablespoons each of Madeira and finely chopped sautéed mushrooms. Bring the sauce to a boil and add 1 large or 2 small truffles, peeled and chopped. Serve with meat or poultry.

Kraftsauce   *Sauce Demi-Glace*

CHOP THE stems and peelings of 6 mushrooms, add them to 1/2 cup dry Sherry, and cook until the wine is reduced to about half the original quantity. Add 2 cups brown sauce and 1 tablespoon meat glaze, or *glace de viande*. Simmer the sauce for 15 to 20 minutes and strain it.

Madeira Sauce   *Madeira Sauce*

REDUCE 4 CUPS *sauce demi-glace* to 3 cups, take it from the heat, and add from 1/4 to 1/3 cup Madeira, or to taste.

Tomatensauce   *Tomato Sauce*

SAUTÉ 1 SMALL onion, chopped, in 1/4 cup butter until it is transparent. Add 1 carrot and 2 stalks of celery, all chopped, 4 sprigs of parsley, and 2 pounds tomatoes, seeded and diced, and stir the vegetables until they are coated with butter. Sprinkle them with 1/3 cup flour and cook them, stirring constantly, for 5 minutes. Add 1/2 cup white wine, 2 teaspoons lemon juice, 1 teaspoon sugar, 1/8 teaspoon ground cloves, a pinch of thyme, and salt to taste. Simmer the sauce, stirring frequently, for 20 minutes. Strain it and add the grated rind of 1 lemon. Correct the seasoning.

Dillsauce mit Saurer Sahne   *Sour Cream Dill Sauce*

SAUTÉ 1 ONION, chopped fine, in 1/3 cup butter until it is lightly puffed and blend in 1/2 cup flour. Add 1 tablespoon finely chopped dill and stir the sauce over low heat for 3 minutes. Gradually add 1 1/2 cups warm beef stock, stirring until smooth, and salt and pepper to taste. Add 1 teaspoon each of lemon juice and sugar and stir in 1 cup sour cream and 3 tablespoons finely chopped dill. Add more beef stock, if the sauce is too thick. Serve with boiled beef.

Paprika Sauce *Paprikasauce*

SAUTÉ 1 ONION, very finely chopped, in 3 tablespoons butter until it is golden. Add 2 tablespoons flour sifted with 1 tablespoon paprika and stir well. Gradually add 1 1/2 to 2 cups beef stock and stir the sauce until it is smooth. Simmer it for 20 minutes, strain it, add 1/2 cup heavy cream, and bring it back to just under a boil.

Madeira Currant Sauce *Madeira-Sauce mit Schwarzen Johannisbeeren*

MELT 3 TABLESPOONS butter, stir in gradually 1 tablespoon flour, and cook the *roux* over low heat for a minute. Slowly add, off the heat, 1 cup stock or 1 cup broth in which ham has boiled and 2 teaspoons each of prepared mustard and vinegar. Return the sauce to the heat, simmer it, stirring, for 10 minutes, and add 3 tablespoons each of currant jelly and Madeira wine. Serve with ham.

Sauce Béchamel or White Sauce *Béchamelsauce oder weisse Rahmsauce*

BRING SLOWLY to a boil 4 cups milk with 6 peppercorns, 1 onion, chopped, 1/2 carrot, 1/2 bay leaf, and a *bouquet garni* and remove the pan from the heat. Sauté gently 1/2 cup chopped lean veal in 2 tablespoons butter for 5 minutes, stirring the veal to keep it from browning. Season it with salt, pepper, and a pinch of nutmeg.

In another saucepan, melt 4 tablespoons butter, blend in 1/2 cup flour, mix well, and cook the *roux,* stirring, for a few minutes. Gradually add the milk mixture, stirring constantly, add the veal, and blend the sauce thoroughly. Cook the sauce over hot water for 1 hour, stirring it from time to time. Strain the sauce through a fine sieve and fleck the surface with small pieces of butter to prevent a film forming.

Sauce Velouté *Weisse Geflügel-Grundsauce*

MELT 1/2 CUP butter in a saucepan, blend in 1/2 cup flour, and cook the *roux* for a few minutes without letting the flour take on color. Add gradually 4 cups hot chicken stock, stirring the mixture vigorously. Add 1/2 teaspoon salt and 1/8 teaspoon white pepper. Cook the sauce, stirring frequently, over very low heat, until it is reduced to two-thirds. Skim it from time to time. Strain the sauce through a fine sieve. If it is not to be used immediately, stir it occasionally as it cools and dot it with bits of butter.

Geflügel-Rahmsauce   Sauce Suprême

COMBINE 2 CUPS chicken stock, 1 cup velouté sauce, 1/2 cup mushroom stems and peelings, chopped, 6 peppercorns, and 1/4 teaspoon salt. Reduce the sauce over high heat to half the original quantity, stirring constantly, and add 3/4 cup cream. Cook the sauce gently for 10 minutes and strain it through a fine sieve. Blend in 2 tablespoons butter, piece by piece, just before serving.

Deutsche Sauce   German Sauce

OVER LOW heat, reduce 3 cups velouté sauce to 2 cups, add 3/4 cup white stock and 1/2 cup mushroom essence, and simmer the sauce for 30 minutes. Correct the seasoning and strain the sauce. Stir in, off the heat, 2 egg yolks beaten with 3 tablespoons cream and reheat the sauce.

Weisse Fasten Grundsauce   Fish Velouté

MELT 4 TABLESPOONS butter in a saucepan and blend in 4 tablespoons flour. Cook the *roux* gently for a few minutes or until it turns golden. Add, little by little, 2 cups fish stock or *fumet*, stirring constantly. Cook the sauce for 15 to 20 minutes and strain it through a fine sieve. Cool it, stirring occasionally, and dot the surface with a little butter to prevent a crust from forming.

Kapernsauce   Caper Sauce

MELT 1/4 CUP butter over low heat. Blend in 1/4 cup flour and gradually stir in 1 1/2 to 2 cups veal or beef stock—or fish stock, if the sauce is to be served with fish. Add 1/2 onion, sliced. Simmer the sauce for 1/2 hour and add more stock, if a thinner sauce is required. Strain the sauce and add 3 tablespoons capers, 1 tablespoon each of chopped parsley and vinegar, and salt, pepper, and sugar to taste. Serve with meat or fish.

Dill Sauce   *Dillsauce*

MELT 1/4 CUP butter over low heat, blend in 1/4 cup flour, and gradually add 1 1/2 to 2 cups veal or beef stock, or fish stock, if the dill sauce is to be served with fish. Add 1/2 onion, sliced. Simmer the sauce over low heat for 1/2 hour and add more stock if a thinner sauce is required. Strain the sauce and add 3 tablespoons finely chopped dill, 1 tablespoon vinegar, and salt, pepper, and sugar to taste. Serve with meat or fish.

Chive Sauce   *Schnittlauchsauce*

MAKE A WHITE *roux* with 3 tablespoons butter and 3 tablespoons flour over low heat and gradually add 1 cup warm cream. Stir the sauce until it is smooth and pour it into the top of a double boiler over simmering water. Add 1 cup hot white veal stock or chicken stock and salt and pepper to taste. Cook for 1/2 hour and add 1/4 cup finely chopped chives. Serve with poultry, vegetables, or soufflés.

Onion Sauce   *Zwiebelsauce*

SIMMER 4 LARGE white onions, sliced, in water to cover until they are tender. Drain the onions, reserving the liquid. Melt 3 tablespoons butter, stir in 3 tablespoons flour, and cook the *roux* for a few minutes, stirring. Add 2 cups of the onion water and 1/2 cup warm white stock. Cook the sauce, stirring, until it is smooth and add the onions. Correct the seasoning. Serve with meat and vegetables.

Cheese Sauce   *Käsesauce*

IN THE TOP of a double boiler, stir 2 cups milk into 2 tablespoons flour, add 2 eggs and a pinch of nutmeg, and cook the sauce over simmering water, stirring, until it thickens. Add 1 cup grated sharp white Cheddar cheese and cook the sauce, stirring, until the cheese melts. Just before serving, fold in 1 cup salted heavy cream, stiffly whipped.

Mustard Sauce   *Senfsauce*

COMBINE AND beat 3 egg yolks, 1/4 cup mild prepared mustard, 3 tablespoons flour stirred with 1/2 cup water, and 1/4 cup white wine in the top of a

double boiler and cook the sauce over hot water until it thickens and increases in volume. Season it to taste with salt, pepper, and a pinch of sugar and beat in 4 tablespoons butter, one at a time, beating thoroughly after each addition. Serve with fish, meat, or eggs.

Kalte Gurkensauce   Cold Cucumber Sauce

PEEL AND CHOP fine 2 firm large cucumbers. Sprinkle them with 1 teaspoon salt and let them stand for 15 minutes. Whip 1 cup heavy cream thick but not stiff. Beat in 3 tablespoons vinegar, 1 teaspoon finely grated onion, and 1/4 teaspoon pepper. Add the cucumber, drained and pressed dry. Correct the seasoning, add 2 tablespoons finely chopped chives, and chill well.

Warme Gurkensauce   Hot Cucumber Sauce

PEEL, HALVE, and seed 2 firm medium-sized cucumbers. Chop them coarsely. Sauté them gently in 1/4 cup melted butter for 20 minutes, or until they are soft and tender. Drain the cucumbers well and press them through a sieve.

Melt 2 tablespoons butter, blend in 2 tablespoons flour, and cook the *roux* gently for 2 minutes, stirring constantly. Do not let it brown. Remove from the heat, add 1 cup scalded milk, stirring constantly, and cook the sauce until it is smooth and thickened. Add the cucumber purée, 1/2 teaspoon each of lemon juice and grated lemon rind, and salt and white pepper to taste. Reheat the sauce, but do not let it boil. Serve over poached sole or salmon.

Hot Horseradish Sauce   *Warme Krensauce*

IN THE TOP of a double boiler, over boiling water, melt 3 tablespoons butter. Blend in 3 tablespoons flour, stirring the *roux* constantly until it is smooth. Gradually add 1 cup warm beef stock—or fish stock, if the sauce is to be served with fish—and 1/2 cup warm milk. Cook the sauce, stirring, over hot water for 20 minutes, adding more liquid as necessary. At serving time, add 1 tablespoon vinegar and correct the seasoning with a little sugar, salt, and pepper. Strain the sauce through a fine sieve and stir in 1/2 to 1 cup freshly grated horseradish. Serve with meat.

Viennese English Bread Sauce   *Wiener englische Brotsauce*

SLOWLY BRING to a boil 2 cups heavy cream, add 1 cup fine white bread crumbs, 2 small onions, and 1/2 teaspoon each of salt and white pepper. Cook the sauce for 5 minutes, remove the onions, and serve at once. Serve with game.

Hollandaise Sauce I   *Holländische Sauce 1*

IN THE TOP of a double boiler over hot but not boiling water whisk 4 egg yolks until they are light and thick. The pan containing the yolks should be warmed by the steam but should not touch the water. Gradually whisk in 1 cup butter, one tablespoon at a time. Do not add another piece until the preceding piece has been incorporated. Add 1 teaspoon lemon juice after 2 tablespoons butter have been added. A tablespoon of boiling water may be beaten in for lightness or if the sauce starts to separate. Finish it with lemon juice to taste. Keep the sauce warm by standing it in a bowl of lukewarm water.

Holländische Sauce 2   *Hollandaise Sauce II*

BEAT 3 EGG yolks and 1 tablespoon warm water in the top of a double
boiler over hot, but not boiling, water, for 3 minutes, or until they are
light and creamy. Remove the pan from the hot water and beat in 1
tablespoon lemon juice and a pinch each of salt and cayenne. Return the
pan to the hot water and add 1 cup soft butter, a little at a time, beating
well after each addition. Continue to beat until the sauce is smooth and
thick. If the hollandaise is not to be used immediately, set it aside in a
warm china bowl, cover it, and keeep it warm at the back of the stove.

Hollandaise Variations

Mousselinesauce—MOUSSELINE SAUCE. To 2 cups thick hollandaise sauce,
add 1/2 cup whipped cream.

Aurorensauce—SHRIMP HOLLANDAISE SAUCE. Substitute shrimp butter for
plain butter in hollandaise sauce.

Cherbourger Sauce—CRAB HOLLANDAISE SAUCE. Substitute crab butter for
plain butter in hollandaise sauce.

Maximiliansauce—ANCHOVY HOLLANDAISE SAUCE. Substitute anchovy
butter to taste for part of the plain butter in hollandaise sauce.

Maltesersauce—MALTESE SAUCE. To 2 cups thick hollandaise sauce, add
1/4 cup orange juice and the zest of 1/2 orange. Use a blood orange if
possible.

Zitronensauce—LEMON HOLLANDAISE SAUCE. Add the zest of 1 lemon to
hollandaise sauce made with 3 egg yolks.

Noisettesauce—HAZELNUT HOLLANDAISE SAUCE. To 2 cups thick hollandaise
sauce, add 1/2 cup finely chopped hazelnuts toasted in butter.

Figarosauce—TOMATO HOLLANDAISE SAUCE. To 2 cups thick hollandaise
sauce, add 1/4 cup sieved tomato pulp and 1 tablespoon minced parsley.

Sauce Divine—SHERRY HOLLANDAISE SAUCE. Combine 2 tablespoons each of Sherry and Sauternes and reduce the wine to half. Whisk it into hollandaise sauce made with 4 egg yolks. Omit the lemon juice and water. Finish with 1/2 cup whipped cream.

Herbed Hollandaise Sauce — Holländische Sauce mit Kräutern

IN THE TOP of a double boiler, over simmering water, whisk 4 egg yolks and a pinch each of salt and white pepper. Do not let the water touch the bottom of the upper section. Gradually add 1/4 pound butter in small pieces, stirring constantly, and continue to stir until the sauce is smooth and thick. Add 1/2 teaspoon each of dill, tarragon, parsley, and chervil, all minced, and grated lemon rind. Take the sauce from the heat and add 2 teaspoons lemon juice and 1/4 cup cream, whipped and salted to taste.

Cucumber Hollandaise — Holländische Sauce mit Gurken

COMBINE 1 TABLESPOON each of water and vinegar in the top of a double boiler and boil the liquid over direct heat for a minute. Add a pinch of white pepper and salt and place the pan over simmering water. Add 3 well-beaten egg yolks and beat the yolks with a wire whisk until the mixture is smooth and light. Add 1 cup butter, piece by piece, beating constantly and being sure each piece is fully assimilated before adding more. When all the butter is added and the sauce is thick, add 1 medium-sized cucumber, peeled and finely chopped, 1 teaspoon each of finely chopped parsley and mustard, and a squeeze of lemon juice. Serve hot, over fish or poultry.

Lobster Sauce — Hummersauce

SAUTÉ 1 CUP diced cooked lobster meat in 2 tablespoons butter for a few minutes. Add 1 shallot, peeled and finely chopped, and keep the mixture warm.

In the top of a double boiler over hot but not boiling water, beat 4 egg yolks with 2 tablespoons fish stock. Whisk in 1 cup butter, as for hollandaise sauce I, and as the sauce thickens, whisk in 6 tablespoons fish stock. Add a dash of lemon juice and salt and pepper to taste. Stir in the warm lobster meat and shallot. Serve the hot lobster sauce with fish and shellfish.

Béanersauce   *Béarnaise Sauce*

COMBINE 1/3 CUP each of tarragon vinegar and white wine, 2 tablespoons each of shallots, parsley, and tarragon, all minced, 4 peppercorns, a pinch of thyme, a quarter of a bay leaf, and salt to taste. Cook over high heat until the mixture reduces to 3 tablespoons. Strain it. Beat 3 large or 4 small egg yolks in the top of a double boiler, over simmering.water, until they are thick and creamy. Do not let the bottom of the pan touch the water; cook the sauce by steam alone and prop the upper section in such a way that some of the steam can escape. Stir 4 teaspoons boiling water into the yolks, a teaspoon at a time, allowing the sauce to thicken between each addition and stirring constantly. Stir in the strained reduced vinegar and when the sauce is smooth take the pan from the heat and beat in with a whisk 1 cup soft butter. Add the butter, a bit at a time. If the sauce should separate, stir in 1 teaspoon boiling water. When the butter is incorporated, add salt and pepper to taste. Finish the sauce with 1 tablespoon each of heavy cream and tarragon and parsley, both minced. Leave the sauce over hot water until it is served. Serve with meat and fish.

Béarnaise Variations

Sauce Choron—CHORON SAUCE. To béarnaise sauce made with 3 egg yolks, add 3 tablespoons reduced tomato sauce.

Tirolersauce—TYROLEAN SAUCE. Add 2 tablespoons grated onion to Choron

Sauce Valoise—VALOIS SAUCE. Add 1 teaspoon *glace de viande,* or meat glaze, to béarnaise sauce made with 3 egg yolks.

Sauce Foyot—FOYOT SAUCE. Add 1 tablespoon tomato paste to Valois sauce.

Sauce Paloise—PAU SAUCE. Add 2 tablespoons chopped mint to béarnaise sauce made with 3 egg yolks.

Herb Butter Kräuterbutter

To 1 1/2 cups creamed butter, add 1 cup finely chopped parsley, salt and pepper to taste, and a few drops of lemon juice and Worcestershire sauce. Turn the butter onto a sheet of moistened parchment paper. Roll the butter in the paper to form a smooth even roll. Turn in the ends to enclose the butter and chill the roll in ice water. Remove the paper and with a knife dipped in warm water slice the butter crosswise into 1/2-inch discs. Lay a disc on any grilled meat, on an opened baked potato, or on broiled fish and serve at once.

Green Herb Butter Grüne Kräuterbutter

BLANCH 9 SPINACH leaves, 1 bunch of chives the size of a finger, and the leaves from 1/2 bunch each of water cress and parsley, for 2 minutes in boiling salted water and drain and dry them. Add 1/2 onion, or 3 shallots, chopped, and the leaves from 3 sprigs each of tarragon, chervil, and dill. Purée the herbs in a blender or mince them and pound them or rub them through a sieve. Add a grating of lemon rind and salt and white pepper to taste and stir the purée into 1 1/4 cups creamed butter. Correct the seasoning and chill the butter.

Anchovy Butter Kalte Sardellensauce

CREAM 3/4 cup butter and add 1 tablespoon lemon juice, the grated rind of 1 lemon, 2 teaspoons anchovy paste, and 1/4 teaspoon pepper. Whip the mixture until it is thoroughly blended and chill it. Serve with fish.

Crayfish, Shrimp, or Crab Butter Krebsbutter

IN THE oven, dry empty well-cleaned shells of cooked crayfish, shrimps, or crabs and pound them in a mortar with butter—about 20 crayfish, 30 shrimps, or 6 crab shells to 1 cup butter. Heat the pounded mixture in the top of a double boiler over very low heat for 10 minutes. Do not let the butter boil. Strain off the butter. Add a little boiling water to the shells and strain this into the butter. Pour the mixture through a cloth into a bowl of ice water and chill it in the refrigerator until the butter hardens on the water. Skim off the butter and pack it in a jar. Store it, covered, in the refrigerator.

Senfbutter   *Mustard Butter*

COMBINE 3 TABLESPOONS prepared mustard and 1 1/2 teaspoons dry mustard with 1 teaspoon lemon juice and add the mixture to 1 cup softened
butter. Add salt and pepper to taste and chill the mustard butter.

Estragonbutter   *Tarragon Butter*

CREAM 1 CUP butter with 2 teaspoons finely chopped tarragon, 1/2 teaspoon lemon juice, and salt and pepper to taste.

Schalottensauce   *Shallot Butter Sauce*

MELT 1/2 CUP salted butter in a small saucepan over low heat without
letting it brown. Add 12 shallots, very finely chopped, and cook them
gently until they are hot. Add 1/2 cup finely chopped parsley and serve
at once, with broiled meats.

Cumberland Sauce   *Cumberland Sauce*

MELT 2 CUPS red currant jelly over hot water and add 1/2 cup Port,
the juice of half an orange and half a lemon, 1 tablespoon finely chopped
and blanched shallots mixed with 1/2 teaspoon each of dry mustard,
and salt and cayenne to taste. Add 3 tablespoons each of slivered and
blanched orange rind and lemon rind and reheat the sauce.

Kalte Ribiselsauce   *Cold Currant Jelly Sauce*

SIMMER THE slivered thin rind of 1 orange and 1 lemon in 1/4 cup water
for 8 minutes. Drain them well and add them to the juice of 1 orange
and 1 lemon. Add 1/2 cup each of Port and red currant jelly, 1 tablespoon Dijon mustard, a pinch of cayenne, and sugar and salt to taste.
Simmer the sauce for 5 minutes. Cool it and serve with cold meat or game.

Kalte Wildsauce   *Cold Game Sauce*

MASH THE yolks of 8 hard-cooked eggs and add 4 tablespoons French
mustard, 1 1/4 cups melted currant jelly, and salt to taste. Purée the mix-

ture in a blender. Add the grated rind of 1 orange and 1 tablespoon orange juice and chill the sauce. Add more orange juice if the sauce is too thick. Serve it with hot venison.

Tangerine Sauce   *Mandarinensauce*

IN THE TOP of a double boiler, combine 12 ounces currant jelly, 2 tablespoons tarragon vinegar, 1 teaspoon dry mustard, and 1/2 teaspoon each of ground cloves and cinnamon. Cook the sauce over gently boiling water for 1 hour, until it thickens. If too thick, add strained orange juice. Add the finely slivered rind of 2 oranges and 1 lemon and 2 tangerines, separated into sections and freed of seeds and membranes, and cool the sauce. Serve with ham.

Cold Raisin Sauce   *Kalte Rosinensauce*

HEAT 1 CUP seedless raisins in 1 cup Port until they are puffed, add 1/2 cup orange juice, the slivered rind of 1/2 orange, and 1/2 cup lump sugar. Simmer until the sugar is dissolved. Add a pinch of salt and more Port to taste. The sauce may be spiced with 1/4 teaspoon each of ground cloves and cinnamon. Serve hot or cold, with meat.

Horseradish Cream Sauce   *Kren Rahmsauce*

WHIP 1/2 CUP heavy cream until it is stiff and add 1/2 cup freshly grated horseradish, 1 teaspoon vinegar, and 1/2 teaspoon prepared English mustard. Add the horseradish quickly or it will turn brown. Season with salt and pepper to taste. Serve at once with fish or meat.

Horseradish Cream   *Meerrettichcreme*

COMBINE 1/2 CUP cream, whipped stiff with a pinch of salt, and 3 tablespoons each of freshly grated horseradish and ground blanched almonds.

Frozen Horseradish Cream   *Gefrorene Krensauce*

INTO 3/4 CUP heavy cream, whipped stiff with a few grains of salt, fold 6 tablespoons freshly grated horseradish, 3 tablespoons orange juice, 3 tea-

spoons grated orange rind, and 3/4 teaspoon sugar. Rinse a chilled mold,
turn the cream into it, and freeze it. Unmold onto a crystal dish and
garnish it with parsley. Serve with hot meat, poultry, game, or fish. The
cream may also be piped in large rosettes with a pastry bag onto wax
paper and frozen.

Apfelkren   *Apple Horseradish Sauce*

WHIP 2/3 CUP cream stiff with 1 teaspoon lemon juice and 1 pinch each
of salt and sugar. Just before serving, grate 1 cored apple and half a
horseradish root, both peeled, and fold them lightly into the whipped
cream. Work quickly, as the apple and horseradish will both darken.
Serve with fish or meat, hot or cold.

Krensauce für Wild   *Horseradish Game Sauce*

ADD 1/2 TEASPOON cinnamon, a pinch of nutmeg, and salt and pepper
to taste to 1 cup Port wine. Reduce over low heat to 2/3 cup. Add 1 cup
melted currant jelly and 1 cup freshly grated horseradish, or reduce the
quantity of horseradish to taste.

Fleischaspik   *Beef Aspic*

SOFTEN 2 ENVELOPES of gelatin in 1/2 cup cold water. Add Sherry to taste
to 2 1/2 cups beef stock and heat the stock to the boiling point. Dissolve
the softened gelatin in the stock, off the heat.

Hühneraspik   *Chicken Aspic*

SIMMER 2 1/2 CUPS chicken stock with 1 onion, sliced, for 10 minutes.
Strain it and stir in, off the heat, 2 envelopes gelatin softened in 1/2 cup
cold stock.

Fischaspik   *Fish Aspic*

HEAT 2 1/2 CUPS strained fish stock to the boiling point. Soften 2 envelopes of gelatin in 1/2 cup cold fish stock. Off the heat, add the softened
gelatin to the boiling stock, stirring until it is entirely dissolved.

Onion Aspic — *Zwiebelaspik*

SIMMER 1 ONION, chopped, in 3 cups clarified chicken or beef stock for 20 minutes. Strain it and stir in, off the heat, 2 envelopes of gelatin softened in 1/2 cup cold stock. Add onion juice and onion salt to taste.

Tarragon Aspic — *Aspik mit Estragon*

SIMMER 3 TABLESPOONS dried tarragon or 1 bunch of fresh tarragon in 1 cup clarified beef or veal stock until the liquid is reduced by half. Strain it and dissolve in it 2 envelopes of gelatin softened in 1/2 cup white Port, light Sherry, or white wine. Add 2 more cups stock. For fish dishes, use fish stock instead of meat stock.

White Wine Aspic — *Aspik mit Weisswein*

BRING 1 CUP clear chicken stock or consommé to a boil and dissolve in it, off the heat, 2 envelopes of gelatin softened in 1/2 cup white wine. Add 1 1/2 cups white wine and salt to taste.

Sherry Aspic — *Aspik mit Sherry*

FOLLOW THE recipe for white wine aspic, substituting Sherry for the white wine.

Chopped Aspic — *Hackaspik*

POUR THE aspic into a shallow pan, such as a jelly-roll pan, and chill it until it is set. Roll up the sheet of aspic and cut the roll crosswise into thin strips. Chop the strips into cubes.

Aspic Sauce for Meat — *Aspiksauce für Fleisch*

BRING 4 CUPS beef stock or consommé and 1 cup wine to a boil and reduce the liquid by half. Soften 2 envelopes of gelatin in 1/2 cup water and dissolve it in the stock, off the heat. Add 1/4 cup chopped parsley, 2 tablespoons tomato purée, 1 teaspoon lemon juice, and salt and pepper to taste. Cool the aspic until it begins to set and pour it over slices of cold meat. Chill until the aspic is firm. Serve with a vegetable salad.

Weisse chaud-froid Sauce   *White Chaud-Froid Sauce*

BRING 1 1/2 CUPS velouté sauce to a boil with 1/2 cup chicken stock or consommé and reduce the sauce by a third, stirring constantly. Gradually add 1/2 cup heavy cream, stirring all the time. Simmer the sauce for 10 minutes and strain it through a piece of cheesecloth. Soften 2 envelopes of gelatin in 1/2 cup stock and dissolve it in the hot sauce, off the heat. Cool the sauce, stirring it frequently to prevent a crust from forming. Use to coat cold chicken or fish.

Braune chaud-froid Sauce   *Brown Chaud-Froid Sauce*

SOFTEN 2 ENVELOPES of gelatin in 1/2 cup cold stock. Combine 2 cups brown sauce with 1 cup stock or consommé, bring the sauce to a boil, and skim it well. Dissolve the gelatin in the sauce. Add 3 ounces Madeira or Sherry and strain the sauce through a fine sieve. Just before it congeals, use the sauce to coat cold foods.

Salatmarinade   *Salad Marinade*

STIR 1 TEASPOON each of sugar and paprika, 1/2 teaspoon each of salt, dry mustard, and crushed celery seed, and 1/4 teaspoon pepper with 1/2 cup tarragon vinegar until the salt, sugar, and mustard are dissolved. Gradually add 3/4 cup olive oil, stirring constantly. Or shake the ingredients in a bottle until the dressing is well blended.

Salatsauce 1   *Salad Dressing I*

IN A WOODEN salad bowl, crush 18 peppercorns with a wooden spoon into a coarse powder. Add 1 teaspoon rough salt and 1/4 teaspoon dry mustard. Stir in 3 tablespoons olive oil and 1 1/2 tablespoons tarragon vinegar. Put lettuce on top of the dressing and chill in the refrigerator. At serving time, stir until all the leaves are coated.

Salatsauce 2   *Salad Dressing II*

STIR 1 1/2 TEASPOONS each of salt and prepared mustard with 1/4 teaspoon black pepper and 1 large clove of garlic, crushed. Add 1/4 cup tarragon

vinegar and stir until the salt is dissolved. Gradually add 3/4 cup olive oil, stirring constantly. Or shake the ingredients in a bottle until the dressing is well blended.

Salad Dressing III — Salatsauce 3

STIR 1/4 TEASPOON salt, a few grindings of black pepper, and 1 teaspoon mild prepared mustard to a smooth cream. Stir in 2 tablespoons vinegar and beat in 6 tablespoons olive oil, drop by drop, as for mayonnaise. This dressing can be made in large quantities and stored. Use 1 1/2 cups olive oil, 1/2 cup vinegar, 4 teaspoons mustard, 1 teaspoon salt, and 1/4 teaspoon freshly ground black pepper.

French Dressing — Französische Marinade

INTO A saucer or shallow bowl, grind about 1/8 teaspoon black pepper over 1/4 teaspoon salt and add 2 tablespoons vinegar, stirring until the salt is dissolved. Beat in 1/4 cup olive oil so gradually that the dressing thickens slightly in preparation. Pour it at once over lettuce leaves and "fatigue," or toss, the salad until every leaf is coated with the dressing. If the dressing has to be prepared in advance, it must be well shaken or stirred before it is used.

Kräutermarinade   *Herb Dressing*

STIR 1 TEASPOON each of salt and sugar and 1/2 teaspoon each of pepper and paprika with 1 tablespoon lemon juice. Add 2 tablespoons minced onion and 1 tablespoon each of minced parsley, chervil, and chives. Add 3 tablespoons each of olive oil and tarragon vinegar. The dressing may also be made with 2 tablespoons each of lemon juice and vinegar.

Zwiebelsauce   *Onion Dressing*

IN A FOOD processor with the steel blade, purée 1/2 onion, 1 shallot, and 1 clove of garlic, all roughly chopped. Add 4 sprigs of parsley, stems removed, and 1 tablespoon Dijon mustard and process for 2 seconds. Add 2 tablespoons each of vinegar and dry white wine, 1 teaspoon salt, and pepper to taste. Gradually add 3/4 cup olive oil and process until the dressing is smooth.

Paprikasauce 1   *Paprika Dressing I*

STIR 2 1/2 TEASPOONS paprika, 1 teaspoon each of salt and sugar, 1/2 teaspoon prepared mustard, and 1/4 teaspoon pepper with 1/3 cup tarragon vinegar until the salt, sugar, and mustard are dissolved. Gradually add 2/3 cup olive oil, stirring constantly.

Paprikasauce 2   *Paprika Dressing II*

COMBINE 2 TEASPOONS paprika, 1 1/2 teaspoons each of salt and dry mustard, 1 teaspoon sugar, and 1/4 teaspoon black pepper. Add 1/2 cup vinegar gradually and stir until the salt and sugar are dissolved. Stir in 3/4 cup olive oil.

Essig Kräutersauce   *Vinaigrette Sauce*

MARINATE 1 TABLESPOON each of shallots, capers, parsley, chervil, and chives, all chopped, in 1 cup olive oil for at least 1 hour. Add 1/2 cup tarragon vinegar, 1 teaspoon salt, and 1/2 teaspoon pepper. Pour the dressing over meat, fish, vegetables, or salad, and rice over the dish 1 hard-cooked egg. (The riced egg may be added to the dressing and 2 table-spoons chopped onion may be substituted for the shallots.)

As a variation, at serving time add to vinaigrette sauce 1 tomato, peeled, seeded, and chopped.

Essig Kräuter sauce, or vinaigrette sauce, is served with many meat, poultry, vegetable, and fish dishes, both warm and cold, in Austria. The most popular are cold boiled beef, boiled new potatoes, herring, and cauliflower.

French Salad Sauce   *Französische Sauce*

BEAT 5 TABLESPOONS olive oil and 3 tablespoons wine vinegar with 2 hard-cooked egg yolks, riced, and a pinch of freshly ground black pepper until the dressing is smooth. Add 2 hard-cooked egg whites, riced, and salt to taste. Serve with any green salad or with cold meat or poultry.

Garlic Salad Dressing   *Knoblauch Salatsauce*

CRUSH 1 LARGE clove of garlic with 1 teaspoon salt and 1/4 teaspoon black pepper and stir in 1 teaspoon prepared mustard. Add a generous 1/2 cup olive oil, 3 tablespoons vinegar, and 1/2 teaspoon dried orégano. Shake the mixture vigorously in a bottle. This dressing is suitable for a green salad or a grapefruit and avocado salad.

Green Sauce   *Grüne Sauce*

COMBINE 1/2 CUP each of water cress, spinach, and parsley, all minced, and 3 tablespoons each of onion and celery, both minced. Blend in 2 tablespoons lemon juice and 1/2 teaspoon salt. Beat in about 1 cup olive oil gradually. The sauce should be thick.

Salad Dressing without Oil   *Salatmarinade ohne Öl*

IN A FOOD processor with the steel blade, purée 1 large tomato, peeled, seeded, and chopped, 1/2 onion, sliced, and 1/2 teaspoon each of dry mustard and snipped dill. Add 3 sprigs of parsley, stems removed, 4 peppercorns, and 1 teaspoon salt and purée until smooth. With the machine running, add 1/4 cup tarragon vinegar, gradually, correct the seasoning, and serve the dressing with mixed greens or sliced tomatoes.

Essigmarinade   *Vinegar Marinade*

COMBINE 1/2 CUP tarragon vinegar, 2 tablespoons olive oil, 1 tablespoon sugar, 1 teaspoon salt, and 1/2 teaspoon pepper. Marinate the salad of your choice in this dressing for at least 1/2 hour and at serving time bind it with mayonnaise.

Kalte grüne Spinatsauce für Fisch   *Cold Spinach Sauce for Fish*

CHOP FINELY 3 small or 2 large shallots. Add 12 sprigs of parsley and 1 bunch of chives, chopped. Add 2 tablespoons lemon juice, 1/4 cup each of white wine and olive oil, and salt and white pepper to taste. Add 1/4 cup cold cooked puréed spinach and chill the sauce. Serve it with any cold fish. It is attractive with cold trout surrounded by tomato slices.

Russische Sauce   *Russian Sauce*

STIR 4 HARD-COOKED egg yolks, riced, with 2 uncooked egg yolks until they are smooth and add 1/2 teaspoon each of tarragon and chervil, both minced, and salt and pepper to taste. Add 1 large or 2 small shallots, minced, and 2 tablespoons mild prepared mustard. Stir the sauce well and add gradually 5 tablespoons olive oil and 4 tablespoons tarragon vinegar. Correct the seasoning and chill the sauce.

Saure Sahnensauce   *Sour Cream Dressing*

HEAT 1 CUP thick sour cream with 2 tablespoons butter until the butter is melted, but do not let it boil. Cool the sour cream and add 3 tablespoons vinegar, 1/2 teaspoon each of paprika and salt, and black pepper to taste. Serve with cauliflower, potato, or cabbage salad.

Basic Mayonnaise   Mayonnersauce

BEAT 3 EGG yolks well and add 1/2 teaspoon each of salt and dry mustard and 1/4 teaspoon pepper. Add 1/2 teaspoon tarragon vinegar and gradually add 1/2 cup olive oil, drop by drop, beating constantly. Add 1/2 teaspoon more tarragon vinegar and beat 1/2 cup more olive oil, drop by drop, into the sauce. Again add 1 teaspoon vinegar and 1/2 cup olive oil, in a thin stream, beating constantly until the mixture is thick and yellow. If the mayonnaise should separate, beat an egg yolk in another bowl and slowly add the curdled mayonnaise, beating constantly.

Viennese Mayonnaise   Wiener Mayonnersauce

IN A FOOD processor with the steel blade put 1 whole egg and 1 egg yolk, both at room temperature. Add 1 tablespoon vinegar or lemon juice, 1 tablespoon Dijon mustard, 1 teaspoon salt, and 1/4 teaspoon freshly ground pepper and process for 3 seconds. With the machine running, add 1 1/2 cups olive oil or 1 cup salad oil and 1/2 cup olive oil in a stream and blend the mayonnaise until it is thick. Chill it and thin it with 1 to 2 tablespoons hot consommé, depending on the thickness required. Salt may be added, depending on the saltiness of the consommé. The mayonnaise may separate if the oil is added too rapidly. Place half of it over boiling water at once and stir in 1 tablespoon hot consommé or vinegar. Beat this mixture gradually into the remaining cold mayonnaise and continue with the preparation.

Chive or Shallot Mayonnaise   Schnittlauch- oder Schallote-Mayonnersauce

To 1 CUP mayonnaise, add 2 tablespoons chopped chives or 3 shallots, minced.

Egg Sauce   Eiersauce

MIX 3 HARD-COOKED egg yolks, riced, with 2 uncooked egg yolks and 1/2 teaspoon vinegar. Gradually beat in enough olive oil to make a thick mayonnaise, about 1 1/2 to 2 cups, 1 teaspoon dry mustard, and salt and pepper to taste. Add 1 teaspoon each of chives, chervil, tarragon, and parsley, all finely chopped, and thin the sauce, if necessary, with cold consommé or stock.

Kräuter Mayonnersauce   *Fresh Herb Mayonnaise*

PLACE 1 1/2 cups thick mayonnaise in the container of a blender with
a generous bunch of chives, the leaves from 4 sprigs of tarragon, and
4 sprigs of parsley. Add the zest of 1 lemon, salt to taste, and more chives
and tarragon, if desired. Cover the container and blend until the sauce
is soft green, about 30 seconds.

Kren Mayonnersauce   *Horseradish Mayonnaise*

FOLD 1/2 cup whipped cream into 1 cup mayonnaise and add the grated
rind of 1/2 lemon and salt to taste. Just before serving, stir in 1/4 cup
freshly grated horseradish.

Zitronen Mayonnersauce   *Lemon Mayonnaise*

IN A BLENDER, blend 1 egg at room temperature, 1 tablespoon lemon juice,
1 teaspoon salt, and 1/4 teaspoon dry mustard for several seconds. With
the machine running, add 1 cup salad oil or a combination of salad oil
and olive oil in a stream and blend the mayonnaise until it is thick. Add
the grated zest of 2 lemons, 1/4 cup grated onion, and 3 sprigs each of
parsley and dill, both minced, and blend well.

Mayonner Senfsauce   *Mustard Cream Sauce*

FOLD INTO 1 cup whipped cream 1/2 cup thick mayonnaise, 2 teaspoons
lemon juice, 1 teaspoon Dijon mustard, and 1/2 teaspoon dry mustard.
Add salt and pepper to taste and chill the sauce. Serve with hot ham.

Remouladensauce   *Rémoulade Sauce*

STIR INTO 1 1/2 cups mayonnaise 1/4 cup finely chopped dill pickle, 2
tablespoons chopped capers, and 1 tablespoon each of tarragon, parsley,
and chervil, all chopped. Add anchovy paste to taste, using a mild paste
from a tube, and salt and pepper. Chill the sauce.

As a variation, add to the finished sauce 3 tablespoons grated horseradish and 1 tablespoon prepared mustard.

Mayonnaise with Rum — *Rum Mayonnersauce*

BEAT I UNCOOKED egg and I riced·hard-cooked egg yolk with 6 table-spoons olive oil, adding the oil drop by drop and beating well. Add I tea-spoon each of dry mustard and sugar. At serving time, stir in I table-spoon rum or arrack and add salt and pepper to taste. Serve with cold meats.

Tartare Sauce I — *Tartarensauce 1*

To 2 CUPS mayonnaise, add I tablespoon each of tarragon vinegar and chopped dill pickle, 2 teaspoons each of onion, parsley, and borrage, all chopped, and I teaspoon each of sharp mustard and lemon juice. Add salt and pepper to taste.

Tartare Sauce II — *Tartarensauce 2*

To I 1/2 CUPS mayonnaise, add I dill pickle, 4 shallots, and 2 anchovies, all finely chopped. Add I tablespoon each of capers, parsley, tarragon, and chervil, all chopped, and I teaspoon mustard. Thin the mayonnaise with heavy cream to taste and add 1/2 teaspoon each of lemon juice and sugar and salt and pepper to taste.

Tartare Sauce with Whipped Cream — *Tartarensauce mit Schlagrahm*

To I CUP mayonnaise, add 2 tablespoons each of tarragon vinegar and minced shallots, I tablespoon minced capers, I teaspoon each of tarragon and chervil, both minced, I teaspoon anchovy paste, and 1/4 teaspoon white pepper. Fold in 3/4 cup stiffly whipped cream.

Green Tartare Sauce — *Grüne Tartarensauce*

PREPARE tartare sauce II, omitting the anchovies, and add 3 tablespoons spinach purée. Add whipped cream to taste instead of heavy cream.

Tomato Mayonnaise — *Andalusische Sauce*

To I CUP heavy mayonnaise, add 1/2 cup each of pimientos, cut into fine julienne, and tomato purée. Add salt and pepper to taste.

Obstsalat Sauce   *Fruit Salad Dressing*

BEAT TOGETHER 1/2 cup each of mayonnaise and sour cream and 1/2 teaspoon each of salt and brandy or wine. Add a grating of fresh black
pepper and chill the sauce. Serve with fruit salad.

Bouquet Garni   *Herb Bouquet*

TO SEASON soups and sauces, the Viennese use the usual herbs and flavor-
ings—celery, parsley or thyme, and bay leaf—but they almost always add
chervil, also.

Croutons   *Croutons*

CUT SLICES of 2-day-old bread into ovals, rounds, strips, cubes, or whatever shapes are needed, and brush the pieces with melted butter. Toast
them on baking sheets in a very slow oven (250° F.) until they are golden
brown. Or sauté them in butter in a skillet until they are golden brown
on both sides.

Anwendung von Kren   *To Use Horseradish*

WHENEVER POSSIBLE, grate fresh horseradish. If prepared horseradish is
used, drain it, press it as dry as possible, and increase the amount called
for in the recipe by one-fourth.

Pilz-Extrakt   *Mushroom Essence*

CLEAN 2 POUNDS mushrooms and chop them. Sprinkle them with 1 teaspoon salt and cook them, without liquid, covered, over low heat for 20
minutes. Drain off the liquid that cooks out of the mushrooms and reserve
it. Simmer the mushrooms again, drain, and reserve the liquid. Add 2 cups
water to the drained cooked mushrooms and simmer them until the liquid
is reduced to 1/2 cup. Combine the two liquids and reduce them until
the essence thickens slightly.

Bread and Sweet Bread

Brot und Germgebäck

VIENNA HAS sent into the world four major products bearing her name. For sheer joy and pleasure, she has given us the Viennese waltz; for substance, she has contributed the *Wienerschnitzel;* for the road, she has contributed the *Wienerwurst,* or just "wiener" for short. And for the daily sustenance of man, she has given us Vienna bread.

The name "Vienna bread" may be applied to all small white breads and fancy loaves, but, to be properly eligible for this title they should be made of rich Vienna bread dough that always yields bread with a beautiful brown crust. Viennese cooks and housewives rarely bake Vienna bread at home, since the bakers' boys bring them oven-warm, crisp loaves every morning along with the latest news. Everyone in Vienna knows that it would take years of practice to perfect the special fold that is needed to make the *Kaisersemmel,* the Emperor's roll, correctly. It is said that the man who devised the *Kaisersemmel,* a round folded roll, was generously rewarded for his invention. Everyone had been trying to invent a roll that could be broken easily in one hand with light pressure. The Viennese, who do try to think of everything, considerately serve *Kaisersemmeln* at dinner parties and in restaurants so that a guest will not need to use both hands and an evil grimace to break a hard roll. Besides the effort it costs, this operation showers the entire area with enormous crumbs. The *Kaisersemmel,* on the other hand, readily breaks apart into five or six sections and leaves no crumbs at all.

When a Viennese hostess prepares for a party that will include open sandwiches, or if she is getting ready for her *Jour,* her special day to entertain, she orders loaves of *Kastenbrot,* box bread, from her baker or bakes them herself in special boxes or enclosed pans. The boxes are contrived in such a way that small round, square, oval, heart- or diamond-shaped loaves can be baked in them, or pieces of different dough can be twisted to make a particolored loaf. Each slice of bread serves for a single open sandwich. It thus has a crisp golden crust all the way around, instead of being without crust because it has been cut from a larger slice.

The sweet doughs and coffeecakes are usually baked at home and are always served with the *Jause,* the late-afternoon meal. In Denmark, people call Danish pastry Vienna bread, *Wienerbrot.* In Vienna, where this kind of pastry actually originated, people called it *Plundergebäck*, and it was the Emperor's favorite pastry. Had the Emperor favored a less popular pastry, the fact would probably have been hushed up. Fortunately he preferred the pastry that has made a name for itself—even though the name varies—around most of the world.

The Viennese version of what Americans call Danish pastry is buttery and flaky, and, made at home or in a Viennese bakery, it can approximate what was the favorite bakery of the Emperor—and all other Viennese. In Vienna, as in Denmark, it is made with a light touch and filled with cheese, fruit, and nuts. It is glazed or iced, and nuts, raisins, or crumbs often decorate the top. Some cinnamon is used, and if other spices are added they are almost undetectable.

Vienna has become famous not only for her bread but for the prowess of her bakers when they undertake extracurricular duties. The exercise of kneading bread apparently made strong soldiers of the bakers, and Vienna had them to thank for defeating Ludwig of Bavaria when he did battle with Frederick the Handsome of Austria. The intrepid bakers also defeated the Sultan Solyman in 1529 at the very gates of the city, when all other troops and professions had failed, and again in 1585, when the undiscouraged Turks came back for more. Apparently the Turkish lust for Vienna was insatiable, since they came back full force in 1683 and settled down outside the city walls to starve her out. It was a watchful baker's journeyman who discovered a Turk tunneling under his oven and gave the alarm that saved the city.

Much of this may be legend, but the Viennese like to believe that it was a baker, who baked his bread in the shape of a crescent—the Mohammedan emblem—who not only warned the citizens that the Turks had actually entered Vienna's gates, but created a very popular new "form" for bread, the famous *Wiener Kipfel.* For certain sections of Viennese society, it is perfectly designed to dip into a cup of coffee.

Vienna Bread and Rolls I — *Wiener Brot und Semmeln 1*

DISSOLVE 2 ENVELOPES of dry yeast with 1 tablespoon sugar in 2 1/2 cups warm water. Whisk in 2 cups flour, 1/2 cup flat beer, 2 tablespoons clarified butter, and 1 tablespoon salt. Set the mixture in a warm place until bubbles break on the surface. Beat in 2 3/4 cups flour to make a soft dough. Cover the dough with a cloth and let it rise in a warm place for 1 hour. Punch it down, cover it, and let it rise in a warm place for about 30 minutes longer.

Turn out the dough on a floured board and knead it well. The dough may be shaped into many forms: plain loaves or rolls, French loaves, round loaves, braids, batons, or twisted batons, as in Viennese coronation loaves. Loaves or rolls should go into the oven 2 3/4 to 3 hours from time of starting dough. Place loaves in greased bread pans, rolls on baking sheets dusted with flour. Brush the tops with Vienna wash. Cover the loaves or rolls and let them rise in a warm place until they are double in bulk. Brush them again with Vienna wash. Bake loaves in a hot oven (400° F.) for 50 minutes. Bake rolls in a very hot oven (425° F.) for 12 to 15 minutes. Cool the loaves or rolls on wire racks. Makes 2 loaves or 30 rolls.

Vienna Bread and Rolls II — *Wiener Brot and Semmeln 2*

SOFTEN 2 ENVELOPES or cakes of yeast in 1 1/2 cups warm water. Add a pinch of sugar and whisk the yeast well. Add 2 cups sifted flour and beat the mixture well with a wooden spoon to make a smooth batter. Sprinkle this sponge with a thin film of flour. Let it rise in a warm place until bubbles appear on the surface, break, and the sponge begins to sink in the middle. Pour over the sponge 1 cup cold milk or water in which 6 tablespoons powdered dry milk have been mixed. Stir in 1 tablespoon each of sugar and salt and add gradually about 4 cups sifted flour. The sponge may not take the entire amount. After enough flour has been incorporated, work in 2 tablespoons shortening.

On a lightly floured board, knead the mixture into a soft dough. The finished dough should be kneaded and folded a few times until it is smooth and dry. Cover the dough with a cloth and let it rise in a warm place for 1 hour, or until cracks appear on the surface. Fold and knead the dough on a lightly floured board or cloth for a few minutes, until it is

smooth. Return the dough to the bowl, cover it, and let it rise for about
20 minutes.

Shape the dough into a loaf or small rolls. Put the rolls on a cloth
lightly dusted with flour and cover them with a cloth. Put the loaf into
a warm greased bread pan. Let the rolls or loaf rise in a warm place
until they are double in bulk. Transfer the rolls to warm greased or
floured baking sheets. Brush the top of the loaf or rolls with cold water.
Bake the rolls in a very hot oven (450° F.) for 12 to 15 minutes, the
loaf for 45 to 50 minutes. Cool them on wire racks. Makes 1 loaf or
2 dozen rolls.

Geflochtenes Brot   *Braided Bread*

MAKE THE dough for *Wiener Brot und Semmeln 2,* Vienna bread and
rolls II. After it has risen, put half the dough on a floured board and cut
it into 4 parts. Roll 3 parts into long pieces, each about 1 1/2 inches in
diameter, and braid them. Fasten the ends securely. Shape the fourth
part of the dough into 3 pieces, each about 1/2 inch in diameter and as
long as the first pieces. Braid these pieces and lay the braid on top of
the first braid. Shape the remaining dough in the same way. Let the
loaves rise, covered, in a warm place for about 1 1/2 hours, or until they
double in bulk. Brush them with beaten egg yolk and bake them in a
hot oven (400° F.) for 15 minutes. Reduce the heat to moderate (350° F.)
and bake the loaves for 45 minutes longer.

Weisses Kastenbrot   *White Box Bread*

MAKE THE dough for *Wiener Brot und Semmeln 2,* Vienna bread and
rolls II, making half the quantity of the recipe. Butter 2 heart-shaped
Kastenbrot pans, box-bread pans. (A heart-shaped box opens down the
middle, each half shaped like half a heart.) Shape the dough into 2 long
pieces. Each piece should half fill a box. Do not let the ends of the dough
taper. Place the dough in the boxes and put on the end pieces, which
secure the halves. Let the loaves rise in a warm place until the boxes are
full. Place the boxes in a moderately hot oven (375° F.) and bake the
loaves for about 25 minutes. Take apart the boxes and cool the loaves
on racks. Box bread may be made in various shapes.

Whole-Wheat Box Bread — *Braunes Kastenbrot*

COMBINE 1/3 TO 1/2 cup sugar, 1 heaping tablespoon rough salt or 1 level tablespoon ordinary salt, 1/3 cup shortening, 1 tablespoon caraway seeds, and 2 cups boiling water. Let the mixture cool to lukewarm.

Into a 1-cup measure put 1/4 cup lukewarm water, 1 teaspoon sugar, and 2 envelopes of yeast and let the yeast bubble until it reaches the top of the cup. Add the yeast to the first mixture, then add 2 well-beaten eggs and stir the mixture. Combine 5 cups whole-wheat flour and 3 cups white flour. Add 4 cups of the blended flour to the yeast mixture and stir the dough until it is smooth. Add the remaining flour and work the dough until the flour is incorporated. Cover the bowl and chill the dough in the refrigerator for 3 hours.

Cut the chilled dough into 4 parts. Rub the hands with shortening and work each piece of dough well, to squeeze out the air. Butter 4 round or square *Kastenbrot* pans, box-bread pans. (Each pan has 2 sections that fit together to enclose the dough completely.) Shape the pieces of dough about the same length as the boxes. Do not let the ends taper. Place the pieces in the pans. They should be about half full. Close the pans and adjust the end pieces, which secure the 2 sections. Let the loaves stand in a warm place for about 1 1/2 hours, or until the dough fills the boxes. Place the boxes in a moderate oven (350° F.) and bake the loaves for 30 minutes, or until they come out of the boxes easily. Remove the boxes and lay the loaves on their sides on a wire rack covered with a towel. Cover them and let them cool.

Twisted Box Bread — *Zweifärbiges Kastenbrot*

COMBINE 1/3 TO 1/2 cup sugar, 1 heaping tablespoon rough salt or 1 level tablespoon ordinary salt, 1/3 cup shortening, 1 tablespoon caraway seeds, and 2 cups boiling water. Let the mixture cool to lukewarm.

Into a 1-cup measure put 1/4 cup lukewarm water, 1 teaspoon sugar, and 2 envelopes of yeast and let the yeast bubble until it reaches the top of the cup. Add the yeast to the first mixture, then add 2 well-beaten eggs and stir the mixture. Add 4 cups unsifted white flour and stir the dough until it is smooth. Add another 4 cups flour and work the dough until the flour is incorporated. Cover the bowl and chill the dough in the refrigerator for 3 hours.

Make a pumpernickel dough. In a warm mixing bowl soften 3 envelopes of yeast in 1 1/2 cups lukewarm water and add 1/2 cup molasses,
3 tablespoons caraway seeds, and 1 tablespoon salt. Stir the mixture well.
Add 2 tablespoons softened butter and 3 cups rye flour and mix well with
a wooden spoon. Add 3 cups sifted white flour and turn out the dough
onto a lightly floured board. Knead the dough until it is smooth, about
8 to 10 minutes. Place the dough in a buttered bowl and turn it until it
is thoroughly coated. Cover the dough with a warm towel and let it rise
in a warm place until it doubles in bulk, about 2 hours.

Take the white bread dough from the refrigerator. Rub the hands
with shortening and work the dough well, to squeeze out the air. Punch
down the pumpernickel dough. Butter a *Kastenbrot* pan, a box-bread
pan, that makes 4 fluted round loaves. (Such a pan has 2 parts: the
bottom has 4 fluted troughs, or compartments, and the lid has 4.) Shape
each bread dough into 4 pieces, each piece the same length as the compartments. Do not let the ends of the pieces taper. Twist the pieces by
pairs into 4 loaves, using a piece of white dough and a piece of pumpernickel dough for each loaf. Place the 4 twisted loaves in the compartments.
Each compartment should be half full. Adjust the lid of the pan and let
the loaves rise in a warm place for about 1 hour, or until they fill the
compartments.

Place the box in a moderate oven (350° F.) and bake the loaves for
35 minutes. Take them from the box and cool them on wire racks.

Wiener Milchbrot   *Vienna Milk Bread*

SOFTEN 2 ENVELOPES or cakes of yeast in 1 cup warm water, add 1 tablespoon malt extract or sugar, and beat well. Beat in 2 cups sifted flour.
Cover the sponge and let it rise in a warm place for 30 minutes. Add
1 cup milk, scalded and then chilled, and stir it in well. Add gradually
about 5 cups flour with 1 tablespoon salt, 3 1/2 tablespoons sugar, and
2 3/4 tablespoons each of lard and clarified butter, mixed together. They
should be at room temperature. When enough flour has been added,
knead the mixture well to make a smooth elastic dough. Cover the
dough and let it rise in a warm place for 1 1/2 hours. Punch it down,
let it rise for 1 1/2 hours, punch it down, and let it rise a third time.
Shape the dough into 2 loaves and place them in warm buttered bread

pans. Cover the loaves and let them rise in a warm place until they double in bulk. Brush the tops with milk or water and bake the loaves in a hot oven (400° F.) for 45 minutes. Cool them on wire racks.

Viennese Coronation Loaf
Krönungsbrot

SIFT AND measure 7 cups flour. Dissolve 2 envelopes of yeast in 1 1/2 cups warm water and whisk in 2 tablespoons malt extract or granulated sugar. Beat in 2 cups flour. Cover the sponge and let it rise until bubbles appear and break, about 3/4 of an hour. Dissolve 2 tablespoons salt and 1/4 cup sugar in 1 1/2 cups milk, scalded and cooled to warm (90° F.). Pour this over the sponge and beat it in. Add gradually 4 cups flour. Work in 3 tablespoons soft fat—lard or butter—and add the remaining cup of flour cautiously, to make a firm dough. Cover the dough and let it rise for 3/4 hour. Punch it down, let it rise again for 3/4 hour, and punch it down. Keep the dough at 72° F. Knead it into a smooth ball on a lightly floured board. Divide the dough into 6 pieces and shape each piece into a baton, an oblong shape with blunt ends. Cross 2 baton pieces at the center and turn them against each other with the thumb and middle finger of both hands to make a ropelike shape. Place the "ropes" in a narrow roasting pan. Cover and let rise until the loaf is double in bulk. Bake in a hot oven (400° F.) for 30 minutes, then, if it seems to be baking too fast, reduce the temperature to slow (300° F.) and bake for 10 minutes longer. Remove the loaf to a wire rack to cool and brush the top with butter. Makes 1 large loaf. For smaller loaves, divide the dough into 10 pieces.

English Vienna Bread
Englisches Wiener Brot

SOFTEN 3 ENVELOPES or cakes of yeast in 2 cups warm water, add 1 tablespoon malt extract or sugar, and whisk them well. Gradually add 4 cups sifted flour. Beat well. Cover the sponge with a cloth and let it rise in a warm place for 45 minutes. Add 2 cups milk, scalded and cooled, and stir in 3 tablespoons sugar, 1 1/2 tablespoons lard, and 1 tablespoon salt. Mix in 5 1/2 cups sifted flour and knead into a smooth dough. Cover the dough and let it rise in a warm place for about 1 hour. Punch it down, let it rise for 3/4 hour, punch it down again, and let it rise for

1/2 hour. Shape it into loaves. Place them in warm greased bread pans, cover, and let rise until they are light. Brush the tops with cold water and bake in a very hot oven (425° F.) for 35 minutes. Reduce the oven temperature to moderately hot (375° F.) and bake until the loaves sound hollow when tapped. Cool on wire racks. Makes 2 loaves.

Kartoffelmilchbrot   *Potato Milk Bread*

SIFT AND measure 8 cups flour. Soften 2 envelopes or cakes of yeast in 1 cup warm water (95° F.) and add 1 egg yolk, 3/4 cup cooked mashed potatoes, 2 tablespoons sugar, and 1 1/2 cups flour. Cover the sponge and let it rise in a warm place until bubbles appear on the surface. Add 1 cup milk, scalded and cooled to warm (90° F.), 1 tablespoon salt, 10 tablespoons sugar, 1/4 cup cooked mashed potatoes, and the grated rind of 1/2 lemon. Beat well and gradually add about 6 cups flour. Add 3/4 cup softened lard when the flour is partly mixed in. Make a smooth but rather stiff dough. Cover it and let it rise in a warm place for 1/2 hour. Punch it down and add 1 pound sultanas. Let the dough rise for 1/2 hour longer, punch it down, and let it rise again for 1/2 hour. Punch it down and shape it into 4 loaves. Or divide it into 8 pieces and make rope-like loaves, as for Viennese coronation loaf. Place the loaves in greased pans and let them rise about 40 minutes, or until they are light. Bake them in a hot oven (400° F.) for 40 to 50 minutes. Cool them on wire racks. The tops of the loaves may be brushed with butter. Makes 2 medium-sized loaves.

Kaisersemmeln   *Emperor's Rolls*

DISSOLVE 1 1/2 ENVELOPES or cakes of yeast in 1 cup warm water and beat in 1/2 tablespoon malt extract or sugar. Whisk these together until they are well blended and beat in 3 cups flour, sifted. Let the sponge rise in a warm place until it begins to drop and a triangular cavity forms in the center. Pour onto it 1 cup milk, scalded and cooled to warm (90° F.). Beat in 3/4 tablespoon salt. Begin to add up to 3 cups sifted flour, incorporating enough to make a firm but not too tight dough. Let the dough rise, covered, until it has doubled in bulk. Punch it down once by folding it.

The shaping of *Kaisersemmeln* is so difficult that it is almost impossible to learn the technique without guidance. The rolls are shaped from pieces of dough the size of small eggs. The bottom of the dough remains unbroken. The sides are pulled out into 5 rough "wings," one after another, and folded into the center with a special twist. The last little "wing" is folded in such a way as to lock the others in place. Shape the rolls as follows: Take the egg-size piece of dough in the left hand and shape it into a round flat roll by holding the thumb of the right hand underneath and with the fingertips making one part of the round flat piece thin and wide enough so that the left thumb can be laid on it. Leave the left thumb in this position until the shaping is finished. With the fingers of the right hand, lift up a fifth of the dough, fold it over the left thumb, and press it with the side of the right hand, close to the left thumb. At the same time, make a counterclockwise movement with the left hand. Repeat the lifting and folding 4 times. Withdraw the left thumb and insert the fifth piece of dough in its place. Seal the ends.

Let the rolls rise on a lightly floured baking sheet. Just before baking them, brush with Vienna wash. Bake them in a very hot oven (450° F.) for 10 to 12 minutes. Just before they come from the oven, brush them again with Vienna wash. Cool them on wire racks.

Pistolets *Folded Rolls*

MAKE THE dough for *Kaisersemmeln,* or Emperor's rolls. Shape the dough into even rounds about 2 inches in diameter and place them on a cloth. Let them rise for 10 minutes. Butter a rolling pin 3 to 4 inches from one end. Lay each round upside down half off the edge of the table. Press the buttered end of the rolling pin firmly along the edge of the table, leaving only a thin transparent film of dough between the two halves. Fold the rolls gently and place them on a buttered baking sheet, the connecting dough film up. Leave ample space between rolls. Let them rise until they double in bulk. Brush them with cold water and bake them, split side up, in a very hot oven (450° F.) for about 12 minutes.

Heiligen Zöpfe *Saint's Plaits*

MAKE ANY preferred roll dough, such as the one for *Krönungsbrot.* When the dough is ready for shaping, shape it into small uniform rounds, 3 to 4 inches in diameter.

Press each round with the heels of both hands alternately until an oval shape with two liplike thick parts and a thin groove in the center is obtained. Pull the thick part opposite you with the fingers of both hands toward the center groove and press it firmly down. Reverse the procedure and pull in the other side. Press firmly with heel of the hand to seal the two thick parts along the center. Roll the elongated dough piece gently into a cylindrical piece with small pointed ends.

Lay 3 elongated pieces together and braid them or lay two pieces across each other at the center and twist to form a rope. Place each plait carefully on a buttered or floured baking sheet, allowing space for them to rise. Let them rise, covered, in a warm place. Brush the rolls with cold water or Vienna wash and bake them in a very hot oven (450° F.) for about 15 minutes. While the rolls are baking, a pan of hot water may be placed on the oven bottom to assure a crisp crust. Cool the rolls on wire racks. Makes 18 rolls.

Vienna Butter Crescents

Wiener Hörnchen

SCALD 1 1/2 CUPS milk and cool it to warm (90° F.). Sift 8 cups flour. Dissolve 2 envelopes or cakes of yeast in 1/2 cup lukewarm water and add the milk and 3/4 tablespoon malt extract. Beat in well 3 cups flour, a cup at a time, with a wooden spoon. Knead the sponge well with both hands. Cover it with a good sprinkling of flour and let it rise for about 1/2 hour, covered with a cloth. Add 2 egg yolks, 1 1/2 tablespoons salt, 1 tablespoon sugar, and 1 teaspoon grated lemon rind. Begin to add the remaining 5 cups flour gradually to make the dough. When 2 cups flour have been added, mix in 2 tablespoons butter softened to room temperature and finish the mixing. Knead the dough well until it is smooth and satiny. Cover it and let it rise in a warm place for 1 hour.

Knead 1/4 cup flour into 1 1/2 pounds butter, shape it into a 6- by 8-inch tile and chill it while the dough is rising. Punch down the dough and roll it out on a lightly floured board to a 1/4-inch-thick rectangle. Place the cold butter in the center, fold over the four sides, enclosing the butter completely, seal the edges, and roll it out again into a rectangle. Fold the dough into thirds and chill it for 20 minutes. Place the dough, narrow end down, on the board and roll it out again into a rectangle. Fold and chill it again. Repeat the turning, folding, and chilling two more times. After the final "turn" chill for at least 1/2 hour.

Bring the dough to room temperature, divide it in half, and roll the pieces as nearly as possible into rounds, each about 1/4 inch thick. Cut each round into 12 pie-shaped wedges with a sharp knife and brush the pieces with melted butter. Beginning at the wide edge, roll up each wedge. Lay the rolled wedges on buttered baking sheets about 2 inches apart. The points of the wedges should be underneath. Bring the ends into half circles, to form crescents. Brush the tops with milk. Let the crescents rise for 3/4 hour. Before baking, brush the tops with cold water. Bake the crescents in a hot oven (400° F.) for about 15 minutes with a pan of hot water in the oven under the rolls while they bake. Brush the baked crescents with Vienna wash and cool them on wire racks.

Bacon Buns

Speck Weckerln

IN A SMALL bowl dissolve 1 envelope dry yeast in 1/3 cup warm milk with 1 teaspoon each of flour and sugar for 15 minutes, or until it is foamy. In a bowl combine 2 2/3 cups all-purpose flour, 1/3 cup lukewarm milk, 1 large egg, 4 tablespoons soft butter, and 1 teaspoon salt, add the yeast mixture, and blend until the mixture forms a smooth dough. Knead the dough on a lightly floured surface for 8 to 10 minutes, or until it is smooth and elastic. Put in a bowl, cover with a cloth, and set the dough in a cold oven with a pan of boiling water. Let the dough rise until double in bulk, about 1 hour. Sauté 1/2 cup each of diced onion and bacon in 1 tablespoon lard until the onion is transparent but not brown and drain the mixture well on absorbent paper. Punch down the dough, roll it out 1/8 inch thick on a lightly floured board, and cut it into 16 rounds with a 3-inch cookie cutter. Pat the filling with absorbent paper and divide it among the rounds. Bring the edges together to enclose the filling, forming buns. Place the buns, seam side down, on a buttered baking sheet and let rise in the turned-off oven with a pan of boiling water for 1/2 hour. Brush with 1 egg yolk beaten with 1 teaspoon milk and sprinkle generously with coarse salt and caraway seeds. Bake in a very hot oven (425° F.) until golden, about 1/2 hour. *(Picture, page 483.)*

Kümmel Salzstängerln   *Caraway Salt Sticks*

SCALD 1/3 CUP milk and let it cool to warm (90° F.). Soften 1/2 envelope of dry yeast in 1/4 cup of the milk with 1 teaspoon each of flour and sugar, cover the mixture, and set it in a warm place for 10 minutes, or until it is foamy. Add 1 1/4 cups flour, 1 egg, lightly beaten, 3 tablespoons butter, softened to room temperature, 1 teaspoon salt, and the remaining milk and blend the mixture, adding more flour, if necessary, to form a soft but not sticky dough. Knead the dough on a lightly floured board until it is smooth and elastic. Let it rise, covered, for 30 minutes, punch it down, let it rise for 30 minutes longer, and punch it down. Let it rise for 20 minutes longer. These salt sticks are rolled out, cut, and rolled up as for crescents but the ends are not bent in. Let them rise, covered, on floured baking sheets. Brush the tops with Vienna wash and sprinkle generously with salt and caraway seeds. Bake them in a hot oven (400° F.) for about 15 minutes. Cool them on wire racks. Makes about 60 miniatures.

Coffee Braid

DISSOLVE 2 ENVELOPES of dry yeast in 1/3 cup warm milk, add 2 tea-spoons sugar, and beat in 3/4 cup flour. Put the sponge in a warm place to rise for 30 minutes.

In a warm bowl, mix 4 3/4 cups flour, 1/2 cup sugar, 1 teaspoon salt, and 1 cup milk, stir in 1 whole egg and 3 egg yolks, and beat until smooth. Gradually beat in 3/4 cup softened butter and the yeast sponge. Beat the mixture with the hand or with a strong beater until it forms a soft smooth dough that will not stick to hands or bowl. Cover the dough and let it rise in a warm place until it doubles in bulk, about 1 hour.

Punch the dough down on a floured board, return it to the bowl, and let it rest for 1/2 hour. Divide the dough into 3 parts and divide each part into 3 pieces of graduated size, so that you have 3 large uniform pieces, 3 medium, and 3 small. Roll the 3 large pieces into strips 20 inches long and braid them together with floured hands. Roll the 3 medium pieces into 18-inch strips and braid them. Paint the first braid with melted butter and lay the second braid on it. Roll the 3 small pieces into 15-inch strips, braid them, and lay them on the second braid. Place the *Striezel* on a baking sheet in a warm place and allow it to rise for about 1 hour. Brush the coffee braid with a mixture of 1 egg yolk and 1 tablespoon water and sprinkle it with pearl sugar. Bake it in a moderately hot oven (375° F.) for about 1/2 hour. Do not cut for 12 to 24 hours. *(Picture, page 482.)*

Vienna Christmas Stollen   *Weichnachtsstollen*

SCALD 1 1/2 CUPS milk and cool it to warm (100° F.). Dissolve 3 enve-lopes or cakes of yeast in 3/4 cup lukewarm water and add 3/4 cup of the cooled milk and 2 cups sifted flour. Cover the sponge with a cloth and let it ripen until bubbles appear on the surface and it is about to drop in the center. Pour the remaining 3/4 cup milk over the sponge. Add 6 egg yolks, lightly beaten, 3/4 cup sugar, and 2 teaspoons salt, and beat until the ingredients are well blended. Add 1 cup flour and beat well. Blend in 1/2 cup softened butter. Add more flour gradually to make a smooth dough, or until 4 to 5 cups have been added. Some flour absorbs more liquid than others. Knead in 2 cups sultanas, 1 1/2 cups almonds, chopped or slivered, 1 cup citron, chopped, and the rind of 1/2 lemon, grated and mixed with 2 tablespoons rum. Knead the dough until the fruits and nuts are dispersed well through it and it is smooth. Dust the top lightly with flour and let it rise in a warm place about 45 minutes. Punch it down and let it stand for 20 minutes.

Divide the dough in half and knead the pieces smooth. Let them stand for 10 minutes. Knead them again lightly and let them stand for 10 minutes longer. Place one ball of dough on a lightly floured board and, with a rolling pin, press down the center of the ball and roll the pin to and fro 4 to 5 times, pressing all the time, to make an elliptical shape, that should be about 12 inches long and 9 inches wide. The center thin strip should be about 1/2 inch thick. Both sides should remain untouched, resembling rather thick lips. Place this rolled-out piece on a buttered baking sheet and brush the thin center part with melted butter. Fold one lip toward the other and on top of it. Press the fingertips down near and below the lips, pulling them somewhat apart. Give a pull away from each end, pointing them inward. The shape should resemble a waning moon. Repeat the process with the second piece of dough. Let the *Stollen* rise, covered, in a warm place until they double in bulk, about 1 1/2 hours. Bake them in a moderately hot oven (375° F.) for 35 to 40 minutes. Do not overbake them. Cool them on racks. Brush them with butter and cover with vanilla sugar. This makes 2 large *Stollen*.

Gugelhupf   *Gugelhupf*

DISSOLVE 2 ENVELOPES of yeast in 1/2 cup warm milk and add 2 tablespoons sugar. Put the mixture in a warm place for 1/2 hour.

Sift 4 cups flour into a warm bowl. Add 3/4 cup sugar, 1 teaspoon salt, 1 teaspoon vanilla, 1 cup raisins, 3/4 cup sliced almonds, and the grated rind of 1 lemon and toss these ingredients to combine them. Make a well in the center of the flour, pour in the yeast mixture, and stir. Incorporate as much flour into the liquid as possible. Stir 4 beaten eggs and 3/4 cup melted butter into the dough, continue to incorporate the flour, and work in gradually about 1/2 cup warm milk, to form a smooth dough. Dust the dough with flour, cover it with a warm towel, and let it rise in a warm place for 2 hours, or until it doubles in bulk.

Turn the dough out on a floured board, punch it down, and shape it quickly into a ring. Put the ring in a well-buttered and floured 10-inch *Gugelhupf* pan. Cover and let the dough rise for 1 hour. Bake the *Gugelhupf* in a moderately hot oven (375° F.) for about 1 hour. If the top browns too quickly, cover it with buttered paper. Dust the cake with powdered sugar and let it stand overnight before slicing. *(Picture, page 485.)*

For holiday breakfasts, bake *Gugelhupf* dough in well-buttered bread pans, slice the cake, toast it, and serve with butter and jam.

Nut Coil   *Nusskuchen*

MAKE THE dough for *Striezel*.

Knead 2/3 cup softened butter and 2 tablespoons flour to a smooth paste. After the *Striezel* dough has rested half an hour, roll it out 1/2 inch thick on a floured board. Spread the dough with the butter-and-flour paste. Fold in the left third and right third of the dough, making 3 layers. Roll it out again, rolling away from you. Give the dough a half turn, so that it lies the long way from left to right, and fold it again in 3 layers. This is a "turn." Let the dough rest in a cool but not cold place for 1/2 hour. Repeat the "turns" twice more and let the dough stand for 1 hour.

Roll the dough out into an oblong, brush it with 2 tablespoons melted butter, and spread it with 1 cup walnuts, chopped, 1/2 cup light brown sugar, and 1/2 cup granulated sugar. Sprinkle the filling with a mixture of 1 teaspoon cinnamon and 1/4 cup powdered sugar and with 2 tablespoons melted butter and roll up the dough. Coil the roll in a spiral in a round 10-inch cake pan, with one end in the center, and let it rise in a warm place for 1 hour. Bake in a moderate oven (350° F.) for 1 hour. Dust the coil with sugar. Let it stand for at least 12 hours and slice thin.

Jam Pockets   *Buchteln*

DISSOLVE 1 ENVELOPE or cake of yeast in 3/4 cup warm water and add 3/4 cup warm milk, 2 tablespoons sugar, and 1/2 cup flour. Let the sponge stand in a warm place until it rises and bubbles, about 1/2 hour.

Sift 3 3/4 cups flour into a warm bowl with 1/2 cup sugar. Make a well in the flour and put in it 3 egg yolks, 1/2 cup soft butter, and the yeast sponge. Sprinkle over the mound the grated rind of 1 lemon. With a wooden spoon, incorporate into the soft ingredients as little flour as possible and work the dough with the hand or a strong beater until it is smooth and glossy. Sprinkle in 1/4 cup more flour as you work, if necessary, to make a dough that can be handled. Cover the bowl with a warm cloth and let the dough rise in a warm place until it doubles in bulk.

Punch the dough down on a floured board and roll it out 1/3 inch thick. Cut 3-inch squares with a floured knife and place on each square a generous teaspoonful of raspberry jam. Fold the 4 corners into the middle and pinch the edges firmly together. Lay the *Buchteln,* folded side down, side by side and touching each other in a generously buttered, deep 10-inch cake pan. Brush each with melted butter as you add it and pour a little more melted butter over the filled pan. Let the *Buchteln* rise in a warm place until they double in bulk. Bake in a moderate oven (350° F.) for about 25 minutes. Turn the *Buchteln* out of the pan and serve hot. *(Picture, page 482.)*

Wiener Brioches *Vienna Brioches*

SOFTEN 2 ENVELOPES of yeast in 1/4 cup lukewarm water and add 1 teaspoon sugar and 1/2 cup sifted flour, beating thoroughly until the mixture is smooth. Let the sponge rise, covered, in a warm place for about 20 minutes. In a large bowl, put 1 1/2 cups sifted flour and add 1/2 cup butter softened at room temperature, 1 tablespoon sugar, 1/4 teaspoon salt, and 1 egg. Beat the mixture with a wooden spoon, adding gradually 1/4 cup milk, scalded and cooled, to make a smooth paste. Add 1/3 cup butter, 2 eggs, and 2 cups sifted flour and beat the paste until it is smooth and no longer sticky. Make a well in the center and add the sponge and 2 eggs. Beat them in and then knead the dough well. Put it in a buttered bowl and let it rise, covered, in a warm place about 1 1/2 hours. Turn it out on a lightly floured board and beat it down with the palm of the hand. Return it to the bowl and let it ripen overnight in the refrigerator.

Turn it onto a lightly floured board and again beat it down with the palm of the hand. Return a fourth of the dough to the refrigerator. Shape the remaining dough into 16 balls about the size of eggs. Put them in well-buttered muffin pans, with cups about 3 inches in diameter. Shape the chilled dough into 16 balls about the size of marbles. Cut a cross in the top of each large ball. Make a hollow in each ball and insert a small ball, to form the crown of each brioche. Let the brioches rise, covered, in a warm place until they double in bulk, about 50 minutes, and brush the tops gently with 1 egg yolk blended with 1 tablespoon cold milk. Bake the brioches in a very hot oven (425° F.) until they are shiny and brown, 30 to 40 minutes. Cool them on wire racks. Makes 16 brioches. The dough may also be shaped into one large and one smaller ball. Put the larger ball in a brioche pan, cut a cross in it, and insert the smaller ball. Bake this large brioche in a hot oven (400° F.) for 45 to 60 minutes.

Belgian Brioches   Belgische Brioche

MAKE THE dough for Vienna brioches. To shape the dough, roll it out 1/2 inch thick on a lightly floured board and cut it into strips 1/2 inch wide and about 10 inches long. Roll up each strip in a spiral and press the end firmly against the roll. Place the brioches in buttered muffin tins. Let them rise for about 1 1/4 hours and brush them gently with 1 egg yolk blended with 1 tablespoon cold milk. Sprinkle them liberally with poppy seed. Bake in a very hot oven (425° F.) for about 25 minutes.

Danish Vienna Bread   Kopenhagener Wienerbrot

SCALD 1/2 cup milk, cool it to warm (90° F.), add 3 envelopes of yeast, 2 tablespoons of sugar or malt extract, and 1 cup flour. Beat the mixture well. Cover the sponge and let it rise in a warm place until bubbles form and it begins to drop in the center. Add to the sponge 1/2 cup crushed ice, 2 eggs, beaten, 1/2 cup sugar, 3/4 teaspoon salt, 1/2 cup cold milk, the grated rind of 1/2 lemon, 1 teaspoon rum, 1/8 teaspoon crushed cardamom seed, 5 1/2 tablespoons softened butter and about 10 cups sifted flour. Use less flour if necessary, but keep the dough smooth and pliable. Knead the dough well on a lightly floured cloth or board and let it rest, covered, for 1/2 hour.

Roll the dough into a rectangle, cover half of it with 12 tablespoons

butter, cut into bits, cover with the other half of the dough, and again roll
the dough into a rectangle. Fold it over like a book and chill it, covered, in
the refrigerator overnight. Use in various forms as desired (see Danish
pastry, below). Bake the dough in a moderately hot oven (375° F. to
400° F.)—never higher. It is rich and burns easily.

Plunder Gebäck 1 — The Emperor's Favorite

Plunder or
Danish
Pastry I

IN A LARGE bowl make a sponge: soften 2 envelopes of yeast in 1/2 cup
warm water or 2 cakes of yeast in 1/2 cup milk, scalded and cooled to
warm (90° F.), and add 1/2 tablespoon sugar and 1 1/2 cups sifted flour.
Beat the mixture well, cover it and let it rise in a warm place until
bubbles have risen all over the surface. Scald and cool 1 cup milk and
add 5 egg yolks, lightly beaten. Add the milk to the sponge with 1 cup
sugar, the grated rind of 1 lemon, 1 tablespoon rum, and 1 teaspoon salt.
Whisk the ingredients together thoroughly. Begin adding gradually 4 1/2
cups sifted flour and with it work in 2 tablespoons softened butter. Make
a smooth pliable dough; be careful not to use too much flour. Keep
at room temperature. Let the dough rest on a floured board for 1/2 hour.
Then roll in 2 cups softened butter as for Danish pastry II. Chill in the
refrigerator, covered, overnight. Shape, fill, and bake the dough as described in the recipes for any of the Danish pastries, below, or the recipe
for Schuberts.

Plunder Gebäck 2

Danish Pastry II

DISSOLVE 2 ENVELOPES of yeast in 1/4 cup cold water or 2 cakes of yeast
in 1/4 cup cold milk. Stir in 2 beaten eggs, 1/4 cup sugar, and 1/2 cup
cold milk. Add gradually 3 cups sifted flour, beating well until all is
thoroughly blended. Knead the dough until it is smooth and glossy. Roll
the dough out on a well-floured board into a square about 1/2 inch thick.
Shape 1 1/3 cups cold butter into a rectangle, less than half the size of the
dough. Place the butter on one half of the dough and fold the other half
over it. Press the edges together. Roll out the dough into a rectangle
about 1/2 inch thick. Fold one third of the dough over the center third
and fold over the remaining third, making three layers. Turn the dough
so that one of the open ends faces front. Roll out the dough again to a

rectangle about 1/2 inch thick, fold, and turn it. Repeat the same process of rolling, folding, and turning twice more. Cover the dough and chill it for 1 hour or more. Shape, fill, and bake the dough as described in the recipes for any of the Danish pastries, below.

Filled Pockets   Plunder Tascheln

ROLL OUT *Plunder Gebäck 2,* Danish pastry II, 1/8 inch thick and cut it into 4-inch squares. Spread the squares with 1 tablespoon of any desired filling, such as prune or apricot. Fold two opposite corners to the center —or all four corners—and press the edges of the dough together firmly. Let the pastries rise on a buttered baking sheet in a warm place until they double in bulk, about 1 1/2 hours. Bake them in a moderate oven (350° F.) for about 20 minutes. Spread the hot pastries with confectioners' sugar icing.

Prune or Apricot Filling   Pflaumen oder Marillenfülle

COMBINE 1 CUP chopped cooked prunes or apricots with 2 tablespoons prune or apricot juice, 1/4 cup sugar, 1 tablespoon lemon juice, 1/2 teaspoon cinnamon, and a dash of ground cloves. Chop the mixture in a food processor. The filling should be a rather dry paste.

Ring with Cheese Filling   Topfenring

ROLL OUT *Plunder Gebäck 2,* Danish pastry II, into a rectangle 1/4 inch thick and spread it with cheese filling. Roll the dough up like a jelly roll, form the roll into a ring, and join the ends. With scissors, cut the ring at 1 1/2-inch intervals two-thirds of the way through. Turn each "slice" so that it lies flat. Let the ring rise on a buttered baking sheet about 1 1/2 hours. Bake it in a moderate oven (350° F.) for about 1/2 hour, or until it is golden. Sprinkle it with confectioners' sugar.

Cheese Filling   Käsefülle

MIX 2 EGG yolks and 2 tablespoons sugar and add 1 cup sieved cottage cheese and enough heavy cream to make a smooth paste that does not run. Grate the rind of 1 lemon over the mixture and add 1/4 cup plumped raisins.

Schuberts *Schuberts*

ROLL *Plunder Gebäck 2*, Danish pastry II, into a rectangle 1/4 inch thick. Spread it with Vienna almond cream or any desired filling to within 1/2 inch of the side opposite to you. Brush this edge with lightly beaten egg yolk. Sprinkle the filling with chopped or slivered almonds. Roll up the dough and seal it well with the egg-brushed part by pulling it gently with the fingertips toward the body of the roll. Cut the roll with a sharp knife into slices 1 inch wide. Place the slices in paper cases set in muffin or bun tins and let them rise in a warm place, covered with a cloth, until they double in bulk. Brush the tops twice with Vienna wash and sprinkle the rolls with almond flakes or pipe a ring of boiled custard around a glacéed cherry set in the center of each. When the rolls are fully risen, bake them in a moderately hot oven (375° F.) for 20 minutes. Remove them in the cups to wire racks to cool. Makes about 40.

Wiener Mandelcreme *Vienna Almond Cream*

CREAM TOGETHER 1 cup butter and 1 cup sugar. Add 3 eggs, one at a time, beating them in well. In a separate bowl mix 2 cups ground almonds with a little cold water to make a smooth paste. Add this paste to the creamed butter and egg. Flavor as desired. This cream will keep a week, covered, in the refrigerator.

Plunderteig *Danish Pastry III*

MIX 1 1/4 CUPS sweet butter with 1/2 cup flour, blending thoroughly. Chill the floured butter. Soften 2 envelopes or cakes of yeast in a little water, then add 1 beaten egg, 1/4 cup sugar, 1 cup cold milk, and 3 1/4 cups flour, beating the dough well and working it until it is smooth and pliable. Roll out the dough on a well-floured board into a 15-inch square. Roll out the chilled floured butter to a rectangle about 6 by 12 inches. Place the butter dough on one-half of the dough, fold over the other half, and press the edges together.

Roll out the folded dough about 1/2 inch thick, fold it in thirds and turn it so that the open end faces front. Roll it out again, fold it in thirds, turn, and repeat the rolling, folding, and turning once more. Chill the dough at once. Roll, fold, and turn the chilled dough three times more.

Chill it again for about 1/2 hour. It is very important to keep the ingredients and utensils cold. Roll out the finished dough and form the pastries below or make other shapes. Place them on a buttered baking sheet and chill them for about 1 hour. Bake them immediately in a hot oven (400° F.) for about 15 minutes.

Danish Pastry Crescents — Plunder Hörnchen

MAKE *Plunder Teig*, or Danish pastry III, and chill it. Cut off a third of the chilled dough and roll it out 1/2 inch thick. Cut it into 3-inch triangles and brush each triangle with beaten egg. Place a tablespoon of almond paste, shaped in a small roll, on the base of each triangle. Cover each triangle with 1 tablespoon finely diced flavored candied fruit and sprinkle them with a little cinnamon sugar. Roll up the triangles and shape them gently into crescents. Brush them with beaten egg and let them rise, covered, on a buttered baking sheet in a warm place until they double in bulk, about 1 1/2 hours. Bake them in a moderate oven (350° F.) for 20 minutes, or until they are puffed and golden. Brush them immediately with apricot glaze.

Almond Paste — Mandelfülle

GRIND VERY fine 1 cup blanched almonds and stir in 1/2 cup sugar. Add 1 beaten egg and beat the paste until it is smooth.

Danish Pastry Twists — Plunder Flechten

MAKE *Plunder Teig*, or Danish pastry III, and chill it. Cut off a third of the chilled dough and roll it out 1/4 inch thick. Brush the dough with beaten egg. Cover it with 1/2 cup finely diced floured candied fruit and sprinkle it with 1 tablespoon cinnamon sugar. Fold dough in half and roll it out 1/2 inch thick. Cut the filled dough into strips 1 3/4 inches by 8 inches. Slit the strips down the center with a pastry wheel, leaving an inch uncut at each end, and twist the strips into various designs of single or double rounds. Arrange the twists on a buttered baking sheet, brush them with beaten egg, let them rise, covered, in a warm place until they double in bulk, about 1 1/2 hours. Bake them in a moderate oven (350° F.) for 20 minutes, or until they are golden. Brush the hot twists with apricot glaze.

Schnecken   *Danish Pastry Snails*

MAKE *Plunder Teig,* or Danish pastry III, and chill it. Cut off a third of the chilled dough, and roll out a rectangle about 12 by 18 inches and about 1/4 inch thick. Brush the dough with 1 egg beaten well with a pinch of salt. Cover it with 1/2 cup finely diced candied fruit and 1/4 cup raisins and sprinkle it with 2 tablespoons cinnamon sugar. Turn over 1/4 inch on one edge and roll up the dough like a jelly roll, rolling it back and forth to make it nicely rounded and smoothing the edges. Cut it into 2-inch pieces, arrange the pieces 4 inches apart on a well-buttered baking sheet, and flatten them lightly. Brush them with beaten egg and let them rise, covered, in a warm place until they double in bulk, about 1 1/2 hours. Bake the pastries in a moderate oven (350° F.) for 20 minutes, or until they are light and golden. Brush the hot pastries with apricot jam thinned with a little hot water.

Germstrudel   *Plunder Dough Strudel*

SCALD AND cool to warm (90° F.) 1 1/2 cups milk. Dissolve 2 envelopes of yeast in 1 cup of the milk and add 2 cups flour, sifted. Dust the sponge with a layer of flour 1/4 inch thick. Cover the sponge and let it rise in a warm place until bubbles form on the top and cracks appear in the flour, about 20 minutes. Watch the sponge carefully. It should not be allowed to drop.

Combine 1 tablespoon salt and 1/2 cup sugar with the remaining 1/2 cup cooled milk, beat in 2 eggs and add a few drops of rum, Sherry, and lemon extract, 1 tablespoon ground cardomom, and 1/4 cup saffron infusion (optional). Sift and measure 4 cups flour.

When the sponge is ready, beat it vigorously with a wooden spoon. Gradually add the flour and the seasoned milk-sugar-and-egg mixture. Work in 1/2 cup softened butter at the last. Knead the dough well, cover it, and let it rise for about 1/2 hour.

With a clean cloth lightly dusted with flour cover a table—a card table is about the right size—that is accessible from all sides. Place the dough on it, dust it with flour, and roll it out 1/4 inch thick. The rectangle of dough should be about 18 by 30 inches. Spread it evenly with a soft cheese filling of 1 pound creamy cottage cheese beaten with 1/2 cup *crème fraîche,* 1 cup sugar, 2 eggs, 1/2 cup raisins, the grated rind of 1/2 lemon, 1/2 teaspoon vanilla, and a pinch of salt. Roll up the strudel, as for apple strudel and let it rise 20 minutes. Bake it in a moderately hot oven (375° F.) for 20 to 30 minutes, or until golden. Serve warm or cold.

Or sprinkle melted cooled butter over the entire surface. Sprinkle 1 cup dried bread or rusk crumbs over half of the dough sheet. Over the crumbs spread any desired filling, roll up the dough like a jelly roll, using the cloth to roll it along. Using a broad spatula, lift the strudel gently onto a buttered baking sheet. Bend it into a horseshoe, if desired. Brush it with melted butter and let it rise. Bake it in a moderately hot oven (375° F.) for 20 to 30 minutes, depending on its size. Remove it to a wire rack and brush it with melted butter. At serving time, dust the strudel with confectioners' sugar and cut it into slices diagonally.

Poppy Seed Filling for Plunder Dough Strudel   *Mohnfülle*

SIMMER A GENEROUS 1/2 pound poppy seeds in a cheesecloth bag in 1/2 cup milk until the seeds are soft. Remove them from the cheesecloth and add 5 tablespoons sugar, 1/4 cup fine cake crumbs, made from plain cake or sweet rolls, 1 teaspoon ground cinnamon, the grated rind of 1 lemon, and 2 tablespoons honey. Spread over the stretched plunder dough, leaving on one edge a 1/2-inch border, brushed with Vienna wash. Roll up the dough toward this border as directed for plunder dough strudel. Seal the dough, place it on a buttered baking sheet, and press it flat gently. Let it rise, brushing it twice with 2 egg yolks beaten with 3 tablespoons water. Bake the strudel as directed.

Walnut Filling for Plunder Dough Strudel   *Nussfülle*

BRING 1 CUP milk to a boil and into it stir 2 cups walnut meats, chopped, 1 cup each of sugar and fine dry bread crumbs, 1 teaspoon rum, 1/2 teaspoon ground cinnamon, the grated rind of 1/2 lemon, and 1 tablespoon melted fat. This makes a firm paste for spreading on plunder strudel dough. Spread, roll, and bake the strudel as directed.

Doughnuts   *Krapfen*

SCALD 2 CUPS milk, add 1/4 cup sugar and 1 teaspoon salt, and cool the milk to warm (90° F.). Soften 2 envelopes or cakes of yeast in 1/4 cup warm water. Pour the scalded milk mixture into a large bowl, add the yeast, 4 cups sifted flour, 1/4 cup oil, and 2 eggs, and stir the mixture well with a wooden spoon. Add 3 more cups flour and beat and stir the dough until it is smooth and comes away from the sides of the bowl. Cover the dough and let it rise in a warm place until it doubles in bulk, about 1 1/2 hours.

Turn the dough onto a well-floured board, roll it out 1/2 inch thick, and cut it into rounds 2 inches in diameter. Place 1 teaspoon strawberry jam on half the rounds, cover them with the remaining rounds, and pinch the edges together. Cut through the two rounds together with a slightly smaller cutter, to seal the edges. Lay the rounds on a floured cloth, cover them with a warm cloth, and let them rise for 1/2 hour.

Fry the *Krapfen,* a few at a time, in deep hot fat (375° F.), at least 3 inches deep, until they are golden brown, turning them once. Drain the *Krapfen,* sprinkle them with confectioners' sugar, and serve them warm. Makes about 24 *Krapfen.*

Wiener Faschingskrapfen   *Vienna Carnival Doughnuts*

SIFT AND measure 5 cups flour. Scald 1 1/3 cups milk and cool it to warm (90° F.). Dissolve 2 envelopes or cakes of yeast in 1/4 cup warm water and add 1/2 cup of the milk, 1/2 tablespoon sugar, and 1/2 cup of the sifted flour. Cover the sponge and let it rise in a warm place until bubbles appear all over the top. In a small bowl set over a pan of hot water beat 8 egg yolks with 1/3 cup sugar and 1 teaspoon salt until they are light. Add 3 tablespoons softened butter, 2 tablespoons rum, and the grated rind of 1/2 lemon. Pour this into the ripened sponge with the remaining warm milk and add about 4 1/2 cups sifted flour. Cover the dough with a cloth and let it rise once. Knead it into a smooth ball and roll it out 1/3 inch thick on a floured board. Use 2 plain round cutters, one slightly larger than the other. With the smaller cutter, just mark half of the surface of the rolled-out dough. With the larger cutter, cut the same number of rounds as those marked. Place 1 teaspoon apricot jam on each of the marked pieces and place the cutout rounds over the jam. Press the edges of the two halves gently together. Cut out each doughnut with the smaller cutter and invert the doughnuts upside down on a warmed cloth-covered board, lightly dusted with flour. Cover them with a cloth and let them rise in a warm protected place until they are very light. Slide the doughnuts upside down into deep hot lard (375° F.). Cover the fryer and fry until the bottom halves are an even golden brown. Turn and finish frying them, uncovered. Drain on wire racks and sprinkle with confectioners' sugar. *(Picture, page 494.)*

Rich Viennese Carnival Doughnuts   *Feinste Krapfen*

SCALD 1 1/4 CUPS light cream and cool it to warm (90° F.). Soften 1 1/2 envelopes or cakes of yeast in 1/2 cup of the warm cream and add 1/4 cup water, 1 tablespoon sugar, and 1 cup sifted flour. Let the sponge rest, covered, in a warm place.

Beat 10 egg yolks with 1 tablespoon each of sugar and rum and the grated rind of 1 lemon, in a bowl placed over a pan of hot water. Add 1/2 cup softened butter. When bubbles appear on the sponge, beat in the egg yolks and remaining scalded cream, beating well. Fold in 2 stiffly beaten egg whites. Begin gradually to add 3 1/2 cups sifted flour. The amount of flour varies, so use caution. Then beat the dough by slapping it with both hands until blisters show. Roll out and fill the doughnuts as for Vienna carnival doughnuts II. The dough may also be cut in strips and each strip folded in the middle and twisted or braided around itself.

Vienna Rusks   *Wiener Zwieback*

SIFT 8 CUPS flour. Soften 2 envelopes or cakes of yeast in 1 cup warm water and add 4 tablespoons soy flour, 2 tablespoons sugar, and 2 cups flour. Let the sponge rest, covered, for 25 minutes in a warm place. Scald 1 cup milk and chill it. Beat into it 1 egg, 6 tablespoons sugar, 2 teaspoons salt, 3 drops of lemon oil, and 1 drop oil of nutmeg. Pour the milk mixture over the sponge and beat it in well. Begin adding 6 cups sifted flour carefully, to make a medium soft dough. Work in 9 tablespoons softened butter. Knead the dough well, cover it, and let it rise for 50 minutes. Punch it down and let it rise for another 30 minutes. Punch it down again and let it rise for 20 minutes longer. Shape the dough into 4 long cylindrical loaves, as for French bread, with blunt ends. Let them rise, covered, on buttered baking sheets. Before baking, pierce each loaf in 3 places with a knitting needle or cake tester. Bake the loaves in a hot oven (400° F.) for 25 to 30 minutes. Do not overbake. Remove the

loaves to racks and store them in a cool airy place for 24 hours. Cut slices
1/4 inch thick and lay them in rows on dry baking sheets or wire racks.
Toast them in a hot oven (400° F.). When the rusks show a golden-brown
tint, turn them carefully and toast the other side. Store in a tight container.

Marienbader Zwieback   *Marienbad Rusks*

DISSOLVE 2 ENVELOPES of yeast in 1/2 cup warm water and add 1/2 cup
warm milk or dissolve 1 cake of yeast in 1/2 cup milk, scalded and cooled
to warm (90° F.). Add 1/2 tablespoon malt extract or sugar and 1 cup
flour. Let the sponge rise, covered, until it is ready to drop in the center.
Beat into it 1/2 cup milk, scalded and cooled, 6 egg yolks, 2 tablespoons rum, 2 1/2 tablespoons sugar, 1/2 teaspoon salt, the grated rind of
1/2 lemon, and 1/4 teaspoon each of ground cloves, mace, and nutmeg.
Add gradually about 4 cups sifted flour, until the dough begins to be
firm, and add 4 tablespoons softened butter. Knead the dough until it is
firm. Let it rise, covered, in a warm place until cracks begin to show.
Punch it down and let it rest for 10 minutes. Shape the dough into 2 long
cylindrical loaves, as for French bread, with blunt ends, and bake them
as for Vienna rusks.

Remove in a thin layer all crusts from the baked loaves. Cut them in
slices 1/8 inch thick. Rub each slice gently in vanilla sugar, on both sides.
Lay the sugared rusk slices on wire racks or baking sheets and toast them
carefully in a hot oven (400° F.). Cool them and store them in a tight
container.

Wiener Streiche   *Vienna Wash*

WHISK 1/2 CUP cold water into 1 egg white and gradually stir in 3 1/2
cups water.

Mehlstreiche für Wiener Brot   *Flour Wash for Vienna Bread*

STIR ENOUGH cold water into 1/4 cup flour to make a smooth paste.
Gradually add 2 cups boiling water, stirring constantly, and stir the wash
until it is well blended.

Pastry and Plain Cakes

Gebäck und Kuchen

OF ALL the European cities, Vienna makes it easiest for the visitor, the *Ausländer,* to orient himself. He cannot miss the wide Ring, an avenue that follows an obvious curve around the inner city, its name changing from Opernring to Burgring and so on with each segment of the circle. It is lined with a double row of chestnut trees and runs where the walls of Vienna once stood.

The Opera stands at Vienna's busiest intersection, where the Kärntnerstrasse crosses the Ring and goes straight to the heart of the inner city, to the Stephansdom—actually just a short eight-block walk. The most important landmark near the beautifully embellished Renaissance opera house, with its open loggia facing the Ring, is Sacher's—home of the famous *Sachertorte*—which lies immediately and conveniently behind it. The visitor turns left as he comes out of Sacher's refreshed by *Sachertorte* with whipped cream, and follows the crowd down the left side of the street for six blocks to Gerstner's, now at Kärntnerstrasse 11 to 15. On his way, he will have passed within a few steps of the Neuer Markt and the Capuchin monastery that houses the imperial vault where the emperors of Austria and the son of Napoleon lie buried.

But first things first. At Gerstner's, the visitor selects his favorite pastries and bakeries, if he can bring himself to make a choice, and he retires to a marble-topped table to eat them with his coffee, chocolate or tea. Sitting at his table, he is in a splendid position to see Vienna and to study the Viennese in one of their favorite and most natural habitats.

After such refreshment and study, and several trips back to the counter for additional confections, he leaves his second Viennese landmark and continues a few steps down the Kärntnerstrasse to the corner of the Graben.

427

He turns left away from the Stephansdom, which he will see on Sunday, past the Stock im Eisen, which he can see when the confectioners are closed, to the Kohlmarkt, where he turns left again to Demel's, at Number 18.

Arrived at his third Viennese landmark, he refreshes himself with an entirely new and equally magnificent choice of pastries and bakeries and again he studies the Viennese around him.

With a good working knowledge of Sacher's, Gerstner's and Demel's, the visitor will know his Vienna. He will discover that when he finally leaves Demel's he can round out his circle by keeping to his left down the Augustinerstrasse until he gets back to Sacher's. The buildings he will see across the street are the Hofburg, the National Bibliothek, and the Albertina, all of which he will return to look at later.

If the visitor has come to Vienna with introductions, or if he wants to look up someone during his stay, he has only to keep his eyes open as he circulates and his friend is bound to show up at one of his three landmarks.

Vienna's bakeries, pastries, and confections are famous; everyone knows them by name as though they were friends. They do not simply point and say, "I'll take that," they order themselves an *Indianer,* a *Kapuziner,* two *Schweinsohren,* pig's ears, and an *Ildefonso.* They patronize the confectioners who make pastries according to their preferences, and in some cases they know how to make their own pastries at home, if necessary. They may discover a small confectionery shop on a side street or they may go to one of Vienna's old and famous ones, but in time every Viennese has a *Konditorei* without which he could hardly imagine his life.

Every confectioner and baker hopes to become renowned for some piece that he himself has devised—a masterpiece of pastry to become his specialty and bear his name. The names Sacher, Pischinger, Zauner, Dobos, and many others have rightly achieved such immortality and have added in their way to the attraction and fame of Vienna.

Pie Dough
Pastetenteig 1

SIFT TOGETHER 2 1/4 cups flour with 1/2 teaspoon salt. In a food processor with the steel blade blend the flour, 1 whole egg, 1 egg yolk, 9 tablespoons cold butter, cut into bits, and 2 tablespoons milk. Add 1 tablespoon olive oil or walnut oil and blend the mixture until it forms a ball. Increase the amount of salt to 1 teaspoon for salty tarts, or reduce it to 1/4 teaspoon and add 1 tablespoon sugar for fruit or dessert tarts. Place dough in a bowl, cover it with a cloth, and let it rest in a cool place for 45 minutes.

Dough for Open Tarts
Pastetenteig 2

MOUND 2 CUPS flour sifted with 1 teaspoon salt on a pastry board and slice 1/3 cup cold butter and 1/3 cup cold lard over the flour. Cut the fat in with a pastry cutter and sprinkle over the mixture enough cold water to bind it. Work the mixture quickly into a rough dough, knead it 2 or 3 times, and chill it for 30 minutes. Halve the dough and roll it out with a floured rolling pin on a lightly floured board. As it will not roll easily, it may be necessary to press it out in the pie plates with floured hands. Line 2 9-inch pie plates with the dough. Turn back the edges and crimp them. Prick the dough, cover the bottom with foil and a little rice, and bake in a very hot oven (450° F.) for 10 minutes.

Tart Paste I
Mürbteig 1

SIFT 4 CUPS flour onto a pastry board and make a well in the center. Put in it 1 1/4 cups butter, cut into large flakes, 1 egg, 2/3 cup cold water, 1 teaspoon sugar, and 2 pinches of salt. Mix the center ingredients until they are well blended. Gradually gather in the flour with the hands and work the mixture gently into a smooth dough. Chill the dough well before rolling it out for baking.

Tart Paste II
Mürbteig 2

SIFT 2 2/3 CUPS flour onto a pastry board and make a well in the center. In it put 1/2 cup sugar, 2 egg yolks, and the grated rind of 1 lemon.

Mix the center ingredients until they are well blended. Add gradually
1 scant cup butter, cut into large flakes. Work the ingredients together,
incorporating the flour as quickly as possible until it forms a smooth dough.
Chill the dough well before rolling it out for baking.

Wiener Mürbteig   *Viennese Sweet Short Paste*

SIFT 3 CUPS flour with 3/4 cup sugar onto a pastry board, sprinkle 1/4
cup ground blanched almonds over it, and make a well in the center.
In it put 1 cup butter, cut into large flakes, 3 eggs, and 1/2 teaspoon
vanilla extract. Mix the center ingredients well, gradually gather in the
flour, and work the mixture quickly and gently into a smooth dough.
Chill the dough well before rolling it out for baking.

Feinster Wiener Mürbteig   *Finest Viennese Short Paste*
or Pâte Sucrée

SIFT 4 CUPS flour with 1 cup sugar onto a pastry board. Spread over the
flour 1 1/4 cups butter, cut into flakes. With the hands, rub the butter
into the dry ingredients until the mixture has the consistency of coarse
meal. Spread out the mixture, sprinkle it with 2 egg yolks, beaten, and
gently work it from the four sides to the center into a smooth dough. Chill
the dough before rolling it out for baking.

Grundteig   *Plain Tart Paste*
or Pâte à Foncer Ordinaire

SIFT 4 CUPS flour with 1 tablespoon sugar and 1/2 teaspoon salt and with
a pastry cutter or two knives, cut in 1 cup butter until the mixture has
the consistency of coarse meal. Spread the mixture on a pastry board,
sprinkle it with 3/4 cup cold water, and gently gather it into a smooth
dough. Chill the dough before rolling it out for baking.

Brandteig   *Pâte à Choux or Cream-Puff Paste*

A PUFF made of *choux paste,* or cream-puff paste, is a *Windbeutel* in
Vienna, and a *Windbeutel*—as everyone knows—is a windbag.

In a small saucepan, bring to a boil 1 cup water, 1/2 cup butter, 1 teaspoon sugar, and 1/2 teaspoon salt. Add all at once 1 cup flour and cook the paste over low heat, beating it briskly and constantly until it is well mixed and leaves the sides of the pan and forms a ball. Remove the pan from the heat and beat in 5 eggs, one at a time. Drop the paste by teaspoonfuls or tablespoonfuls onto a buttered baking sheet or press it through a pastry tube, allowing space between the puffs. Bake the puffs in a very hot oven (425° F.) for 15 to 18 minutes, reduce the heat to moderately hot (375° F.), and bake them until they are brown. Cool them and fill them, if desired.

Coffee Cream Puffs   *Kaffee Brandteigkrapfen*

THE VIENNESE like to make little cream puffs that look rather like coffee beans. Bake puffs in the shape of coffee beans, split them, and fill them with whipped cream flavored with triple-strength coffee. Ice them with fondant icing flavored with triple-strength coffee.

Puff Paste I   *Blätterteig 1*

SIFT 2 CUPS all-purpose flour onto a pastry board. Make a well in the center and in it put 1/4 cup water and 3/4 teaspoon salt. With the fingertips work the water into the dry ingredients. Mix quickly and add 1/4 cup more water with 1 tablespoon rum as the water is absorbed. The paste should be about the same consistency as butter—firm but not hard. Let it stand in a cool place for 15 minutes.

Place the paste on a lightly floured board and pound it out with the fists into a rectangle about 1/4 inch thick. Shape 1 cup firm, but not hard, sweet butter into a flat square cake about 1 inch thick and place it in the center of the paste. Fold the paste over the butter to enclose it in an envelope of paste. Roll the folded paste away from the body into a long rectangle. Roll it as thin as possible without letting the butter break through. Fold it in thirds: bring one side over the center third and fold the other side over the first. Turn the dough package so that one of the side edges faces you. This rolling, folding, and turning is called a turn. Make another turn and chill the dough for 20 minutes. Make 2 more turns and chill the dough again for 30 minutes. Make 2 final turns— 6 turns in all. Chill the dough before rolling and cutting it for baking.

Blätterteig 2

SIFT 2 CUPS all-purpose flour and 1 teaspoon salt into a bowl and work 1/4 cup shortening into the dry ingredients. Gradually add 1/2 cup ice water mixed with 2 teaspoons lemon juice. Mix quickly and lightly, using the hands, to make a dough with about the same consistency as butter, firm but not hard. Chill it for 15 minutes.

Work 1/4 cup sifted all-purpose flour into 1 cup sweet butter lightly with the fingers to make a firm but pliable dough.

Roll out the chilled flour dough on a lightly floured board into a rectangle about 1/4 inch thick. Shape the butter dough into a flat square cake about 1/2 inch thick and place it in the center of the flour dough. Fold the upper flap of dough down to cover the butter and fold the lower flap of dough up over the upper flap, making 3 layers and completely covering the butter. Turn the layered dough so that one edge faces you and roll it away from the body to make another long rectangle. The dough should be rolled as thinly as possible without letting the butter break. Fold the rectangle of dough into thirds in the same way and turn it so that one of the side edges faces you. This rolling, folding, and turning is called a turn. Make another turn and chill the dough for 20 minutes. Make 2 more turns and chill the dough again. Make 2 final turns— 6 turns in all. Chill the dough for 15 minutes before rolling and cutting it for baking.

Schokolade Plätzchen

TOAST 1 2/3 CUPS shelled hazelnuts in a slow oven until the skins have cracked and the nuts are lightly browned. Rub off the skins with a rough cloth and in a food processor with the steel blade grind the nuts fine.

Cream 2/3 cup butter with 5 ounces semisweet chocolate, melted and cooled. Add 1 1/4 cups confectioners' sugar, sifted, and the ground hazelnuts. Chill the mixture for 10 minutes. It should not be too cold. Shape it into 1-inch balls with sugared hands. The dough will be sticky and soft. Place the balls about 2 inches apart on 2 baking sheets lined with baking paper. Set the sheets in a cool place until all the balls are completed.

In a very slow oven (225° F.) bake the rounds for 10 minutes, turn off the oven, and leave the sheets of rounds in the oven for 12 hours.

Melt 3 ounces semisweet chocolate over warm water, stir it well, and pipe, or spoon, a small chocolate rosette onto the center of each round. Let the cookies stand in a cool place for 30 minutes, or until the chocolate is firm.

Apricot Rounds   *Spitzbuben*

CUT 1 1/2 CUPS butter into 3 cups all-purpose flour sifted with 1/2 cup sugar. Add 1 teaspoon vanilla and work the ingredients into a smooth dough. Chill the dough thoroughly. Roll it out as thin as possible on a lightly floured board and cut out rounds with a 2-inch fluted cutter. Cut a 1-inch center out of half the rounds. Bake rings and rounds on an unbuttered baking sheet in a moderately slow oven (325° F.) for 15 minutes. Dust the hot rings with sugar, spread the rounds with apricot jam, and lay the rings on them. Sprinkle the jam with chopped blanched almonds. Make about 48.

Suvaroffs   *Suvaroffs*

CUT 3/4 CUP butter into 1 1/2 cups flour, add 1/3 cup sugar, and work the mixture into a smooth dough. Roll it out 1/4 inch thick and cut it with a small round cutter. Cut the centers out of half the rounds. Bake them on a lightly buttered baking sheet in a moderate oven (325° F.) for 12 to 15 minutes, or until they are faintly yellow and dry. Sprinkle them with vanilla sugar while they are warm and sandwich a ring and round together with a little strained raspberry jam. Use very little filling; Suvaroffs should be less than 3/4 inch high. *(Picture, page 492.)*

Vanilla Crescents   *Vanillekipferl*

HAVE ALL the ingredients for this recipe as cold as possible and work in a cool place.

Cut 1 cup less 2 tablespoons butter into 2 1/2 cups all-purpose flour sifted with 1/2 cup sugar. Add 1/2 cup blanched ground almonds, 2 egg yolks, and 1/2 teaspoon vanilla and work the ingredients into a smooth

dough. Chill the dough for at least an hour. Roll the dough into strips
the thickness of a finger and cut the strips into 2-inch pieces. Roll out
each piece until it is 3 inches long and curve it into a crescent. Bake the
crescents on a buttered baking sheet in a slow oven (300° F.) for about
20 minutes, until they are dry and very faintly colored. Sprinkle a plate
heavily with vanilla sugar. With a spatula carefully transfer the warm
crescents to the plate and sprinkle them with more vanilla sugar. Makes
about 60.

Eichenblätter   *Oak Leaves*

STIR 1 1/2 CUPS sifted flour with 2 cups almonds, finely ground, and
1 cup sugar. Stir in 1/4 cup browned butter and 4 lightly beaten egg
whites. Spread a thin layer of the mixture through an oak-leaf stencil
onto a well-buttered and floured baking sheet. Remove the stencil and
bake a test leaf in a moderately hot oven (375° F.) for 15 minutes, or
until it is brown. If the leaf spreads a little after the stencil is removed
and comes up easily from the baking sheet, proceed with the rest of the
batter. If the edges do not spread, add more egg white, lightly beaten,
and test again. The dry ingredients are sufficient for 4 large egg whites,
or 5 to 6 small ones. Make a test leaf after the fourth and fifth egg

white so that the exact proportion can be found. When there is too much egg white, the leaves spread out and lose their outlines. Take the leaves from the baking sheet with a spatula while they are still warm, and let them cool. Glaze the flat sides of the leaves with a thin layer of coating chocolate and mark the ribs and veins with a knife before the chocolate sets.

Coating Chocolate — Couverture

USE *couverture,* or coating chocolate, which may be obtained from a candy shop. If it is not, add melted cocoa butter to melted sweet cooking chocolate until the mixture will spread easily. Keep the chocolate soft over warm water.

Viennese Cubes — Wiener Würfel

CREAM 1 1/4 CUPS softened butter with 3/4 cup fine granulated sugar. Add 3 beaten egg yolks and the juice and grated rind of 1/2 lemon and beat the mixture until it is light. Sift 3 3/4 cups flour with 1/2 teaspoon salt and stir it in gradually to make a smooth dough. Roll out the dough 1/3 inch thick on a lightly floured board and cut it into 1-inch squares with a pastry wheel. Place the squares on a buttered baking sheet and brush the tops with a beaten egg yolk. Bake them in a moderate oven (350° F.) until they have become golden-brown puffed cubes, about 20 minutes.

Wednesday Cakes — Husarenkrapfen

CREAM 9 TABLESPOONS butter with 2 egg yolks, 1/2 cup sugar, 1/2 teaspoon vanilla extract, and the grated rind of 1/2 lemon. Dust 1 1/2 cups flour over the mixture and incorporate it gradually to make a smooth dough. Form the dough into balls the size of walnuts, place them on a buttered baking sheet, and indent each ball deeply with the handle of a wooden spoon or a thimble. Paint the edges of the indentation with 1 beaten egg and sprinkle them with chopped blanched almonds and coarse sugar. Bake the cakes in a moderate oven (350° F.) for 20 minutes, or until they are golden. Cool the cakes and fill the indentations with strained raspberry or apricot jam or fill them before baking.

Mandelplätzchen *Almond Short Wafers*

CREAM 1/2 CUP softened butter with 1/4 cup sugar. Add 1/2 teaspoon lemon juice and 1/4 teaspoon grated lemon rind and cream the mixture until it is fluffy. Gradually stir in 1 cup flour sifted with 1/4 teaspoon salt to make a smooth dough. Roll out the dough 1/8 inch thick on a lightly floured board and cut it into small diamonds with a pastry wheel. Brush the wafers with lightly beaten egg white and sprinkle them with 1/2 cup sliced almonds, finely chopped. Bake them on a buttered baking sheet in a moderate oven (350° F.) until they are delicately brown, about 15 minutes.

Halbmonde *Half Moons*

SOFTEN 3/4 CUP butter, stir in 2 generous cups flour, 1/2 cup sugar, and 1/2 teaspoon vanilla, and work the mixture into a soft dough. Roll out the dough, cut it with a crescent cutter, and bake the crescents on a buttered baking sheet in a moderately hot oven (375° F.) until they are light yellow, about 12 minutes.

Butterrosetten *Butter Rosettes*

CREAM 1 1/4 CUPS butter with 1/2 cup sugar, add 2 1/2 cups flour, 1/4 cup ground almonds, and 1 teaspoon vanilla extract. Work the mixture into a smooth dough and pipe it through a star tube onto an unbuttered baking sheet. Press a little piece of almond in the center of each rosette. Bake them in a moderate oven (350° F.) for 15 or 20 minutes, or until they are light golden.

Walnuss Gebäck *Walnut Cookies*

IN A FOOD processor with the steel blade blend 1 3/4 sticks butter, 2 1/2 cups flour, 1 cup chopped walnuts or hazelnuts, 3/4 cup confectioners' sugar, sifted, and 1 teaspoon vanilla extract until the mixture forms a smooth paste. Pat the dough into a ball and chill it for 20 minutes. Roll the dough into sausages as thick as a heavy pencil, cut it into 3-inch lengths, and shape the lengths into crescents. Bake the cookies on a baking sheet lined with parchment paper in a moderate oven (350° F.) for 10 minutes and dredge them with vanilla sugar when they have cooled slightly.

"S" Cookies — *Kringel*

CREAM 1 CUP butter with 1 cup sugar, add 1 egg beaten with 1 tablespoon brandy, and stir the mixture well. Add 2 cups flour sifted with 1 teaspoon baking powder and work it into a smooth dough. If it has become too soft to handle, cool it slightly. Pipe the dough through a cookie press or pastry bag onto a buttered baking sheet in "S" shapes. Bake them in a hot oven (400° F.) for 9 minutes, or until they are lightly yellowed and dry.

Linzer Tarts — *Linzer Gebäck*

CREAM 1 CUP butter with 1/2 cup sugar until it is light and foamy. Add 2 cups flour sifted with 1/4 teaspoon salt and make a smooth dough. Roll out the dough 1/4 inch thick and cut it into rounds with a 3-inch fluted cookie cutter. Cut the centers out of half of the rounds with a small fluted cutter. Bake rings and rounds in a moderately hot oven (375° F.) for 10 minutes, or until they are lightly browned.

Cool the cookies, spread the rounds with drained apricot or strawberry jam, and place a ring on each. Put a little more jam in the hole. Dust the "tarts" with confectioners' sugar.

Miniature Florentines — *Florentiner*

BOIL 1/2 cup sugar, 3 1/2 tablespoons butter, and 2 1/2 tablespoons each of honey and heavy cream, stirring constantly, for 5 minutes. Stir in 2/3 cup sliced almonds and 3 tablespoons minced candied orange peel. Remove from the heat and drop 1/2 teaspoons of the dough onto parchment-paper-lined baking sheets. Bake in a hot oven (400° F.) for 5 minutes, even the edges with a cookie cutter dipped in cold water, and bake for 5 minutes more, or until golden. Let stand on the sheet for 2 minutes before transferring to a rack to cool completely. Brush the smooth backs with 8 ounces semisweet chocolate, melted. Let dry, brush on a second coat, and make a zigzag pattern with the tines of a fork on each cookie.

Mutzemandeln *Almonds*

CUT 1 1/8 CUPS butter into 4 cups flour, make a well in the center, and add 1 1/4 cups sugar, 1/4 teaspoon baking powder, and 1 large or 2 small eggs. Add the grated rind of 1 lemon or 1/2 teaspoon vanilla extract and work the mixture into a stiff dough. Let it rest for 1/2 hour and roll it out 1/2 inch thick. Cut overlapping circles with a cookie cutter, to make small lozenges or almond shapes. Fry the "almonds" in deep hot fat (375° F.) until they are brown. Drain them well and dust them with powdered sugar while they are hot.

Mandelringe *Almond Rings*

CREAM 1 1/3 CUPS butter with 1 cup confectioners' sugar and add 4 cups flour sifted with 1/4 teaspoon salt and 2 eggs beaten in 1/4 cup milk. Add the grated rind of 1 lemon and work the mixture into a smooth dough.

Roll out the dough 1/8 inch thick and cut it into rounds with a fluted cookie cutter 2 1/2 to 3 inches in diameter. Cut out the centers with a smaller cutter, to make rings. Paint the rings with 2 beaten eggs and turn them over carefully onto 1 1/2 cups chopped almonds, so that the tops of the cookies are entirely covered. Bake them on a buttered baking sheet in a moderate oven (350° F.) until they are golden, about 18 minutes.

Hohlhippen *Tuiles*

BEAT 4 LARGE or 5 small egg whites stiff with a pinch of salt. Gradually add 1 1/2 cups sugar, beating the meringue until it is glossy. Dust over it 1/2 cup flour and fold it in just long enough to incorporate it well. Fold in 1 1/2 cups almonds, blanched and thinly sliced, 1/3 cup melted butter, and 1 teaspoon vanilla extract.

Put mounds of the mixture on a baking sheet, using 2 heaping table-spoonfuls for each mound and placing them far apart. Flatten them as much as possible with the back of a spoon and bake them in a slow oven (300° F.) for about 6 minutes. *Tuiles* are delicate and ovens differ, so watch them carefully. They should be brown around the edges and pale in the center. Test one by lifting the corner; if it holds together, the *Tuiles* are done. Lift them carefully with a spatula and hang them over a broomstick or rod. Do not try to handle more than 6 at a time, as they become too brittle to bend. Reheat them in the oven to soften them, if necessary. If the first batch of *Tuiles* sticks, increase the butter to 1/2 cup. This may be necessary because the size and consistency of eggs vary. Store the *Tuiles* in a tightly covered container.

Macaroons   *Makronen*

GRIND 1 1/3 CUPS blanched almonds as fine as possible. With a wooden spoon, work in 2 cups confectioners' sugar. Gradually work in 3 or 4 egg whites, one at a time, until the mixture is soft but not liquid. Add almond extract or grated lemon rind to taste. Let the dough rest 8 hours. Pipe the macaroons onto a paper-lined baking sheet, in any size desired, and let them dry again for 1 hour. Sprinkle them lightly with sugar. Bake them in a slow oven (300° F.) for 8 minutes, increase the temperature to moderately hot (375° F.), and bake until they are brown, about 5 minutes more. Slide the paper onto a damp cloth, to loosen the macaroons.

Potato Dough   *Kartoffelteig*

COMBINE AND work into a dough 1 cup sifted flour, 1/2 cup butter, 1 cup grated Parmesan cheese, 1/2 teaspoon salt, and 1/2 cup cold boiled riced potatoes, tightly packed. Roll out the dough, fold it in thirds, and chill it for 1/2 hour. Roll it out again, sprinkle it with 2 tablespoons grated Parmesan cheese, and fold it in thirds in the opposite direction. Chill the dough for 1/2 hour, roll it out, sprinkle it with cheese, and fold it in thirds once more in the opposite direction. Chill the dough before rolling and cutting it for potato discs and potato sticks.

Potato Sticks   *Stangen*

ROLL OUT potato dough 1/8 inch thick on a lightly floured board and cut it into strips 1/2 inch wide and 8 to 10 inches long. Lay the sticks on an unbuttered baking sheet, paint them with egg yolk, sprinkle them with Parmesan cheese, and bake in a moderate oven (350° F.) for 15 minutes. Serve hot. Makes about 12.

Plätzchen   *Potato Discs*

ROLL OUT potato dough 1/8 inch thick on a lightly floured board and cut it into rounds with a 1-inch scalloped cutter. Press a hazelnut into each round, sprinkle with salt, and bake the discs on an unbuttered baking sheet in a moderate oven (350° F.) for 15 minutes. Serve hot. Makes about 24.

Schinkenkipfel   *Ham Crescents*

COMBINE AND work into a smooth dough 1 1/2 small potatoes, or 1/4 pound, boiled, riced, and cooled, 2 cups flour, 3/4 cup butter, 2 egg yolks, and 1/2 teaspoon salt. Roll out the dough 1/6 inch thick, cut it into 5-inch squares, and cut the squares diagonally into triangles. Add just enough heavy cream, about 3 tablespoons, to 3/4 cup finely ground ham to make a paste, and add 1 tablespoon pickle relish and salt to taste. Place 1 tablespoon ham paste on each triangle and roll up the triangles from the long side. Bend the rolls into crescents and paint them with 2 egg yolks beaten with 1 tablespoon water and 1/4 teaspoon salt. Bake the crescents on a buttered baking sheet in a hot oven (400° F.) for 30 minutes, or until they are golden.

Salzstangen 1   *Potato Salt Sticks*

CUT 1/2 CUP butter into 1 cup flour and add 1 1/2 small potatoes, or 1/4 pound, boiled, riced, and cooled, and 1 teaspoon salt. Work the mixture into a smooth dough and chill it for 15 minutes. Roll out the dough less than 1/4 inch thick and cut it with a pastry wheel into strips 1/2 inch by 6 inches. Paint the strips with beaten egg and sprinkle them generously with coarse salt. Bake them in a moderate oven (350° F.) until they are golden, about 15 minutes. Serve with soups, salads or cocktails.

Salzstangen 2   *Salt Sticks*

SIFT TOGETHER 1 1/2 cups flour, 1/4 teaspoon double-acting baking powder, and 1/2 teaspoon salt. Cut in 1/2 cup less 2 tablespoons butter, add 2 egg yolks and 1/4 cup heavy cream, and work the ingredients quickly into a smooth dough. Chill it for at least 2 hours. Roll out pieces of dough the size of walnuts on a lightly floured board into pencil-thin sticks about 14 inches long. Paint them with an egg yolk beaten with 1 teaspoon water and sprinkle them with freshly ground salt and caraway, poppy, or sesame seeds. Bake the sticks on an unbuttered baking sheet in a moderate oven (350° F.) for 15 minutes. The sticks should be pale in color though the ends will brown. They will loosen from the baking sheet when they are done. Makes about 30.

Viennese Cigarettes $\mathcal{W}iener\ \mathcal{Z}igaretten$

SIFT TOGETHER 1 1/2 cups sifted flour, 1 teaspoon salt, and 1/4 teaspoon paprika. Toss the flour with 1 cup finely grated Swiss cheese, cut in 1/2 cup butter, and work in 3 tablespoons cream to make a smooth dough. Chill the dough for 1/2 hour.

Roll the dough out into a rectangle on a pastry board lightly sprinkled with part of a mixture of 1/2 cup each of flour and grated Parmesan cheese. Sprinkle the dough with more flour and Parmesan cheese and fold it in thirds. Roll it out, sprinkle again with flour and cheese, and fold in thirds in the opposite direction. Roll out, sprinkle, and fold it once more. Chill the dough for 15 minutes.

Roll the dough out 1/8 inch thick and cut it into strips 3/4 inch wide and 10 inches long. Wrap each strip in a spiral around a well-buttered stick about the size of a pencil. Brush the dough with an egg yolk beaten with 1 teaspoon water and roll the sticks in grated Parmesan cheese. Bake them on a lightly buttered baking sheet in a moderately hot oven (375° F.) for 20 minutes. Carefully draw out the wooden sticks while the "cigarettes" are hot. Makes about 20.

Nut Roll $\mathcal{N}ussrolle$

SIFT TOGETHER 2 cups flour, 1 teaspoon double-acting baking powder, and 1 teaspoon salt. Add 1/2 cup grated Cheddar cheese and cut in 1/2 cup butter. Add 1/2 cup cream and work the ingredients into a smooth dough. Chill it for 1/2 hour.

Mix together 1 egg, 6 stuffed green olives, finely chopped, 4 anchovies, washed, dried, and finely chopped, 1 cup chopped almonds, and 1/2 teaspoon salt. Roll the dough on a lightly floured board into a rectangle about 1/4 inch thick and spread it with this filling. Roll it up and chill for 15 minutes. Brush the roll with an egg yolk beaten with 1 teaspoon water and bake it in a slow oven (300° F.) for 30 minutes. Brush it again with egg and sprinkle it with grated Parmesan and with blanched slivered almonds. Bake the roll 15 minutes longer and slice it. Serve it hot.

Haselnuss Salzgebäck   *Hazelnut Salt Rounds*

SIFT TOGETHER 2 1/2 cups flour and 1/2 teaspoon salt, cut in 3/4 cup butter, and work in 1 egg yolk and enough ice water—about 2 tablespoons —to make a smooth dough. Chill the dough for at least 1/2 hour. Roll the dough out 1/8 inch thick on a lightly floured board, cut small rounds with a fluted cutter, and paint the rounds with an egg yolk beaten with 1 teaspoon water. Sprinkle the rounds lightly with salt and cinnamon and thickly with 1 cup finely chopped hazelnuts. Bake the rounds in a moderate oven (350° F.) for 15 minutes. Makes about 6 dozen.

Salzschiffchen   *Salt Barquettes*

LINE TINY *barquette* molds with the dough for *Haselnuss Salzgebäck*, eliminating the final dusting of salt, cinnamon, and nuts, and bake the shells in a moderate oven (350° F.) for 15 minutes. Combine 3 tablespoons cream cheese, 5 tablespoons butter, 1 tablespoon each of finely chopped parsley, chives, and water cress, 1 teaspoon prepared mustard, 1/4 cup minced ham, and salt and pepper to taste. Pipe this filling into the little baked shells through a pastry bag fitted with a small tube. This amount should fill about 4 dozen shells.

Käsebeilage für Salate   *Cheese Bakery for Salads*

SIFT 1 CUP flour with 1 teaspoon each of double-acting baking powder and salt, add 1 cup chilled cream, and stir in 1/2 cup grated Parmesan or Romano cheese. Knead the mixture until it is smooth and pliable. Roll pieces of it between the hands to form marble-sized balls, set them on a baking sheet in a cool place, and let them rest for 20 minutes.

Fry the balls in deep hot vegetable oil (375° F.) for 6 minutes, or until they are crisp and delicately brown. Drain them on absorbent paper and serve them hot.

Wood Strawberry Barquettes   *Walderdbeerschiffchen*

SIFT 2 CUPS flour onto a pastry board, make a well in the center, and in it put 1/2 cup sugar, 2 egg yolks, and the grated rind of 1 lemon. Work the egg yolks into the dry ingredients with a wooden spoon and then, with the hands, incorporate into the yolks as much more of the sugar and flour as possible. Cut 7/8 cup chilled butter into thin slices and lay them on top of the mixture. With the hands, work in the butter just as quickly as possible, to make a smooth dough. Chill it in the refrigerator for at least 2 hours. Roll out the dough on a lightly floured pastry board to a scant 1/4-inch thickness. Press the dough into buttered oval fluted tartlet or *barquette* molds and trim the edges. Bake the pastry shells in a moderate oven (350° F.) for 15 minutes, or until they are golden brown. Or you may cut the dough with a 3-inch fluted cookie cutter, press it over the backs of buttered muffin tins, and bake the pastry shells for 10 to 12 minutes. Handle the fragile little *Schiffchen* very carefully. Fill them with sugared wood strawberries or with raspberries, pipe sweetened whipped cream over the fruit with a pastry tube, and garnish with a row of berries. Depending upon the size of the molds, this recipe should make about 30 *Schiffchen*.

Traum des Herzens   *Heart's Dreams*

MAKE *Wiener Mürbteig,* or Viennese sweet short paste, roll it out, and cut it with a large heart-shaped cutter. Bake the hearts until they are golden. Cool them and pipe a border of *Schaummasse,* or meringue, on each heart and bake them in a slow oven (250° F.) until they are dry and light golden. Line the hearts with a thin layer of apricot glaze and fill them with seedless grapes mounded high in the center. Pour an apricot glaze over the grapes and let it set.

Himbeerkuchen   *Raspberry Cake*

ROLL OUT *Mürbteig 2,* tart paste II, 3/16 inch thick and line a flan ring or straight-edged cake pan with it. Roll the edges in to make a 1/4-inch double border and flute or indent the border with a spoon. Line the tart shell with wax paper, fill it with rice or dried beans, and bake it in a moderately hot oven (375° F.) until it is golden, about 30 minutes. Remove the rice and paper, cool the shell, and remove the flan ring. Spread the shell with 2/3 cup raspberry jam. Cover the jam with a layer of fresh raspberries or pile them high in the shell. Use at least 1 1/2 cups. Melt 3/4 cup red currant jelly and pour it over the raspberries while it is hot. Let the tart cool. Serve the tart plain or with sweetened whipped cream.

Apfeltorte mit Meringue   *Meringue Apple Cake*

ON A PASTRY board, cut 1/2 cup butter into 2 cups sifted flour sifted with 1 teaspoon baking powder and 1/4 teaspoon salt. Add 1/2 cup sugar mixed with 1/4 teaspoon cinnamon and mix the ingredients well. Make a well in the center and drop in 1 egg yolk. Work the dough with the hands until it is stiff and chill it for 20 minutes. Roll it out and line the bottom of a buttered spring-form pan, allowing the dough to extend 1 inch up the sides. Line the dough with 2 pounds apples, peeled, cored, and thinly sliced. Arrange them in overlapping layers with 1/4 cup raisins spread over the first layer. Sprinkle with sugar only if the apples are very tart. Bake the *Torte* in a moderately hot oven (375° F.) for 20 minutes, and let it cool.

Sift together 1/2 cup sugar, 1/4 cup sifted flour, and 1/8 teaspoon salt. Place the mixture in the top of a double boiler over boiling water, gradually stir in 1 1/2 cups scalded milk, and cook the icing, stirring constantly, for 15 minutes. Stir in 1 slightly beaten egg and continue to cook the icing, stirring constantly, for 3 more minutes. Let the icing cool and stir in 1/2 teaspoon heavy rum and 1/4 cup chopped toasted almonds or hazelnuts. Frost the *Torte* with the nut icing. Beat 1 egg white stiff with 3 tablespoons sugar and pipe a line of the meringue about an inch from the rim of the cake. Make a rosette in the center. Dust the *Torte* with sieved confectioners' sugar and brown the meringue in the oven. Remove the sides of the pan. Serve the *Torte* cold, with a fresh dusting of confectioners' sugar.

Open Apple Pie   *Apfelpastete*

COMBINE 2 1/2 CUPS flour, 6 tablespoons butter, 1 egg yolk, and 3 tablespoons cold water to make a pie crust. Roll it out and line an 11-inch pie plate with it. Fill the bottom with 6 apples, peeled, cored, and sliced, and cover with 1/2 cup orange marmalade. Blend 1 1/2 cups crushed macaroons with 6 tablespoons sugar and sprinkle them over the marmalade. Pour 1/2 cup melted butter onto the tart. Bake it in a hot oven (400° F.) for 10 minutes, then reduce the heat to slow (325° F.) and bake for 30 minutes longer. Serve it hot, with whipped cream flavored with almond extract.

Fruit Flan   *Obstkuchen*

SIFT 1 1/2 CUPS flour onto a pastry board and make a well in the center. In it place 4 egg yolks, 1/2 cup butter, broken in pieces, and 5 tablespoons sugar. Work the mixture thoroughly with the fingers, adding a little ice water to hold the dough together, if necessary. Roll it out, place a flan ring on a baking sheet, and put the dough over the ring, or use a spring-form pan. Press the dough down carefully. Do not let the edges overhang the ring. Prick the dough with a fork. Put rice or dried peas on a piece of wax paper in the shell and bake it in a moderate oven (350° F.) until it is brown. Cool it and remove the ring.

Cut 2 pounds plums in half and remove the stones. Fill the cooled tart shell with 1 1/2 cups whipped cream flavored with vanilla extract.

Lay the plums over the cream, skin side up, and strew them with 1/2 cup slivered almonds.

Topfenkuchen *Cheese Cake*

SIFT 2 1/2 CUPS sifted flour onto a pastry board, make a well in the center, and into it put 1/2 cup sugar, 1 cup softened butter, 2 egg yolks, and 2 teaspoons grated lemon rind. Quickly work the center ingredients into the flour to make a smooth dough, adding a little more flour, if necessary, to facilitate handling. On a lightly floured pastry board roll out the dough into a rectangle about 11 by 17 inches. Line a baking sheet with the dough and bake it in a moderate oven (350° F.) for about 15 minutes, or until it is half done. Let the pastry shell cool.

To 1 1/2 cups sieved cottage cheese add 4 egg yolks and 2 teaspoons grated lemon rind. Beat 4 egg whites very stiff, gradually adding 1/2 cup sugar when they have slightly stiffened. Fold the beaten egg whites and 2 tablespoons flour into the cheese mixture and spread the cooled pastry shell with the cheese filling. Sprinkle the cake with 1/2 cup each of raisins and slivered blanched almonds. Bake the *Topfenkuchen* in a very slow oven (275° F.) for about 45 minutes, let it cool, and cut it into large squares.

Kirschkuchen *Cherry Cake*

STIR TOGETHER 1 cup each of softened butter and sugar, and 5 or 6 egg yolks, depending on their size. Add 3/4 cup ground almonds, 6 pieces of stale bread, soaked in milk and pressed dry, 2 pounds stemmed pitted black cherries, 2 tablespoons kirsch, 4 tablespoons heavy cream, and 1/4 teaspoon cinnamon. Fold in 5 or 6 stiffly beaten egg whites. If the batter is too moist, add another slice of stale bread. Pour the batter into a buttered spring-form pan and bake it in a moderate oven (350° F.) for 1 to 1 1/4 hours. Dust the *Kirschkuchen* with sugar and cool it.

Römisches Gebäck *Raspberry Cones*

INTO 1 1/3 CUPS flour beat 6 tablespoons water, 2 egg yolks, 1 pinch each sugar and salt, and 1 teaspoon vegetable oil, in the order given.

Heat a *Pasteten* iron in hot fat and dip it into the batter to 1/4 inch from the top. Lower the iron into deep hot fat (375° F.) and fry the *Pastete* until it is golden, about 2 minutes. Remove the *Pastete* from the iron and repeat the operation until all are done. Fill the *Pasteten* with fresh raspberries and sweetened whipped cream. Omit the sugar when the *Pasteten,* or pastries, are to be filled with vegetables.

Apricot Pockets   *Tascherln*

ROLL OUT *Mürbteig 2,* tart paste II, 1/8 inch thick and cut it into 5-inch squares. Lay 2 teaspoons apricot jam on each square. Beat an egg with 3 tablespoons water, paint the edges of each square, fold them in half, and press the edges together. Paint the tops of the pockets with beaten egg and dust each with 1/2 teaspoon chopped hazelnuts and sugar to taste. Bake the pockets on an unbuttered baking sheet in a moderate oven (350° F.) until they are golden, about 18 minutes.

Viennese Pastry Envelopes   *Wiener Liebesbriefe*

CREAM TOGETHER 2/3 cup each of sweet butter and cream cheese. Beat in 2 egg yolks, one at a time, and work in 1 1/3 cups flour to make a smooth dough. Roll it out on a floured board 1/8 inch thick and cut it into 2 1/4-inch squares. Place 1/2 teaspoon apricot jam in the center of each square. Fold the four corners to the center, pressing the edges together firmly, forming a tight little envelope for the jam. Bake the "love letters" on a buttered baking sheet in a slow oven (300° F.) until they are lightly browned, about 20 to 25 minutes. Dust them with confectioners' sugar while they are hot. Serve warm or cold.

Lemon Rings   *Kränzchen*

BRING 3/4 CUP water to a boil with 14 tablespoons butter (1 cup minus 2 tablespoons), add 1 cup plus 2 tablespoons flour all at once, and cook the mixture, stirring constantly, until it leaves the sides of the pan. Take it from the heat, cool it slightly, and beat in 5 eggs, one after an other, as for *choux* paste. Add 1 teaspoon baking powder and put the paste in a pastry bag. Dip a sheet of parchment paper into hot fat. Pipe 6 circles 3 to 4 inches in diameter onto the paper and pipe a second ring on top of the first, to make a high circle. Slide one or two at a time into deep hot fat (375° F.) and fry them until they are puffed and golden. After the rings have burst open, turn them once. Drain them well.

Into 3/4 cup sifted confectioners' sugar stir just enough of a mixture of 3/4 warm lemon juice and 1/4 warm rum so that very faint "stirring" lines remain in the surface of the sugar. Pour this lemon icing over the puffed *Kränzchen*. Only the tops should be iced.

Spritzkrapfen   *Puffed Doughnuts*

IN A large skillet (do not use an enamel pan), simmer 1 1/8 cups milk, 1/2 cup butter, 1 tablespoon sugar, and a pinch af salt until the butter is just melted. Remove the pan from the heat and add 1 1/4 cups sifted flour all at once, mixing it in quickly. Return the pan to the heat and cook the dough, stirring constantly, for 5 to 8 minutes. The dough must cook even after it leaves the sides of the pan. Turn the dough into a bowl, let it cool slightly, and beat in 6 eggs, one at a time, mixing thoroughly.

Using the largest fluted tube of a pastry bag, pipe the dough in rounds or figure eights onto well-buttered heavy paper. Carefully turn the paper over and drop it into deep hot fat (375° F.). The piped *Krapfen* will loosen and the paper can be removed. Fry the *Krapfen* for 6 to 8 minutes. They will turn themselves over as soon as one side is done. Skim them from the fat with a slotted spoon, sprinkle them with powdered sugar, and serve them hot, with warm vanilla sauce. Makes 18 *Spritz-krapfen*.

Rum Rosinenkrapfen   *Rum Raisin Fritters*

CUT 1 CUP butter into 4 cups flour until the mixture resembles rough sand. Dissolve 1/4 teaspoon salt in 3/4 cup ice water and add to the flour-butter mixture as much of the liquid as necessary to make a firm dough. Let the dough rest in a cool place overnight.

Chop 1/2 cup raisins and marinate them in rum to cover until they are soft. Chop 1 cup walnuts, or 1/2 cup each of walnuts and hazelnuts, and add 1 cup sugar, 1/2 cup dried macaroon crumbs, and the raisins.

Add 1 egg and just enough of the rum to make a firm, cohesive mixture.

Roll out the dough and, with a cookie cutter, cut it into 4-inch rounds. Place about 1 1/2 tablespoons of the filling in the center of each round. Paint the edges with egg yolk, fold the rounds, and press the edges together very firmly.

Fry the *Krapfen*, a few at a time, in deep hot fat (375° F.) until they are golden, let them cool, and dust them with powdered sugar. Makes about 24 *Krapfen*. Serve with ice cream sauce.

Prune Fritters — *Schlosserbuben*

GRADUALLY STIR 2 cups white wine into 2 cups flour, add a pinch of salt, and set the batter aside. Drain 1 pound cooked prunes, about 36. The prunes should not be too soft. Substitute a blanched almond for each prune pit and skewer each prune with a wooden pick to secure the almond. Dip the prunes in the wine batter. Fry them at once in deep hot fat (375° F.) until they are golden brown. Drain the prunes on absorbent paper and roll them in a mixture of 1/2 cup each of grated sweet chocolate and sugar. Serve the prunes on the picks.

Sponge Roll — *Biskuitrolle*

BEAT 8 EGG yolks with 1 cup sifted confectioners' sugar until they are light and creamy. Gradually add 1 1/4 cups sifted flour and fold in 6 stiffly beaten egg whites. Add 1/4 cup butter, melted and cooled. Pour the batter 1/3 to 1/2 inch deep onto buttered paper in a jelly-roll pan. It is important to spread the batter absolutely evenly in the pan. Bake the sponge in a hot oven (400° F.) for 7 to 8 minutes. Turn it onto a cold surface and draw off the paper. Let it cool and spread it with any butter cream. Roll it up carefully and spread the outside with any fondant or butter cream. Chill the roll and slice it diagonally.

Coffee Log — *Mokka Baumstamm*

IN THE TOP of a double boiler over very low heat beat 5 eggs and 3/4 cup sugar for 15 minutes, or until the mixture has tripled in volume. Remove the pan from the heat, add 1/2 teaspoon vanilla, and continue to beat for 5 minutes longer.

Sift together 2/3 cup sifted flour, 1/3 cup potato starch, and 1/4 teaspoon baking powder and fold the flour into the egg mixture. If the batter is not entirely smooth, beat it for no more than a minute. Line a buttered 11- by 17-inch jelly-roll pan—a baking sheet with shallow sides—with heavy paper or parchment, butter the paper, and spread the batter evenly in the pan. Bake the cake for 25 minutes in a moderate oven (350° F.). Loosen the edges of the cake and invert it at once on a lightly sugared towel. Remove the paper, trim the edges off the narrow ends, and spread the cake evenly with coffee butter cream. Roll the cake up lengthwise as tightly as possible. Wrap the roll in paper and chill it.

Arrange the *Baumstamm* on a serving platter, cut off a 2-inch slice, and lay this piece at an angle with the roll to simulate a branch. Fill a pastry bag fitted with a half-moon tube with mocha butter cream and pipe parallel ridges close together down the length of the roll. Pipe similar ridges onto the "branch." Make a swirl now and then to resemble a knothole and stick pistachio nuts in it. Leave the ends of the trunk and the end of the branch uncovered, and decorate the cake with angelica, candied leaves, and violets. Chill the *Baumstamm* well and cut it in diagonal slices.

Mokka Buttercreme

Mocha Butter Cream for Coffee Log

MELT 2 OUNCES sweet baking chocolate and 1/2 cup butter over hot water. Add 1/2 teaspoon each of triple-strength coffee and vanilla and 1 1/2 cups sifted confectioners' sugar and stir the cream until it is smooth.

Kaffee Buttercreme

Coffee Butter Cream for Coffee Log

CREAM 3/4 cup butter, add 1 cup sifted confectioners' sugar and 2 egg yolks, and beat the mixture well, using an electric beater if possible. Stir in 1/4 cup triple-strength coffee and 1 tablespoon kirsch. If the cream separates, beat in 2 or 3 teaspoons hot water.

Sylviarollen

Almond Rolls

GRIND 3/4 CUP blanched almonds, add 1/3 cup sugar and 2 tablespoons flour, and carefully fold in 4 egg whites beaten stiff with 2 tablespoons sugar. Butter and flour a baking sheet and spread the batter thinly in 4-inch squares, using a stiff paper stencil if desired. Leave enough space between the squares to allow for spreading. Dust a 1-inch strip of finely shaved blanched almonds down the center of each square and bake the squares in a slow oven (300° F.) for 15 to 20 minutes, or until they are lightly browned. Roll each square at once over a wooden stick to form a hollow tube 4 inches long and about 3/4 inch in diameter and lightly press the seam. Do not attempt to bake more than 4 squares at once, and, if they become too brittle to handle, return them to the oven to soften.

Pipe each tube half full of mocha butter cream and fill the other half with chocolate butter cream, to which pistachio nuts may be added.

Mocha Wedges   *Vindobonaschnitten*

BEAT 9 EGG yolks with 3/4 cup sugar until they are light and foamy and fold in 3 stiffly beaten egg whites. Add 9 tablespoons flour mixed with 6 tablespoons finely ground blanched almonds. Add 3 tablespoons melted butter mixed with 2 tablespoons chocolate, melted and cooled. Spread the batter in a narrow buttered cake pan, about 16 inches long, and bake the cake in a moderately hot oven (375° F.) for 40 minutes, or until it tests done. Let the cake cool and split it into 3 layers. Or bake the cake for 15 minutes in a shallow baking pan lined with paper and cut it into 3 strips while it is hot.

In the top of a double boiler over hot but not boiling water, beat 3 egg yolks and 2 eggs with 1 cup sugar until the mixture is thick. Take it from the heat and continue to beat it until it is cold. Add triple-strength coffee to taste, about 2 to 3 tablespoons, and carefully stir in 1 1/2 cups creamed butter. Chill the cream until it will spread well. Fill and ice the cake with this coffee butter cream and make waving ridges with a pastry comb or a wide fork. Cut the cake diagonally in a zigzag pattern to form triangular wedges. Sprinkle the top and back of each wedge with chocolate shot or toasted chopped hazelnuts or almonds. Chill the cake.

Pink Cakes   *Rosa Törtchen*

PREPARE THE batter for Genoese spongecake base I. Bake the cake in a large shallow buttered pan for 40 to 45 minutes, or until it leaves the

sides of the pan. Let it cool. Cut the cake into 2-inch rounds with a cookie
cutter and sandwich four rounds together with raspberry jam. Glaze the
little cakes with pink rum fondant icing and pipe onto each a rosette of
whipped cream.

Donauschnitten   *Danube Strips*

BEAT 8 EGG yolks with 6 tablespoons sugar until they are thick and yellow.
Whip 8 egg whites until they are half stiff and gradually dust in 6 tablespoons sugar, beating until the whites are stiff. Pour the yolks carefully onto the whites. Gradually dust 1 1/3 cups flour over the mixture,
adding 4 tablespoons at a time, and fold the mixture once after each
addition of flour. Pour the batter 1/4 inch deep into two 11- by 17-inch
buttered jelly-roll pans and bake the sheets in a moderate oven (350° F.)
for 12 to 16 minutes, or until they are golden and shrink from the sides
of the pan. Cut each sheet at once into 3 even strips lengthwise, and lift
the strips carefully from the pans. The strips become brittle as they cool.
Retain the best strips for the top and spread the other 5 with chocolate
butter cream. Lay them one on another. Trim the sides of the strips evenly
and cover them with the butter cream. Dust them with 1 1/2 cups finely
chopped toasted hazelnuts or almonds and glaze the top with chocolate
icing. Mark the top crosswise with a knife at 1 1/2 or 2 inch intervals.
Pipe a ribbon of chocolate butter cream down the long edges of the
stacked strips and pipe a rosette of the cream in the center of each
marked slice. Place a whole toasted hazelnut or almond in each rosette.
Chill the cake until it is needed. To serve, slice it crosswise at the marked
lines. Each slice will have a rosette in the center.

Indianerkrapfen   *India Puffs*

BEAT 9 EGG yolks with 1/3 cup sugar until they are light and foamy.
Fold in 10 egg whites beaten stiff with 1/2 cup sugar and dust in 1 1/4
cups flour sifted with 2/3 cup potato flour. Pipe the batter onto paper
in half rounds the size of half a small orange or pipe it onto buttered
wooden Indianer molds. Dust the cakes lightly with flour and bake them in
a moderately hot oven (375° F.) until they are dry and golden, leaving
the oven door open just enough to allow the steam to escape. Remove

the *Krapfen* from the paper or molds and cool them. Hollow out the flat sides with a spoon. Spread half the shells with apricot glaze and let them dry. Pour chocolate fondant icing into the unglazed shells and pipe sweetened whipped cream into them. Cover them with the glazed halves and serve at once.

Bishops' Bread — *Bischofsbrot*

CREAM 3/4 CUP butter with 1/2 cup sugar until light and beat in 6 eggs, one at a time, adding 1 teaspoon flour with each egg. Sift 1 teaspoon baking powder with 1 1/3 cups flour over 1 cup raisins and 1/2 cup each of chocolate bits and slivered blanched almonds and fold the mixture into the butter mixture. Pour the batter into a buttered and floured 9- by 5- by 3-inch loaf pan. Bake in a moderate oven (350° F.) for about 65 minutes, or until it tests done. Let the cake stand for at least 24 hours and serve in very thin slices.

Health Cake — *Gesundheitskuchen*

BEAT 4 EGG yolks light and creamy with 2/3 cup sugar. Add a pinch of salt and the grated rind of 1 lemon. Sift 2 1/2 cups sifted cake flour with 4 teaspoons baking powder. Stir the flour into the egg yolks alternately with 3 tablespoons heavy cream mixed with 1/2 cup milk. Add 1/2 cup floured raisins and fold in 4 egg whites, beaten stiff. Pour the batter into an 8-inch tube pan, buttered and dusted with 1/2 cup shaved almonds. Bake the cake in a moderate oven (350° F.) for 1 hour.

Loaf Cake — *Teekuchen*

BEAT 1 CUP butter until it is creamy. Beat in 1 2/3 cups sugar gradually and beat the mixture until it is very light and creamy. Add 5 eggs, beating thoroughly after each addition. Continue beating until the batter is very light. Fold in 2 cups cake flour, 1 teaspoon lemon juice, and 1/2 teaspoon grated lemon rind. Pour the mixture into 2 well-buttered and floured narrow Viennese box molds or into 1 loaf-cake pan. Bake the cake in a moderate oven (350° F.) for 1 1/2 hours. Let it cool for 10 minutes before turning it out on a rack. The cake is better if it stands until the next day. Sprinkle the top with confectioners' sugar.

Blitzgebäck 1   *Lightning Cake I*

CREAM A GENEROUS 1/2 cup butter, stir in 2/3 cup sugar, and add 3 eggs, alternating with 3 additions of 5 tablespoons flour each. Add 1/2 teaspoon vanilla and spread the mixture 1/3 inch deep in a well-buttered baking pan. Dust it with 2/3 cup chopped hazelnuts. Bake it in a moderate oven (350° F.) for 15 minutes, or until it is golden. Cut the bakery into "fingers" at once and dust them with vanilla sugar.

Blitzgebäck 2   *Lightning Cake II*

BEAT 1/4 CUP butter with 2/3 cup sugar. Add 3 eggs, 2 tablespoons milk, and 1/2 teaspoon vanilla, and stir the mixture until it is smooth. Add gradually 1 1/3 cups flour sifted with 1 teaspoon baking powder and 1/2 teaspoon salt. Pour the mixture into a 13- by 9-inch buttered baking pan and strew it with 2/3 cup slivered almonds. Bake the cake in a moderately hot oven (375° F.) for 12 to 15 minutes, or until it shrinks from the sides of the pan and is golden. Cut it at once into 1 1/2-inch squares and dust them with vanilla sugar.

Der Hausfreund   *Friend of the Family*

BEAT 4 EGGS with 1 1/4 cups sugar until they are light and foamy. Add the grated rind of 1 lemon and stir in 2 1/4 cups flour. Spread the batter 1/3 inch thick in a heavily buttered baking pan and strew it with 1/3 cup slivered almonds. Place the pan on a baking sheet and bake the cake in a moderate oven (350° F.) until it is lightly golden, about 15 minutes. Cut it at once into 1 1/2-inch squares or triangles and take them from the baking sheet while they are hot. Dust them with vanilla sugar.

Praline Cakes *Grillagekugeln*

MAKE A MACAROON batter as for *Kaisertorte 1* but bake the batter in 18 small rounds instead of 1 large one.

Beat 4 egg yolks light and foamy with 1/3 cup sugar. Beat 6 egg whites stiff, gradually adding 1/4 cup sugar. Carefully fold the egg whites with 1 cup sifted flour into the yolks. Pour the batter into 18 small muffin tins, and bake the cakes in a moderate oven (350° F.) for 20 minutes, or until they test done. While the cakes are warm, hollow out the top of each with a spoon, let them cool, and fill each with 1 brandied cherry and as much praline butter cream as possible. Invert the cakes onto the macaroon bases and press them down firmly. Spread the top and sides of each cake with enough praline butter cream to conceal the macaroon base and sprinkle the little cakes with coarsely chopped praline powder.

Sugar Squares *Jourkonfekt*

BOIL TOGETHER 1 cup each of sugar and water for 5 minutes. Add the juice of 1/2 lemon. Stir 1/3 cup rice flour or potato starch to a paste with 1/2 cup water and pour it gradually into the sugar syrup, stirring constantly over low heat until the mixture is thick and transparent. Remove the paste from the heat and add the grated rind of 1/2 lemon and 1/2 cup slivered blanched almonds. Flavor the paste with 1 teaspoon lemon, pineapple, or raspberry extract, or rose water, and color it with a few drops of suitable vegetable coloring. Beat the paste well and turn it out onto a pastry board heavily dusted with sifted confectioners' sugar. Roll out the paste into a rectangle 1 inch thick, dust it with confectioners' sugar, and cut it into small squares. Dry the squares in a very slow oven (200° F.) for about 15 minutes, until they feel solid to the touch.

Stuffed Chocolate Figs *Schokoladefeigen*

CUT THE stems from 1 pound large soft dried figs. Slit the figs and cut and widen a pocket in each fig. Heat 1/2 cup heavy cream in an enamel saucepan and add 4 ounces sweet cooking chocolate, shaved or softened over hot water. Let the mixture boil up once, stirring constantly to prevent the chocolate scorching. Stir it until it is cold. Put the pan over ice if desired. Add 1/2 teaspoon vanilla extract or a dash of dark rum. Fill the figs with the mixture and reshape them. Melt 2 ounces sweet chocolate over hot water. Dip the figs into the chocolate, coating them half way. Dry them on a wire rack or on wax paper at room temperature. Put each fig in a fluted paper cup.

Kapuziner   *Kapuziner*

TOAST 2/3 cup almonds, blanched and shaved, on a baking sheet in a slow oven (300° F.) for 15 minutes, until they are golden brown. Melt 5 ounces sweet chocolate in the top of a double boiler over hot water and stir in 1 tablespoon butter and 1/2 teaspoon rum, orange bitters, or vanilla extract. Remove the pan from the heat and stir in the almonds. Drop the chocolate-coated almonds by spoonfuls onto wax paper. Let the *Kapuziner* cool and chill them until they are hard. Serve them in individual fluted paper cups. Makes about 30.

Glasierte Früchte und Nüsse   *Glazed Fruit and Nuts*

COMBINE 2 CUPS sugar, 1 cup water, and 1/4 teaspoon cream of tartar and cook the syrup, without stirring, to the hard-crack stage, or until a candy thermometer registers 290° F. Remove the saucepan from the heat and place it in cold water, to lower the temperature quickly. Place the pan in hot water to prevent the syrup from hardening. Use any small fruits, such as grapes and cherries, and unbroken nut meats. Be sure the fruits are completely dry. Quickly dip the fruits and nuts in the syrup, a few at a time, and remove them with a slotted spoon to a marble slab or an oiled enamel surface. Glazed fruit does not keep well. It is best glazed in cold weather and should be served immediately.

For chocolate-dipped strawberries, melt 4 ounces sweet chocolate over hot water, stirring, and dip the strawberries into it, holding them by the hulls and dipping them to within 1/4 inch of the hulls. Let the dipped berries dry on wax paper. *(Picture, page 493.)*

Torten

S*chön, schöner, am schönsten:* a positive, a comparative, and a superlative with which to say beautiful, more beautiful, and most beautiful. Not content with a mere superlative, the Viennese have a super-superlative, a plus ultra, the *allerschönste,* the most beautiful of them all. In this case it means the hollow Viennese meringue *Torte* elaborately decorated and filled with strawberries and whipped cream.

The most beautiful of all the *Torten* depends basically on two simple ingredients and a little practice with a pastry bag and tube. The *Torte* to begin and end all *Torten* is the *spanische Windtorte,* the Spanish wind cake. Just why egg whites beaten with sugar, which most people call a meringue, should be called Spanish wind in Vienna is one of those culinary mysteries that no one can explain.

When Frau Baronin planned for a Spanish wind cake she always started with a trip to her son's desk. This, needless to say, entailed a complete straightening up of the desk, in the course of which she found what she was looking for, his compasses, and borrowed them for the better preparation of her *Torte.* A Spanish wind cake was largely a matter of design, layout, and careful drafting—truly an architect's *Torte,* made with precision and a working knowledge of engineering. The Spanish wind cake consists of egg whites and sugar, no more and no less, a simple formula. With the compasses, Frau Baronin drew 6 circles on 6 pieces of parchment paper, five of them measuring nine inches in diameter and one an inch smaller. She knew that the circumference of a circle is roughly three times its diameter and six times its radius. Fortunately it was one of those sentences that stay with anyone who learns them once, like "Thirty days hath . . ." and *"Die Muschel erinnert an das Rococo*—the shell brings to mind the rococo."

Frau Baronin cut out her circles. She piped a flat disc of meringue onto the first circle, meringue rings onto the next four, and onto the last a disc decorated with such a wild elaboration of *Schnörkel,* shells, and curlicues that she was obviously being influenced by her ability to recognize rococo when she saw it. The six sheets went into a slow oven for the day or for as much time as she could allow and dried out to a creamy white instead of actually baking.

Taken from the oven, the four cooled rings were detached from their parchment papers and placed on the solid bottom—a simple rule of a proper foundation for the coming superstructure. Frau Baronin filled in the four rings with fresh meringue, as a mason cements a wall, and having smoothed it with a trowel-like blade, she piped rosettes around the bottom, which were not functional but gave a lovely look to the *Torte*. She also ornamented the smooth sides with bas-reliefs and ended with a cornice inspired by the baroque architecture of Vienna. This masterpiece of design and construction went back into the oven to dry out a second time. On one occasion, she had forgotten it and let it dry out for three days. It turned out to be more perfect than ever before.

Before it was to be served, Frau Baronin had her final pleasure. She marinated strawberries in maraschino, she crushed stale macaroons and toasted hazelnuts, she searched out a candy here and a bit of praline there. (Her *Torten* were never the same, but they never failed to be fascinating.) She folded everything into sweetened whipped cream and cooled her beautiful baroque meringue shell. She piped in the cream, interspersed it with strawberries, and quickly added a little shaved bitter chocolate, an inspired afterthought. When the lid went on and the Spanish wind cake, the most beautiful of all the cakes, went onto a cake stand and so to the table, even her son, who had not been able to find a thing in his orderly desk for the last three days, forgave her.

Vienna is justly famous for her *Sachertorte,* invented within the inner city, for the *Linzertorte* that came to her from a baker in Linz on the Danube, for the *Dobostorte* that came from Hungary, and for the many and incomparable *Torten*— all of them *die allerschönsten.*

Cake Batters   *Biskuit-, Sand-, und Schaum-Massen*

The 12 following Viennese cake batters may be prepared by the warm or the cold method. When the eggs and sugar are beaten together over simmering water, the cake is lighter than it is when the eggs are separated and the beaten whites are folded into the yolks. The batters can be baked in sheets in shallow baking pans and cut into long strips to make Schnitten, *or slices. For* Torten, *they can be baked in a spring-form pan and cut into layers on the following day or after they are cold; or the layers can be baked in separate cake pans, usually 9-inch pans. The batters can also be baked in cake molds. Large sheets of the basic cakes are spread with filling, assembled, and cut into layered pastry squares.*

Genoese Spongecake Base I   *Warme Biskuitmasse 1*

IN THE TOP of a double boiler over simmering water, beat 8 eggs and 1 1/3 cups sugar until they rise to 3 times their original volume, about 8 minutes with an electric beater. Take the mixture from the heat and beat it until it is cold. Dust in 2 1/2 cups flour gradually and stir in 1/4 cup butter, melted and cooled. Pour the batter into well-buttered and floured cake pans or a spring-form pan and bake the cake in a moderate oven (350° F.) until it is golden and tests done, about 60 minutes in a spring-form pan. Let it cool. Cut, fill, and ice it as directed.

Genoese Spongecake Base II   *Warme Biskuitmasse 2*

IN THE TOP of a double boiler over simmering water, beat 6 eggs with 1 cup sugar until they rise to 3 times their original volume and flow from the end of the beater in a thick stream. Take the mixture from the heat and beat it until it is cold. Stir in the grated rind of 1/2 lemon and sift in gradually 1 2/3 cups flour. Pour the batter into well-buttered and floured cake pans or a spring-form pan and bake in a moderate oven (350° F.) until it tests done, about 25 to 30 minutes for a single cake, less for small molds. Let it cool. Cut, fill, and ice the cake as directed.

Chocolate Spongecake Base   *Schokoladen Biskuitmasse*

BEAT 8 EGG yolks and 1 cup sugar over heat as for Genoese spongecake and then beat the mixture until it is cold. Mix in gradually 1 1/2 cups flour sifted with 1/2 cup cocoa and stir in 1/3 cup butter, melted and cooled. Bake as for Genoese spongecake. Use this cake base for *Torten, Schnitten,* and pastries. Cut, fill, and ice the cake as directed.

Sandmasse   *White Cake Base*

CREAM 1 CUP and 2 tablespoons butter in a warm bowl with 1 1/4 cups sugar, a pinch of salt, and the grated rind of 1 lemon. Add, one by one, 5 egg yolks and 1 tablespoon each of lemon juice and rum. Beat until the sugar is dissolved. Beat the 5 egg whites very stiff with a pinch of salt and fold them into the yolk mixture, alternating with 2 2/3 cups cake flour, sifted twice with 1 teaspoon double-acting baking powder. Bake in a buttered and floured spring-form or cake pan in a moderate oven (350° F.) until it is golden and tests done, about 60 minutes. Let it cool. Cut, fill, and ice the cake as directed.

Sachermasse   *Chocolate Cake Base*

CREAM 8 1/2 TABLESPOONS butter with 1/3 cup sugar and gradually beat in 7 egg yolks. Add 8 tablespoons or 4 ounces semisweet chocolate, melted and cooled, and stir in 1 cup plus 1 tablespoon flour. Beat 7 egg whites with 1/4 cup sugar until stiff, fold them into the chocolate mixture, and bake in a buttered and floured spring-form pan in a moderate oven (350° F.) for 1 hour, or until it tests done. Cool and glaze as directed on *page 466.*

Kaltgerührtes Biskuit 1   *Biscuit Cake Base I*

STIR 6 EGG yolks with 1/3 cup sugar until they are light and creamy and add the grated rind of 1 lemon. Fold in 6 egg whites beaten stiff with 1/3 cup sugar and gradually sift in 1 1/3 cups flour. Pour the batter into buttered cake pans or molds or into a spring-form pan and bake the cake in a moderate oven (350° F.) for 50 or 60 minutes, or until it tests done. Cool it. This cake base is heavier than Genoese spongecake. Use it for *Torten, Schnitten,* and pastries. Cut, fill, and ice the cake as directed.

Kaltgerührtes Biskuit 2   *Biscuit Cake Base II*

STIR 8 EGG yolks with 3/4 cup sugar until they are light and creamy, and add 1 teaspoon vanilla extract or the grated rind of 1/2 lemon. Stir in 1 1/2 cups flour and fold in 8 stiffly beaten egg whites. Pour the batter into well-buttered cake pans or a spring-form pan and bake the cake in a moderate oven (350° F.) for 50 to 60 minutes, or until it tests done. Let it cool. Cut, fill, and ice the cake as directed.

Walnut or Hazelnut Cake Base — *Nussmasse*

STIR 8 EGG yolks with 1/3 cup sugar until they are light and creamy and add the grated rind of 1/2 lemon and 1/2 teaspoon vanilla extract. Fold in 8 egg whites beaten stiff with 1/3 cup sugar and gradually fold in a mixture of 1/4 cup flour, 1/2 cup finely grated walnuts or hazelnuts, 2/3 cup dry cake crumbs, and 1/4 cup melted and cooled butter. Pour the batter into well-buttered and floured cake pans or into a spring-form pan and bake the cake in a moderate oven (350° F.) until it is golden and tests done, about 60 minutes in a spring-form pan. Let it cool. Cut, fill, and ice the cake as directed.

Almond or Hazelnut Genoese Cake Base — *Mandelbiskuit*

CREAM 5 EGG yolks with 1/2 cup sugar and stir in 1/4 cup each of ground almonds and flour. Add 3 stiffly beaten egg whites and the juice of 1/2 lemon. Bake in a buttered cake mold or pan in a moderate oven (350° F.) until it tests done. Use this almond base for *Torten, Schnitten,* and pastries. Cut, fill, and ice the cake as directed. Hazelnuts may be substituted for almonds.

Praline Cake Base — *Grillagemasse*

IN A SMALL iron skillet, simmer 1/3 cup sugar until it turns golden brown and add 1/2 cup blanched almonds, or hazelnuts with their skins rubbed off. Pour the mixture onto an oiled marble or enamel slab and let it cool until it is brittle. Crush it to a coarse powder with a rolling pin. Stir 7 egg yolks with 1/4 cup sugar until they are light and creamy. Fold in 7 egg whites beaten stiff with 1/4 cup sugar and add 1 1/2 cups flour mixed with the praline powder. Pour the batter into buttered cake or loaf pans or into a spring-form pan. Bake the cake in a moderate oven (350° F.) until it tests done, about 50 to 60 minutes in a spring-form pan. Let it cool. Use this praline cake base for *Torten, Schnitten,* and pastries. Cut, fill, and ice the cake as directed.

Nuss Schaummasse   *Japonais Cake Base*

MIX 1 2/3 CUPS sugar with 2 scant cups very finely ground unblanched almonds and 1/4 cup flour. Fold in 7 stiffly beaten egg whites and pipe the mixture in 9-inch circles onto buttered and floured baking sheets. Bake the circles in a slow oven (300° F.) until the layers are dry and lightly browned, about 1 hour. Let them cool. This batter can be made with half almonds and half toasted hazelnuts. Fill and ice as directed.

Schaummasse   *Meringue*

BEAT 8 EGG WHITES until they are half stiff. Gradually add 1 cup sugar, beating until the meringue is very stiff. Fold in 1 cup more sugar and pipe the meringue through a pastry bag in flat spirals onto 9-inch circles drawn on heavy brown paper. Begin each spiral in the center. Or spread the meringue with a knife or use it as the recipes require. Bake the meringue layers on baking sheets in a very slow oven (225° F.) for about 45 minutes, or until they are cream colored but not brown and the paper pulls off easily. Change their positions in the oven, if necessary, to insure even baking. Leave the door ajar, if necessary, to lower the heat. Remove the paper and dry the meringues in a barely warm oven for 2 hours. Let them cool. Fill and ice them as directed.

Viennese Orange Cake   *Wiener Orangentorte*

MAKE GENOESE spongecake base II and cut it into 2 layers. Fill it with
1 cup curaçao butter cream and glaze the top and sides with orange
fondant icing. Decorate the sides with chocolate shot before the icing sets.

Nut Cake   *Nusstorte*

MAKE 3 LAYERS of walnut cake base and fill them with 1 1/2 cups coffee
butter cream. Ice the top and sides with mocha fondant icing and decorate
the top with walnuts before the icing sets.

Biedermeier Cake   *Biedermeiertorte*

MAKE JAPONAIS cake base, using hazelnuts instead of almonds and adding
to the batter 2 tablespoons each of grated chocolate and flour. Bake the
cake in 3 layers, or cut it into 3 layers, and fill it with 1 cup sweetened
whipped cream. Cover the sides and top with 1 cup sweetened whipped
cream, flavored with rum to taste, and pipe onto the cream a border,
lattice, and center decoration of chestnut purée flavored with rum. Use
about 1 1/2 cups purée.

Chocolate Cake   *Schokoladentorte*

MAKE CHOCOLATE cake base and flavor it with 2 tablespoons coffee
essence. Bake it in 3 layers or cut it into 3, and fill it with 1 1/2 cups
chocolate butter cream. Ice the top and sides with chocolate fondant
icing and decorate the top with 3/4 cup coffee butter cream piped in
rosettes.

Praline Cake   *Grillagetorte*

MAKE PRALINE cake base and bake it in 3 layers or cut it into 3 layers.
Fill it with light mocha butter cream, spread the butter cream on the
sides and top of the cake, and decorate the cake with piped rosettes of

butter cream. Press a toasted hazelnut into each rosette. Use 2 1/2 cups butter cream.

Johann-Strauss-Torte — *Johann Strauss Cake*

MAKE BISCUIT cake base II and cut it into 5 layers. Sprinkle them with a few drops of brandy and fill them with 2 cups whipped cream sweetened with 1/4 cup vanilla sugar. Make 1 1/2 cups praline butter cream and tint half of it pink with vegetable coloring. Spread the top of the cake with the untinted cream and the sides with pink. Decorate the top with a border and lattice of chocolate butter cream.

Erdbeercremetorte — *Strawberry Cream Cake*

MAKE GENOESE spongecake base I and cut it into 3 layers. Press 1 1/2 cups strawberries through a sieve with 2/3 cup confectioners' sugar and flavor the purée with maraschino to taste. Fill the cake with the strawberry purée and pipe rosettes on the top and sides with 3 cups sweetened whipped cream. Decorate each rosette with a strawberry.

Esterhazy-Torte — *Esterhazy Cake*

MAKE ALMOND GENOESE cake base and bake it in 6 layers. Fill them with 2 cups chocolate butter cream. Brush the cake with apricot glaze and ice it with vanilla fondant. Immediately pipe lines of melted chocolate across the top, 1/2 inch apart, and draw a knife blade across the lines in opposite directions to decorate the glaze with the Esterhazy design.

Russische Torte — *Russian Cake*

MAKE BISCUIT cake base II and cut it into 3 layers. Fill them with 1/2 cup apricot marmalade mixed with 1/4 cup chopped candied cherries. Pipe *Schaummasse,* meringue, made of 3 egg whites and 7 1/2 tablespoons sugar through a large fluted tube over the top and sides of the *Torte,* covering it completely. Stud the meringue with 1/2 cup slivered almonds and bake the cake in a slow oven (300° F.) until it is golden and the meringue is stiff.

Hunyadi Cake · *Hunyadi-Torte*

MAKE JAPONAIS cake base with hazelnuts and almonds, bake it in 1 layer, and cut it into 3 rounds. Fill the cake with 1 1/2 cups sweetened whipped cream. Ice the top and sides with chocolate fondant icing and decorate the cake with red candied cherries.

Schönbrunn Cake · *Schönbrunner Torte*

MAKE JAPONAIS cake base, adding to the batter 2 tablespoons grated chocolate and 1 tablespoon rum. Bake the cake in 3 layers or cut it into 3 layers, and fill it with 1 1/2 cups whipped cream sweetened with 1/4 cup vanilla sugar. Flavor 2 cups sweetened whipped cream with rum and pipe rosettes over the top and sides of the *Torte*. Sprinkle it with 1/2 cup chocolate shot.

Coffee Cream Cake · *Kaffeecremetorte*

MAKE JAPONAIS cake base with hazelnuts and almonds and bake it in 2 layers or cut it into 2 layers. Fill it with 1 cup coffee butter cream and ice the top and sides with 1 cup chocolate butter cream. Decorate the top with a border of chocolate shaped like coffee beans.

Valery Cake · *Valerie-Torte*

MAKE HAZELNUT Genoese cake base and bake it in 3 layers or cut it into 3 layers. Fill them with 1 1/2 cups rum butter cream. Ice the *Torte* with 1 1/2 cups chocolate butter cream and pipe rosettes of butter cream around the edge of the top and in the center.

Sachertorte 1   *Sacher Cake I*

BEAT 1 CUP butter with 1 cup sugar until light and beat in 9 egg
yolks, 3 at a time. Add 8 ounces semisweet chocolate, melted and cooled,
and mix well. Fold 9 stiffly beaten egg whites into the batter and sift in
2 cups flour as the egg whites are folded in. Bake the cake in a buttered
and floured spring-form pan in a moderate oven (350° F.) until it tests
done. Remove the rim and let the cake rest for 1 to 2 hours. Spread the
top and sides of the cake with a thin layer of apricot glaze and ice the
entire *Torte* with chocolate fondant icing. In Vienna, the *Torte* is served
with sweetened whipped cream. *(Picture, page 495.)*

Sachertorte 2   *Sacher Cake II*

CREAM 1/2 CUP butter with 3/4 cup confectioners' sugar and add 6 egg
yolks beaten until light with 3/4 cup confectioners' sugar. Add 4 ounces
semisweet chocolate, melted and cooled, 2 teaspoons vanilla, and 1 cup plus
2 tablespoons flour. Fold in the 6 egg whites beaten until very stiff with
2 tablespoons sugar. Pour the batter into a well-buttered spring-form pan
and bake the *Torte* in a moderate oven (350° F.) for about 1 hour. Test it
for doneness after 45 minutes. Let the cake cool in the pan, preferably
overnight. Next day, cut the cake into 2 layers. Fill it with apricot glaze
and spread the top and sides with the glaze. (The authentic *Sachertorte*,
however, is left uncut, as in *Sachertorte 1*, and is not filled but simply
spread with apricot glaze.) Spread chocolate fondant icing over the glaze.
Serve the cake with sweetened whipped cream.

Doboschtorte   *Dobostorte*

CREAM 2/3 CUP butter with 1/4 cup sugar. Gradually add 5 egg yolks and
1 teaspoon vanilla extract. Fold in 5 egg whites beaten stiff with 1/2 cup
sugar and dust in 1 cup flour. Butter and flour the backs of six 9-inch cake
pans or the bottom plates of spring-form pans and spread them as thinly
as possible with the batter. Bake the layers in a moderate oven (350° F.)
for 10 minutes, or until they are golden. Remove them from the tins with
a sharp knife and let them cool. Trim the layers evenly and reserve the
best one for the top. If any are too high in the center, cut them down

with a large knife. If possible, let the layers rest in a dry place for 4 to 12 hours.

In the top of a double boiler over simmering water, beat 1 cup sugar with 4 eggs, 3 egg yolks, and 3 ounces semisweet chocolate, grated, to a thick smooth cream. Chill the chocolate cream, add 1 tablespoon triple-strength coffee and 1 teaspoon vanilla extract, and beat in 1 1/2 cups creamed butter. Boil 3/4 cup sugar and a few drops of water in a skillet until the syrup turns yellow and boil it, stirring, until it turns golden. Pour the caramel immediately onto the best layer, spread it quickly with a knife, and mark it in radiating lines into serving portions. Fill the layers with the chocolate cream, place the glazed layer on top, and spread cream on the sides of the *Torte*. Sprinkle the sides thickly with chopped toasted hazelnuts.

Emperor's Cake I   *Kaisertorte 1*

GRIND 1 2/3 CUPS blanched almonds and pound them in a mortar to a paste. Work in 1 1/4 cups sugar, 3 tablespoons brandy, 1 teaspoon almond extract, and 2 unbeaten egg whites, one at a time. Fold in 3 stiffly beaten egg whites and 1 tablespoon flour. The mixture should be moist enough to pipe easily, but it should not run. Draw a 12-inch circle on a piece of brown paper, pipe the batter through a pastry tube evenly onto the circle, and bake the macaroon in a very slow oven (250° F.) for 30 minutes. Strip off the paper and let the cake cool. Moisten the paper, if necessary, to loosen it.

Beat 3 egg yolks with 2/3 cup sugar until light and foamy, and add 3/4 cup almonds, blanched and ground, 1 teaspoon grated lemon rind, and the juice of 1 lemon. Beat 3 egg whites very stiff and fold them with 3/4 cup sifted cake flour into the egg yolk mixture.

Pour the batter into a buttered 10-inch spring-form pan and bake the cake in a moderately hot oven (375° F.) for 25 minutes, or until it tests done. Cool the cake and split it in half. Spread the macaroon with thick seedless raspberry jam and cover the jam with one of the cake halves. Spread it with more jam and top with the second cake layer. Frost the cake with lemon fondant icing, tinted, if desired, with a few drops of yellow vegetable coloring. Pipe large rosettes of vanilla butter cream on the macaroon border and on the edge of the cake, and dust the rosettes on the border with 1/2 cup powdered sweet chocolate.

*K*aisertorte 2   *Emperor's Cake II*

BEAT 5 EGG YOLKS until light and creamy with 3 tablespoons confectioners' sugar and 1 1/2 teaspoons each of vanilla extract and rum. Add 1/4 cup butter, melted, and 2 1/2 ounces semisweet chocolate, melted and cooled. Fold in 5 egg whites, beaten stiff with 1/2 cup sugar, and 1 cup toasted almonds, blended to a powder with 1/3 cup flour. Bake the batter in a buttered and floured 8-inch spring-form pan in a moderate oven (350° F.) for 30 minutes, or until it tests done.

Cut the cake into 3 layers and assemble them with 1 recipe chocolate butter cream, as for butter cream cake below, leaving only the top uniced. Melt 2/3 cup, or 3 ounces, lump sugar in 2 tablespoons hot water. Bring it to a boil, remove from the heat, and stir in 1 1/2 ounces semisweet chocolate, melted. Add 1 drop oil and stir until smooth. Pour the icing on the center of the cake and spread it into a 6-inch round with a knife. Make a circle in the center with a 3-inch cutter and bring the remaining butter cream up to it. Cover the cream with 3/4 cup toasted sliced almonds.

*B*uttercremetorte   *Butter Cream Cake*

IN A LARGE bowl, beat 4 egg yolks with 1/4 cup hot water until they are light and foamy and gradually beat in 1/4 cup sugar. Beat 4 egg whites with 1/8 teaspoon salt and 1/4 cup sugar until they are stiff, invert the whites onto the yolks, and add the grated rind and juice of 1/2 lemon. Sift 1 1/4 cups sifted flour with 1 1/2 teaspoons baking powder and 1/8 teaspoon salt. Sift it over the egg whites, and fold all together gently. Pour the batter into a buttered spring-form pan lined with buttered brown paper and bake the cake in a moderately hot oven (375° F.) for 35 to 40 minutes. Let the cake cool and remove the sides of the pan, leaving the cake on the bottom of the pan. When the cake is completely cool, cut it into 3 layers. Paint the bottom and middle layers with a thin coat of apricot marmalade.

Cream 1 1/2 cups softened butter with 1/3 cup sifted confectioners' sugar. Beat 4 egg yolks until they are light and gradually beat in 1 cup sifted confectioners' sugar and 1/2 teaspoon vanilla. Carefully combine the 2 mixtures and beat the icing until it is smooth. Beat in 1/2 cup semisweet chocolate, melted and cooled, and continue to beat the cream until it is smooth. Do not overbeat or it will separate.

Cover the 2 glazed layers with the butter cream. Place the layers on

top of each other, cover with the third layer, and cover the sides of the cake with the butter cream. Brown 1/2 cup blanched chopped almonds and 1 teaspoon sugar in 1 teaspoon butter, drain them, and sprinkle the sides of the cake with the almonds. Spread a thin layer of the butter cream over the top and mark it with 8 or 16 radiating lines. Pipe the remaining butter cream through a fluted tube in a border on the top edge of the cake and along the radiating lines. Place 8 or 16 whole blanched almonds between the lines. Pipe a small ring of butter cream in the center of the cake and fill it with 1 teaspoon apricot marmalade.

Geneva Cake   *Genfer Torte*

IN THE TOP of a large double boiler, over simmering water, beat 1 cup sugar with 8 eggs and 4 egg yolks with a wire whisk until the mixture triples in volume and runs from the whisk in a thick stream. Remove the pan from the heat and, in a cool place or over a basin of ice water, beat the mixture until it is cold. Combine 2 cups sifted flour and 1 cup grated blanched almonds, loosely packed, and sprinkle the mixture over the sugar and eggs, a little at a time, folding it in gently. Add 1/2 cup melted and cooled butter and pour the batter into a buttered spring-form pan. Bake the cake in a moderate oven (350° F.) for about 50 minutes, or until it is brown and tests done. Cool the cake and split it into 2 layers. Return 1 layer to the spring-form pan and chill it, keeping the most perfect layer for the top.

Bring to a boil 1 cup milk and 1/2 cup sugar, remove it from the heat, add 1/2 teaspoon vanilla extract, and beat in 3 egg yolks. Dissolve in the mixture 1 envelope gelatin softened in 1/4 cup strong cold coffee. Cool the mixture and add 1 cup heavy cream, whipped. As soon as it starts to set, pour it onto the chilled cake base. Chill the cake again until the cream is half set and cover it with the top layer. Chill the cake for 2 hours, or until it is entirely firm. Spread the sides of the *Torte* thinly with mocha butter cream and sprinkle the cream with 1 cup toasted flaked almonds. Cover the top with a perfect sheet of white sugar icing. Pipe a border of mocha butter cream around the top of the cake and lines across it in a grill pattern.

Rigo Jancsi Hotel Goldener Hirsch   *Rigo Chocolate Cake*

BEAT 6 EGGS AND 3/4 cup sugar with an electric hand mixer in the top of a double boiler over simmering water for 10 minutes. Take from heat and beat until cold. Stir in 18 tablespoons flour, 3 tablespoons unsweetened cocoa, and 7 tablespoons butter, melted and cooled. Bake in two 8- by 8- by 2-inch buttered and floured cake pans in a moderate oven (350° F.) for 25 minutes, or until done. Cool the layers and brush one with apricot glaze.

Pour 1 1/2 cups chocolate fondant over one layer. Melt 13 ounces sweet chocolate with 3 1/2 ounces cocoa butter, combine with 2 1/4 cups heavy cream, and whip until stiff. Pour the mousse on the second layer. Pipe 3/4 cup heavy cream whipped stiff with 1/4 cup confectioners' sugar on the mousse and chill both layers. Take layers from pans, cut the iced layer into sixteen 2- by 2-inch squares, lay them on the second layer, and cut through the mousse to make sixteen 2- by 2-inch cubes. *(Picture, page 488.)*

Orangentorte   *Orange Cake*

BEAT 2/3 CUP sugar with 6 egg yolks until they are light and foamy. Add 2/3 cup blanched ground almonds and the grated zest and juice of 2 small oranges. Fold in 10 egg whites beaten stiff with 3 tablespoons sugar and gradually fold in 1/2 cup flour and 2 tablespoons butter, melted and cooled. Bake the batter in 3 buttered cake pans in a moderately hot oven (375° F.) for about 40 to 50 minutes, or until they test done. Cool the layers. Fill them with sweetened whipped cream, flavored with orange curaçao. Ice the *Torte* with orange fondant icing.

Heat 1 cup sugar with 6 tablespoons water and, when it reaches a boil, dip 24 to 30 orange sections into the glaze. Remove the sections and drain them well. Lay them in a circle around the rim of the *Torte,* overlapping.

Punsch Cake   *Punschtorte*

IN THE TOP of a double boiler over simmering water, combine 6 eggs, 1/2 cup sugar, and the grated rind of 1 lemon. Beat the mixture until it rises and is light and smooth, and continue to beat it until it is hot. Remove the saucepan from the steam and beat the mixture until it is entirely cold. Gently stir into the egg mixture, bit by bit, 1 1/2 cups sifted flour. Line the bottom of an unbuttered spring-form pan with heavy paper and pour in the batter. Bake the *Punschtorte* in a moderate oven (350° F.) for about 35 minutes, or until it tests done. Invert the pan and let the cake cool. Turn the pan upright and cut the edge of the cake loose with a knife. Detach the rim and bottom of the pan and carefully pull the brown paper off the cake. If possible, let it rest for several hours or overnight.

Cut the cake into 3 layers, lay the bottom layer on the bottom of the reassembled spring-form pan, and spread it thinly with apricot jam or orange marmalade. Cut the center layer into small even cubes, reserving the trimmings and edges. Heat 1/2 cup orange marmalade in a saucepan with 1/3 cup heavy rum and a few drops of red food coloring or 1 tablespoon grenadine. Add 2 tablespoons sugar and continue to heat the mixture until the sugar is melted. Add more rum if the marmalade is very thick. Soak the cake cubes in this mixture until they are saturated and place them on the glazed cake layer.

Crush the scraps and trimmings of the second layer with 1/4 cup finely chopped blanched almonds, 1/4 cup crushed macaroon crumbs, any remaining rum mixture, and enough sugar and rum to bind them into a paste. With this mixture fill the edges and cavities between the saturated cubes. Spread the cut side of the remaining layer of cake with apricot jam or orange marmalade and lay it jam side down on the cake. Place a weighted plate on the cake to bind the second layer together. Let the *Torte* rest about an hour. Remove the weight and spring-form from the *Punschtorte* and ice it with a rum-flavored pink fondant icing. The top is sometimes decorated with candied orange peel.

Fürst Metternich-Torte   *Prince Metternich Cake*

CREAM 1 1/2 CUPS softened butter with 1 1/2 cups sugar. Add 1/2 teaspoon each of vanilla and rum and 1 teaspoon triple-strength coffee and gradually beat in 6 eggs. Sift together 2 1/3 cups sifted flour, 1 1/2 teaspoons double-acting baking powder, and 1 tablespoon cocoa. Fold the flour mixture gradually into the batter mixture to make a smooth batter.

For a more beautiful cake, omit the cocoa, divide the batter in half, and stir 2 tablespoons cocoa into one half. Line the base of a 10-inch spring-form pan with baking paper and butter and flour the paper. Spread 1/6 of the batter on the paper and bake the layer in a moderate oven (350° F.) for 15 minutes, or until it tests done. Bake 5 more layers in the same way, to make 6 rounds in all. If preferred, the cake may be baked in seven 9-inch cake pans. Use a spatula to spread the batter evenly in the pans. Cool the layers.

Cream 1 cup butter with 1 1/2 cups sifted confectioners' sugar and 1 tablespoon cocoa. Stir in 3 tablespoons dark rum and the grated rind of 1 orange. Fill the cake with this butter cream and spread the sides. Sprinkle the sides with 1/2 cup chopped toasted hazelnuts.

Melt 4 ounces sweet baking chocolate and 1 tablespoon butter over hot water. Add 4 tablespoons rum and 2/3 cup sugar and stir the icing until it is smooth. Spread the top of the *Torte* with this icing and decorate it with whole hazelnuts.

Vindobonatorte   *Mocha Cake*

STIR 8 EGG yolks with 1 cup sugar until they are light and creamy. Add 1 1/2 cups sifted flour very gradually and fold in 8 stiffly beaten egg whites. Add 1/2 cup butter, melted and cooled, folding it in only enough to blend all the ingredients. Pour the batter into 4 well-buttered and floured cake pans and bake the layers in a moderate oven (350° F.) for about 15 minutes, or until they test done. Cool the layers. Make about 4 cups mocha butter cream and fill and ice the cake. Sprinkle the cream with 1 cup slivered toasted almonds. Put the remaining butter cream into a pastry bag fitted with a fluted tube. Pipe a row of large rosettes around the outside edge of the top and lay 1 chocolate coffee bean on each rosette. Cover the top of the *Torte* completely with rosettes, one next to the other. Chill the cake until serving time.

Hazelnut Cake   *Haselnusstorte*

IN A LARGE bowl, beat 4 egg yolks, 2 eggs, 6 tablespoons hot water and 1 1/2 cups sugar until the mixture is light and foamy. Gradually stir in 1 cup sifted flour and the grated rind and juice of 1/2 lemon, and fold in 4 egg whites beaten stiff enough so they do not slide when the bowl is tilted. Sprinkle the batter with 1 1/4 cups ground hazelnuts and fold them in gently. Divide the batter between 3 well-buttered cake pans and bake the cakes in a moderately hot oven (375° F.) for 45 minutes. Let the layers cool.

In the top of a double boiler, over simmering water, beat 2 eggs with 2/3 cup sifted confectioners' sugar until it is thick and stands in peaks and remove it from the heat. Stir in 1 1/2 teaspoons heavy rum and 1/2 teaspoon vanilla and beat the icing until it is lukewarm. Gradually beat in 1 1/4 cups creamed butter. If it should curdle, place the icing over hot water and stir it until smooth. Fill and ice the cake with this butter cream. Just before serving, whip 1 cup cream and pipe rosettes over the entire top. Place a toasted hazelnut in each rosette.

Hazelnut Meringue Cake   *Haselnuss Schaumtorte*

COMBINE 2 SCANT cups confectioners' sugar with 2 cups ground hazelnuts and 2 tablespoons cornstarch. Fold the mixture gently into 8 stiffly beaten egg whites and pour the batter into 2 well-buttered and floured 9-inch cake pans. Smooth the tops with the flat of a knife and bake the cakes in a slow oven (275° F.) for 1 1/2 to 1 3/4 hours, or until they begin to shrink from the sides of the pan. Remove them from the pans and let them cool.

Make simple mocha butter cream. Spread a thin layer on one layer of cake and pipe small rosettes around the outside edge. Spread a very thick layer of the butter cream on the second layer and place the first on it. The cake should resemble a three-layer cake: two layers of pastry and one equally thick layer of butter cream. Spread the sides of the cake with butter cream and chill it.

Sonntags Haselnusstorte — Sunday Hazelnut Cake

STIR 9 EGG yolks with 3/4 cup sugar until they are light and creamy. Add 1 cup hazelnuts and 3/4 cup almonds ground together. Fold in 9 stiffly beaten egg whites and pour into 3 well-buttered 9-inch cake pans. Bake the cake in a moderate oven (350° F.) until it tests done. Cool the cake and sprinkle each layer with 3 tablespoons maraschino. Fill the layers with 3/4 cup thick raspberry jam and cover the entire cake with a layer of sweetened whipped cream 1/4 inch deep. Pipe 2 cups mocha butter cream in radiating lines on the top of the cake and loops on the sides and pipe a circle on the center of the top. Fill the circle with raspberry jam. Pipe whipped-cream rosettes around the top of the cake and bottom and place a toasted hazelnut in each rosette.

Feinste Nusstorte — Walnut Cake

IN A LARGE mixing bowl, beat 6 egg yolks with 3 tablespoons sugar until they are light and foamy. Stir in 2/3 cup walnuts, finely ground, and 1/2 teaspoon vanilla. Carefully fold in 6 egg whites beaten stiff with 6 tablespoons sugar and sprinkle 2/3 cup finely ground biscuit or cooky crumbs and 1/4 cup sifted flour over the batter. Stir the batter once and pour 1/4 cup melted and cooled butter in a thin stream over the whole surface. Stir the batter again and divide it among 3 well-buttered cake pans. Bake the layers in a moderately hot oven (375° F.) until they test done. Test for doneness after 25 minutes. The cakes should be moist. Cool the layers for at least 3 hours.

Cream 1 cup butter with 1 cup sifted confectioners' sugar and stir in 2 tablespoons rum, a pinch of cinnamon, the grated rind of 1/2 lemon, and 1 cup grated walnuts. Fill the cake with this walnut butter cream. Ice the top and sides with simple chocolate icing and decorate the cake with sugared walnut halves.

Almond Cake $\mathcal{M}$andeltorte

BEAT 8 EGG yolks with 1/4 cup sugar until the mixture is very light and creamy and add 3/4 cup blanched ground almonds, 1/2 cup cookie crumbs, 1/2 teaspoon almond extract, and the grated rind of 1 lemon. Beat 8 egg whites until they are stiff with 1/4 cup sugar. Fold the egg whites into the yolk mixture and turn the batter into a deep spring-form pan oiled and dusted with powdered sugar. (If a deep pan is not available, tie a collar of buttered paper around the rim of the pan to allow room for the cake to rise.) Bake the *Torte* in a moderate oven (350° F.) for 1 hour, or until it tests done. Unmold the cake and let it stand for 24 hours. Cut it horizontally into 1/2-inch layers and fill and ice it with chocolate rum butter cream.

Make a plain rum cream: Cream 1/4 cup butter with 1/2 cup or more sifted confectioners' sugar and add 1 tablespoon rum. Pipe the cream in rosettes onto the cake and decorate it with almonds.

Nesselrode Cake $\mathcal{N}$esselrode-$\mathcal{T}$orte

CREAM 1/2 CUP butter and gradually add 1/2 cup sugar and 3 tablespoons melted chocolate. Add 5 egg yolks and stir the batter lightly until it is creamy. Fold in 5 egg whites beaten stiff with 1/2 cup sugar. Sprinkle 1/2 cup ground blanched almonds over the batter and fold them in gently with 3/4 cup sweet chestnut purée. Bake the *Torte* in a well-buttered spring-form pan in a moderate oven (350° F.) for 45 minutes. Let it cool.

Cut the cake into 3 layers and glaze 2 layers with 1/3 cup raspberry jam, strained and thinned with 1 tablespoon maraschino. Beat 1 cup chestnut purée, made with chestnuts cooked in milk, with 3 tablespoons sugar and fold in 2 cups whipped cream. Fill the glazed cake layers with the chestnut cream and re-form the cake. Spread the sides of the cake with chestnut cream and sprinkle them with 1/2 cup riced cooked chestnuts. Spread the top with a smooth layer of simple chocolate icing. Ring the base with *marrons glacés* dipped halfway into the chocolate icing.

Strawberry Meringue Cake $\mathcal{E}$rdbeerschaumtorte

MEASURE 1 SCANT cup egg whites. Beat them at high speed with an electric beater, gradually adding 3/4 cup sugar, until the meringue does not slide when the bowl is tipped. Fold in another 3/4 cup sugar. Fill a pastry bag fitted with a 3/16-inch fluted tube with half the meringue. Draw three 9-inch circles on 3 sheets of heavy brown paper. Starting in the center, carefully fill two of them with a piped meringue spiral. The rows of meringue should just touch and the outside row should follow the outline exactly and be of an even thickness so that it does not become brittle and break. Using a 1/4-inch fluted tube, pipe the remaining meringue in a spiral 6 inches in diameter onto the third brown paper circle. Pipe the 1 1/2-inch border with two rows of tall adjoining rosettes, or alternating rosettes and arabesques. Or spread a thin layer of meringue with a knife and pipe rosettes on top of it.

Bake the meringue layers on 2 baking sheets in a very slow oven (225° F.) for about 45 minutes, until the meringue is cream colored but not brown and the paper pulls off easily. Change the position of the meringues, if necessary, to ensure even baking. You may leave the oven door ajar slightly to lower the heat. Remove the paper and dry the meringues in a warm oven for at least 2 hours.

Lightly brown 1 1/2 cups plain vanilla cookie-crumbs in 1/4 cup butter. Add enough maraschino, about 1/4 cup, to make a soft but not runny

476

paste. Slice 1 pint strawberries thickly. Spread them on a cloth, sugar them lightly, and sprinkle them with maraschino. Whip 2 cups heavy cream, gradually adding 1/2 cup confectioners' sugar, add 1/2 teaspoon vanilla extract, and fold in 3/4 cup chopped toasted hazelnuts.

Cover the 2 plain meringue layers with the cookie-crumb paste and arrange the sliced strawberries on them. Place one of the layers on a cake plate on 4 overlapping squares of wax paper that can be drawn out after the cake is decorated. Cover this layer with one-third of the whipped cream, place the second layer on top, and cover it in the same manner. Place the third layer on top and spread the sides of the *Schaumtorte* smoothly with the remaining whipped cream. Dust the sides with dried cookie-crumbs, chopped toasted hazelnuts, or crushed meringue crumbs. To make meringue crumbs, beat 2 egg whites very stiff with 1/2 cup sugar, spread the meringue on a baking sheet, and bake it in a very slow oven (225° F.) until it is golden. Crush the baked meringue with a rolling pin.

In the top of a double boiler over boiling water, melt 2 ounces bitter chocolate, add 1 teaspoon vegetable oil or cocoa butter, and stir until the chocolate will flow from a spoon or pastry bag in a thin line that holds its shape without spreading. Make a crisscross pattern on the 6-inch-round center of the top layer. Serve the *Schaumtorte* at once, cutting it with a sharp pointed knife, as a blunt knife crushes meringue. Raspberries may be substituted for strawberries.

Spanish Wind Torte   *Spanische Windtorte*

MAKE SCHAUMMASSE, or meringue cake base. Draw 5 perfect 9-inch circles on heavy brown paper and one 8-inch circle. In one 9-inch circle, pipe meringue in a spiral, starting at the center and filling the circle. Pipe a border of meringue about 1-inch wide on each of the four remaining 9-inch circles. Fill the 8-inch circle with a spiral of meringue and then pipe arabesques and rosettes over it. This will be the lid of the cake.

Bake the meringue rings and circles in a very slow oven (225° F.) for 45 minutes, or until they are cream colored and the paper pulls off easily. Leave the oven door ajar, if necessary, to keep the heat low. Remove the paper and return the meringue rings and circles to an oven that is barely warm. Dry them for as much as 2 hours. Let them cool.

Repeat the recipe for *Schaummasse*. Paint the rings with this fresh meringue and assemble them on the solid meringue disc to make a shell.

Smooth the side of the shell with meringue and pipe large arabesques onto it. Pipe rosettes around the base. Dry the decorated shell again in a barely warm oven. Let it cool. Just before serving, fill the shell with sweetened whipped cream and strawberries and cover with the lid.

Blättertorte   *Leaf Cake*

WORK INTO a smooth dough 2/3 cup sugar sifted with 1 1/3 cups sifted flour, 5 hard-cooked egg yolks, riced, and 3 uncooked egg yolks. Shape the dough into 3 balls and roll them as thinly as possible into 3 even rounds. Bake the rounds on a buttered baking sheet in a moderate oven (350° F.) until they are golden. Beat 4 egg whites partially stiff, gradually add 1/3 cup sugar, and continue to beat until the whites are stiff. Fold in 1/4 cup drained raspberry jam and cover 2 of the cake rounds with the meringue. Assemble the rounds, and pipe a circle of whipped cream, about 3/4 cup, sweetened to taste, onto the center of the top round about 2 inches from the edge. Fill the circle with 1 cup fresh raspberries.

Biscotten-Torte   *Ladyfinger Cake*

THIS TORTE must be prepared the day before it is served. Cream 3/4 cup butter with 1/4 cup sugar, add 1/3 cup finely ground blanched almonds, 6 tablespoons heavy cream, and 2 tablespoons triple-strength coffee. Line a spring-form pan with white paper. Dip *Biscotten,* ladyfingers, in rum diluted with water and sweetened to taste. Cover the bottom of the pan with *Biscotten,* cutting them to fit. Spread them with half of the coffee cream, add a second layer of rum-flavored *Biscotten,* spread them with most of the remaining coffee cream, and add a third layer of *Biscotten.* Fill in the edges with coffee cream. Store the cake in a cool place overnight. Three hours before serving time, remove the sides of the pan and pipe 2 cups sweetened whipped cream over the cake. Decorate it with 1/2 cup toasted hazelnuts and freeze it for 3 hours.

Biscotten   *Ladyfingers*

BEAT 6 EGG yolks with 2/3 cup sugar until they are light and creamy. Fold in 9 egg whites beaten stiff with 1/2 cup confectioners' sugar. Dust 1 1/2 cups flour over the batter and fold it in carefully. Pipe the batter through a pastry bag onto baking paper in even "fingers." Dust them well with confectioners' sugar shaken through a fine sieve. Bake them at once in a moderately hot oven (375° F.) until they are done, about 15 minutes. Loosen them from the paper immediately and let them dry for 24 hours.

Hazelnut Rum Linzer Cake

SIFT 1 3/4 CUPS flour with 1 teaspoon double-acting baking powder onto a pastry board and make a well in the center. In the well place 3/4 cup sugar, 2 eggs, and 2 tablespoons rum and grate the rind of 1 lemon over all. With a wooden spoon, incorporate as much flour as possible into the liquid ingredients. Cut 3/4 cup chilled butter into thin slices and lay them on the flour mixture. Grate 1 cup toasted and skinned hazelnuts and sprinkle these over the butter. Incorporate all the ingredients into a smooth dough, working as quickly as possible, and chill in the refrigerator for 1/2 hour.

Cut the dough in half and press one part on a floured pastry sheet to a scant 1/4 inch. Butter a 10-inch flan ring set on the baking sheet or line a 10-inch spring-form pan with the dough. Allow the dough to extend only about 1/4 inch up the straight sides of the pan. Spread the shallow unbaked pastry shell with 1 cup strawberry jam thinned with 2 teaspoons rum.

Place the second half of dough in a cookie press or pastry bag with a plain tip and pipe it across the jam in plain strips long enough to cover the *Torte*. Paint the rim of the pastry shell with a lightly beaten egg white. Lay strips of dough across the jam, 3/4 inch apart. Press the ends of the strips onto the rim and lay a second set of strips across the *Torte* in the opposite direction, to make a lattice. Paint the rim again with egg white and use a strip of dough to edge the *Torte*, covering all the ends of the strips. Paint the lattice and the edging with 1 egg yolk beaten with 1 teaspoon water.

Bake the *Torte* in a moderate oven (350° F.) for 50 minutes, or until it is golden brown. As *Linzertorte* burns easily, it is best to place it on second baking sheet in the oven. Let the *Torte* cool and sift over it confectioners' sugar in which a vanilla bean has been buried for several days or weeks. Allow the *Linzertorte* to ripen for 2 or 3 days before serving it. Serves 8.

*L*inzertorte   *Linzer Cake*

CREAM 14 TABLESPOONS butter with 1/2 cup sugar and add 3 egg yolks
and the grated rind of 1 lemon. Fold in 2 cups flour and 1 1/3 cups toasted
and skinned hazelnuts, ground. Chill the dough for 30 minutes. Press a
1/4-inch-thick layer of the dough into a 10-inch-diameter spring-form pan,
lined with baking paper, and shape a 1/4-inch rim up the sides of the pan.
Fill this shallow base evenly with 2/3 cup raspberry jam. Roll the remaining dough into rolls as thick as a heavy pencil and cross five rolls in each
direction to form a lattice over the jam. Press a last roll of dough around
the edge of the pan to cover the ends of the lattice, crimp the edge decoratively, and fill with more jam where needed. Bake in a moderately hot oven
(375° F.) for 35 minutes, or until it is lightly browned. Cool, remove the
rim, and sprinkle with confectioners' sugar. *(Picture, page 486.)*

*P*ischingertorte   *Pischinger Cake*

COOK 1 1/2 CUPS sugar with enough water to cover, about 3/4 cup. Let
the syrup boil up once, remove it from the heat, and let it cool. Melt
7 ounces sweet cooking chocolate over hot water and let it cool. Stir in
1 cup hazelnut praline powder and moisten with some of the cooled
sugar syrup. The mixture dries quickly and must be moistened several
times. Spread this filling over 4 *Karlsbader Oblaten,* wafers that can be
purchased in specialty food shops. Sandwich the *Oblaten,* top them with
a fifth wafer, and press them down. This is a very thin cake. Chill it.

Butter the top of a double boiler and in it melt 4 ounces sweet chocolate
over hot water, stirring until it is smooth. Pour a narrow ribbon of melted
chocolate around the rim of the *Torte* and let it flow evenly down to cover
the sides. Pour the rest of the chocolate in the center of the *Torte* and tilt
the cake so that the icing spreads over the entire top. Let it dry at room
temperature. Chill the *Torte* again. Cut the *Torte* in narrow wedges
to serve. In Vienna, wedges of *Pischingertorte* can be bought singly. Each
wedge is chocolate-covered.

Waffle sandwich wafers may be used instead of *Oblaten.* Spread 7
wafers, laid side by side, with half the filling mixture, cover with 7 more
wafers, and spread these with the rest of the filling. Top the long cake
bar with 7 more wafers and ice it as for the round *Torte.* Cut the bar in
1/2-inch slices to serve.

On the Graben, The Column of the Pe

Jam Pockets and Coffee Braid   *(recipes, pages 415 and 413)*

Salt Bakery

(recipes, pages 339 and 411)

Apples in Robes
Hotel Schloss Dürnstein

(recipe, page 507)

Gugelhupf

(recipe, page 414)

Linzertorte   *(recipe, page 480)*

Emperor's Omelet

(recipe, page 517)

Rigo Jancsi Hotel Goldener Hirsch   (*recipe, page 470*)

Salzburger Nockerln
Hotel Goldener Hirsch

(recipe, page 516)

489

Apple Strudel

(recipe, page 507)

Apple Strudel

(recipe, page 507)

Peach in Champagne
with Suvaroffs

(recipes, pages 539 and 433)

Chocolate-Dipped
and Glazed Strawberries

(recipe, page 456)

Coffee and *Krapfen* at Café Sirk (*recipe, page 423*)

494

Sachertorte from the Hotel Sacher   *(recipe, page 466)*

Pistachio Ice Cream Cake   *Pistazieneistorte Stephanie*

BEAT 8 EGG yolks with 3/4 cup sugar until they are creamy, add 1 1/2 cups sifted flour, and fold in 8 stiffly beaten egg whites. Pour the mixture into a 10-inch spring-form pan lined with buttered paper and bake the cake in a moderately slow oven (325° F.) for about 1 hour, or until it tests done.

Next day, split the cake into 2 or 3 layers, sprinkle the layers with sugar, and fill them with about 2 quarts pistachio ice cream. The ice-cream layers should be almost as thick as the cake layers. The top layer should be cake. Return the cake to a spring-form pan and freeze it.

Boil 2 cups water with 1 cup sugar for 5 minutes and in this sugar syrup simmer small whole peeled pears for 20 minutes, or until they are soft. Cool and chill them.

Sprinkle 2 cups strawberries with kirsch to taste, marinate them for about 20 minutes, and bind them with thick raspberry sauce—melted strained raspberry jam flavored with kirsch.

Arrange the chilled pears in a ring around the top of the cake and fill the ring with the strawberries. Remove the sides of the pan, set the cake on a serving platter, and with a pastry bag quickly pipe vertical adjoining rows of sweetened whipped cream on the sides of the cake. Pipe whipped cream around the base of the cake and sprinkle the cream with chopped pistachios. Serves 12.

Pears on Buttercake   *Arenberg Birnen*

IN THE TOP of a double boiler, over gently boiling water, beat 8 eggs and 1 cup sugar with a whisk until they triple in volume. Remove the eggs from the heat and continue beating until they are cold. Slowly add 2 cups sifted flour, folding it in gently with a spoon. Melt 1/2 cup butter, let it cool, and pour it gradually into the batter. Pour the batter into 12 well-buttered round molds, but do not fill the molds to the top. (Or, bake the cake in a large sheet and cut it into rounds.) Bake the cakes in a moderate oven (350° F.) until they test done, about 30 to 50 minutes, depending on their size. Remove them from the molds.

Place 1 whole stewed pear on each cake round, pour over *mousseline* sauce, and chill them. Decorate the pears with a piped spiral of chocolate butter cream and pour apricot sauce around the base. Serves 12.

A Sitting Room in the Former Viennese Apartment of Federico Pallavicini

Ronny Jaques

Glasuren und Füllen
Icings and Fillings

Wiener Buttercreme
Viennese Butter Cream

Boil 3/4 cup or 3 1/2 ounces lump sugar with 1/3 cup water to the thread stage, or until a candy thermometer registers 234° F. Immediately beat the hot syrup into 4 well-beaten egg yolks and continue beating until the mixture is cold and thick. Beat the mixture gradually into 1 cup creamed butter. Flavor according to the following suggestions. Makes 2 cups.

Vanillebuttercreme 1—VANILLA BUTTER CREAM I. Add 2 teaspoons vanilla while stirring the butter cream cold.

Schokoladebuttercreme—CHOCOLATE BUTTER CREAM. Add 2 to 4 ounces melted and cooled chocolate to the finished butter cream.

Schokolade-Grillagebuttercreme—CHOCOLATE PRALINE BUTTER CREAM. Add 1/4 cup praline powder to chocolate butter cream.

Kaffeebuttercreme—COFFEE BUTTER CREAM. Cook the sugar with 1/3 cup strong coffee instead of water.

Mokkabuttercreme—MOCHA BUTTER CREAM. Cook the sugar with 1/3 cup strong coffee instead of water and add 3 tablespoons triple-strength coffee while stirring the butter cream cold.

Mokka-Grillagebuttercreme—MOCHA PRALINE BUTTER CREAM. Add 1/4 cup praline powder to mocha butter cream.

Grillagebuttercreme—PRALINE BUTTER CREAM. Add 1/4 cup praline powder to the finished butter cream.

Fruchtbuttercreme—FRUIT-FLAVORED BUTTER CREAM. Add fruit juices and flavoring to taste while stirring the butter cream cold.

Likörbuttercreme—RUM, BRANDY, OR LIQUEUR BUTTER CREAM. Add flavoring to taste while beating the sugar syrup into the yolks.

Vanilla Butter Cream II   *Vanillebuttercreme 2*

WITH AN ELECTRIC hand mixer, beat 8 egg yolks and 1 cup sugar in the top of a double boiler over barely simmering water until light and thick. Add 4 ounces semisweet chocolate, melted and cooled. Take from heat, beating constantly until the mixture is cold. Cream 1 2/3 cups butter and beat it into the yolks with 2 teaspoons vanilla. Chill the butter cream until it is firm enough to spread evenly.

Chocolate Rum Butter Cream   *Schokolade-Rumbuttercreme*

WITH AN ELECTRIC HAND MIXER, cream 1 cup and 2 tablespoons butter with 3 egg yolks. Add gradually 1 cup sifted confectioners' sugar, 3 ounces sweet chocolate, melted, and 1 teaspoon each of vanilla and rum. Spread the cream with a spatula dipped in hot water.

Chocolate Hazelnut
Butter Cream   *Schokolade-Haselnussbuttercreme*

TOAST 1/4 CUP shelled hazelnuts in a hot oven (400° F.) for 10 to 12 minutes, or until they are lightly browned. Rub off the skins with a rough cloth and chop the nuts finely. Cream 1 1/2 cups butter and add 2 teaspoons vanilla extract or rum. Boil 1 1/2 cups sugar with 2/3 cup water in an enamel saucepan until the syrup spins a thread or a candy thermometer registers 234° F. Immediately pour the sugar syrup into 8 well-beaten egg yolks and continue to beat the mixture until it is very thick and cold. Add the creamed butter to the cold syrup very gradually, stirring only until it is blended, and add 5 ounces melted and cooled semisweet chocolate, 1 teaspoon triple-strength coffee, and the chopped hazelnuts. Do not overstir as the butter cream will separate; but if it does, add a little more butter. Chill the butter cream until it reaches spreading consistency.

Simple Mocha Butter Cream   *Mokkabuttercreme*

CREAM 3/4 CUP sweet butter until it is very light and fluffy, stir in 2 well-beaten egg yolks, and gradually add 2 1/2 cups sifted confectioners' sugar sifted with 2 tablespoons dry cocoa. Beat the icing until it is light and add enough cold triple-strength coffee to make it the right consistency for spreading.

Fondant   *Fondant*

COMBINE 3 CUPS sugar and 1/8 teaspoon cream of tartar in a heavy saucepan, add 1 cup boiling water, and stir until the sugar dissolves. Cook the
syrup without stirring to the soft-ball stage, or until a candy thermometer
registers 236° F. Wipe off the sugar crystals on the inside of the pan with
a fork wrapped in a damp cloth. Immediately remove the fondant from
the heat and pour it onto a marble or enamel surface. Work it with a
spatula until it is cool and then knead it into a smooth mass as quickly
as possible. Pack the fondant in an airtight container and store it in the
refrigerator.

Fondantglasur   *Fondant Icing*

WARM FONDANT in the top of a double boiler over simmering water to
spreading consistency, about 100° F. on a candy thermometer. Do not allow
the water to touch the upper pan. Thin the fondant to the desired consistency with boiling water. It may be flavored with vanilla or almond
extract or another flavoring or with any liqueur. To ice a *Torte,* pour the
fondant icing onto it and quickly tilt it, to spread the icing. Rewarm the
fondant if it becomes too stiff to spread.

Schokoladefondantglasur   *Chocolate Fondant Icing*

WARM 2 CUPS fondant over hot water to spreading consistency and add
up to 1/2 cup melted sweet chocolate, depending on the color and flavor
desired. Thin the fondant with water, if necessary.

Mokkafondantglasur   *Mocha Fondant Icing*

WARM 1 CUP fondant over hot water to spreading consistency and add
2 ounces chocolate, melted and cooled to lukewarm, and 1 tablespoon
triple-strength coffee.

Zitronenfondantglasur   *Lemon Fondant Icing*

WARM 1 1/2 CUPS fondant over hot water to spreading consistency. Color
it pale yellow with a few drops of yellow food coloring and add 2 tablespoons lemon juice.

Pink Rum Fondant Icing   *Rosa Punschglasur*

HEAT 1 1/2 CUPS fondant over hot water to spreading consistency. Color it pale pink with red food coloring and add 1 teaspoon heavy rum.

Orange Fondant Icing   *Apfelsinenfondantglasur*

WARM 1 CUP fondant over hot water. Thin it with a little orange juice and orange curaçao to spreading consistency.

Simple Chocolate Icing   *Schokoladeglasur*

BRING 1 CUP heavy cream to a rolling boil. Stir in 1 pound semisweet chocolate, chopped or grated, and stir until almost melted. Take from heat and stir until smooth. Use when it is almost cold or refrigerate and warm over hot water to spreading consistency when needed.

Confectioners' Sugar Icing   *Glasur*

GRADUALLY ADD 2 tablespoons hot milk to 3/4 cup confectioners' sugar and beat the icing until it is smooth. Flavor it with vanilla extract or lemon juice to taste.

Apricot Glaze   *Marillenglasur*

HEAT APRICOT jam over hot water, thin it with a little water, and flavor it, if desired, with apricot brandy to taste.

Praline Powder   *Grillagepulver*

COOK 1 1/4 CUPS sugar in a heavy skillet, stirring, until the sugar has dissolved and turned brown. Add 1 cup unblanched almonds, pour the mixture onto an oiled enamel or marble surface, and let it cool and harden. Break the praline into coarse or fine powder with a rolling pin or in a food processor. Hazelnuts may be used instead of almonds.

Hazelnut Praline Powder   *Haselnussgrillagepulver*

HEAT 1/2 CUP shelled hazelnuts in a hot oven (400° F.) for 10 minutes.

With a rough cloth, rub off the brown skins. Any that do not come away easily can be rubbed off after the nuts are toasted. Toast the nuts in the oven about 10 minutes longer, or until they are golden brown. Shake them once or twice to prevent scorching. Boil 1 cup sugar with 3 tablespoons water and 1/8 teaspoon cream of tartar in a heavy pan over low heat, without stirring, until the syrup takes on color. Add the toasted hazelnuts and continue to boil the syrup until it is golden brown. Pour the mixture at once onto a marble slab or lightly buttered pan. Let it cool and chill it until it hardens. Pulverize the praline with a rolling pin.

Grillagecreme   *Praline Cream*

MAKE PRALINE powder with 3/4 cup sugar, 1/2 cup unblanched almonds, and 1/2 cup hazelnuts. Cream 3/4 cup butter well with 2/3 cup sifted confectioners' sugar and 2 egg yolks. Melt 4 ounces sweet chocolate over hot water and stir in 2 tablespoons cream and 1/2 teaspoon each of triple-strength coffee and vanilla extract. Combine the chocolate and butter mixtures, beat the cream until it is smooth, and stir in the praline powder. Chill the cream before using it.

Vanillezucker   *Vanilla Sugar*

STORE 2 POUNDS confectioners' sugar in a tightly covered container with 4 fresh vanilla beans, bent in several places. Replace the sugar as it is used and the beans when they have lost their aroma. Or mix 1 tablespoon vanilla extract with 3 1/3 cups confectioners' sugar, dry the sugar well, and rub it through a fine sieve. Store it covered.

Kaffee-Essenz   *Triple-Strength Coffee or Coffee Essence*

To MAKE strong coffee for flavoring, bring to a boil 1/2 cup water and dissolve in it 2 tablespoons powdered coffee.

Süsse Kastanienpüree   *Sweet Chestnut Purée*

FOR PASTRIES and desserts, cook peeled chestnuts as for plain chestnut purée but in milk instead of in stock and do not add butter or seasonings.

Desserts

Mehlspeisen und
Süss-Speisen

F WE REALLY are what we eat, as Brillat-Savarin
stated, then the Viennese are among the sweetest
people in the world. A dinner in Vienna does not end quietly with light
refreshing fruit or just with coffee; it works itself gradually up to a climax
of a *Mehlspeise,* a dessert that includes flour. Some hostesses always offer
a choice of desserts at dinner: a *Mehlspeise* and a *Süss-Speise,* a dessert
without flour. Since the guests are mostly Viennese, it goes without saying
that they choose both desserts and then sit patiently in the salon until
midnight in the hope that fresh fruit with whipped cream will be served
or that a *Torte* will suddenly appear to round out the evening. They are
seldom disappointed.

In America, the word "dessert" is usually felt to include all the sweets
served at the end of a meal, whatever they are. The Viennese divide
desserts into two broad categories: those that contain flour and those that do
not. The first category, the *Mehlspeisen,* originally included cakes, pastries,
and *Torten* as well as pancakes, soufflés, puddings, and strudels. Now, however, the cakes, pastries, and *Torten* are thought of as *Bäckerei,* "bakery,"
and all the remaining desserts that contain flour, no matter how little,
claim the name *Mehlspeisen.* The second category, the *Süss-Speisen,* includes the fruits, creams, ices, *bombes,* mousses, and puddings.

Desserts are never simple, whatever their category. A plain cake is
listed as a tea bakery or *Gesundheitskuchen,* a health cake. Anyone search-
ing for a light, unpretentious little dessert in a Viennese cookbook would
probably have to turn to the chapters devoted to the feeding of children
and invalids. There he would find plain rice pudding, without the almonds
and whipped cream that would make it into a proper and acceptable

503

Süss-Speise. The fruit jelly would lack the liqueur flavoring, and the *Auflauf,* the soufflé, would lack the brandied peaches.

Many *Mehlspeisen* are also eaten as a main course, or even as the only course at a meal. A *Kaiserschmarrn* with compote or a German pancake with apples or with applesauce is often served with nothing else. A meal without a meat course is far more thinkable than a meal without a *Mehlspeise.*

The Viennese take pride in their innumerable *Mehlspeisen,* from the Emperor's favorite *Kaiserschmarrn* through their airiest *Nockerln,* which qualify as a *Mehlspeise* only by grace of the dusting of flour that goes into them. A well-trained Viennese cook should have three hundred and sixty-five desserts at her fingertips, and every home should have its own recipes, handed down from generation to generation. Frau Müller, who may curtsy to Frau Baronin, still believes that her own strudel dough is thinner and her *Schmarrn* is lighter than any that may be set before her betters. Frau Baronin gives in to all her Resi's whims rather than face the ghastly possibility of having her cook go to another Viennese employer with Frau Baronin's precious secret recipes, including those for desserts, locked in her memory, if not in her suitcase.

Viennese children, who are always told "*Nicht naschen—*don't nibble," are traditionally disobedient in this one matter, and they invariably raid the *Mehl- und Süss-Speisen.* During the day, they also sniff and peek a good deal so that they can whisper to their father when he comes home from his office, "*Heute gibt's Kastanienreis—*today there is chestnut rice." He, in turn, can regulate his consumption of all that precedes the *Mehlspeise* by his fondness for that day's dessert. To be forewarned is to be forearmed, an important consideration where *Mehlspeisen* are concerned.

As the social stations rise—from the workman who comes home to look into every pot on the stove to the gentleman who reads the menu from a china menu card to the titled prince whose major-domo reads him the menu and wine list while he is being shaved—every Viennese knows roughly how much appetite to keep for each course. No hostess would want her guest of honor to turn to her with bitter accusation after a lovely dinner and say, "You didn't tell me there were going to be plum dumplings!"

Apples in Maraschino
Äpfel in Maraschino

PEEL AND core 6 large baking apples and arrange them in a baking dish. Mix 3/4 cup water with 4 1/2 tablespoons apple jelly and pour it around the apples. Bake them in a moderate oven (350° F.) for 30 minutes, or until they are tender. Carefully remove the apples to a serving platter. Reduce the water in which the apples baked by half. Add 1/4 cup maraschino and chill the sauce.

Fill the centers of the apples with 1/3 cup apricot jam mixed with 1 tablespoon freshly squeezed lemon juice. Pour the sauce over the apples and garnish each with a red cherry.

Baked Apples
Äpfel in Wein

PEEL AND core 6 large baking apples. Fill their centers with 1 tablespoon each apple jelly. Arrange the apples in a baking dish just large enough to hold them. Pour 1 cup white wine around the apples and bake them in a moderately hot oven (375° F.) for 30 minutes, or until the apples are tender. Remove them carefully to a hot platter and serve at once with warm wine sauce, *Weinschaumsauce,* and Suvaroffs or other small pastry.

Apple Porcupine
Apfel Igel

CUT 9 PEELED and cored apples in half across. Dissolve 1 cup sugar in 1 cup water and cook 9 apple halves in the syrup until they are just tender. Remove them carefully and set them aside. Boil the remaining apple halves in the syrup to a thick apple purée. Fill the apple halves with 3/4 cup apricot marmalade mixed with 2 tablespoons Calvados. Combine the apple purée with 1/4 cup apricot marmalade and the juice and grated rind of 1/2 lemon. Arrange the apple halves on an ovenproof serving platter, round side up, to form a mound. Smooth the purée mixture between and over the apples. Beat 4 egg whites with 1/4 cup confectioners' sugar until they are stiff, spread them over the apple mound and dust it with confectioners' sugar. Stud the mound closely like a porcupine with 3/4 cup blanched slivered almonds. Bake the meringue in a slow oven (300° F.) until it is lightly browned.

Apfelpüree *Applesauce*

STEW 8 LARGE cooking apples, peeled, cored, and quartered, in very little water until they are soft. Drain them well and blend or process them into a smooth purée with 1/3 cup each of brown sugar and white wine, 1 tablespoon lemon juice, and a pinch each of ground cloves and cinnamon. Serve the applesauce hot or cold sprinkled with 1/2 cup chopped toasted almonds. It may also be served with meat.

Streuselmus *Applesauce with Crumb Topping*

PEEL, CORE, and quarter 8 firm apples. Simmer the apples until they are soft in 3/4 cup each of water and apple juice or soft cider. Drain them and put them through a sieve or blender. Cool the apples and season them to taste with sugar mixed with cinnamon. Add the grated rind of 1 lemon and 2 to 3 tablespoons heavy cream, put the sauce in a serving dish, and chill it. Brown 4 tablespoons each of dried bread or cookie crumbs, chopped almonds, and sugar in 3 tablespoons butter, stirring constantly, as the crumbs turn dark suddenly. Cool the mixture and crumble it over the applesauce just before serving.

Apples in Robes I   *Äpfel im Schlafrock 1*

INTO 2 CUPS flour, cut 1 cup butter and 1 cup cream cheese. Work this into a smooth dough with 1 egg yolk and chill it. Cut 3 large, peeled and cored apples into 3/8-inch round slices with the hole in the center. Mix 4 tablespoons sugar with 1 teaspoon cinnamon. Roll out the dough on a floured board to 3/16-inch thickness and cut it into rounds a little larger than the apple slices with a glass or large cookie cutter. Place an apple slice on each round and fill the center with the sugar and cinnamon mixture. Mix 1/4 cup raisins and 1/4 cup slivered almonds with the remaining sugar and cinnamon, and pile it on top of the apple slices. Cover each apple slice with a second, larger round of dough and press the edges down well. Bake them on a buttered cookie sheet in a moderately hot oven (375° F.) for 15 minutes. Serve with a sauce made of equal parts of softened vanilla ice cream and whipped cream.

Apples in Robes   *Äpfel im Schlafrock Hotel Schloss Dürnstein*

HOLLOW A LITTLE from the insides of 6 carefully peeled and cored apples and fill each apple with 3 tablespoons lemon or orange marmalade. Into 3 cups flour cut 2/3 cup butter, sprinkle it with 3 tablespoons water, and 1 egg beaten with 2 tablespoons sugar, and blend the mixture quickly into a smooth paste. Roll the pastry out thin, cut it into 6 squares, and wrap the apples in them, sealing the edges with beaten egg white. Paint the tops of the apples with egg white and bake on a baking sheet in a moderately hot oven (375° F.) for 40 to 45 minutes. Dust them with powdered sugar.

For the sauce, combine 1 cup butter, 1 cup sugar, 1 egg yolk, and 1/2 cup brandy. Cook the sauce over low heat, stirring it vigorously until the sugar is melted, and serve it at once. If the sauce is to be served cold, omit the egg yolk. *(Picture, page 484.)*

Apple Strudel   *Apfelstrudel*

SIFT 2 CUPS all-purpose flour onto a pastry board, make a well in the center, and in it put 1 egg well beaten in 2/3 cup lukewarm water, a dash of salt, and 1 tablespoon melted butter. Work these gradually into the flour and knead the dough until it comes away from the board clean and is silky and pliable. Shape the dough into a small loaf and let it rest on a floured board for 1 hour, covered with a warm bowl.

Cover a table that is a yard or more across with a cloth. Sprinkle it with flour. Roll out the dough as large as possible and quickly transfer it on the back of your hands to the center of the dusted cloth. This sheet of dough has to be stretched over the back of the hands until it is as large as the table. Reach under the dough with your hands, palms down, make fists of your hands, and draw them toward you, bending your wrists upward. Pull gently but steadily with the backs of your hands, working around until the evenly pulled dough covers the table, with only a narrow thicker edge hanging down. Brush the dough with 1/4 cup melted butter.

Spread over the dough 1 cup toasted bread crumbs, 6 Greening apples, peeled, cored, and thinly sliced, and 1 cup each of sultana raisins and blanched slivered almonds. Sprinkle the filling evenly with 1 1/2 cups sugar and 1 teaspoon cinnamon, and grate the rind of 1 lemon over it. Trim off the hanging edges of dough. Gently lift the cloth from one end and let the strudel roll itself up. Slide it onto a buttered baking sheet, bend it into a horseshoe, and brush it generously with 1 cup melted butter. Bake the strudel in a hot oven (400° F.) for 45 minutes to 1 hour, or until it is golden brown. Sprinkle it generously with confectioners' sugar and serve it hot. *(Pictures, pages 490 and 491.)*

Kirschenstrudel *Cherry Strudel*

SUBSTITUTE 2 POUNDS or 3 cups pitted black sweet cherries for the apples in the recipe for apple strudel.

Mürber Apfelstrudel *Apple Strudel with Short Crust*

CUT 1 CUP butter into 2 1/2 cups flour, add 1/2 cup sugar, a pinch of salt, 2 egg yolks, and 2 tablespoons each of milk and white wine. Mix the dough rapidly and chill it for 1 hour.

Roll the dough into an oblong. Place 6 apples, peeled, cored, and thinly sliced, down the middle lengthwise. Sprinkle the apples with 1/2 cup sugar, 1/4 cup each of raisins and blanched slivered almonds, the grated rind of 1 lemon, and the juice of 1/2 lemon. Fold the two sides of the dough over the filling in the center and seal the overlap with egg white. Transfer the strudel to a baking sheet, bend it into a horseshoe, and paint the top with egg white. Bake it in a hot oven (400° F.) for 1/2 hour, until it is golden. Serve it hot, generously sprinkled with sugar.

Apricots and Almonds in Cider — Marillen und Mandeln

SOAK 1 PACKAGE dried apricots overnight in enough cider to cover. Boil the apricots in the cider until they are soft and add 2 tablespoons butter and 2 tablespoons sugar. Sprinkle them with 1/2 cup blanched slivered almonds. Serve warm or cold.

Viennese Cherries — Wiener Kirschen

COOK 1 POUND pitted sweet cherries in water to cover until they are tender but not too soft. Melt 1/2 cup black currant jelly over low heat. Add 1/4 cup kirsch, mix it well, and add the cooked cherries, well drained. Shake the cherries in the sauce until they are well coated. Chill them and serve cold.

Cherries on Skewers — Kirschenspiesschen

SKEWER 1 1/2 POUNDS pitted large black cherries, putting about 8 cherries on each skewer, leaving the ends free. Stir 1 1/2 cups flour, 1/2 cup beer, 1/4 cup each of water and brandy, and 1/4 teaspoon salt with a wooden spoon until the mixture is smooth and fold in 2 egg whites beaten stiff. Dip the skewered cherries into the batter and fry them in deep hot fat (380° F.) until they are brown. Roll them immediately in 1 cup confectioners' sugar mixed with 1/4 teaspoon cinnamon until they are heavily coated. Place them on a cooky sheet under the broiler for 5 minutes to glaze the sugar. Serve at once on the skewers.

Poached Cherries — Piz Palü

PIT 1 POUND cherries and poach them in their own juice with 1/4 cup each of water and melted currant jelly. Drain the cherries well, retaining the juice, and divide them into 6 individual portions. Pour 2 tablespoons warm kirsch over each portion, and serve flaming. Add 1/4 cup slivered blanched almonds to the juice as a sauce for the cherries.

Dolce di Castagne — Chestnut Roll

COMBINE 1 CUP milk, 1/2 cup water, and 1/4 cup sugar and in it cook 2 pounds peeled chestnuts, covered, for 20 to 30 minutes, until they are tender. The nuts may be placed on a low trivet to prevent their sticking to the pan. Put the hot chestnuts through a food chopper at once.

Gradually stir into the chestnut purée a mixture of 2/3 cup cream, 1/2 cup powdered sugar, and 1/3 cup kirsch or cherry brandy. Add 1/4 cup ground blanched almonds and whip the paste. It should be very thick. The mealiness of chestnuts varies; add a little more kirsch and cream if necessary. Chill the paste and whip it again.

Spread the paste in a square 1/2 inch thick on buttered brown paper and chill thoroughly on a baking sheet in the refrigerator. Spread the paste with 2/3 cup orange marmalade and chill it again. Lift one edge of the brown paper and, with a knife, loosen the paste from the paper and roll up the sheet of paste as you would a jelly roll, smoothing it with the knife as you roll it. Smooth the finished roll and chill it. Spread the roll with marmalade and cover all except the two ends with 1/2 cup shaved blanched almonds. Arrange the *dolce* on a chilled serving platter and keep

it cold. At servingtime, pipe around the roll with a pastry tube 1 cup heavy cream whipped with 1/4 cup powdered sugar. Dot the cream with large black or brandied cherries.

The *dolce di castagne* may also be made in a loaf mold lined with buttered paper. Press a layer of chestnut paste into the mold, spread it with marmalade, add another layer of paste, spread with marmalade, and top with a final layer of paste. Pack each layer firmly and chill it before proceeding. Unmold the confection carefully, smooth it with a knife, spread it with marmalade, sprinkle with shaved blanched almonds, and garnish with whipped cream and cherries.

Fruit Maltese — *Obst Maltaise*

SEPARATE INTO sections 1 grapefruit and 2 oranges and remove the seeds, pith, and membrane. Arrange the fruit in a crystal dish, pour over it 1/4 cup maraschino, and sprinkle it with slivered orange rind and powdered sugar to taste. Chill the fruit thoroughly and serve it with a topping of 6 stale macaroons crushed and added to 1 cup sweetened whipped cream.

Peaches Stuffed with Almonds — *Pfirsiche mit Mandeln*

COMBINE 1/2 CUP confectioners' sugar, 1/2 cup blanched almonds, ground to a thick paste, and 1/4 cup dark rum. Peel, halve, and stone 6 peaches. Fill the cavities with the almond paste and re-form the halves into whole peaches. Melt 1/2 cup butter in a baking dish, add the peaches, and sprinkle them with 1/2 cup vanilla sugar. Bake the peaches, covered, in a moderate oven (350° F.) for 15 minutes, or until they are soft. Serve them hot or cold, with sour cream flavored to taste with sugar and rum.

Peaches Meringue — *Pfirsichmeringue*

POACH 4 PEELED, halved, and stoned peaches in 1 cup wine until they are just soft. Arrange the peaches in a shallow ovenproof dish and pour the wine over them. Beat 2 egg whites with 1/2 cup confectioners' sugar until they are stiff. Cover the peaches with the meringue and bake it in a slow oven (300° F.) until it is golden. Serve immediately.

Birnen Alma

Pears in Port

HEAT 1 CUP Port wine, 1/2 cup freshly squeezed orange juice, and the grated rind of 1 orange in a saucepan over low heat. Add 4 fine large pears, peeled, cored, and halved lengthwise. Poach them gently in the wine sauce until they are medium soft. Remove the pears from the heat, arrange them in a serving bowl, pour the sauce over them, and chill.

Zwetschkenknödel

Plum Dumplings

RICE 6 HOT boiled potatoes onto a pastry board and add 2 cups flour sifted with 1/4 teaspoon salt. Make a well in the center, add 1 egg, and work the ingredients into a soft, light dough. Roll out the dough 1/4 inch thick, cut it into 2 1/2-inch squares, and fold each square around a small blue German plum, smoothing each into a perfect round. Simmer the dumplings in salted water for 15 minutes. Remove them with a slotted spoon and serve with buttered Holland rusk crumbs, browned butter, and a sprinkling of sugar.

Marillenknödel

Apricot Dumplings

PIT APRICOTS and replace the pits with lumps of sugar. Substitute the stuffed apricots for plums in the recipe for plum dumplings.

Kirschenknödel

Cherry Dumplings

SUBSTITUTE 3 BLACK cherries for each plum in the recipe for plum dumplings.

Mirabellenkompott

Plum Compote

WIPE 12 LARGE or 24 smaller greengage plums, halve them, and remove the stones. Crack the stones and add the skinned kernel to the plums. Add water to cover, about 2 cups, and sugar, about 1/2 cup, depending on the sweetness of the fruit. Simmer the plums gently over low heat for 10 to 15 minutes, until they are soft. Remove them from the syrup, let them cool, and chill them.

Add the juice of 1/2 lemon to the cooking syrup. Reduce the syrup slightly, add the slivered rind of 1 lemon, an equal amount of slivered grapefruit rind, 1 tablespoon crème de menthe, a drop of green vegetable color, and sugar to taste. Chill the syrup, pour it over the plums, and garnish the dish with a ring of chilled lingonberries or cooked cranberries. Serves 12.

Port Wine Prune Whip   *Pflaumen mit Portwein*

SOAK 1 1/4 CUPS dried prunes in water for 12 hours. Add 3/4 cup sugar and cook the prunes until they are tender. Drain them, add 1 cup Port and cook them for 10 minutes more. Remove the stones and purée the prunes in a blender or food processor. Add sugar and Port to taste and fold in 1/2 cup cream, whipped stiff. Serve the prune whip topped with 1/2 cup cream, whipped, sweetened with 3 tablespoons confectioners' sugar, or to taste. Sprinkle over the whipped cream 1/4 cup toasted slivered almonds.

Strawberry Pineapple Compote   *Erdbeerananas*

WASH AND hull 1 quart ripe strawberries. Retain 6 large strawberries for garnishing and press the rest through a fine sieve twice, to make 1 cup strawberry purée. Peel, core, and slice thinly 1 fresh ripe pineapple. Arrange the slices on a chilled serving platter. Add 1/4 cup kirsch to the strawberry purée and pour it over the pineapple. Garnish each serving with one whole strawberry. Serve chilled.

Strawberry Omelet   *Erdbeer Omelett*

WASH AND HULL 1 pint strawberries. Cut them in half, sugar them lightly, and set them aside for 15 minutes. Beat 4 egg whites stiff, gradually adding 4 tablespoons sugar. Beat 3 egg yolks with 3 tablespoons sugar until creamy and combine the mixtures. Melt 1 1/2 tablespoons butter in a frying or omelet pan, add the egg mixture, and let it brown, half covered, for 10 minutes. Slip the omelet onto a hot platter, add the strawberries, fold it over, and serve it sprinkled with confectioners' sugar.

Erdbeermeringue　　　*Strawberries Meringue*

ARRANGE 1 QUART large ripe strawberries, washed and hulled, in the bottom of a shallow ovenware dish. Sprinkle them with 1/4 cup Curaçao. Pipe a border of meringue made by beating 2 egg whites stiff with 1/4 cup confectioners' sugar. Bake the meringue in a hot oven (400° F.) until it is brown. Serve at once.

Schokoladekoch　　　*Chocolate Soufflé*

BEAT 6 EGG yolks with 3/4 cup sugar until they are light. Add 1/2 cup cake flour gradually and stir until it is smooth. Add gradually 1 cup milk and cook in the top of a double boiler over hot water, stirring constantly, for 5 minutes. Add 5 ounces grated semisweet chocolate and stir until it thickens. Remove the mixture from the heat and cool it. Add 2 teaspoons vanilla and fold in 8 egg whites, stiffly beaten. Bake the soufflé in a buttered and sugared ovenware dish in a moderately hot oven (375° F.) for 50 to 60 minutes, or until it is puffed. Serve with a sauce made by folding 1 cup heavy cream, whipped, into 1 pint softened vanilla ice cream.

Haselnussauflauf　　　*Hazelnut Soufflé*

BEAT 5 EGG yolks with 1/4 cup sugar until they are light. Add 1/4 cup flour and a pinch of salt, stirring well. Gradually beat in 1 cup hot scalded milk, and cook the mixture in the top of a double boiler over hot water, stirring constantly, until it thickens and coats the spoon. Remove it from the heat and cool it. Add 1 cup hazelnuts, grated and browned in 3 tablespoons butter, and 1 tablespoon rum. Fold in 6 egg whites beaten stiff. Bake it in an ungreased baking dish set in a pan of hot water in a moderately hot oven (375° F.) for 45 minutes, or until the soufflé is puffed and golden.

Beat 1 cup softened coffee ice cream with 1 tablespoon heavy rum. Fold in 1/2 cup heavy cream, whipped and sweetened to taste. Serve the sauce with the soufflé.

Lemon Soufflé

MELT 2 TABLESPOONS butter, blend it well with 2 tablespoons flour, and add 1/2 cup sugar, 1/3 cup each of cream and lemon juice, 2 table-spoons grated lemon rind, and 1 pinch salt. Cook, stirring constantly, until the mixture is smooth and thick, about 6 minutes. Take it from the heat, stir in 5 lightly beaten egg yolks, and cook the mixture for a minute, but do not let it boil. Let it cool. Fold in 5 egg whites, beaten stiff. Bake the soufflé in a moderate oven (350° F.) in an unbuttered baking dish set in a pan of hot water for 40 minutes, or until it is puffed and golden.

Cointreau Soufflé with Oranges
Orangenauflauf

MELT 4 TABLESPOONS butter, blend it well with 4 tablespoons flour, and cook the mixture for a few minutes, stirring constantly, until it starts to turn golden. Gradually stir in 1 cup scalded light cream and 1/3 cup sugar and cook it for about 5 minutes. Remove it from the heat and gradually beat in 4 egg yolks. Add 6 tablespoons Cointreau, cool, and fold in

515

6 egg whites, stiffly beaten. Cover the bottom of a generously buttered and sugared soufflé dish with orange sections marinated in Grand Marnier. Pour the batter over the oranges, set the dish in a pan of hot water, and bake the soufflé in a moderately hot oven (375° F.) for 45 minutes, or until it is puffed and golden. Serve at once.

Schneenockerln   Nockerln with Vanilla Cream Sauce

BEAT 6 EGG whites until they form soft peaks. Add gradually 1 cup sugar, continuing to beat until it makes a stiff meringue. Divide into 6 equal portions. Bring 3 cups milk to a boil with 1 teaspoon vanilla and drop the *Nockerln* into it. Simmer them, covered, for 4 minutes, turn them, and continue cooking them, uncovered, for about 2 minutes longer. Lift them from the milk with a slotted spoon and lay them on a cloth to drain. Stir 3/4 cup sugar into 3 egg yolks, add the simmering milk, and whisk the mixture into a thick creamy sauce over low heat. Add more vanilla to taste and chill the sauce. Arrange the *Nockerln* on a glass dish or on individual dessert plates and pour the vanilla cream sauce over them. Serve cold.

Salzburger Nockerln Hotel Goldener Hirsch   Salzburger Nockerln

WARM SLIGHTLY a 12-inch gratin dish and brush it lightly with butter. Beat 5 egg whites until almost stiff, gradually add 3 tablespoons sugar, and beat until stiff. Sprinkle 1 tablespoon flour over the whites and fold it in gently. Beat 3 egg yolks with the grated rind of 1 lemon and fold the mixture gently but thoroughly into the whites. Quickly divide the mixture into 4 large portions and arrange the portions in the buttered dish, smoothing the sides with the back of a spoon and shaping the *Nockerln* into the highest possible peaks. Bake the *Nockerln* in a moderately hot oven (395° F.) for 15 minutes, or until they are lightly golden. Sprinkle the tops with powdered sugar. *(Picture, page 489.)*

Egg Puffs with Cream · Grinzinger Omeletten

IN THE TOP of a double boiler, beat 4 egg yolks lightly with a fork and add 2 tablespoons sugar and 1 tablespoon flour. Put the pan over simmering water and gradually add 1/2 cup milk, stirring constantly. Cook the custard, stirring, until it thickens. Add 1/2 teaspoon vanilla extract and let it cool. Beat 4 egg whites stiff with 1/2 teaspoon salt and fold them a little at a time into the custard. Pour the mixture into 3 buttered pans 6 inches in diameter and bake the "puffs" in a moderate oven (350° F.) for about 20 minutes, or until they are puffed and a light golden brown. Cover each "puff" with apricot jam or currant jelly and top with 1/2 cup whipped cream flavored lightly with vanilla extract.

Emperor's Omelet · Kaiserschmarrn

SOAK 2/3 CUP raisins in 2 ounces brandy. Stir 6 tablespoons sugar into 6 egg yolks. Add 1 cup heavy cream, stirring constantly, and gradually add 1 1/2 cups flour, stirring until the batter is smooth. Fold in 6 stiffly beaten egg whites. Pour the mixture into a wide buttered pan and bake in a moderately hot oven (375° F.) about 30 minutes, until golden. Tear the omelet into large chunks with two forks, add 1/2 cup butter, the raisins, and 1/3 cup sugar to the pan, and sauté the chunks on top of the stove, turning them, until they are coated with butter and sugar. Sprinkle with confectioners' sugar and serve with plum sauce. *(Picture, page 487.)*

German Pancake · Deutscher Pfannkuchen

BEAT 3 EGGS with 3 tablespoons flour, 1 tablespoon sugar, and 6 tablespoons milk. Pour the batter into a large generously buttered skillet and bake it in a hot oven (425° F.) for 8 minutes. Reduce the heat to moder-

ately hot (375° F.) and bake it for 8 minutes longer, or until the pancake puffs up above the sides of the pan and turns a delicate brown.
Place the pancake on a platter, sprinkle it with the juice of 1/2 lemon,
3 tablespoons sugar, 1/4 teaspoon cinnamon, and 1/4 cup melted butter.
Roll the pancake and dust it with powdered sugar. Serve at once, with
applesauce, if desired.

Palatschinken   *Rolled Pancakes with Jam*

STIR 1 TABLESPOON brandy into 1 cup apricot or strawberry jam.

Sift into a bowl 1 cup flour with a pinch of salt. Stir in 2 tablespoons
sugar and, gradually, 1 cup milk, to make a smooth batter. Add 2 eggs
and stir until the batter is again smooth.

Heat a 9-inch skillet and pour in just enough melted butter to cover
the whole surface when the pan is tilted. Pour in enough batter to cover
the pan thinly but completely. Cook the *Palatschinke* over medium heat
until the underside is lightly browned and the pancake is firm. Turn the
pancake with a spatula or wide knife and brown it lightly on the other
side. Transfer the first *Palatschinke* to a warm plate, butter the pan again
and pour in the batter for the second *Palatschinke*. While it is browning,
spread the entire surface of the first *Palatschinke* with a thin coating of the
apricot or strawberry jam. Roll it up neatly, place it on an ovenproof or
silver platter, and keep it hot in a slow oven (250° F.). Repeat this procedure until all the batter is used, laying the *Palatschinken* side by side or
stacking them like logs. Dust the finished *Palatschinken* generously with
vanilla sugar.

Erdbeerpalatschinken   *Strawberry Pancakes*

MAKE 18 SMALL dessert pancakes, *Palatschinken,* and saturate them with
orange Curaçao. Fold them and arrange them in 6 groups of 3 each, on
a serving platter. Pour over them 1 1/2 cups cooked and well-drained
strawberries. Sprinkle them with 1/4 cup each of finely chopped toasted
almonds and chopped nougat. Sweeten whipped cream and press it into
rosettes through a pastry bag fitted with a rose tube. Freeze the rosettes
for at least 1 hour. Garnish each serving of the strawberry pancakes with
a rosette and serve them at once.

Cottage Cheese Pancakes　　　　　　　　*Topfenpalatschinken*

CREAM 1/2 cup butter. Add 3/4 cup sugar, 1/4 teaspoon salt, 1 teaspoon vanilla, and the grated rind of 1 lemon. Add 3 egg yolks, one at a time, stirring the mixture well. Add 1 1/2 cups well-drained cottage cheese and 3/4 cup each of raisins and sour cream.

Stir 1 1/2 cups milk with 1 cup water, 1 1/2 cups flour, and 1/4 teaspoon salt until the batter is smooth. Add 2 eggs and 1 egg yolk and beat it until it is smooth. In an omelet pan heat just enough butter to cover the surface. Pour in enough batter to make a large thin pancake. Cook it over medium heat, turning it once, until it is lightly browned on both sides. Keep the pancakes hot in the oven as they are cooked. There should be about 12.

Spread them quickly with the cheese mixture, roll them up, and lay them next to each other in an ovenware serving pan. Pour over them a mixture of 3 cups milk well beaten with 2/3 cup sugar and 2 whole eggs. Bake them in a moderate oven (350° F.) until they are lightly browned, about 25 minutes. Serve at once.

Beignets Soufflés　　　　　　　　　　　*Brandkrapfen*

BRING TO a boil 1 cup milk, 1/2 cup butter, 3 tablespoons sugar and 1/4 teaspoon salt. Add 1 cup flour and stir the mixture with a wooden spoon until the flour is incorporated and the paste leaves the sides of the pan. Remove the paste from the heat, add 1 teaspoon grated lemon rind, and let it rest a few minutes. Beat in, one after another, 4 eggs, incorporating each thoroughly before the next is added. With 2 spoons, form 1 1/2-inch balls and fry a few at a time in deep hot fat (375° F.) until they are delicately brown. The *Krapfen* will turn of their own accord if there is enough room in the fryer. Drain the *Krapfen* well and sprinkle them with vanilla sugar. Serve them at once, without sauce or with whipped cream or vanilla ice cream sauce II.

Snowballs　　　　　　　　　　　　　*Schneeballen*

CUT 1/2 cup butter into 2 2/3 cups flour until the mixture is fine. Make a well in the center and drop in 1 egg beaten with 4 egg yolks, 1/2 cup white wine, and a pinch of salt. Work the ingredients quickly into a smooth dough and let it rest in a cool place for 1 hour. Roll out the dough 1/8 inch thick, or less, if possible, and cut it into rectangles 4 by 5 inches. With a pastry wheel make 6 parallel cuts through the dough lengthwise, to within about 1/2 inch of the left and right edges. Weave the handle of a wooden spoon through the cuts and lift it, to open out the strips. Bunch the rectangle loosely into a ball and arrange it in two tea strainers wired together to make a frying basket. The "snowballs" should be large. Fry them in deep hot fat (370° F.) until they are golden. Drain them on absorbent paper, sprinkle them with vanilla sugar, and let them cool. Serve them cold, with raspberry sauce or wine sauce.

Goldnudeln Karneval   *Golden Noodle Nest*

MIX TO a smooth paste 4 cups flour, 1/4 cup milk, 8 egg yolks, 2 whole eggs, 1/2 teaspoon vanilla, and a pinch of salt. If the eggs are small, it may be necessary to add a little more milk. Divide the dough in half and roll it out very thin. Let the two pieces dry for 15 minutes. Cut one piece into "noodles" 8 inches long and 1/4 inch wide. Cut the other piece into "noodles" 8 inches long and 1/8 inch wide. Boil the wider strips in salted water for 15 to 20 minutes and drain them well. Fry the thinner strips in deep hot fat (375° F.) for about 10 minutes, or until they are golden, and drain them well. Shake the boiled strips with 3 tablespoons butter, arrange a layer of them on a serving platter, and sprinkle them with sugar and hazelnuts, chopped and browned with butter in a very slow oven (250° F.). Arrange a layer of fried strips on the nuts and sprinkle them with more sugar and nuts. Repeat the layers, to form a mound, until all the strips are used, sprinkling each layer with additional sugar and nuts. Use about 3/4 cup each of sugar and nuts.

In the top of a double boiler, over gently boiling water, beat together 1/2 cup each of white wine and sugar, 3 egg yolks, and a squeeze of lemon juice until the sauce has risen and is pale and foamy, about 5 minutes with an electric beater. Pour the sauce over the strips on the serving platter and serve at once.

Almond Pudding   *Mandelpudding*

CREAM 1 CUP butter until it is light and fluffy and gradually work in 6 egg yolks, 1 cup almonds, blanched and ground, 3/4 cup sugar, and the grated rind of 1 lemon. Fold in 6 stiffly beaten egg whites and pour the mixture into a buttered pudding mold. Steam it, covered, for 1 hour in boiling water, adding more water as necessary. Unmold the pudding.

Combine 1 cup vanilla ice cream and 4 tablespoons dark rum and fold in 1 cup heavy cream, whipped stiff. Chill the sauce and serve it separately.

Apple and Almond Pudding   *Apfelspeise*

LINE A BUTTERED baking dish with 1/3 cup crushed macaroons. Cover this in turn with 2 apples, thinly sliced, 1/2 cup buttered bread crumbs, 1/4 cup each of raisins and slivered almonds, 1/3 cup sugar, 1/2 teaspoon cinnamon, the grated rind of 1/2 lemon, and 1/3 cup melted butter. Repeat the process, starting with the macaroons, and cover all with a final 1/3 cup crushed macaroons and 1/3 cup melted butter. Bake the pudding in a moderate oven (350° F.) for 30 minutes or until it is golden brown. Serve warm, with melted vanilla ice cream sauce I.

Apple Rice Pudding   *Apfel Reispudding*

PLACE 1 1/4 CUPS rice in a saucepan with just enough cold water to cover. Bring it to a boil and boil it for 5 minutes. Pour the rice into a strainer and rinse it with cold water. Return the rice to the saucepan with 3 cups milk and 1/4 teaspoon salt and cook it until almost all the milk is absorbed. Let the rice cool.

Lay 6 tart cooking apples, peeled, cored, and sliced, in the bottom of a large buttered baking dish and sprinkle them with 3 tablespoons sugar, 1 teaspoon cinnamon, the grated rind of 1 lemon, and a pinch of powdered cloves.

Cream 2 tablespoons butter with 2 tablespoons sugar and gradually stir in the cold rice and 5 egg yolks. Add more cinnamon and sugar to taste, and the finely chopped rind of 1 lemon. Fold in the egg whites, stiffly beaten, and pile the rice mixture over the apples in the dish. Sprinkle it with 1/4 cup sugar and 1/4 cup slivered almonds and bake it for 1 hour in a moderately hot oven (375° F.).

Apfel Adele   Apple Pudding with Hazelnuts

SOAK 8 SLICES of white bread, free of crusts, in 1 cup light cream. Cream 2/3 cup butter and stir in 3 egg yolks and 1/3 cup sugar. Combine the soaked bread with the egg yolks and stir them well with 1 cup ground hazelnuts, 1/4 cup heavy cream, and the grated rind of 1/2 lemon. Fold in 3 egg whites beaten stiff with 1/3 cup sugar. Pour half of the mixture into a buttered soufflé dish. Cover it with an overlapping layer of 1 pound apples, peeled, cored, and sliced, and dust the apples with 1/4 cup sugar mixed with 1 teaspoon cinnamon. Pour the remaining batter over the apples. Bake the pudding in a moderately hot oven (375° F.) for 40 minutes. Serve with fresh raspberry sauce.

Arme Ritter   Poor Knights

CUT 6 SLICES of stale bread into large rounds and sauté them in 4 tablespoons butter until both sides are golden. Dust them with a mixture of 4 tablespoons sugar and 1/4 teaspoon cinnamon. Spread a thin layer of apricot marmalade on each slice and sprinkle them with 1/2 cup roughly ground walnuts. Bake the rounds in a moderate oven (350° F.) for 5 minutes. Serve hot.

Götterpudding   Ambrosial Pudding

BEAT 8 EGG yolks with 3/4 cup sugar until they are light and foamy and stir in 3/4 cup ground unblanched almonds and 1/3 cup grated bittersweet chocolate. Fold in 8 stiffly beaten egg whites. Make 1 cup coarse bread crumbs, free of crusts, from a day-old loaf of pumpernickel. Toast the crumbs slowly with 1/4 cup butter in a very slow oven (225° F.) until they are crisp and dry. Carefully fold the crumbs into the pudding mixture, pour it into a well-buttered mold, and cover the mold. Steam the pudding for 3/4 hour in a covered kettle in boiling water that comes halfway up the sides of the mold. Add more boiling water to the kettle, if necessary, to maintain this depth. Unmold the pudding and serve it with sweetened cream whipped only until it thickens and flavored with rum or vanilla extract.

Hungarian Pudding — *Ungarischer Pudding*

ADD 7 TABLESPOONS butter and 1 teaspoon salt to 1 cup simmering milk. Reduce the heat. When the butter melts, add a scant 3/4 cup flour all at once and stir briskly until the paste leaves the sides of the pan and forms a ball. Remove the pan from the heat and beat in 3 tablespoons sugar. Cool the mixture slightly and beat in 4 egg yolks, one at a time, beating briskly after each addition. Add the grated rind of 1 lemon and cool the mixture. Fold in 4 stiffly beaten egg whites and pour the batter into a well-buttered and floured mold. Set the mold in a pan of hot water and bake the pudding in a moderate oven (350° F.) for 1 hour. Unmold it immediately and serve at once, with raspberry sauce and raspberries.

Chestnut Pudding — *Karnevalpudding*

CUT CROSSES on the flat sides of 1 pound chestnuts and heat the nuts in a moderate oven (350° F.) for 8 to 10 minutes, or until the edges of the

shells have rolled back and are brittle. Peel the nuts and boil them with 1/2 cup sugar in water to cover until they are soft, about 20 minutes. Pull off any remaining inner shells and rice the chestnuts, setting aside 1/2 cup riced chestnuts for later use. Stir into the chestnuts 6 tablespoons butter, 1/2 cup sugar, 4 egg yolks, and 2 tablespoons cocoa. Add 1/3 cup flour and fold in 4 stiffly beaten egg whites. Pour the mixture into a well-buttered pudding mold, cover the mold, and steam it in a covered kettle of boiling water for 3/4 hour. The water should reach halfway up the mold. Unmold the pudding and pour over it a mixture of 1/2 cup apricot jam heated with 1/2 cup dark rum. Sprinkle the reserved 1/2 cup riced chestnuts over the pudding.

Mohr-im-Hemd   *Moor in a Shirt*

IN A LARGE bowl, cream 2/3 cup butter. Soak 8 slices of rich white bread in 3/4 cup heavy cream. Add them to the butter, stir well or use an electric beater. Add 9 eggs and 4 egg yolks, 3/4 cup blanched almonds, ground, 3/4 cup sugar, and 4 ounces bittersweet chocolate, melted over hot water. Beat the mixture well, adding more sugar if a sweet pudding is preferred. Pour the mixture into a well-buttered 2-quart mold, using a tall one, if possible. Cover or seal the mold and place it in a kettle of boiling water. The water should come halfway up the mold. Steam the pudding for 1 1/2 hours, adding more boiling water to the kettle if necessary. Whip 2 cups heavy cream stiff with 1/2 cup confectioners' sugar. Unmold the pudding on a serving platter and surround it with swirls of whipped cream. Serve at once. Serves 12.

Reismeringue   *Rice Dessert with Meringue*

COOK 1 CUP washed rice in a double boiler with 2 cups hot water and 1/2 teaspoon salt for 30 minutes without removing the cover.

In a saucepan mix 3/4 cup sugar with 2 tablespoons softened butter. Heat it slowly, stirring constantly until it is lightly browned. Add the juice of 1 lemon and 1 orange and 4 tablespoons light rum. Cook, stirring, until the mixture becomes a well-blended syrup. Carefully fold in the cooked rice, mixing it lightly with a fork until the rice grains are coated with the syrup. Cover the bottom of a buttered baking dish with a 1 1/2-inch layer of the rice mixture and follow with a 1/4-inch layer of apricot jam. Using the remaining rice mixture and 1 cup apricot jam, make alternate layers, ending with a layer of rice. Whip 3 egg whites until they are stiff and fold in 3 tablespoons sugar, 1/2 teaspoon vanilla extract, and 1/4 teaspoon salt. Swirl the meringue over the rice in peaks, and bake it in a moderate oven (350° F.) until it is a light golden brown.

Rice Trautmannsdorf with Strawberries   *Reis Trautmannsdorf*

PUT 1 1/2 CUPS rice in a saucepan, cover it well with water, bring it to a boil and cook for 5 minutes. Drain the rice thoroughly and combine it with 2 cups hot milk in the top of a double boiler. Add a pinch of salt and 1/2 teaspoon vanilla and cook it over boiling water for 30 minutes, stirring occasionally. Dissolve in the hot rice 1 envelope of gelatin softened in 1/4 cup milk. Add 1/2 cup sugar and 1 tablespoon maraschino, and cool the rice. Before it begins to set, fold in 1 1/2 cups heavy cream, whipped. Pour it into a tiered mold rinsed in cold water and chill it for 2 hours. Unmold the rice on a chilled platter. Garnish the mold with perfect whole strawberries. Serve whipped cream and crushed strawberries separately.

The rice may also be served with raspberries.

Hazelnut Cream   *Mecklenburger Haselnusscreme*

BEAT 8 EGG yolks with 1 cup sugar until they are light and creamy. Place them in a double boiler over boiling water and gradually stir in 2 cups milk. Cook the mixture until it starts to thicken. Remove it from the heat and stir in 1 teaspoon vanilla and 1/2 teaspoon rum. Soften 3 tablespoons gelatin in 1/4 cup milk and stir it into the hot custard mixture until the gelatin is dissolved. Cool the mixture and chill until it begins to set. Stir in 1 cup toasted chopped hazelnuts and fold in 2 cups heavy cream, whipped. Pour the mixture into an oiled mold and chill it thoroughly for at least 2 hours. Unmold the cream on a silver platter. Pipe whipped cream rosettes around it and set 1 toasted hazelnut in each.

Schokolademus   *Chocolate Mousse*

BEAT 6 EGG yolks with 1/2 cup sugar until they are light and thick. Add 10 ounces melted semisweet chocolate and 1/2 teaspoon each of vanilla and rum and continue to beat the mixture until it is smooth. Add 3/4 cup softened butter, a little at a time, and fold in 6 stiffly beaten egg whites. Add 1/2 cup chopped walnuts. Pour the mixture into an oiled mold and chill it for at least 6 hours. Serve with whipped cream.

Kaffeecreme   *Coffee Mousse*

SOFTEN 2 ENVELOPES of gelatin in 1/2 cup cold water. Combine 1 cup confectioners' sugar, 1 cup milk, and 4 teaspoons coffee essence and cook the mixture over boiling water until it is hot. Add the gelatin and cook it, stirring, until it is dissolved. Cool it, stirring from time to time to prevent a crust from forming. When it is cold, add 1 tablespoon rum and beat it until it is light. Fold in 2 egg whites, beaten stiff, and 2 cups heavy cream, whipped until it stands in soft moist peaks. Pour the mousse into an oiled mold and chill it thoroughly for at least 2 hours. Unmold it on a large serving platter. Serve with almond sauce.

Mokkamus   *Mocha Mousse*

BEAT 2 EGG yolks until they are light and very pale. Combine 1 1/2 cups sugar and 1 cup strong coffee. Cook the syrup rapidly until it makes a soft ball (250° F. on the candy thermometer). Remove the syrup from the heat and immediately stir it into the yolks. Add 1/4 cup heavy cream and 2 teaspoons coffee essence and beat the mixture until it is cold. Fold in 2 egg whites, beaten stiff, and 2 cups heavy cream, whipped. Pour the mousse into a mold rinsed in cold water and chill it for 2 hours. Dust it with praline powder and serve with hot brandied peaches.

Pfirsiche mit Kaffeecreme   *Peaches with Coffee Cream*

SOFTEN 1 ENVELOPE of gelatin in 1/2 cup water. In the top of a double boiler, over boiling water, heat 1 cup milk with 1 1/4 cups confectioners' sugar and 2 tablespoons triple-strength coffee. Add the gelatin and stir until it is dissolved. Cool the mixture and add 1 tablespoon dark rum. Before it starts to set, fold in 2 egg whites, beaten stiff. Fold in 2 cups heavy cream, whipped until stiff with 1/4 cup sugar. Pour the cream into an oiled ring mold and chill it for at least 3 hours. Invert it onto a serving platter and fill the center of the ring with peaches, peeled, sliced, and sprinkled with rum. Serve with whipped cream.

Cheese Cream

BEAT TOGETHER two 8-ounce packages cream cheese and 1 cup heavy cream until the mixture is light and frothy. Beat in, one at a time, 4 egg yolks. Add 1 teaspoon vanilla and confectioners' sugar to taste and fold in 4 stiffly beaten egg whites. Press the cream into a mold rinsed in cold water. Freeze it for 2 hours. Unmold it and surround it with fresh raspberries or wood strawberries.

Raspberry Mousse *Himbeermus*

COOK 1 CUP milk in the top of a double boiler with 4 lightly beaten egg yolks and 3 tablespoons sugar, stirring, until the custard coats a spoon. Take it from the heat and beat in 1 tablespoon maraschino and 1/2 teaspoon vanilla. Chill the mixture and add it to 2 cups raspberries, crushed. Fold in 2 cups heavy cream, whipped, and 4 egg whites, beaten so stiff that they do not move when the bowl is inverted. Chill the mousse in a serving dish or in an oiled mold for at least 4 hours, and serve it with raspberry sauce.

Strawberry Mousse

WASH AND hull 1 quart strawberries. Reserve a few perfect berries and purée the rest of the berries. Add 1/2 cup sugar and the juice of 1/2 lemon or 1/2 cup white wine, stir the mixture, and chill it. Soften 2 envelopes of gelatin in enough water to cover and dissolve it in 1/2 cup boiling water, off the heat. Cool the gelatin mixture and beat it with the strawberries until it is light. Fold in 2 cups heavy cream, whipped stiff, and pour the mousse into an oiled mold. Chill it for at least 2 hours. Unmold it onto a chilled platter and garnish it with the remaining strawberries.

Reicher Mann   *Rich Man*

SOAK 8 MACAROONS in 1/4 cup brandy and chill them. Cream 1/2 cup butter with 1/2 cup confectioners' sugar and add 1/4 cup each of toasted ground almonds and Sherry, 2 hard-cooked egg yolks, and 2 egg yolks. Add 1/4 cup *crème fraîche* and blend until smooth and thick. Put the soaked macaroons in a chilled crystal bowl and pour the blended mixture over them. Top with 1/2 cup heavy cream, whipped, and decorate it with slivered toasted almonds. Chill the dessert.

Wiener Götterspeise   *Food of the Gods*

COMBINE 1 CUP macaroon crumbs with 2 tablespoons rum beaten with 1 egg yolk and 2 tablespoons sugar. Fold the mixture into 1 cup heavy cream, whipped stiff, and pour it into a rinsed mold. Place the mold in the freezing compartment of the refrigerator for 2 hours. Wash and hull 1 quart strawberries, dip them in rum, and roll them in confectioners' sugar. Unmold the cream and surround it with the strawberries.

Black Bread Crumbs with Cherries   *Götterfreude*

REMOVE THE crust from 1 loaf of four-day-old pumpernickel and crush it, making 3 cups of fine crumbs. Combine 1/4 cup maraschino, 1/4 cup cherry jam, and 2 tablespoons kirsch with the crumbs. Place a 3/4-inch layer of the mixture on the bottom of a serving dish, and pipe a layer of whipped cream over it. Continue with alternating layers of the crumb mixture and whipped cream, piping the whipped cream in swirls on the top layer. Arrange 3/4 cup drained and pitted sweet black cherries over the cream. Serve thoroughly chilled.

Pineapple Bombe   *Eisbombe Romanoff*

TO 2 QUARTS vanilla mousse add 1/2 cup each of chopped *marrons glacés,* drained, crushed stale macaroons, and chopped green pistachio nuts. Line a chilled 2 1/2-quart *bombe* mold with a thick layer of the mixture, spreading it with a spatula as evenly as possible, and chill the mold again. To the remaining mixture add 1 cup finely diced fresh pineapple that has been saturated with kirsch and fill it into the center of the mold. Cover the mousse with buttered wax paper, adjust the cover of the mold, and bury the *bombe* in ice or freeze it for 2 to 3 hours. Dip the *bombe* in hot water and unmold it. Serve it with apricot sauce made by heating 1 cup thick apricot marmalade in the top of a double boiler and flavoring it with kirsch to taste.

Vanilla Mousse   *Vanillemus*

DISSOLVE 1 1/2 CUPS sugar in 1 cup water and cook the syrup rapidly for 5 minutes. Cool it. Beat 8 egg yolks in the top of a double boiler and whip in the syrup gradually. Add some fine seeds from a vanilla bean and cook the custard over hot, but not boiling, water, stirring constantly, until it becomes thick and creamy. Replace the hot water in the double boiler with ice cubes and beat the custard until it is cold. Add 1 teaspoon vanilla and fold 3 cups heavy cream, whipped until stiff, into the cold custard. Fill a mold with the mixture. Cover the mousse with buttered wax paper, adjust the cover of the mold, and bury the mold in ice or freeze it in the refrigerator for 2 or 3 hours. Unmold the mousse and garnish it lavishly with whole fresh raspberries. Serve it with *Rosa Törtchen,* pink cakes.

Orangenchaudeau   *Orange Sabayon*

PLACE 3 EGG yolks, 1/3 cup each of orange juice and Cointreau or Curaçao, and 3 tablespoons sugar in the top of a double boiler. Beat or whisk the mixture over simmering but not boiling water until it is light and rises in a froth to 3 times its bulk. Serve at once in stemmed glasses with a dusting of grated orange rind.

Weinchaudeau   *Wine Sabayon*

IN THE top of a 1 1/2-quart double boiler, combine 4 egg yolks, 1/3 cup granulated sugar, and 1 cup Chablis or Moselle. Have ready near the stove 6 large Champagne or punch glasses and a ladle, for *chaudeau* rises suddenly. Place the top of the double boiler over gently boiling water and beat the mixture steadily with a rotary beater until it becomes light and creamy and rises to the top of the pan. Stop beating long enough to ladle off a glassful and continue to beat and ladle off the *chaudeau* until all the glasses are filled. Serve the *chaudeau* at once.

Kirschencreme   *Kirsch Cream with Cherries*

POUR 1/2 CUP kirsch over 1 pound stoned cherries and marinate them for at least 2 hours, stirring at intervals. Beat 4 egg yolks with 1/2 cup granulated sugar until they are light and creamy. Heat, but do not boil, 1 cup light cream with 1/2 teaspoon vanilla and pour it over the egg yolks and sugar. Cook the mixture in the top of a double boiler over gently boiling water until it coats a spoon. Let it cool and chill it thoroughly. After 1 hour, add 1/4 cup kirsch and fold in 1 cup whipped cream. Chill the cream in the refrigerator, stirring it frequently until it is needed. Serve it in chilled glasses with the cherries and their marinade poured over.

Süsse Saucen
Dessert Sauces

Almond Cream Sauce
Mandelcreme

GRIND 1 CUP blanched almonds until they are very fine. Pound them in a mortar with 1/2 cup superfine sugar. Add 1/4 teaspoon each of almond extract and grated orange rind and continue to pound until all the ingredients are well blended. Transfer the mixture to a saucepan and add 2 egg yolks beaten with 1 cup heavy cream. Cook the mixture, beating constantly, over low heat until it is frothy. Do not allow it to boil. Serve at once. Add more cream for a thinner sauce.

Apple Wine Sauce
Apfel Weinschaum

IN THE TOP of a double boiler, beat 4 eggs with 1/2 cup sugar until they are light and creamy. Add 1 cup apple cider or sweet apple wine, 3 tablespoons flour, and 2 tablespoons lemon juice and beat the mixture over simmering water until it is light and has doubled in volume. Take the sauce from the heat and beat it until it is cold. Serve at once.

Spiced Cherry Sauce
Kirschensauce

COMBINE 3 CUPS pitted black Bing cherries and their juice with 1 1/2 cups sugar, 1/3 cup vinegar, and 1/2 teaspoon each of cinnamon, ground cloves, ground ginger, and allspice. Simmer the sauce for 25 minutes. Serve it hot, over vanilla pudding.

Mocha Sauce I
Mokkasauce 1

BOIL 1 CUP strong black coffee with 1 cup sugar for 5 minutes. Remove it from the heat and stir in 4 ounces melted sweet chocolate and 2 tablespoons butter. Beat the sauce until it is smooth. Add 1 teaspoon each of vanilla, rum, and finely chopped candied orange rind, and a pinch of salt. Beat in additional sugar to taste. The orange rind may be omitted.

Mokkasauce 2 *Mocha Sauce II*

MELT 2 OUNCES bitter chocolate in 1 cup strong coffee and add sugar to taste. Chill the syrup. Fold in 1 cup heavy cream, whipped stiff, and add 1/2 cup crushed walnuts. Chill the sauce. Serve with coffee mousse.

Marillensauce 1 *Apricot Sauce I*

IN THE TOP of a double boiler, melt 1 cup apricot jam and add 2 cups apricot purée and sugar to taste, if desired. Add 1 cup finely slivered blanched almonds. Cook the sauce over gently boiling water for 1 hour. At serving time, add 2 ounces apricot brandy, 1 teaspoon lemon juice, and 1/4 teaspoon almond extract.

Marillensauce 2 *Apricot Sauce II*

HEAT 3/4 CUP apricot jam with 1/2 cup apricot juice until the jam is dissolved. Add 2/3 cup almonds, blanched and slivered, and 2 tablespoons sugar. Just before serving, add 1/2 cup apricot brandy. Serve hot or cold.

Musselinsauce *Mousseline Sauce*

BEAT 4 EGG yolks with 1/2 cup sugar and 1/2 egg white until the mixture is smooth, add 1/2 cup flour, and beat the mixture smooth again. Bring to a boil 1 1/2 cups milk and add 1 teaspoon vanilla. Gradually pour the milk into the egg mixture, stirring constantly. Simmer the sauce for 2 minutes, stirring constantly. Cool and chill it. Fold in 1 cup heavy cream, whipped with 1/4 cup sifted powdered sugar, and beat the sauce gently until it is smooth.

Mandelsauce *Almond Sauce*

BEAT 2 EGG yolks with 3/4 cup powdered sugar until the mixture is creamy. Beat in 1/3 cup heavy rum and fold in 1 cup heavy cream, whipped. Add 3/4 cup chopped toasted almonds.

Peach Sauce  *Pfirsichsauce*

SCALD, PEEL, and slice 6 peaches, retaining all the juice. Crack the stones, remove the meats, and add them to 1/2 cup almonds. Scald the meats and almonds, remove the skins, and slice the nuts. Sprinkle 3/4 of the peach slices with 2 tablespoons confectioners' sugar and the juice of 1/2 lemon. Purée the remaining peach slices until smooth and heat the purée with 1/2 cup each of honey and light rum until the honey is dissolved. Stir the mixture well and add the sliced peaches with their juice and the almonds. Serve the sauce hot, over simple frozen desserts and puddings.

Raspberry Sauce *Himbeersauce*

COMBINE 1 PINT fresh raspberries, 3/4 cup sugar, and 1/4 cup white wine over low heat, stirring with a wooden spoon until the berries are soft. Purée the berries in a food processor or blender. Strain to remove the seeds. Return the sauce to the stove and heat it with 1/2 cup currant jelly, a few drops of lemon juice, and sugar to taste. The sauce may be thickened with 1/2 cup heavy cream, whipped.

Rum Sauce *Rumsauce*

HEAT TOGETHER for 5 minutes 1 cup each of heavy cream and dark brown sugar and 1/4 cup each of rum and butter. Pour 1/2 cup triple-strength coffee into the cream mixture, stirring constantly, and cook the sauce for a few minutes, without letting it come to a boil. Serve the sauce warm, with frozen desserts.

Strawberry Port Wine Sauce *Erdbeersauce*

BRING 1 CUP strawberry juice to a boil and stir in 1 tablespoon cornstarch blended with 1/4 cup cold water. Cook the sauce, stirring constantly, until it thickens. Add 1 cup Port and cook the sauce, stirring, until it is clear and thickened. Add 1 cup washed and hulled strawberries. Serve with ice cream or pudding.

Vanillesauce   *Vanilla Sauce*

LIGHTLY BEAT 2 or 3 egg yolks with 1/3 cup sugar. Stir in 1 teaspoon flour. Scald 1 1/2 cups milk with a small piece of vanilla bean and add the milk little by little to the egg yolk mixture, stirring well. Cook the sauce over very low heat, stirring constantly, until it almost reaches the boiling point. Remove the vanilla bean and strain the sauce. Cool it, stirring it vigorously at first and then occasionally, to prevent a crust from forming.

Gefrorene Sauce 1   *Vanilla Ice Cream Sauce I*

STIR TOGETHER 2 cups softened vanilla ice cream and 2 beaten egg yolks. Fold 1 cup cream, whipped stiff, into the ice cream and stir in 2 tablespoons rum. Chill the sauce.

Gefrorene Sauce 2   *Vanilla Ice Cream Sauce II*

BEAT 2 CUPS softened vanilla ice cream until it is smooth. Fold in 1 cup heavy cream, whipped, and beat the sauce just long enough to make it smooth.

Weinschaumsauce   *Wine Sauce*

IN THE TOP of a double boiler, beat 4 eggs with 1/2 cup sugar until they are light and creamy. Add 1 cup white wine, 3 tablespoons flour, and 2 tablespoons lemon juice and beat the mixture over simmering water until it is light and has doubled in volume. Take the sauce from the heat and beat it until it is cold. Serve at once.

Drinks

Getränke

SMALL BOYS in Vienna are much more apt to be given a nip of wine at their father's knee than the knowledge that is usually acquired there. Needless to say, the nip is only given after the boy has eaten a piece of plain bread, and it is invariably followed by a lecture: "That, my son, was Oppenheimer Goldberg—Feinste Auslese 1947, whereas this—" after another piece of bread —"is Oppenheimer Schlossberg 1947—Spätlese." As a result of this early training, many of the young Rudolfs and Ottos know a Pommard from a Montrachet before they know their multiplication tables.

For a time, the Viennese child may be incomprehensible to playmates from the *Ausland*. A boy might play a splendid game of soccer, then refuse a cold *Gespritzer* on the ground that he could detect the cork, while the rest of the team would be drinking soda pop. But no child can become an adult Viennese full of knowledge, traditions, and whims, most of which he laughs at himself, if he has not first been a Viennese child and suffered the full impact of his father's loving training in man's domain, the wine cellar.

No Viennese father would descend to his cellar to see to his wines or to select a bottle without taking his son along. He would instruct the boy in matters of temperature and humidity, and lecture on vintages and *Auslesen,* grape selections, as he went. The son would not object as much as might be expected, since the same thing was happening to his friends and he rather hoped to sit at the head of his own table one day and roll a golden wine around the side of his glass with a blissful expression as he had seen his father do.

Every year, provided it promised to be a good year, the father and his son went on a wine-buying trip. They went down the Danube to Hungary to reserve some Tokay from the side of the Carpathian wine hills that the father told his son would yield the best wine. They traveled to Germany, to the Rheingau on the right bank of the Rhine, to set aside the wine of their choice, they crossed to Rheinhesse and from there to the Bavarian Palatinate. The father lectured his son every inch of the way, and both tasted and thought and tasted again with expressions that were ludicrously similar. If possible they went to France, a journey which, at least in the eyes of the son, nothing short of a trip to Hollywood could equal. The years that promised to be good were usually the hot dry years, and the trips became immediately memorable for the heat waves and discomforts. As the years rolled by and the wine fulfilled its promise, there were always the anecdotes to remember. The father could always recall that in 1911 *his* father had suffered six blowouts on the hot parched roads of Germany, and they had then been stranded for a week in a famous vineyard, since his father affected a huge Renault landaulet for which enormous spare tires had to be sent from France. The week had obviously been well spent since his father's cellar and his own cellar for years had borne tribute to the perfections of 1911, blown-out tires and all.

The Austrian wines, both red and white, made mostly from Riesling and Traminer grapes, were light and refreshing. The wine-buying trip ended with selections in Austria, the last of which they made in the Viennese suburb Gumpoldskirchen where Austria's best known white wine is grown. They went up to the Hohe Warhe and out to Krems for white wines, to Vöslau and Baden for red wines, and came home at last via Grinzing, Sievering, and Nussdorf, right within the city limits, where they tasted the new wine and bought a little old.

The ladies of the family, both young and old, drank the wine when it came to the table, sometimes years later, and listened to the accounts of heat and dust and reports of unusual amounts of cold German beer that had been consumed in the search for wine. They rarely went along on the wine-buying trips, and if they did, they kept entirely quiet—since a wine tongue, with all its ramifications, was a man's boast, and one he busily tried to develop in his son.

The Viennese do not chill punches with a block of ice. They pack the bowl in chopped ice, on the theory that when it melts it does less harm on the outside of a punch bowl than on the inside.

They also mix their punches or Bowlen, according to the number of bottles the recipes involves and not the number of guests involved. If more punch is needed, they repeat the Bowle recipe rather than doubling the quantity to begin with.

Champagne Punch   *Champagnerbowle*

To 1 BOTTLE Champagne add 1 cup Sherry, 1/2 cup Curacao, 1 tablespoon bar syrup, 1 wide strip of dark green cucumber peel, and 1 split of soda. Serve very cold.

Cold Duck I   *Kalte Ente 1*

POUR 2 BOTTLES chilled Moselle and the juice of 1 lemon over 8 lumps of sugar which have been rubbed on the rind of a lemon. Add a dash of Angostura bitters, 6 lemon slices, cut paper thin and seeded, and 1 bottle chilled Champagne.

Cold Duck II   *Kalte Ente 2*

RUB 12 PIECES lump sugar on the rind of 2 lemons and place them in a chilled bowl. Add 1 bottle white Port and the juice of 3 lemons. Put in the bowl a large block of ice (an exception to the rule above) and add 1 bottle chilled Champagne at serving time.

Posse   *Landsturm*

STEEP THE finely slivered rind of 4 lemons, from which all the white pulp has been removed, in 2 bottles Rhine wine, covered, for 8 hours. Add 2/3 cup sugar and chill the mixture. Add 1 bottle chilled Champagne at serving time.

Danzig Punch   *Krambambuli*

POUR 1 BOTTLE Burgundy into a silver punch bowl, lay a screen or metal mesh across the bowl, and arrange 1 pound lump sugar on it. Saturate the sugar with warm brandy or rum and flame it. Add brandy or rum with a long-handled silver spoon (do not pour it from the bottle) until all the sugar has run down into the wine. Cool the drink and add 1 to 3 bottles of Champagne to taste. Serve very cold.

Oberstleutnant   *Lieutenant Colonel*

CHILL 6 PEACHES, peeled and sliced, for 30 minutes in a large bowl. Add 2 bottles light-bodied red wine and chill the punch for 15 minutes. Add 1/2 bottle red Burgundy, chill the punch again for 15 minutes, and add 1 bottle Champagne at serving time.

Je länger, Je lieber   *The Longer, The Dearer*

COMBINE 1 BOTTLE Hochheimer, or any Rhine wine, 1 bottle Champagne, and 1 bottle Swedish punch. Serve very cold.

Waldmeisterbowle   *Woodruff Bowl*

CHILL 2 BOTTLES light Rhine wine, 2 bottles Moselle, and 2 bottles Champagne. Open 1 bottle Moselle before chilling and pour off 2 cups of wine. Steep 1 1/2 cups fresh or 1/2 cup dried woodruff in the Moselle, at room temperature. Clean 3 pints strawberries and divide them into two equal

amounts, putting the larger berries together, and chill these until needed. Dust the smaller strawberries with 1/2 cup sugar, pour over them 1 cup brandy and enough Moselle to cover, and chill them.

At serving time, strain the wine from the woodruff into a chilled punch bowl, discarding the woodruff. Add the unsugared strawberries. Discard any wilted sugared berries and add the rest, with their marinade, to the bowl. Add the chilled white wine and the Champagne. To serve, place af few of the most perfect strawberries in each glass and ladle in the vine. Pack the punch bowl in ice, but do not put ice in the punch.

May Wine *Mai Bowle*

STEEP 1/2 CUP dried woodruff *(Waldmeister* or *Herzensfreud)* in 2 bottles Rhine wine and 1 bottle red wine for 30 minutes. Add 2 tablespoons sugar, or to taste, and strain the liquid over 2 cups hulled and sugared strawberries in a chilled punch bowl. Pack the bowl in chopped ice and add 1 bottle chilled Champagne and the strained juice of 1 orange.

Peaches in Champagne *Pfirsiche in Champagner*

THIS IS an old Viennese recipe for an inexpensive and refreshing drink. Scald and peel 6 peaches, place them in 6 tall Champagne glasses, and pierce each peach 30 times with a fork. Borrow 3 bottles chilled Champagne from a friend and pour it over the peaches. Eat the peach with the last glass of Champagne. *(Picture, page 492.)*

Peach Punch *Pfirsichbowle*

SCALD 6 LARGE or 9 small peaches, skin them, and cut them into thin slices, reserving the stones. Sprinkle 1 cup powdered sugar over them, add 2 cups brandy, and chill them for 15 minutes. Crack the peach stones and remove the almonds. Squeeze off the brown skins and add the almonds, chopped, to the peaches. Add 2 bottles cold Rhine wine and chill the mixture for 15 minutes longer. Pour the wine with the peaches into a punch bowl set in cracked ice and add 2 bottles chilled Champagne. The peach bowl must be prepared quickly and in small quantities, so that the punch can be served before the peaches turn brown. If more punch is required, prepare a second bowl while the first is being served.

Ananasbowle 1 *Pineapple Punch I*

SUGAR 1 PEELED and sliced pineapple and pour over it 2 bottles Moselle. Chill the mixture and add to it, at half-hour intervals, 1 bottle each of white Port, Sherry, and Chablis, 1/2 bottle Curaçao or any orange liqueur, and 1 bottle Champagne. Serve at once.

Ananasbowle 2 *Pineapple Punch II*

POUR 1 BOTTLE each of Port, red Bordeaux, and Rhine wine over 1 pineapple, peeled and sliced, and 2 cups lump sugar. Chill and add 2 bottles chilled Champagne at serving time.

Ananasbowle 3 *Pineapple Punch III*

MARINATE 1 PINEAPPLE, peeled and sliced, in 1 bottle Moselle for 1 hour. Simmer the pineapple peel with 1 cup sugar in water to cover for 30 minutes, and reduce the syrup to 1/2 cup. Chill it and strain it over the fruit. Chill the bowl and add 1 bottle each of chilled Champagne and Moselle.

Malteserinnen 1 *Dames of Malta I*

To ANY pineapple punch, add half a vanilla bean while the pineapple marinates. Remove the bean at serving time.

Malteserinnen 2 *Dames of Malta II*

To THE punch cup in which pineapple punch is served, add 1 small scoop very firmly frozen vanilla ice cream the size of a walnut.

Malteserritter *Knights of Malta*

POUR 2 BOTTLES each of red Burgundy and Sauternes over 1 pineapple, peeled, sliced and sugared. Serve chilled.

Parisertrank *Parisian Punch*

MARINATE 1 CUP hulled strawberries in 1/2 cup Curaçao for 1/2 hour. Pour over 2 bottles red Bordeaux, and serve without chilling.

Strawberry Punch .... *Erdbeerbowle*

CLEAN AND hull 1 quart fresh strawberries and sprinkle over them 1 1/2 cups powdered sugar, the juice of 2 lemons, and 4 ounces brandy. Chill the strawberries, covered, for 2 hours. Boil together 3/4 cup each of sugar and Rhine wine until the syrup spins a thread, or until a candy thermometer registers 230° F., and let it cool. Add to the strawberries the sugar syrup, the rest of the bottle of wine, and 1 more bottle chilled Rhine wine and let them marinate for 15 minutes. Pour the punch into a silver or crystal punch bowl set in cracked ice and add 2 bottles chilled Champagne. Serve the punch in chilled glasses. Do not add ice to the bowl.

Admiral .... *Admiral*

HEAT 1 BOTTLE red Burgundy in the top of a double boiler, over simmering water, with a stick of cinnamon and a 2-inch piece of vanilla bean. Add 6 egg yolks, beat until the mixture is foamy, and serve it while it is still hot. Serve to an Admiral in order to insure promotion.

Glow Wine .... *Glühwein*

HEAT 3 BOTTLES light-bodied red wine, 2 cups sugar, a small stick of cinnamon, and 3 cloves to just below a simmer. Add a paper-thin slice of lemon to each cup and serve at once.

Nose Warmer .... *Nasenwärmer*

BRING 2 BOTTLES light-bodied red wine and 1 bottle brandy to just below a simmer. Stir in 1/3 cup sugar and add 3 lemons, free of seeds, and 3 seedless oranges, all cut into thin slices. Reheat the mixture, flame it, and serve it while it is still flaming. Add more brandy if necessary for a good flame.

Life Saver .... *Lebensretter*

HEAT TOGETHER 1 bottle Port and 1/2 bottle Cognac, add sugar to taste, and serve the drink hot. Recommended for fainting spells.

Klabautermann *Hobgoblin*

HEAT TOGETHER 2 1/2 cups each of Port and water, and 3 tablespoons sugar. Add 1/2 bottle brandy, heat until the mixture simmers, and serve it hot.

Bischof *Bishop*

HEAT TO the boiling point 2 bottles red Burgundy, 1 3/4 cups sugar, 1/2 teaspoon cinnamon, and the rind of 2 oranges. Serve the drink hot.

Kardinal *Cardinal*

STEEP THE rind of 2 oranges, scraped free of white pulp, 1/2 teaspoon cinnamon, 3 cloves, and sugar to taste in 2 bottles claret or white wine for 24 hours. Serve the drink cold.

Papst *Pope*

HAVING SCALED the ecclesiastic hierarchy from the Bishop to the Cardinal, we come to the Pope.

Rub several lumps sugar on the rind of an orange, place it in a bowl, and add 3 oranges, cut into thin slices, a stick of cinnamon, and 3 cloves. Add 3 bottles of Tokay and steep for 24 hours. Serve without chilling.

Feingespritzer *Champagne Spritzer*

FILL a large glass 1/3 full of chilled Champagne, add 3 ice cubes, and fill the glass with chilled Rhine wine. Add a jigger of red Burgundy.

Gespritzer *Spritzer*

FILL A LARGE glass half full of chilled Rhine wine, add 3 ice cubes and fill the glass with soda.

Strohwitwer *Grass Widower*

CHILL A LARGE silver beaker, fill it half full with hulled and sugared strawberries, and fill the beaker with chilled Champagne.

Cock-a-Doodle-Doo   *Kikeriki*

SHAKE WITH ice 1 part each of Moselle and Port with 1/2 part soda. Drink very cold just when the rooster sounds his first *Kikeriki*.

Egg Brandy   *Eierkognak*

BEAT 6 EGG yolks with 3 tablespoons vanilla sugar—powdered sugar in which a vanilla bean has been stored—until they are light and foamy. Bring 2 cups milk to a boil with 1 3/4 cups sugar and pour it very slowly, in a thin stream, into the egg yolks, stirring constantly. Continue to stir until the mixture is cool. Add 1 cup brandy, mix well, and store the egg brandy, tightly covered, in the refrigerator.

Ambrosia   *Ambrosia*

PURÉE 1 QUART strawberries, hulled and washed, in a processor with 1/2 cup superfine sugar and the juice of half a lemon. Add 1 teaspoon vanilla and chill the fruit. Add 1 bottle Sauternes and 1 cup heavy cream, and serve, especially for ladies.

Glückliche Ehe   *Happy Marriage*

To 4 CUPS hot chocolate, add 1 1/2 cups strong coffee and 1 cup Cognac. Add sugar to taste and just before serving fold in 1 cup heavy cream, whipped.

Barsirop   *Bar Syrup*

COMBINE 3 CUPS sugar and 1 cup water and boil the syrup for 5 minutes. Use it to sweeten drinks. Keep it in the refrigerator, tightly covered.

Schokolade   *Hot Chocolate*

IN THE TOP of a double boiler, over hot water, melt 4 1/2 ounces chocolate. Stir in 1/3 cup sugar and 1/3 teaspoon salt. Add slowly 1 1/4 cups boiling water and blend the mixture. Add 2 1/4 cups scalded milk. Simmer the chocolate for a few minutes and beat it with a wire whisk until it is frothy. Add 1 scant teaspoon vanilla extract. Serve the hot chocolate in a pitcher and serve whipped cream separately.

Türkischer Kaffee   *Turkish Coffee*

GRIND COFFEE beans in a Turkish coffee mill, which reduces them to a powder as fine as flour. Allow 6 tablespoons water, 2 tablespoons sugar, and from 1 to 2 teaspoons coffee powder per person.

Combine the water, sugar, and coffee in a copper Turkish coffee pot and bring the mixture to a boil. Take the pot from the heat and stir the coffee well. Return it to the heat and let it boil up once. Remove it immediately and let the grounds settle. Repeat the boiling up and settling procedure twice more. Cover the pot and let it stand for 2 minutes, add 2 to 3 teaspoons cold water and let the coffee settle a minute longer. Pour it into cups. The coffee will remain slightly foamy.

The Viennese prefer lump sugar to granulated. They allow 6 tablespoons water, 2 large lumps sugar, and 1 heaping coffee spoon of coffee powder per person. Their Turkish coffee cups are smaller than after-dinner coffee cups.

Menus
&
Memoirs

Das Menü

To THE PEOPLE of a monarchy, a picture or description of a royal princess learning how to cook was always more reassuring than a report on her brother's training in affairs of state. No one in Vienna ever wanted the reins of the household to leave the hands of the *Hausfrau,* whether she lived in the Hofburg or in Vienna's simplest home. If her station in life prevented her from giving her home and her table full attention, then at the very least she was expected to take an interest in determining the daily menu. Here it was essential that she know how to cook, even if she never had to prove her proficiency, so that she would not order a dinner that required three ovens simultaneously or a meal that included more than one item fried in deep fat. She must also be able to answer that burning question: "*Was essen wir heute*—what will we have today?"

Viennese menus differed from those of other countries. Soups, *Vorspeisen* (first-course dishes), vegetables, and salads played a more important part than they did in places where meat was more plentiful. Almost all the salads, vegetables, and cheese dishes could also be served as first courses, and many of the *Vorspeisen,* in turn, could be substituted for the main course. The love of the Viennese for sweets also changed their approach to menu making, since they frequently chose the dessert or pastry first and then composed their meal to go with it. In America, the question is what to have after the roast; in Vienna, the question is what to eat before the *Mehlspeise,* the dessert. If they couldn't think of anything they liked better than *Palatschinken* or *Kaiserschmarrn,* they were quite capable of making twice as much of the dessert and serving it with compote or fruit as a meal in itself. The menu in Vienna usually

547

started with soup and led gradually upward to the dessert. It never started at the top and tapered off to an inconspicuous little dessert.

Although conversation proceeded throughout dinner, it was interspersed with pauses and silences during which the diners concentrated on eating the food while it was hot. Guests expected side dishes, *Beilagen,* at dinner parties and ate them in strange and wonderfully individual ways. A guest at dinner might find himself cut off from his compote or sherbet, which he wanted to eat as an accompaniment to the roast, by a barricade of glasses, little stands for his cutlery, cucumber salad, and a porcelain menu. Under such circumstances, a long-armed guest would stab a peach with his fork and bring it back into his mouth, juice and all, with lightning speed. His conversation with the lady on his left, indicated because his compote was stationed on the outer left reaches of his place, would naturally suffer slightly as a result of these maneuvers, but it would be punctuated with slight bows of appreciation on her part and a happy sense of achievement on his. She, on the other hand, having been equipped by nature with what the Viennese evasively called *ein schönes Dekolleté* and the French call *une jolie poitrine*—a sort of natural ledge—was able to reach over and bring her compote up under her chin. She held it, along with her serviette, in her left hand, her little finger extended with infinite refinement, and spooned it with the help of her other extended little finger across the three-inch distance to her mouth without mishap.

When the *Beilagen* and main dishes were removed, there was always a slight straightening up. The *Mehlspeise* was due—*hoffentlich eine Torte, hoffentlich eine Creme*—every heart had its hope for a favorite dessert.

The menu might be made by the *Hausfrau* and her Resi, but not without a directive or two from the *Hausherr* before he left for his *Bureau* in the morning. He took care of his affairs or the affairs of his clients conscientiously, giving only part of his mind to what was cooking at home. When he returned home in the late afternoon, he came with his entire system adjusted to the dinner he expected. A Viennese husband prepared for *Kalbfleisch* could not be given chicken. He never accused his wife, as husbands did in the *Ausland,* with "But that's what I had for lunch," since he had come home for lunch and a short nap. But he could say, *"Das ess' ich nicht, ich hab' mich auf Kalbsbraten eingestellt*—I won't eat it, I'm adjusted for veal." The menu was always *die Hauptsache,* the most important thing. Anyone could learn to cook, but only the *Hausfrau* knew that the *Hausherr* was adjusted to *Marillenknödel* on that particular day, preceded by a *tournedos* and followed by a long rest.

Menus

Frühstück BREAKFAST

Coffee with Cream
Vienna Brioche
Butter Curls
Greengage Preserve

Gabelfrühstück SECOND BREAKFAST

Sherry
Asparagus Pastry Roll
Profiteroles with Anchovy Butter

Mittagessen LUNCHEON

Spinach Tart
Mixed Compote
Coffee

Jause HIGH TEA

Tea with Rum
Gugelhupf
Walnut Cookies

Abendessen DINNER

Cobenzl Eggs
Consommé
Asparagus Maltese
Wienerschnitzel
German Cucumber Salad I   New Potatoes
Rolled Pancakes with Jam
Turkish Coffee

White Wine

Souper LATE SUPPER

Sachertorte with Whipped Cream   Wood Strawberries
Champagne

549

Der Neue Stilton

T HERE WERE many essential things that Herr
Baron was always without. He never owned
a pair of rubbers or, for that matter, anything really sensible, but, like
his father before him, he was never without his Stilton cheese. When it
arrived from England each year, after weeks of correspondence and negoti-
ation, he planned a quiet evening at home to start it on its last lap to
perfection. Young Eduard Karl and Mauserl were allowed to stay up
for the good of their education and so that their father could borrow
all the implements he needed from Eduard Karl, who owned a well-
equipped tool chest and workbench.

Herr Baron could never undertake a simple task in his home without
involving everyone and everything in the operation. Eduard Karl produced
a perfectly adequate hammer and chisel, but Herr Baron had to try some
knives, a mallet, and a whetstone; by the time he had opened the solid
wooden box, several kitchen and storeroom drawers had been emptied.
But nothing Herr Baron ever did was completed until he had used Frau
Baronin's manicure set.

When he finally unearthed the cheese, concealed under layers of sound
British packing, the children were always disappointed. There stood a
large discolored cheese, over which their father exclaimed rapturously,
which everyone had to look at and admire. Even the porter and his wife,
who had carried the case upstairs, were rewarded with a chance to look
at it. Each year a proper and worthy receptacle had to be found to hold
the cheese, and it had to be one the household could do without for six
months. Resi produced the ideal container, but it looked too much like
a pail to Herr Baron, who felt that his Stilton was being treated without
piety. He would not consider a crock brought for the purpose since he
had a brand-new theory that earthenware lent a slight flavor of its own
to the cheese. Finally, with a heavy heart, Resi gave up her deep boiler.

She would not be able to simmer jars of mushrooms for the winter, and she herself had a brand-new theory that the cheese would ultimately lend a slight flavor of its own to the boiler.

A lid was cut from the cheese, an operation which required more knives and all remaining household hardware, and soft old linen was found to lay between the cheese and the enamel of the boiler. This effort necessitated taking apart the linen closet and three trunks in the attic, but saw the Stilton into its final resting place. Herr Baron quickly solved the problem of boring the cheese by using Eduard Karl's gimlet and grips. From the children's angle, this was the pleasantest part of the procedure, since wonderful corkscrew curls of cheese came winding up and out as their father bored the holes. They were allowed to eat these curls, although their father couldn't understand children who wanted so much as to taste unripened Stilton. He sometimes wondered whether perhaps his children were taking after Frau Baronin's side of the family. Herr Baron suddenly discovered that Franz was missing, and all Stilton operations were stopped until Franz, who was making for his bed, came downstairs again. When

he inquired what Herr Baron wanted, Herr Baron replied, "I want you here." After all, he was preparing his Stilton, an hour during which Franz should have known the Baron would want all of his family and staff around him.

The careful opening of the bottle of Port and the filling of the holes in the cheese—there were as many holes as there was cheese when Herr Baron got through—disrupted and involved all that had remained untouched in the house. Frau Baronin's manicure set came out so that her Sollingen nail scissors could be used to cut the old lead cap from the bottle, and the Port was strained, in case a little sediment had been stirred up, and her oldest handkerchief served for that. The cheese was filled, the carefully cut cheese lid was replaced, more soft linen was found to cover it, and the lid went back onto Resi's boiler. Franz and Resi went to bed; they would face the house in the morning. Meanwhile, Herr Baron solved his last problem; where to keep the cheese. One of his Stiltons had spent a winter in the pantry, until the scent was too much for the maid; one had spent a winter in the music cabinet, and had to be moved when it became quite obvious that something other than sheet music was spending the winter there. Herr Baron felt so strongly about his Stilton that Frau Baronin did not take it amiss, although she refused, when he suggested her wardrobe in the dressing room. The children had fortunately just gone to bed when Herr Baron hit on the schoolroom as a totally new storage place for his cheese. It would be cool, concealed in a cabinet with old schoolbooks, and by the time the children realized it was there, they might have swung over to his side sufficiently to put the good of the Stilton ahead of all other considerations.

Menus

Cheese Fritters with Tomato Sauce
Onion Salad
Applesauce with Crumb Topping
Coffee

White Cheese Soup
Caraway Salt Sticks
Water Cress and Onion Salad
Food of the Gods
Coffee

Ham and Cheese Balls
Spinach Pudding with Mushroom Sauce
Sliced Tomatoes
Fruit Compote
Miniature Florentines
Coffee

Mushroom Fritters
Tartare Sauce
Spinach and Water Cress Salad
Cheese Palmiers
Viennese Cherries
Coffee

Menus

Smoked Salmon with Thin Black Bread
Cheese Soufflé in Tomatoes
Adam and Eve Salad
Coffee
Gespritzter

Iced Tomato Soup with Wine
Egg and Chicken Liver Salad
Garnished Liptauer Cheese
Thin Bread and Cheese Pastries
Fruit
Coffee

Figs with Westphalian Ham or Salami
Mushroom Onion Tart
Spinach and Water Cress Salad
Molded Russian Cheese
Coffee

Convent Pudding
Spring Radish and Cucumber Salad
Strawberry-Pineapple Compote
Gugelhupf Slices
Tea

Die Kur

CHESTERFIELD SAID, "Whatever is worth doing at all, is worth doing well." The Viennese used to apply this principle to their yearly *Kur,* changing it ever so slightly: "Whatever is worth eating at all is worth doing the cure for in September."

Spurred on by visions of the next winter's temptations at the table and controlled by the necessity of fitting into their London smoking jackets and Paris gowns, all good Viennese not only made the "cure," they also made a *Vorkur,* the *Kur,* and a *Nachkur*—a before, during, and after cure. Since they all made it together under the most attractive conditions possible, any suffering attached to the loss of twenty or thirty pounds was shared and consequently was much easier to bear. Under these conditions, it might almost be said that the cure was a pleasure. The first few days were always the hardest; the *Kurgäste,* the cure guests, usually spent the pre-cure period in solitary confinement in their darkened bedrooms—ostensibly they were gathering their strength, but actually they were losing a few pounds from sheer boredom. This procedure would make the first official weighing-in a little less of a shock and would enable them to look upon the whole cure with optimism, since there was no denying that they were already well under way. After the *Vorkur,* the Viennese could relax, since the entire place was going to make it a point to massage, rejuvenate, manipulate, pummel, rest, and reduce them. The guests participated to a certain extent, but the real responsibility lay with the spa.

The waters, no matter how disagreeable, must of course be taken regularly each morning and each evening. But how delightful to rise early, wear a becoming Paris creation, and promenade. What a pleasure to hold a finely cut crystal cup with a frivolous lace napkin and sip hot spring water through a glass straw to the strains of the "Radetzky March," played by the Stadt Kapelle with full brasses and the crash of cymbals and tympani! There was so much to see that the Kapellmeister always con-

555

ducted with his back to the orchestra and his face to the *Kurgäste*. Facing this way, he could note prominent military officers, for whom he played regimental marches, and stars from the Volks Oper, for whom he played tunes from the latest operetta. He could bow to guests of long standing and keep his eye out for anyone incognito who might be taking the waters for a touch of distinguished gout.

After the promenade along the colonnade came the first breakfast, taken at one of the restaurants located just the proper distance from the heart of town so that any calories that might be gained there would be burned up on the walk back. Tables were set in the restaurant gardens and waitresses brought Karlsbad's famous coffee and paper-thin slices of pink Prague ham. There were trays of fruit and, inevitably, Karlsbad zwieback. The invigorating air and short walk gave the guests' healthy appetites, but empty stomachs could crave in vain. The restaurant was only equipped to feed "cure" guests, not tourists.

Frau Baronin had promenaded and breakfasted in an extremely chic creation and Herr Baron had sported the last word in white flannels. But from eleven to twelve they could be seen with their fellow *Kurgäste* of both sexes (though this distinction was hard to make) in most unflattering smocks, without stays or foundations, working their slow way through the *Zander-Saal*, the gymnasium, from rowing machine to saddle, from the pummeler to the camel.

The indignity of being strapped by an attendant to a thigh-rolling machine was offset by the pleasure of seeing Frau Grafin, with more points in her tiara and more fat on her hips, being strapped to a double-chin vibrator. Machines were placed in sociable proximity. A lady could lie on her back on a black leather divan with a leaded strap across her waist while double rollers ran up and down her back, causing first her feet and then her head to bob rhythmically, and carry on a jerky conversation with a gentleman whose arm was being flung in circles as though he were pitching a baseball. Eminent professors pulled weight-lifting machines, bankers bicycled side by side with ladies who had only recently been carrying them away with magnificent performances in Ibsen dramas. The Viennese took the Zander institution with complete seriousness. Nothing would have induced them to see one another in less than bandbox perfection at home, but in Karlsbad they calmly viewed one another wrapped in shapeless towels and slithering around in paper scuffs.

A brisk massage followed Zander. The masseurs were not imported Swedish gymnasts, they were respected Herr Doktors who massaged gentle-

men and ladies scientifically, even if painfully, in tiny cubicles separated only by flimsy partitions. Had the massages been less strenuous and the Herr Doktor less venerable, the eavesdropping would probably have been more enthusiastic. As it was, the whisper of Brunhilde's (or Frau X's) latest romance fell flat when she could be seen unglamorously bobbing up and down next door on a horseless saddle.

In the middle of the day the guests rested in their shady rooms; then they all met again at the *Moor* and *Mineral* baths. A *Moorbad* meant that the *Kurgäste* lowered themselves into wooden bathtubs filled with a substance so closely resembling mud that only the thought of the active mineral properties it contained made the ordeal possible. Once the bather was in the hot *Moor*, such a fine steaming went on that it compensated amply for all the endless dinners and receptions of the last winter and the winter to come. For the fainthearted there were *Moorumschläge,* mud compresses that were brought steaming hot to the *Gäste* in their rooms.

After the baths came walks through the incredibly beautiful and mani-cured woods to romantically located benches and rustic bowers, with little follies at every notable view. Every unusual event that had ever taken place in Karlsbad was commemorated in a little tea house. For instance, the spot where Stephanie had waited was called *Stephaniewarte* ... the spot where the stag leapt over the gorge was the *Hirschensprung*. Just what incident inspired the *Klein Versailles,* the little Versailles, no one knows, except that infinitesimal Versailles would have been more apt. The guests took their weary way back for the afternoon waters and for *Musik.*

At a point when the day should actually have been over, it started. No Viennese could suffer hardships and lose two pounds without regaining one of them as pleasantly and deliciously as possible. Herr Baron and Frau Baronin ordered a carriage, a *Zweispänner* with rubber tires, and two old *Rappen,* black horses, who had been drawing them for years. The coachman, old Peperdl, had driven their grandfathers. Old as Peperdl was and weak as Herr Baron was, the two always got down and walked on the uphill stretches.

They drove through the lovely quiet evening to Hans Heiling or to any of the many restaurants they had to choose from. They were beyond the limits of Karlsbad and the *Kur,* beyond restrictions and schedules, they were off on their own to eat their favorite of all favorites—*blaue Forelle.* The restaurant, which had to be built next to or over a trout stream, was equipped with a large wood-and-wire cage. Into it the restaurateur and the waiters dropped the living trout they caught during the day. These trout were no unsporting hatchery product—they were game fish from the icy streams, held comfortable prisoners for a day on an extra diet so that their last hours would be happy. Herr Baron and Frau Baronin knew that only fish plunged into boiling water from their natural habitat with scarcely a moment's delay and so brought to their table could be brilliant blue, tender, and superb. They ate it with reverence and gusto and crisp cucumber salad, new potatoes, and cold fresh butter, with a placid cow imprinted on it. They drank a bottle of cold light wine, waved to their Herr Doktor, who knew where to go and what was good, and finished their meal with some of the matchless native fruit. Herr Baron sighed over a plate of *Emmentaler* and a seidel of light beer that went past him to the Herr Doktor's table, but there was no sadness—the drive home was all downhill.

The *Kur* was so strenuous that it necessitated the *Nachkur,* a gradual recovery from starvation, a slow putting on again of five pounds, in itself a most enjoyable occupation. The cure having taken off from twenty to thirty pounds, the *Nachkur* stopped the dizzy spells and lessened the spots before the eyes. During the fall in Vienna, all sudden illnesses and unexpected collapses were very simply diagnosed: the patient was suffering from, or even went so far as to die of, the cure.

Menus

Jellied Consommé with Green Grapes
Mushroom Soufflé Rudolfina with Tomato Sauce
Lettuce Salad
Mocha Wedges
Coffee

Cauliflower Polonaise
Spinach and Water Cress Salad
Pears Alma
Suvaroffs
Coffee

Eggs Stuffed with Crab Meat Mimosa
Broccoli Roll with Cheese Sauce
Tomato, Artichoke, and Endive Salad
Viennese Cherries
Bishops' Bread
Coffee

Balkan Chlodnik
Spinach Soufflé Caroline with Mushroom Sauce
Cheese Sticks ·
Apples in Robes
Coffee

Menus

Water Cress and Ham Salad
Asparagus Holstein
Sliced Peaches

Jellied Consommé
Wiener Zwieback
Water Cress and Apple Salad

Mushrooms with Rice and Almonds
Baked Tomatoes
Fruit Salad

Cold Roast Beef
Cucumber Salad
Iced Black Cherries

Thin Prague Ham
Green Bean and Shrimp Salad
Apricot Compote

Spring Radish and Cucumber Salad
Blue Trout
Wood Strawberries

Cauliflower and Ham
Green Salad
Raspberries

Cabbage Salad
Green Eggs
Grapes

Der Ausflug

EVEN THE most beautifully brought-up Viennese children got out of hand when an *Ausflug* was brewing in the household. When Franz and Ferdinand put on their green baize aprons and started on an endless round of trips up to the attic and down to the cellar, when wine baskets and binoculars, fitted hampers and butterfly nets accumulated in the hallways, when Resi roasted and baked and Herta took the plaids from the camphor and beat them thoroughly and noisily in the courtyard, when Frau Baronin sent for her dirndls, then everyone—including the parents and the dogs—went completely to pieces with the delirium of the moment.

Preparations for the outing were not simply a matter of packing food and drink. An *Ausflug* required *Lederhosen,* leather breeches, and *Lederhosen* required lean, sunburned knees. Herr Baron had to time his last skiing trip so that his knees would still be brown for the first *Ausflug.* His unpretentious little Tyroler hat, apparently no different from those that covered every head in Austria, had to go back to Habig, Vienna's most renowned hatter, to be reblocked, and the hard-won *Gemsbart,* the little chamois-hair brush that decorated it—a trophy of the hunt—had to be adjusted. Herr Baron laid aside formalities along with his striped trousers. His native costume meant release and relaxation—also, it became him very well.

Frau Baronin might keep her sawdust-filled muslin dress form at Drecoll in Paris, but this stratagem was a frivolity compared to the importance of fitting into her dirndl. She quickly organized four "apple days" before the *Ausflug,* to insure the perfect fit of the skintight bodice. She abandoned her smart pompadour for the twisted braids of the simpler rustic hair style, and she unearthed her beautiful old peasant jewelry and her white Loden shepherd's cape.

For some long-forgotten reason, which no one questioned, an *Ausflug,*

561

a "flight out," could not be planned within normal bounds. Three or four elaborate and beautifully arranged courses suited to outdoor eating were unthinkable. The menu had to assume the proportions of a restaurant bill of fare, with several choices for each course. There had to be *Vorspeisen,* or first-course dishes, of fish as well as of shellfish and eggs. The main course had to include a selection of game, beef, and birds, salads, a selection of fruit, vegetables, and rice, and desserts a choice of both pastries and creams as well as the omnipresent *Torte.* On top of all this, the fruits of the season were gathered by the children and added to the menu. Certain preparations were made to accommodate this battery of food most advantageously—little *barquettes* and shells were baked to hold the *Walderdbeeren*—the wood strawberries that the children would pick— and the chilled *Bowle* lacked only the fresh *Waldmeister,* or woodruff, also to be supplied by the children when they arrived at the outing spot. Aspects not only of seasonal perfection but of geographical suitability affected the menu planning. If an *Ausflug* went to the Danube, a *Linzertorte* and a light Klosterneuburger wine were essential; if it went to Baden, the occasion called for *Badener Krapfen*. No opportunity for including more food could be missed. The making of the menu became doubly complicated since, on an *Ausflug*, everyone was allowed to order his *Leibspeise*, his favorite dish. Frau Baronin loved cold trout, Herr Baron would start with crayfish and follow it with a rare filet of beef, interrupting his meal only to taste a little of the trout and a little of everything else. The children always insisted on mandarin oranges stuffed with pheasant mousse, less out of passion for the dish than delight in the name. They had long since conjured up a magnificently bearded old mandarin who lived exclusively on pheasant mousse, and each year they revived him and his insatiable appetite. Out of respect for Frau Baronin, everyone ate a slice of her special *Linzertorte*. If they had no room left for any more food, they would play a strenuous game before proceeding to the desserts.

When the preparations were well under way, Herr Baron always said, "*Also*—where shall we go this year?" This was a delightful game: everyone suggested a different place, from mountainous Semmering to Krems, on the Danube. The family discussed every location in happy detail and weighed all pros and cons seriously. They could play this game quite safely, since they all knew perfectly well that they would end by going to Dürnstein. They had gone there ever since Herr Baron, as a little boy, had discovered a marked resemblance and a deep sympathy between himself and Richard Löwenherz, the Lion-Hearted, who had lain imprisoned there in a deep dungeon, in 1193.

After the location was settled, the day had to be set. This matter also inspired endless discussion, since complicated factors like aspic entered into the calculations. The *Ausflug* could not possibly take place before the wood strawberries were ripe and the cyclamen was in bloom, it could not be before there was spring in the air and just enough warm sunshine so that everyone could play *Blinde Kuh* (blind cow, a romantic blindman's buff), but not so much sunshine that the carefully prepared aspics would run or the ice around the *Bowle* would melt.

With the choice finally made, Resi, Franz, and Ferdinand spent most of the eve of the *Ausflug* counting, checking, and worrying; the *Ausflugsmahl* had taken three full days to cook and would take half a night to pack. Visky and Zoda dug themselves into the hampers so that they wouldn't be forgotten, someone remembered the cameras, everyone forgot the films. The cars came around early and were packed and repacked with the voluble assistance of every Viennese who happened to be passing. The *Herrschaft*—the master and mistress—rode in the first car, the children with part of the equipment in the second. Franz and Ferdinand followed in the third car, holding the fragile baked food and the delicate aspics and suffering over what might have been forgotten and the safety of the silver. As paper plates and cups were unheard of, and china was impractical, the feasters set out their precious food on silver and heavy crystal service, which they packed in velvet-lined cases for the journey. The caravan stopped to rendezvous with other cars full of guests, all of whom had brought along a little something to eat.

The *Ausflug* left the city and wound its way through the beautiful vineyard-covered and wooded hills along the Danube. At Dürnstein they climbed the hill to the ruins of the old castle and spread their feast on the finest linen, choosing a level spot against a sunwarmed wall of the old foundations. Far below them lay the road on which Blondel traveled in search of his king. How Richard heard Blondel's song or how he managed to answer it is not known, since the road and the dungeon were far apart and the sinister Hadmar II kept careful watch over the royal crusader. After the children had gathered the woodruff, they made little baskets of leaves pinned together with twigs to hold the strawberries. They picked cyclamen to decorate the cloth and made wreaths of wild flowers for all the feminine heads. Franz and Ferdinand set out sauces and whipped cream, which they had brought in jars, and they found shady spots to store the ice-packed dishes and the *Bowle*. The climb and the fresh air made it possible for everyone to eat a little of everything—it would have been tragic to return to Vienna and realize that one had missed a taste of the duck or hadn't had a crumb of the *Torte*. It was understood that everyone ate a normal portion of the dish he had chosen and just a taste of everybody else's dishes. Games after luncheon helped everyone to avoid falling asleep, and a small fire was always elegantly laid with kindling, paper, and wood that had been neatly packed and brought from Vienna. Over this blaze Franz made coffee, for which he even had brought the water, since everyone believed firmly that only Viennese water could produce proper coffee. When the sun set over the Danube and family and friends looked across at the meadows and hills on the other side and heard the faint ringing of the cowbells, they knew exactly where they would go when Herr Baron said "*Also*—" next year.

Menus

Marinated Shrimps   Salt Sticks
Mandarin Oranges with Pheasant Mousse
Cold Zucchini Salad
Wood Strawberry Barquettes

Green Eggs
Lobster Salad
Thin Rye-Bread Sandwiches
Tomato, Artichoke, and Endive Salad
Chocolate Cake   Mixed Fresh Berries
Champagne

Iced Cucumber Yoghurt Soup   Salted Melba Toast
Cold Stuffed Trout with Shallot Mayonnaise
Cold Filet of Beef in Crust
Wood Strawberries   Linzertorte
Woodruff Bowl

Assorted Stuffed Eggs
Cold Water Cress Soup
Cold Saddle of Roast Lamb
Mushroom, Potato, and Radish Salad
Herbed and Minted Mayonnaise
Sliced Oranges   Almond Short Wafers
Coffee

Ein Lunch Debout

ABOUT FOUR hundred and eight years after the discovery of America, the Viennese began to accept the fact by allowing a few well-chosen Americanisms to slip into their language. This process did not result in their using fewer French words; it only meant that some very recherché trilingual combinations came forth. Everyone might live according to *Seinem Code d'Honneur,* but the most popular way for a hostess to stay smartly abreast of the times, in three easy words, was to give *Ein Lunch Debout*—preferably early in the season.

The French words were always pronounced properly, but the English ones were frequently unrecognizable. Lunch became anything from "Lontsch" or "Loonsh" to "Lünch," complete with umlaut and a hard "ch." No matter how serious the mispronunciation might be, *Ein Lunch Debout* was infinitely smarter than a *Mittagessen Assis* or a *Stand-up Déjeuner.* It was also in many respects the ideal way of entertaining; the hostess did not have to check silver and the table leaves against her guest list, nor did she have to stoop to the dreadful indignity of renting red velvet and gilded chairs. As long as she had enough floor space, if her dining room would allow thirty-six people to stand and move about gracefully, and if there was still sufficient room for the footmen to circulate with ease, she could give *Ein Lunch Debout.* This occasion had a further advantage: No guests could stand for as long a period as they could sit, and the lunch would break up promptly—which a *Lunch Assis* could not be depended upon doing.

Standing was absolutely compulsory—the invitation clearly stated *Debout.* It was unheard of for a guest to capture an attractive lady and take her off to two comfortable chairs in a quiet corner of the *Bibliothèque.* Such liberties with etiquette were Americanisms that Vienna simply did not accept, hence they could not possibly occur.

At a luncheon where the guests were seated, the menu usually bulged with innumerable side dishes and accompaniments. Depressing displays of cutlery and glassware made the guests wonder whether they would be home before evening. The main course might suddenly involve the guest with an icy sherbet on his left, a cup of steaming bouillon beyond the sherbet (despite the fact that the meal had started with a soup three courses earlier), cucumber salad in front, a compote on his right, and a footman behind. Beyond the compote, his wineglasses were only just within his reach. In order to leave room on the table for all the side dishes, guests had to be seated so far apart that they either had to raise their voices or lean alternately to the right and left, at a dangerous angle, in order to make conversation—in three languages, if possible.

Frau Baronin, a born hostess, knew perfectly well that *Ein Lunch Debout* was the answer: four courses, no side dishes, no knives, no complication—standing room only. In fact, it became a leisurely moving about from group to group, a circulation of conversation. A guest could shine with a single new story repeated for the benefit of each new group and, at the end of the *Lunch*, there would not be a single guest who could go home and report to all of Vienna, within the hour, "She seated me next to that *unmögliche* Parvenu (impossible upstart)."

A fine line was also drawn between a Buffet Luncheon and *Ein Lunch Debout*. At the Buffet, the hostess had to arrange an impressive display of food and, if she did not provide formal seating, she had to accept the fact that her guests would search out their own. They had been known in a pinch to make do with her priceless spinet or to use her fragile *étagère* as a sort of shooting stick. The *Lunch Debout* stood in the cleared dining room, was served from the sideboard by the staff without previous ostentatious exposition, and the guests went home when their legs ached, a development that usually coincided with the coffee-drinking.

The thoughtful hostess always planned her *Lunch Debout* to follow one of the pleasant pastimes in which the Viennese indulged in the middle of the morning. It could follow a Philharmonic concert, the opening of an exhibition, a recital, or one of the delightful dancing classes that met at eleven each day. Here, too, the discovery of America made itself felt —although there was no question of public acceptance, habituées could arrange for private instruction in the Hesitation from the more talented members of Austria's aristocracy. Of course, any talents that might be discovered in this direction were doomed to go unapplauded; at best they could be whispered to a friend. To like ragtime, let alone dance it

with a stranger, was the sort of thing no one would want Mother to hear about.

Frau Baronin always timed her first *Lunch Debout* to follow the opening performance of the Spanish Riding School in the Imperial Palace. She liked her guests to come fresh and inspired from one of the few events that still reflected the glory of the monarchy. The Viennese still had an emperor in their Hofburg to love and cherish, and they still had the magnificent silvery white stallions of the royal stud that had carried every Hapsburg through peace and battle from the sixteenth-century reign of Ferdinand I to Franz Josef. Nothing was too good for the matchless Lippizaner that originally came from Spain and were named for Lippiza, the small town near Trieste where they were bred and trained. After they had gradually changed from coal-black foals to snow-white stallions, the most splendid were chosen to make their home with their king in Vienna. There, in the six-storied splendor of the white-and-gold riding school, no less beautiful than the grand ballroom, they performed the intricate jumps and pirouettes of the *haute école*. Although the Lippizaners could be seen at stud farm in Lippiza and in the Hofburg stables, it was only amid their own beautiful surroundings in Vienna, to the strains of Vienna's finest orchestra, that they rose to the Levade and the final jump of the Mezair. The luncheon guests always sat in the box beside the royal box at the end of the magnificent columned sweep of the Reitschule, the famous Riding School. Their hearts thrilled to see each perfect Capriole and the flawless rhythm of the Quadrille performed in ballet precision by horses and riders. They were proud of the superb animals and the long history of the royal stud that had produced Florian, the Emperor's horse.

Frau Baronin could hardly resist the temptation to make her *Lunch Debout* all white and gold and chocolate brown, but she always withstood such *Geschmacklosigkeiten* (manifestations of poor taste), although she served the white and brown Arenberg pears on her gold luster plates. The menu had to be planned so that everything could be eaten with the right hand while the left held the plate and the serviette. Wineglasses were passed between courses and marked a sort of intermission during which the groups shifted about. After a cup·of hot soup came a wonderfully attractive fish course, served from a large flat platter over which a twisted trellis of puff pastry was laid. The trellis was baked separately and the kitchen staff held their breath until the fragile pastry was safely in place. A cold white wine made its appearance while plates were removed and the meat course was served. The arrangement of the platters had to be particularly beautiful since they passed so intimately among the guests. Frau Baronin either had to select a ragout of meat for her one-handed guests, or the meat had to be so tender that it could be cut with a fork. She did not even consider the former: Who could eat a ragout after watching the *haute école?* She selected noisettes of whitest veal, surrounded by filled mushrooms and garnished with almonds and lemons. A glass of Champagne was followed by a cup of Turkish coffee—one guest was leaning against the wall by now.

With the coffee came a noticeable changing from foot to foot; it was not surprising that almost all the guests left immediately. They headed for home and a comfortable chair or the nearest *Kaffeehaus. Debout* was all very well, but they would all have their five o'clock tea sitting down.

Menus

Figs with Prosciutto
Green Rice
Stuffed Tomato Salad
Assorted Cheeses
Fruit and Nuts
Coffee

Clear Consommé with Almonds
Ham and Noodle Squares
Apple Salad
Port Wine Prune Whip
Coffee

Asparagus with Lemon Crumbs
Paprika Veal Cutlets
Potato Baskets
Hazelnut Soufflé
Coffee

Cauliflower with Green Pea Sauce
Cold Loin of Veal with Caper Sauce
Mixed Green Salad
Egg Puffs with Cream
Coffee

Asparagus Maltese
Sautéed Veal Cutlets
Black and White Salad
Wood Strawberry Barquettes
Coffee

Squab Soup
Cheese Strips
Asparagus Holstein
Rice Dessert with Meringue
Coffee

Cold Chicken Soup with Curry
Viennese Filet of Sole   Potato Balls
Tournedos Béarnaise
Spinach and Water Cress Salad
Fruit Sherbet   Half Moons

Paradise Soup
Lobster in Puff Pastry Gregor
Noisettes of Veal with Pâté
Mushrooms Stuffed with Peas   Broccoli Roll
Pears on Buttercake   Apricot Sauce
Coffee

Rice Ring with Shrimps
Dill Sauce
Clear Consommé with Sherry
Spit-Roasted Stuffed Capon
Viennese Wax Beans
Apple Porcupine

Brussels Sprouts Salad
Consommé with Croutons
Roast Saddle of Lamb
Potatoes with Chestnuts
Orange Sabayon

Der Jour

E VER SINCE the period when it was proof of good breeding to substitute a French word for its German equivalent, Ladies in Vienna have had their Day—and elegantly called in their *Jour*.

While Parisians made an art of the *salon*, Londoners were *"at home,"* and we held "open house," the Viennese *Jour* became a delightful institution characterized by a complicated etiquette and by magnificent food.

Every house had its own jealously guarded recipe for *Jourbrot, Jourgebäck*, and *Jourtorte*, and every lady who lived in the magic *Jour* cycle had thirty days in which to recover from her last *Jour* and prepare for her next one.

Very Important Ladies automatically kept the same *Jour* from year to year, and in some cases even bequeathed the dates to their daughters, who thus carried on the tradition from generation to generation. Less influential Ladies had to compete with each other every autumn for the desirable days for the approaching season, which they called *la saison*, of course. The contest was not settled without near bloodshed and heartbreak. Calendars, friends, servants, and even soothsayers had to be consulted, promises were made and broken, tears were shed. No one willingly took Friday and everyone wanted Saturday. No two prominent *Jours* could fall on the same day. No one wanted to precede or follow a long-established, famous *Jour*—and for good reason. Frau von Demel's carefully constructed *Fürst Metternich Torte* and her renowned cheese *palmiers* might fall completely flat if they had to follow a brilliant *Jour* at the Seherr-Thosses.

In this initial skirmish, normally friendly Ladies cajoled, flattered, teased, and frequently hated each other, although even at the height of the struggle they dared not risk the satisfaction of an insult, lest their own *Jours* be cut in retaliation. When the *Jourkalender* was finally settled, every Lady in Vienna had her Day—her very own until the following year.

After the *Jours* had been allotted, work really began. The guest lists had to be fully revised; there were always names to be deleted and new ones to be added. All during the fall months, chefs, cooks, and even the Ladies themselves tested new recipes and tried to improve old ones. By the time the leaves had fallen from the chestnut and linden trees and fires were being laid in the porcelain stoves, all Vienna was preparing for the formal pleasures of the large *Jours* and the inimitable *Gemütlichkeit* of the small ones.

Numerous *Jour* cards had to be written and delivered by hand. In the old days the Ladies rode about the streets of Vienna and waited in their carriages while the footman went upstairs to deliver the cards, their corners bent to show that the Lady herself was below. These longed-for visitations caused great commotion. The children and household staff rushed to the windows to report on the fashion of Frau Hofrätin's hat or on the latest addition to her equipage. If Frau Baronin absent-mindedly opened her parasol and thereby prevented the careful inspection of her toilette from above, she suffered for it later.

Chic automobiles replaced some horse-drawn carriages in the cobbled streets of Vienna, but the *Jour* cards were still delivered by the

footmen—with corners unbent, for the personal touch was gone. This was, however, a great convenience to the footmen, who simply met in a centrally located *Kaffeehaus* and exchanged cards over a sociable cup of coffee.

The favored families displayed the eagerly awaited cards proudly: they represented the interlocking, though widely divergent, circles of social life, intellectualism, and gastronomy—heavily sugared—that were Vienna.

A *Jour* card was—and indeed still is—a visiting card with the *Jour* day inscribed by hand in the lower right-hand corner. The legend "Second Saturday" meant that the Lady would be at home, surrounded by her family, food, and footmen, to all the fortunate recipients of her *Jour* card, on the second Saturday of every month from November to April, from five until eight o'clock—and that after eight, she would be at home to her intimates and their gossip. It would be perfectly proper, the recipients knew, to attend one, two, or all the *Jours,* but to attend none of them would be an unforgivable insult, a cut. Although the perennial *Jour*-goer started the rounds in November, really important personages graced with their august presences only the December and January *Jours.* Hostesses saved their prize delicacies for these climatic *Jours.*

The correct response to a *Jour* invitation was a *Jour* invitation. A *Jour* for a *Jour* was an honored Viennese maxim. Single gentlemen and *Ausländer,* unable to return the hospitality in kind, replied with flowers and/or a call—this of such brief duration that they kept on their gloves. The proud possessor of a *Jour,* on the other hand, could use it to discharge all social obligations. Wherever the Lady with a *Jour* went, to a *Déjeuner, Après Souper, Dîner,* or *Lunch Debout,* she had only to say to any new and interesting people she met, "I'll see you at my *Jour,* of course." Even if the season was well advanced, she could send a *Jour* card.

Jour bookkeeping was very simple. A large silver salver waited in the anteroom for the visiting cards of the departing guests. The numbers of cards grew to imposing heights and were as carefully hoarded as are the Christmas cards on our American mantels today. At the end of the season, the daughter of the house counted the cards and checked them against the original guest list. If she found no visiting card to correspond with a name on the list, her parents emphatically crossed the name from next year's list and from their hearts.

Each month the *Jour* guests ate and drank of their hostess' best, and each month the hostess went to her guests' *Jours* and ate and drank of their best in return. All this happy reciprocity encouraged great inventiveness in the kitchen. No hostess would have let it be said of her anchovy-caviar *profiteroles* or her *flûtes enchantées* that they were old hat. Every lady perfected her *têtes de nègres* and her *Punschringelchen* until they could not be surpassed. She spent months plotting her menus for the entire season according to the prescribed ritual. There were always three kinds of *Bäckerei*—salt "bakery," cheese "bakery," and sweet "bakery"—a *Torte*, and a *pièce de résistance*. There was a plain cake for Jourists who were dyspeptic—and who can blame them? And no *Jour* was complete without myriad open sandwiches to bewitch the eye, homemade candies, *Jourkonfekt*, Turkish cigarettes, and Turkish delight.

Although one also served coffee, Sherry, and even liqueurs, the true *Jourgetränk* was tea. The tea tray always bore, in addition to sugar, cream, and lemon, two very small and elegant decanters of cobalt or ruby crystal filled with rum and with Cognac. Many of the guests laced their tea with spirits, and the bottles were frequently refilled, though they were never replaced by larger ones. The footmen passed beautifully arranged trays of food in a stipulated order: first salt and cheese "bakeries" to whet the thirst and appetite, then sandwiches and *Jourbrot*, then sweet "bakery" and *Torten*. The food was not displayed as it is on our buffets, nor was it served from a central table. The footmen replenished the trays and teapots in the kitchen and periodically filled empty plates and teacups. No one ever knew how much food had been prepared, or could guess whether the supply was running low, but *Jour* hostesses became so adept at appraising the season that even without cards of acceptance they knew how many guests they could expect. There could never be more guests than names on the list, since there was no such thing as an uninvited guest. The hostess, unharassed by the necessity to "pour," sat at the left of the most honored guest, in the center of the inner circle. Most of the guests were seated and in true European fashion were introduced to each other and clasped hands in greeting.

The *Jour* still exists in Vienna, although, *natürlich*, it has done the inevitable: it has become the *Cocktailjour*. The *Jour* guests enjoy Pink Ladies and Specials, Slings and Sours, all of them extremely sweet. The food at a *Cocktailjour* is still very much the same. Nothing could prevent a Viennese hostess from preparing one of the beloved *Torten* when guests are expected. The *Jour* still starts with tea and sweet "bakeries," to satisfy tradition, and goes on to salt "bakeries," *Joursandwiches*, and *Schnitten* and *Bissen* of every kind. *Kartoffelchips* are much admired. And finally, Vienna still being Vienna, the guests happily follow several *Jour-Special-Martinis* with *Sachertorte*.

Tea with Rum, Lemon, Sugar, or Cream

Cheddar Cheese Pigs	Cheese Sticks
Ham Crescents	Cheese Palmiers
Liver Pâté Sandwiches	Thin Cucumber Sandwiches
Sliced Stuffed Roll	Asparagus Pastry Roll
Viennese "Cigarettes"	Hazelnut Salt Rounds
Half Moons	Apricot Pockets
Suvaroffs	Linzer Tarts
Prince Metternich Cake	Danube Strips
Strawberries	Fresh Figs

Cheese Palmiers	Almond Cheese Cookies
Potato Discs	Cheese Canapés
Open Anchovy Sandwiches	Rolled Water Cress Sandwiches
Sandwich Loaf	Open Sliced-Egg Sandwiches
Ham Pockets	Nut Roll
Lightning Cake I	Walnut Cookies
Vanilla Crescents	Wednesday Cakes
Dobostorte	Raspberry Cake
Raspberries	Plum Compote

Menus

Tea with Rum

Gugelhupf

Fruit Flan

Vienna Bread

Danish Pastry

Jam Pockets

Nut Cake

Tea with Lemon

Loaf Cake

Vanilla Crescents

Butter Curls and Apricot Preserve

Bishops' Bread

Kapuziner

Coffee Braid

When the Viennese ate dinner in the middle of the day, Jause, *or high tea, often merged into the* Abendessen, *the evening meal.*

Tea with Cream

Coffee Braid

Cherry Cake

Stuffed Rolls

Vienna Butter Crescents

Butter Curls and Honey

Deep-Fried Poached Eggs

Blackberries

Tea with Brandy

Schuberts

Miniature Emperor's Rolls

Butter Curls and Honey

Black Cherry Preserve

Loaf Cake

Eggs Parmesan

Fresh Figs

Menus

Iced Coffee
Almond Rings
Praline Cake
Raspberry Ice
Chilled Sliced Peaches
Punschtorte
Orangeade
Bonbons

Gespritzter
Sweet Palmiers
India Puffs
Rum Raisin Fritters
Lemon Ice
Kaisertorte II
Raspberry Juice
with Sparkling Water
Stuffed Chocolate Figs

Chocolate with Whipped Cream
Apricot Pockets
Raspberry Cones
Almond Rolls
Orange Ice
Viennese Orange Cake
Lemonade
Glazed Fruit

Coffee
Sweetened Cottage Cheese on Black Bread
Danish Pastry with Poppy Seed Filling
Linzertorte
Berries with Thick Cream
Cherry Cake
Butter Milk
Candied Orange Rind

Menus

Oysters with Herbs
Stuffed Eggs with Anchovies
Open Sardine Sandwiches
Iced Celery and Cucumbers
Potato Discs
Cheddar Cheese Pigs
Smoked Eel with Black Pepper

Smoked Salmon Cornucopias
Cheese Sticks
Radishes   Celery
Open Tartare Sandwiches
Eggs Stuffed
with Goose Liver Pâté
Marinated Mushrooms
Nuts
Prosciutto around Melon Cubes

Filled Artichoke Leaves
Ham Pockets
Herring in Sour Cream
Ripe Figs
Smoked Sturgeon on Black Bread
Cheese Palmiers   Salted Almonds
Iced Celery and Carrot Sticks
Cucumber Cups

Mushroom Onion Tart
Open Tongue Sandwiches with Horseradish
Artichoke Bottoms with Shrimps
Bird's Nest Salad   Thin Black Bread
Assorted Stuffed Eggs
Salted Hazelnuts

Apfelstrudel

N<small>O CONCERT PIANIST</small> ever sacrificed her finger-nails to her career with greater dedication than Frau Baronin did to her *Apfelstrudel*. She filed them down without regret. What were a few fingernails and an upset household compared to a golden strudel? It was even worth the minor estrangement that always developed between herself and Herr Baron—a sort of unavoidable fringe evil of strudel making.

All Viennese husbands had a finely developed sixth sense that propelled them rapidly from the house on any pretext whatever when certain rites were going to be practiced there. Herr Baron was especially sensitive in these matters. He had unexpected calls to the outer city when a *Kaffee-klatsch* seemed to be brewing. He was occupied with *Ausländer* when the furs were going to be put away in camphor, and he developed acute indispositions when the ceilings were due to be washed. But Herr Baron fled farthest fastest when he felt the imminence of an *Apfelstrudel*-pulling.

The strudel atmosphere could be sensed for days before the ritual actually took place. Herr Baron knew what lay in store the moment Frau Baronin showed a tendency to save small confectioners' boxes and bits of string; next came a dreamy look and whispered sessions with Resi who always concealed under her apron the apples she brought for in-spection. For some reason, everything had to be done with the utmost secrecy, the strudel had to be an *Überrashung,* a surprise, a sensation.

Espionage, counterespionage, and the sixth sense flourished. Franz re-ported a basket of greenings under the corridor stairs. Herr Baron looked at his wife's hands and knew the time had not yet come. The apples were probably for applesauce. As the greenings improved and Frau Baronin looked more and more bemused, Herr Baron was not the only man in the household whose sixth sense started to work. The problem was to devise pretexts that would suddenly and emphatically remove all the men from the house, but which would at the same time permit them to return in time for dinner. Herr Baron ended by composing a telegram to himself. He sent it on the morning after Frau Baronin, having gone to the linen closet for the oldest, softest damask tablecloth, had quietly cleared the dining room and filed down her nails. Not only Herr Baron knew he would receive a summons to the country; all the men in the house knew they were going to be called away. The footman invariably rushed to the beside of one of his aunts. The boys found they had to stay in school to make up studies, and the porter had an errand across town. Only Resi, Fräulein, Frau Baronin, the porter's wife Frau Jüpsel, and Anna stayed home. Mauserl also stayed to watch, wide-eyed, and pull a gray little strudel of her own out of the trimmings.

These intrepid women were closely knit by the mutual enterprise they had undertaken; they were collaborators and colleagues. They spent the morning peeling, coring and slicing apples, with Mauserl to watch. Frau Baronin, who loved to peel apples, cut the whole peel in a single long wonderful green curl. They soaked raisins in brandy, mixed cinnamon with sugar, scalded and slivered almonds, grated bread crumbs, and clarified butter. Frau Baronin always made two strudels—perfect golden horseshoes that tasted even better when they were heated for the second time. With all the furor of the preparation, it was better to go through it twice in one day than to repeat the whole operation a few weeks later.

The dining room slowly filled with strudel ingredients. First came the large bowls of finely sliced apples, each slice cut as large as possible, the bowls of raisins, sugar and cinnamon, almonds, and browned bread crumbs, and a great bowl of melted butter. Then there were always a lemon grater and beautiful yellow lemons, and several new white feather brushes made of goose quills.

Up to this point, all was calm. The gentlemen of the house could just as well have stayed at home. Then the moment arrived when the dough came out from under the warm bowl where it had rested for an hour and was laid in the center of the table. Someone gave it a few rolls with the rolling pin to spread it just large enough so that Resi, Frau Jüpsel, Frau Baronin, Fräulein, and Anna could get their five pairs of hands under it. Then, holding their fists under the dough with the palms down, they suddenly started to work their hands in a motion that pulled the dough towards them. No one could stop working, everyone had to keep her own section just as thin as the rest. The dough could not be put down and picked up again. Mauserl held her breath, everything became electric; the men had known what they were about when they had devised their excuses.

If the dough had torn (it never did), hysteria would probably have set in. As it was, the women finally dropped the tissue-thin sheet and drew their hands out from under it, and everyone wanted to collapse. But there was no time for that: the dough would dry. It was quickly sprinkled, strewed, dribbled, and dusted with all the ingredients, evenly distributed. Then came the marvel of marvels. The ladies picked up the edges of the table cover on one side and gently lifted it so that the strudel started to roll up. (Mauserl had to grow up before she would believe that the table cover was not baked in with the strudel.) The long strudel roll was bent into a horseshoe. Then came a problem: it had to be transferred to a large baking pan. Five pairs of hands again went under it. It moved onto five pairs of forearms, and, with unexpected maneuvering, suddenly went into the pan. Painted once more with butter, it went into the oven. Half the day's torture was past. The second strudel followed hard upon the first. At last, late in the afternoon, both were completed, sprinkled with sugar, and hidden.

Men started to return to the house. Herr Baron even brought a gift. The dining room was rearranged, the table was set. Guests had been asked for the evening. The two strudels went back into the oven to be heated. By this time, the bottoms were marvelously caramelized. When they were served, the dinner guests were overcome with delight. They had suspected, they had hoped—but how could they be sure that the dough had not torn and a *bombe* for dessert been hastily substituted?

With the eating of the strudel, the estrangement melted away. Herr Baron produced his gift; and as the guests departed, each received a little confectioners' box containing a piece of strudel and tied with a piece of string. Anyone who has from four to ten hands can make a strudel, but only a Viennese knows enough to eat it reheated—for breakfast next morning.

Menus

Marinated Mushrooms
Bouillon with Egg
Roast Goose
Viennese Fried Potatoes
Cucumber Salad
Apple Strudel
Coffee

Tomato Surprise
Cold Wine Soup
Chicken in Spinach
Rice
Green Salad
Apple Strudel with Short Crust
Coffee

Herring in Sour Cream
Consommé with Filled Pancakes
Roast Veal with Pea Purée
Potato Balls
Green Salad
Cherry Strudel
Coffee

Quartett

IN VIENNA, where culture is spelled with a capital "K" and everyone prides himself on his knowledge of *Literatur* and *Musik,* no self-respecting family would be without its own Quartet.

There are young couples who may have to start with a Trio or even a Duet, but they will not rest until they have their own Quartet. Once having achieved a Quartet, no self-respecting family could ever again be satisfied with less than four instruments. There are some who boast Quintets and even Sextets, but this can only be regarded as snobbery, since few salons can accommodate the sound produced by six energetic strings, let alone a large enough audience to listen to it. Some families only play in their friends' Quartets, and very poor relations only listen, but everyone participates in the musical evenings that are so essential in the *Kulturstadt Wien.*

The trick, of course, is to snare a really first-class First Violin—the Second Violin, the *Bratsche,* and the Cello will follow. The players may be extremely talented amateurs or famous professionals: a good cellist from the *Philharmoniker* will enjoy playing with the *Bratschist* from the *Musikverein.* Under no condition may a family member play unless he or she is an outstanding musician. A talented and attractive First Violin with a presentable wife will be sought after by every hostess in Vienna, and it stands to reason that he will play in Frau Hofrat's Quartet far more readily if the Councillor and Frau Hofrat ask distinguished guests to listen to him and serve a delicious dinner after the music. No one could expect him to play even for the most appreciative audience if he had to eat a tough bird afterward.

Quartets meet monthly or possibly every other month. The musicians are the same, but the program, the audience, and most important, the dinners, are different. Before arranging her menus, Frau Hofrätin invites the First Violin and his wife to an intimate little dinner. This not only acquaints him with the caliber of her cook and whets his appetite for pleasures to come, but it gives Frau Hofrätin an opportunity for adjusting her menus to his programs. The First Violin thinks in terms of a well-arranged program of chamber music for the winter; Frau Hofrätin thinks in terms of a well-balanced series of menus that tastefully conform with the musical program, and that allow suitable opportunities to produce her specialties. She hopes for an evening of Mozart so that her matchless *Salzburger Nockerln* will be appreciated, she hints for Dvorák and Smetana so that her *Rehrücken* in sour cream can be included. The First Violin suggests Tchaikovsky or possibly Borodin, and Frau Hofrat is dismayed: her beef Stroganoff does not compare with her paprika chicken. But she welcomes his suggestion of an evening of Béla Bartók: The music may be rather advanced for her audience and annoying to the people in the apartment above, but her spicy Hungarian *gulyás* will compensate for everything.

She excels in fish pudding and is delighted when Herr Hofrat, who is of course well up on *Musik* and glad of an opportunity to show the First Violin that he isn't dealing with a musical imbecile, suggests Grieg. The First Violin, who does not know about the fish pudding, which Frau Hofrat serves with cucumber salad, is not enthusiastic. He loves his Haydn and would also like the posthumous Schubert piece in D. This reference depresses the Hofrätin, who likes to think of the living.. . . . Dvorák, whom she adores, springs to mind. How about Quartet in F Major Opus 96? The wife of the First Violin abruptly changes the subject to César Franck. Fortunately they are eating a really first-class carp and both the First Violin and his wife feel that musical concessions can be made where the table leaves no room for criticism. Frau Hofrätin is inspired to address the First Violin as "Meister," and immediately gets her way with Dvorák, for which she gracefully concedes him César Franck, and wonders desperately where she can lay her hands on a large and well-aged Belgian hare.

Quail follow the carp, and the little dinner party is a great success. The Brahms evening is planned in greatest musico-gastronomic harmony. Although Brahms wisely came to live in Vienna, he was born in Hamburg, so the first course could be a perfect *Krebssalat,* and the rest of the dinner completely Viennese. It might even include some of Brahms's favorite dishes. The Italian evenings of Boccherini, Paganini, and Scarlatti arrange themselves smoothly around a *pollo alla romana* and *dolce di castagne.*

There is no problem about Debussy and Ravel, because Herr Hofrat has given the Hofrätin a first edition of Escoffier that she will consult. This leaves only the spring evenings to plan and one or two programs to arrange in case the Quartet should become a Trio through an unforeseen cancellation—or a Quintet because of an eminent musical guest. The final planning is done over black coffee. Bruckner is included for Vienna's sake, Beethoven, and Hugo Wolf. A Bach trio will provide for any emergency, and if there should be a second mishap Frau Hofrat has the beautiful Chopin trio and her cauliflower *polonaise* up her sleeve. The Brahms, Beethoven, and Mendelssohn quintets will be held in reserve for visiting musicians. If a string should fail them at the last moment, Schumann's Quartet in E flat for piano and strings can be substituted, with Herr Hofrat at the piano.

Now all is settled—only the Russians are left. They agree to start the next season with the new Prokofiev and some Shostakovich—that leaves the whole summer free to practice *Kulich* and save for *Kaviar*.

The Meister goes home in mellow mind to test the timing. He will send in a sort of timetable for Frau Hofrätin's cook to use, so that she can begin to serve each dinner at just the right moment after the applause. The strings meet to run over their parts and Frau Hofrätin sends out her invitations. Politeness demands punctuality and her guests arrive promptly. It would be uncultivated to keep musicians waiting and far too uncomfortable in the *Vorzimmer* to sit out the first number there.

Musik comes first—*Kultur* requires *Musik* on an empty stomach. The Quartet starts at six. There is great concentration; nods and little indications from the guests show that they know every note. The daughter of the house follows breathlessly in her *Partitur*. As the *Musik* continues, with little *Pausen* full of "ohs" and "ahs" and discreet applause, the interest of the guests and possibly even of the musicians seems to turn to thoughts of dinner, of which they may become slightly aware as a faint aroma drifts through the strains of the last number.

The musicians are lauded with a glass of Sherry, and then to dinner: the First Violin on Frau Hofrätin's right, the wife of the First Violin next to Herr Hofrat. The guests and musicians are uplifted by musical conversation and anecdotes, and by a dinner calculated to hold fast the First Violin, so that he will not be lured to Frau Sektionschef's Quartet next year.

Menus

Crayfish Salad
Chicken Consommé
Sautéed Veal Cutlets
Green Noodles
Small Glazed Onions
Salzburger Nockerln
Coffee

Balkan Chlodnik
Squab Chickens
with Paprika Sauce
Buttered Noodles
Lettuce Salad
Schneeballen   Raspberry Sauce
Coffee

Cold Wine Soup
Zucchini with Dill
Fish Pudding   Lobster Sauce
Cucumber Salad
Chestnut Roll
Coffee

Cauliflower Polonaise
Cream of Green Pea Soup
Blue Carp
New Potatoes
Cabbage Salad
Chocolate Cake
Coffee

587

Herr Ober

THE PROPER time for the summer exodus from Vienna was very simply decided. When the Court left the city, everybody else left the city too, happy in the implication that the simultaneous departure was no coincidence. Later, when there was no longer a court to follow and no army to join nor any other suitable occupations for gentlemen, many Viennese had to work. This necessity often meant, horror of horrors, going into industry or, even worse, into finance. Husbands could no longer retire to their hunting boxes, or to their little follies, nor could they accompany their wives and children to the mountains. Instead, they were left behind in a deserted city to work in their offices all day and dine at their favorite restaurants in the evening.

The staff usually accompanied the family to the *Schloss,* or villa, where they spent July and August, while a nameless charwoman was left behind to take care of the one room that remained open in the apartment for the sole use of the head of the house.

The deserted Viennese husband was thrown entirely upon his own resources, and those had to be away from the house since everything inside the house—from the chandeliers to the pictures on the walls—had been wrapped in muslin or in slip covers made of a classic off-white fabric as universal as mattress ticking, and as uninteresting. The Viennese never considered gay summer slip covers of flowered chintz: The well-managed home was taken apart, beaten, cleaned or washed, and wrapped in labeled off-white slip covers. For no reason other than unreasonable tradition, all beds and bedding were disassembled, slip covered, and carried into one bedroom, while all dressers were carried into another, and all chairs into a third. For the summer, at least, most Viennese homes looked like closed furniture stores. Silk-covered walls were draped with yards of the protecting cloth, portieres were fitted into their own clearly labeled sacks, which were then hooked into the curtain rings. Doors were locked.

Somewhere in all this ghostly unlighted desolation, a little island of life remained for the man of the house. He called this haven his *Jung-gesellenwohnung*—bachelor quarters—but even here he had to face the white wrappings everywhere. They left him a rug on the floor, but they enclosed it in a white duck carpet cover for him to stumble over all summer. They put covers on his lamps so that he could hardly see, and they covered his chairs, not with the beautifully tailored, zippered covers of today, but with loose, shapeless wraps that made the furniture un-recognizable (unless one read the printed labels) and quite impossible to sit on. They covered the headboard and the footboard of his bed, and the poor man even had to unwrap his closet before he could reach his clothes. They also left him a smell of tar and camphor strong enough to drive him from his home early each day and to keep him away as late as possible each night. This arrangement had the advantage that he never saw the charwoman, who came late and left early, and it also forced him to try out restaurants until he found one that suited him so well that he could spend most of his summer evenings there.

The restaurant had to be pleasant, the food had to be good, and, most important of all, there had to be a sympathetic Herr Ober, a head-waiter who took the abandoned husband's plight to heart and filled the gap left by his departed family. Viennese husbands were gallant, romantic, and dashing—*fesch,* in a word—but they were also spoiled, pampered, and coddled. At table, especially, most of them became tyrants. As the summer progressed, the relationship between the employees of the restau-rant and Herr Baron became, in a one-sided way, extremely intimate. Herr Ober listened to letters from the Baron's family, he was initiated into family secrets, and he learned every detail of Herr Baron's state of health and digestion. He knew that Frau Baronin disliked *Punschtorte* and that, in spite of the happy relationship between the Baron and his wife, she refused even to be present when he ate raw beef, which he adored. Herr Ober understood perfectly that his patron was having a gastronomical fling: A man separated from his family was bound to want a *Wiener Rostbraten,* a rib steak, buried under fried onions, and might even go so far as to have *Punschtorte* on top of it. Herr Ober knew at once when there was no letter from Frau Baronin, and he helped to prepare the heart-shaped *Nusstorte* that Herr Baron sent to her by special courier for her birthday. A headwaiter who would not concern himself with these matters, who would recommend strawberries after cucumber salad with-out remembering that this combination was fatal for Herr Baron, deserved

to lose a client. Herr Baron did not know the headwaiter's name. If he had passed Herr Ober on the street, wearing a hat and street clothes, he would not have recognized this man, the same man to whom he had just confided the state of his liver. But in his customary place in the restaurant, moving among his patrons, he was Herr Ober, Herr Baron's closest summer friend.

Next in command was Alfred, the *Speisenkellner*. He did not enjoy Herr Baron's confidence; on the contrary, he confided in the Baron. Alfred contemplated making a proposal, and Herr Baron amused himself while his dinner was being served with a little experienced advice on courting. Next to the Baron's heart after Herr Ober came the *Kellermeister*—the wine steward—resplendent in his apron and chain. Here again, no names were known, but any two men of the world who had in common the love of wine could become warm friends. Last of all was the *Piccolo,* the little *Piccolo* in his tiny handed-down full-dress suit, not tall enough to hold Herr Baron's coat for him, but quick to bring water or a light for his cigarette, quick to catch the coin that was always tossed to him and to salute his patron's *Guten Abend*. In addition to Herr Baron's close summer friends, there was an enigmatic and beautiful man in a fez and shalwar (Oriental trousers) who brewed thick, sweet Turkish coffee and smiled a warm, white-toothed smile. Herr Baron did not speak Turkish and Timur spoke no German, but even these two came to feel congenial.

The moment Herr Baron arrived, Herr Ober gave him a bulletin from the kitchen. The veal was white . . . like a dream. Would Herr Baron consider it with mushrooms? Just so . . . let's see . . . Herr Baron wasn't going to spoil all the fun by capitulating so soon. Perhaps . . . but maybe today required something just a little lighter. Herr Baron had thought about cold Rhine salmon and hot *Palatschinken* all afternoon, but that didn't mean he would come right out and ask for it. They had to work around to it slowly, in mouth-watering steps. No final decisions could be made until the dessert had been selected. Contrary to the system in all other countries, most Austrians consider dessert the most important course and plan the rest of the dinner around it. If a heavy dessert tempted Herr Baron, he and Herr Ober might have to revise their plans completely. When the menu was settled, the wine steward came quietly to the table with his embossed leather-bound book, they opened the magic volume together, and Herr Baron told the *Kellermeister* what he was going to have for dinner. The wine steward always had something that would be perfect with the menu. His Berncasteler was at the peak or his Tokay was. . . . Only a discreet gesture could show how absolutely superb it was. Herr Baron had to call back the Herr Ober and revise his plans slightly. If the Tokay was really as perfect as the wine steward claimed, he would change his dessert to a *Creme* and his salad to cress.

When the food was served, Herr Ober went through all his paces. He boned fish and birds with a stroke—he carved to perfection. He finally presented the garnished plate, tensely watched Herr Baron through the first taste, and after a reassuring nod or smile from the Baron, he retired. The wine steward, who had been chilling the wine or allowing it to breathe, depending on its character, drew the cork deftly, smelled it, rolled his eyes to heaven, poured off the first thimbleful, and let the wine run slowly into Herr Baron's glass. He, too, stayed to see the first swallow go down. Herr Baron always took the glass from his lips and raised it to the wine steward, a silent *prosit,* a tribute to a perfect bottle of wine. Later in the evening, Herr Ober and the wine steward enjoyed a similar dinner, with which they finished the remains of Herr Baron's bottle.

Herr Baron walked home to his white-draped apartment, enjoying the memory of the dinner he had eaten and of the dinners he had planned and discussed with his friend the Herr Ober, but had not eaten. He wondered contentedly whether the duck would have been better than the *poularde* or the peaches better than the pears.

Menus

Stuffed Mushrooms with Jellied Mayonnaise
Consommé Elizabeth
Rib Steak with Onions
Beet Salad
Rolled Pancakes with Jam
Coffee

Crayfish Salad
Paprika Veal Cutlets   Spätzle
Braised Cucumbers
Hazelnut Rum Linzer Cake
Turkish Coffee

Cream of Green Pea Soup Rigoletto
Roast Guinea Hens with Water Cress
Noodles with Bread Crumbs and Brown Butter
Punschtorte
Turkish Coffee

Beef Consommé with Farina Dumplings
Lentil Salad
Garnished Beefsteak Tartare   Thin Buttered Black Bread
Cheese and Apples
Beer

Spinach Soup Leopold
Orange and Endive Salad
Saddle of Veal with Paprika Sauce
Braised Cucumbers
Viennese Fried Potatoes
Ambrosial Pudding
Coffee

Lemon Trout
Lemon Mayonnaise
Spit-Roasted Stuffed Capon
New Potatoes
Steamed Asparagus
Vanilla Mousse
Raspberry Sauce
Almond Short Wafers
Coffee

Green Pea and Shrimp Tart
Squab Chickens with Egg Sauce
Green Salad
Pineapple Bombe
Apricot Sauce
Suvaroffs
Coffee

Potato and Tongue Salad
Thin Buttered Black Bread
Queen of Chickens
Assorted Vegetables
Coffee Mousse
Oak Leaves
Coffee

593

Der Heurige

THE EVER-ILLOGICAL and beloved Viennese may house only the most precious vintages in their own cellars and their palates may be educated to appreciate only the noblest wines, but when the first green bush appears from under the eaves of a vintner's house in the little suburb of Grinzing, they are off—as one man—to the *Heurige* to drink Grinzinger.

In German the word *heurig* means "this year's" or just "this." It is most often used in describing *heurige Kartoffeln,* new potatoes, words without romance or music. But Vienna speaks an enchanted language of her own. There, *Heurige* means the fragrant, fresh, new wine of Grinzing and all that surrounds the lighthearted, carefree drinking of it. It means the place, the wine, and the age-old customs. The Viennese go to the *Heurige* and they drink *Heurige* and they call it all by the single word. It means *Schrammelmusik* and zither playing; it means the indescribable atmosphere, the *Stimmung,* the charm, the green wine hills, and the first taste of the cold, pale golden wine. It means the effect of the wine, different from that of any other, and the feeling of gaiety and happiness, of romance and enchantment. It means the traditional vendors who carry their heavy wooden trays of sweets and confections through the village from *Heurige* to *Heurige.* It means good food—*Wiener Backhendl, Grinzinger Salat,* and *kalter Aufschnitt*—it means Vienna and spring.

The green bush that signals that a vintner is pouring new wine is a small bunch of evergreen boughs tied to the end of a staff and hung out from his low white house. The moment it is in view, word travels fast and far that Poldi's or Franzl's wine is ready, and every heart in Vienna begins to sing. From Jani the shoemaker's assistant right up to Herr Graf and Frau Gräfin there is no one in Vienna who is going to miss the *Heurige.* It is said that a passing stranger once observed, "There must be a hole in heaven—over Grinzing."

594

Heurige cannot be bottled transported; it must come straight from the casks in the vintner's cellars to the tables set out in his garden. Since the *Heurige* cannot go to the Viennese, the Viennese, with Mohammed's wisdom, go to the *Heurige*. They go right out to the grape arbor at the back of the vintner's little house and, while they happily drink, Grinzinger grows green on the wine hills behind them.

Ever since the first vintners poured out their new wine to avoid taxes and discovered that the young golden wine was, in fact, a gold mine, there have been established procedures which are still followed. Originally, all the vintners drew lots, and each hung out his green bush only after the casks of the *Heurige* next in line before him had been drained dry. But as the taste for the new wine grew, it was possible for several vintners to hang out their bushes at the same time. Thus Jani and his Resl could find a primitive *Heurige* to suit their simple tastes, while Herr Graf and Frau Gräfin went to the *Heurige* that their fathers and grandfathers had patronized before them. Fortunately the vintner always provided a son and heir to the vineyard, while the Graf and Gräfin produced an heir to the title, so the noble family could go on for generations with a *Heurige* that they considered practically their own.

Austria is the only country in the world that grows many of its best wines within the city limits of its capital. Jani and Resl, who couldn't possibly afford more than a few tumblers of wine, packed their sausage, bread, and cheese in a rucksack and walked out to Grinzing. They chose a *Heurige* that provided only the wine and the rough wooden tables and benches in the garden; itinerant musicians might stop to play *heurigen Lieder* and pass the hat for coppers before they moved on. Jani and Resl sat arm in arm in a garden that overlooked Vienna. They watched the sun setting and they ate their heavy slabs of black bread and sausage. They drank the delicious new wine from thick tumblers as casually as they would have drunk water, and they saved their last coppers for the sugar-men whose tempting trays were piled high with traditional confections. There were always little sticks strung with sugared dates and figs, which were sold by the stickful. For those who could afford such sweets, there were wedges of *Pischingertorte,* little chocolate confections wrapped in foil. The wine was cheap and the Viennese were born musicians. Many brought their own guitars, and all linked arms and sang as the magic of the evening drew them together.

Herr and Frau Müller went out to Grinzing by horsecar, from which they alighted at the last stop on the Grinzinger Platz. They walked

up one of the steep cobbled streets that wind through the wine hills of
Vienna's suburbs and chose a slightly more pretentious *Heurige,* one with
a large garden, with lanterns and checkered tablecloths, a *Heurige* with
four musicians. They selected a *Heurige* that served just enough food to
counteract the effect of the wine and to enable the guests to stay from
late afternoon through the long evening without bringing their own supper.
The Müllers could request their favorite songs from the musicians, who
went from table to table, and they could order any of the numerous *kalte
Aufschnitte,* large tempting platters of cold meats. These became increas-
ingly elaborate when Herr Müller ordered a *feiner* (or even a *sehr feiner*)
kalter Aufschnitt. Feiner meant the addition of butter rosettes and salads,
sehr feiner always meant a little goose liver pâté. When the vintner's
wife was enterprising, the Müllers could order *Cobenzl* eggs, named for
the hill behind Grinzing, and *Sülze.* They invariably missed the last horsecar back to the inner city at midnight so that they could walk home with
the musicians.

Herr Graf, on the other hand, approached the whole thing quite differ-

ently. He was, after all, a connoisseur of wines and pleasure. Having kept
a careful eye out for the days of sunshine and the days of cloud or rain
during the previous spring and summer, he knew just about what to
expect of his *Heurige*. He had also gone out during the winter to spend
a few quiet, pleasant evenings with Pepi and Mina Huber, his family
vintners, to determine how the young wine was coming along. He had
sat in the small low-ceilinged room with its warm tile stove and lovely
old guitar. He had enjoyed a pipe and tasted the new, as well as some
very good old wine.

When the wine was ready and the day was set, Herr Graf and Frau
Gräfin invited their guests. Pepi Huber was not only a good vintner, he
had the added advantage of a strong baritone voice and a repertoire that
included all the beloved old songs, and he could accompany himself on
the guitar. Herr Graf engaged a zither player to entertain while Pepi was
drawing the wine, for he considered the ensemble required for *Schrammelmusik* too pretentious. Pepi Huber's Mina knew what was wanted from
her. She fattened her pullets and slowly dried golden rolls for perfect
bread crumbs. She churned butter, and when the day finally came, she
prepared crisp, juicy *Wiener Backhendl* and served it with an enormous
Gurkensalat and *heurige Kartoffeln*. Her dessert was invariably the same.
Ever since Oskar Pischinger, Vienna's famous nineteenth-century confectioner, had contrived his *Pischingertorte,* it had been the accepted *heurigen* sweet. Mina made the richly filled *Torte* herself.

The Graf and his guests enjoyed their *Heurige* as sincerely and simply
as Jani and Resl enjoyed theirs. They loved the primitive garden with its
benches and long table, the scent of lilac and linden in bloom mingled
with the delicious fragrance of *Backhendl,* the soft twang of the zither
and Pepi Huber's *Lieder,* and they looked forward to the *Heurige* all
year. For all of them it was a part of Vienna that could not be imitated
anywhere—to drink new wine in the landscape that has produced it, in
Grinzing, an ageless, unchanged Grinzing.

Menus

Eggs Stuffed with Sardines
Goulash Soup
Apples in Robes
Coffee

Poor People Salad
Calf's Liver Dumplings
Onion Sauce
Apple Sauerkraut
Emmenthal Cheese
Thin Black Bread
Beer

Garnished Liptauer Cheese
Oven-Dried Vienna Bread
Cold Viennese Fried Chicken
Grinzing Salad
Pischingertorte
Coffee

Stuffed Mushrooms
Balkan Soup
Cottage Cheese Pancakes
Coffee

Lentil Soup with Red Wine
Garden Beef Platter
Horseradish Cream
Tomato and Green Bean Salad
Potato Balls
Linzertorte

Russian Salad
Cheese Palmiers
Coffee Mousse
Assorted Cheeses
Thin Breads and Crackers

Mushroom Soufflé over Dilled Shrimps
I Know Everything Salad
Apple Strudel with Short Crust
Coffee

The Betrothal

Die Verlobung

THE ENTIRE apartment smelled of Eau de Cologne
—*Kölnisches Wasser*—a clearly decipherable
message to one and all that Frau Hofrat had awakened with a headache
and that she must on no account be disturbed by those members of her
family who were to blame for it. The accusation inherent in the scent gave
Herr Hofrat a strong feeling of guilt. Having achieved an impressive station
in life, as well as a title and a most impressive goatee, he could no longer
be said ever to *slink*, but his silent departure from the apartment, on a
wave of Joseph Maria Farina's famous concoction, closely resembled sneak-
ing. The boys left for school the moment the first whiff seeped under their
door, and the maid found work that had to be done in the most remote
room. The Hofrätin's daughter and the cook, Lutz and Teckla—both
newly betrothed and ecstatic brides-to-be—remained happily unaware of
the ominous scent around them. In the dream world they had entered,
no practical considerations mattered: the endless details of engagements
and weddings, the planning of festivities, and the making of complicated
menus played no part. Frau Hofrat had to carry the full burden of the
Verlobung, Hochzeit, and *Ausstattung*—the betrothal, wedding, and all-
important trousseau—without Teckla's help. Teckla had her mind and her
elbows deep in her own hope chest. Added to these difficulties was the
constant danger that the maid would succumb to the epidemic and announce a third engagement.

The letter formally requesting Lutz's hand had come and been answered;
the proposal call had been made and returned; cards had been left with
all relatives and connections, and Lutz wore on her left hand the simple
gold band that would be transferred to her right hand by the bridegroom
after being blessed at the altar. Frau Hofrat would gladly have dispensed
with this charming sentimentality in exchange for a diamond engagement
ring. Teckla's hand was similarly adorned, thus making it almost impossi-

ble for her to knead dough and bake bread. Nothing could be undertaken that might impair the yellow luster of her ring.

Herr Geheimrat, the father of the bridegroom, had met with Herr Hofrat for the formal arrangements and clarification of the bride's expectations. These coincided so closely with Herr Geheimrat's rough calculations of the position that he expressed himself satisfied. Since young Doktor Karl was an only son, and Herr Geheimrat a successful advocate, there was no need of further discussions regarding the bridegroom's outlook. Not mentioned but tacitly taken into account was the fact, also, that Frau Geheimrat was a *geborener* Schmidt—that is, nee Schmidt—which meant solid assets in industry. All things considered, it might be said to be, on both sides, perhaps not an absolutely brilliant but certainly a satisfactory match. To make matters even pleasanter, the Geheimrat and the Hofrat and their wives allowed their negotiations to be influenced by the charming circumstance that, in addition to all other good reasons for the match, the young couple also seemed to love each other.

Just so with Teckla. Her ad in the marriage column had swelled the Hofrätin's mail, and for days she oversalted the roast and undersalted the soup. Most disgraceful of all, her last *Torte* was *sitzengeblieben*—it didn't rise at all—probably the final factor that induced Frau Hofrat's headache. After several rendezvous in various *Kaffees* and at street corners, Teckla had quickly made her choice. The happy man was a veterinarian with a small practice in the provinces. Teckla's savings would enable him to buy several pieces of equipment; with these, he felt, he could so far increase his earnings that he would be able to afford a wife. Teckla was perfectly happy because her ability to cook had never been mentioned, and she felt loved for herself alone—and for the enlarged practice that would result from the union.

Frau Hofrat, having escaped to a darkened room, could not escape her fate. She and she alone would have to give the *Verlobungsfest,* send out the notices, buy the *Ausstattung.* Lutz was so young that they had been letting down the hems of her skirts rather than hemming sheets for her. Frau Hofrat had to plan the *Tees* for the young, the *Après Soupers* for the adults, the large reception, and the dinners. She moaned in agony; Herr and Frau Geheimrat would attend most of the functions, so she could not resort to preparing one menu and repeating it over and over again. She would have to produce her entire repertoire, including the *Kalbsrücken,* saddle of veal, and the cold lemon trout, all in two months, with the help of a cook who had lost her touch. The children wanted to marry in

June, and, naturally, so did Teckla. And there sat Frau Geheimrat with a confirmed old-maid cook in the kitchen, and convention required of her only a dinner party for four—*four!*—Lutz, Karl, the Geheimrat, and Frau Geheimrat, a charming, intimate little dinner, with a well-roasted and garnished *poularde,* a compote, and a pudding. Frau Hofrat, on the other hand, might have to stage as many as eighteen functions, haunted all the while by the ominous prospect of another small daughter growing up.

At the moment of Frau Hofrat's deepest despair, the maid announced Herr Gumprecht, the veterinarian. He was calling, if not actually to ask Frau Hofrat for the hand of Teckla, at least to wait upon her with his respects. The Hofrätin arose. She steadied herself with a whispered *noblesse oblige:* She felt far more animosity toward the man who was going to take her cook away from her than she felt toward Doktor Karl, who was marrying her daughter. In spite of her headache, Herr Gumprecht won her over immediately with a stiff bunch of flowers and the sincere admiration he expressed for her favorite poodle.

Frau Hofrat could not but give her blessings, though she sorrowed for the *Hühner in Spinatsuppe,* the *Feinschmeckersalat,* and the *Eisbombe Romanoff* that would in future be wasted in the provinces while she would have to make do with any young woman the newfangled employment agency· sent her. Herr Gumprecht agreed to put off his wedding day until Lutz had safely departed on her own wedding trip to Paris. Frau Hofrat, in return, was so carried away that she rashly offered a small X-ray machine as a wedding present.

Overawed by this generosity, Teckla produced an edible *Jause* after the call, and Frau Hofrat managed to start a trousseau list that made it look as though she were equipping a small hotel rather that her daughter.

Lutz arrived in time to decide on featherbeds rather than comforters, button-on sheets rather than tuck-ins, square pillows rather than oblong, Alençon rather than Valencienne lace, and please, please, please, a toaster, a mixer, and a beater—*und alles Amerikanisch!* She also chose squab chickens in cream for the intimate first *Verlobungs* dinner, paprika chicken for the distant relatives, and an *Indian* for the last dinner for the less intimate friends. Some people supposedly called *Indians* turkeys—a ludicrous idea when every child in Vienna knew they were *Indians.*

Herr Hofrat returned, sniffing, at five. Prepared for the worst, he was delighted to find the Hofrätin up and well, and the fumes of *Kölnisches Wasser* completely evaporated. After dinner he let Frau Hofrat read him the lists and begin schooling him in his duties as the goateed *Vater der Braut.*

Menus

Smoked Eel Platter

Thin Black and Rye Bread

Warm Salt Sticks

Dilled Butter Curls

Emmenthal Cheese

Sherry

Coffee

Asparagus Pastry Roll

Filets of Sole with Tomatoes

Green Salad

Chilled Fruit

Hazelnut Salt Rounds

Sherry

Coffee

Skewered Mushrooms

Rice and Tomato Salad

Thin Buttered Rye Bread

Dried Fruit and Nuts

Sherry

Coffee

The Wedding

Die Hochzeit

As Luzetta's wedding day drew nearer and nearer, Frau Hofrat was forced to cross her Rubicon, or at least her Danube, in search of Frau Marie, Vienna's ubiquitous and overbearing wedding-day cook. Like her colleague, Jour-Ludwig, Frau Marie had built up a reputation as a specialist, and she went from house to house to help with the preparation of the *Hochzeitsgabelfrühstück,* the wedding luncheon, a single unpronounceable word.

Frau Marie may not have been as essential to the wedding as the bride and the groom, but she came only a step behind them in her own estimation of the proper protocol, and way ahead of the mother of the bride. Frau Hofrat had hoped to do without Frau Marie, but as she looked at Teckla and saw that strong pillar of society, the Viennese cook, collapse before her eyes, she realized that a cook in love was worse than no cook at all and that Frau Marie would have to take over. Odious and ignominious as this might be, it was better than worrying about Teckla, who thought only of Herr Gumprecht, her fiancé.

Frau Marie and her helpers listened to the reading of the marriage banns each Sunday in church and studied the wedding announcements. As new banns were read and new announcements published, Frau Marie ticked them off on her calendar. Long before Frau Hofrat had made her decision, Frau Marie already had Luzetta's name written across Saturday, June twenty-seventh, in her engagement book. She had also written down exactly what she would prepare for the wedding, a fact of which Frau Hofrat was still happily unaware.

Frau Hofrat, always the Modern Mother, had asked Luzetta for her preferences, and Lutz in turn consulted with Karl and came up with a wonderful menu of all their favorite dishes, their *Leibspeisen*. Not that either of them would eat very much, but they wanted their friends to eat what they themselves liked best.

603

Equipped with Lutz's list, an umbrella, and some very definite mental reservations, Frau Hofrat set out for Floridsdorf across the Danube on what she innocently thought of as an exploratory sortie. She found Frau Marie fully armed with a menu, a marketing list, a bill, and a contract, in a small house which would obviously never see one of Frau Marie's own weddings. The conflict lasted only a few minutes. Frau Marie fired off a long list of her past and future weddings and ended with the name of a ducal house, doubtful but effective, as she handed over her contract, her fountain pen, and her ultimatum: "No additions." Frau Hofrat capitulated. She signed where she was told, took her copy, and silently went away. She stopped at a *Kaffeehaus,* something she had never done before, and ordered an *Eierkognac* to quiet her nerves while she read Frau Marie's menu.

Mercy, it began with *Ragoutsuppe* and went on to *Fischmayonnaise.* It now became quite clear that Frau Hofrat had been eating Frau Marie's wedding luncheons for years, and that Lutz had to have something quite different. Frau Hofrat went straight to Herr Hofrat's office —something that she had never done before either—and had him compose a letter to renegotiate the menu.

With the full weight of the law and of beautifully engraved very heavy white paper behind it, Herr Hofrat's letter not only changed the menu but forced an addition—peppermints.

When Frau Marie and her staff arrived to take over Teckla's kitchen, they encountered none of the usual resentment. Teckla whiled away the time calculating whether she could herself afford to have Frau Marie prepare her wedding luncheon the next week; perhaps she would even make a special price, since Teckla was in a way a member of the trade.

No matter how often Frau Hofrat weeded out and rearranged the list, she could not get the wedding luncheon guests down to less than twenty-seven. Twenty-six members of the laity and Herr Pfarrer, for whom she hardly considered it necessary to produce a single lady, especially since she had run out of single ladies some time ago. She hoped for an enormous attendance at church and for at least nine cancellations for the luncheon. She could just seat eighteen comfortably in the dining room and had to have a table set up in the large salon in order to seat twenty-seven. To add to her troubles, Frau Marie had come equipped with garlands of white flowers to weave around Lutz's and Karl's chairs, which seemed a *Geschmacklosigkeit,* a lapse of taste, to Frau Hofrat. Teckla considered it all absolutely rapturously beautiful and mentally set aside another layer of her life's savings so that she, too, could crush white flowers when she sat down to her wedding feast.

Frau Marie brought along as part of her contract the great cakes, slices of which would be delivered to the homes of all the Viennese who had an interested share in Lutz. This group would include her old governess, the seamstress, and Herr Eddy, who always came to the house to shampoo her hair. Frau Marie provided the small boys who delivered the cakes and, no doubt, a list of her own addresses. The boys carried away the great cakes, while the bride's cake in Vienna was just a *Torte,* beautifully prepared but with no tiers and no embellishments.

According to tradition, Lutz should have remained blushingly ignorant of the place Karl had chosen for their honeymoon, but since she had to pose for her *Ausreise* picture and sign her applications, she could not help discovering that they were going to leave the country. In her heart of hearts, she hoped for Paris, but all young Viennese are trained to respect their husbands and she would not have dreamt of expressing a preference.

Although Karl's parents had urged him to go to the Semmering, or, at most, to Salzburg for his honeymoon, Karl had disregarded all advice. From the moment he squared his young shoulders and walked alone without his father, the Herr Geheimrat, through the portals of the Wagon-Lits office, often passed but never entered, and reserved accommodations to Paris for himself and his wife, his Frau Gemahlin, he was a man. He was almost tearful with joy and his knees shook, but he was an independent man capable of taking his Lutz to Paris, which he suspected was the place to which she wanted most to go.

The *Hochzeit,* the high time, of Karl and Luzetta was celebrated without pomp and with great dignity. They were married at the Minoriten Kirche at eleven o'clock by Herr Hofrat's third cousin, Pfarrer Michael. Herr Hofrat remembered him only as a very mischievous boy and was rather startled to find him middle-aged and worthy, though still with a twinkle in his eye. The orchestra in the organ loft played Bach, and Luzetta, dressed in simple white and accompanied only by her two witnesses, exchanged rings with Karl and repeated her vows in a clear young voice.

The day was beautiful and the young *Brautpaar,* the bride and bridegroom, drove home in a smart carriage, which forced the guests who came by car to drive three times around the Ring in order to arrive after the wedding party. When Lutz entered the building the porter touched his cap and said "Frau Doktor," since in Vienna the titles and accomplishments of the husband are given to his wife, in direct address, in preference to his name.

Frau Marie had done her work well: the thorns had been removed from the white roses around the bridal chairs and her luncheon, which started with *Brautsuppe* instead of *Ragoutsuppe,* went on to such an assortment of unexpected dishes that no one ever dreamt she was behind the whole thing. The fish course was hot, there was no mayonnaise at all, and the filet of beef was almost too beautiful to disturb. Teckla confiscated the bouquet of vegetable flowers that garnished the top in the hope that she could keep it fresh for a week, and the mocha *Torte* was only just large enough to go around for the second helpings that Pfarrer Michael initiated. While the guests drank coffee, Luzetta changed into the tailored suit that every bride in Vienna, winter or summer, has to wear.

When they finally arrived at the *Bahnhof,* and there before them stood the big polished, steaming Wagon-Lits, Frau Doktor burst into tears of happiness.

Consommé with Filled Pancakes

Salt Bakery

Cold Brook Trout   Fresh Herb Mayonnaise

Roast Turkey with Turkish Stuffing

Duchess Potatoes

Geneva Cake

Peaches in Champagne

Coffee

Chicken Soup with Curry

Steamed Asparagus

Hollandaise Sauce

Spring Rhine Salmon in Aspic

Garden Beef Platter

Horseradish Cream

Vindobonatorte

Strawberry Punch

Coffee

Artichoke Bottoms with Shrimps

Consommé Elizabeth

Chicken Talleyrand

Potatoes Anna with Cheese

Endive Salad

Moor in a Shirt

Coffee

Oranges with Avocado Dressing

Open Sandwiches

Herring Salad

Thin Buttered Pumpernickel

Swedish Platter

Strawberry Mousse

Walnut Cake

Landsturm

Coffee

Menus

Clear Consommé with Sherry
Pompanos with Anchovies
Cucumbers with Horseradish Cream
Potato Balls
Filet of Beef in Crust   Madeira Sauce
Spanish Wind Torte
Peach Punch
Coffee

Clear Consommé
with Emperor's Garnish
Individual Salmon Mousse
Lemon Mayonnaise
Stuffed Prague Ham
Pineapple Rings
with Glazed Chestnuts
Potato Balls   Glazed Onions
Vanilla Crescents
Weinchaudeau

Assorted Stuffed Eggs
Cold Carp with Walnuts
Lemon Mayonnaise
Squab Chickens in Aspic
Endive and Lentil Salad
Vindobonatorte
Pineapple Bombe
Champagne Punch
Coffee

Melon Balls with Orange Sauce
Cream of Chicken Soup with Chestnuts
Potato Salt Sticks
Cold Loin of Veal with Caper Sauce
Asparagus in Aspic
Black and White Salad
Viennese Orange Cake
Happy Marriage
Coffee

Stille Nacht, Heilige Nacht

The adage "children should be seen but not heard" rigidly prevailed in Vienna for eleven months of every year. On December first, however, the situation was reversed. From then on, until Christmas, the children were rarely seen but almost constantly heard practicing "Stille Nacht, Heilige Nacht" as a Christmas Eve surprise for their parents and the family's guests. Even though Herr Baron and Frau Baronin had similarly surprised their own parents each year and knew, from painful weeks of the children's practicing, that their little Elizabeth Maria would never reach the last high F of the carol, they were always moved to tears on Christmas Eve when the children stood in front of the candlelit tree and raised their squeaky little voices.

The moment the ordeal ended, for the performers as well as for the audience, everyone relaxed. Herr Baron distributed parcels to his guests and family and, once these had been opened and admired, everyone helped the children play with their gifts. In Vienna St. Nicholas always visited the children on his feast day, December sixth, to ask them whether they had been good. Traditionally, he was tall, stern, and rather skinny— although his dimensions differed in different homes—and his annual visit did much to insure discipline throughout the year. If the children were able to give a good account of themselves, as they invariably could, he asked them for their list of wishes. Wondering whether he would bring everything they wanted kept the children in a mood of alternate hope and despair for the eighteen days before Christmas. In spite of all their doubts, he not only fulfilled every wish but always added a few marvelous surprises that even the best child would not have dared to hope for. St. Nicholas even brought Frau Baronin everything her heart desired: She found the beautiful baroque pearls, the trained bullfinch, and, miracle of miracles, the *Amerikanische Eis-Machine,* the ice-cream freezer, among her gifts. Possibly this generosity occurred because she too had been good or possibly because she had given St. Nicholas, alias the Baron, just a little hint.

The children's Fräulein, who had lived through the whole year for her one great moment, accompanying the children's singing on the piano, returned to reality and the immediate responsibility of watching the candles on the Christmas tree. Having been delegated not only to watch but also to act at once in an emergency, she stood ready behind the tree, a candle snuffer on a broomstick in one hand and a large pail of water in the other. She stayed constantly and courageously on the watch for the flare of a flame or the smell of burning pastry.

Frau Baronin's tree was always trimmed beautifully, elaborately, and deliciously with Christmas baked specialties and confections of every kind. With the exception of the old wax angel that came out of its box to adorn the top of the tree each year, the household was not burdened with the cumbersome storage of Christmas ornaments. The angel passed from generation to generation, and everything else came fresh and crisp from the kitchen, to be gradually eaten off the tree as the holidays progressed.

They prepared baked delicacies of the kind that aged well and even improved with time. Although the tree was gradually stripped of decoration and often became quite bare, with only the inedible angel and a few unreachable pretzels at the top, it always stood until the Feast of the Three Kings on January sixth. When it was taken down, the last morsels were divided among the children, and the angel returned to its old velvet-lined black leather case.

The *Heilige Abend*, the Holy Evening, was a time for parents and children, for close and dear friends, and for rejoicing and happiness. Frau Baronin never asked more than twenty-four guests to her buffet. She did not want to share this evening with acquaintances; it was the occasion she loved most in all the year and it should be reserved for the people dearest to her. She planned every detail carefully, supervised every step of the preparations, and spent weeks with Resi, baking and storing the food that would be given away to the poor while her own buffet was in progress.

During the opening of the presents, one of the footmen was sent out of doors to survey the heavens. As soon as he found the evening star, assisted by a hint from the kitchen, he came back to announce dinner and the breaking of fast. Vienna could always be depended upon to produce a white Christmas, but not always one with a clear starry sky. An experienced footman had to know how to find the evening star even through falling snow.

When the adults went to dinner, the children were allowed to select one gift to take to bed. Frau Baronin, realizing that Eduard Karl couldn't sleep comfortably with skis or a fortress with a drawbridge, had rushed out at the last moment to buy a soft toy. But in the end, there were always tears, and Eduard Karl retired with an enormous papier-mâché railroad tunnel, and Elizabeth Maria, Mauserl for short, took the new green leather suitcase that had her own initials on it—an achievement that left her starry-eyed for weeks. Young Rudolf chose his extremely frightened English cocker spaniel puppy, named Christmas, to take to bed.

Frau Baronin's formal buffet dinner started the three consecutive holidays that Vienna needed to celebrate Christmas adequately. Traditionally there had to be a carp or some kind of shellfish for the wealthy and a lesser fish for the poor, but rich and poor alike ate nine dishes on Christmas Eve, the last of which had to be an apple. Everyone cut his apple across and, if he did so without cutting through a seed, a wonderful fortune lay in store. If he cut a seed, the future looked just a little less bright.

Mindful of the importance of nine dishes on her menu, Frau Baronin started with a hot soup. Next came a cold lobster salad, the top gaily decorated with bright red crayfish standing on their tails. No Viennese household was complete without carefully cleaned and lacquered crayfish shells to garnish the fish course. When the shells were not in use, they were put away in cotton wool and they might even find their way into a daughter's hope chest.

Frau Baronin chose as main dishes a glazed capon with individual capon aspics and asparagus, and a carp surrounded by cornucopias of fish mousse. The decorated capon and carp adorned the buffet table, but she served her guests only the individually prepared portions. She would not dream of asking them to eat a slice of dry meat. She had a compote of greengage plums and a vegetable pudding. There were a salad, a pistachio ice-cream *Torte,* and, ninth and last, a beautiful red apple for every guest. The dinner was gay and full of warmth, the table was beautifully set, and everyone cut the apples without mishap. Some of the guests drove through the snowy streets to St. Stephen's Cathedral for midnight mass, where they solemnly celebrated the Nativity. Others stayed on to await their return and the serving of the holiday *Punsch.*

All Viennese shared the celebration with the poor. They set candles in their windows and, wherever a light burned the poor were sure of a welcome. Every ring of the doorbell was greeted with joy and generosity. Since the Viennese believed that the Christ Child stopped at every door, they would never allow anyone to leave empty-handed.

When the churchgoers returned, Herr Baron took over. He served hot punch, and the guests made the first inroads on the Christmas tree cookies. Friends and acquaintances stopped in to wish everyone *Frohe Weihnachten* and the musicians played waltzes until dawn. The trained bullfinch felt more and more at home and finally contributed his own talents to the evening. He whistled clearly, precisely, and very remarkably "Stille Nacht, Heilige Nacht."

On Christmas Day, the *Erste Feiertag,* the whole family went to eat a huge meal and celebrate with Herr Baron's mother. Next day, on the *Zweite Feiertag,* they went to feast at the home of Frau Baronin's mother, and on the *Dritte Feiertag,* December twenty-seventh, there was a large party for less intimate friends and acquaintances.

Herr Baron and Frau Baronin reminded each other that next year they wanted the children to surprise them with Gounod's "Ave Maria," and they retired on the evening of the twenty-eighth with the comforting thought that in Vienna Christmas comes but three and a half days a year.

Christmas Eve Dinner

Consommé with Salty Orange Macaroons
Blue Carp
Potato Balls
Cucumber Salad
Roast Pheasant with Grapes
Glazed Chestnuts
Mushroom Rice
Hazelnut Rum Linzer Cake
Red Apples
Coffee

Christmas Day Buffet

Pheasant Soup
Lobster Salad Heligoland
Capon in Aspic with Asparagus
Christmas Ham with Tomatoes and Tangerine Sauce
Molded Vegetable Pudding
Truffle and Avocado Salad
Pistachio Ice-Cream Cake
Red Apples
Coffee

Menus

New Year's Eve Buffet

Caviar
Cold Lemon Soup
Crab Meat in Potato Cheese Ring
Cold Duck Bristol
Oranges Filled with Lingonberries
Millionaire Salad
Pastries and Confections
Champagne
Coffee

New Year's Eve Dinner for Two

Artichokes with Chestnut Purée
Périgord Sauce
Sautéed Tournedos
Herb Butter
Potato Baskets
Water Cress and Apple Salad
Vanilla Mousse
Suvaroffs
Coffee

Consommé with Salty Orange Macaroons
Pheasant with Mushrooms and Sour Cream
Lemon Sherbet
Noodles with Bread Crumbs
Cabbage Salad
Salzburger Nockerln
Coffee

Melon Balls with Orange Sauce
Quail in Tart Shells
Cauliflower with
Julienne of Ham and Truffles
Shoestring Potatoes
Hazelnut Soufflé
Suvaroffs
Coffee

Onion and Caviar Boats
Partridge with Chestnuts
Brown Rice with Grapes
Small Glazed Onions
Vanilla Mousse   Rum Sauce
Tuiles
Coffee

Lemon Trout
Saddle of Venison with Port Wine
Stuffed Mushrooms   Potato Dumplings
Lingonberries
Celery Salad   Sour Cream Dressing
Viennese Carnival Doughnuts   Wine Sauce
Coffee

Recipe Index

*All recipes, unless otherwise noted, are for six persons. When reference
is made within a recipe to a second recipe, consult the index.*